GEORGE B. KLIPPERT

CANADIAN

BUSINESS

LAW

PRINCIPLES IN ACTION

Canadian Cataloguing in Publication Data

Klippert, George B.
  Canadian business law : principles in action

Includes bibliographical references and index.
ISBN 0–03–921676–4

1. Commercial law – Canada. I. Title.

KE919.K58 1987   346.71′07   C86–094350–X

Publisher: Richard Kitowski
Managing Editor: Edie Franks
Copy Editor: Peter Scargall
Cover and Interior Design: Brant Cowie
Artist: Pronk and Associates
Cartoons: Roy Condy
Typesetting and Assembly: Q Composition Inc.

1 2 3 4 5 91 90 89 88 87

TO MY PARENTS

PREFACE

The Case Study of Rinehart Software Ltd.

Throughout the book reference will be made to Rinehart Software Ltd. — a hypothetical Canadian company with its headquarters in British Columbia and a subsidiary company operating in Ontario.

The technique employed is to discuss selected areas of law and then to provide illustrations based on the business activity of the company. This bridge allows a transition between the theory and the practice. Problems for discussion included in each chapter require the reader to apply the legal elements of the discussion to answer specific questions or problems. Many of the problems are directly related to the operation of the company.

The Use of a Hypothetical Computer Company

It is not an easy task to make the law live on the printed page. Legal problems in a business setting arise out of the interaction of people with one another or other companies. The challenge is to approximate the reality of a business setting. The model adopted is the creation of a hypothetical Canadian computer company, which was selected for several reasons. (i) The growth of high technology has created many new jobs in North America, and the trend is that more jobs in this industry will be created in the future. (ii) A businessperson working for a non-computer firm will likely use computers and software during his/her career, and the legal problems surrounding these uses will require resolution. (iii) The rapid technological changes in the computer industry illustrate some of the fundamental problems of law trying to adapt and provide solutions. (iv) The diversity of legal problems is arguably greater in the computer business, and this complexity allows a greater appreciation of the potential range of legal problems than might be found in other industries.

The Functional Approach to Business Law

A business student does not take a law course for the same reason that a law student takes a course on creditor's remedies. Most commerce students do not expect to become a lawyer. Instead there is a reasonable expectation that a business law course will provide the student with knowledge about how law operates in a business context. As a business executive, there are many day-to-day decisions that have legal implications. A conceptual framework is required to allow a student to identify those legal decisions that can be adequately handled without the use of a lawyer from those that require the specialized expertise, skill, and knowledge a lawyer possesses. In other words, when the president of the company, the sales manager or personnel manager makes certain types of decisions, there must be a basic awareness of certain legal principles. Also, those legal principles will often shape the scope and number of options available in a business context.

The treatment of legal principles is based on the notion that, like business itself, the law is a process. Principles of law are not static abstraction, and cannot be safely placed in compartments that give the appearance that they are self-contained and isolated. In essence, a functional approach requires the student to understand the legal process in an ever-changing business context. The businessperson is a problem-solver and decision-maker who must appreciate the potential legal consequences of his or her decisions.

Law is more than a system of rules, and lawyers are more than mere technicians who mechanically apply or interpret the rules. Business executives must take into account the sociological, psychological, and political consequences of their decisions, and increasingly, they expect their lawyers to adopt a similar approach. A legal solution, however, is not always the best answer. Such lawyers must be able to shift from a rule-oriented world to one in which principles of accounting, marketing, and management become viable decision-making alternatives. For the business executive, the determination of how to use a lawyer and what to expect of a lawyer is a very important skill.

Basic Tenets

There are a number of premises underlying these basic tenets that form the philosophy of this book.

Knowledge of Business Students

Most business students have elected to work roughly in the same environment and they already share a knowledge about a number of variables in that environment. As the students are taking a business law course, there is a shared interest about the relationship of that subject to their prior knowledge and the knowledge that will be subsequently acquired.

Placing the Law in Perspective

Most students find it easier to read, understand, and remember a story than an abstract discussion of the story's idea, plot, and characterization. One way to learn about law in context is to illustrate in story form various situations in which people who are managing a company find themselves. There are many ways to tell the story of Rinehart Ltd. Each situation, in point of detail, will have different emphases, characters, locations, entanglements, and motives. The story, for the most part, is explained by using chapter illustrations, discussion problems, and examples. This allows for continuity throughout the book.

This book chooses to tell one long narrative about a single software computer company located in Vancouver, British Columbia. Within the context of the story we will soon discover that law is a process made up of many separate events. The process is defined by the events that occur between the company officers, shareholders, directors, suppliers, wholesalers, distributors, and consumers. Law becomes a part of the process of doing, thinking, and believing for all of these connected individuals, the company, and other individuals and institutions. At times there will be an outward appearance of legal rules that appear to be solid, firm, immutable, and objective; but we must also be prepared to consider the constant shifts, adjustments, contradictions, and re-evaluations caused in this environment.

Flexibility of the Law

There is probably no such thing as the term "business law"; it is at best a vague generality. With equal conviction it might be stated that all law is business law, because many relationships, confrontations, and events in the environment require a business executive to consider some aspect of law. As the type, size, structure, and goals of businesses may differ substantially, no business law code could ever be self-contained. The goal is to demonstrate that the law in the business environment is often open-ended and cannot be comprehensively understood by reading a single text.

Selecting Business Law

Lastly, writing a business law text is as much a matter of exclusion as well as of inclusion of law. An attempt has been made to include classical topics in conjunction with more recent developments such as intellectual property, business torts, and professional responsibility. This provides the business student with a balanced perspective. The software business of Rinehart Ltd. is a good basis for learning the basic elements of copyright, patent, and trade secrets. Even though only a few business students may ultimately work for a software company, the selected principles — including the modern ones — will have a general application to the broad spectrum of businesses.

The Role of Rinehart's In-House Lawyer

One technique used in the text is to consider the legal options available to Ms. Julia Bach, Rinehart's in-house lawyer. She is responsible, as an employee, for handling the company's legal planning and problems.

The view of business law through the eyes of an in-house lawyer is often different from that of a lawyer practising in a law firm. The in-house, or company lawyer, is an employee. She has merely one "client". At times, the in-house lawyer may have trouble deciding who the client is: the executive officers? the board of directors? the shareholders? She may also be approached by employees of the company regarding legal problems arising from their job or from their private lives.

A company with an in-house lawyer may also use the services of outside lawyers. The decision to go outside the company is often, though not exclusively, made by the company lawyer. As a general rule, an outside lawyer will be consulted in three circumstances: (i) The time-pressure problem: when the company lawyer has other demands on her time, an outside lawyer can be assigned certain responsibilities. (ii) The company lawyer may lack the expertise to competently advise the company on a legal question concerning tax, trade regulation, securities legislation, or property. (iii) The company lawyer may have the time and expertise, but the opinion of an outside lawyer may be required to satisfy the independence requirement demanded by a third party, or the management, the board of directors, or shareholders of the company.

The Organization of Rinehart Software Ltd.

Background of Rinehart Ltd.

The company has fifty employees in the Canadian operation, with the head office located in Vancouver, British Columbia. Worldwide there are two hundred employees of the company and its subsidiaries. Rinehart Software Ltd., as suggested by the name, is in the business of developing, testing, and distributing software programs for home and commercial computers.

The company has wholly owned subsidiaries in Ontario (QueTech Ltd.), Delaware (Rinehart Software [U.S.] Ltd.), and England (Rinehart Limited [England]).

The Product Line

There are two main markets for the company's products: the general computer owner market and the specific user market. The former is called a horizontal market and the latter a vertical market. The main distinction is that products in the horizontal market are directed toward major segments of the personal and commercial computer user market. Products in this market must also compete with similar products produced by other companies with the same market. A videogame, for example, is a horizontal market product. The vertical product, on the other hand, is designed to meet the specific applications required by a particular industry. A law office systems software product is an example of a vertical market product. The same law office, however, may also use a horizontal product such as an accounting program, as it is made for a wide spectrum of businesses.

The products developed by Rinehart Software Ltd. and its subsidiary companies include the following software packages.

VIDEOGAMES
The company is the owner of three entertainment videogames: *Space Attack, Fight of the Titans*, and *Epic Encounters*. The company has sub-licensed *Space Attack* to West-Game Worlds, Inc., which is a major distributor of videogames in the United States. Five new videogame programs are currently being developed by the Research and Development Department.

E.E.C. ACCOUNTING SYSTEM
Through the English subsidiary, Rinehard Limited (England), the company has developed and distributed a number of accounting software

products for use in the Common Market countries. The product systems provide for payroll, accounts receivable and payable, sales and production orders, and fixed and capital system analyses. The products have been sold to retail shops, manufacturers of cars, ships, and electronic equipment, newspaper and magazine publishers, and airlines.

LAW OFFICE MANAGEMENT SYSTEM

This is a software package of programs for law offices and individual lawyers that allows for record keeping, client accounting, billing, time records, accounts receivable, and office expenses — including overheads and salaries.

REAL ESTATE INVESTMENT SYSTEM

This system is for banks, real estate companies, insurance companies, pension managers, and private real estate investors. The system provides pricing, inflation and tax indexes, transaction histories, price charting, mortgage interest analysis, transactional cost analysis of commissions, fees, and legal and accounting expenses.

HOME MATH TUTOR

This system is designed as an educational learning tool for children aged twelve to sixteen. It uses graphic images, sound, colour, and animation to teach math skills. As part of the venture into the educational learning programs, the company is currently considering a scheme to introduce "Learning Shoppes" as part of its educational package. The Learning Shoppes would be independent franchises that would teach children and adults how to use computers by using the educational software produced by the company. Part of this plan will be to develop an educational line of software that will be attractive to students. One of the benefits of the Learning Shoppes is that it will diversify the company's product to include specialized services. Another benefit is that it will introduce a younger generation to the product line of the company. This may serve as a marketing device in the future.

PUBLISHER'S NOTE TO INSTRUCTORS AND STUDENTS

This text book is a key component of your course. If you are the instructor of this course, you undoubtedly considered a number of texts carefully before choosing this as the one that will work best for your students and you. The authors and publishers of this book spent considerable time and money to ensure its high quality, and we appreciate your recognition of this effort and accomplishment.

If you are a student, we are confident that this text will help you to meet the objectives of your course. You will also find it helpful after the course is finished as a valuable addition to your personal library. So hold on to it.

As well, please don't forget that photocopying copyright work means the authors lose royalties that are rightfully theirs. This loss will discourage them from writing another edition of this text or other books, because doing so will simply not be worth their time and effort. If this happens, we all lose — students, instructors, authors, and publishers.

And since we want to hear what you think about this book, please be sure to send us the stamped reply card at the end of the text. This will help us to continue publishing high-quality books for your courses.

ACKNOWLEDGMENTS

The author gratefully acknowledges the contribution of many people over the past four years — colleagues, students, reviewers of the draft manuscript, and the professionals at Holt, Rinehart and Winston of Canada — for their counsel, advice, and critiques. Special appreciation is owed for the efforts of Johanna Bates, University of Calgary; Steven Enman, Acadia University; John Kelly, Seneca College; David Terrell, Camosun College; George Cummins, Memorial University of Newfoundland; Gerald Smeltzer, the University of British Columbia; Bliss A. White, of Blake, Cassels & Graydon, each of whom reviewed drafts of the manuscript. Sally Gunz, University of Waterloo, provided invaluable suggestions on both drafts, and from the beginning believed in the project and provided much encouragement along the way. My publishers, Holt, Rinehart and Winston of Canada, contributed the considerable talent, energy and commitment of Jackie Kaiser, Michael Roche, Richard Kitowski, and Edie Franks, to whom I owe a debt of gratitude.

George B. Klippert
Toronto, Ontario

Contents

PART SEVEN
LEGAL ETHICAL PROBLEMS IN THE BUSINESS ENVIRONMENT

Part I

THE LAW OF CONTRACTS

1 THE NATURE OF CONTRACTS

Contract Law and Usage

A contract is a promise or set of promises that is enforceable against the person or company giving the promise or promises. A promise must be supported by consideration. Consideration results when, for instance, there is an exchange of promises, or a promise is exchanged for money or something of value, such as land, a car, a software program. Contract law is largely based on the common law. Common law refers to the doctrines and principles created and applied by judges and reported in their decisions. A breach of contract is the failure to perform as promised. The breach will cause economic injury to the party deprived of the

FIGURE 1.1 **CONTRACT DISPUTE RESOLUTION**

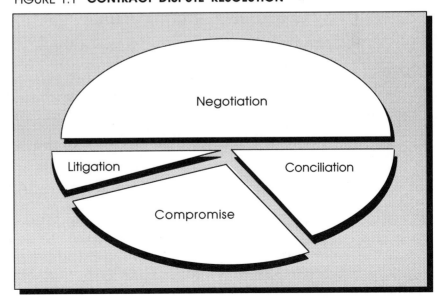

promised performance. The injured party may enforce remedies against the contract breaker.

The most common form of remedy is for damages, which may be defined as monetary compensation. For example, Rinehart pays Charles Smith $10 000 for his promise to deliver a software program on December 1st; then, on December 1st, Charles Smith writes that he has no intention of delivering the promised program. The contract is enforceable. Mr. Smith has made a promise — a promise that was made in return for Rinehart's actual payment of $10 000 (which is called consideration) — and that promise has been breached. The injury caused by Mr. Smith's breach is at least $10 000. The damages awarded to Rinehart may not be, however, limited to that sum. Rinehart may have suffered further economic loss: it may have made a contract with a third party based upon the delivery of the Smith software. Damages would then include this economic loss as well.

How is legal knowledge about contract law relevant to the day-to-day business transactions made by those inside a company? One answer is to be found in the crucial planning stages. It is at this time — before the actual contract is made — that contract law provides the most valuable use. For instance, Julia Bach, Rinehart's in-house lawyer, will include clauses that determine the scope of the obligation to perform a contractual promise. There may be certain contingencies — uncertain future events that Rinehart may want the other party to agree excuses the company from performance of a promise (e.g., a strike by the union or a work stoppage). Another example is a clause that limits the other party's remedy in the event that Rinehart's performance of the promise is defective.

The Business of Contracting

Empirical studies in the United States and England show that the law of contract is not the most important factor in the exchange of promises made between business executives. The promises between companies for materials, supplies, and distribution of goods and services are commonly called commercial transactions. The promises between the manufacturer, distributor, and retailer with the consumer who buys and uses the goods and services are commonly called consumer transactions.

NON-LEGAL FACTORS
The studies in commercial transactions suggest that many non-legal factors such as trade custom, business reputation and standing, and personal association of individuals within the companies play an important role. It is no surprise that these factors should play an important role in business. Further, the courts consider these factors in applying contract rules to a case. The law of contract, and the business environment in

which contractings occur, is constantly changing. In Alberta, for instance, the concept of "usage" is enshrined in legislation governing the sale of goods.

Private negotiations   Business executives are less inclined among themselves to insist on the strict letter of a written contract. The focus, in the event of a disagreement about the commercial contract, is more likely to be resolved through private negotiation. Litigation is the rare exception to the rule. For example, Professor Macaulay found that business executives view their transactions as "orders" that can be "cancelled" rather than "contracts" and "breach of contracts".[1] A later study by Beale and Dugdale was consistent with Professor Macaulay's findings.

These later researchers found that business executives do not approach their transactions with others from a formalistic or legalistic perspective. As there are other devices, contracts are not generally needed.[2] The Ontario Law Reform Commission in 1979, reporting on proposed changes to the Sale of Goods Act, found:

> Although commercial lawyers would readily recognize the problem areas that we have identified, it must be admitted that there is little evidence that the business community feels equally keenly about the need for a revised Sale of Goods Act. There appears, rather, to be a fairly pervasive feeling that legal rules are not very relevant in the conduct of everyday business relationships, and that such difficulties as may arise from time to time can be resolved amicably and without resort to the courts.[3]

Non-speculative goods and services   The evidence suggests that there are few lawsuits over business contracts in non-speculative goods and services; and moreover, that few business executives read the fine print on the back of their suppliers' forms. In Rinehart Ltd., the production employees and the sales force have the goal of making and selling as much of their product as they can. These people do not have an appetite to approach each transaction as a potential legal problem waiting to happen. They are more concerned with creating business relations with their suppliers and distributors based on mutual trust.

THE PERSONAL RELATIONSHIP

Professor Macaulay points out the importance of the personal relationships among people working for companies that desire to exchange goods and services. The continuing nature of these relationships is a crucial factor in doing business efficiently. Company officers may have social contacts and serve on common trade boards. There may be an interconnection in terms of common directors, or the seller may own shares in the buyer's company. The predominant theme in business is to gain a reputation that promotes the continuing business relationship between the parties. A legalistic approach may soon damage or destroy such values.

CONCILIATION THEME

Professors Friedman and Macaulay have expressed a conciliation theme in this fashion:[4]

> Businesses of all kinds have tended to develop stable economic relationships. Therefore, the two businesses involved in any kind of deal are likely to be interlocked beyond the fact of a particular contract. No one disagreement would justify jeopardizing a total relationship. Personal relationships may exist across all levels of the two organizations involved. Executives, for example, are likely to know each other socially: one behaves differently with friends than with strangers. Today, if not in the past, most people in most kinds of businesses share a norm of honoring commitments unless there is an extraordinary reason not to.

Planning in the Company's Interest

It would be a mistake to conclude that contracts and the law of contract are unimportant in the business context. It is in the interest of a company to carefully plan a transaction, especially where the potential for legal problems appears to be great, where there is a significant monetary investment, or where there are trade secrets or confidential information to protect. The nature of the company's product is also a relevant consideration in determining whether to contract. Where the product is standard and can be tested to ascertain if it works as warranted, the potential for substantial loss because of defective goods is less. The highly specialized product designed exclusively for the buyer presents a greater degree of risk in the event of design or product defect.[5]

It is one thing to acknowledge that business executives place a high value on non-legal factors in their commercial contract dealings; at the same time, it would be unwise to conclude that the non-legal factors are the exclusive basis of such dealings. The business executive must understand the basic principles of contract law; that a person should keep promises is at the heart of both contract law and social relationships. Thus, it would be a mistake to assume that the contract principles are created in a social void.

Although an appreciation of contract law is understood by most business executives, it is rarely called upon. However, when dealing with "strangers", the business executive is likely to exercise greater care in planning dealings and to keep in mind the law of contract. This follows because there is no history of dealings to call upon.

The Freak Case

A major problem in the study of contract law is the distortion that the reported decisions are representative of most contract dealings. In reality, most of the reported cases have little to do with the commercial transactions carried on by a company such as Rinehart Ltd. Professors Friedman and Macaulay observe that the most appellate judgments are "atypical or freak business transactions; economically marginal deals both in terms of the type of transaction and amounts involved; high-stake, zero sum speculations; deals where there is an outsider interest that does not allow compromise; and family economic transactions."[6]

The study of contract law by a business executive is akin to the study of pathology by a medical student. There is a risk of losing perspective. Diseased or abnormal body tissue becomes the norm rather than the exception. The reality is that most transactions between companies (and most body tissue) are vital and healthy, and function quite well without the intervention of lawyers. Thus, in the chapters that follow, we will consider the types of transactions that can go wrong. We will also address the consequences attached to them by the law of contract. In the very rare circumstances where coercive force of the law is invoked, there is a basic understanding that can be drawn upon to make an informed choice.

The Process of Making a Contract

The process of making a contract may be defined as all the negotiations and dealings between the parties before they have exchanged promises that are legally binding. The substantive rules of contract may be defined as: the common law principles that determine under what circumstances a legally binding agreement is created, performed or breached; and the remedies available in case of breach.

The processing of formal contracting provides insight into the areas where a company elects to use a contract and the law of contract to plan a particular transaction. We have discovered that this process is not widely used by a business. Nonetheless, there is merit in understanding this process and the contractual principles that form part of that process.

Rinehart Ltd. will, at times, rely on the law of contracts as creating a legal mechanism for exchange of their goods and services, and for the acquisition of goods and services from others. In an economy that is largely composed of private businesses, the activities of commerce are conducted through the medium of private exchange. Of course not all of these exchanges follow the rules of contract law.

The traditional approach to the law of contracts has been to focus on the substantive principles of the law. The general framework of study is typically loaded with major emphases on contract formation principles, the necessity for written contracts in certain situations, the restrictions imposed by the privity of contract doctrine, and compensation principles. The challenge is to focus on the relevant contractual principles in the process of contracting. The approach of studying the abstract principle is rarely of value to the practical consideration that will face a business executive.

The goal, therefore, is to forge an appreciation of both the process and the substantive rules. This interrelationship will provide a greater awareness of the type of problems actually encountered in the business world. It is appropriate to recall the words of the great English lawyer Sir Frederick Pollock who wrote in 1921: "Legal rules exist not for their own sake, but to further justice and convenience in the business of human life; dialectic is the servant of their purpose, not their master."[7]

The Standard Form Contract

We have discussed the informality with which business executives view contracts. The notions of "contracts" as "orders" that may be "cancelled" to preserve the underlying business relationship are important and real. In modern business, most repetitive business dealings are covered by "standard form contracts". A standard form contract is a generic contract drafted to apply to all transactions of a similar nature. There may be hundreds or even thousands of similar transactions. For example, the consumer licence contract between Rinehart and a consumer of the company's software is the same in each instance.

The treatment and enforcement of the terms of the contract may vary depending on whether the buyer is a stranger to the company or an old, valued supplier. Rinehart's lawyer ensures the standard form contract is favourable to the company's interest. Where the other party has equal or near equal bargaining power, then it may challenge the terms of Rinehart's contract and negotiate different ones. As the empirical research indicates, these tailor-made agreements are rare. But to say that they are rare is not to suggest that they are unimportant. In terms of economic interest, the fortunes of the company may rise or fall on the terms of an important distribution or supplier contract.

Julia Bach, as inside counsel, will play a pivotal role in advising, drafting, and negotiating contracts for the company. In addition, she will ensure the necessary formalities for execution, and, where necessary, registration or disclosure of certain types of contracts. Generally, the contracts are generated as a means of implementing the business transactions of the company. There are many decisions where Ms. Bach will be asked to provide her legal expertise and to translate the business decision into a contract.

The General Counsel and Secretary of IBM Canada Ltd., Mr. Grant G. Murray, has written that his company processes approximately 60 000 sales contracts annually.[8] The overwhelming majority of these contracts are "standard form" contracts prepared by the legal department of IBM. In total, IBM uses 205 standard form contracts.[9] The standard form contract means that, for instance, everyone who purchases an IBM typewriter signs a contract with exactly the same terms and conditions. Presumably a large portion of these contracts are between IBM and its consumers. The advantage of the standard form contract in these circumstances is that it permits the company to treat each consumer in the same manner.

From a business point of view, it is revealing that, in over twenty years as General Counsel to IBM Canada, Mr. Murray is able to conclude: " . . . I cannot remember a single instance where a customer has tried to repudiate a deal or has resisted a claim for payment on the grounds that there was no valid contract or that the contract contained contradictory terms."[10] When disputes arise, the issue is usually one of interpretation of a clause in the contract.

Illustration of Business Contracts

For purposes of illustration, we will consider three different types of contracts used by the company. Each contract will illustrate the involvement of management in the decision-making process, and the connection of the in-house counsel in that process. Included are both the standard form contracts and the contracts specially negotiated and drafted for a particular commercial transaction.

Commercial Transaction

The decision to license another company to sell the company's Law Office Management System in Alberta would be made by the Vice-President of Marketing. This agreement would be, in most instances, a standard form contract. The Software Licence and Marketing Agreement contained in Figure 1.2 has been entered into between Rinehart Ltd. and Acrodrome Ltd.

FIGURE 1.2

SOFTWARE LICENCE AND MARKETING AGREEMENT

THIS AGREEMENT made as of this 10th day of March, 1987, by and between Rinehart Ltd., a British Columbia Corporation with its principal office in Vancouver ("Rinehart") and Acrodome Ltd., an Alberta Corporation with its principal office in Calgary ("Distributor").

1. Licence

(a) In consideration of Distributor's performance of its obligations herein, Rinehart hereby grants to Distributor, subject to the condition in subparagraph (b), an exclusive licence ("Licence") (i) to sub-license in the Territory the Software products to end-users who have executed the Licence Agreement ("Customers"); (ii) to demonstrate the use of the Software Products in connection with advertisement, promotion, and sub-licensing of the Software Products pursuant to Paragraph 2; (iii) to make copies of the Software Products for use by Customers; and (iv) to merge the Software Products into other software systems or adapt the Software Products for use in conjunction with other software systems, provided, however, that no such merger or adaptation of any Software Product shall be attempted to be made without Rinehart's prior written approval and no disposition of any merged or adapted Software Product shall be made until Distributor has submitted it to Rinehart and Rinehart has approved in writing such merged or adapted Software Product. Rinehart shall be under no obligation to approve the merger or adaptation of any Software Product. Rinehart shall retain complete ownership of all right, title, and interest in and to all merged or adapted Software Products. Distributor shall not make any use or disposition of any Software Product or of any merged or adapted Software Product except as expressly provided in this Agreement.

(b) In the event that Distributor fails to make at least 150 dispositions of Software Products during any six (6) month period during the term of this Agreement, the Licence granted hereunder shall become non-exclusive. In the event that Distributor fails to make at least 75 dispositions of Software Products during any six (6) month period during the term of this Agreement, Rinehart may, in its sole discretion, terminate this Agreement at any time pursuant to paragraph 8(b). Each such disposition will be deemed to occur on the earlier of (i) execution by a Customer of Licence Agreement in respect of a copy of a Software Product, and (ii) a copy of a Software Product leaving the possession of Distributor regardless of terms of payment by the Customer and regardless of credit risks or losses ("Date of Disposition").

(c) Distributor agrees to include on all copies of Software Products licensed hereunder all copyright and proprietary notices found on the original Software Products provided by Rinehart to Distributor hereunder without modification or obliteration.

(d) Distributor will not enter into a Licence Agreement on behalf of Rinehart with any third party if it appears likely that such third party will not honour its obligations thereunder. Distributor will adopt such reasonable screening and monitoring procedures as Rinehart may suggest from time to time to gauge the suitability of third parties as Customers and their compliance with the Licence Agreement. Distributor will promptly inform Rinehart of any breach of the Licence Agreement of which it becomes aware.

2. Marketing of Software

Distributor will use its best efforts to actively advertise, promote, and sub-license the Software Products throughout the Territory during the term of this Agreement. Distributor agrees to use in connection with the Software Products only advertising and promotional material that Distributor previously has submitted samples of to Rinehart for approval and that Rinehart had not disapproved of in writing within thirty (30) days after its receipt of such samples. Distributor agrees to make no representation or warranty in connection with the Software Products other than those representations and warranties expressly contained in the Software Products or this Agreement.

3. Limited Warranty

(a) Rinehart does not warrant that the functions contained in the Software Products will meet Customer's requirements or that the operation of the Software Products will be uninterrupted or error free.

(b) However, Rinehart warrants the disk(s) or diskette(s) on which Rinehart furnishes the Software Products to be free from defects in materials and workmanship under normal use for a period of ninety (90) days from the date first above written. This limited warranty extends only to Customers.

(c) EXCEPT AS EXPRESSLY PROVIDED ABOVE, THE SOFTWARE PRODUCTS ARE PROVIDED "AS IS" WITHOUT WARRANTY OF ANY KIND, EITHER EXPRESSED OR IMPLIED, INCLUDING, BUT NOT LIMITED TO THE IMPLIED WARRANTIES OF WORKMANSHIP AND FITNESS FOR A PARTICULAR PURPOSE.

(d) SOME JURISDICTIONS DO NOT ALLOW THE EXCLUSION OF IMPLIED WARRANTIES, SO THE ABOVE EXCLUSION MAY NOT APPLY TO DISTRIBUTOR AND ITS CUSTOMERS. THIS WARRANTY GIVES DISTRIBUTOR AND ITS CUSTOMERS SPECIFIC LEGAL RIGHTS AND DISTRIBUTOR AND ITS CUSTOMERS MAY ALSO HAVE OTHER RIGHTS THAT VARY FROM JURISDICTION TO JURISDICTION.

4. Limitation of Remedies

(a) Rinehart's entire liability and the exclusive remedy of customer shall be the replacement of any disk or diskette not meeting Rinehart's "Limited Warranty".

(b) IN NO EVENT WILL RINEHART BE LIABLE TO DISTRIBUTOR OR CUSTOMER FOR ANY DAMAGES, INCLUDING ANY LOST PROFITS, LOST SAVINGS OR OTHER INCIDENTAL OR CONSEQUENTIAL DAMAGES ARISING OUT OF THE USE OR INABILITY TO USE SUCH SOFTWARE PRODUCTS EVEN IF RINEHART OR AN AUTHORIZED RINEHART REPRESENTATIVE OR AGENT HAS BEEN ADVISED OF THE POSSIBILITY OF SUCH DAMAGES, OR FOR ANY CLAIM BY ANY OTHER PARTY.

(c) SOME JURISDICTIONS DO NOT ALLOW THE LIMITATIONS OR EX-CLUSION OF LIABILITY FOR INCIDENTAL OR CONSEQUENTIAL DAM-AGES SO THE ABOVE LIMITATION OR EXCLUSION MAY NOT APPLY TO DISTRIBUTOR OR CUSTOMER.

5. Confidentiality

Distributor agrees and acknowledges that the Software Products embody confidential and proprietary information (hereinafter the "Confidential Information") owned by Rinehart. Confidential Information shall not include any information that can be demonstrated by Distributor to have been in the public domain prior to disclosure thereof to Distributor or that becomes part of the public domain by publication or otherwise through no fault of or negligent or unauthorized act or omission of Distributor; or that Distributor lawfully receives from an independent third party not previously employed by Rinehart or who acquired such information through no breach of any obligation to Rinehart; however, no combination of any information shall be excluded from Confidential Information because any specific information would be excluded. Distributor, including its employees, shall not disclose, make available, provide copies or summaries in any form of, or commit any act or omission that would impair or depreciate the confidential nature or value of, the Confidential Information. Distributor may disclose Confidential Information to only those supervisory employees who need to know such information to carry out their duties on behalf of Distributor.

6. Proprietary Rights

Rinehart shall have the right to apply for, prosecute, obtain, maintain, defend, and enforce Rinehart's rights to and interests in the Software Products in such countries, and in such manner, as Rinehart may in its sole discretion determine. Distributor will have no rights to or interest in the Software Products except as expressly granted in Paragraph 1 of this Agreement. Distributor will not acquire or attempt to acquire any proprietary rights to the Software Products or any merger or adaptation thereof other than pursuant to subparagraph 1(a). Distributor will assist Rinehart in obtaining protection in the Territory for the Software Products and all mergers or adaptations thereof.

7. Fees

Distributor will pay Rinehart (i) in respect of each disposition of the Software Products furnished to Distributor a Licensing Fee in the amount of $2000 per month; (ii) in respect of each annual renewal fee accepted by Distributor for providing telephone support and enhancements, an Annual Renewal Fee in the amount of $1000; and (iii) in respect of each disposition of the data entry program a Data Entry Program Fee in the amount of $150.00.

8. Term and Termination

(a) This Agreement, unless sooner terminated, shall be effective for five (5) years from the date first written above.

(b) Subject to the provisions of Paragraph 3, either party may terminate this Agreement effective upon (and only upon) any anniversary of this Agreement by delivering written notice thereof to the other party at least ninety (90) days prior to such anniversary. Also, in the event either party materially fails to perform its obligations under this Agreement, the other party shall have the right to terminate this Agreement upon thirty (30) days' written notice provided that the other party does not rectify such breach within that time. Finally, Rinehart shall have the right to terminate this Agreement in the event that the Distributor files a petition for voluntary bankruptcy, has a petition for involuntary bankruptcy filed against it (which petition is not withdrawn within sixty (60) days of filing), is unable to pay its debts as they become due including but not limited to the payments required under this Agreement, or ceases to actively function as a business.

9. Severability
The provisions of this Agreement shall be severable, and if any provision of this Agreement shall be held or declared to be illegal, invalid or unenforceable, such illegality, invalidity or unenforceability shall not affect any other provisions hereof, and the remainder of this Agreement disregarding such invalid portion shall continue in full force and effect as though such void provisions had not been contained herein.

10. Waiver
The waiver of either of the parties hereto of any breach of any provision hereof by the other party shall not be construed to be either a waiver of any succeeding breach of any such provision or a waiver of the provision itself.

11. Entire Agreement
This instrument contains the entire agreement between the parties hereto with respect to the subject matter hereof and supersedes and cancels any and all previous written or oral understandings, agreements, negotiations, commitments, and any other writings or communications in respect of such subject matter. This Agreement may not be released, discharged, abandoned, changed or modified in any manner except by an instrument in writing signed by a fully authorized officer of each of the parties.

12. Binding Agreement
This Agreement shall inure to the benefit of and be binding upon the successors and assigns of Rinehart and Distributor provided, however, that the Distributor may not assign any of its rights, duties or obligations hereunder by operation of law or otherwise without the prior written consent of Rinehart.

13. Construction
The language used in this Agreement shall be deemed to be language chosen by both parties hereto to express their mutual intent, and no rule of strict construction against either party shall apply to any term or condition of this Agreement.

14. Nature of Relationship
Nothing herein shall be construed to place the parties in a relationship of partners, or joint venturers, or of agency, and neither party shall have the power to obligate or bind the other in any manner whatsoever.

Research and Development Business Decisions

In the case of special research projects, Rinehart Ltd. will often employ the services of a consultant. The consultant brings to the project expertise and skills, and eliminates the need to hire an additional employee. An example of a consulting contract is contained in Figure 1.3. It should be noted that the consultant may be an individual who or a firm that provides computer experts on a consulting basis. Carefully note the specific interest that Rinehart seeks to protect in this contract.

FIGURE 1.3

SOFTWARE CONSULTING AGREEMENT

THIS AGREEMENT, effective this 18th day of November, 1987, between Rinehart Ltd., a British Columbia Company with its principal office in Vancouver ("Customer") and Lindsay Software Distributors Ltd., an Ontario Company with its principal office in Toronto ("Consultant").

WITNESSETH:

WHEREAS, CONSULTANT is ready, willing, and able to develop software to permit Customer's Dental Office Management System program ("Program") to be used in networked computer systems and customer desires to obtain such software;

NOW, THEREFORE, in consideration of the mutual covenants and agreements of the parties hereto and other good and valuable consideration, the receipt and sufficiency of which are hereby acknowledged, it is hereby mutually agreed as follows:

1. Services

acceptance

Subject to the terms and conditions set forth herein, Consultant agrees to furnish the consulting services necessary to perform all of the tasks specified herein.

2. Phase I

(a) Commencing on December 15, 1987, Consultant shall develop and submit for Customer's approval a detailed model of the Systems that shall include: (i) a network operating system; (b) supervisor programs to control the interface between the network operating system and Program; and (iii) a library of routines to allow each individual Program that is connected to the Systems to access all centralized data in the system. The Systems shall be completely compatible with I.B.M. and Apple personal computers (hereinafter collectively referred to as the "Microcomputers"). The Systems shall permit any number of Microcomputers to be linked together (i.e., networked) for centralized data collection on a hard disk. The speed of screen changes on each Microcomputer shall not be affected by changes in the number of Microcomputers networked in the System.

(b) Commencing on January 18, 1988, Consultant shall develop and submit for Customer's approval detailed recommendations for all hardware required to network the Microcomputers in accordance with paragraph 2(a) so as to provide for centralized data collection on a hard disk and to permit proper execution of the Systems.

(c) A model of the Systems acceptable to Customer, as specified in paragraph 2(a), and hardware recommendations acceptable to Customer, as specified in paragraph 2(b), shall be submitted to Customer by Consultant on or before March 30, 1988.

3. Phase II

(a) Following Customer's acceptance of Phase I, Consultant will develop and submit for Customer's approval source and object code necessary to implement the Systems developed under Phase I as well as Systems documentation, including systems maintenance instructions, sufficient to allow Customer personnel to service and update the Systems. With the co-operation of Customer, Consultant will fully test the Systems.

(b) Consultant will provide training for Customer personnel sufficient to fully familiarize such personnel with the design, implementation, operation, service, and maintenance of the Systems.

(c) Complete Source and object code and documentation acceptable to Customer shall be submitted to Customer by Consultant on or before July 1, 1988.

(d) Consultant shall provide maintenance and updates for the Systems for a period of two years from the date of execution hereof.

4. Fees

Within ten (10) days after completion of the tasks specified in Phase I hereof to the satisfaction of Customer, Customer will pay Consultant a fee not to exceed One Hundred Thousand dollars ($100 000). Within ten (10) days after completion of the tasks specified in Phase II hereof to the satisfaction of Customer, Customer will pay Consultant a fee not to exceed Seventy-Five Thousand dollars ($75 000) and a royalty of eight percent (8%) of Customer's gross sales of the Systems.

5. Warranty

Consultant warrants and represents that the Systems will perform in accordance with the model and specifications developed pursuant to paragraph 2(a). If at any time the Systems fail to meet any of the applicable specifications or to perform in accordance with the model, Consultant will promptly make consulting services available to Customer, at Consultant's expense, for the purpose of correcting any deficiency provided that Customer gives Consultant written notice specifically identifying any such deficiency, and makes available to Consultant sufficient documentation and data to enable Consultant to confirm the existence of the deficiency within ten (10) days of such notice, Customer may withhold royalties until the deficiency is corrected.

6. Property Rights

All programs, including both source and object code versions, and all program documentation relating thereto, including but not limited to the model and all specifications, developed by consultant hereunder shall belong to Customer. Consultant shall not copy, use, or authorize others to use such programs and program documentation except in connection with rendering services to Customer in accordance with this Agreement; provided, however, that nothing herein contained shall preclude Consultant from using in programs that it may hereafter develop for itself or third parties — subroutines that may be incorporated by Consultant in the Systems so long as such subroutines individually or in the aggregate do not utilize or perform any of the unique features of the Customer's Systems.

7. General

(a) This Agreement and the Non-Disclosure Agreement between the parties hereto contain the full understanding of the parties hereto with respect of the specific subject matter hereof and supersede and cancel all other previous agreements, negotiations, commitments, discussions, and writings in respect of such subject matter. No representations, promises, or understandings that are not expressly set forth herein are binding upon any of the parties. This Agreement may not be released, discharged, abandoned, changed, or modified in any manner except by an instrument in writing signed by a duly authorized representative of each of the parties. Neither the course of conduct between the parties nor trade usage shall act to modify or alter the provisions of this Agreement.

(b) This Agreement shall be construed and the legal relations of the parties hereto shall be governed in accordance with the laws of the Province of British Columbia, Canada.

(c) The provisions of this Agreement shall be severable, and the invalidity or illegality of any provisions of this Agreement shall not affect the validity or legality of the remaining provisions.

(d) The waiver by either the parties of any breach of any provisions hereof by the other party shall not be construed to be either a waiver of any succeeding breach of any provision or a waiver of the provision itself.

(e) This Agreement, and all rights and obligations hereunder, shall inure to the benefit of and shall be binding upon subsidiaries, affiliates, successors, or assigns of the parties hereto; provided, however, that neither party shall assign nor transfer this Agreement in any manner without the prior written consent of the other party, which consent shall not unreasonably be withheld.

(f) If Consultant commits a breach or threatens to commit a breach of its agreement contained herein, Customer shall have the right and remedy in addition to any others that may be available, at law or in equity, to have the agreement contained herein specifically enforced by any court having equity jurisdiction, together with an accounting thereof, it being acknowledged and agreed that any such breach or threatened breach will cause irreparable injury to Customer and that money damages will not provide an adequate remedy. Such injunction shall be available on an immediate, *ex parte* basis, without the posting of any bond or other security, and Consultant hereby consents to the issuance of such injunction.

(g) Neither party shall be considered an agent for the other party, nor shall either party have authority to bind or obligate the other to third parties.

(h) This Agreement will terminate one year from the date of execution unless Consultant fails to comply with any term or condition of this Agreement, in which event Customer may terminate this Agreement by giving Consultant written notice of termination effective upon receipt thereof by Consultant.

The Consumer Licence Agreement

In the third illustration, we will examine an "end-user" contract. In this contract, each consumer of the company's videogame software will enter into a contract for the use of the product. As there may be thousands of such contracts, again Ms. Bach will have drafted the standard form contract establishing the terms and conditions binding the purchasers of their software products. The contract in Figure 1.4 is often referred to as "Shrink-Wrap Contracts". The distinctive feature of the shrink-wrap contract is, by the terms of the contract, that the buyer of the software consents to be bound by the terms of the contract drafted by the seller by tearing off the cellophane wrapping that envelopes the software.

In all three examples, the business decision has been converted into a legally binding contract between the company and the other party. Throughout this section on contract law we will refer back to these contracts to illustrate the application of the legal principles underlying the law of contract.

FIGURE 1.4

RINEHART LICENCE AGREEMENT

CAREFULLY READ ALL THE TERMS AND CONDITIONS OF THIS AGREE-
MENT PRIOR TO BREAKING THE DISKETTE SEAL. BREAKING THE
DISKETTE SEAL INDICATES YOUR ACCEPTANCE OF THESE TERMS
AND CONDITIONS.

If you do not agree to these terms and conditions, return the unopened diskette
package and the other components of this product to the place of purchase and
your money will be refunded. No refunds will be given for products that have
opened diskette packages or missing components.

1. Licence

You have the non-exclusive right to use the enclosed program. This program
can only be used on a single computer. You may physically transfer the program
from one computer to another provided that the program is used on only one
computer at a time. You may not electronically transfer the program from one
computer to another over a network. You may not distribute copies of the program
or documentation to others. You may not modify or translate the program or
related documentation without the prior written consent of Rinehart.

YOU MAY NOT USE, COPY, MODIFY, OR TRANSFER THE PROGRAM
OR DOCUMENTATION, OR ANY COPY EXCEPT AS EXPRESSLY PRO-
VIDED IN THIS AGREEMENT.

2. Back-up and
Transfer

You may make one (1) copy of the program solely for back-up purposes. You
must reproduce and include the copyright notice on the back-up copy. You
may transfer and license the product to another party if the other party agrees
to the terms and conditions of this Agreement and completes and returns a
Registration Card to Rinehart. If you transfer the program, you must at the
same time transfer the documentation and back-up copy or transfer the documentation and destroy the back-up copy.

3. Copyright

The program and its related documentation are copyrighted. You may not copy
the program or its documentation except as for back-up purposes and to load
the program into the computer as part of the executing program. All other copies
of the program and its documentation are in violation of this Agreement.

4. Term

This licence is effective until terminated. You may terminate it by destroying
the program and documentation, and all copies thereof. This licence will also
terminate if you fail to comply with any term or condition of this Agreement.

You agree upon such termination to destroy all copies of the program and documentation.

5. Limited
   Warranty

THE PROGRAM IS PROVIDED "AS IS" WITHOUT WARRANTY OF ANY KIND. THE ENTIRE RISK AS TO THE RESULTS AND PERFORMANCES OF THE PROGRAM IS ASSUMED BY YOU. SHOULD THE PROGRAM PROVE DEFECTIVE, YOU (AND NOT RINEHART OR ITS DEALERS) ASSUME THE ENTIRE COST OF ALL NECESSARY SERVICING, REPAIR OR CORRECTION. FURTHER, RINEHART DOES NOT WARRANT, GUARANTEE, OR MAKE ANY REPRESENTATIONS REGARDING THE USE OF, OR THE RESULTS OF THE USE OF, THE PROGRAM IN TERMS OF CORRECTNESS, ACCURACY, RELIABILITY, CURRENTNESS, OR OTHERWISE; AND YOU RELY ON THE PROGRAM AND RESULTS SOLELY AT YOUR OWN RISK.

Rinehart does warrant to the original licensee that the diskette(s) on which the program is recorded be free from defects in materials and workmanship under normal use and service for a period of ninety (90) days from the date of delivery as evidenced by a copy of your receipt. Rinehart warrants to the original licensee that the hardware components included in this package are free from defects in materials and workmanship for a period of one year from the date of delivery to you as evidenced by a copy of your receipt. Rinehart's entire liability and your exclusive remedy shall be replacement of the diskette not meeting Rinehart's limited warranty and that it is returned to Rinehart with a copy of your receipt. If failure of the diskette has resulted from accident, abuse, or misapplication of the product, then Rinehart shall have no responsibility to replace the diskette under this Limited Warranty. In the event of replacement of the diskette under this Limited Warranty, the replacement will be warranted for the remainder of the original one (1) year or 30 days, whichever is longer.

THE ABOVE IS THE ONLY WARRANTY OF ANY KIND, EITHER EXPRESSED OR IMPLIED, INCLUDING BUT NOT LIMITED TO THE IMPLIED WARRANTIES OF WORKMANSHIP AND FITNESS FOR A PARTICULAR PURPOSE THAT IS MADE BY RINEHART ON THIS RINEHART PRODUCT. THIS WARRANTY GIVES YOU SPECIFIC LEGAL RIGHTS AND YOU MAY ALSO HAVE OTHER RIGHTS THAT VARY FROM PROVINCE TO PROVINCE.

NEITHER RINEHART NOR ANYONE ELSE WHO HAS BEEN INVOLVED IN THE CREATION, PRODUCTION, OR DELIVERY OF THIS PROGRAM SHALL BE LIABLE FOR ANY DIRECT, INDIRECT, CONSEQUENTIAL, OR INCIDENTAL DAMAGES ARISING OUT OF THE USE, THE RESULTS OF USE, OR INABILITY TO USE SUCH PRODUCT EVEN IF RINEHART HAS BEEN ADVISED OF THE POSSIBILITY OF SUCH DAMAGES OR

CLAIM. SOME PROVINCES DO NOT ALLOW THE EXCLUSION OR LIM-
ITATION OF LIABILITY FOR CONSEQUENTIAL OR INCIDENTAL DAM-
AGES SO THE ABOVE LIMITATION MAY NOT APPLY TO YOU.

6. Update Policy

In order to be able to obtain updates of the program, the licensee and persons
to whom the program is transferred in accordance with this Agreement must
complete and return the attached Registration Card to Rinehart. IF THIS REG-
ISTRATION CARD HAS NOT BEEN RECEIVED BY RINEHART, RINE-
HART IS UNDER NO OBLIGATION TO MAKE AVAILABLE TO YOU ANY
UPDATES EVEN THOUGH YOU HAVE MADE PAYMENT OF THE AP-
PLICABLE UPDATE FEE.

7. Misc.

This licence agreement shall be governed by the laws of the Province of British
Columbia and shall inure to the benefit of Rinehart Ltd., its successors, administrators, heirs, and assigns.

8. Acknowledgement

YOU ACKNOWLEDGE THAT YOU HAVE READ THIS AGREEMENT, UN-
DERSTAND IT, AND AGREE TO BE BOUND BY ITS TERMS AND CON-
DITIONS. YOU ALSO AGREE THAT THIS AGREEMENT IS THE COM-
PLETE AND EXCLUSIVE STATEMENT OF AGREEMENT BETWEEN THE
PARTIES AND SUPERSEDES ALL PROPOSALS OR PRIOR AGREEMENTS,
VERBAL OR WRITTEN, AND ANY OTHER COMMUNICATIONS BE-
TWEEN THE PARTIES RELATING TO THE SUBJECT MATTER OF THIS
AGREEMENT.

Nature of a Contract

One of the principal values of contract law is based on the freedom of
private parties to decide whether to enter a contract on the terms offered
or whether to contract at all.

The Theory of Private Autonomy

This is known as the theory of private autonomy[11]. The theory is based
on the notion that private parties within the economy have the power
to choose with whom, when, and on what terms to alter their legal
relations. Once two or more parties agree to this legal relation, they
assume that the law will provide them with legal recourse. The overwhelming number of contracts never require the intervention of the
courts to settle a dispute between the parties. Most parties perform their

contractual obligations, and the viability of doing business assumes individual compliance of what was agreed.

There is a fundamental policy that underscores contract and commercial transactions. Professor Vaver has expressed the policy in the following fashion: " . . . given justifiable reliance upon the existence of a promise by one party to the knowledge of another, a court will do its utmost to protect the party acting on the faith thereof against a change of heart in the other."[12]

The practical reality of contracts is this notion of reliance on the promise of another. Although, traditionally, the Anglo-Canadian law has paid lip service to the requirement of consideration as an essential ingredient of a contract, as Professor Vaver has pointed out, the modern trend is less concerned with such technicalities. At the root of contract law is the notion of allowing private parties to individually exploit (subject to certain exceptions) their own self-interest, and providing at the same time a climate of certainty and predictability that their expectations will be fulfilled.

Basic Definitions and Terms

There are a number of basic definitions and terms that will assist us in understanding the purpose, function, and scope of the contract law. In the agreements contained in Figures 1.2 through 1.4, the draftsman has used a number of legal terms that define the rights of the other party against Rinehart. Although we will refer to these contracts throughout the contract chapters, select clauses from them as illustrations, and raise questions about the nature and scope of the rights and obligations contained in them, at this point, we will confine our attention to the legal terminology used.

OFFER, ACCEPTANCE, AND CONSIDERATION

The formation of a valid and enforceable contract requires the elements of offer, acceptance, and consideration. However, the words "offer" and "acceptance" are rarely found in a written contract, and do not appear in the contracts set forth in Figures 1.2, 1.3, or 1.4. The underlying assumption is that Rinehart, by communicating the contract to the other party, has "offered" it. When the other party of the contracts in Figures 1.2 or 1.3 signs the contract without any changes, he/she has "accepted" the contract. In the case of Figure 1.4 contract, the acceptance of Rinehart's terms is the buyer's opening of the "shrink-wrapper".

Offer   An offer, which is made by the offeror, contains all the terms in a concrete and definite fashion that the offeror demands in order to sell or buy goods, services, or property. The offer is made to the offeree

FIGURE 1.5 **ELEMENTS OF THE CONTRACT**

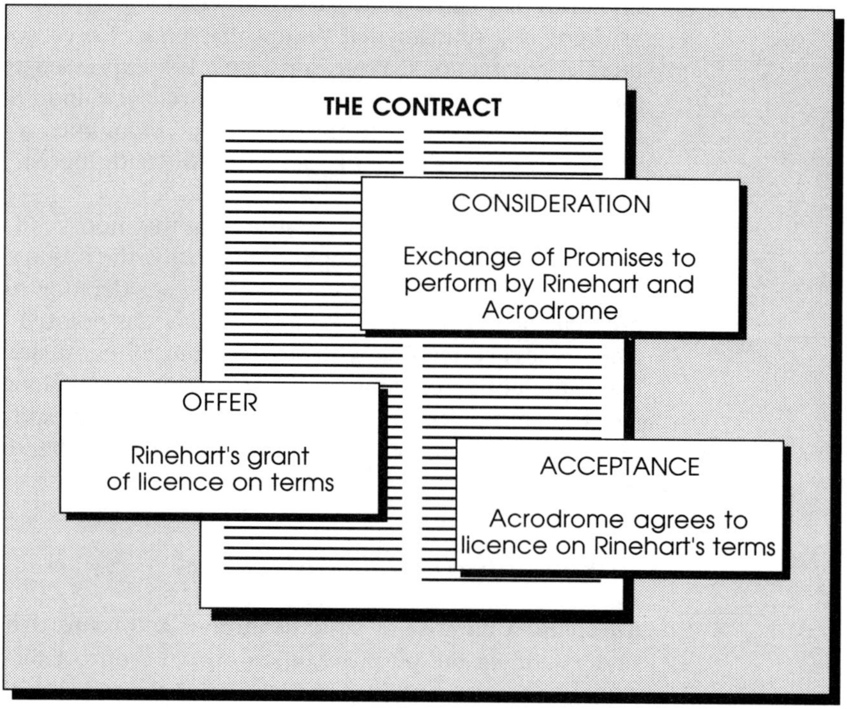

THE CONTRACT

CONSIDERATION

Exchange of Promises to
perform by Rinehart and
Acrodrome

OFFER

Rinehart's grant
of licence on terms

ACCEPTANCE

Acrodrome agrees to
licence on Rinehart's terms

who then can either accept or reject the terms made by the offeror. Where the offeree replies with a new or different set of terms for contracting, this is called a counter-offer and the onus then shifts to the original offeror to accept or reject them.

Acceptance   An offer standing alone does not make a contract. The offer must be accepted by the party to whom it has been communicated. Rinehart, in the case of the Software Licence and Marketing Agreement (Figure 1.2) intends only to enter a contract with Acrodrome Ltd. For example, if by accident the contract was delivered to another company that inserted its name, this would not be an "acceptance" of Rinehart's "offer". The offer is intended only to be made to Acrodrome Ltd., and only that party may accept it. Acrodrome Ltd. would, in most instances, accept the offer by signing the contract.

Until there is an agreement on the terms of contracting, there is no legally enforceable contract between the parties. Once the offer is accepted, then the contract answers the crucial questions concerning the business relationship between Rinehart and Acrodrome. For instance, the contract has a specific period of duration, e.g., five years. The compensation arrangement between the parties is defined in clause 7, which deals with "fees".

Consideration   The doctrine of consideration is designed, at least in part, to separate informal arrangements such as the promise to make a gift from promises that are intended to bind the parties exchanging them. It would be extremely rare to find a business contract failing for lack of consideration. In the Software Licence and Marketing Agreement (Figure 1.2), the consideration of Acrodrome is the performance of all of its obligations under the contract.

For instance, one obligation imposed on Acrodrome is its promise to use its best efforts to promote Rinehart's software in a specified territory. (See clause 2.) There are many more obligations imposed in other clauses of this contract. In return for the performance of Acrodrome's contractual obligations, Rinehart grants Acrodrome an exclusive licence to sell Rinehart software products. This exclusive licence is Rinehart's consideration. Each party has given something of benefit or value in return for something of benefit or value to the other. This is the essence of consideration.

The traditional definition of consideration is contained in the following passage:

> A valuable consideration, in the sense of law, may consist either in some right, interest, profit, or benefit accruing to the one party, or some forbearance, detriment, loss, or responsibility given, suffered, or undertaken by the other. [Courts] will not ask whether the thing which forms the consideration does in fact benefit the promisee or a third party, or is of any substantial value to any one. It is enough that something is promised, done, forborne, or suffered by the party to whom the promise is made as consideration for the promise made to him.[13]

Licence   This is a common term in software contracts. A licence is a limited or restricted right to use or sell the property of another party. For example, **A** may sell his car to **B**. In this instance, **A** has relinquished all rights and interests in the car. In the outright sale, **B** has exclusive title. On the other hand, **A** may have rented his car to **B** for two weeks at $200 per week. During this two-week period, **B**'s right is paramount. At the end of that period, however, unlike the outright sale, **A** has a right to the return of the car. This is the model that lawyers have attempted to modify for software manufacturers, and, in large part, rests upon certain assumptions about the application of copyright law of software products. By licensing the software, the manufacturer retains more "control" over the use (and misuse) of the software.

Warranty Warranty is another term that appears in the Rinehart contracts. A warranty is a seller's obligation about its title to the property sold or licensed, or the quality, condition, or quantity of the goods sold. In the Rinehart Licence Agreement (Figure 1.4), the company, as seller, attempts to eliminate any "warranty" about the quality or condition or performance of its software. The attempt is to shift the risk of the buyer's loss in using the software onto the buyer's shoulders.

Severability The term severability (Figure 1.2, clause 9) is a pair of "legal scissors" that directs to remove any provision of the contract that might make the entire contract unenforceable. For instance, we will assume that on policy grounds a judge would hold the limited warranty in clause 3 as unenforceable. Rather than the entire contract falling with this clause, the severability provision allows the remaining provisions of the contract to remain enforceable and binding.

Binding Agreement Clause 12 of Figure 1.2 is titled "binding agree-ment", and sets forth the extent to which third parties may obtain a benefit under the contract. Rinehart might be the target of a hostile take-over bid by the **XYZ** Company. Clause 12 expressly states that **XYZ** Company, as Rinehart's successor, is entitled to the benefit of the contract. Instead, the **XYZ** Company might have taken over Acrodrome Ltd. In that case, **XYZ** Company is not entitled to the benefits of the exclusive dis-tributorship of Rinehart's software without Rinehart's written consent.

Types of Contracts

Express contract An express contract is an understanding that cre-ates a legally binding and enforceable set of mutual rights and obligations. In a legal sense, it contains all the essential ingredients required to form a contract: offer, acceptance, and consideration. The express contract may be reduced to written form or may be oral. The three contracts set out above are examples of written express contracts. The hallmark of the express contract is the explicit verbalization of the terms of the transaction in such a fashion as to make them specific, definite, and concrete.

Implied contract An implied contract occurs in the absence of such explicit verbalization and is implied in fact from the parties' conduct and the circumstances surrounding the bargain. The dividing line between the non-written express contract and the implied-in-fact contract often becomes blurred in a given factual setting.

In *Canadian Co-operative Implements Limited v. Lou Petit Trucking Ltd.* case,[14] the plaintiff owned a machine used for snow removal, and allowed the defendant to take possession of the machine on a "demon-stration" basis. The intent of the plaintiff was to sell the defendant the

FIGURE 1.6 **TYPES OF CONTRACTS**

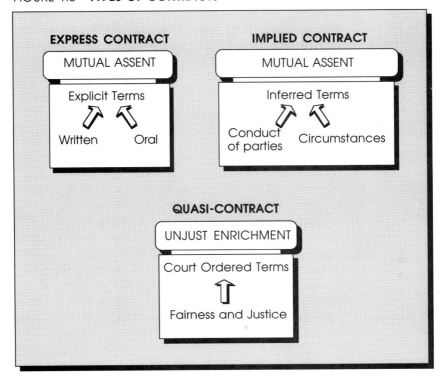

machine. The sale was not completed at the time of delivery because of the mechanical difficulties in the machine. The defendant took possession in October 1977. The intent of the defendant was to purchase the machine if it proved to be satisfactory. When the defendant continued to retain possession of the machine for a number of months, the plaintiff sent invoices charging them for the rental use of the machine. The evidence indicated that the defendant recognized his/her liability to the machine owner for the use of the machine.

The court found that between November 21, 1977, and February 10, 1978, the defendant allowed the City of Winnipeg to use the plaintiff's machine for snow removal and received nearly $18 000 from the City. But the defendant argued that he had no liability to pay the plaintiff any rental for using the machine. That is, he argued that they had no contract. The basis of their agreement was solely limited to a free trial use of the machine on a demonstration basis. There was no evidence of an express agreement as to the payment of rent at the time the defendant took possession of the machine. Moreover, there was no written agreement covering rent between the parties.

Clearly there was a contract respecting the demonstration use of the machine. But was there a contract entitling the plaintiff to compensation for the use of their machine after the demonstration period? If so, is the contract an express or implied-in-fact contract? The court found that both parties intended the demonstration period to terminate at the end of November 1977. From the conduct of the plaintiff submitting written invoices demanding rental payment and the defendant using the machine on a commercial basis after receiving a demand for payment, the court concluded there was an express agreement on the basis of the plaintiff's regular monthly rental for the machine. Given these facts, the court might have inferred from the conduct and circumstances of the parties that there was a contract implied-in-fact.

Quasi-contract   There is a third category of potential liability sometimes termed "quasi-contract". This category is often pleaded where the express contract is defective or unenforceable or there is insufficient evidence to justify the finding of a contract implied-in-fact. The modern trend is to dispense with the term quasi-contract because the term misleads one into believing that liability is based on contract principles. In place of quasi-contract, the courts presently use the term "unjust enrichment", which is defined as liability to compensate a party who has furnished a benefit but cannot establish a valid contract. In a case such as *Canadian Co-operative*, the court may employ unjust enrichment as an alternative, non-contractual basis of liability.

Unjust enrichment is discussed in the following passage from *Canadian Co-operative*:[15]

> If I had not found there was an agreement by the defendant to pay for the use of the machine, I would have imposed liability on the defendant on the basis of unjust enrichment. The basis of the principle of unjust enrichment is set out in the text *Unjust Enrichment* (1983 Ed.) by George B. Klippert at pp. 37–8 as follows: 'The control devices underlying the principle of unjust enrichment in Canadian law might be reformulated in the following fashion:
> (i) that the defendant received a benefit at the plaintiff's expense,
> (ii) evidence of volition in the receipt or retention of the benefit,
> (iii) that the benefit was not voluntarily conferred, and
> (iv) that the benefit is unjustly retained by the defendant.'

Thus, in the absence of a common intention to contract for the machine, liability is imposed on the grounds that by using the machine the defendant obtained a benefit — the payment from the City of Winnipeg — the defendant obtained the benefit at the plaintiff's expense and continues to retain it, and the plaintiff expected to receive payment for use of the machine. In these circumstances, the benefit is unjustly retained by the defendant and the law will impose an obligation on him to compensate the plaintiff for that benefit.

Problems for Discussion

1. Why isn't it in the interests of a company to negotiate detailed contracts with their suppliers?

2. What is the relationship between the unwritten law of business practice and the law of contract?

3. What are the recurring terms in the Rinehart contracts (Figures 1.2, 1.3, and 1.4)? *warranty, termination*

4. What is the main distinction in business perspective between a commercial and consumer contract?

5. Explain the apparent contradiction between the statement by the General Counsel of IBM that 60 000 contracts are made each year with the empirical research of Macaulay, and Beale and Dugdale that formal, legalized contracts are the exception to the rule.

6. How does the offeree of the Rinehart Licence Agreement (Figure 1.4) accept the terms of the contract? How is acceptance different from that for the Distributor in Figure 1.2 or the Consultant in Figure 1.3?

7. What is the purpose in Figure 1.4 of clause 8 titled "Acknowledgment"?

8. Assume that the contract (Figure 1.4) is enclosed in the software in such a fashion that it cannot be read before it is purchased. The consumer, therefore, reads the terms only after paying for the software. What implications does this have for the enforceability of the terms of the contract against the consumer?

9. What terms form the offer and acceptance in Figure 1.2?

10. Where is the consideration for the contracts in Figures 1.2, 1.3, and 1.4? (In particular, compare the drafting technique to cover the consideration issue in Figure 1.3.)

11. Distinguish quasi-contract from unjust enrichment.

12. What is the relationship between the law of contract and unjust enrichment?

Chapter 1 Notes

1. Macaulay, "Non-Contractual Relations in Business: A Preliminary Study," *American Social Review*, Vol. 28 (1963), pp. 55, 61. See also, Beale and Dugdale, "Contract Between Business Men: Planning and The Use of Contractual Remedies," *British Journal of Law & Society*, Vol. 2 (1975), p. 45.
2. *Ibid.*, p. 62.

3. "Report on Sale of Goods," Ontario Law Reform Commission, Vol. 1, (1979), p. 25.
4. Friedman and Macaulay, "Contract Law and Contract Teaching: Past, Present and Future," *Wisconsin Law Review*, Vol. 805 (1967), pp. 815–16.
5. See, note 3, *supra*, at footnote 2.
6. *Ibid.*, p. 817.
7. Pollock, *Principles of Contract*, 9th ed. (1921), Preface.
8. Murray, "A Corporate Counsel's Perspective of the 'Battle of the Forms' ", Ziegel, ed., Papers and Comments delivered at the 9th Annual Workshop on Commercial and Consumer Law (1981).
9. *Ibid.*, p. 146.
10. *Ibid.*, p. 148.
11. See Fuller, "Consideration and Forms," *Columbia Law Review*, Vol. 41 (1941), p. 799.
12. Vaver, "Battle of the Forms: a Comment on Professor Shanker's Views," Ziegel, ed., Papers and Comments delivered at the 9th Annual Workshop on Commercial and Consumer Law (1981), p. 138.
13. *Hamer v. Sidway*, (1891) 27 N.E. 256 (Ct.App.N.Y.).
14. (1983) 27 Man.R.(2) 177 (Man.Q.B.).
15. *Ibid.*, p. 181.

2 FORMATION OF THE CONTRACT

Manifestation of Mutual Assent

In Canadian law, a contract is formed when two or more parties show their mutual assent. The key phrase "manifestation of mutual assent" is derived from the overt acts of the parties, i.e., their conduct, oral or written statements. Mutual assent is determined by an objective standard. In other words, it is what the parties actually said or did, rather than their "motives" for saying or doing something — such as signing a contract. For example, when the President of Lindsay Software Distributors Ltd. signs a software consulting agreement (Figure 1.3), it shows an objective intention to bind the company to the contract. At the same time, the President of Lindsay may have thought to himself: "I'm signing this contract as a practical joke. Tomorrow, I'll tell the people at Rinehart and we can all have a big laugh." This subjective intention, i.e., the unexpressed motive to "play a joke" is ignored, and Rinehart is entitled to rely on the objective intention, i.e, the signing of the contract by an authorized officer, and hold Lindsay to the contract.

Mutuality of Assent

Assent occurs when one party makes an offer to another who accepts the offer. The mutuality of assent results because the party making an offer manifests intent to contract, and the party accepting the offer manifests intent by accepting the offer. Typically, parties manifest their mutual assent by either making a promise or rendering a performance. The promise or performance forms a binding contract upon acceptance of the offer.

For example, in the Software Consulting Agreement (Figure 1.3), both Rinehart and Lindsay Software Distributors make written promises about the software program. Rinehart's assent to its promises is derived from the written agreement that its lawyer drafted and forms an offer to Lindsay. Similarly, Lindsay's assent to the Software Consulting Agreement is derived from conduct that indicates acceptance of the Rinehart offer. For example, an officer of Lindsay who signed the contract would be manifesting the intention of the company to be bound. Mutuality is present because both Rinehart and Lindsay have assented to be bound by the identical contract.

Communication of Assent

Communication of the parties' intention is essential to the formation of a binding contract. The general rule is set forth in *Thierry v. Thierry*:

> The intention of a person can be ascertained by another only by means of outward expressions either words or acts as a nod or the fall of the hammer at an auction; and for the purpose of agreement there must be a communication of intention between them by means of such expressions. Accordingly the law judges of the intention of a person by outward expressions only and it judges of an agreement between two persons exclusively from those expressions of their intentions which are communicated between them, unless there is a duty to speak in which event a party may become bound by his silence. Consequently an intention not expressed or not communicated or communicated to a third person is, in general, inoperative and immaterial to the question of agreement.[1]

The Acceptance Rule

An acceptance must be absolute and unequivocal. This rule, however, is modified by the caveat that "it is equally clear that such an acceptance need not be in express terms and may be found in the language and conduct of the acceptor."[2] Instead of a formalistic approach, the courts evaluate the acceptor's language. As a matter of construction, a determination is made as to whether the language amounts to an unequivocal acceptance. For example, assume that the President of Lindsay, Page Hall, wrote at the bottom of the contract: "I disagree with the $100 000 amount in clause 4, and want $150 000 instead" — and then signed his name to the contract. Hall has not accepted Rinehart's offer, but has made a new and different offer.

In some cases, an examination of the communications between the offeror and offeree indicate an absence of intention to conclude a contract. The requirement of an absolute and unequivocal acceptance allows the court to determine whether the parties intended their communications to be the basis for negotiations for a future contract.[3] The main concern is whether there is clear evidence that the parties have agreed upon the terms of a contract.

Where the offer is silent on what the acceptor must do for acceptance, then his conduct will be the equivalent to acceptance.[4] For example, Lindsay might accept the software consulting agreement by starting to work on developing the software. But Lindsay must bring notice of its conduct to the attention of Rinehart. It is not enough for Lindsay to put the written contract on the shelf, and then to secretly start to work on the project and expect a court to find that this amounts to acceptance and binds Rinehart to the contract.

The Period of Time to Accept

Once the offer has terminated, the acceptor has lost his power to accept the offer. The offer may be terminated in a number of circumstances: (i) lapse of time; (ii) revocation by the offeror; (iii) rejection; (iv) counter-offer; (v) death or incapacity of the offeror or offeree.

LAPSE OF TIME

The time during which an offer remains open for acceptance is based on either an express limitation imposed by the offeror, or on a reasonable period after the offer has been made. For instance, the offeror may state that the offer is open for a period of ten days from communication to the offeree. Should the offeree "accept" the offer on the eleventh day, there is no contract between the parties. The power to accept the offer has lapsed and the offer no longer has legal existence.

In the absence of an express time limitation, the courts treat the duration of the offer as existing for a reasonable time. What is a reasonable time is a question of fact and is resolved by considering the relevant circumstances at the time the offer was made and the acceptance attempted.[5] Among the factors considered by the court are: the purpose of the contract and parties, trade usage and custom, and prior dealings between the parties.

For example, assuming the Software Consulting Agreement (Figure 1.3) did not have a time limitation for Lindsay's acceptance, it is likely that Lindsay would have a relatively short period of time for acceptance. That contract requires Lindsay to furnish services in a highly competitive and fast-changing marketplace. But the period would likely be shorter if the offer were a commodity such as gold, which changes value on the international markets by the hour.

REVOCATION

The offeror may communicate to the offeree — before acceptance is made — that he/she has revoked the offer. A revocation is the cancellation or withdrawal of an offer prior to acceptance. This voids the offeree's power of acceptance.

The power of revocation is lost where the offeror has made the offer under seal, or where the offeree has been granted an option that operates to keep the offer open. For example, Rinehart pays Henry Gear $1000 for a ninety-day option to purchase a warehouse in London, Ontario, at a price of $350 000. What Rinehart has "bought" with the option is a right to "accept" Gear's offer to sell for $350 000 during a ninety-day period, and Gear has sold for $1000 his right to cancel or withdraw his offer until the expiration of that period.

REJECTION

The offeree's power of acceptance is lost when he rejects the offer.[6] The rejection is the manifestation of the offeree's unwillingness to contract with the offeror. Evidence of rejection may be expressed or implied from the conduct or words of the offeree. The rejection is effective to terminate the offer at the moment it is received by the offeror. Thus, where the offeree mails his rejection, and two days later (after a change of heart) telephones his acceptance of the offer, there is a contract if the offeror has not received the rejection. The mailbox rule states that a mailed acceptance is not effective until actual delivery to the offeror. Although the acceptance letter is in transit, the offeree can communicate either his acceptance or rejection of the offer at any time before the letter is delivered to the offeror.

COUNTER-OFFERS

A counter-offer is a continuation of the bargaining or negotiating process. The offeree wants a contract with the offeror but not on the terms set forth. The counter-offer, like the rejection, terminates the offer. But unlike the rejection, the counter-offer gives the original offeror the power to accept the counter-offer and thus agree to the new terms proposed.

In an earlier example, the President of Lindsay, Page Hall, wrote in a clause at the bottom of the Software Consulting Agreement. This hand-written addition to the contract changed the amount of Lindsay's fee from $100 000 to $150 000. The effect of the change was to present Rinehart Ltd. with a counter-offer. Rinehart would then have to decide whether to accept Lindsay's counter-offer or not.

DEATH OR INCAPACITY

The power to accept an offer terminates upon the death or incapacity of the offeror or offeree. One explanation of the rule is based on the historical ground that common law judges required a "meeting of minds" to form a contract. Death prevents actual mental assent. But most contracts are enforceable against the estate of the deceased offeror or offeree. Also, a binding option is enforceable against the estate of the party granting it. In most cases, however, the courts have been unwilling to construe an offer by a person who dies as continuing to be an offer by his estate.

Similarly, the incapacity of the offeror or offeree will normally terminate the power of acceptance. For instance, the intervening mental illness of the offeror would terminate the offeree's power of acceptance.

Battle of the Forms

The battle of the forms describes the "paper" war involving the exchange of standard form contracts — each with different terms — between sellers and buyers of goods and services. For example, Rinehart Ltd. delivers a copy of the Software Consulting Agreement (Figure 1.3) to Lindsay. An officer of Rinehart Ltd. has signed on behalf of the company. Lindsay returns a copy of the agreement that is drafted in different language and contains some different terms. An officer of Lindsay has signed on behalf of that company. This is a common occurrence in many business transactions. It is not surprising, therefore, to find that a considerable body of case law has emerged to define the rights and obligations of parties who are combatants in the battle of the forms.

The Mirror Image Rule

The mirror image rule developed by the common law courts required that both parties bargaining for goods or services must agree on every term before there is a binding contract. Where one party offers to contract on one set of terms and the other counter-offers on terms that deviate, then there can be no contract. The Lindsay change of the fee amount is a good example. There is no contract between Rinehart and Lindsay because they disagreed on one term.

The rationale for the rule is the need to ensure that the parties have true consensus *ad idem*, i.e., mutual consent to the terms of the agreement. The minds of the parties must meet. This will not occur if, for example, one or both parties are still negotiating for better terms.[7]

The common law rule was strict. No contract was made where the offer and the acceptance were inconsistent. Of course, it is possible that the offer is written and the acceptance is oral. If the oral acceptance mirrors the written offer, there is a contract. The offer can be accepted by conduct, unaccompanied by either an oral or a written acceptance.[8]

Application of Mirror Image Rule

The mirror image rule has been called a "paradigm of legal formality".[9] The formality results from placing the offer and acceptance side by side and looking to whether the terms mirror one another. Where the acceptance contains terms that do not mirror the offer, it becomes a counter-offer. If the original offeror performed on the basis of the counter-offer, he would be deemed to have accepted the terms of the counter-offer and his original offer would have been spent. Controversy over the arbitrariness or unfairness of the mirror image rule has continued for many years.

Perhaps the best view[10] is one of reasonableness, i.e., whether the parties have proceeded on the basis that they are contractually bound even though they have not agreed to all the essential terms of the bargain. The courts will also protect the justifiable reliance of one party who, on reliance on a promise, makes substantial expenditure of time, capital, and labour to the knowledge of the person who has made the promise.

THE EFFECT OF CONFLICTING FORMS

The effect of conflicting forms was discussed in *Tywood Industries Ltd. v. St. Anne-Nackawic Pulp & Paper Co. Ltd.*[11] In that case, the defendant company (buyer) invited the plaintiff company (seller) to tender for the sale of storage tanks. An agreement was reached as to specifications and price, and three storage tanks were delivered to the defendant. The defendant stopped payment for the third tank complaining about deficiencies in operation. The plaintiff then sued for the balance owing them under the contract, and the defendant applied for an order staying the action on the grounds the contract contained a clause providing for arbitration of disputes. The issue was whether in the exchange of standard forms the defendant's form incorporating an arbitration clause became the contract between the parties.

Each party attempted to impose its terms on the other. In holding that the arbitration clause in the defendant's standard form did not apply, the court stated:[12]

> I have the greatest doubt that the plaintiff put its mind to the question at all. Certainly it tried (perhaps not consciously) to impose its non-arbitrable condition upon the defendant when it quoted its price originally, it at no time acknowledged the supremacy of the defendant's terms. On the other hand, the defendant (again perhaps not consciously) did try to impose the arbitration term in the purchase orders, but it drew no particular attention to the term. Nor did it complain when the plaintiff failed to return the vendor's copy of the purchase orders with an acknowledgment of the terms sought to be imposed. This was a commercial transaction and terms might well have been expected, but the conduct of both parties seems to me to indicate that neither party considered any terms other than those found on the face of the documents (i.e., the specifications and the price) important. What was important to both was the consummation of the business deal that had been arranged between them.

In the United States, the emphasis is on "the bargain of the parties in fact".[13] The factual bargain requires an inquiry beyond the written documents exchanged between the parties, and includes their course of dealing and custom of the trade. It has been argued that this loose, open-ended approach to finding an in-fact-bargain between the parties promotes important values underlying commercial transactions: "good faith, conscionability, commercial reasonableness and realism."[14] The American position begs an important issue: whether the mirror image rule has indeed systematically invalidated factual bargains. The case law indicates that, by and large, this has not occurred.

The Anglo-Canadian view, however, is based on the foundation that these values can be achieved by applying the conventional rules of the common law. Thus, Lord Diplock in *Gibson v. Manchester City Council*[15] applied the conventional rule to the documents relied on as forming a contract between the parties. On this basis, the so-called offer, which provided that the vendor "may be prepared to sell", was found fatal to finding that the letter constituted a contractual offer. The conventional approach is to consider the writing and determine whether there is a contract.

ABOLITION OF THE MIRROR IMAGE RULE

In the United States, the mirror image rule has been abolished.[16] One observer noted that "the whole thrust of section 2-207 is the prevention of the unfair 'surprise and hardship' that occurs under a mechanical application of the mirror image rule."[17] Another point of view on the section is that in place of the formal common law rules of offer and acceptance, the legislation adopts an open-ended standard requiring the court to determine if from the "gist of the parties' communications" they intended to contract.[18]

The statutory abolition does stop either the offeror or offeree from using the appropriate "magic language" to contract out of the legislation and make the mirror image rule apply to their contract.[19]

Most legal commentators acknowledge that business people do not read printed forms; and if they read them, they probably do not understand the printed terms. Thus, what should the court do when a seller includes a printed term that expressly makes the buyer's acceptance conditional on agreeing to different or additional terms imposed by the seller? The courts employ either an unconscionability or surprise rule to make the harsh terms unenforceable against the offeree. The question remains as to whether a counter-offer is effective.

DICKERED TERMS

Parties to a contract typically negotiate certain terms of their exchange. These dickered terms include the price, quantity, and financing. The non-dickered terms include exclusionary clauses, liquidated damages clauses, and arbitration clauses. These non-dickered terms are often found in the boiler-plate provisions in a standard form contract. "Boiler-plate" is a term applied to contract language that is used most often by a company for a large number of consumer transactions. Rinehart's Licence Agreement (Figure 1.4) includes clauses on "warranty" and "copyright", among other terms, that are included in every sale of the software to a consumer. There is no bargaining with the consumer over these clauses.

In most cases these boiler-plate clauses are neither read nor understood by the party entering into the contract. In Chapter 8, we will examine the Canadian cases that have held that where the terms of the printed form are so bizarre or unreasonable as to catch the non-drafting party by surprise, they are not enforceable. A similar rule may be found in the United States.[20]

Unilateral Contracts

A bilateral contract results from an exchange of promises between the offeror and offeree. A unilateral contract depends upon the offeree performing a particular act requested by the offeror. Whether the acceptor of the offer is required to make a promise or perform an act is generally a matter of interpretation. The courts, however, lean in favor of bilateral contracts "since in a bilateral contract both parties are protected from a period prior to the beginning of performance on either side — that is from the making of mutual promises."[21]

In the unilateral contract, there is no contract until the acceptor has performed in accordance with the tenor of the offer. "In 'unilateral contracts' the offeror contemplates not the creation of mutual promises, but the dependence of his own promise upon the offeree's performance of 'an act'."[22]

There is a major distinction between the unilateral and bilateral contract at the moment of formation of the contract. The bilateral contract is formed at the moment the promises are exchanged between the offeror and offeree. The unilateral contract, however, which can only be accepted by complete performance, is formed only after the acceptor has acted. The courts have taken a pragmatic approach to fit the facts of particular cases into the classical theories of offer, acceptance, and consideration. One court has observed the difficulty of applying these theories to the many common daily forms of contracting, e.g., "sales at auction; supermarket purchases; boarding an omnibus; purchasing a train ticket; tenders for the supply of goods; offers of rewards; acceptance by post; warranties of authority by agents; manufacturers' guarantees; gratuitous bailments; bankers' commercial credits."[23]

Illustration A common example of a unilateral contract is the offer for reward. Rinehart Ltd. offers a reward for information leading to the conviction of anyone unlawfully copying one of their copyrighted software programs. Jones, a software pirate, duplicates without permission a copy of Real Estate Investment System and sells it to Smith. Bates, a colleague of Smith, who has read the offer-of-reward ad placed by Rinehart Ltd. in a computing magazine, learns of Jones' activity. He phones Ms. Bach and provides her with information about the Jones and Smith transaction. Jones is later convicted of theft. Bates is entitled to claim the $1000 reward. The contract has been formed on the basis of Bates' performance, which operates as an acceptance of the Rinehart offer.

The Defence of *non est factum*

In some cases, a person might claim that he is not bound by the contract because when he accepted the offer he either didn't read the contract, or, if he did read it, he did not understand it. The argument rarely succeeds. The party taking this position normally relies upon the doctrine of *non est factum*. However, the courts have been cautious in applying the doctrine. The term *non est factum* is given meaning in the following passage:

> Their Lordships wish to add that, in a case where the person executing a deed is neither blind nor illiterate, where no fraudulent misrepresentation is made to him, where he has ample opportunity of reading the deed, and such knowledge of its purport that the plea of *non est factum* is not open to him, it is quite immaterial whether he reads the deed or not. He is bound by the deed, because it operates as a conclusive bar against him — not because he has read it or understands it, but because he has chosen to execute it.[24]

The effect of a successful *non est factum* defence is to render the entire contract void. The contract is said to be void *ab initio*, i.e., from the beginning. The burden of establishing a successful *non est factum* defence is difficult. The courts have formulated the burden of proof in the following fashion:

> What has to be established, if the plea of *non est factum* is to succeed, is that the misrepresentation which caused the signature was a misrepresentation of the character and class of document in question, and not a misrepresentation simply as to its contents. The distinction is not easy to define because the character and class of a document may be said in one sense to depend on its contents, so that a misrepresentation of the contents inevitably involves a misrepresentation of the character and class.[25]

A car dealer requested a customer on a hire-purchase agreement to sign what he called a release note clearing the customer from liability on the automobile. Actually, the customer signed an indemnity form making the customer a surety in the resale of the automobile to another party. The surety was not enforceable on the grounds of *non est factum.* Similarly, where the defendant was asked to sign a paper represented to deal with insurance and in fact signed a guarantee of another's debt, the plea of *non est factum* succeeded.

Problems for Discussion

1. Both parties were in the business of renting heavy earth-moving equipment. The defendant had a project to drain a marshy piece of ground. They contacted the plaintiff and requested immediate delivery of a dragline crane. The agreement was made over the telephone; a formal contract was not signed, nor was there any mention of specific terms. Both parties used an industry-approved standard form contract, however, that included specific terms covering the use and care of the rented machinery. In prior transactions, the parties had used such standard forms with one another, and a term of that agreement provided that the party renting the machinery was liable to indemnify the owner against all expenses in connection with the use. The defendant, in this case, however, using the crane without signing the standard form contract, had an accident and the crane sank into the marshy ground. The plaintiff contended that the indemnity term of the standard form contract applied even though the defendant had not signed it and had not, over the telephone, agreed to an indemnity term. Assume the damage to the crane was not the result of the defendant's negligence. Is the plaintiff entitled to enforce the indemnity clause in this case? See *British Crane Hire Corporation Ltd. v. Ipswich Plant Hire Ltd.*, (1974) 1 All E.R. 1059 (C.A.).

2. Rinehart Ltd. placed an order for 2000 diskettes with the **MTZ** Company. The diskettes were used by Rinehart Ltd. for the videogames *Space Attack* and *Fight of the Titans*. Within one week, Rinehart began receiving complaints from consumers that the games did not operate properly. A later analysis by the Research and Development Department indicated a latent defect in the diskette. Rinehart Ltd. seeks compensation from **MTZ** arising from the loss in using the diskettes. **MTZ** Company defends on the basis that after receiving the order from Rinehart Ltd. they sent a printed form that included this clause:

> Due to the variable conditions under which these goods may be transported, stored, handled, or used, Seller hereby expressly excludes any and all warranties, guaranties, or representations whatsoever. Buyer assumes risk for results obtained from use of these goods, whether used alone or in combination with other products. Seller's liability hereunder shall be limited to replacement of any goods that materially differ from the Seller's

sample order on the basis of which the order for such goods was made.

Rinehart Ltd. conceded that they did not protest **MTZ**'s attempt to limit its liability, and paid for the diskettes after they were received. It is also conceded that Rinehart Ltd. had notice of this clause when they accepted the goods. What is the basis of the contract between the parties? Is exclusionary clause part of that contract? See *Roto-Lith, Ltd. v. F.P. Bartlett & Co.*, 297 F.2d 497 (1st Cir. 1962).

3. In the battle of the forms, are there separate considerations that apply to the seller's attempt to impose an arbitration clause in the printed form sent to the buyer who has placed an order? See *Tywood Industries v. St. Anne-Nackawic Pulp & Paper*, (1979) 100 D.L.R. (3d) 374 (Ont. H.C.); and *Doughboy Industries Inc.*, 17 A.D. (2d) 216, 233 N.Y.S. (2d) 488 (S.C., App. Div. 1962).

4. Rinehart Ltd. entered into negotiation with Gilbert Turner Ltd. for the lease of a warehouse. Rinehart Ltd. desired a five-year lease of the warehouse, which was to be used for storage of inventory. During the negotiations, Rinehart Ltd. emphasized that the warehouse would require substantial alterations, including a "clean room" for the storage of diskettes. The parties agreed to the term and the rent, but negotiations continued on Rinehart Ltd.'s request for an option to purchase. Meanwhile, in anticipation of the lease, Gilbert Turner Ltd. began to make a number of alterations to the warehouse. Later, through no fault of either party, the negotiations broke down and Rinehart Ltd. was unwilling to sign a lease. Gilbert Turner Ltd. claimed the expenses incurred in altering the warehouse according to the specifications demanded by Rinehart Ltd. Is Rinehart Ltd. liable to pay the cost of the renovations? See *Brewer Street Investments Ltd. v. Barclays Woollen Co. Ltd.*, (1954) 1 Q.B. 428 (C.A.).

5. Is the decision in *Tywood Industries Ltd.* consistent with the mirror image rule of the common law? Is it important that the clause in issue is a risk-shifting provision? What onus is placed on the party placing a risk-shifting provision such as a disclaimer, exemption, arbitration or exclusionary clause in the contract. See *Curtis v. Chemical Cleaning & Dyeing Co.*, (1951) 1 K.B. 805 (C.A.)? Is there a distinction between consumer and commercial transactions when the court determines the enforceability of such a clause? (See *O'Connor Real Estate Ltd. v. Flynn*, (1969) 3 D.L.R. (3d) 345, 356 for the quote from Denning's judgment.)

6. What arguments can be advanced against the approach adopted by the Court of Appeal of New York in *Poel v. Brunswich-Balke-Collender Co.*?

Chapter 2 Notes

1. (1956) 18 W.W.R. 127, 131 per Martin, C.J.S.
2. *Dawson v. Helicopter Exploration Co.*, (1955) 5 D.L.R. (3d) 404, 413 (S.C.C.).
3. See *Harvey v. Perry*, (1953) 1 S.C.R. 233 (S.C.C.).
4. See *Hamilton Gear & Machine Co. v. Lewis*, (1924) 3 D.L.R. 367, 369-70 (Ont. S.C.).
5. See *Restatement of the Law of Contracts*, 2nd ed., Vol. 1. (1981), s. 41(2); and Waddams, *The Law of Contracts*, (1977), pp. 71–72.
6. Restatement, *supra*, s.38(1).
7. See *Harvey v. Perry, supra*, note 3, p. 242.
8. See for example, *Saint-John Tug Boat Co. Ltd. v. Irving Refining Ltd.*, (1964) S.C.R. 614 (S.C.C.).
9. Baird and Weisberg, "Rules, Standards, and the Battle of the Forms: A Reassessment of s.2-207", (1982) 68 *Virginia L. Rev.*, pp. 1217, 1231.
10. See *Vaver, "Battle of the Forms: A Comment on Professor Shanker's Views"*, Vol. 4 *Can. Bus. Law. J.* pp. 277, 279.
11. (1979) 100 D.L.R. (3d) 374 (Ont. H.C.).
12. *Ibid.*, p. 377.
13. U.C.C. s. 1-201(3).
14. Murray, "Section 2-207 of the Uniform Commercial Code: Another Word About Incipient Unconscionability", 39 *Univ. Pitts. Law Rev.* pp. 597 & 600.
15. (1979) 1 All. E.R. 972 (H.L.).
16. U.C.C. s. 2-207(1), (2).
17. Murray, "The Standardized Agreement Phenomena in the Restatement (Second) of Contracts", 67 *Cornell L. Rev.* 735, 751.
18. Baird and Wiesberg, *supra* note 9, p. 1237.
19. See Shanker, "Contract by Disagreement!?" (Reflections on U.C.C. 2-207) (1976) *Commercial Law J.* pp. 453 & 457.
20. See Restatement (Second) of Contracts s. 237 (2), (3) (Tent. Draft No. 5, 1970).
21. *Williston on Contract*, Vol. 1, at 76–77, cited with approval by the Supreme Court of Canada in *Dawson v. Helicopter Exploration Co.*, (1955) 5 D.L.R. 404, 411.
22. *Controlled Parking Systems Ltd. v. Sedgewick*, (1980) 4 W.W.R. 425, 430 (Sask.Dist.Ct.).
23. *New Zealand Shipping Co. v. A.M. Satterthwaite & Co.*, (1975) A.C. 154, 167, (1974) 1 All E.R. 1015 (P.C.).
24. *Cashin v. Cashin*, (1938) 1 All E.R. 536, 545 per Lord Maugham.
25. *Muskam Finance, Ltd. v. Howard*, (1963) 1 All E.R. 81 (C.A.).

3 CONSIDERATION

Tests for Consideration

Consideration is an essential ingredient of a contract. It may be generally defined as promises that have legal consequences. The main legal consequences for this type of broken promise are either to award the innocent party money compensation for his loss, or to compel the promise breaker to perform his promise. In this chapter, our main focus is on the "tests" used by the courts to determine whether there is the consideration required to form a contract.

Consideration has had three different legal definitions. It is important to examine each definition. The flexibility (or alternative rigidity) of our definition operates to expand or constrict the types of transactions that a court will label a contract. The more flexible and open-ended our definition of consideration, the more *discretion* a court has to conclude that a party's particular words or conduct amounted to a contractual promise.

FORMULATION #1
One English authority defines consideration in connection with the making of promises as "the price paid by the plaintiff for the defendant's promise . . . ."[1] Payment is not restricted to money alone: Payment can also come in the form of a product or service.

FORMULATION #2
Another equally influential English scholar supports the conventional meaning of consideration: "Consideration is either some detriment to the promisee (in that he may give value) or some benefit to the promisor (in that he may receive value)."[2]

FORMULATION #3
The last formulation has had considerable influence in Anglo-Canadian law, and is found in *Thomas v. Thomas*,[3] where Patterson J. said: "Con-

sideration means something which is of some value in the eye of the law, moving from the plaintiff; it may be some detriment to the plaintiff, or some benefit to the defendant; but at all events it must be moving from the plaintiff."

The third formulation has operated to effectively prevent third parties who were the recipients of a promise but had not furnished consideration from enforcing the contract. Thus, where Alison paid money to Ben for Ben's promise to work as a software engineer for Rinehart Ltd., and Ben breaches his promise, Rinehart Ltd. could not successfully sue Ben. Rinehart Ltd. fails because they did not provide consideration for Ben's promise. There are two promises at issue: (i) the promise the plaintiff received from the defendant; and (ii) the promise moving from the plaintiff to the defendant. The promisee must demonstrate that consideration (e.g., a product or service) moved from him/her to the defendant. Without such evidence the action based on the defendant's promise will fail.

In the commercial context, where the parties exchange standard form contracts, the problem of consideration rarely surfaces. There are several reasons for the absence of the problem. First, regardless of the formulation of consideration adopted, the courts are making judgments about what type of promises are enforceable. In the business context, promises are invariably intended to be enforceable. Starting with this presumption, the defendant-businessperson will have difficulty defeating the plaintiff-businessperson's claim for breach of contract on the grounds that the promise enforced by the plaintiff is unsupported by consideration. A second reason is that this class of contracts, which is usually professionally drafted, expressly recites the consideration for the transaction. Generally, these recitals are the mutual reciprocal promises between the parties.

Most consideration problems are found outside commercial transactions. The vast majority of modern disputes arise in instances of informal promises unsupported by consideration. **A** promises to make a gift to **B** and later changes his mind. As there is no consideration supporting **A**'s promise, **B** cannot enforce it. Often, there is a family or personal connection between the parties in such circumstances. There is, however, the occasional spill-over into the business context.

Illustration   The president of Rinehart Ltd., Paul Faber, allowed his nephew, John, to work for the marketing department for a two-week period prior to Christmas. John approached his uncle and requested the chance to learn first hand how to launch a marketing campaign. John, a third-year commerce student, agreed to work for "free" for the two-week period. After the two weeks, his uncle promised to pay him $500 for his excellent contribution to the marketing campaign. On New Years' Day, John and his uncle had a falling out. His uncle now refuses to pay the $500. John would fail to enforce the contract because there is no consideration to support his uncle's promise to pay the $500.

The reality of the marketplace makes this problem remote. The motives of business people, however, are generally clear. When the issue of consideration does arise in a commercial context, it generally concerns promises or representations made after the written contract is signed. A business transaction is rarely static. Circumstances, markets, and costs fluctuate, and one party may have a compelling reason to modify his/her performance or that of the other party. During the course of performance, the parties may agree to alteration or extensions. Are these promises outside of the contract enforceable? In the last section of this chapter, this issue will be discussed under the heading of Equitable Estoppel.

At this juncture, it is useful to examine the oral modification of contractual promises. The basic issue is whether modifications of an existing contract are supported by consideration and thus enforceable. A good example of the problem is found in *Gilbert Steel Ltd. v. University Construction Ltd.*[4] In this case, the plaintiff was contractually obliged to deliver fabricated steel to the defendant. The defendant planned to erect apartment buildings on three sites. Before the plaintiff began construction on one of the sites, the steel mill owners raised the price of steel.

Later the prices were increased again. An oral agreement reached between the parties required the defendant to pay a price higher than in the original contract. Later, the plaintiff sued for damages based on breach of the oral agreement. The defendant's contention was that there was an absence of consideration to support the oral agreement. Wilson J.A. gave the following judgment for the Ontario Court of Appeal:

> Counsel for the defendant submitted at the trial that past consideration is no consideration and that the plaintiff was already obliged before the alleged oral agreement was entered into to deliver the steel at the original prices agreed to in the written contract of October 22, 1961. Where then was the *quid pro quo* for the defendant's promise to pay more?
>
> Counsel for the plaintiff sought to supply this omission from the evidence of Hersz Tenebaum who, during the course of discussions which took place in September, 1970, with a view to a contract for the supply of steel for the second building at the University site, asked whether the plaintiff would give him "a good price" on steel for this building. Plaintiff's counsel argued that the promise of a good price on the second building was the consideration the defendant received for agreeing to pay the increased price on the first. The trial Judge rejected this submission and found the oral agreement unenforceable for want of consideration.
>
> The consideration for this new oral agreement, submitted Mr. Morphy [Counsel for the plaintiff], was the mutual agreement to abandon the previous written contract and to assume the obligations under the new oral one. Mr. Morphy submitted to the Court for its consideration two lines of authority, the first line illustrated by the

leading case of *Stilk v. Myrick*, (1809) 2 Camp. 317, 170 E.R. 1168, in which the subsequent agreement was held to be merely a variation of the earlier agreement and accordingly failed for want of consideration, and the other line, illustrated by *Morris V. Baron & Co.*, (1918) A.C. 1, in which the subsequent agreement was held to have rescinded the former one and was therefore supported by the mutual agreement to abandon the old obligations and substitute new. Mr. Morphy invited us to find that the oral agreement to pay the increased price for steel fell into the second category. There was, he acknowledged, no express rescission of the written contract, but price is such a fundamental term of a contract for the supply of goods that the substitution of a new price must connote a new contract and impliedly rescind the old.

I am not persuaded that either of the parties intended by their discussions in March, 1970, to rescind their original contract and replace it with a new one. Indeed, it is significant that no such plea was made in the statement of claim which confined itself to an allegation that 'it was orally agreed in March 1970 that prices as set forth in the said contract (i.e., of October 22, 1969) would be varied. . . . ' Accordingly, consideration for the oral agreement is not to be found in a mutual agreement to abandon the earlier written contract and assume the obligations under the new oral one.

In summary, I concur in the findings of the trial Judge that the oral agreement made by the parties in March, 1970, was an agreement to vary the written contract of October 22, 1969, and that it must fail for want of consideration. . . .

The defendant in the *Gilbert* case made a promise to pay the increased price for the steel. Why wasn't this new promise to pay a higher price binding? The answer is generally explained on the basis that there was absence of new consideration. The essential aspect of the *Gilbert* case is the pre-existing obligation of the plaintiff to deliver the steel at a price already fixed under the original contract. The policy ground underlying the decision in this case is clear. The change of economic circumstances may allow one party to blackmail the other to agree to a new price or fail to get what was promised under the original contract.

Illustration   Mr. Anderson, a computer engineer, signed a consulting contract with Rinehart Ltd. on March 1st for a one-year period. He was assigned responsibility to lead a research team. The team's mandate was to develop a new telephone communicating program. In October, as the research reached a crucial stage, Mr. Anderson informed the President of Rinehart Ltd. that, unless his compensation was increased 50 percent, he would take employment with another software company in Toronto. The President was informed that Mr. Anderson's services were essential to the successful completion of the project. On this basis, the President agreed to Mr. Anderson's demand. Later, after the project was completed, Rinehart Ltd. informed Mr. Anderson that he would be compensated in accordance with the written contract. He then sued the company to enforce the oral promise for the 50 percent increase. Is there consideration for the October promise by the Company? On the basis of the *Gilbert* case, it is highly unlikely that Mr. Anderson's action would succeed. There is an absence of consideration to support the President's subsequent promise.

Benefit and Detriment as Consideration

The term "detriment", although not free from doubt, means in most situations the existence of economic loss.[5] Consideration has been defined in terms of detriment to the promisee. Placing benefit and detriment together, the general rule is that the consideration must be either a benefit to the promisor or a detriment to the promisee. In the typical business contract, there will be both a benefit to the promisor, i.e., he/she receives money, services or goods, and a detriment to the promisee, i.e., he/she gives up his/her money, services or goods. The exchange of these promises supplies the consideration necessary to make the contract binding.

The detriment to the promisee, however, standing alone, is sufficient consideration, provided that the promisor has agreed to it. Lord Ellenborough said: "A consideration of loss or inconvenience sustained by one party at the request of another is as good a consideration in law for a promise by such other as a consideration of profit or convenience to himself."[6]

Illustration   The President of Rinehart Ltd. asks his nephew, John, to drop Finance 101 halfway through the term. He also promises John $1000 for John's promise to drop the course. John honours his promise and drops Finance 101. He has thus supplied consideration for his Uncle's promise of $1000.

The traditional benefit/detriment approach has been criticized because the ultimate question as to whether there is a consideration goes unanswered.[7] The traditional definition, therefore, begs the real question as to what types of consideration make a promise legally enforceable. Consideration in the example given above, for instance, is in the form of an action by John. Benefit and detriment as a formulation, therefore, leaves undisclosed the answer as to why the courts enforce certain promises but not others.

Adequacy of Consideration

It is well established that the courts will not judge the adequacy of the consideration in determining whether the disputed contract is binding. A contract by Rinehart Ltd. to purchase diskettes for $1.75 each from the **MXZ** Company does not lack consideration even though it might be proved that diskettes of the same kind and quality could be purchased from other companies for $1.00 each.

In commercial transactions, the courts will not use the doctrine of consideration to unwind bad bargains. The parties in such transactions must judge for themselves the economic risks and benefits at the time the contract is made. Our economic system would soon run into disruption if the consideration needed to make a contract binding was tested on the fairness of the economic value given for goods and services. This general rule, however, in recent years has come under increasing pressure as the courts and provincial legislatures have expanded the scope of unconscionability.

The refusal to judge the adequacy of the consideration opens up the way for the parties to recite that nominal consideration, i.e., $1.00, is the price for the performance, goods, or property purchased. Nominal consideration is infrequently used in commercial transactions. Instead, nominal consideration enables private parties to convert a gratuitous promise into a binding contract. Thus, **A** signs a contract to transfer a car to **B**, his son, for $1.00. If the father later changes his mind, the son can enforce the father's promise, which is supported by the $1.00 consideration even though the market value of the car is $16 000.

Bilateral Contracts

In many business contracts, the consideration is not the payment of money or the delivery of goods and services but the *promise* to pay for goods or services in return for the seller's promise to deliver goods or perform services. This exchange of promises between the seller and buyer makes the contract immediately binding. The contract, in these circumstances, is enforceable before the actual performance of the promises. Much of contract law is explained on the basis that the courts seek to protect a party who has received such a promise from loss or disappointment arising from the failure of the other party to carry out his/her promise.

Not every promise, however, will be sufficient consideration to make the contract binding. The major exceptions include: (i) obscure, vague or indefinite promises, i.e., we are not sure what, if anything, has been promised; (ii) the promise may be based on a mistake of law or unlawful under a statute or regulation; or (iii) the party demanding a promise of payment may be under a pre-existing obligation either in a prior contract or by law to perform a service or deliver goods.

The sufficiency of the consideration is not tested solely by the exchange of the promises. The court, at the same time, must decide if the performance of the promise is sufficient consideration.[8] The promise is only as good as the acts of performance contained in it. Otherwise, a promise by Alison to pirate the software owned by Ben, and then deliver the pirated copy to Chuck would be sufficient consideration.

Illusory Consideration

Illusory consideration means the party making the promise has really promised nothing. The best example is where the party promises a performance if he feels in the mood. Thus, a software engineer who signs a consulting contract to the effect that he/she will work for Rinehart Ltd. for a period of one year, provided that he/she feels the project assigned to him/her has good "karma", has left the entire question of performance to his/her subjective discretion. In the words of Corbin such a promise is "like the mirage of the desert with its vision of flowing water that yet lets the traveller die of thirst; there is nothing there."[9]

In essence, the illusory promise is another example of insufficient consideration, perhaps fitting best into the category of a vague or indefinite promise. Whether the illusory promise fits into the theoretical framework, the consequences are abundantly clear: such a promise is not enforceable. Thus, a lawsuit by Rinehart Ltd. against the software engineer would fail for lack of consideration even though the return promise to pay the defendant is good consideration.

The illusory promise also destroys any mutuality of obligation between the parties. Mutuality means that both parties are under a contractual obligation. This is not an uncommon theme in contract law, as there is a taint of unfairness, which the courts attempt to prevent. The man who says his wife is married but he is not may be making a tasteless social joke. The man who says **B** is bound by a contract to perform services but he is not bound to compensate **B** may find that the joke is on him. He will not be able to successfully enforce the contract against **B**.

The line between the illusory promise and true mutuality of obligation becomes fuzzy when the court attaches the label "option" contract to the transaction. Thus, Rinehart Ltd. may promise to buy all the diskettes it requires from **MXZ** Ltd. for $1.75 each. **MXZ** Ltd. agrees to sell as many of the diskettes at the price as Rinehart Ltd. should need. Is the promise made by Rinehart Ltd. illusory? They have not committed themselves to buying a fixed amount. It may be that during a given period of time they have no need for additional diskettes.

The promise, however, is enforceable on the basis that, given the nature of Rinehart Ltd.'s business, they will consume diskettes. On the other hand, if an oil exporter or a shoe manufacturer made a similar promise to **MXZ** Ltd., the promise would probably be illusory as they do not require diskettes for the main operation of their businesses. Although, under these facts, Rinehart Ltd. has a considerable amount of discretion under the contract, it is not the same as the consulting software engineer who performs only if he/she feels the karma is right. To do business, Rinehart Ltd. must have a supply of diskettes.

There may be legitimate commercial reasons to ensure such a future supply at a fixed price. Certainly, the courts would hold there is mutuality of obligation between the parties, notwithstanding the uncertainty of the exact number of diskettes Rinehart Ltd. will buy.

The Contract Seal

Many rules in modern law are rooted in historical common law traditions. The operation of the seal is such a tradition. Like the rituals at Stonehenge, the use of the seal is the hallmark of an ancient ceremony that a modern mind only vaguely understands. In ancient England, where reading and writing were limited to very few, the wax seal placed at the foot of a contract was a required formality to transfer land. The seal placed on the document was a public pronouncement that the person fixing it staked his reputation and honour to abide by the agreement. Scanting a sealed document for consideration would have been to miss this essential point.

Today, seals are still used, though they lack the coat-of-arms and lions that often adorned the ancient seals used by nobility. They are circular, red, adhesive stickers placed next to the name of the parties signing the

FIGURE 3.1 **THE ANCIENT SEAL**

British Patent, 1867.
Photo courtesy of Roy Scheaffer, Law Society of Upper Canada

contract. The use of the seal eliminates the defence that the contractual promise is unsupported by consideration. Thus, Alison can agree to give Ben a new car without any corresponding obligation on Alison to pay for the car, and the sealed contract is enforceable by Ben against Alison.

Promissory Estoppel

The doctrine of promissory estoppel provides a means to circumvent the unfairness and harshness of the doctrine of consideration. This doctrine owes its existence to the more flexible, discretionary jurisdiction of "equity". The tradition of equity — indeed, in England, there once were separate equity courts called Chancery Courts — is to emphasize good faith and bona fides, and to prevent oppression and injustice. Another formulation of promissory estoppel is equitable estoppel. For our purposes, the terms are interchangeable. In the following passage from Lord Cairns' judgment in *Hughes v. Metropolitan R. Co.*,[10] the application of promissory estoppel is discussed:

> It is the first principle upon which all Courts of Equity proceed, that if parties who have entered into definite and distinct terms involving certain legal results — certain penalties or legal forfeiture — afterwards by their own act or with their own consent enter upon a course of negotiation which has the effect of leading one of the parties to suppose that the strict rights arising under the contract

FIGURE 3.2 **THE MODERN SEAL**

will not be enforced, or will be kept in suspense, or held in abeyance, the person who otherwise might have enforced those rights will not be allowed to enforce them where it would be inequitable having regard to the dealings which have thus taken place between the parties.

The modern view of promissory estoppel can be traced to Lord Denning's judgment in the *High Trees* case.[11] In this case two companies entered into a ninety-nine year lease from September 29, 1937. The defendant, a subsidiary of the plaintiff, entered possession of the block of flats and commenced sub-letting them to third parties. The rent reserved under the head lease was £2500/a. With the beginning of World War II, it became clear that the defendant would have difficulty finding tenants for the block of flats. Negotiations then commenced between the parties over the rent reserved in the head lease, i.e., the consideration for granting the defendant the ninety-nine year term lease.

On January 3, 1940, the parties agreed to reduce the ground rent of £2500 to £1250/a. Eighteen months later, the lease was repudiated by one of the parties. The plaintiff in the action sought to recover the difference between the rent that the defendant originally agreed to pay and the rent actually paid under the January 3rd agreement. The issue was whether the January 3rd promise by the plaintiff to accept £1250 was enforceable. If it were, then the action to recover the full rent under the original lease would fail.

Strictly as a matter of contract law, unaided by equitable principles, the plaintiff was entitled to recover the portion of the rent withheld by the defendant under the January 3rd agreement. Lord Denning's judgment found for the defendants and said:[12]

There has been a series of decisions over the last fifty years which, although they are said to be cases of estoppel are not really such. They are cases in which a promise was made which was intended to create legal relations and which to the knowledge of the person making the promise, was going to be acted on by the person to whom it was made, and which was in fact so acted on.... In each case the court held the promise to be binding on the party making it, even though under the old common law it might be difficult to find any consideration for it. The courts have not gone so far as to give a cause of action in damages for the breach of such a promise, but they have refused to allow the party making it to act inconsistently with it....

Subsequent decisions have added two conditions to the applications of the doctrine of promissory estoppel: (i) that the party asserting the defence can show he/she relied upon the promise; and (ii) that the party making the promise can revert to the original contract terms upon providing reasonable notice.

Illustration The terms of the exclusive licensing agreement (see Figure 1.2) expressly prohibit a customer from modifying the licensed software. Under the termination and default provisions of the contract, a customer who modified the software breached the contract and Rinehart Ltd. has the right to terminate the agreement. Moreover, an express section of the contract provides "No modification, amendments, or waivers of any of the provisions or terms of this Agreement shall be effective unless the same shall be made in writing and manually signed by an officer of Rinehart Ltd. and a duly authorized representative of the Customer."

On March 10th, the Vice-President in charge of Research and Development for the company, received a telephone call from a customer who had licensed software under the Rinehart Ltd. standard form contract. The customer, InvestTeck Ltd., has a licence to use Rinehart Ltd. Real Estate Investment System. An officer of InvestTeck explained that they had received a contract to provide investment service for a major insurance company. The company, however, demanded that modification should be made to the actuary tables contained in the software so as to comply with the laws of New York State. Subsequently, correspondence was exchanged and there were additional telephone conversations between the two officers. On August 4th, Vice-President of Rinehart, Sam Sones, phoned the officer at InvestTeck Ltd., Lisa Richards, and gave the "go ahead" for the proposed modifications.

Later, the relations between the two companies deteriorated. Ms. Bach discovered that the modifications made by her company officer were not in compliance with the licence agreement, and gave InvestTeck Ltd. formal notice of termination of the agreement. InvestTeck Ltd. refused to return the software, arguing that there were no grounds for termination. The success of InvestTeck Ltd.'s defence will turn on two grounds: first, whether the doctrine of promissory estoppel applies to override the express contractual provision restricting the manner in which the parties can modify the contract; second, whether factually, InvestTeck Ltd., given the contract with a third party, can now resume its original position under the Rinehart contract.

Problems for Discussion

1. Instead of the doctrine of consideration or promissory estoppel, should promises be made enforceable on the grounds that the parties, as honourable persons, bound themselves to carry out their bargain? This position was adopted in the eighteenth century by a leading English judge, Lord Mansfield, who said in *Hawkes v. Saunders*, (1782)

1 Cowp. 289, 290: "Where a man is under a moral obligation, which no Court of Law or Equity can enforce, and promises, the honesty and rectitude of the thing is a consideration . . . the ties of conscience upon an upright mind are sufficient consideration." Within sixty years, Lord Mansfield's view was expressly repudiated in *Eastwood v. Kenyon*, (1840) 113 E.R. 482. Formulate an argument for or against the view of Lord Mansfield.

2. D.&C. Builders Ltd. contracted to do work on the premises owned by Mr. Rees. The final bill came to £746 13s. Mr. Rees paid £250 on account. Later, when the builders attempted to collect the balance of £480, they ran into delays with Mr. Rees. D.&C. Builders Ltd. was near bankruptcy at the time, and it was imperative that they collect the money owed. Mr. Rees' wife sought to compromise the outstanding amount by offering to settle the bill for £300. Given the financial position of the builders, they had little choice, and accepted the £300. Mrs. Rees requested that they sign a receipt that provided: "Received the sum of £300 from Mr. Rees in completion of the account. Paid, M. Casey." Later, the builders sought to recover the balance of over £180 still unpaid by Mr. Rees, who defended on the basis of the signed receipt. Is the promise to forgive the balance of the unpaid debt enforceable against the builders? See *D.&C. Builders v. Rees*, (1966) 2 Q.B. 617, (1965) 3 All E.R. 837 (C.A.). Also see *Foakes v. Beer*, (1884) 9 A.C. 605 (H.L.) the leading case on the effect of paying a lesser sum in satisfaction of a larger debt.

3. Why does the doctrine of consideration have little importance in commercial contracts?

4. What is the consideration for the contract in Figure 1.3 and Figure 1.4?

5. Can you distinguish the results in the *Gilbert Steel Ltd.* case with Lord Denning's judgment in *High Trees*?

6. Consider whether clause 8 in Figure 1.4 effectively precludes a party to the Rinehart Ltd. contract from successfully raising either the *Gilbert* or the *High Trees* case.

7. What is the distinction between the Adequacy of Consideration and the Sufficiency of Consideration?

8. Why isn't a contract to buy all the diskettes that Rinehart Ltd. requires in a given year from a manufacturer an illusory promise?

9. A software engineer under a consulting contract with Rinehart Ltd. is orally promised an additional $10 000 bonus if he/she finishes a research project assigned to him/her two months after he/she starts his/her job. The software engineer completes the project but the

company refuses to pay the bonus on the basis there was no consideration for the promise. Is this promise enforceable against Rinehart Ltd.?

10. Before the promises are enforceable, must the consideration be evidenced in writing?

Chapter 3 Notes

1. Cheshire and Fifoot's *Law of Contract*, 9th Ed., p. 66.
2. Treitel, *The Law of Contract*, 6th Ed. (1983), p. 52.
3. 2 Q.B. 851.
4. (1976) 67 D.L.R. (3d) 606 (Ont.C.A.).
5. Corbin, *Contracts*, Volume 1 Ed. (1952), p. 181.
6. *Bunn v. Guy*, (1803) 4 East 190.
7. Corbin, *supra* note 5, at 183; Cheshire and Fifoot's, *supra* note 1, p. 65.
8. Corbin, *supra* note 5, pp. 208-10.
9. *Ibid.*, p. 211.
10. (1877) 2 A.C. 439, 448 (H.L.).
11. *Central London Property Trust Ltd. v. High Trees House Ltd.*, (1947) 1 K.B. 130 (Q.B.).
12. *Ibid.*, p. 134.

4 FACTORS DESTROYING CONTRACTUAL CONSENT

Introduction

In general, the manifestation of assent to contract must be freely and voluntarily given. When this is not the case, the contract can be either void, i.e., of no validity from the beginning, or voidable, i.e., where one party has grounds to set aside a contract after it was made. In the case of void, there never was a contract between the parties. A voidable contract, on the other hand, means that although a contract was made, there is a basis for prematurely ending the contract. This principle assumes certain conditions and qualities about the "free will" of the parties involved, as well as of the identity and subject matter of the contract.

A common allegation is that the use of wrongful pressure by the defendant prevented the plaintiff from truly consenting to the terms of the contract. The crucial element is the legitimacy of the pressure used by the defendant. In Canadian law, the courts have evolved rules to test the degrees of coercion of the will. Not all coercion will render the contract void or voidable. Certain types of mistakes will also have the same legal effect on enforceability of contractual promises.

Commercial morality is the implicit reason for holding that certain types of conduct will vitiate consent. Traditionally, the courts have looked with disfavour on deception, dishonesty, oppression, and unfairness. Also, outside of the commercial transaction, the weak, the infirm, and poorly educated have been accorded protection against gross overreaching by others who contract with them. Thus, the set of rules as to what is "fair and proper" advantage taking between businesspersons does not necessarily apply in consumer or non-commercial transactions. The courts are required to delicately balance the demand for certainty and predictability in the enforcement of contracts with the desire to ensure that minimum standards of fair and proper conduct are observed.

Duress

In many commercial transactions there may be evidence of commercial pressure. On the other side of the line is economic duress. The problem, however, has been to define where to draw that line.

Illustrations

The following two problems illustrate the fine line between permissible and impermissible commercial pressure.

Illustration   Rinehart Ltd. undertakes the development of an "artificial intelligence" computer system for international currency trading transactions. The lending institution is willing to finance the development but only on terms of a 5 percent equity interest in the company. No other institution is willing to make the investment risk. The "single opportunity" of financing greatly enhances the lending institution's bargaining position. Is it coercion that destroys Rinehart Ltd.'s contractual consent to form a contract? It is likely that a Canadian court would hold the pressure was permissible. The balance might be tipped in favour of Rinehart Ltd., however, if there was evidence to indicate that it was custom of the lending industry to discourage such transactions.

Illustration   Ben, a software engineer assigned to a software design project (as in Figure 1.3) informs the project leader that he wants an immediate 30 percent increase in compensation. If the project leader refuses, then Ben will sabotage the software system. Although the total economic cost incurred by the engineer is less than that of the lending institution, there is major legal difference between the two cases. The engineer's demand is an illegitimate threat, i.e., the physical destruction of property; the lending institution, which has no pre-existing relationship with the company, has offered terms — from a position of strength — on which they will do business with the company.

Common Law Categories

The common law definition of duress was limited. One category was duress of the person. Where one party was wrongfully imprisoned or had a gun placed to his head, then duress of the person vitiated his consent and the contract was void. Another common law category was duress of goods. The actual or threatened seizure of a person's goods, unless the owner agreed to pay a sum of money, was a type of pressure that rendered the transaction involuntary.

Modern Guidelines to Duress

The common law categories have been expanded to include other types of conduct that amount to practical compulsion. However, the conduct that destroys a person's free will is difficult to frame in a general rule. There are two general guidelines: (i) illegitimate pressure or wrongful conduct is used by the defendant; and (ii) the plaintiff demonstrates that as a result of the pressure he/she had to either submit to the demand or suffer harm personally or to his/her family or business.

Two cases illustrate the difficulty of applying even the most general guidelines to a specific case.

Case #1 *R. v. Premier Mouton Products Inc.*[1]   In this case, a taxpayer was requested to pay excise tax on his product. In his view, the tax was inapplicable to his product. The tax department, however, insisted on its interpretation, and threatened to close up his business unless the tax was paid. The taxpayer paid following the threat and later sued the government to recover what he continued to assert was a wrongfully assessed tax. The Supreme Court of Canada in this case agreed with the taxpayer that the conduct amounted to duress or compulsion.

> [T]he payments made were not prompted by the desire to discharge a legal obligation, or to settle definitely a contested claim. The pressure that was exercised was sufficient, I think, to negative the expression of the free will of the respondent's officers, with the result that the alleged agreement to pay the tax has no legal effect and may be avoided. The payment was not made voluntarily to close the transaction.[2]

Case #2 *Morton Construction Co. Ltd. v. Hamilton*[3]   In this Ontario Court of Appeal case, a municipality threatened that unless a contractor repaired certain sidewalks it would not consider the contractor for future contracts. The contractor protested that they were not obliged under the existing contract to make the requested repairs. But the threat to lose future business caused the contractor to do what was requested. The court found that the municipality was entitled to make a threat of that nature and carry it out.

Illegitimate Commercial Pressure

In commercial transaction cases, the courts have attempted to define illegitimate commercial pressure. In many commercial situations, there will be inequality of bargaining power. One company has greater resources, a monopoly on a product or service, or a substantial market segment. If inequality of bargaining power was the sole test for illegitimate commercial pressure, then such a company could never enforce a contract with another. That is obviously not the law. Instead, the courts are more concerned with the means by which such a company exercises its enormous power. Intervention by the courts turns on whether there has been an abuse of power by the large corporation, labour union, public utility or government. Such a finding makes the contract between the parties voidable.

An example of illegitimate commercial pressure is found in *Universe Tankships of Monrovia v. International Transport Workers Federation.*[4] In that case, a Liberian tanker owner employed a crew at substantially less than the rate contained in the International Transport Workers Federation collective agreement. When the ship arrived in an English port, a union representative gave the master a demand for $162 per crew member payable to the union welfare fund. Until the money was paid, the ship was "blacked" and couldn't leave port. After about eleven idle days in port, the owner agreed to pay the sum demanded by the union. After the ship left England, the owner sued the union to recover the money paid. The House of Lords observed that the union admitted that the continued "blacking" of the ship would have financially catastrophic consequences for the owners, which amounted to coercion of the shipowner. As a result, the shipowner recovered the money paid to the union and the contract between the union and shipowner was avoided.

Undue Influence and Unconscionability

Commercial transactions between businesspersons are generally immune from a successful argument based on undue influence or unconscionability. A consumer transaction, or a commercial transaction where one of the parties has very slight knowledge of business matters or is under recognized disability, may be avoided on this basis. As is the case with duress, inequality of bargaining power alone is insufficient to engage the doctrine of undue influence or unconscionability. Also, like duress, a successful argument of undue influence or unconscionability allows the victim to avoid the contract and recover benefits conferred on the other party.

Basic Distinctions

The distinction between undue influence and unconscionability is defined by the British Columbia Court of Appeal in *Morrison v. Coast Finance Ltd.*:[5]

A plea of undue influence attacks the sufficiency of consent; a plea that a bargain is unconscionable invokes relief against an unfair advantage gained by an unconscientious use of power by a stronger party against a weaker. On such a claim the material ingredients are proof of inequality in the position of the parties arising out of the ignorance, need or distress of the weaker, which left him in the power of the stronger, and proof of substantial unfairness of the bargain obtained by the stronger. On proof of the circumstances, it creates a presumption of fraud which the stronger must repel by proving that the bargain was fair, just and reasonable.

In England, Lord Denning has held that there is a common thread running through undue influence, unconscionability, and related doctrines, i.e., inequality of bargaining power. Lord Denning said in *Lloyds Bank Ltd. v. Bundy*:[6]

> Gathering all together, I would suggest that through all these instances there runs a single thread. They rest on "inequality of bargaining power". By virtue of it, English law gives relief to one who, without independent advice, enters into a contract on terms which are very unfair or transfers property for a consideration which is grossly inadequate, when his bargaining power is grievously impaired by reason of his own needs or desires, or by his own ignorance or infirmity, coupled with undue influence or pressures brought to bear on him by or for the benefit of the other.

In Canada, there is support for this general approach to the unconscionable contract. Some background is necessary to understand the historical roots to the doctrines of undue influence and unconscionable bargains.

Undue Influence

The doctrine of undue influence was narrow in early common law. The court presumed undue influence arose in transactions between parties occupying a certain legal status. Thus, a fiduciary who purchased land, goods, or services from the beneficiary to whom he owed an obligation of trust and confidence was presumed to have used undue influence. Similarly, the relationships of guardian and ward, parent and child would raise the presumption. Once the presumption was raised, then the trustee, guardian, or parent would have the burden of showing the fairness of the contract. Also, to rebut the presumption normally required evidence that the "weaker" party had had the benefit of independent advice before entering the contract.

Unconscionability

Factors used to judge unconscionability include: (i) whether the defendant may fall within a class of poverty, ignorance, ill health, low level of education; (ii) whether the exchange received by the claimant under the contract was grossly inadequate in comparison to the property or goods transferred to the defendant; (iii) whether the plaintiff received independent legal advice; and (iv) whether the defendant abused his/her power in bargaining for the exchange.

Figure 4.1 illustrates the general approach taken by Canadian courts to unconscionability cases.

GROSS IMBALANCE IN THE EXCHANGE

The threshold question is whether there is a gross imbalance in the exchange between the parties. In Chapter 3, we discussed the general rule that a court does not judge the adequacy of consideration; in the unconscionability cases, the adequacy becomes an essential issue. The amount to be paid for land, goods, or services may be substantially below market. Other elements in the exchange may also be unfairly weighted to one party. For instance, one party may reserve a right to terminate the contract on a basis grossly unfair to the other. Thus, the unconscionability issue can be resolved solely on the basis of a gross imbalance in the exchange. In the absence of such evidence, there is a further possibility of success based on either inequality of bargaining power or abuse of power.

INEQUALITY OF BARGAINING POWER

In this category of unconscionability, the court looks at the status, condition or behavior of the person asserting unconscionability. Unless the person who is poor, infirm, illiterate, or the subject of a fiduciary relationship has had independent legal advice, there is a possibility of the court's holding the contract unconscionable. The claimant must prove a grievous impairment by reason of his health, education, or economic condition.

ABUSE OF POWER

In the final category of unconscionability, the courts include parties with equal bargaining power. Nonetheless, the party asserting unconscionability must prove that illegitimate means of persuasion were used by the defendant in negotiating the contract. Unlike the economic duress cases, where the pressure is not used to achieve a contractual exchange, the unconscionable contract is assailed because the means used to effect the unfair exchange were wrongful in the view of the court.

CASE ILLUSTRATIONS

It is not uncommon for a case to contain facts that fit into more than one of the unconscionability categories. An example of both inequality of bargaining power and gross imbalance in the exchange is found in *Harry v. Kreutziger*.[7] A poorly educated native Indian man sold his fishing boat to the defendant for $4500. He claimed that the true value of his

FIGURE 4.1   **BASIS FOR UNCONSCIONABILITY**

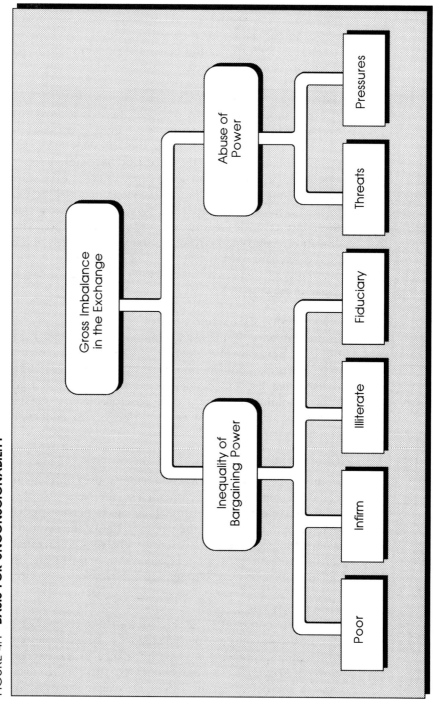

boat was $16 000. The contract to sell the boat was unconscionable even though the claimant could have sought independent advice but did not, could have refused to deal with the purchaser, and could have torn up the cheque given to him by the purchaser.

The majority of the court, following *Lloyds Bank v. Bundy*, held that a presumption of fraud had been established and the stronger party had failed to demonstrate that the contract was fair and reasonable. In a separate judgment, Lambert J.A. said such a case is resolved by asking whether the transaction, seen as a whole, is sufficiently divergent from community standards of commercial morality that it should be rescinded."[8]

Where the advantage-taking is within the context of a commercial contract such as franchise contract, it is substantially more difficult to raise the presumption of fraud. Thus, in *Jirna v. Mister Donut*,[9] the plaintiff — a franchisee, i.e., a person given an exclusive right by contract to market and sell goods under a specific name, failed to recover secret profits made by the franchisor, i.e., the person who granted the exclusive right to market and sell donuts as "Mister Donut". The franchisor received kick-backs from suppliers of ingredients. Under the franchise contract, the franchisee was obliged to purchase from only these suppliers which had been approved by the franchisor.

The abuse of power category was successfully invoked by the franchisee in *A & K Lick-A-Chick Franchises Ltd. v. Cordiv Enterprises Ltd.*[10] In this case, all the parties were experienced businessmen. The defendants operated a "Lick-a-Chick" franchise in New Waterford, Nova Scotia. In the spring of 1978, Brushett and Rossi decided to purchase the interest of the franchisor in A & K Lick-a-Chick Franchises Ltd. (A & K). Brushett had grand plans to expand the franchise operation. He met with the defendants and told them of his plans to open ten additional outlets. Also, he told the defendants of a number of financial advantages that would accrué to them once he became the franchise owner. At this first meeting, the defendants signed a preliminary agreement with Brushett.

After Brushett's group purchased the franchise, Mr. Brushett met the defendants in New Waterford on July 18, 1978. At that time he handed them a twenty-six page franchise agreement. Brushett did not give them time for their lawyer to review the agreement. He also made a number of representations about finding a purchaser in the event of termination of the agreement, the big money behind the Brushett group, and the threat of operating a competing outlet across the street unless they signed. The defendants signed the franchise agreement. Brushett's grand plans failed to materialize and the number of pre-existing outlets dropped in the first year. On February 25, 1980, the defendants, through their lawyer, wrote a letter to Brushett terminating the franchise agreement. Brushett sued for specific performance of the franchise agreement, i.e., a court order compelling the defendant to perform their contractual promises, or alternatively for damages.

The judgments of Lord Denning in *Lloyds Bank v. Bundy*, and Lambert J.A. in *Harry v. Kreutziger* were considered by the court:[11]

... It seems to me that these two concepts are slightly different approaches to the same principle. A finding of inequality of bargaining power cannot be made in isolation but must be relative to those standards which constitute the norm. Therefore, a transaction can be said to be unconscionable if it is sufficiently divergent from community standards or manifests a substantial inequality of bargaining power between the parties.

In the present case the defendants felt that they were bound to enter into the franchise agreement because of the commitment made in the preliminary agreement. They were apprehensive as to their future in the fast food business and this apprehension was fueled by Brushett's threats to "open up across the street". They were subject to high pressure tactics and were effectively prevented from seeking independent advice. As I have already stated, they also perceived themselves to be in a substantially inferior bargaining position to Brushett. For these reasons I have no hesitation in finding that the meeting of July 18th which concluded with the execution of the franchise agreement was in total an unconscionable transaction and cannot be permitted to stand.

The importance of A & K Lick-A-Chick Franchise Ltd. is the application of the doctrine of unconscionability to a commercial transaction between businessmen. This expands the traditional approach, which combines the inadequacy of the bargain with evidence of misrepresentation, substantial disability, lack of education or ignorance, or breach of a fiduciary relationship.

Statutory Approaches to Unconscionability

The commercial contract cases are less common than those involving consumer contracts. Many provinces have legislation directed toward establishing rules applicable to the unconscionable consumer contract. For example, an unfair practice prohibited under the Ontario Business Practice Act[12] includes:

[A]n unconscionable consumer representation made in respect of a particular transaction and in determining whether or not a consumer representation is unconscionable, there may be taken into account that the person making the representation or his employer or principal knows or ought to know:

(i) that the consumer is not reasonably able to protect his interest because of his physical infirmity, ignorance, illiteracy, inability to understand the language of an agreement or similar factors,

(ii) that the price grossly exceeds the price at which similar goods or services are readily available to like consumers,

(iii) that the consumer is unable to receive a substantial benefit from the subject-matter of the consumer representation,

(iv) that there is no reasonable probability of payment of the obligation in full by the consumer,

(v) that the proposed transaction is excessively one-sided in favour of someone other than the consumer,

(vi) that the terms or conditions of the proposed transaction are so adverse to the consumer as to be inequitable,

(vii) that he is subjecting the consumer to undue pressure to enter into the transaction.

Compare the statutory approach in Ontario with that found in the United States where the doctrine of unconscionability has been incorporated into the Uniform Commercial Code section 2-302, which provides:

(1) If the court as a matter of law finds the contract or any clause of the contract to have been unconscionable at the time it was made the court may refuse to enforce the contract, or it may enforce the remainder of the contract without the unconscionable clause, or it may so limit the application of any unconscionable clause as to avoid any unconscionable result.

(2) When it is claimed or appears to the court that the contract or any clause thereof may be unconscionable the parties shall be afforded a reasonable opportunity to present evidence as to its commercial setting, purpose and effect to aid the court in making the determination.

There is also an Official Comment to section 2-302, which explains its purpose. Part of the comment is reproduced below:

This section is intended to make it possible for the courts to police explicitly against the contracts or clauses which they find to be unconscionable. In the past such policing has been accomplished by adverse construction of language, by manipulation of the rules of offer and acceptance or by determinations that the clause is contrary to public policy or to the dominant purpose of the contract. This section is intended to allow the court to pass directly on the unconscionability of the contract or particular clause therein and to make a conclusion of law as to its unconscionability. The basic test is whether, in the light of the general commercial background and the commercial needs of the particular trade or case, the clauses involved are so one-sided as to be unconscionable under the circumstances existing at the time of the making of the contract. Subsection (2) makes it clear that it is proper for the court to hear evidence upon these questions. The principle is one of the prevention of oppression and unfair surprise ... and not of disturbance of allocation of risks because of superior bargaining power. ...

STANDARD FORM CONTRACTS AND UNCONSCIONABILITY

The role of the standard form contract is often of importance in resolving the issue of unconscionability. In one case, the two factors considered by the court in an unconscionability case were: (i) whether the contract was a printed standard form drawn by the defendant and; (ii) whether the parties had entered into any negotiation.[13] The fear is that the standard form contracts may result in an abuse of power by the one drafting it. In the consumer contract case, the court is more open to the argument that the fine print, in difficult legal language, contained unreasonable or oppressive terms. The mere fact that a standard form is used may be some evidence of the inequality of bargaining power between the parties.

A standard form contract that contains a non-negotiable price that is excessive opens an argument that the contract is unenforceable against the consumer. The oppression, however, may not be limited to the excessive amount paid for goods or services. Other clauses such as penalty or limitation on remedies or exorbitant interest charges on financing indicate unconscionability. The classic case is the exemption clause hidden away in the fine print of the standard form of consumer contract. It is reasonably clear that the consumer will be able to avoid the clause based on unconscionability. Whether the rationale is abuse of power, inequality of bargaining power, or surprise, the oppressive terms in a consumer contract are prime targets for the application of the doctrine of unconscionability. All these rationales are used by the court to justify a decision that there has been a defect in the formation of the contract, and that a manifestation of assent is excluded to one or more terms or the entire contract.

Illustration Rinehart Ltd. has decided to franchise its Learning Shoppes. The company was approached by Mr. and Mrs. King. Mr. King is a former school teacher. His wife holds an M.B.A. and worked for an insurance company as a supervisor. They expressed a keen interest in buying a franchise for the Sudbury area. Neither party, however, has had either previous business experience or computer background.

On August 2nd, Mr. Hodge, a representative of the company, called upon the Kings at their home in Sudbury. He brought along the standard form franchise agreement that was thirty pages in length. A large part of the agreement was in technical, legal jargon. The price of the franchise was $75 000, which the Kings planned to raise by mortgaging their house and taking a personal loan guaranteed by Mr. King's father. Mr. Hodge left the contract with the Kings for two days. On August 5th, he called upon them again. At this meeting, they signed the agreement with some brief discussion about some of the terms. During the discussions, Mr. King disclosed that he was an alcoholic. He insisted the problem was under control. Mr. Hodge took Mr. King's statement at face value.

By September 1st, the Kings had raised $25 000 by taking a second mortgage on their house. The bank lent the Kings the balance of $50 000 on a promissory note. The note was guaranteed by Mr. King's father, who was told that unless he signed, his son and daughter-in-law would not get the loan. Mr. King also told his father, in the presence of the bank manager, that unless the guarantee was signed, he and his wife might be sued by Rinehart Ltd. on the contract signed August 5th. Mr. King, Sr. then signed the guarantee in the presence of the bank manager who was an old and trusted personal friend. The elder Mr. King is seventy-eight years old, and his only asset is the $75 000 equity that he has in his house.

In October, the franchise was opened by the Kings. They had been given a one-week seminar on inventory, display, and sales by the company. However, within eight months, owing mainly to the Kings' inexperience in marketing, the business sustained substantial losses. Mr. King had started drinking heavily again. Rinehart Ltd. then served a notice of termination, which under the terms of the franchise, could be given in the event a franchisee suffered a loss for three consecutive months. A liquidated damages clause entitled the company to receive $5000 in damages as a result of the expenditure in training the franchisee, and finding and training new franchisees to take over the operation, as well as the loss of good will and reputation in the community resulting from the termination.

In November, the mortgage company foreclosed on the Kings' house to enforce the second mortgage. And the bank sued on the $50 000 loan and guarantee, naming both the Kings and Mr. King's father in the action. Were one or more of the contracts unconscionable? It is unlikely on the basis of these facts that the franchise agreement was unconscionable. The Kings, however, could argue "surprise" on the liquidated damages clause. Assuming that argument succeeds, that clause could be eliminated from the contract. Mr. King's father, however, has a stronger case. Based on the *Bundy* case, there is a greater likelihood the bank could not enforce the guarantee against the elder Mr. King.

MISREPRESENTATION

A misrepresentation occurs when one party (the representor) makes a statement of material fact that he/she knows or ought to know is false, and that statement induces the other party (the representee) to make a contract with him/her. The intervention of the courts to avoid a contract in these circumstances is premised on similar lines to their unconscionability jurisdiction. Misrepresentation is another example of a rough-and-ready means of ensuring a minimal degree of integrity, fairness, and ethics in contractual dealings. To this end, the court has developed a number of rules required to establish a misrepresentation case: (i) a false statement; (ii) of a material fact; (iii) intended to induce the representee to contract; and (iv) being unaware of the falsity of the statement, the representee is in fact induced to make the contract.

Misrepresentations prevent the necessary free consent required to make a binding contract. The courts have drawn distinctions based on the knowledge of the representor. There is fraudulent misrepresentation when the representor knows of the deception practised on the representee. This is the category of the "con artist", the "rogue", or the "crook" — all terms that indicate that the representor is a dishonest person.

Another category of misrepresentation is that of negligent misrepresentation. Generally, the negligent misrepresentor has failed in some duty arising out of relationship with the representee. The innocent misrepresentation is done without fraud, without a special relationship existing between the representor and representee, and without negligence.

Essential Elements

We will consider the three categories of misrepresentation after first reviewing the basic nature of the principle that appears in all three categories.

FALSE STATEMENT

A false statement may be defined as: a positive statement communicated through either the representor's words or conduct, that deceives the representee into believing as a fact. For example, Ben sells a software spreadsheet program to John, an accountant. Ben represents to John that this problem can be given "voice commands" and is compatible with John's personal computer.

Both representations are false. A false representation standing alone is insufficient. The statement must be dissected to determine whether the retailer was making a statement of fact, giving an opinion, or making a trade "puff" — a statement such as: This spreadsheet is one of the best in the market. It is more of an opinion than a fact. In the example, the retailer made specific representations about an important attribute of the spreadsheet.

AS TO FACT

As a general rule, the representor must have made a representation as to a fact and not merely expressed an opinion. A fact is some condition or state that exists in the present and does not rest upon contingencies that may occur in the future. Assume that Ben tells John, the accountant-customer, that the spreadsheet has a first-rate graphic capacity. In fact, the software has only limited graphics and has been returned by approximately 20 percent of all customers because of a "bug" in the graphic mode. Ben then adds that in the future an accountant who fails to use such an advanced program may be negligent.

Are these positive statements substantially different from the statement above? Or has Ben merely asserted an opinion or trade puff? As to the latter statement, which attempts to predict future developments, it is reasonably clear that the customer would not have a clear action based on misrepresentation.

Each statement must be analysed to determine whether the representor was expressing an opinion or asserting a fact. The line between a fact and an opinion is not always easy to discern. Indeed there may be overlap. Bowen L.J. observed in *Smith v. Land and House Property Corporation*:[14]

> It is often fallaciously assumed that a statement of opinion cannot involve statement of fact. In a case where the facts are equally well known to both parties, what one of them says to the other is frequently nothing but an expression of opinion. . . . But if the facts are not equally well known to both sides, then a statement of opinion by the one who knows the facts best involves very often a statement of material fact, for he impliedly states that he knows facts which justify his opinion.

MATERIALITY AND INDUCEMENT

It is often said that the misrepresented fact must be material and induce the representee to make the contract. "A misrepresentation, to be material, must be one necessarily influencing and inducing the transaction and affecting and going to the very essence and substance."[15]

An illustration is John, the accountant, who asks whether the spreadsheet software program has an electronic mail capacity. He is told that the program has this capacity, and, based on the representation, he buys it. When he starts up the program in his office, he discovers there is no electronic mail component, and misses sending an urgent message to a client in Toronto.

The contract, under these facts, induced by a material misrepresentation of fact, is voidable. Once the contract is avoided, as we see later, the accountant has an action against Ben, the retailer in tort — a civil action to recover compensation for harm to a person or his property in contract to recover for a breached promise — for his out-of-pocket expense plus damages arising out of the missed message to the Toronto client.

On the other hand, if John, the accountant, was a computer buff and knew Ben, the retailer, was making a false statement, an action based on misrepresentation would fail. Simply, with John's knowledge of the falsity of the statement, he was not induced by it to buy the software. What would be the case if nothing was mentioned about the electronic mail feature of the program, but that there was a representation to that effect inside the package? Also, suppose that Ben did not know of the accountant's intention to use the program for electronic mail. There is then no misrepresentation that induced the accountant to make the contract. Misrepresentation after the fact does not prevent the formation of the contract.

Fraudulent Misrepresentation

To stamp a person as a fraud requires a heavy burden of proof. Some have suggested it approaches the criminal burden of beyond a reasonable doubt. The allegation of fraud casts a stigma that may ruin a business or professional career. In the unconscionability section, we discussed the presumption of fraud. That was a different matter. A presumption of fraud can be created in the absence of wrongdoing, and operates merely as a burden-of-proof-shifting device. Actual fraud means there is evidence of misconduct or dishonesty on the part of the defendant.

There is, however, no one agreed-upon meaning of fraud. In the widest sense, it encompasses "all kinds of unfair dealing and unconscionable conduct."[16] In the misrepresentation cases, the court must find evidence that the representor knew or ought reasonably to have known that he was telling a lie.[17] What about the half-lie? A statement that is partially true and partially false falls in the same category.

As one commentator has explained: "If a representor honestly believes his statement to be true, he cannot be liable in deceit, no matter how ill-advised, stupid, credulous or even negligent he may have been."[18]

Nothing short of compelling evidence of dishonesty will suffice. Thus, the representor who has sold himself "a bill of goods" about his goods, service, or land will escape the label of fraud. The retailer who knows that the software spreadsheet program does not contain an electronic mail feature, and makes that representation of fact to induce a sale, has made a fraudulent misrepresentation.

In *Fundy Chemical*,[19] an action for fraud and deceit was brought against the vendor of real property. The vendor represented that certain material piled on the land made "excellent fill". He neglected, however, to tell the purchaser one important fact — the so-called excellent fill was radioactive waste! The purchaser later spread the material on the land and placed a warehouse addition and cable storage area on it. Also, part of the material was removed to other land owned by the purchaser and used as fill.

In fact, the slag material contained twenty times the maximum thorium content set by the Atomic Energy Control Board, and required a licence for the possession and removal of such material. The vendor knew the law and the nature of the slag material at the time that he made the representation to the purchaser; yet he kept the fact of the radioactive nature of the fill a secret from the purchaser. That is, he did not expressly tell the purchaser that the material was free from a radioactive substance. Nonetheless, the trial court found a fraudulent representation had been made and allowed substantial damages against the vendor. Reliance was placed on the early case of *Tapp v. Lee*,[20] where Chambre J. said:

> An action on the case for deceit is an action well known to the law,
> and I cannot agree in the argument which has been used for the

Defendant, that such actions ought to be confined to representations which are literally false. Fraud may consist as well in the suppression of what is true, as in the representation of what is false. If a man, professing to answer a question, selects those facts only which are likely to give a credit to the person of whom he speaks, and keep back the rest, he is a more artful knave than he who tells a direct falsehood.

Innocent Misrepresentation

In the absence of fraud, the misrepresentation will be classed as innocent. The representor did not know that his representation was false and was not negligent in making the statement. At one time, *all* non-fraudulent misrepresentations were classed as innocent misrepresentation. That is not the law today, however.

The main distinction between a fraudulent and innocent misrepresentation is the scope of remedies available to the representee. Determining the representor's remedies for innocent misrepresentation is complicated. The common law courts first ascertained whether the misrepresentation was a term of the contract, or an inducement to enter a contract where the terms were accurately represented. In the former case, the representee would have an action for breach of contract, and in certain cases recission of the contract coupled with an action against the representor for benefits conferred under the contract. In the latter case, the representee was entitled to avoid an innocent misrepresentation of the effect of a term contained in a contract.

Statutory provisions in the *Sale of Goods Act* and in the Business Practices or Trade Practices legislation further define and limit the application of the common law remedies.

An example of innocent misrepresentation concerning the effect of a contractual term is found in *Jaques v. Lloyd D. George & Partners Ltd.* [21] The principle of this case has been expressly approved by the Supreme Court of Canada. [22]

In *Jacques*, the owner of a café wanted to sell his business. In October 1965, he was approached by a real estate agent (his previous agent had been unsuccessful in selling the business) who offered to assist him. The agent told the café owner: "If we find a suitable purchaser and the sale goes through, you will pay us £250." He then produced a standard form contract for the vendor to sign. One term of the contract provided that the vendor would pay at least £250 should the agent be instrumental in introducing a person willing to sign a document capable of becoming a contract to purchase.

In December 1965, the agent brought along a prospective purchaser who made an offer in writing to the vendor. The offer was conditional upon the purchaser obtaining the consent of the vendor's landlord to an assignment of the lease. The landlord refused to make the assignment on the grounds that the purchaser was not a suitable person for the business. The purchase fell through. The agent claimed the right to retain the £250 deposit given by the purchaser as commission under the agency contract. The vendor said he had been told the commission was payable only if the purchase was completed. The agent relied upon the terms of the contract that were inconsistent with his earlier statements. Lord Denning found for the vendor, observing:[23]

> An estate agent cannot rely on the printed form when his representative misrepresents the content or effect of it. In *Dennis Reed Ltd. v. Goody*, the representative said it was "merely a routine matter" when he asked the seller to sign. In the present case he said: "If we find a suitable purchaser and the deal goes through, you [pay] £250." That is equivalent to a representation that the usual terms apply. It was a misrepresentation of the effect of the document. No person can hold another to a printed form which has been induced by misrepresentation, albeit an innocent misrepresentation. I well remember Scrutton L.J. in *L'Estrange v. F. Graucob Ltd.* saying with emphasis: "in the absence of fraud . . . or, *I will add, misrepresentation*, the party signing it is bound."
>
> Applying this other principle, I think that the agent misrepresented the effect of the document, and for this reason it can and should be avoided. . . .

Negligent Misrepresentation

The traditional rule had been that no action for damages would lie unless the misrepresentation was fraudulent. Thus, an innocent or negligent misrepresentation would not support a claim for damages. This inevitably placed considerable pressure on the representee to show that the representor knew his misstatement was false, or was reckless to the truth or falsity of the statement. However, this narrow interpretation was first questioned by the House of Lords in *Nocton v. Lord Ashburton*.[24]

In 1963, the House of Lords decision in *Hedly Byrne & Co. Ltd. v. Heller & Partners, Ltd.*,[25] opened the way for a damage action for negligent misrepresentations. In that case, the House of Lords for the first time acknowledged that a misrepresentation by one in a special relationship with the representee would give rise to a tort action for damages.

In *Hedly Byrne*, the plaintiffs were advertising agents. Easipower Ltd. placed a substantial advertising order with the plaintiffs. The plaintiffs were personally liable to the television company and newspapers that carried these ads in return for payment. To reduce their risk of default by Easipower Ltd., the plaintiffs contacted their own bank, which, in turn, wrote to Easipower's bankers to inquire into the financial stability of the company. The plaintiffs wanted to know whether Easipower Ltd. would be a good credit risk for an advertising contract for £8000 to £9000.

The company's bank replied with the disclaimer "For your private use and without responsibility" that the company was respectably constituted. This information was passed on to the plaintiffs through their own bank. Relying on the company's bank representation, the plaintiffs went through with the advertising contracts. Easipower Ltd. defaulted, and the plaintiffs lost over £17 000. They then sued the bank for damages based on negligent misrepresentation.

The bank escaped liability because of the disclaimer of "without responsibility". But the principle was established that an action on negligent misrepresentation could be founded so long as there was a "special relationship" between the parties. Such a special relationship arose where the persons provided professional services to clients who relied upon their expertise in making accurate statements. This would cover lawyers, accountants, architects, real estate agents, and similar professionals who hold themselves as having special skills.

The law of negligent misrepresentation is complicated by the Pigeon J. judgment in *J. Nunes Diamonds Ltd. v. Dominion Electric Protection Co.*:[26]

> The basis of tort liability considered in *Hedley Byrne* is inapplicable to any case where the relationship between the parties is governed by a contract, unless the negligence relied on can properly be considered as "an independent tort" unconnected with the performance of the contract. . . .

The timing of the misstatement is crucial in an action found on negligent misrepresentation. Where the misstatement leads to the making of a contract, a tort action will lie against the representor who made the negligent misrepresentation. Similarly where the parties already have a contract, unless there is evidence of an independent tort unconnected with the contract, the representee will not have an action in tort. The test of whether the misstatement is connected with the performance of the contract is: "Would these representations have been made if the parties had not been in the contractual relationship in which they stood?"[27]

In *Nunes Diamonds*, a contractual claim would have been of little value. Under the terms of the contract, the representee was limited to liquidated damages of $50. Therefore, unless the representee could base an action on tort, the actual losses suffered from the negligent misrepresentation were not recoverable. Also, on the facts the trial court judge found that there was no evidence of breach of contract by the representor.

The problem of remedies for negligent misrepresentation is shown in the following illustration.

Illustration   Rinehart Ltd. uses telecommunication hook-ups to communicate with its subsidiary companies. Many sensitive messages are relayed, including technical research and development data. The President of the company is concerned about the possible wrongful interception of this information by third parties. A company called Tele-Secure Ltd. is contacted. This company is in the business of supplying hardware and software that allows the user to scramble and unscramble information sent over modems.

PROBLEM #1

The President of Tele-Secure Ltd., Joan Allen, states to the President of Rinehart Ltd. that not even her best computer "hackers" could breach the security system contained in their hardware and software scramblers. She further stated no one had ever breached the system without setting off an alarm built into the system. After this representation, Rinehart Ltd. enters into a contract for the Tele-Secure Ltd. system. In the standard form contract drawn by Tele-Secure Ltd. there were these provisions: (i) It is agreed by and between the parties hereto that Tele-Secure Ltd. is not an insurer, and in the case of failure of the system, its liability hereunder is limited to and fixed at the sum of $500 as liquidated damages. (ii) No conditions, warranties, or representations have been made by Tele-Secure Ltd., its officers, servants, or agents other than those endorsed hereon in writing.

Six months later, Rinehart Ltd. discovers that a valuable trade secret sent with the Tele-Secure Ltd. system was intercepted by a competitor. The wrongful use of that information has cost Rinehart Ltd. $25 000. In these circumstances, there is a reasonable probability that Tele-Secure Ltd. would be liable in a tort action for damages based on their president's negligent misrepresentation.

PROBLEM #2

The facts are the same except for two crucial differences. The President, Joan Allen, did not make any precontractual representation concerning the ability of others to breach the system. After the contract was executed, a computer engineer assigned by Tele-Secure Ltd. to install the system told the President of Rinehart that the system was "absolutely invulnerable" and "could never be penetrated by someone on the outside". As in *Nunes Diamonds*, it is unlikely that Rinehart Ltd. would succeed in damages for breach of contract given that there was no warranty. Although there would be a stronger case for fundamental breach of contract, i.e., Rinehart Ltd. did not get what they had bargained for, we will assume that the system was not defective but that the intruder "picked the lock" by a means not known or anticipated by companies such as Tele-Secure Ltd. In the absence of contract liability, is there a claim in tort? Based on *Nunes Diamonds*, the tort action would fail on the grounds that the computer engineer would not have made his claims but for the contractual relationship between his employer and Rinehart Ltd.

Mistake

Parties entering a contract may make errors or have misunderstandings about matters involving the contract. The law of mistake defines the legal consequences of such errors and misunderstandings. That leads us to the initial question: What, according to common law principles, constitutes a mistake? This question has created a cottage industry of legal texts and articles, each suggesting different means of classification and putting different emphasis on the nature, scope, and consequences of mistake. There is neither space nor time to follow the fine threads of the many arguments on the innumerable themes, or variation on themes, making up the law of mistake. Our concern is limited to mistakes in the formation of a contract. To this end, we will briefly survey a few of the major classifications of mistakes that have the effect of destroying contractual consent. Once assent to the contract is lost, formation of the contract is prevented.

Mistake as to Assent to a Contract

Each party may misunderstand what the other intends; they are at cross-purposes. The buyer believes he/she is contracting for one thing while the seller believes the contract is for something else. In such a case neither party is aware of the other's mistake.

Illustration A business executive, Gary Sebert, inexperienced in computers, contracts with a computer retailer for the Rinehart spreadsheet software program. The retailer sells him a program called Rindheart Spreadsheet Program; this program is manufactured in Hong Kong and is substantially inferior to the Rinehart Ltd. product. Neither the seller nor the buyer of the software is to blame for the misunderstanding. Nonetheless, the product that one wants to buy and the other to sell are radically different. How can there be a contract formed with such a basic misunderstanding?

A leading English case illustrating the problem is *Raffles v. Wichelhaus*.[28] In that case the plaintiff agreed to sell the defendant 125 bales of Surat cotton, which was to arrive from Bombay on a ship called *Peerless*. As it turned out, there were two ships called *Peerless* sailing from Bombay. One was to leave Bombay in October and the other in December. The defendant buyers said that they intended to take delivery of the cotton from the *Peerless* that left Bombay in October. The plaintiff seller said he intended the *Peerless* that set sail in December. As the plaintiff intended one ship and the defendant a different one, there was no consensus *ad idem*. As a result, the buyer could not recover damages because the seller failed to deliver the cotton from the *Peerless* sailing in October. Similarly, the seller could not recover damages because the buyer refused to take delivery of cotton on the December sailing of the second *Peerless*.

If each party meant a different thing, how can there have been a meeting of the minds? The answer is that there cannot be a contract in these circumstances.

Mistake as to Subject Matter

In the illustration above, we considered an example of mistake as to identity of the subject matter. Such mistakes may also include errors as to the existence of the subject matter. The buyer contracts to buy a Rinehart word processing program and the seller accepts that order; but Rinehart does not produce a word processing program. The contract is void because the subject of the contract does not exist.

As a general, rule a mistake about the quality of the subject matter will not prevent the formation of a contract. This is true even though the quality and value of the thing sold are closely interrelated. A buyer would be willing to pay $75 000 for a painting by Emily Carr. If, however, it was discovered by both seller and buyer that the painting was done by Joe Citizen, and that Joe Citizen's paintings sell for no more than $1000 each, the mistake would not prevent the formation of the contract.[29]

What happens when the point is reached where the mistake as to quality is so fundamental that, had the parties known the true quality, they would not have made the contract? Even so the contract is not nullified. In one celebrated case, a company made a contract to pay a managing director £30 000 compensation for the loss of his job. Later the company learned that the managing director, owing to misconduct, could have been dismissed without compensation. The company sued to recover the £30 000 and lost. The House of Lords held the common mistake did not nullify the contract.[30]

Mistake as to Quality

In most cases where there is a mistake as to quality, there is a contract. The buyer who receives the product with substantial defects in quality is left to sue for breach of contract based on the representation or warranty attached to the product. Here the parties are not at cross-purposes over the identity of the thing sold. The mistake is about some feature or quality about which they both agree is the subject of the contract.

Illustration   Rinehart Ltd. sells a word processing program for IBM PCs and Apple computers. The company has an initial order for 10 000 copies of the program from a software distributor, **AJI** Technical Products Inc. After the standard form contract is signed, **AJI** runs a test on the program and discovers a number of substantial defects. The documentation is only ten pages and is virtually useless. Also, the program has no capacity to copy files, search and replace, or write to other devices, and the formatted output leaves in all the format commands. **AJI** refuses to accept delivery of the 10 000 diskettes of the program on the basis they are not getting what they contracted for. It is likely that a court would hold that there is a contract between the parties. However, based on these different quality facts, **AJI** would have remedies for breach of contract against Rinehart Ltd.

Mistake as to Identity of a Person

As a general rule, a mistake as to the identity of another person will prevent the formation of a contract. In the typical case, one party has lied or disguised his/her identity to mislead the other. Then this rogue transfers the goods obtained under the contract to a third party and disappears. The consequence of the mistake rule, in these circumstances, is particularly serious for a third party who buys the goods from the rogue. If the original contract was never formed, then no title ever passed to the rogue. Thus, the third party would not obtain title in the transaction with the rogue.

The original owner of the goods has an action for conversion against the innocent third party. On the other hand, where the contract is voidable (rather than void), the innocent third party is able to take good title from the rogue. Therefore, an important distinction exists between a mistake of identity and a mistake as to an attribute of identity. In the former case, the contract is not void.

In the mistaken identity cases, the reasoning is familiar: There is no consent to deal with a person of a different identity. The problem has been to distinguish between a mistake as to identity and a mistake as to some attribute of identity. The distinction is not always easy to apply. A person's identity is a series of attributes.

Illustration Ms. Bach engages the services of John Wallis, who holds himself as a lawyer qualified to practice law in New York City. Ms. Bach has asked for a legal opinion on corporate status of a distributor of software in New York State. After Ms. Bach receives the opinion, she discovers that Mr. Wallis is not a lawyer, and is not qualified to practise law in New York or any other state. Here the identity as "lawyer" is absolutely crucial from Ms. Bach's point of view. A legal opinion from a non-lawyer would be worthless. In this case, it is likely there would be no contract between the parties. Ms. Bach only consented to contract with a lawyer.

Assume, however, that Mr. Wallis was a qualified lawyer with only one year of experience. There would be a contract even though Ms. Bach mistakenly believed that he had practised corporate law in New York for twenty years. The nature of the mistake is of importance. Did Mr. Wallis cause the mistake by improper concealment or suppression of the material fact concerning his years of experience? Evidence of such concealment would amount to fraud and invalidate the contract.[31]

Mere silence alone with regard to the material fact will not invalidate the contract. Even this proposition of the common law might be questioned today. It is clear that the courts condemn the use of an artifice or disguise by the seller of goods or services for purposes of concealing defects or flaws. The policy of the law is to prevent wrongful advantage-taking through lies, deceptions, and unfair dealing. In the words of Grange J.: "The intention of the non-mistaken party is of importance and may, indeed, in many circumstances be paramount."[32]

Where goods or services are sold on credit, the seller has an economic interest in ensuring that the buyer can ultimately honour his/her obligation to pay. A buyer who is dishonest may attempt to mislead the seller into making a mistake about risk to selling to him/her on credit. The deception may take the form of the buyer assuming another identity. In these circumstances, does the law of mistake render the contract void? In most cases it does not.

There are reported cases where the buyer has assumed the identity of a movie star or well-known, reliable person. The deceptions caused the seller to make a mistake about the buyer's financial resources to pay for goods or services received on credit. The law is clear that there is a contract. A mistake of attribute such as the financial resources of the other person will not nullify the consent to contract with that person.

Mistake as to Value

Parties to a contract attach a value to the goods or services exchanged under the contract. The buyer may miscalculate the price he/she is willing to pay for 10 000 word processing programs. The miscalculation may result from his/her mistaken view on the number of willing consumers who will purchase the program or the number or quality of competing word processing programs. This type of mistake is not a grounds for holding the contract is void or voidable. The risk of buying and selling any product is, in part, accurately assessing its value. The law of mistake does not avail the person who has, through his/her own error, paid too much for goods or services. There are instances, however, where the court, based on equitable principles, has intervened to relieve a party who has agreed to receive an excessively low value for a thing sold. By and large, these cases are not commercial cases between businesspersons.

There may be an attribute of a product that the buyer mistakenly assumes exists and believes that there is no risk in the product lacking such an attribute. In these circumstances, the courts may intervene on behalf of the buyer. Thus, the buyer of the 10 000 diskettes of Rinehart Ltd. word processing program may mistakenly assume that it can be used on IBM PCs. He/she discovers, in fact, that the program is only compatible with Zorba 2000. If the substance of what the buyer has contracted for is an IBM PC word processing program, and the price has been fixed on that basis, then the mistake goes to the very substance of the contract.

The buyer would not have made a contract on the basis of a program for the Zorba 2000.

Mutual and Unilateral Mistake: Identity and Subject

In a mutual mistake case both parties have made an error about the other's intentions. A software retailer agrees to sell the Rinehart Ltd. word processing program on the assumption the customer wants Apple software. The customer, in fact, wants to buy a word processing program for an IBM PC Neither the retailer nor the customer is aware of the misunderstanding of the other. They have both made a mistake about what the other party intends. A binding contract would not exist in such a case.

The traditional test employed by the courts is whether a reasonable person would believe the terms offered by the other party. If on an objective view a reasonable person would conclude that there was a contract, then the mistake will not vitiate the consent required to form a contract. Another test adopted in Canada places emphasis on whether or not the mistake was fundamental. The problem is that the term "fundamental" is less a legal test than a conclusion applied to underlying assumptions of the parties — a conclusion that can be made without any genuine analysis.

In a unilateral mistake case, one party is aware of the mistake the other party has made about the subject matter of the contract or the identity of the person being contracted with. Thus, where the retailer knows the customer wants an IBM word processing program and that the Rinehart Ltd. word processing program will not operate on a IBM PC, there is a case of unilateral mistake. Indeed, in such cases there is often evidence that the seller misrepresented the product to the customer. As we have earlier seen, a fraudulent misrepresentation prevents the formation of a binding contract. What is the result in the absence of misconduct by the non-mistaken party? The non-mistaken party will not generally be allowed to take advantage of the other's mistake. The rationale is based on the notions of fair dealing and unconscionable conduct.

Mistake of Fact/Mistake of Law

It is well established that a mistake of law will not be a grounds for nullifying or rescinding a contract. Only mistakes of fact will be the basis for preventing the formation of a contract. Moreover, a person who pays money under a mistake of law has no right to recover it.[33] In many cases, it is difficult to justify allowing the defendant to retain the money mistakenly paid to him in these circumstances.

There is, however, no bright-line distinction between mistake of fact and law. In some instances, there is an overlap between law and fact. The courts have circumvented the unfairness of the mistake of law rule by finding that there was a mistake as to private rights arising from a misinterpretation of a document or statute. This is merely one example of the bewildering number of exceptions to the mistake of law rule that enables the court to grant relief.

The basis of the mistake of law rule comes from the English case of *Bilbie v. Lumley*.[34] Legions of cases have followed the general principle that every person is presumed to know the law. In reality, where fairness and equity demand intervention, the Canadian courts have intervened and treated the mistake of law, through the device of an exception, in the same matter as a mistake of fact. Many commentators have argued that the distinction should be abolished. The British Columbia Law Reform Commission has urged the abolition of the rule for that province.

Problems for Discussion

1. Rinehart Ltd. entered a contract for software development consulting services with Acrodrome Ltd. on October 1, 1987. Under the terms of the contract, Acrodrome provided two software engineers to prepare detailed specifications and plans for a Canada-wide telecommunication system. The project is the subject of a general contract between Rinehart Ltd. and the Canadian government. The sub-contract between Rinehart Ltd. and Acrodrome incorporates, by references, the terms of the main contract, including a provision that allows the government's chief engineer or Rinehart Ltd.'s project head to alter, modify, or change specification in the software design. In late December, Rinehart Ltd.'s project head made alterations to the specification being developed by Acrodrome Ltd.

   These changes would involve considerably more money and time for Acrodrome Ltd., which protested the alterations as adding extra work. The President of Rinehart Ltd. said the alterations were permitted under the contract. Acrodrome Ltd. disagreed with that interpretation, saying this was more work than they had agreed to perform. The President replied that unless Acrodrome changed the specification and incorporated them into the software, they would call in another software firm to do the job and deduct the cost against the amount owed to Acrodrome Ltd. under the contract. As Acrodrome Ltd. was facing financial difficulty, they had no choice but to agree with Rinehart Ltd.'s demand or face bankruptcy. After the contract was completed, Acrodrome claimed Rinehart Ltd. was obliged to pay them for the "extra work". Does Acrodrome Ltd. have a good cause of action? See *Peter Kiewit Sons' Co. of Can. Ltd. v. Eakins Const. Ltd.*, (1960) S.C.R. 361, 22 D.L.R. (2d) 465 (S.C.C.).

2. Jones took his I.B.M. P.C. into **JWX** Computer Ltd. for repairs. He was having trouble with disk drive **A** loading software into memory. He explained the problem to a clerk at the desk. He was then asked to sign a receipt. When Jones asked why he had to sign the receipt, the clerk explained: "You're responsible for any damage to disk drive **A**. They are tricky to fix and if we try, and make things worse, then we're not liable." The receipt contained a clause that read: "This computer is accepted on condition that the company is not liable for any damage howsoever arising, or delay." Three days later, **JWX** Computer Ltd. was broken into and Jones' computer was stolen. **JWX** Computer Ltd. relies on the printed contract to deny any liability for Jones' loss. Jones argues the contract was misrepresented to him. Can he recover for the loss of his computer, valued at $2000? See *Curtis v. Chemical Cleaning and Dyeing Co.*, (1951) 805 (C.A.).

3. Whitney Smith, an accountant, read an advertisement for the Lindley Personal Computer. The advertisement represented that computer as follows: (i) the hottest computer system to hit the market in five years; (ii) far more powerful than the current 16-bit 80888 found in most other computers; (iii) perfect for the professional accountant or lawyer; (iv) user friendly; you'll be working flat out on our system in 6 hours; (v) the Lindley will increase your productivity by at least 50%. The following day Smith purchased a Lindley Personal Computer from **JWX** Computer Ltd. for $8000. Rinehart Ltd., on an agreement with Lindley, Inc., distributed the computer in Canada. This was a name familiar to Smith and one of the reasons that he bought the computer. The purchase was made one month before the start of the tax season.

   The Lindley proved to be an absolute failure. The documentation was poor and, after two weeks, the computer was still not functioning properly. Smith's business began to fall off rapidly as clients took away their accounts. By the end of the tax season, Smith had lost nearly half of his business as a result of the attempted computerization of his office. Smith was unfamiliar with the characteristics and performance of computers and relied on **JWX** Computer Ltd.'s skills and judgment in representing what was the best buy for an accountant. The manufacturer's warranty excluded the seller from liability other than repairing or replacing any defective part of the computer. All other warranties, express or implied, were excluded. Smith seeks advice as to whether he has any action against **JWX** Computer Ltd., Rinehart Ltd., and Lindley, Inc. for the damage to his business. See *Murray v. Sperry Rand Corporation*, (1979) 96 D.L.R. (3d) 113 (Ont. H.C.).

4. Ms. Harvey, the bank manager of the N.B. Bank, approved the loan of $50 000 to James Lewis, a computer engineer. Mr. Lewis used this money as venture capital to establish Exotic Software Ltd. The purpose

of this company was to create and market a software aimed at farmers who breed exotic animals. It was a speculative venture, but Mr. Lewis had a good track record in developing software for Rinehart Ltd. during the two years that he was employed with the company. The company provided him with a letter of introduction and a high recommendation for his software development skills and expertise. In June 1986, Mr. Lewis fell into arrears on his loan to the bank. He began canvassing the area for potential investors in his company. He met Mrs. Jones, a fifty-nine-year-old widow whose only substantial asset was her house in Toronto. Her annual income was $10 000. She was impressed by Mr. Lewis and made an appointment with Ms. Harvey to borrow $25 000 to invest in his company. Ms. Harvey expressed great enthusiasm about the Lewis venture. She said that it was a good chance for her to make some money. But she did not tell Mrs. Jones that Mr. Lewis was in arrears on his $50 000 loan to the bank.

As she had known Ms. Harvey for about five years and had relied on her advice before, Mrs. Jones borrowed the money and lent it to Mr. Lewis. Six months later, Exotic Software Ltd. went bankrupt and Mr. Lewis disappeared. Does she have an action against the bank? See *Harvey v. Bank of Nova Scotia*, (1984) 27 C.C.L.T. 298 (Ont.H.C.).

5. Rinehart Ltd. offered to sell 5000 copies of their videogame software to a Royal-Soft Distributors Ltd. In the past, the two companies had done business. On this occasion, an employee of Rinehart Ltd. made an error in calculation. He quoted the price at $7 per diskette; in fact, the wholesale price was $10 per diskette. Later, Royal-Soft Distributors Ltd. accepted delivery of the product and issued a cheque to Rinehart Ltd. for $35 000, which contained the notation "paid in full". We can assume from the previous dealings that Royal must have known an error was made. Once the error was discovered, Rinehart Ltd. sent a new invoice to Royal for an additional $15 000. Royal refused to pay, claiming that they had a contract for $7 per diskette. Discuss Rinehart Ltd.'s position. See *Hartog v. Colin & Shields*, (1939) 3 All E.R. 566.

6. John Jones gave a presentation of what he described as his new "Pirates of Lions Bay" videogame to Research and Development Vice-President Sam Sones, who was also in charge of acquisitions. Rinehart Ltd. decided to purchase the copyright of the game from Jones for $5000 cash and royalties of 4 percent on all copies of the game sold by Rinehart Ltd. After paying Jones the $5000, it was discovered that Jones did not own copyright in "Pirates of Lions Bay". His nephew, Harold, had created the game and owned the copyright to it. At the time Jones made the contract with Rinehart Ltd., he believed that he could buy his nephew's copyright for $200. The nephew, however, read about the Rinehart sale in the newspaper and refused to sell to his uncle.

Rinehart seeks to recover the $5000 paid to Jones; but he claims that they have a contract. Does the mistake prevent the formation of the contract? Can Rinehart Ltd. recover the money from Jones? See *Couturier v. Hastie*, (1856), 5 H.L. Cas. 673 and *Roche v. Johnson*, (1916) 53 S.C.R. 18, 29 D.L.R. 329 (S.C.C.).

7. Rinehart Ltd. received an order for 5000 copies of their word processing program from a New York company called Complete Software Distributors Ltd. The letterhead of Complete Software indicated that it was a major software distributor for the East Coast. The diskettes were shipped to Complete on credit terms. Payment was due ninety days after delivery. After the ninety days expired, Rinehart Ltd. discovered that Complete was a company established by an impecunious person named Howard Rogue. Rogue has sold the 5000 diskettes to Data Soft Distributors in New Jersey. Data Soft Distributors had no connection with Rogue other than this one sale. Can Rinehart Ltd. successfully sue Data Soft Distributors for conversion? Assume that Anglo-Canadian law applies. See *King's Norton Metal Co. Ltd. v. Edridge, Merrett & Co. Ltd.*, (1897) 14 T.L.R. 98; and compare with *Cundy v. Lindsay*, (1878) 3 App.Cas. 459. For a more recent case, see *Lewis v. Averay*, (1972) 1 Q.B. 198.

8. In the legislative approach to unconscionability is there a difference between the Ontario and American (U.C.C.) legislation? How does this legislative approach compare with the one found in the common law? To what extent is the unconscionability jurisdiction an invitation for the courts to rewrite and set aside commercial and consumer transactions? Are our judges in a good position to make informed judgments about the commercial background and needs of an industry or trade? Why is it important to maintain a distinction between commercial and consumer contract in the application of the unconscionability principles?

Chapter 4 Notes

1. (1961) S.C.R. 361, 27 D.L.R. (2d) 639 (S.C.C.).
2. *Ibid.*, p. 642.
3. (1961) O.R. 154, 31 D.L.R. (2d) 323 (C.A.).
4. (1982) 2 W.L.R. 803 (H.L.).
5. (1965) 54 W.W.R. 257, 259, 55 D.L.R. (2d) 710 (B.C.C.A.).
6. (1975) Q.B. 326, (1974) 3 All E.R. 757, 765 (C.A.).
7. (1978) 95 D.L.R. (3d) 231 (C.A.).
8. *Ibid.*, p. 241.
9. (1973) 40 D.L.R. (3d) 303 (S.C.C.).
10. (1981) 119 D.L.R. (3d) 440 (N.S.S.C., Trial Div.).
11. *Ibid*
12. *S.O. 1974, c. 31.*

13. See *Davidson v. Three Spruces Realty Ltd.*, (1978) 79 D.L.R. (3d) 481, 482 (B.C.S.C.).
14. (1884) 24 Ch.D. 7,15.
15. *Hinchey v. Gonda*, (1955) O.W.N. 125, 127 (Ont.H.C.).
16. *May v. Platt* (1900) 1 Ch. 616.
17. See *Derry v. Peek*, (1889) 14 App.Cas. 337, 374.
18. Cheshire and Fifoot, *Law of Contract*, 9th ed. 256.
19. *C.R.F. Holdings Ltd. et al. v. Fundy Chemical International Ltd., et. al.*, (1981) 21 B.C.L.R. 345 (B.C.S.C.), varied (1982) 33 B.C.L.R. 291 (B.C.C.A.), reheard on quantum of damages (1983) 39 B.C.L.R. 43 (B.C.S.C.).
20. (1803) 3 Bos & P. 367, 127 E.R. 200, 203.
21. (1968) 1 W.L.R. 625 (C.A.).
22. *Canadian Indemnity Co. v. Okanagan Mainline Real Estate Board*, (1970) 16 D.L.R. (3d) 715, 720 (S.C.C.).
23. *Supra*, note 21, p. 630.
24. (1914) A.C. 932 (H.L.).
25. (1964) A.C. 465; (1963) 2 All E.R. 574 (H.L.).
26. (1972) 26 D.L.R. (3d) 699, 727-28 (S.C.C.).
27. *Ibid.*, p. 728.
28. (1864) 2 Hurl. & C. 906.
29. See *Leaf International Galleries*, (1950) 2 K.B. 86.
30. *Bell v. Lever Brothers Ltd.*, (1932) A.C. 161; (1931) All E.R. 1 (H.L.).
31. See *Smith v. Hughes*, (1871) L.R. 6 Q.B. 597.
32. *Brooklin Heights Homes v. Major Holdings*, (1977) 80 D.L.R. (3d) 563 (Ont. H.C.).
33. *Hydro Electric Commission of Township of Nepean v. Ontario Hydro* (1982) 132 D.L.R. (3d) 193 (S.C.C.).
34. (1802) 2 East 469, 102 E.R. 448.

5 THIRD PARTY CONTRACTS

Privity of Contract

It has been well established since the nineteenth century that a stranger to a contract has neither the benefit of the contract nor can he/she be sued on it. Privity of contract means that the enforcement of contractual benefits is restricted to persons who are party to a contract and have furnished consideration. A person who has neither furnished consideration nor is a party to the contract is a stranger or third party. The window of contractual rights and remedies is closed to the third party. For over one hundred years, the Canadian and English courts have limited contractual enforcement solely to parties who can demonstrate that they are in privity of contract with the person sued.[1]

Privity of contract is a good example of a legal abstraction that distracts judges from the real flesh and blood reality of risk allocation.[2] The Canadian privity rule is mirrored in the earlier, more rigid and formalistic mould of English law. Little of the recent English case law, which has sought to interject a degree of flexibility to the privity of contract rule, has been accepted in Canada. The following illustration indicates the practical problem presented by the privity of contract rule.

Illustration   Rinehart Ltd. entered into a software development consulting services contract with Acrodrome Ltd. Under the terms of the contract, Acrodrome Ltd. will supply a software engineer for development of a Canadian-wide telecommunication system. Rinehart Ltd. promises to pay $5000 for the software engineer's services to the Royal Bank. Acrodrome Ltd. owes the Royal Bank $5000. The effect of the contract is the assignment, i.e., where one party transfers his/her benefit under a contract to a third party, by Acrodrome of their compensation due from Rinehart directly to the bank. When Rinehart Ltd. pays the Royal Bank the $5000, then Acrodrome's debt to the bank will be discharged.

After the completion of the contract, the President of Acrodrome Ltd. directs Rinehart Ltd. to pay the $5000 directly to Acrodrome Ltd. This is done by Rinehart Ltd. Does the Royal Bank have any right to sue Rinehart Ltd. for the $5000? As a third party or stranger to the Rinehart-Acrodrome contract, the Royal Bank cannot enforce the promise made by Rinehart Ltd. to Acrodrome Ltd. to pay the bank. There is no privity of contract between the Royal Bank and Rinehart Ltd., the promisor. Only the promisee, Acrodrome Ltd., is entitled to sue on Rinehart Ltd.'s promise to pay the $5000.

Application of the Privity of Contract Rule

The Canadian Law

Most Canadian commentators have condemned the privity of contract rule as applying form over substance. The rule may cause injustice and frustrate the intention of the parties to the contract. The prime example is found in the Supreme Court of Canada decision in *Greenwood Shopping Plaza Ltd. v. Beattie.*[3]

In *Greenwood Shopping Plaza* (the landlord), the owner of a shopping centre leased space to Neil J. Buchanan Limited (the tenant). The tenant opened a Canadian Tire store on the leased premises. Two employees of the tenant, Beattie and Pettipas, were engaged in erecting racks in the garage and storage area. While negligently using welding equipment, the employees caused a fire and substantial damage resulted to the shopping centre.

In the name of Greenwood Shopping Plaza, the landlord's insurance company sued the two employees of the tenant. This is an example of subrogation, which means that one party — in this case an insurance company — stands in the same legal position as the landlord. The insurance company has every right of action against the tenant's employees that the landlord would have had. The insurance company, under the terms of the insurance contract, has compensated the landlord for his loss, and has an express right to recover that compensation from the persons who caused the loss.

The employees defended the action on the grounds that, under the lease, the landlord was required to insure the buildings and expressly waived their right to grant subrogation to the insurer in the event of loss. The landlord failed to obtain the insurance as contemplated in the lease, and failed to arrange a waiver of subrogation with its insurer. The landlord's insurer argued, however, that the employees were not privy to the lease and could not rely on it.

The Court of Appeal of Nova Scotia held that the tenant, in making the lease with Greenwood, had intended that the insurance provisions would cover its employees' liability resulting from negligence. That is, the tenant intended to confer a benefit on third-party employees even though they were not parties to the lease. The Supreme Court of Canada reversed. Following *Tweedle v. Atkinson*, this court held that the employees were not parties to the lease and could not rely upon the insurance provisions to defend the negligent action commenced by the landlord's insurer. None of the common law exceptions to the privity of contract were held to apply.

Two commentators have considered the *Greenwood* case and concluded:[4]

> The most distressing thing about the judgment in *Greenwood* is the fact that the Court does not seem to care about the result. Yet the effect of the judgment is either to frustrate the efforts of the landlord and tenant to arrange between themselves how the cost of insurance will be borne (by forcing the tenant to indemnify his employees and, thus casting the loss on him) or put the loss on individuals who would never have appreciated the need to carry their own personal insurance and are now caught by surprise in a way that is . . . unfair and unnecessary. . . .

This pattern has become entrenched in Canadian law. Thus, in another Supreme Court of Canada decision, *C.G.E. v. Pickford-Black Ltd.*,[5] stevedores — those who work on docks, loading and unloading ships — negligently loaded heavy electrical equipment on a ship. As a result, the cargo was damaged at sea. The contract, in the form of a bill of lading — the receipt given by the person who transports or forwards goods — was entered into between the shipper and the carrier and contained an exemption clause limiting liability for damage to the cargo. Such a clause places the burden of acquiring insurance coverage for the cargo on the shipper. The stevedores argued they were also entitled to the benefit of the exemption clause in the bill of lading.

The Supreme Court of Canada, following the House of Lords,[6] held that the stevedores could not escape civil liability to pay damages for their tort by relying on the bill of lading exemption clause. There was, in other words, no privity of contract between the shipper and the stevedores, and the exemption clause in the contract between the shipper and the carrier did not apply to them.

English Trend Toward Flexibility

While affirming the common law doctrine, the English House of Lords has performed some fancy side stepping to avoid the doctrine. A good example of the abstraction of the privity of contract rule's clashing with commercial reality is contained in *The New Zealand Shipping Co. Ltd. v. A.M. Satterthwaite & Co. Ltd.* [7] The shipper, which manufactured drilling equipment, was issued a bill of lading by the carrier, which agreed to deliver the equipment to the consignee (buyer) in Wellington, New Zealand. The New Zealand Shipping Co., which was in the stevedore business, carried out all the stevedoring work as agents for the carrier in New Zealand. The day the consignee became the holder of the bill of lading, the equipment was damaged by the stevedores. The question was whether the stevedores could claim the benefit of the exemption clause contained in the bill of lading entered into between the shipper and the carrier.

> The bill of lading expressly provided ... that every exemption, limitation, condition and liberty herein contained and every right, exemption from liability, defence and immunity of whatsoever nature applicable to the Carrier or to which the Carrier is entitled hereunder shall also be available and shall extend to protect every such servant or agent of the Carrier acting as aforesaid and for the purpose of all the foregoing provisions of this Clause the Carrier is or shall be deemed to be acting as agent or trustee on behalf of and for the benefit of all persons who are or might be his servants or agents from time to time (including independent contractors as aforesaid) and all such persons shall to this extent be or be deemed to be parties to the contract in or evidence by this Bill of Lading. . . .

The House of Lords held that the stevedores were entitled to have the benefit of the exemption clause contained in the bill of lading. In Lord Wilberforce's judgment, he observed that: "The whole contract is of a commercial character, involving service on one side, rates of payment on the other, and qualifying stipulations as to both. The relations of all parties to each other are commercial relations entered into for business reasons of ultimate profit." In other words, by the terms of the contract, the parties were allocating risk in a commercial transaction. In the same fashion as in the *Greenwood* case, the landlord had accepted the obligation to insure the tenant's premises in the event of fire. Clearly the result in the *New Zealand Shipping* case accords with the actual expectations of the parties to the contract. There is no surprise; indeed, applying the privity of contract rule would have caused surprise.

By exempting the carrier and its agents, the shipper elected either to take the risk of loss over the amount contained in the bill of lading or to purchase insurance to cover the possibility of loss. The House of Lords was mindful that allowing the shippers to succeed against the stevedores would enable them to shift their loss to the agents, servants, and independent contractors of the shipper while at the same time receiving a shipping freight rate based on an exemption of liability across the board. The decision represents an important departure from the more rigid approach taken by the House of Lords in *Midland Silicones Ltd. v. Scruttons Ltd.*[8]

Exceptions to the Doctrine of Privity

The doctrine of privity is riddled with exceptions. In practice, it is easy for the experienced draftsman to avoid the problem. As a result, it is the inexperienced person who becomes caught in the ancient trap and must thrash around in the courts for years trying to fit the case within one of the established exceptions. For the most part, the exceptions operate as an escape hatch for a court that wants a convenient means of avoiding the privity rule without actually abolishing it.

Agency

In some instances, an agent will contract on behalf of his principal with a third party. In this case, the contract is actually between the principal and the third party. The key to the agency exception is the authority of the agent to enter a contract on behalf of his principal. Even where the agent lacks authority, it is possible for the principal to ratify the actions of his agent and take the benefit of the contract. Thus, agency is an important means for business to circumvent the privity of contract rule.

Illustration   Acrodrome Ltd., as a disclosed agent and with express authority, contracts on behalf of Rinehart Ltd. with a software engineer, John Howard. Under the terms of this employment contract, executed by both Acrodrome Ltd. and Mr. Howard, it is agreed that he will provide his engineering skill and expertise to develop a Canadian-wide telecommunication system for Rinehart Ltd. The term of the employment contract is six months. Mr. Howard receives his compensation directly from Rinehart Ltd.

One month after beginning his work at Rinehart Ltd., Mr. Howard repudiates the contract and takes employment with another software company for increased compensation. In these circumstances, Rinehart Ltd. would have a direct action for breach of contract against Mr. Howard. Because of the agency relationship between Acrodrome and Rinehart, the privity of contract argument would fail.

Restrictive Covenants

The English courts developed an exception to the privity rule for restrictions attached to use of land. A restrictive covenant on land, e.g., owner agrees never to build a fence higher than eight feet, would bind successors in title, who had knowledge of the covenant. It was not a defence that the successor in title was not a party to the original contract creating the restriction. Judicial enforcement of the contract was premised on the new owner's notice, actual or constructive, of the restriction. There were other limitations on these exceptions, including the restriction that it had to be for the benefit of adjacent land.

With respect to the land cases, a nineteenth-century English court in *De Mattos v. Gibson*[9] applied the same principle of pre-existing contractual restrictions to a chattel. In Canadian law, however, there is an indication that this extends to liability against a third party who has knowledge of a restriction and acts to interfere with the performance of the contract. There is some controversy in Canadian law about the extent to which this exception will be applied in a case involving a chattel, which is defined as moveable, personal property. Similarly, English authority[10] indicates that restrictions on the use or dispositions of chattels are not generally enforceable against third parties. The direction is toward the development of tort liability to restrain wrongful interference with the contractual relations of others.

Illustration   Rinehart Ltd. distributes its word processing programs through a wholesaler, TransCanada Compute Ltd. The distribution agreement between the parties provides that the price to TransCanada for bulk sales of the product (more than twenty copies) to a Canadian company for business use is $125 per copy. The price for distribution to retail computer stores for consumer use is $250 to TransCanada. The packaging and documentation for the product is different in each case. Rinehart Ltd. has discovered that an Ontario company, Canal Street Products, has been buying the word processing programs from TransCanada for $125 and retailing them to the public for $250. The retail price is $375 at a computer store. Rinehart Ltd. brings an action to restrain Canal Street from continuing to sell the word processing programs for $250 each. Canal Street Products, although not a party to the contract between Rinehart and TransCanada, was aware of the pricing provisions.

On the basis of *Trudel v. Clairol Inc. of Canada*,[11] the Rinehart Ltd. action would likely succeed in Ontario. The result, however, is not free from doubt. In reaching their decision on similar facts, the court quoted with approval a passage from the lower Quebec court that relied substantially on French authority, namely: "In France, contractual prohibitions have given rise to judgments against third parties who have knowingly participated in the exporting of the protection. . . The same binding effect is recognized in respect of third parties to fix the resale price. . . ."[12] In light of the common law fixation with privity of contract, it remains open for the Supreme Court of Canada to apply the *Trudel* judgment in a case arising from a common law jurisdiction.

Trusts

Establishing a trust requires that one party — the trustee — has agreed to hold the benefit of a promisor's contractual promise — the trust property — on trust for a third party — the beneficiary's. The beneficiary, or third party, has a right to enforce this promise through the trustee. If the trustee refuses to protect the beneficiary's promise, then the beneficiary is entitled to sue the promisor and the trustee as defendants.

The law of trusts provides an old established method to avoid the privity doctrine. But the courts apply the trust concept strictly. For example, in the *Greenwood* case, the Supreme Court of Canada refused to hold that the two employees who negligently caused the fire in the shopping centre were trust beneficiaries of the landlord's promise to insure. This decision was reached on the grounds that the landlord and tenant could have altered the insurance provisions of the lease without the consent of the employees.

The trust device has the potential to be a convenient fiction employed by the court to prevent an injustice.[13] The express trust is based on actual intention to create a trust. A constructive trust is based on a court-imposed obligation to hold property in trust because justice and fairness would be violated if the defendant were allowed to keep the property for his own benefit and enjoyment. The doctrine of constructive trust, as it has evolved in Canadian law, provides a further potential inroad to the privity rule. Although to date there has been little success in using the constructive trust — which is imposed to prevent unjust enrichment — in this fashion.

Nonetheless, a more enlightened use of the constructive trust in other areas of the law indicates that this may be a fruitful area of development in the future. In contrast to the modern constructive trust, the traditional Anglo-Canadian trust requires evidence of intention to create a trust. One position is that there must be an intention by the promisee to benefit a third party. So long as the courts continue to insist upon evidence of actual intention to create a trust, the trust exception will not be of substantial benefit to businesspersons attempting to avoid the privity rule. This follows from the fact that in most instances involving contracts in a business context it would be difficult, if not impossible, to prove an express intention to create a trust. Businesspersons do not want the heavy burdens and complex obligations attached to a trust. Courts recognize that in most matters of commerce between businesspersons, an extension of trust law would disrupt and make uncertain business transactions.

Assignment

It is well established that the promisee can assign the benefit of a promise to a third party. The third party can then enforce the promise against the promisor. The assignment of benefits under the contract does not infringe the privity of contract rule.

Illustration Rinehart Ltd. contracts to deliver 5000 copies of a videogame to Royal-Soft Distributors Ltd. Two days later, Royal-Soft Distributors Ltd. assigns its right to receive shipment of the videogames to Acrodrome Ltd. The right to receive the shipment is called a *choses in action* — from the French "la chose", which means "the thing". The assignment transfers Royal-Soft's right to receive delivery to a party who is a stranger to the original contract. Royal-Soft Distributors Ltd. is the assignor and Acrodrome Ltd. the assignee under the assignment. The law is settled that an assignment of a right to receive goods under a commercial contract is valid and enforceable.[14] Rinehart Ltd. may object to the assignment; it may not want to deal with Acrodrome Ltd. After all, Rinehart Ltd. expressly chose Royal-Soft Distributors Ltd. as the buyer of their product.

An assignment will not be valid against Rinehart Ltd. where there is evidence that the effect of the assignment is to expose the company to different business risk or additional burdens. For example, evidence that Acrodrome Ltd. was unable to pay the purchase price of the product would invalidate the assignment.

Collateral Contracts

For this exception to apply, there must be two independent contracts. The collateral contract is either an oral or written agreement made prior, contemporaneously, or subsequently to the main contract. The rule is that, where the collateral contract is either prior or contemporaneous with the main agreement, it is valid and enforceable in the absence of any conflict between the terms of the collateral and main contract. Where the collateral contract is subsequent to the main contract, then it is invalid, even though it is consistent with the main contract.

It should be emphasized that the finding of the second or collateral contract often smacks of a fiction to do justice where the privity of contract rule would otherwise intervene. The first, or main, contract might be an agreement to sell a product and is made between the retailer and the consumer. The collateral agreement for the manufacturing warranties is between the manufacturer and the customer. Thus, the customer has made "two" contracts, although it is unlikely that the average consumer would be aware that he had a separate contract with the manufacturer.

The collateral contract exception is important in the enforcement of warranties made by manufacturers. Typically, Rinehart Ltd.'s software would be sold through retail outlets. The contract of sale is between the consumer and the retailer. Thus Rinehart Ltd., as a third party to that contract, might argue that privity of contract precludes the enforcement of any warranty communicated to the consumer. But the courts have now allowed the manufacturer to hide behind the privity rule.[15]

In Canada, the same approach is found in *Murray v. Sperry Rand Corp.*[16] where a farmer, Mr. Murray, bought a defective forage harvester and sued the manufacturer, distributor, and the dealer. A sales brochure given to the farmer by the salesperson contained representations about, among other things, the "fineness of the cut". When the farmer began to use the harvester, he found that it did not meet the descriptions contained in the brochure. Many attempts to adjust the machine to reach the promised level of performance failed to increase its efficiency.

The result was a disaster for the farmer, who ultimately lost his crop, sold the machine, and gave up farming. The court held that the sales brochure prepared by the manufacturer was a sales tool intended to induce consumers to purchase the harvester. Mr. Murray was able to convince the court that the "sales brochure" was a collateral contract, which the manufacturer had broken, resulting in damages to him and that he was entitled to compensation for his loss.

Another explanation of the case is that there was a collateral warranty between the consumer and the manufacturer. Another, more far-reaching explanation is that the absence of a contractual relationship does not preclude an action for breach of warranty where a third party has given a warranty and, on the basis of the warranty, the buyer has entered into a contract with the retail seller of the goods. The best explanation, however, is that the plaintiff was enforcing a collateral contract with the harvester manufacturer.

Also, collateral contract exception applies where the consumer pays for the software by using a credit card. Although the contract is between the consumer and the retailer, the credit card company has an enforceable collateral contract with the retailer. The consideration is the credit card company's promise to pay the retailer.

Statutory Exceptions

Provincial legislatures have expressly altered the privity rule in a number of specific instances. In most cases, it is evident that, without legislative intervention, a serious injustice would result and the intentions of the parties would be frustrated. Moreover, the conduct of commerce would be seriously hampered unless certain third party rights were enforceable. Legislation further indicates the rigidity of the privity of contract rule and the hit-and-miss nature of the court-made exceptions. The legislatures, in turn, can be equally criticized for not directly abolishing the common law rule.

In England, the Law Revision Committee urged abolition in these terms: "Where a contract by its express terms purports to confer a benefit directly on a third party, it shall be enforceable by the third party in his own name subject to any defences that would have been valid between the contracting parties."[17] The recommendation, however, was never acted upon in England. In Canada, there has been a piece-meal approach to legislative reform. What follows is a brief illustration of some of the legislative changes in Canada.

INSURANCE

In a policy of insurance, the parties to the contract are the insurance company (the insurer) and the insured. The ultimate beneficiary of the policy, in particular a life insurance or automobile insurance policy, is often not a party to the contract. The privity of contract rule, for example, would prevent a beneficiary under a life insurance policy from obtaining the proceeds from the insurer on the death of the insured.

The substantial injustice of such a result is evident in *Vandepitte v. Preferred Accident Insurance Corp. of New York.*[18] In that case, the insured held a policy on his automobile with an insurance company. The policy expressly provided that the insurer would indemnify not only the insured but any person operating the automobile with his permission. The insured's daughter, who drove his car with permission, was in an automobile accident and another person was injured.

The injured person sued the insurance company directly. The company succeeded in asserting that they were not liable because the insured's daughter was not in privity of contract. The value of any rule that flies directly in the face of justice must be seriously questioned. Such an outrageous application of the rule was soon remedied by the legislature in British Columbia.

Legislation in most provinces now expressly allows the third party beneficiary to recover against the insurer. In Ontario, for example, the beneficiary is deemed to be a party to the insurance contract and to have consideration for it.[19]

LABOUR RELATIONS

It is common practice for a union to negotiate and execute a collective agreement on behalf of its members with a company. An employee, who is a member of the union, may seek to enforce the collective agreement. The doctrine of privity, however, before legislative intervention, stood as an obstacle to enforcement of collective agreements by employees.[20] To apply the privity of contract rule to collective agreements would strip unions of their most meaningful role, i.e., negotiation of a single contract containing rights and benefits for all employees. It was left to provincial legislatures to make the political judgment that unions play a positive role and that collective agreements are deserving of enforcement. In Canada, this is reflected in provincial legislation. In Ontario, for example, the *Labour Relations Act*[21] expressly makes the collective agreement binding on the employees.

NEGOTIABLE INSTRUMENTS

Negotiable instruments such as cheques, letters of credit, and promissory notes could not exist under the shadow of the privity rule. Negotiability means that a third party who has purchased the instrument has enforcement rights against the original maker. Commerce requires efficient means of financing for businesses. Not surprisingly, the negotiable instruments have been excluded from the privity rule. Federal legislation provides for protection of third-party rights and powers in the case of bills of lading and bills of exchange.[22] There is also provincial legislation for certain types of negotiable instruments.[23]

CONSUMER WARRANTIES

An important piece of legislation in Saskatchewan, New Brunswick, and Quebec allows third parties to enforce consumer warranties. In other jurisdictions, such as Ontario, the courts have sought to intervene on behalf of consumers.

Illustration: Jones, who buys the Rinehart Ltd. word processing program from **JWX** Computer Ltd., a retailer of software, later sells the program to his friend Smith. After one month of use, Smith finds a malfunction in the program and wants to enforce the manufacturer's warranty against Rinehart Ltd. In Ontario, Smith, notwithstanding the absence of privity of contract, is entitled to bring an action based on the warranty against Rinehart Ltd.[24]

Problems for Discussion

1. In the *Greenwood* case, did the Supreme Court of Canada place too little emphasis on the allocation of insurance responsibility, by the terms of the lease, on the landlord? Is the philosophy contained in *Greenwood* consistent with Lord Wilberforce's judgment in *The New Zealand Shipping Co. Ltd. v. A.M. Satterthwaite & Co. Ltd.?*

2. If the privity of contract rule has caused injustice and hardship, why hasn't the Supreme Court of Canada abolished it? What would be some of the potential adverse consequences of a blanket reversal of the rule?

3. **AJW** Computer Ltd. entered into a contract with Acrodrome Ltd. under which they promised to retail the Rinehart Ltd. word processing pro-

gram for $379 and to pay $25 in liquidated damages for each breach of the promise to Rinehart. **AJW** Computer Ltd. has repeatedly breached the promise to Acrodrome. Ms. Bach is considering suing **AJW** Computer Ltd. for the liquidated damages. Will the privity of contract defence apply? See, *Dunlop Pneumatic Tyre Co. v. Selfridge & Co.*, (1915) A.C. 847 (H.L.).

4. Rinehart Ltd. has negotiated to acquire an Alberta software company called TrivCard Software Ltd. A term of the proposed contract requires Rinehart Ltd. to pay Mr. Noble $10 000/a until his death, and after his death, to pay Mr. Noble's widow the sum of $10 000/a from the anniversary of death. Mr. Noble, who is President and the majority shareholder of TrivCard, will execute the acquisition agreement on behalf of his company. Ms. Bach, on behalf of Rinehart Ltd., has been asked to determine whether this promise is enforceable by either Mr. Noble or, upon his death, his widow. It should be noted that Mrs. Noble is the executrix of her husband's will and is a shareholder in TrivCard. Does the privity of contract rule preclude enforcement? See *Beswick v. Beswick*, (1968) A.C. 58, (1967) 2 All E.R. 1197 (H.L.).

5. In May, 1983 Ms. Bach's father opened a joint account for himself and Ms. Bach at the Commerce Bank. The opening deposit was $50 000. Between May, 1983 and the death of Ms. Bach's father on April 9, 1986, there were no further deposits or withdrawals. At the request of the Royal Trust, the executor of the father's estate, the Commerce Bank paid over the $50 000. Ms. Bach brings an action against the Commerce Bank for the $50 000. The Commerce Bank argues that she was not in privity of contract and had no right to the funds. Discuss whether this defence by the Commerce Bank will succeed. See *McEvoy v. Belfast Banking Co., Ltd.*, (1935) A.C. 24 (H.L.)

Chapter 5 Notes

1. *Tweedle v. Atkinson*, (1861) 1 B. & S. 393, 121 E.R. 762.
2. See Swann and Reiter, "Developments in Contract Law: the 1979-80 Term," (1981) 2 S.C.L.Rev. 125, 133-34.
3. (1980) 2 S.C.R. 228, 111 D.L.R. (3d) 257 (S.C.).
4. *Supra*, note 2, at 135.
5. (1971) S.C.R. 41, 14 D.L.R. (3d) 372.
6. *Midland Silicones Ltd. v. Scruttons Ltd.*, (1962) A.C. 446.
7. (1975) A.C. 154, (1974) 1 All E.R. 1015.
8. *Supra*, note 6.
9. (1858) 4 De. G. & J. 276, 45 E.R. 108.
10. *Port Line Ltd. v. Ben Line Steamers Ltd.*, (1958) 2 Q.B. 146.
11. (1975) 54 D.L.R. (3d) 399 (S.C.C.).
12. *Ibid.*, p. 403.
13. See *Les Affreteurs Reunis S.A. v. Leopold Walford (London) Ltd.*, (1919) A.C. 801.

14. See *Tolhurst v. Associated Portland Cement Co.*, (1903) A.C. 414 (H.L.).
15. See *Shanklin Pier Ltd. v. Detel Products Ltd.*, (1951) 2 K.B. 854 (K.B.).
16. (1979) 5 B.L.R. 284.
17. 6th Interim Report (Cmnd. 5449), Section D.
18. (1933) A.C. 70 (P.C.).
19. See *Insurance Act*, R.S.O. 1980, c. 218, section 213.
20. See *Young v. Canadian Northern Railway*, (1931) A.C. 83 (P.C.).
21. R.S.O. 1980, c. 228, s. 50.
22. See *Bills of Lading Act*, R.S.C. 1970, c. B-6, section 2; and *Bills of Exchange Act*, R.S.C. 1970, c. B-5, section 74.
23. See, e.g., *Warehouse Receipts Act*, R.S.O. 1980, C. 528, section 6.
24. See *Consumer Products Warranties Act*, R.S.S. 1978, c. C-30, s. 14.

6 CONTRACT PERFORMANCE

Meaning of Performance

As a general rule, performance means that the promisor has strictly discharged his contractual obligations. A court judges the party's performance with a strict standard. The party, whose performance is at issue, must have discharged all the contractual obligations found in the express or implied terms of the contract. Failure of performance means that the party who did not receive all that the other party promised him/her is entitled to recover damages for breach of contract.

FIGURE 6.1 **TESTING STANDARD OF PERFORMANCE**

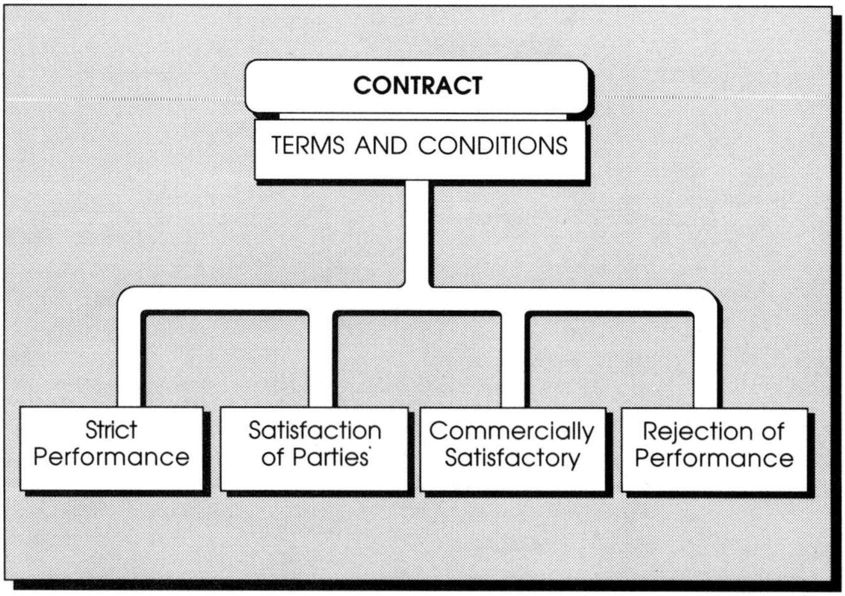

CONTRACT

TERMS AND CONDITIONS

| Strict Performance | Satisfaction of Parties | Commercially Satisfactory | Rejection of Performance |

The Standard of Performance

Contract lawsuits, however, are the exception. Most contracts are fully performed to the satisfaction of the parties. Each party has received the benefits that he/she contracted for and discharged his/her obligations as the price for the benefits. The "strict" standard of performance, however, gives way to the more realistic "to the satisfaction of the parties" standard in practice. The courts themselves recognize the less-exacting standard in many cases. The complex commercial contract often precludes exact performance of every obligation to the strict letter of the agreement. This tension between "strict" or "exact" performance and "satisfactory" or "substantial" performance is found in a number of cases. The term performance requires further elaboration.

Types of Performance Obligations

In Figure 1.2, the performance obligations placed on the distributor are multiple and complex. For example, the distributor has distribution quotas (clause 1(b)), an obligation to place copyright and proprietary notices on copies of the software sold (clause 1(c)), and restrictions on the dissemination of confidential information (clause 5). The essence of the contract, however, is the distributor's obligation to sell Rinehart's product. The contract drafter has created a mechanism for effective distribution of Rinehart's software by defining the performance obligations of the distributor. In addition to the quota requirement, the distributor is required to use "best efforts" to advertise and promote the software (clause 2). The "big stick" to ensure the distributor's satisfactory performance is Rinehart's right to terminate the five-year term of the agreement on thirty days notice.

The Marketing Agreement in Figure 1.2 illustrates that performance of a contract may continue over a long period of time. Regulation of performance is not left to chance. Both Rinehart and the distributor have announced, in advance, what is meant by performance and the consequences of inadequate performance. Similarly, in the Software Consulting Agreement (Figure 1.3) the contract carefully divides performance by the consultant into two phases, and payment by Rinehart is dependent upon completion of each stage to its satisfaction (clause 4).

Turning to the consumer contract (Figure 1.4), there is no on-going relationship between the consumer and Rinehart once the software has been sold. This contract is primarily concerned with imposing obligations on the consumer as to the use of the software. The performance obligation placed on Rinehart is carefully limited. In the event that the consumer discovers the software is defective, the remedies against Rinehart are specifically limited and defined.

The contracts in Figures 1.2 and 1.3 fall within the continuing service category. Rinehart is "buying" the services of a distributor to sell its product, and the services of a consultant to create its product. The core of each contract is found in the nature, scope, and mechanism that allows Rinehart to monitor the contract performance of the other party. In contrast, the contract in Figure 1.4 is for the sale of consumer goods to the general public. This is the end of the chain begun in the contracts found in Figures 1.2 and 1.3. At this juncture, it is the consumer who has a great interest in ensuring that Rinehart has performed according to the advertising for a particular software product. But when the tables are turned, Rinehart carefully limits the consumer's right to pursue remedies for defective performance against them.

The Contractual Right to Reject Performance

Non-performance occurs where, for instance, the consultant has completed Phase I of the software project, according to Rinehart, but, nevertheless, Rinehart refuses to pay the fee. The breach of contract entitles the consultant to recover damages against Rinehart. On the other hand, the approval of the consultant's performance might become a way to avoid a breach of contract action. Is such a clause that allows the recipient of services or goods to say that the performance was unsatisfactory, a valid, enforceable term?

The courts have upheld such clauses. There is a caveat: The party rejecting the services or goods under such a clause must act with honesty.[1] Honesty is defined in terms of good faith. The Canadian courts apply this "good faith" test to determine whether the rejection was based on legitimate business grounds or on a hidden agenda such as a market down-turn.[2]

Illustration   Two months after Rinehart entered into the Software Consulting Agreement (Figure 1.3) with Lindsay Software Distributors Ltd., a major employer of engineers announced a layoff of 1500 engineers in British Columbia. As a result, consulting firms in that province have reduced the compensation of newly hired engineers. Rinehart has been approached by Direct Computer Consultants Ltd. which has offered to perform the same service as Lindsay for 25 percent less compensation. Ms. Bach is asked by the President whether Rinehart can terminate the consulting contract if the detailed model is unsatisfactory to Rinehart. Given these facts, it is likely that Ms. Bach would advise Rinehart that a court would view termination as "bad faith", and that Lindsay would probably succeed in a breach of contract action.

Limitation on Strict Performance Obligation

Not all commercial contracts contain a provision allowing the buyer to be final arbiter of whether the performance is satisfactory. In such a case, a problem that may surface is whether the party furnishing the goods or services has fully carried out his/her performance obligation.

Illustration Rinehart has contracted with Arnold Press Ltd. for the printing and binding of the documentation included with its software. Rinehart specified in the printing contract that the paper to be used was to be "Paris" bond. The paper actually used by Arnold Press Ltd. was "London" bond. There is no difference, however, between the two types of paper except the name. Anyone examining the documentation would be unable to determine whether "Paris" or "London" bond had been used.

Arnold Press Ltd. printed an order for $75 000 on the "London" bond. Ninety days after delivery of the printed material, Rinehart discovered that "London" bond had been used. Prior to this discovery, Rinehart shipped most of the documentation obtained from Arnold Press Ltd., along with the software, to its distributors.

These facts raise the issue of how strictly a party must comply with the exact definition of performance contained in the contract. There is authority that suggests that Arnold Press Ltd. is not in breach of contract even though its performance deviated from the precise terms of the contract.

In *Jacob and Youngs v. Kent*,[3] the plaintiff contracted to build an expensive country house for the defendant. One of the specifications required that "standard pipe" of Reading manufacture was to be used for the plumbing. The plaintiff's subcontractor substituted Cohoes pipe for Reading. The only distinguishing factor between the two pipes was the name stamped on the pipe. Once the pipe was installed it was encased behind walls. To have required the plaintiff to replace Reading pipe for the Cohoe would have resulted in substantial demolition of the completed house.

Cardozo J. held that the plaintiff was entitled to recover. "The question is one of degree, to be answered, if there is doubt, by the triers of facts. . . ." The court refused to adopt a formula which would distinguish between important and trivial deviations in performance. Instead an open ended standard was accepted. "We must weigh the purpose to be served, the desire to be gratified, the excuse for deviation from the letter, the cruelty of enforced adherence. Then only can we tell whether literal fulfillment is to be implied by law as a condition." Cardozo J. did, however, draw a firm distinction between the intentional, or willful contract breaker and the unintentional, trivial contract breaker. As for the former, the court would hold that exact performance according to the letter of the contract was required. The justification is based on the ancient rule that a man cannot be allowed to take advantage of his own wrong.[4]

Dependent and Independent Promises

The definitions of dependent and independent promises are rooted in ancient English law. Where the promise is independent, the promisee can sue without proving that he/she has performed his/her promises to the promisor. Conversely, where the promise is dependent, the action will fail unless the promisee can demonstrate that he/she has performed as required by the contract.

Whether a promise is dependent or independent depends upon the intentions of the parties and the circumstances of the contract. The court asks whether the parties intended that performance by one party was dependent upon the performance of the other. In addition to intention, factors such as the nature of the contract, customs of the industry, and the history of the relationship between the parties are relevant.

In the consumer contract (Figure 1.4) — a typical bilateral contract for the sale of goods for cash — the promises of both the retailer and the consumer are dependent. The software is sold to the consumer on the condition of payment and the payment is made condition to the receipt of the software. In the words of Corbin, the promises are dependent where "... the duty of rendering performance of one promise is conditional upon the antecedent performance of the other, or of a tender of such performance ...."[5]

There is a common-sense reason for favouring dependent promises. By making the promises dependent, each party has some insurance against the default of the other. This security function acts as an incentive for the other to perform. The failure to perform justifies the other party in withholding his/her performance. This leaves open the question of which party is required to perform first. Often the sequence of performance is contained in the contract. In the typical consumer transaction, where the seller hands over the software and the buyer hands over cash, the performance is simultaneous.

Conversely, independent promises strip the parties of any security for the return performance required of the other. Not surprisingly, independent promises are rare in commercial contracts. The one instance where they still appear is in leases of real property. The rule remains that a tenant's obligation to pay rent is independent of the landlord's obligation to, say, make repairs. In other circumstances, independent promises are generally confined to limited categories: i) where the promises occur at times or depend on events disconnected with one another; or ii) where there is clear intention by the parties not to link a duty to perform to the other's performance.[6]

Historically, there was a presumption, in absence of evidence to the contrary, that promises were dependent. The modern rule, however, presumes that mutual promises are dependent. This accords with the expectations of those in the business community. It is the rare case where those entering into a contract for goods and services would desire or intend the law to cast their mutual promises into separate orbits.

Conditions and Promises

In some cases it is unclear from the language of the contract whether the parties intended to extract a promise from the promisor or to make the promise conditional on some future and uncertain event or fact. An example of a condition is found in Clause 4 respecting Rinehart's obligation to pay fees to the consultant (Figure 1.3). Even though the consultant has fully performed according to the specification, Rinehart has made payment of the fee conditional upon the company's satisfaction of the completed tasks. Until Rinehart indicates that the completed task is satisfactory, the company has no duty to pay the consultant.

Assume that Figure 1.3 had been drafted placing an obligation on Rinehart to pay once the consultant completed Phase I of the project. After completion, the consultant would be entitled to enforce Rinehart's promise. The failure of Rinehart to pay in these circumstances would amount to a breach of promise and subject them to damages.

Clause 4, however, by interjecting the satisfaction condition, prevents the consultant from acquiring any immediate right to payment once the work is completed. The condition operates to qualify Rinehart's duty of immediate performance even though the consultant has fully performed his obligation. By taking the position that the tasks completed by the consultant were not satisfactory (assuming good faith) Rinehart is excused from the obligation to pay the fee.

Conditions Precedent and Subsequent

Parties to a contract utilize express conditions to assign risk of non-performance. These express conditions enable the parties to determine what their respective rights and obligations will be upon the happening or non-happening of such a fact or event. But it is impossible to plan for every possible contingency that may occur. To plan for every foreseeable contingency would make the contract an enormously long and complex document, and even then gaps in the planning would unexpectedly arise. On a simple cost-benefit analysis it is clearly not in the economic interest of the parties to spend weeks, if not months, considering how to draft terms to cover every conceivable fact or event that might affect the risk undertaken by each.

As a result, gaps are likely to occur in the final drafted contract once it is tested against the reality of actual performance. When such a gap appears in the contract, the courts attempt to allocate the risk on the basis of what the parties would have intended had they put their minds to the problem at the time of contracting. In this section, we will consider the express conditions used by parties to allocate important risks in the contract.

Conditions are generally divided between conditions precedent and conditions subsequent. A condition precedent operates to qualify an immediate duty to perform under a valid contract until the occurrence of some fact or event. Thus, Clause 4 in Figure 1.3 contains a condition precedent to Rinehart's duty to pay the consultant for work completed under the two phases of the project. There can be no breach of Rinehart's contractual duty until the condition of satisfaction is met.

A condition subsequent operates to terminate the promisee's right to immediate performance under the contract; the promisor's obligation is ended by the happening of a specified event or fact. A convenient distinction is that a condition precedent suspends performance whereas a condition subsequent terminates the performance obligation.[7]

The Software Licence and Marketing Agreement (Figure 1.2), Clause 1(b), contains a condition subsequent: "In the event the Distributor fails to make at least seventy-five dispositions of Software Products during any six-month period during the term of this Agreement, Rinehart may, in its sole discretion, terminate this Agreement at any time pursuant to paragraph 8(b)." The non-fulfillment of the Distributor's sales quota provides grounds for termination. A true condition subsequent would terminate the contract automatically. In the Software Licence and Marketing Agreement, the draftsman has avoided automatic termination in favour of vesting Rinehart with a power to end the contract upon the happening of the condition.

Clause 1(b) can be regarded as an express allocation of termination rights between the parties. Although such clauses are generally enforceable, it is open for the distributor to argue either that the clause is not justified on commercial grounds or that there has been bad faith in exercising the clause. There are other judicial techniques to avoid the consequences of termination clauses, including the waiver and forfeiture jurisdiction of the court.

There are two conflicting themes: i) freedom of contract; and ii) judicial avoidance of contractual terms. A consistent trend in Canadian law is the willingness of the courts to intervene based upon general notions of fairness, justice, good faith, and reasonableness.

The potential for judicial intervention is not an excuse for a party to ignore a forseeable contingency. As the Rinehart commercial contracts illustrate, the use of conditions is an essential device for allocating business risks. Failing to include such a clause, however, may lead a court to conclude that Rinehart has assumed the risk of, for example, the distributor's inability to sell software products over the five-year term of the distribution agreement.

Constructive Conditions

The term "constructive" is a well-known weasel word in the law. It is used to modify contract, trust, and condition. In each case, under the guise of "constructive", the court sets out to do justice, and the actual intentions of the parties play little, if any, role in this process. An express condition, e.g., Figure 1.3, Clause 4, in contrast, rests on the manifestation of assent of the parties to the contract. Similarly, an implied-in-fact condition arises by the nature of the thing promised. Thus, in Figure 1.3, Clause 3(b), the consultant promises to train Rinehart personnel. It would be an implied-in-fact condition that Rinehart select employees for training and instruct them to be available to the consultant who will train them. It is implied-in-fact because Clause 3(b) does not expressly require such action from Rinehart. Rinehart's obligation arises from the very nature of what has been promised.

A constructive intention is based on the court's view, given the factors of justice and equity of the case, of what the parties would have intended had they put their minds to a fact or event that has subsequently occurred.

The Software Consulting Agreement (Figure 1.3) with slight modification provides a further illustration.

Illustration Assume that the consultant is a person rather than a company, and that he/she has given an express promise to develop a piece of software for Rinehart. Two months into the project, the consultant is taken seriously ill and can not perform his/her tasks under the contract. The Agreement is silent on the effect of the consultant's non-performance because of illness. Is Rinehart entitled to damages for breach of contract against the consultant? It is likely that the court would find that the physical well-being of the consultant is a condition to the consultant's obligation to develop the software. But the contract is silent. Using the constructive condition as a device to achieve a fair and just result, the court would impose the physical well-being condition. The rationale would often be that this "constructive condition" accords with the intention of the parties.

Timing of Performance

In most commercial contracts the parties set forth the time sequence for performance. Specific dates are often employed. Under the Software Licence and Marketing Agreement, six months has been chosen as the period in which the distributor must sell seventy-five software products (Figure 1.2, clause 1(b)). In the Software Consulting Agreement (Figure 1.3), clause 2(a) provides that the consultant must submit to Rinehart a detailed model of the system on December 15, 1987.

In addition to a specific date, period of performance, or other formula, the parties may agree that "time is of the essence". Such a clause is of particular importance in volatile markets. The effect is to make certain that the time limit is strictly observed. The consultant who submitted the detailed working model of the system on December 16, 1987 would be in breach of contract if a "time is of the essence" clause had been included in the Software Consulting Agreement. Rinehart would be entitled to rescind the Software Consulting Agreement even if the consultant could demonstrate the one-day delay had not caused any harm or loss.

In the common law there was a presumption that time was of the essence in contracts of the sale of goods and mercantile contracts. The modern rule has dispensed with this presumption and leaves the court to determine, from a construction of the contract, whether time is of the essence.[8] The courts now ask whether there is an express or implied term of the contract that makes time of the essence.

In the event that the commercial contract is silent on the timing of performance, the court will impose a "reasonable time" qualification. The reasonableness of the time will be affected by the nature and subject matter of the contract, industry standards for timing, and the economic conditions of the market place. In the past, the time of the essence rule imported a higher degree of urgency in all contracts. Modern courts, however, have been more flexible to defining the "time boundaries" for performance consistently with the factors listed above.

Substantial Performance

The common law rule was strict and rigid: Payment under the contract required the performer of service to completely perform. Anything short of complete performance fell short of meeting the condition precedent for payment. The modern rule prevents injustice and unfairness by making, in certain instances, the recipient of the benefit of substantial performance liable to pay the performer compensation.

The substantial performance doctrine is dependent upon a number of rules. For example, where the plaintiff has abandoned the contract, his claim is denied. In the leading English case, *Sumpter v. Hedges*,[9] the contract called for the contractor to build two houses and stables for £565. After the contractor had completed work on the project worth about £333, he ran out of money and was unable to complete the work. The contractor sued the owner for the value of the work completed. The trial court judge found the contractor had abandoned the contract, and denied recovery. On Appeal, the trial court judgment was affirmed.

The courts attempt to balance two policies: i) the enforcement of contractual obligation; and ii) the relief of unjust enrichment. In *Sumpter v. Hedges*, the balance was tipped to strictly enforcing the contractual obligation of the contractor. To have permitted the contractor relief would have ignored his conduct. In the substantial performance case, the claimant may seek relief based on restitution and the underlying principle of unjust enrichment. But the contract and the conduct of *both* parties plays an important part in the decision to allow unjust enrichment recovery against the party receiving substantial benefits under the contract.

A modern Canadian illustration of the substantial performance doctrine is found in *Kemp v. McWilliams*.[10] In this case, there was a contract to paint a house. After a substantial amount of work had been completed by the painter, a dispute erupted with the owner. The owner refused to advance money owed under the contract to the painter. The painter sued the owner based on the theory of restitution and claimed that he was entitled to the reasonable fair market value of the work done. The historical, technical term for such a monetary claim for services performed is *quantum meruit*.

The court held the painter was entitled to his *quantum meruit* recovery. Unlike the *Sumpter v. Hedges* case, the painter had not intentionally abandoned the contract. He was forced into that position because of the failure of the owner to advance money. An important factor was the work done, which, in the view of the court, resulted in a substantial benefit to the owner. In both cases, i.e., *Sumpter* and *Kemp*, the plaintiff had improved the defendant's real property through the expenditure of labour and materials. In principle, the doctrine of substantial performance "applies not only to building contracts, but to all contracts for the construction of chattels according to plans and specifications."[11] The plaintiff must demonstrate that he/she has strictly performed in all the essentials necessary to fulfill the design and specifications contained in the contract.

Does the same principle apply in the case of the consultant and distributor in their contracts with Rinehart? The substantial performance rule is excluded by the terms of the contract in each case. By inserting in Clause 4 (Figure 1.3) completion to the satisfaction of the customer, Rinehart has created a condition precedent. Unless the condition has been waived by Rinehart, it might be argued that the consultant is not entitled to recovery for work done on the detailed model of the systems in the absence of Rinehart's satisfaction.

One justification for leaving the distributor empty-handed is that he/she expressly assumed the risk of no payment for full performance under Clause 4. Consequently, he/she should not be in a better position by rendering substantial performance that does not satisfy the company. Another rationale is the absence of any benefit conferred on the company unless Rinehart is satisfied with the consultant's work. On the other hand, were Rinehart to use the consultant's work for the benefit of the company while maintaining that it was unsatisfactory, this would be bad faith, and Rinehart would be liable to compensate the consultant.

The personal satisfaction clause may not always allow the buyer to hide behind the cloak of his own subjective standards. Two types of contracts must be distinguished. Where the work to be done is of such a nature that it cannot readily be determined by objective standards, then the subjective taste of the buyer under a personal satisfaction clause will prevail. Thus, a painter who agrees to paint a portrait of the buyer subject to a clause that the buyer is not liable to pay unless the portrait meets his/her personal satisfaction will fall into this category. No objective standard can be applied to hold that the painter has substantially performed.

A contract where the promisee undertakes to perform work involving operative fitness, mechanical utility, or structual completion, the personal sensibilities of the promisor are of less importance. An objective standard is applied and thus prevents the promisor from arbitrarily withholding his/her approval unless there is reasonable justification. Which category does the Software Consulting Agreement fall into? It is likely that a court would find that this contract falls into the second category and the court would refuse to allow Rinehart to escape liability unless a satisfactory reason were provided to reject the work done by the contractor.

What chance of success does the distributor have under the Software Licence and Marketing Agreement of arguing Rinehart is disentitled from terminating the contract (Figure 1.2) under Clause 1(b) based on the doctrine of substantial performance? The distributor's evidence is that in the prior six-month period they sold seventy-two of Rinehart's software products. They claim recovery based on substantial performance of the contract. This argument would likely fail. A distinction exists between a claim for the value of service performed and a claim to prevent termination under an express clause. In the latter case, Rinehart has not retained the benefit of sales made by the distributor: Rinehart has terminated the contractual basis on which the distributor is entitled to make future sales.

Discharge of Performance

Agreement Between the Parties

The parties to a contract may later agree to alter, modify, or vary the performance of one or both. Something in the original deal may have been radically changed halfway through the contract. Often, some supervening event has made the performance by one party more costly and difficult than originally anticipated. In order to keep the deal alive, the parties agree to recognize the impact of the supervening event and make a new agreement about performance in light of that event.

The effect of the second agreement is to discharge the performance obligation contained in the original contract. The key is the *agreement* to change the original performance obligation. One party cannot unilaterally change the nature or scope of his/her performance under the contract. The main categories of changing performance are: substituted

FIGURE 6.2 **METHODS OF DISCHARGE**

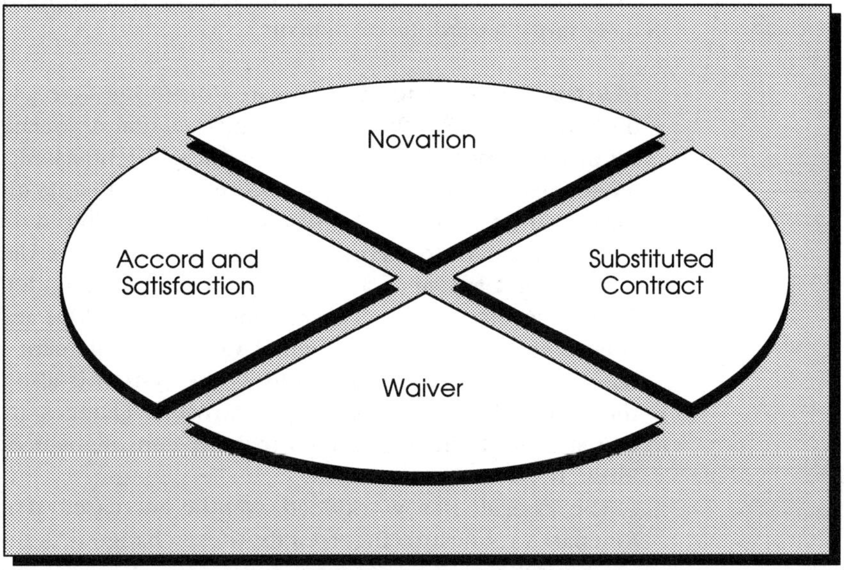

contract, novation, accord and satisfaction, and waiver. Each of these means of changing the performance will be considered separately.

SUBSTITUTED CONTRACT

The parties to the contract may agree to a substantial modification of one or more terms. The new terms become binding on the parties and the inconsistent terms are rescinded. It depends on the nature of the subsequent agreement whether or not the other terms of the original contract remain in force. The substituted contract is often the result of some unanticipated circumstance or event that places higher costs or burdens of performance on the promisee.

The substituted agreement must be supported by consideration in order to be valid and enforceable. A promise to pay for what the promisor is already entitled to receive under the original contract will not be sufficient consideration to support the substituted agreement. In essence, there must be evidence of mutual consent to rescind the original contract along with new consideration, such as the promisor's consent to pay an amount higher than that contained in the original contract. This additional amount must generally be coupled with the promisee's promise to perform additional work.

The element of duress is often an important factor in the circumstances leading to the substituted agreement. Where the promisee threatens to break the original contract and a substituted agreement with a higher payment is made, this new promise is invalid. The duress argument may be used if evidence that new conditions or circumstances not originally expected by the parties has made the promisee's performance substantially more hazardous or difficult.

Illustration   After the Software Consulting Agreement was executed on November 18, 1987, the Canadian Dental Association issued a new set of guidelines on the reporting duties of dentists. Along with the new guidelines, the Association has recommended that its members purchase the Epson QX-10 computer system. Epson has offered the computer with a major discount to the members of the Association. Under the Software Consulting Agreement, the consultant is obliged under Phase I (Clause 2(a) to develop a system compatible with only IBM and Apple personal computers. However, the Dental Office Management System program will fail in the market place unless the system is also compatible with the Epson QX-10. Moreover, the recent changes in guidelines will increase the training seminars that the consultant is obliged to give in Phase II.

The consultant's work load will be increased if it complies with Rinehart's request to incorporate these changes. As the consultant was not bound, under the original contract, to take into account the Epson QX-10 or the new guidelines, any substituted fee structure under Clause 4 would be a valid, substituted contract. Moreover, it would not be duress for the consultant to refuse doing these additional tasks in the absence of a new agreement with a higher rate of compensation.

NOVATION

Novation occurs when the parties to the original contract agree for good and sufficient consideration to substitute a new party for one who is bound by the contract. The new party is normally undertaking the original debtor's payment obligation to the creditor. This arrangement is based on the mutual consent of the original and new parties to the contract. The original debtor must consent to withdraw from the contract, the new debtor must agree to assume the original debtor's obligations, and the creditor must consent to release the original debtor and to the assumption of the substituted debtor as a party to the contract.

Illustration   Rinehart's distributor has sold software products to **JWX** Computer Ltd. on credit terms. Under the terms of the contract, **JWX** Computer Ltd. has agreed to pay $4000 over a twelve-month period with interest charges set at 15 percent. Two months after receiving delivery of the software, **JWX** Computer Ltd. is sold, as an ongoing concern, to Baxter Computers Ltd. Baxter Computers Ltd., in its contract with **JWX** Computer Ltd., has agreed to assume the debt to the distributor. Both **JWX** and Baxter notify the distributor of the sale and of Baxter's agreement to assume the unpaid balance of the $4000 debt. A novation takes place when the distributor agrees to release **JWX** Computer Ltd. from the original contract and accept Baxter Computers Ltd. as its debtor. The novation discharges **JWX** Computer Ltd. from any further obligation to pay under the original contract.

ACCORD AND SATISFACTION

An accord and satisfaction discharges a contractual obligation. In *Bank of Nova Scotia v. Maclellan*,[12] the following definition of accord and satisfaction was approved:

> Accord and satisfaction is the purchase of a release from an obligation, whether arising under contract or tort, by means of any valuable consideration, not being the actual performance of the obligation itself. The accord is the agreement by which the obligation is discharged. The satisfaction is the consideration which makes the agreement operative.[13]

In the *Maclellan* case, a husband and wife divorced. Prior to the divorce they had a promissory note with the bank. The outstanding balance owing was $2440.55. The ex-husband left town and the bank sought payment from the wife. The wife's solicitor proposed a settlement of the outstanding debt on the following terms: She would pay $610.13 and assist the bank in attempting to locate her ex-husband so that the bank could recover the balance of the debt. The bank agreed to discharge the wife's debt based on this offer. Later, the bank argued it was not bound by the settlement because there had been no consideration. The court found the promise to attempt to locate her ex-husband was enough to meet the test of consideration.

Fresh consideration is an essential ingredient to make the accord valid. In a typical case, for example, where the debtor offers to pay a lesser sum as settlement of the debt, and the creditor agrees to accept that sum, the creditor is not bound by the settlement. Writing "paid in full satisfaction of my debt" on the back of a cheque will not bar the creditor from cashing the cheque and suing for the balance outstanding. There can be no true accord unless both parties freely agree to it. Threats and coercive action will render the accord invalid.[14]

WAIVER

The Supreme Court of Canada, in *Turney v. Zhilka*,[15] defined waiver as follows:

> All that waiver means . . . is that one party to a contract may forego a promised advantage or may dispense with part of the promised performance of the other party which is simply and solely for the benefit of the first party and is severable from the rest of the contract.

Waiver often appears where one party to the contract has inserted a condition precedent and later decides to forego the benefit of that condition. The legal questions posed by the waiver rule have been troublesome and have divided the Supreme Court of Canada. For example, in *Barnett v. Harrison*,[16] the court considered a contract that provided that in the event certain conditions were not satisfied the contract was null and void. The purchaser attempted to waive a condition that required municipal approval of an application to develop certain land. The land was being bought under a contract of sale.

Dickson J. held that allowing the purchaser to waive the condition amounted to rewriting the contract. The parties agreed that noncompliance with the conditions would render the contract null and void. Moreover, the court was concerned that allowing waiver would invite the purchaser to treat the contract as an option to purchase and, in the event that the land increased in value, waive compliance and take his speculative profit.

Illustration   Rinehart is entitled to terminate the Software Licence and Marketing Agreement (Figure 1.2) in the event that the distributor fails to make at least seventy-five dispositions of software in a six-month period. Assume that the distributor makes only fifty dispositions within a six-month period. Clearly, the condition is solely for the benefit of Rinehart and is severable by Clause 1. By waiving the quota requirement under Clause 1(b), the distributor is still bound by the contract even though the condition has not been satisfied. Moreover, by virtue of Clause 10, the waiver does not preclude Rinehart from insisting on the condition for future six-month periods.

Discharge by Frustration

The doctrine of frustration is a judge-made rule that has the effect of discharging prospective performance obligations under a contract. The early English cases, however, did not recognize a supervening event that made performance impossible even though the subject matter of the contract had been destroyed. The contractual obligation to perform was absolute. Unless the parties specifically addressed the contingency in the contract, the impossibility of performance brought on by external forces, and not the fault of the promisor, was not a defence to an action for damages based on breach of contract.[17]

The modern doctrine of frustration is traced to Blackburn J.'s judgment in *Taylor v. Caldwell*.[18] In that case a fire destroyed a music hall. The music hall, prior to the fire, had been rented to a party who had intended to use it for concerts. The fire occurred before any concerts were held. In these circumstances, the owner of the music hall was held discharged from the contract and absolved from any damages suffered to the other party based on his failure to perform. After the *Taylor* case, the harsh rule of absolute contracts was abandoned by the English courts. The Canadian law of frustration draws heavily from this modern English trend.

Several important points should be kept in mind. First, the frustration doctrine only rarely applies to the commercial or consumer transaction. Second, along with the common law, there have been statutory attempts to define and determine the effect of frustration. Third, there is controversy over the test applicable to determine frustration. Finally, the nature of judicial relief in frustration cases may work a hardship or injustice on the party who has made expenditures in reliance on the contract and who is no longer entitled to call upon the other party to perform.

MEANING OF FRUSTRATION

The challenge for the courts has been to develop a credible definition of frustration that excuses performance in certain cases. Examples of supervening events or circumstances that may frustrate the contract are: the outbreak of (or the ending of) war or hostilities; legislation that changes planning or zoning requirement; the decision of government to exercise expropriation powers; the physical destruction of the subject matter of the contract; and death or incapacity in a personal service contract.

At the same time, the courts have been careful to avoid expanding the doctrine to discharge performance that has become economically more difficult, impractical, or less profitable. A large number of the reported frustration cases involve the sale, lease, or development of real property, and charterparties. A charterparty is an agreement between a ship-owner and a merchant for the use of the ship and the safe transport of goods.

Usually, some supervening event or circumstance has made the main purpose impossible or destroyed the adventure the parties sought to achieve. Some fundamental assumption shared by the parties has subsequently disappeared. In these circumstances what happens to the obligations to perform under the contract?

The Canadian courts, like the English courts, have developed theories of frustration. Our courts will confine the application of the doctrine to a reasonably narrow category of cases. The generally accepted theory of frustration is based on implying a term in the contract that operates as a condition to the party's performance. This implied term discharges the party's obligation to perform if a particular state of circumstances no longer exists. This approach was originally adopted by Blackburn J. in the *Taylor* case, where an implied condition was held to excuse the music-hall owner's performance because the destruction by fire of the hall had made his performance impossible. The Canadian courts have approved the "implied term" approach.[19] The implied term approach leaves open the grounds justifying the court's decision to add a new term to the contract.

The implied term, however, is not based on the subjective intention or views of the parties. Instead, the courts have evolved a reasonable person test: what reasonable persons in the position of the parties would have agreed if they had put their mind to the contingency. Another formulation requires the court to ask whether reasonable persons would have intended the performance obligation to be binding given the altered conditions.

The nature of the contingency or supervening event is crucial. There are two basic rules. First, the supervening event must strike at the root or underlying assumption of the contract. "In other words the principle applies also where there is 'cessation or non-existence of an express condition or state of things going to the root of the contract'."[20] The implied term is not incorporated where performance is merely difficult; the basic foundation of the contract must have been destroyed.

Second, the supervening event must be beyond the control of the parties. It is important to distinguish, therefore, between some unexpected external force or event and an event caused by one or both of the parties. Moreover, if the specific event is expressly governed by the contract or contemplated by the parties, the doctrine of frustration is unavailable. Professor Fridman has observed that: " . . . the contract may provide specifically for its termination in stated circumstances: no term can therefore be implied to allow termination in other circumstances."[21]

Other explanations for the operation of frustration can be found in the cases. It is sometimes said that the supervening event has caused a total failure of consideration and for that reason discharged further performance. Another alternative to an implied term is based on the court exercising discretion to relieve contract performance in order to achieve a just, fair, reasonable solution.[22] In the decision by Duff J. in the *Canadian Govt. Merchant Marine Ltd.* case, there is a formulation of the "just solution" approach for the case of commercial contracts — a recent Canadian authority for the "just solution" approach as a replacement for the traditional "implied term" approach.[23]

EFFECT OF FRUSTRATION

The effect of frustration at the common law was to leave the losses where they fell upon the discharge of the contract. The discharge prevented either party from suing for breach of contract. The problem, however, was what remedy, if any, should be available to a party who had incurred expense in anticipation of performance, performed services, paid money, or delivered goods? A case of unjust enrichment is compelling where, for example, the buyer has paid a deposit of $10 000 for the delivery of machinery and the seller's obligation is discharged because of frustration.

In such circumstances, the House of Lords, in the leading case of *Fibrosa Spolka Akcyjna v. Fairbairn Lawson Ltd.*,[24] held that the deposit made by a buyer under a commercial contract to purchase machinery could be recovered. The theory used to support recovery was that there had been a total failure of consideration; that is, the buyer had paid $10 000 to the seller. The buyer failed to receive *any* benefit for this sum under the contract. Even though the *Fibrosa* case marks an important advance, it has certain limitations.

First, unless there was total failure of consideration, no recovery was permissible. Thus, if the buyer had received one machine valued at $500 prior to the supervening event, he lost the remaining $9500. Second, the total failure of consideration rule fails to take into account the expenditures undertaken by the seller in reliance of the contract. Those expenses could not be recovered and were borne entirely by the seller. The court refused to apportion any loss in such circumstances. Apportionment means dividing the loss between the seller and the buyer. The delivery of a single machine to the buyer, applying apportionment rules, would not eliminate the buyer's claim, but merely reduce the amount of the claim by the value of that machine. It has taken the intervention of legislation in both Canada and England to provide a fairer and more just resolution of the apportionment of loss problem.

SELF-INDUCED FRUSTRATION

A well-embedded principle of law states that a party cannot take advantage of its own wrongdoing. Where the frustrating event has been induced by one of the parties to the contract, its performance under the contract will not be excused. The same principle applies where both parties have contributed through their conduct to cause the intervening event that frustrates the contract. The burden of proving self-induced frustration lies on the party asserting that the intervening event was caused by the other party to the contract.

Illustration   The consultant claims that the Software Consulting Agreement has been frustrated. Rinehart learns the basis of the consultant's argument is on the loss of the service of its chief design engineer. The engineer was fired by the consultant halfway through Phase I of the project. The dismissal arose as a result of a dispute over payment to the engineer for overtime work. It is clear that without the engineer it would be impossible for the consultant to perform the contract. In this case, it is likely that a court would hold that the supervening event, i.e., the dismissal of a "key" employee by the consultant, induced the frustration of the contract. As a result, the consultant would be liable in damages to Rinehart.

LEGISLATION

Most Canadian provinces have enacted legislation modelled on the *English Law Reform (Frustrated Contracts) Act*, 1943.[25] The main impact of the legislation is to modify the common law rule that prevents recovery of benefits or apportionment of losses and expenses arising out of frustrated contracts. In British Columbia, for example, there is a provision for equal division of the loss between the parties.[26] The legislation does not apply to all contracts. Exceptions include contracts for insurance, charterparties, sale of goods, and contracts with express terms covering the event.

The effect of the legislation is to provide new remedial tools for judges to apply where a contract is frustrated. The total failure of consideration rule from *Fibrosa* is abrogated. Thus, money paid prior to the frustrating event can be recovered even though the payor has received some benefits under the contract. The payee, in return, is entitled to retain an amount equal to the value of the benefits conferred on the payor. Also, the payee's expense may be set off against the money paid. The English legislation provoked no litigation until 1979.[27]

The second major source of legislative modification is found in provincial Sale of Goods legislation. A number of conditions must be fulfilled before the *Sale of Goods Act* applies. First, the contract of sale must be for "specific" goods. Second, the goods must have existed at the time of contracting. It is doubtful that the legislation would apply if the goods never came into existence. Third, the goods must have perished. The legislation does not define perish, and controversy has arisen over whether or not stolen goods have "perished", and whether or not all the goods, as opposed to part of the goods, must have "perished". Fourth, there is the concept of fault to contend with. Fault means a "wrongful act or default" but leaves open the issue of whether or not negligence is included in the definition. The goods must have perished without the fault of either the seller or the buyer. Lastly, the legislation applies only to agreements to sell. In such an agreement, the title to the goods is retained by the seller. Conversely, in a contract of sale, the property in the goods passes to the buyer and the legislative solution for frustration does not apply. An agreement to sell governed by the *Act*, assuming the above conditions are met, is avoided in the event of frustration.

Problems for Discussion

1. Why have the Canadian courts developed a "good faith" test for cases where one party has reserved a contractual right to accept performance that is satisfactory to them? What economic interest is being served?

2. Did Cardozo J. rewrite the contract in *Jacob and Youngs v. Kent*? Do you agree that there is justification for judicial intervention in such cases?

3. In what circumstances would a court find the parties made independent promises? See *Tito v. Waddell (No. 2)* (1977) Ch. 106; and *Fearon v. Aylesford*, (1884) 14 Q.B.D. 792.

4. In the case of dependent promises, how do the courts decide who has the obligation to perform first?

5. Explain the distinction between a condition and a promise. What interest is being served by inserting a condition to performance?

6. What is the difference on prospective performance duties between a condition precedent and condition subsequent?

7. Distinguish between an implied-in-fact condition and a constructive condition.

8. Is the substantial performance rule consistent with the general principle that parties must strictly perform in accordance with the contract? Is it possible to insert a term in the contract that will protect the promisor from being liable under the rule?

9. Rinehart Ltd. received a cheque from a distributor for software delivered. The amount owed is $10 000. The distributor has written on the back of a cheque for $7000 the words "cashing this cheque operates to fully discharge all payment obligations to Rinehart Ltd. for software received." If Rinehart Ltd. cashes the cheque, are they barred from recovering the balance of $3000?

10. In the contracts contained in figures 1.2 and 1.3, there is a provision for the effect of waiver. Why has Rinehart included this term?

11. What events or circumstances might frustrate the Software Consulting Agreement (Figure 1.3)?

12. Is it open to argument that the "implied term" and the "just solution" approach to frustration lead to the same result in practice?

13. What is the justification for limiting the scope of the frustration doctrine?

14. What gaps has legislation filled in the common law doctrine of frustration?

Chapter 6 Notes

1. Fridman, *The Law of Contract*, (1976), p. 456.
2. Waddams, The *Law of Contracts*, (1977), p. 312.
3. (1921) 129 N.E. 889 (N.Y.C.A.).
4. See *Hong Kong Fir v. Kawasaki Kisen Kaisha Ltd.*, (1962) 2 Q.B. 26 (C.A.).
5. Corbin on "Contract" (1952) One Volume Ed., p. 602.
6. See, e.g., *Kingston v. Preston*, (1773) 99 E.R. 437 (K.B.).
7. Fridman, *supra* note 1, p. 273.
8. *Ibid.*, p. 458-60; Waddams, *supra* note 2, pp. 370-71.
9. (1898) 1 Q.B. 673 (C.A.).

10. (1978) 87 D.L.R. (3d) 544 (Sask.C.A.).
11. See *Harrild v. Spokane School Dist.*, (1920) 112 Wash. 266, 192 p. 1 (S.C.Wash.).
12. (1977) 78 D.L.R. (3d) 1 (N.S.S.C. App.Div.).
13. *British Russian Gazette Ltd. v. Associated Newspapers, Ltd.*, (1932) 2 K.B., 616, 643-4.
14. See *D. & C. Builders v. Rees*, (1966) 2 Q.B. 617, 3 All E.R., 837.
15. (1959) S.C.R. 598 (S.C.C.).
16. (1975) 57 D.L.R. (3d) 225 (S.C.C.).
17. See *Paradine v. Jane*, (1647) Aleyn 26; 82 E.R. 897.
18. (1863) 3 B. & S. 826, 122 E.R. 309.
19. See *Canadian Govt. Merchant Marine Ltd. v. Canadian Trading Co.*, (1922) 64 S.C.R. 106, 68 D.L.R. 544 (S.C.C.).
20. *Australian Dispatch Line v. Anglo-Canadian Shipping Co.*, (1940) 4 D.L.R. 104, 107.
21. Fridman, *supra* note 1, at 491.
22. *Constantine (Joseph) SS. Line v. Imperial Smelting Corp. Ltd.*, (1942) A.C. 154, 186, per Lord Wright.
23. *Capital Quality Homes Ltd. v. Colwyn Construction Ltd.*, (1975) 9 O.R. (2d) 617, 61 D.L.R. (3d) 385 (Ont.C.A.).
24. (1943) A.C. 32; (1942) 2 All E.R. 122 (H.L.).
25. 6 & 7 Geo. 6, c. 40.
26. See *The British Columbia Frustrated Contracts Act* 1974, section 5(3).
27. See *B.P. (Exploration) Libya Ltd. v. Hunt*, (1979) 1 W.L.R. 783; aff'd (1981) 1 W.L.R. 236, (1982) 1 W.L.R. 253.

7 REMEDIES FOR BREACH OF CONTRACT

Breach

Before we launch into the question of what remedies are available to an injured party who has suffered a loss resulting from a breach of contract, attention must be focussed on the concept of "breach". Our analysis requires defining the meaning of "breach", considering the effect of breach, and determining the remedial options open in the event a breach occurs or is threatened to occur.

Breach of contract is the non-performance by the promisor of some contractual promise without any lawful justification supporting his non-performance. There are three categories of breach: i) repudiatory breach; ii) anticipatory breach; and iii) defective or negligent performance.

One common link in all cases of breach is the importance of the term of the contract that one party refuses or fails to perform. In Anglo-Canadian law, the promisor's repudiation must deprive the promisee of his main benefit under the contract. Repudiation is treated as a serious matter. The remedy available to the promisee reflects the gravity of the promisor's conduct or inaction, and the remedy is termination of the contract. This remedy, unlike damages — an award of money, specific performance — an order compelling the defendant to do something, or an injunction — an order compelling the defendant *not* to do something, is not contained in a court decree. The innocent promisee takes it upon himself to terminate the contract because of the promisor's repudiation.

Litigation requires time, patience, and money. The parties need to know on short notice whether the contract continues or ends. Placing repudiation in the hands of the innocent promisee is based on a fundamental notion of fairness. Once the breach has deprived the innocent party substantially of what he/she had bargained for, it would be grossly unfair to allow the defaulter to demand his/her performance.

Before we take the plunge we should check the depth of the legal pool. More than one breach of contract action has been lost for the simple reason that the court did not view the defendant's conduct or inaction as causing a breach of contract. Many hours of pre-trial discovery — the process by which each party to the litigation is entitled to obtain documents and ask questions of potential witnesses — may be needed to establish which party is at fault. Often the parties exchange accusations that the contract was broken off because of something that the other did.

A major portion of the litigation may turn on factual findings made by the judge or jury who is left to decide what, based on the evidence adduced, actually happened; only then is a conclusion as to fault made. What this means is that the "innocent party" to the breach had better be right in his/her judgment that the other side has committed a breach amounting to repudiation. If the innocent party miscalculates, then by refusing to perform based on his/her assessment of "fault", the innocent party will be liable for damages. Assuming the promisee is on solid ground, the law provides the innocent party with several options.

The innocent party may accept the repudiation which discharges him/her from any further duty to perform under the contract. The next step is usually to sue the offending promisor for damages. Although in the appropriate case he/she may wish to invoke an equitable remedy — specific performance and injunctions are the most common remedies — by either compelling the promisor to perform, or by stopping the promisor from continuing the breach.

Notwithstanding the breach, the promisee may elect to affirm the contract. Affirm means to keep the contract alive as opposed to taking immediate legal action or accepting the repudiation as putting an end to the contract. Such a decision depends on the promisee's business judgment about the future economic benefits that may result from keeping the mutual performance obligation alive. The effect of affirmation is to maintain the future performance obligations required of each party.

Affirmation of the contract is not a waiver by the promisee of his/her right to recover for his/her economic loss arising from the breach. The promisor's breach is neither forgotten nor forgiven in law. Furthermore, the promisee's affirmation will not usually deprive him/her of his/her damage claim against the promisor.

Repudiatory Breach

One party to the contract commits a repudiatory breach when his/her performance is due but he/she fails or refuses to perform. For instance, under the terms of the Software Consulting Agreement (Figure 1.3), Clause 2, the consultant is required to develop and submit for Rinehart's approval a detailed model of certain software to be used in the networked computer system. The due date is December 15, 1987. On December 19th, the consultant notifies Rinehart that it has been unable to make

FIGURE 7.1 **ELEMENTS OF REPUDIATORY BREACH**

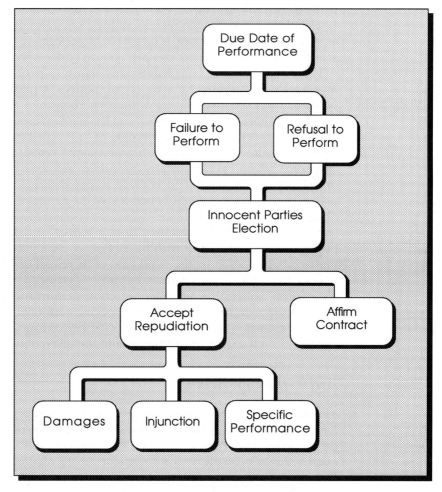

the system compatible with the IBM and Apple personal computers. Further, it has failed to develop the detailed model as required under the contract. This is an example of failure to perform.

The consultant's conduct may not necessarily be a matter of bad faith or of market forces souring its deal. The consultant may simply lack the technical skill and expertise to perform its end of the contract.

The failure of performance will likely have injured Rinehart and will entitle it to damages as compensation for the loss of the consultant's performance. By the terms of the contract, Rinehart is not limited to compensatory damages. Under Clause 7(f) (Figure 1.3), the parties have agreed that Rinehart is entitled to compel the consultant's performance. We will examine this clause in the section on specific performance in some detail. Here it is enough to indicate that Rinehart's right to specific performance will depend on a number of factors beyond the clause itself. One such factor is the consultant's ability to perform. If the consultant, as suggested in the example, is incapable of performing owing to lack of skill and expertise, an order compelling it to perform would be fruitless.

The consultant, however, may simply refuse to perform. The refusal may have been fathered by a variety of motives. A personal falling out between the executive officers of the two companies; the consultant's obtaining a more lucrative contract and lacking the resources to perform both; a disagreement over the meaning of "a detailed model of the Systems". Regardless of the motive, the consultant's refusal to perform, barring some lawful excuse such as frustration, amounts to a repudiatory breach. Again, the consultant is liable to pay damages. An order compelling performance is doubtful because of the nature of the consultant's obligations under the contract.

A repudiatory breach resulting from a refusal or failure to perform provides the injured party with the option of ending the contract. The unilateral notification by the consultant of its refusal or failure does not operate to terminate the contract. By virtue of clause 7(f), the consultant has express notice that, upon its breach of performance, Rinehart Ltd. reserves the right to seek a decree of specific performance. While there is a contractual right to insist on specific performance, the actual receiving of such a court order falls within the discretion of the court.

Anticipatory Breach

An anticipatory breach occurs where one party, prior to the due date for performance, gives notices that it will either fail or refuse to perform on the fixed date. For example, on December 1, 1987, the consultant notifies Rinehart that it refuses to submit the detailed model of the Systems on December 15th. What options are open to Rinehart? Rinehart can "wait and see" if the consultant actually commits the breach by failing to submit the detailed model on December 15th. This time might be used to negotiate an extension, depending on the nature and seriousness of the performance difficulties experienced by the consultant. The second alternative is for Rinehart to accept the anticipated breach, terminate the contract prior to December 15th, and sue for damages. A final alternative is contemplated in Clause 7(f). Rinehart elects to keep the contract alive and sue for specific performance that would compel the consultant to perform on December 15th. As has already been suggested, there is in a contract for personal service considerable risk of failure in pursuing the specific performance option.

The acceptance of the anticipatory breach must be followed by a clear, positive statement. Conduct that might indicate the innocent party still considers the contract in force may prevent recovery of damages prior

FIGURE 7.2 **ANTICIPATORY BREACH**

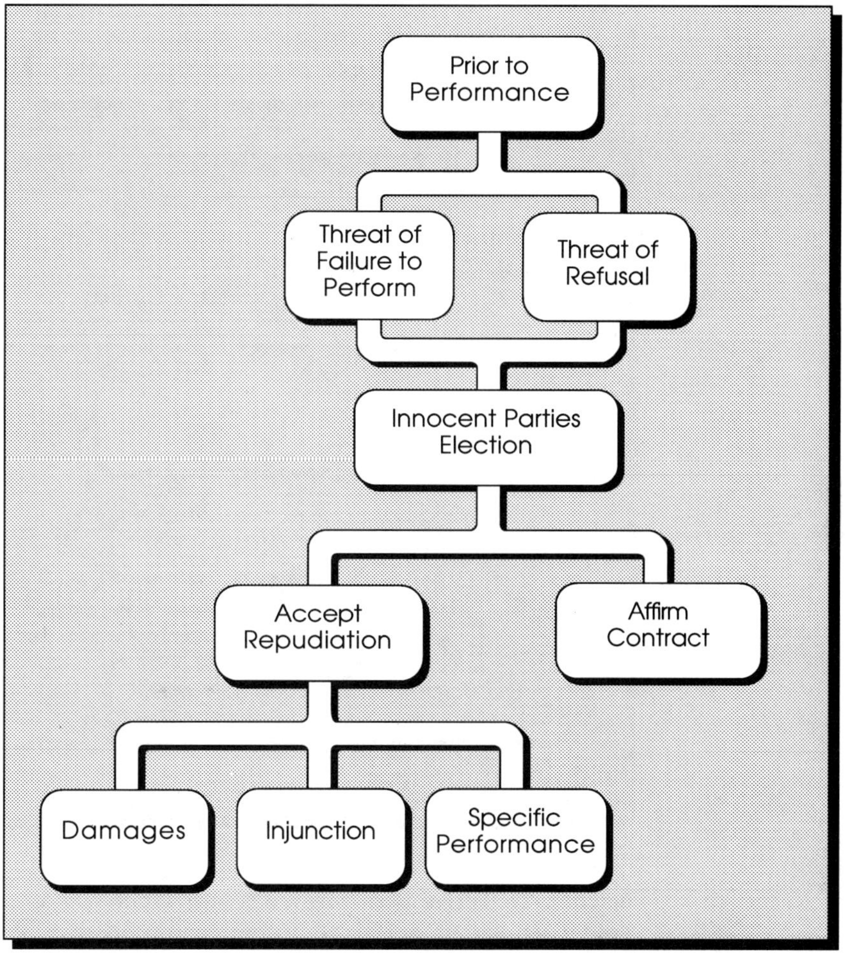

to actual breach. The main lesson is that the innocent party should act immediately and unequivocally to exercise its option to accept the anticipatory breach. The clearest route is a formal notice of acceptance of the anticipated repudiation followed by the filing of a lawsuit. At the point of acceptance, the innocent party is relieved of any further performance obligations it may have under the contract to the defaulting party. Finally, in the legal action commenced prior to the contract date for actual performance, the defendant cannot defend on the grounds that the action is premature.

DEFECTIVE OR NEGLIGENT PERFORMANCE

Defective or negligent performance results when the services performed or the goods delivered have a substantial qualitative or quantitative de-

FIGURE 7.3 **DEFECTS IN GOODS OR SERVICES**

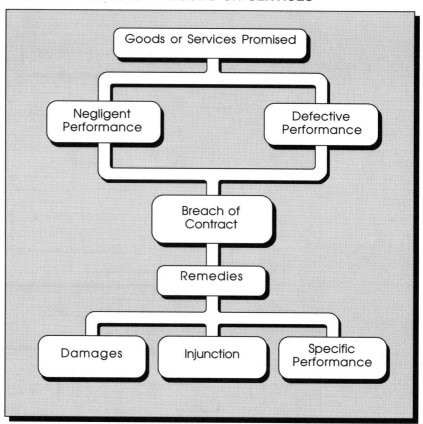

ficiency. Defective performance results where the consultant has delivered a detailed model of the system that is only partially compatible with the IBM personal computer. The effect is similar to non-performance. Rinehart has not received what it had bargained for under the Software Consulting Agreement.

Defective goods or services are of considerable concern in consumer transactions. Given the disparity of bargaining power between the manufacturer and the consumer, and the fact that the manufacturer drafts the contract, it is not surprising that every attempt is made to limit liability for defective products or services. Rinehart is no exception; the wide umbrella of protection against consumer suits is a standard clause in the company's Licence Agreement (Figure 1.4). Specifically, Rinehart seeks to impose strict limitation on the consumer whose software fails to work. In Clause 5, for example, the contract provides that "The program is provided 'As Is' without warranty of any kind. The entire risk as to the results and performances of the program is assumed by you." The clause shifts the full risk of defective or negligent performance of the software to the consumer.

The line between defective performance and failure of performance is sometimes blurred. Take for example the Software Licence and Marketing Agreement (Figure 1.2). It might be argued that Rinehart has provided for termination of the contract based on either the failure or defect of performance by the distributor. This is done through the condition precedent found in Clause 1(b). In essence this clause provides that where the distributor has failed to make at least seventy-five sales of the software products in a six-month period, the licence to sell becomes non-exclusive. The reason for the distributor's failure to perform may be the poor quality of its sales force. Alternatively, the sales force, though of a high quality, may have stiff competition from other distributors with a better product. It would be difficult to characterize the non-performance as "defective" in the latter case.

The main conclusion to be drawn from the Rinehart "contracts" is the attempt to shift the risk of defective or negligent performance. In the consumer contract, the risk is expressly placed on the shoulders of the buyer. The typical consumer has little bargaining power to negotiate a more equitable allocation of the risks. In the commercial transaction, the stronger party, i.e., Rinehart, which is now on the buying end, has effectively shifted the risk of non-performance onto the consultant and distributor. By expressly defining performance and detailing the consequences of non-performance, Rinehart has built into the contract tailored monitoring devices to assess the quality and quantity of performance.

Fundamental Breach

The doctrine of fundamental breach applies to both consumer and commercial transactions. For example, a consumer buys the Rinehart word processing program but the program is defective. The format function works imperfectly causing the printer to skip every other line of text; the boldface command operates to delete text; the line spacing breaks down causing lines to overwrite other lines. It might not be totally useless; so, the consumer's total failure consideration would not succeed, however, even though this is not what he/she bargained for.

The consumer's argument would be founded on fundamental breach of the contract. The argument would follow that, because the inability of the software to perform is so basic to the contract itself, the contract has been fundamentally breached. (One would hope that the argument would not be prepared on such word processing software! An exhibit might prove exceedingly useful at trial, however.) It is then for the court to decide whether Rinehart has fundamentally breached the contract by supplying a grossly defective word processing program. In each case, the question of fundamental breach turns on the seriousness of the breach.

The courts are guided by the seriousness of the loss to the injured party or the degree of recklessness or deliberateness of the breaching parties' conduct in causing the breach.

The bad news for the consumer is that a fundamental breach does not automatically preclude the breaching party from asserting that damages are limited or excluded by a specific term in the breached contract. The court applies a rule of construction to determine whether the language of the clause covers the particular facts surrounding the breach.

Once there has been a breach of contract, the innocent party is relieved from any further performance. Typically, the innocent party seeks to recover damages arising from the breach. In some contracts, breach is anticipated, and there is an attempt to liquidate damages, or a limitation or exclusion of damages. Such a contractual term has caused difficulty for the courts. The innocent party may argue that the effect of the breach is to terminate the contract, including the term liquidating or excluding damages. This argument will likely fail. The courts have distinguished between the discharge of further performance obligations on the innocent party and discharge or termination of the contract between the parties.

Illustration   On March 2, 1985, Rinehart licensed to Allyn and Harding, Barristers & Solicitors in Toronto, the Law Office Management System. The actual sale was made through a software dealer, Bragg Computer and Business Equipment. All the negotiations occurred between Mr. Allyn, on behalf of the law firm, and Mr. Bragg, on behalf of his company. Rinehart had no direct contact with the buyer. After a trial run of the system, Mr. Allyn made the decision to purchase. The formal licence agreement drafted by Ms. Bach, Rinehart's in-house counsel, provided in part:

1.   No Warranties by Licensor. Licensee has selected both (a) the software and (b) the dealer of the software. Licensor makes no representations or warranty and there are no conditions (expressed, implied, statutory, or otherwise) except as expressly stated herein, as to any matter whatsoever including without limitation, the condition of the software, its merchantability or its fitness for any particular purpose.

2.   Claims against the Dealer. If the software does not operate as represented or warranted by the dealer, or is unsatisfactory for any reason, Licensee shall make claim and any complaint thereto solely against the licensee and shall, nevertheless, pay Licensor all rent payable under this licence. Licensor hereby agrees to assign to Licensee, solely for the purpose of making and prosecuting any such claim, all of the rights that the Licensor has against the dealer for breach of warranty conditions or any other representation respecting the equipment.

3. Entire Agreement. This instrument (clauses 1-29) constitutes the entire agreement between licensor and licensee. Licensee understands and agrees that neither the dealer nor any salesman nor any other agent of the dealer is an agent of Licensor. No salesman or agent of Licensee is authorized to waive or alter any term or conditions of this licence printed hereunder or add any provisions hereto. Any representation as to the equipment or any other matter by the dealer shall in no way affect Licensee's duty to pay the rent and perform its other obligations as set forth in the licence.

The Law Office Management System software proved to be defective. Rinehart has offered to supply a non-defective program. But Allyn and Harding has refused the offer, claiming breach of contract by Rinehart. The law firm further claims that as a result of the breach, it has lost approximately $20 000 in billings; those billings cannot be recovered. The outstanding rent owing to Rinehart under the agreement is $2500. Rinehart sued Allyn and Harding for $2500 under the licence, and Allyn and Harding counterclaimed for $20 000 in damages. The law firm argues that based on the doctrine of fundamental breach that the licence agreement, including the exemption clause, is no longer in force. Consequently, it no longer has any obligation to pay the outstanding rent and is entitled to recover its damages.

In a similar case, the Ontario Court of Appeal[1] found for the licensor. The legal basis for the decision was derived from an earlier decision of Wilson J.A. (as she then was).[2]

Where there is a fundamental breach of contract by a party in whose favour is drawn an exclusionary clause, the effect of the clause generally depends on the construction of the contract, and this in turn depends on whether it is fair and reasonable for the exclusionary clause to survive a fundamental breach.

In *Canadian-Dominion Leasing Corp. Ltd.*,[3] the court concluded:

In our view, having regard to all the circumstances of the case, including the dealings between the parties and their clear intent as expressed in the language they have used, the "no warranties" clause in the lease set out heretofore in this judgment was applicable notwithstanding the breach might be regarded as fundamental. The facts come squarely within the relevant contractual language.

Remedies

History has left us with two categories of remedies. The English common law courts' jurisdiction was limited to granting damages to the victim of a contract breach. The Chancery Courts, until the mid-nineteenth century, lacked jurisdiction to award damages. Instead, these courts developed a system of equitable remedies. By assuming personal jurisdiction over the person of the defendant or his/her property, the Chancery issued orders governing the defendant's conduct or the use, transfer, or other disposition of his/her property. Enforcement of Chancery's order was done through contempt power. Failure to comply with the Chancery's order left the subject of the order liable to a fine or imprisonment.

Although Chancery developed a number of equitable remedies, we will limit our discussion to two: specific performance and injunction. Modern courts in Canada and England have merged the historical jurisdiction of common law and chancery into a single, unified court system. Today, a Canadian judge has the option of either awarding damages or granting a request for an injunction or specific performance. With unification of the court system, the old problem of when one remedy is more appropriate in a given case has now disappeared.

Damages

THE NATURE OF COMPENSATION

The basic theory of damages is to provide monetary compensation to the plaintiff who has suffered a loss resulting from the defendant's breach of contract. Damages are awarded on the basis of the plaintiff's loss. Failure to prove the harm has caused some measurable economic loss will, at best, leave the plaintiff with nominal damages, i.e., one dollar. Is it proper

FIGURE 7.4 **THE BASIS OF COMPENSATION**

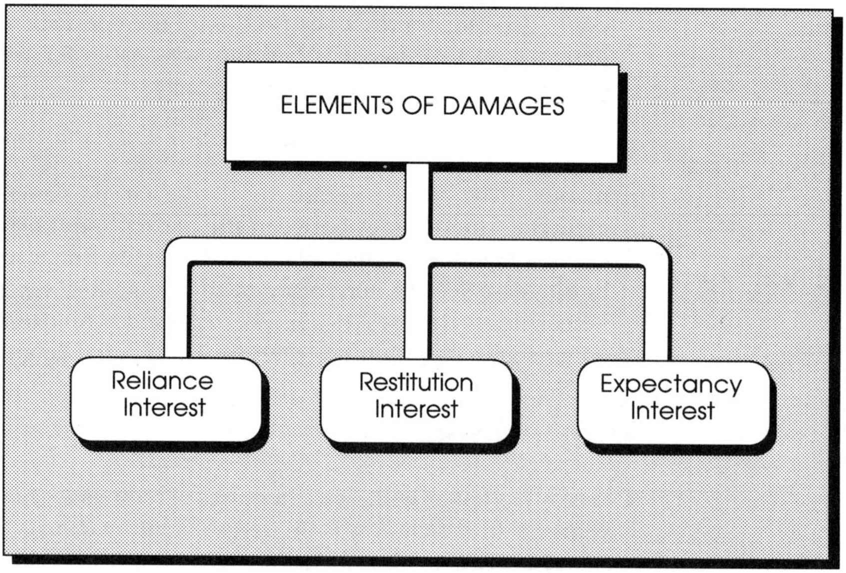

that the breaching party who has committed an undisputed breach pays only one dollar? At the heart of damages is the notion that the court compensates the plaintiff; if the plaintiff has suffered no measurable loss to his/her business, property, or person, the court will not punish the defendant by requiring him/her to pay a "fine" to the plaintiff. Breach of contract is a civil action. Imposing a penalty on the defendant would mean the court has crossed the line between civil and criminal remedies.

The classic formulation divides the compensation principle into three categories of protected interests: i) restitution interest; ii) reliance interest; and iii) expectation interest.[4]

RESTITUTION INTEREST

The plaintiff, after the contract is made, confers a benefit on the defendant who has failed to perform his/her end of the bargain. In such a case, it is said that the defendant has been unjustly enriched at the expense of the plaintiff. The compensation principle is tailored to recover the defendant's gain rather than the plaintiff's loss. In the simple case of the consumer who prepays $250 to a dealer for Rinehart's Word Processing Program, and the dealer fails to deliver, there is both a loss to the plaintiff and concurrently a gain to the dealer. The consumer by claiming the prepaid purchase price is seeking to protect his/her restitution interest.

An important common law limitation restricted recovery to cases where there had been a total failure of consideration. The classic case was non-delivery of goods to a buyer who had prepaid the purchase price or put up a deposit. The buyer was allowed to recover a money judgment. The nature of the action was historically called quasi-contract and the plaintiff used an action called money had and received. The Canadian courts regard such actions as restitutionary, based on the principle of unjust enrichment. In certain cases, such as bankruptcy of the seller, the buyer may enforce a constructive trust for the prepaid sum. Unlike a personal judgment for money, the constructive trust treats the seller as a "trustee" and the money paid by the buyer as "trust property". As the buyer has a continuing equity in the money, the other creditors enforcing claims against the seller's bankruptcy estate cannot look to the money subject to the constructive trust to satisfy their claims.

The restitutionary interest takes on added importance where a contractor has substantially performed his/her end of the contract before the owner commits a breach of contract. By accepting the repudiation of the contract, the contractor is entitled to base his/her claim on *quantum meruit*, i.e., the reasonable fair market value of the benefit conferred. In the United States, it has been held that "where a contract has been rescinded for prevention of performance, the plaintiff may recover the reasonable value of what he has done or supplied under the contract, even though such recovery may exceed the contract price."[5] In Canada, it is more likely that the courts would be influenced by the contract price in awarding *quantum meruit* recovery. For example, Ben, our consulting engineer, is to receive $10 000 for his professional services. Rinehart Ltd. breaches the contract after Ben has already received $8000 in payment. Ben, however, can prove that the benefit of his work for Rinehart Ltd. was $50 000. The question is whether Ben's restitutionary interest is limited to the value of his services by the contract price or whether he is entitled to the true market value of the services to Rinehart. A Canadian court would limit Ben's award to $2000 in this case.

But in the American case of *Boomer*,[6] the contractor recovered $258 000 compensation in *quantum meruit*. Had the contractor fully performed he/she would have received only an additional $20 000 compensation under the contract. If this case were followed in Canada, then Ben would be able to recover $42 000 against Rinehart Ltd.

RELIANCE INTEREST

The reliance interest protects the plaintiff who, in relying upon the defendant's promise to perform, has incurred expense. For example, the distributor, under the Software Licence and Marketing Agreement, may have invested substantial sums training personnel to sell Rinehart's software products and advertising Rinehart's products. Rinehart's wrongful termination of the Agreement exposes the distributor to the loss of these substantial out-of-pocket expenses made in reliance on its contractual right to distribute Rinehart's software products.

The distributor's harm resulting from Rinehart's breach is the wasted expense incurred as a preliminary to performance. Compensation of the distributor based on the reliance interest allows the distributor to be placed in the same financial position it occupied prior to making the expenditures under the contract. In this case, the distributor would produce receipts, records, bank statements, letters, and oral testimony to establish the amount expended on training employees and on advertising. This amount becomes the "damages" that Rinehart would then be required to pay.

This category might be difficult to distinguish from the restitution interest in certain cases. Much depends upon the interpretation of "benefit" to the defendant. The restitution interest allows recovery of benefits conferred on the defendant. Reliance interest is based on the loss of necessary expenditures made by the plaintiff. Although the expenditures to train the distributor's personnel are probably of no benefit to Rinehart, the advertising expenditures might be.

EXPECTATION INTEREST

Each party enters into the contract expecting to benefit from the performance of the other. When the defendant fails to perform, the plaintiff has lost the benefit of the promised performance. The ability to sue for damages protects the plaintiff's expectation interest by compensating him/her for the value of the lost performance. The damages are intended to place the plaintiff in the same economic position as if the defendant had performed under the contract.

The consultant under the Software Consulting Agreement (Figure 1.3) may not have conferred a benefit on Rinehart or expended any money in reliance on the Agreement; nonetheless, assuming that Rinehart wrongfully terminates the Agreement, the consultant is entitled to compensation for its loss of expectancy. In many breach of contract cases, the plaintiff is seeking to recover damages to compensate his/her expectation interest in the contract. Unlike the first two interests, here damages act as a deterrent to breach of contract.

Damages, although civil in nature, may appear to impose a form of punishment for the contract breaker. But this point should not be pushed too far. It is well-established that damages are based on compensation of the plaintiff and not punishment of the defendant. This explains the rule that punitive damages are not awarded in breach of contract cases. In some cases, the contract breaker may be economically better off paying damages based on the lost expectation of the promisee; in most cases the spectre of such a claim is an incentive for the promisor to carry out his/her promise and perform.

By dispensing with evidence of any actual out-of-pocket loss, the promisee is given a means of enforcing his/her business deal. One rationale of the expectation interest is that it is simply a legal means to promote the carrying out of commercial agreements. In theory, the expectation interest will strip the promisor of any profit gained through non-performance. By taking the profit out of contract breaking, the courts show that our legal system takes the enforcement of agreements or promises seriously. There is an expectation that promises ought to be performed. The law merely provides expression and forums for the realization of this shared expectation.

The plaintiff decides which category of compensation would be claimed against the defendant. He/she is entitled to claim either lost profit or wasted expenditure, but not both.[7]

MEASURING DAMAGES

In the case of restitution interest, the measure of damages is the value of the benefit conferred on the defendant. In the case of money, there is no problem in quantification. With goods and services, the court determines the fair market value of what was furnished to the defendant. The reliance interest compensation claim generally presents few quantification problems. The plaintiff merely proves the actual expense incurred.

Difficulties, however, emerge when the compensation is based on the plaintiff's expectancy interest. The court must quantify the value of the lost performance to the plaintiff. The denied or defective performance may involve goods, services, property, or money. For our purposes we are primarily concerned with goods and services. How does the court arrive at a value of goods and circumstances?

In the case where goods or services are withheld by the promisor, damages are calculated on the basis of the difference between the contract price and the market price prevailing at the time of the breach. This is generally the quantification rule applied by the courts since the mid-nineteenth century case of *Barrow v. Arnaud*.[8]

In the case of defective goods or performance of service, the damages are based on the cost to the promisee of correcting the defect. Where the cost of remedying the defect is grossly higher than the difference between the value of what was received and what can be bought in the marketplace, then the promisor is restricted to the latter method of damage assessment.[9]

MITIGATION OF DAMAGES

Along with the right of the plaintiff to claim compensation for loss, he/she must show corresponding responsibility to take reasonable measures to minimize the loss arising from the promisor's breach.[10] The mitigation of damages rule places a duty on the promisee to take such action as is necessary to reduce the quantum of damage as a result of the breach. The rule is explained by Laskin C.J. in *Red Deer College v. Michaels*:[11]

> The parameters of loss are governed by legal principle. The primary rule in breach of contract cases, that a wronged plaintiff is entitled to be put in as good a position as he would have been in if there had been proper performance by the defendant, is subject to the qualification that the defendant cannot be called upon to pay for avoidable losses which would result in an increase in the quantum of damages payable to the plaintiff. The reference in the case law to a "duty" to mitigate should be understood in this sense.
>
> In short, a wronged plaintiff is entitled to recover damages for the losses he has suffered but the extent of those losses may depend on whether he has taken reasonable steps to avoid their unreasonable accumulation.

One explanation, in the sale of goods case, is that mitigation of damages prevents the plaintiff from sitting back in a volatile market, where the price is fluctuating, and play a market speculation game on the back of the defendant. The following illustration demonstrates the operation of the mitigation of damages rule.

Illustration   Rinehart contracted to buy 5000 diskettes from Dillon Distributors Ltd., a supplier of computer diskettes. The contract called for Dillon to deliver the diskettes on February 2, 1986. Rinehart was obliged to pay $50 000 upon receipt of the shipment. On February 3rd,

Rinehart is informed that Dillon is unwilling to make the delivery. During the interval between the making of the contract and the seller's performance date, the price of diskettes in the marketplace had risen to $12 each, or $60 000 for 5000. On February 4, Rinehart bought 5000 diskettes from another distributor for $60 000. Rinehart's lost expectation, i.e., diskettes at $10 each, forms the basis for compensations in damages. The measure of the lost expectation is the difference between the contract price and the prevailing market price. Damages are, therefore, $10 000.

Alternatively, assume Rinehart was aware that the price of diskettes would continue to rise throughout February. On March 2, 1986, the price of diskettes had increased to $15 each, and on that date Rinehart bought 5000 diskettes at this price. Is Rinehart entitled to recover $25 000 in damages against Dillon?

The *prima facie* measure of damages is the difference between the contract price and the market price for diskettes on February 2, the date of the breach; the additional loss, which Rinehart could have prevented, cannot be recovered against Dillon. Rinehart's delay in buying substitute diskettes is unreasonable. In each case it is a question of fact whether or not the plaintiff acted reasonably under the circumstances to mitigate the defendant's loss. The reasonable promptness rule laid down by the courts is designed to prevent the accumulation of the plaintiff's loss.

REMOTENESS

The rule of remoteness places a legal ceiling on the economic consequences flowing from a breach of contract. In the above illustration concerning the sale of diskettes to Rinehart, the seller's failure to deliver might set up a chain reaction. Rinehart, we will assume, urgently required the diskettes to prepare software for a major software consumer fair in Toronto on February 14. Dillon, however, was unaware of the fair or the purposes for which Rinehart had planned to use the diskettes.

Several of Rinehart's distributors had been informed the programs would be sent to them in advance for sale at the fair. As a result of the breach, the software programs could not be sent to the distributors. Rinehart claims as head of damage the following: the loss of good will with its distributors; the loss of sales to consumers at the fair; and the loss of its competitive market position in the highly competitive software market. These losses are in addition to the difference between the contract price and the market value of the diskettes at the date of breach. Is Rinehart entitled to these additional items of damage?

The answer to this problem lies in the classic English case of *Hadley v. Baxendale*,[12] where Alderson B. explained the remoteness rule:

> Where two parties have a contract which one of them has broken, the damages which the other party ought to receive in respect of such breach of contract should be such as may fairly and reasonably

be considered either arising naturally, i.e., according to the usual course of things, from such breach of contract itself, or such as may reasonably be supposed to have been in the contemplation of both parties, at the time they made the contract, as the probable result of the breach of it. Now, if the special circumstances under which the contract was actually made were communicated by the plaintiffs to the defendants, and thus known to both parties, the damages resulting from the breach of such a contract, which they would reasonably contemplate, would be the amount of injury which would follow from the breach of contract under these special circumstances so known and communicated.

In *Hadley v. Baxendale*, a shaft in a mill broke, causing a closure of the mill. An employee of the mill was sent to the engineers who had built the machine. The engineers told him that in order to make a new shaft they needed the old broken one for a pattern. Also, the engineers promised that if the shaft were delivered by noon it would be ready by the next day. The broken shaft was sent to the engineers' works in Greenwich, but owing to some delays, constructing the new shaft was delayed several days. The mill owner then sued the engineers for the lost profits from the mill arising from the delay. Based on the above rule, the engineers were held not liable for the mill owner's lost profits. It is likely that liability for the profits would have been imposed had the engineer been informed that any delay in building the new shaft would delay the opening of the mill and result in loss of business.

Sellers of goods and services are taken to forsee the ordinary purpose to which the buyers would use them. The doctrine of remoteness operates as a brake on damages that arise because the buyer has some specialized use unknown to the seller. Thus, the seller of diskettes in the above illustration would not likely contemplate that Rinehart required the diskettes for immediate use at a software fair, and that the failure to deliver the diskettes would cause a chain of economic calamities far beyond buying similar diskettes at a higher price in the open market. It is a question of fact whether the particular loss suffered was in the reasonable contemplation of both parties.

Equitable Remedies

In addition to the common law remedy of damages, the innocent party to a breach of contract has a number of equitable remedies at its disposal. Because the party suffering a loss from another's breach of contract is entitled to damages as a matter of right, it is said that equitable remedies are discretionary. For instance, a plaintiff whose own conduct is unreasonable, unfair, or dishonest might be denied an equitable remedy even though the defendant has clearly broken his/her promise to perform.

A common request is for the court to compel the defendant to perform his/her end of the contract. Such an order or decree is called specific performance. Another common request is to have the court order the defendant to stop breaching the contract and resume performance. Such an order or decree is called an injunction. The advantage of the equitable remedies of specific performance and injunction is that the promisee receives what he/she bargained for under the contract, and not a money judgment in substitution for non-performance.

Until the *Judicature Act*,[13] equitable remedies were administered by a separate court called the Chancery Court. The other main court, the common law court, lacked jurisdiction to provide any remedy other than monetary damages. After that legislation, the jurisdiction was merged into one court with authority to impose either damages or equitable remedies. A general rule that has survived the *Judicature Act* was that an equitable remedy was available only where damages were inadequate to compensate the plaintiff for actual or threatened loss.

Specific Performance

The effect of a decree of specific performance is to compel the defendant to perform in accordance with the contract. The decree blocks the breach of contract and gives the promisee his/her bargained-for exchange. The initial rule is that damages will not adequately compensate the plaintiff in the event that the promisor breaches the contract. For instance, in most cases involving the sale of goods, damages are an adequate remedy. But a different rule applies to the sale of land. No parcel of land or a house, no matter how ordinary to the eye, is like any other parcel of land or house. Land is unique. A seller who refuses to complete the sale can be compelled by a decree of specific performance; similarly, a buyer who refuses to complete can be compelled to buy at the suit of the seller.

GOODS

Unless the goods are unique, the buyer who has been refused delivery under the contract of sale can buy replacement or substitute goods from another supplier. Damages are assessed on the basis of the difference between the cost of the goods under the contract and the cost of buying replacement goods from the alternative supplier.

The common law recognized, however, that certain goods were "unique", which meant there was no substitute for them. A contract to sell an Emily Carr oil painting would fall into this class. The buyer cannot find a substitute for this painting; there is only one in existence. Another common example is family heirlooms. A necklace, ring, or chair that has been in the same family for generations has a particular history of personage and usage attached. Another necklace, ring, or chair that might be substituted lacks such attributes. Thus, a court will find the goods unique and order specific performance of a contract.

There is a growing trend to recognize a broader category of goods labelled "commercially unique". This fictional device allows the courts greater flexibility in shaping a remedy to fit the equities of a particular case.[14] The *Sale of Goods Act* in force in England and Canada expressly provides for the application of the specific performance remedy where there is a sale of specific or ascertained goods. There is controversy in Canada as to whether or not the statutory provisions — imposed by the common law "uniqueness" rule — have indeed substantially expanded the remedy of specific performance beyond its limited scope.[15]

A software dealer who promises to sell a copy of the Rinehart Word Processing Software and fails to deliver will be liable in damages. The buyer would fail to obtain a decree of specific performance. The reason is the abundance of other software dealers from which the buyer could obtain the same program. Even assuming the Rinehart program was unavailable from another dealer, unless there were some highly distinctive features contained in the Rinehart software, a court would find another word processing program that would be an adequate replacement. The buyer's remedy would be the difference between the dealer's price for the Rinehart word processing program and the substituted one bought from another dealer.

PERSONAL SERVICE CONTRACTS

As a matter of principle, the courts refuse to order specific performance of personal service contracts. Such an order gives the unpleasant appearance of sanctioning the slave driver's whip. An employee who walks off the job cannot be compelled against his/her will to continue to work for the employer. Rinehart may have hired a specially qualified software engineer for a project on a two-year contract. After three months on the job, the engineer informs the company of his/her decision to quit. Even though the engineer will be liable in damages, the court will not force him/her back to the computer terminal with a decree of specific performance.

It may be possible for Rinehart, in effect, to compel performance of the employment contract where there is a term providing that the engineer promises not to work for anyone else for the two-year period. In such a case, upon breach, the court might enjoin (by issuing an injunction) the employee from working for another company. The employee then has the option of remaining idle as a software engineer for the duration of the contract, or to return and work for Rinehart.[16]

THE CONSTANT SUPERVISION RULE

The courts have traditionally avoided granting a decree of specific performance of a contract that requires constant, on-site supervision to ensure that the promisor is performing his/her contractual duties. Closely connected with the constant supervision rule is the problem arising from a contract where the promisor's duties involve discretionary, subjective, or artistic factors.

The Software Consulting Agreement (Figure 1.3) provides an example of these problems. In Phase I of the project, the consultant's detailed working model must include, among other things, a network operating system and a library of routines (Clause 2(a)). In Phase II, the consultant is required to submit source and object codes (Clause 3(a)). Assume that the consultant refuses to complete either Phase I or II of the project. Rinehart then invokes Clause 7(a), which provides that the contract is specifically enforceable. Will the court grant an order of specific performance against the consultant?

The problem of supervision and enforcement of the order presents considerable difficulty to the court. Is the consultant in breach of the order if Rinehart is dissatisfied with the library of routines or the source or object code? These are the types of questions the courts attempt to avoid. Short of the court hiring a computer expert to stand at the side of the consultant, a decree of specific performance would be difficult to monitor. Even assuming that such a court-appointed expert is looking over the consultant's shoulder, given the many different ways that the consultant might develop the library of routines or the source or object code, reasonable minds might differ on whether the consultant's work was in breach of contract. The fact that the contract expressly states that the consultant agrees to such an order does not strip the court of the standard discretion to withhold the specific performance remedy.

DISTRIBUTORSHIP AND OTHER LONG TERM SUPPLY CONTRACTS
The courts have begun to realise the special and distinctive features contained in a contract between a supplier and distributor.[17] The Software Licence and Marketing Agreement (Figure 1.2) provides a good illustration of the use of a specific performance order to keep open the line of supply between the supplier and the distributor. Under this Agreement, the distributor, Acrodrome Ltd., is given an exclusive right to licence Rinehart's software in a particular territory. A refusal to deliver the software under the contract would disrupt the distributor's business. There is no alternative source for the Rinehart software. Although the distributor might find alternative software from another supplier, its customers may have associated the distributor with Rinehart software and require only that software in their business or home. As a result, the customer would go to another Rinehart distributor and the original distributor's business may suffer irreparable harm. The trend in North America has been to grant a distributor a decree of specific performance of the distributorship agreement against the supplier.

Injunction

An injunction restrains the defendant from threatening or continuing a breach of a contract. In effect, the injunction states: "Cease and desist from the breach or be held in contempt of court and subject to either a fine or imprisonment." The injunction is a negative command in the language "Thou shall not" and the specific performance order is a positive command in the language "Thou shall". Both equitable remedies are discretionary, which allows the court to take into account circumstances bearing on the issues of hardship or unfairness.

In certain cases, the effect of the injunction may be the same as a decree of specific performance. For instance, assume that Rinehart wrongfully terminates the Software Licence and Marketing Agreement. The distributor wants the flow of software re-established. How does the distributor go about getting the court to remove the wrongful termination? One avenue, as we have seen above, is to compel Rinehart to carry out its obligations under the Agreement by issuing a decree of specific performance. Another avenue is an injunction that orders Rinehart to stop breaching the contract. Whichever route is taken, the essence of the order is the same: It opens up the supply of software from Rinehart to the distributor. The court, while recognising that the true effect is to give the plaintiff specific performance of the contract,[18] looks at the substance or effect of the order, and in the appropriate circumstances, is willing to grant an injunction.

Considerable controversy has followed the early English case of *Lumley v. Wagner*,[19] where an English impresario contracted with a singer to perform exclusively at a London theatre and not for anyone else. The singer breached the contract and agreed, with another party, to sing at Covent Garden. The impresario succeeded in obtaining an injunction against the singer from carrying out her engagement at Covent Garden. There are two important qualifications for an injunction to be granted. First, the employment contract must contain a negative covenant barring the employee from working for another employer during the term of the contract. Second, the negative covenant must not be so wide as to prevent the employee from working altogether.

Thus, in a contract between Rinehart and a software engineer that provides that during the two-year term the engineer will not work for another software development company in Vancouver, can Rinehart invoke to enjoin the engineer to keep his/her promise? But Rinehart could not expand the negative covenant to prevent the engineer from working at *any* job in Vancouver. The latter covenant would give the engineer the option of welfare or working at Rinehart. The courts will not allow an employer to enforce such an option on an employee.

Problems for Discussion

1. Ms. Bach, in examining the insurance coverage for the head office, discovered that a newly leased warehouse area was not covered for fire insurance. She phoned the insurance agency that had placed the original coverage on Rinehart's facilities. The agent, Mr. Thomas, promised to add fire insurance coverage immediately to the policy at an additional premium of $475 per year. One month later, Ms. Bach had not received written confirmation of the additional fire insurance. She phoned Mr. Thomas, who assured her the policy would be placed that day. Four months later, a fire occurred in the warehouse and $40 000 worth of software was destroyed. It turns out that Mr. Thomas neglected to place the fire insurance. Rinehart has sued Thomas Insurance Agency for this loss. Mr. Thomas has defended the action on the basis that Ms. Bach was guilty of contributory negligence in not following up with the insurance agency during the four-month period. Discuss whether the fault of the promisee will act to reduce the damage award entered against the promisor who has breached his contract to place fire insurance coverage. See *Cosyns v. Smith*, (1983) 146 D.L.R. (3d) 622 (Ont.C.A.).

2. The defendant, Park Computer Diskettes, supplied 5000 diskettes to Rinehart. The diskettes were used by Rinehart for purposes of manufacturing its software programs. The diskettes, however, proved to be defective and, as a result, Rinehart was forced to meet thousands of claims from dissatisfied customers. Rinehart also lost the profits from its future business as a result of the defective diskettes. The defendant claims that awarding the loss of contemplated future profits is too remote because only a vague estimate could be made. Assume that the law of Ontario applies, including the *Sale of Goods Act*, R.S.O. 1980, c. 462, section 51(2). See *Canlin Ltd. v. Thiokol Fibres Canada Ltd.*, (1983) 142 D.L.R. (3d) 450 (Ont.C.A.) and *Richmond Wineries Western Ltd. v. Simpson*, (1940) S.C.R. 1, (1940) 2 D.L.R. 481 (S.C.C.). Discuss whether the loss of profits in this case is a direct and natural consequence of Park Computer Diskettes' breach of contract.

3. Clarke Building Contractor agreed to build a warehouse for Rinehart (to replace the one destroyed in the fire). The warehouse was to cost $250 000. After construction was complete, Rinehart discovered a number of deficiencies in the warehouse construction. An independent appraiser estimated that the cost to remedy the defects would be $50 000. Later, Rinehart sold the warehouse and land for $350 000. The estate agent representing Rinehart said a sale in the rising real estate market would allow the warehouse to be valued at $250 000

and the land at $100 000. The subsequent sale confirmed the estate agent's valuation. After the sale, Clarke sued Rinehart for the unpaid balance of $25 000 owing under the construction contract. Rinehart then counterclaimed against Clarke for $50 000 as damages for breach of contract. Is the proper measure of damages the cost of performance or the difference in value resulting from the defective performance? See *Eldon Weiss Home Construction Ltd. v. Clark*, (1983) 39 O.R. (2d) 129 (Ont.Co.Ct.).

4. Rinehart's Ontario subsidiary company, QueTech Ltd., prepared a tender for a software contract with the Law Society of Upper Canada. The Law Society invited tenders from software development companies for a computer system that would allow them to keep track of disciplinary matters, issue billings to solicitors and barristers, and analyse the investment of interest received on lawyer's trust accounts. The bid prepared by QueTech Ltd. provided for a profit of $50 000 on the contract. The bid was then delivered to Purolator Courier Ltd. with instructions to deliver the bid the following morning to the Law Society. Purolator, however, failed to deliver the bid, and the contract for the software development was awarded to another company. It is clear that if QueTech Ltd.'s bid had been delivered, QueTech would have received the contract. QueTech Ltd. sues Purolator Courier Ltd. for $50 000 damages, i.e., its lost profit.

Purolator defends the lawsuit on the basis of an exemption clause in the standard form contract signed by QueTech. The exemption clause provided: "Unless specifically agreed to in writing, the carrier will not: i) be liable for any special, consequential, or other damages for any reason whatever including delay in delivery, ii) transport any goods declared to have a value in excess of $250. Enquiries for the carriage of goods valued at over $250 and insurance charges in such event should be directed to the carrier's closest regional office." QueTech Ltd. claims that the exemption does not apply because of the doctrine of fundamental breach. Discuss. See *Cathcart Inspection Services Ltd. v. Purolator Courier Ltd.*, (1983) 139 D.L.R. (3d) 371 (Ont.C.A.). Would the result be the same if QueTech Ltd. had used a telegram to deliver the bid and CN, through negligence, delivered the bid one day too late? See *B.G. Linton Construction Ltd. v. C.N.R.*, (1974) 49 D.L.R. (3d) 548 (S.C.C.).

5. Acrodrome Ltd., after entering into the Software Licence and Marketing Agreement with Rinehart Ltd. on March 10, began to complain of delays in receiving software program shipments from Rinehart. The evidence indicates that in July, Rinehart was diverting software from Acrodrome's territory (Western Canada) to distributors in Eastern Canada and the Northeastern United States. As a result, Acrodrome started losing business because it could not fill orders. Ultimately, the lack of supply of software put Acrodrome out of business. In the subsequent lawsuit against Rinehart, Acrodrome claimed entitlement

to recover the expenses incurred in carrying out its business as a Rinehart distributor. Rinchart Ltd. argues that Acrodrome is only entitled to nominal damages. The evidence indicates that Acrodrome's inefficient management structure, lack of experienced employees, and high salaries and overhead costs made the distributorship a losing proposition from the start. Further, Rinehart argues that its breach of contract saved Acrodrome from incurring further losses. Discuss whether or not the court should consider that the plaintiff is suing on a losing contract and, taking into account the breach action, whether or not it is an attempt to shift the bad bargain onto the defendant. See *Bowlay Logging Ltd. v. Domtar Ltd.*, (1978) 4 W.W.R. 105, 117 (B.C.S.C.).

6. In the event that the promisor has fully performed his/her end of the contract, but during the course of performance committed several breaches that amount to a fundamental breach of the contract, is it too late for the promisee to rescind the contract and sue for *quantum meruit* recovery? See *Morrison-Knudsen Co., Inc. v. B.C. Hydro and Power Authority (No. 2)*, (1978) 4 W.W.R. 193, 85 D.L.R. (3d) 186 (B.C.C.A.).

Chapter 7 Notes

1. *Canadian-Dominion Leasing Corp. Ltd. v. George A. Welch & Co.; O'Connor Office Machines Ltd., Third Party*, (1982) 33 O.R. (2d) 826 (Ont.C.A.).
2. *Chomedy Aluminum Co. Ltd. v. Belcourt Construction (Ottawa), Ltd.,* (1979) 24 O.R. (2d) 1, 97 D.L.R. (3d) 170, affirmed sub. nom. *Beaufort Realties (1964) Inc. v. Chomedy Aluminum Co. Ltd.*, (1980) 2 S.C.R. 718, 116 D.L.R. (3d) 193 (S.C.C.).
3. *Supra*, note 1.
4. Fuller and Perdue, "The Reliance Interest in Contract Damages," (1936) 46 *Yale L.J.* 52, 573.
5. *Boomer v. Muir*, 24 P.2d 570, 574 (Cal.Dist.Ct.App. 1933).
6. *Ibid.*
7. *Anglia T.V. v. Reed*, (1972) 1 Q.B. 60, (1971) 3 All E.R. 690 (C.A.).
8. (1846) 8 Q.B. 595; 115 E.R. 1000.
9. Trietel, *Law of Contract*, 6th ed. (1983), pp. 711-12.
10. See *Asamera Oil Corp. Ltd. v. Sea Oil & General Corp.; Baud Corp. N.V. v. Brook*, (1979) 1 S.C.R. 633, 89 D.L.R. (3d) 1 (S.C.C.).
11. (1975) 57 D.L.R. (3d) 386, 390 (S.C.C.).
12. (1854) 9 Exch. 341, 156 E.R. 145.
13. 36 & 37 Vict. c. 66.
14. Waddams, *The Law of Contracts*, p. 426.
15. Compare Waddams, *ibid.*, pp. 426-27 with Fridman, *The Law of Contract* (1976), pp. 596-97 and Trietel, *supra*, note 9, pp. 766-68.
16. See *Warner Brothers Pictures Inc. v. Nelson*, (1936) 3 All E.R. 160, (1937) 1 K.B. 209.
17. See 'Study No.4,' Reiter & Swann, eds., *Studies in Contract Law* (1980), pp. 100-07.
18. See *Sky Petroleum Ltd. v. VIP Petroleum Ltd.*, (1974) 1 All E.R. 954 (Ch.Div.).
19. (1852) 1 D.M. & G. 604.

8 THE STANDARD FORM CONTRACT

Introduction

The importance of standard form contracts in daily commerce has been acknowledged by a number of commentators. A typical view of the importance of such contracts is found in this passage:[1]

> Standard form contracts probably account for more than ninety-nine percent of all the contracts now made. Most persons have difficulty remembering the last time they contracted other than by standard form; except for casual oral agreements, they probably never have. But if they are active, they contract by standard form several times a day. Parking lot and theater tickets, package receipts, department store charge slips, and gas station credit card purchase slips are all standard form contracts.

Sellers and buyers often resort to preprinted forms containing standardized terms sometimes called "back of order conditions" (as they appear on the reverse side of the document) that outline the primary obligations between the parties. These conditions include i) warranties, i.e., promises as to condition, quality, or fitness of goods; ii) liquidated damages, i.e., a fixed sum of money agreed upon in advance as compensation to the innocent party in the event of breach of the contract; iii) exclusionary clauses, i.e., a total or partial exclusion of liability to pay damages for certain types of contract breaches; and iv) arbitration provisions, i.e., a prior agreement that the parties will submit their contractual disputes to one or more lay persons (rather than a court) for resolution.

In consumer transactions, however, the buyer is often more concerned with the price, quantity, and delivery of the goods. These elements form the primary obligations between the parties. The same is true for most commercial transactions between businesspersons. The secondary terms that deal with issues of potential liability, in the event of failure to perform or defect in the performance, are found in the fine print on the standard form. Their enforcement or validity arises on the allegation of some breach of the primary obligations.

In this chapter, it is convenient to divide our discussion between commercial and consumer transactions where the standard form is used. The evolving rules and standards applied by the courts or found in legislation make an implicit assumption about the different bargaining power, expectations, customs, expertise, and business goals contained in commercial and consumer transactions. The perception of the essential differences often explains the approach of the courts and commentator in analysing the contract.

The Binding Nature of Standard Form Contracts

One party — usually the manufacturer — drafts the standard form contract for use in consumer transactions. The manufacturer, of course, seeks the benefit of terms favourable to its interest. For his or her part, the consumer can be expected to marshall arguments against the enforceability of all or part of the standard form contract.

The consumer contract has attracted the colourful metaphor of the jungle:[2]

> But power, like greed, if it does not always corrupt, goes easily to the head. [Thus] the form-agreement tends either at once or over the years, and often by whole lines of trade, into a massive and almost terrifying jug-handled character; the one party lays his head into the mouth of a lion — and expectation (not infrequently solid) that it will be a sweet and gentle lion.

The courts have developed many devices defusing the snare that has caught the consumer. A clause may be found "ambiguous" and the court can then construe it against the drafter. The clause may be said to be inconsistent with another clause, and again the result goes against the drafter. An entire clause may be struck down. Later in this chapter, we will examine the basis on which the courts justify in holding a particular clause in a standard form contract not to be binding.

The Traditional Approach

Traditionally, the courts have played a hands-off role. The underlying assumption of that policy was simply non-interference. The courts have labelled their non-interference policy "freedom of contract". This doctrine gathered considerable force in England during the nineteenth century, and the echo of that doctrine still resounds in modern Canadian decisions. An example of the traditional English position illustrates the enormous power reserved in the hands of the "contracting" parties, although in fact there was probably very little bargaining.

The English position that the document once signed is binding in the absence of fraud or misrepresentation is found in *L'Estrange v. F. Graucob, Ltd.*[3] In the same case, Maugham L.J. stated that the law was beyond dispute. A party who had signed a contract was bound even though he had not read it and did not know its contents.[4] In that case, the company successfully defended a suit brought by a buyer who alleged that the goods sold were unfit for the purposes for which they had been sold. A broad exemption clause barred her action. The exemption clause provided that "any express or implied condition, statement, or warranty, statutory or otherwise not stated herein is hereby excluded." Compare this with the exemption clause in the consumer agreement reproduced in Figure 1.4.

Modern Canadian Approach

In Canada, there is a continuing controversy as to the application of *L'Estrange*. In *Delaney v. Cascade River Holidays*[5], the British Columbia Court of Appeal decided, even though the seller was negligent, that the exclusionary clause was correctly applied consistently with the rule in *L'Estrange*. In the 1980s, an interventionist, regulatory attitude developed in Parliament and the courts. The hands-off role gradually has been replaced with a hands-on role.

It has been pointed out that many of the judicial doctrines, which form the basis for intervention into the bargain, mask important policy decisions not articulated by the courts.[6] One commentator has concluded that "Through a great variety of techniques, the courts have paid lip service to contract law in theory, and have ignored it in practice."[7]

The courts, for example, have "implied terms" in the contract, read expressed terms of a contract in a fashion favourable to the non-drafter, used the notion of repugnancy to exclude undesirable terms, and revamped the doctrine of fundamental breach so as to exclude limitations on remedies provided to the party suing on the contract. Where the standard form contract contains written terms — one party, with a pen, by hand, writes in entirely new terms or alters existing printed terms — and the hand-written terms are inconsistent with the printed terms, the court gives more weight to the written terms.[8] The judges themselves, however, may disagree as to whether any inconsistencies exist.[9] Under ordinary circumstances, the rule excluding the printed term only applies when it is consistent with the written term.

Basis of Judicial Intervention

An examination of Canadian contract reveals that the basis of judicial intervention can be roughly divided into general categories: i) preventing "surprise", ii) controlling oppression, and iii) exercising broad discretionary power.

The standard form contract is an attempt to regulate and control the risk factor in the mass production and distribution of goods and services. The supplier of the goods and services seeks to minimize what one commentator has labelled the "juridical risk", or "irrational factors", that might influence a judge or jury to side with the "little person" against the "corporate giant".[10] The party with the inferior bargaining power has no choice but to accept the terms. This take-it-or-leave-it position excludes any possibility of a factual bargain between the parties. Where the drafter of the standard form contract has a monopoly or its competitors use the same terms, the consumer has no effective bargaining position.

The consumer transaction is compared with the ordinary commercial transaction. In the latter case, there is "frequently a sense of formality in the transaction, and ... a full opportunity for the parties to consider the terms of the proposed contract submitted for signature."[11] In contrast, the standard form consumer contract is "invariably carried out in a hurried, informal manner."[12]

FIGURE 8.1 **GROUNDS FOR INTERVENTION**

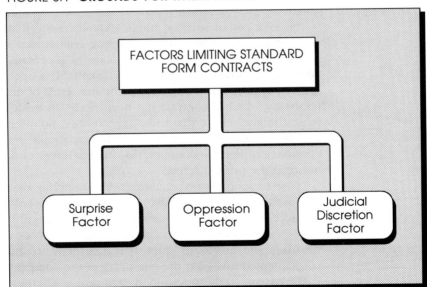

The Surprise Element

The surprise element translates into a duty imposed by the court on the drafter of the standard form contract to put the other party on notice as to any unusual or onerous terms in the contract. One example where intervention was justified on this basis, at least in part, is found in *Davidson v. Three Spruces Realty Ltd.*[13] where the plaintiffs deposited valuables for safekeeping with the defendant. The defendant was in the business of renting safety deposit boxes and bulk storage space. A party in such a business is known as a "bailee" and his customers as "bailors". At the time of contracting, the bailors were asked to sign a standard form contract drafted by the bailee. One of the terms of the contract excluded the bailee's liability in the event that the bailor's goods were lost, stolen, destroyed, or injured in any way. Negligence in the safekeeping of the store valuables was expressly excluded under the contract.

The bailors' goods were stolen while in the bailee's possession. In the action brought for the loss of the goods stored, the bailee defended on the basis that, by contract, the bailors had agreed to waive such an action against the bailee. The court held that the defence failed and the bailee was liable. One of the factors stressed by the court in reaching this decision was that a copy of the contract had not been given to the bailors and neither was the contract read to them nor was the exclusionary clause drawn to their attention. The surprise element was compounded by evidence that the bailee told them it was not necessary to insure the stored goods. A reasonable inference could be drawn from that statement that adequate precautions were taken by the bailee to safeguard their goods.

The element of surprise might extend to the matter in which the consumer enters into a legally binding relationship with the seller. A court might view as surprise the means of acceptance of the Rinehart consumer contract, i.e., opening the diskette. It is open to argument that surprise applies not only to the particular terms of the contract but the means by which a contract has been made. In most instances, the lay person might believe that to be contractually bound requires the "signing" of a document. It is likely, however, should a court require the consumer to sign the contract, that the consumer of the software would not read the printed terms.

These terms function primarily as a risk-shifting device. Any defect or flaw in the software that causes loss or harm is shifted to the buyer; with the exception of a limited warranty and replacement of the diskette, the company has substantially reduced the potential scope of liability to those who buy and use its product. Is it a surprise to shift liability for the consequential loss onto the consumer of the company's software?

The answer to this question in each case is whether or not the drafter of the standard form contract has gained an unfair surprise. The doctrine of unconscionability (see Chapter 4) is often the basis for upsetting the risk-shifting term of the contract. The legal conclusion is that the buyer is not bound by the term because it is unlikely that he/she read it, or if he/she did read it, that he/she would not reasonably be expected to understand the effect of the term. Because the products of mass production and marketing are sold by salespeople who themselves understand little more than the average consumer, it is unlikely that the element of surprise can be effectively eliminated through the actual person making the sale.

There is Canadian authority for the proposition that "when a contract of a common type contains special onerous and unusual provisions it is the duty of the party in whose interest such provisions are inserted to see that they are effectively called to the attention of the other party under the penalty of their being held not binding upon the latter party."[14] There is a presumption, then, that a contract will not contain unreasonable or oppressive terms, and, if it does, the party seeking to enforce them must demonstrate that he/she called them to the attention of the party signing the contract and that he/she agreed to be bound by the terms.[15]

In the *Tilden* case, the Ontario Court of Appeal held that:[16]

> In modern commercial practice, many standard form printed documents are signed without being read or understood. In many cases the parties seeking to rely on the terms of the contract know or ought to know that the signature of a party to the contract does not represent the true intention of the signer, and that the party signing is unaware of the stringent and onerous provisions which the standard form contains. Under such circumstances, I am of the opinion that the party seeking to rely on such terms should not be able to do so in the absence of first having taken reasonable measures to draw such terms to the attention of the other party, and in the absence of such reasonable measures, it is not necessary for the party denying knowledge of such terms to prove either fraud, misrepresentation or non est factum.

The contrary view, based on the traditional English position, has been followed by the British Columbia Court of Appeal in *Delaney*.[17] In that case, the deceased had signed a standard form contract excluding liability of a company offering rafting trips down the Fraser River in British Columbia. The deceased drowned on the rafting trip. His estate claimed the employees of the company negligently caused his death. In an action for damages, the company successfully argued that the exemption clause barred the claim. In reaching this conclusion, the British Columbia Court of Appeal followed the traditional rule found in *L'Estrange*.

In the view of the two-member majority, the traditional rule stopped short of placing an obligation of drawing the terms to the attention of the seller in a consumer transaction. Thus, in Canada, the courts are split on the continued application of the rule in *L'Estrange*. It can be argued that the better, more progressive approach is reflected in *Tilden*. This decision of the Ontario Court of Appeal has gathered support in a number of subsequent Canadian cases.[18]

The Oppression Factor

The oppression factor assumes a degree of domination exerted by the drafters of standard form contracts over those who desire to buy the goods and services of the drafter. Given the drafter's complete control over the content of the standardized form, his/her profit motive, unless constrained by competition (unlikely in our highly regulated economy) or by legislative restraints, invariably will generate excessively one-sided terms.

ABSENCE OF BARGAINING POWER
The oppression factor may also apply when disagreements arise over the interpretation of the terms of the contract. The drafter, given his superior position in the transaction, may seek to interpret the contract in the most favourable possible fashion, which gives the other party few options: either accede to the interpretation imposed or end the contract. In Chapter 4, under the heading of Duress, considerable attention was devoted to considering the types of situations in which the court finds oppression and the type of relief granted in such cases. At this point, it is sufficient to demonstrate that oppression applies to the factors creating the contractual relations and the factors concerning contract performance. In the latter case, as a general rule, Canadian law is less willing to intervene.

There is overlap between the oppressive nature of terms arising from an imbalance in the equality of bargaining and the surprise factor. Thus, in another Tilden case, *Tilden Rent-A-Car Co. v. Chandra*,[19] the consumer was able to escape liability for damage to a car that he had rented from Tilden even though he had signed a contract containing terms that had made him liable. Those terms, in the view of the court, were "stringent and onerous" and they had not been drawn to the attention of the consumer; he had not read them, and no reasonable drafter of such a contract could reasonably believe, under those circumstances, that the consumer had consented to them.

At the heart of the oppression issue is the absence of bargaining that goes on between the parties to a consumer transaction. Oppression, however, may also be an important factor in a commercial transaction. Not all commercial enterprises have equal bargaining, or indeed, in given markets, any bargaining power at all. In England, Lord Denning was a leading proponent of active judicial intervention in such cases. The guise of controlling the oppression factor in such contracts was the doctrine of fundamental breach of the contract. Under that doctrine, the contract was said to not exist and the terms excluding liability fell with the contract. In *Levison v. Patent Steam Carpet Cleaning Co. Ltd.*, Lord Denning said:

> The other means of getting round the injustice of these exemption or limitation clauses is by means of the doctrine of fundamental breach. . . . I think that a special solution is required: because in these standard forms the party with the strong bargaining power would always be able to insert words wide enough to exempt him from any liability or to limit his liability to a negligible figure. . . . If a party uses his superior power to impose an exemption or limitation clause on the weaker party, he will not be allowed to rely on it if he has himself been guilty of a breach going to the root of the contract.[20]

Lord Denning is blunt about his attitude toward the standard form contract in consumer transactions, and sees the law as providing a means of "getting around" the perceived injustice of certain terms. Rather than construe the exclusionary clause to determine whether it covers the specific facts of the case, Lord Denning was willing to impose his own solution — a rule of law that would strike down such clauses, even though by their language they clearly covered the type of alleged liability complained of by the consumer. Although these views have not been accepted by the English courts in general, there is evidence that Lord Denning's views have found fertile soil in Canada.[21]

In Canada, where the court views the clause as clearly unfair and unreasonable, the tendency is to find that the drafter of the standard form contract has "abused" the doctrine of freedom of contract. In this watchdog role, the court uses the common law to ensure that such abuses do not adversely affect the consumer's right to seek redress in the courts.[22]

CONTRACTS OF ADHESION

The hallmarks of such a contract are: i) standardized terms that apply to a large number of similar transactions involving different persons; ii) the contract is drafted by the party offering goods or services in the marketplace; iii) the other party to the contract has little, if any, power to alter or modify the terms of the contract that favour the drafter; iv) the terms and conditions drafted are not easily comprehended by the other party to the transaction.[23] At the heart of the contract of adhesion is the almost total absence of equal bargaining power between the party offering goods or services and the consumer buying the goods or services. The problem was articulated by Francis J. in *Unico v. Owen*:[24]

The consumer-credit market is essentially a process of exchange, the general nature of which is shaped by the objectives and relative bargaining power of each of the parties. In consumer goods transactions there is almost always a substantial differential in bargaining power between the seller and his financier, on the one side, and the householder on the other. That difference exists because generally there is a substantial inequality of economic resources between them, and of course, that balance in the great mass of cases favours the seller and gives him and his financier the power to shape the exchange to their advantage. Their greater economic resources permit them to obtain the advice of experts; moreover, they have more time to reflect about the specific terms of the exchange prior to the negotiations with the consumer; they know from experience how to strengthen their own position in consumer-credit arrangements; and the financier-creditor is better able to absorb the impact of a single imprudent or unfair exchange.

The basic argument articulated against the contract of adhesion is based on the premise that standard form contracts are not truly based on the consumer's consent to the terms. Instead, the consumer, if he/she wants to buy the goods or services of the seller, is compelled to contract on the standard form contract terms presented to him/her. The consumer has an absence of choice; there is no other option but walking away from the transaction altogether. In this world of pre-bargained, non-negotiable contracts, the consumer has no individual power to correct unfairness in the terms imposed by the seller.

Discretionary Judicial Power

The courts have often exercised their power on broad discretionary grounds either to intervene and rewrite contractual terms or find contractual terms not enforceable. Because the courts hold this trump card, it becomes exceedingly difficult to predict whether or not a particular contract or term in a contract will have created the binding rights and obligations originally intended under the contract. The two case studies will focus on the use of exclusionary clauses and penalty or liquidated damage clauses in a contract. Both often operate as risk-planning devices. They are placed in a contract so as to allow the party drafting the standard form to predict in advance the nature and scope of his/her potential liability under the contract with the other party.

THE EXCLUSIONARY CLAUSE
The case study of the exclusionary clause provides some insight into the role exercised by the court over standard form contracts. The main

purpose of the exclusionary clause is to shift responsibility for the loss or damage that may arise from the use of a product. The loss may range from economic loss of an opportunity to the death of the person using the product. Given the potentially wide range of unforeseen events or circumstances that might arise in a particular case, the seller attempts, in general language, to exclude totally, or substantially limit, his/her potential liability to the buyer of his/her product.

An example of an exclusionary clause may be found in the consumer transaction (Figure 1.4):

> Neither Rinehart nor anyone else who has been involved in the creation, production, or delivery of the program shall be liable for any direct, indirect, consequential, or incidental damages arising out of the use, the results of use, or inability to use such product even if Rinehart has been advised of the possibility of such damages or claim.

The purpose of the exclusionary clause is to minimize the possibility of a consumer suing the company because the software has resulted in a loss. The contract attempts to limit the consumer's remedy to replacement of the diskette. Assuming the enforceability of the exclusionary clause, Rinehart's potential exposure to the risk of a large damage action has been substantially reduced.

Illustration   A consumer buys a Rinehart Ltd. software program for purposes of doing his/her financial statements and preparing his/her tax return. Assume that because of a bug in the program, the taxpayer makes an error on the return and pays substantially less tax than is owed, and Revenue Canada, catching the error, later levies a penalty of $2000 against the consumer-taxpayer. The consumer-taxpayer contends that but for the bug in the Rinehart tax program, the error would not have been made. He/she then wants to hold the company liable for the penalty payable to Revenue Canada.

Avoidance of exclusionary clauses   What techniques can the consumer's lawyer use to avoid the application of the exclusionary clause? One technique is called fundamental breach. This technique entitles the consumer to put an end to the contract.[25] Once the contract terminates, then the exclusionary clause ceases to have effect. The House of Lords in *Photo Production Ltd. v. Securicor*,[26] however, held that an exclusionary clause survived a breach of contract by the party that had drafted the contract. The determination of the issue in that case turned on the "reasonableness" of the exclusionary clause contained in a contract between "two equal parties" where the risk of the party performing the service was intended to be modest.

The English approach is to restrict the circumstances in which the courts will hold that the exclusionary clause does not apply. It is opposed to a broadly based discretion for the court to find the exclusionary clause can be avoided in every case of breach. Instead, the House of Lords clearly indicated that the doctrine of fundamental breach provided the courts with a rule of construction, e.g., based on the intention of the parties. Using this rule, the court asks whether or not the clause has excluded liability for a breach going to the root of the contract.

Rules applied to an exclusionary clause case   There is an important distinction between employing a rule of construction and a rule of law in the exclusionary clause cases. One commentator has expressed the difference in the following fashion:[27]

> If one argues that fundamental breach is a rule of construction only the courts must assess the contract objectively to see whether the parties intended to exclude liability for a breach going to the root of the contract, but if one argues that fundamental breach is a rule of law then the courts may ride roughshod over the contract and invoke the "presumed intention" of the parties as justification for doing as they wish.

The Canadian exclusionary clause   The Supreme Court of Canada in *Beaufort Realties (1964) Inc. and Belcourt Construction (Ottawa) Ltd. v. Chomedey Aluminum Co. Ltd.*[28] expressly approved of the House of Lords decision in the *Photo Production* case. However, the result of *Beaufort* is quite different, and provides a good illustration of judicial intervention. In *Beaufort* there was no evidence of "surprise" or "imbalance" of equality of bargaining between the parties. Each party was a company and had negotiated a contract. Contained in the contract was an exclusionary clause that provided:

> Article 6. The Subcontractor hereby waives, releases and renounces all privileges or rights of privilege, and all lien or rights of lien now existing or that may hereinafter exist for work done or materials furnished under this Contract, upon the premises and upon the land on which the same is situated, and upon any money or monies due or to become due from any person or persons to Contractor, and agrees to furnish a good and sufficient waiver of the privilege and lien on said building, lands and monies from every person or corporation furnishing labour or material under the Subcontractor.

The right to exclude a lien was expressly authorized by statute in Ontario.[29] Later the main contractor could not pay the subcontractor and the subcontractor filed a lien against certain property owned by the main contractor. It is difficult to understand how the subcontractor could argue, based on the very specific language in Article 6, that he/she had reserved the right to file a lien in the event of non-payment. Indeed, a lien could only be filed in this eventuality. But the subcontractor argued that failure to make payments as due under the contract resulted in a fundamental breach and the effect of such a breach was to eliminate the effect of the exclusionary clause. Nonetheless, the Supreme Court of Canada held that the subcontractor was not bound by the clause because of the main contractor's fundamental breach.

Contrasting *Beaufort Realties* with the House of Lords decision in *Photo Production* indicates an important difference in the approach to contracts. The English position illustrates an increased commitment to dividing the law between commercial and consumer contracts. Legislative changes in English law may well be responsible for, or at least have accelerated, the distinction between the basis of treating exclusionary clauses in commercial contracts as opposed to consumer contracts. In Canada, the courts are less inclined to adopt this distinction.[30] It has been suggested with considerable force that the Court in *Beaufort* apparently "missed an essential feature of the Law Lords' judgment [in *Securicor*], namely that between freely contracting parties the clear language of an exclusionary clause should be respected."[31]

Survival of an exclusionary clause   The test of whether an exclusionary clause survives fundamental breach is set forth in *Chomedey Aluminum Co. Ltd. v. Belcourt Construction (Ottawa) Ltd. et al.*[32] by the Ontario Court of Appeal:

> Where there is a fundamental breach of contract by a party in whose favour is drawn an exclusionary clause, the effect of the clause generally depends on the construction of the contract, and this in turn depends on whether it is fair and reasonable for the exclusionary clause to survive a fundamental breach.

The test provides an ad hoc approach to the contract. The court had regard to all the circumstances of the case, including the events following the signing of the contract and their intent as evidenced by the written terms, and had to decide whether the exclusionary clauses survived. In some cases, there is little analysis and merely a short conclusion about the continued existence or cessation of the clause.[33]

Beneath the language of the Canadian cases is an unarticulated policy: The Canadian courts will not allow one party to exclude another party's access to the courts through the use of exclusionary clauses. The reason for an exclusionary clause is to define precisely, in advance, what remedies will be available in the event of breach. The Canadian cases, however, provide no clear indication as to when the clause is enforceable.

PENALTY CLAUSES

Another example of the Canadian judiciary intervening and setting aside terms of a contract negotiated between parties of equal bargaining power, and where surprise was not an issue, may be found in *H.F. Clarke Ltd. v. Thermidaire Corp. Ltd.* In an exclusive distributorship contract there was a clause that established the measure of liquidated damages in the event of breach of contract. The plaintiff had broken two terms of the contract by selling competitive products other than those of the defendant's, as well as the covenant against post-contract competition. The defendant, after the breach, elected to terminate the contract and the plaintiff, the alleged breaching party, brought an action for damages claiming wrongful termination. The defendant counterclaimed for damages under the breached covenant. The plaintiff, on the counterclaim, contended that the liquidated damages clause in the contract constituted a "penalty" because the formula for assessing damages unreasonably increased their liability to compensate for the breach. If the liquidated damages clause were a "penalty" then it was not enforceable, but if the clause were a genuine attempt by the parties to pre-estimate the loss as best they could within their special knowledge of the circumstances, it was not a penalty, and enforceable. The trial and appellate level courts held the liquidated damages clause to be enforceable.

In the Ontario Court of Appeal, the court considered the disparity between the $92 000 estimated actual loss and the possibility of $200 000 that would result from applying the gross trading profit formula contained in the liquidated damages clause, and concluded:[34]

> the employment of a formula geared to sales of competitive products during the prohibited period was adopted by two keen business firms as the best method of determining the loss resulting from a breach of the covenant — a covenant into which they entered with their eyes open. . . . The parties knew and appreciated these factors and chose this method to establish compensation for a loss, the amount of which was difficult to determine and, no doubt, very costly to establish.

But the Supreme Court of Canada disagreed and reversed the Ontario Court of Appeal. Exercising equity jurisdiction for relief against penalties, Laskin C.J. concluded that intervention was based on "a manifestation of concern for fairness and reasonableness". Despite what bargain the parties might make respecting a liquidated damages clause, the court always retains its jurisdiction to make an independent determination of whether or not the enforcement of the clause is reasonable in the circumstances.

Under the facts of that case, Laskin C.J. placed considerable emphasis on the disparity between the estimated actual loss and the damages calculated on the basis of the liquidated damages formula. He concluded that the clause was a penalty because it was a "grossly excessive and punitive response to the problem to which it was addressed; and the fact that the appellant subscribed to it, and may have been foolish to do so, does not mean it should be left to rue its unwisdom.[35]

In a later Supreme Court of Canada decision in *Elsley et. al. v. J.G. Collins Insurances Agencies Ltd.*,[36] Dickson J., without referring to *H.F. Clarke Ltd.*,[37] stated:

> It is now evident that the power to strike down a penalty clause is a blatant interference with freedom of contract and is designed for the sole purpose of providing relief against oppression for the party having to pay the stipulated sum. It has no place where there is no oppression.

Problems for Discussion

1. Are judges qualified to determine what clauses in a standard form are "unreasonable" so as to invoke the obligation to call them to the attention of the other party to the contract?

2. Isn't reasonableness closely tied with the type of business in which the contract is being used?

3. What steps should Rinehart Ltd. take to ensure that its consumers are not surprised by the terms of the Licence Agreement?

4. Would the average consumer of computer software understand the meaning of the exclusionary clause in the Licence Agreement?

5. Are the terms of the Licence Agreement "onerous and unusual provisions"?

6. Is the surprise argument merely a means of ensuring that consumers are not bound by certain types of terms that they have not consented to at the time of contracting?

7. Is the Rinehart Ltd. Licence Agreement a contract of adhesion (Figure 1.4)? Is the Commercial Contract in Figure 1.2 a contract of adhesion? How would you distinguish between the two contracts on this issue?

8. Is the nature of oppression connected with the specific contractual terms contained in the document or with the relative absence of bargaining power? If the latter, is it ever possible for a powerful company to draft and enforce an exclusionary clause in a lawsuit with a consumer?

9. Does it follow that inequality of bargaining power will inevitably lead to onerous terms imposed on the consumer?

10. Does the inequality of bargaining power between Rinehart Ltd. and the engineer in the Consultant Contract (Figure 1.3) make it unenforceable?

11. Do you agree with the judicial attitude expressed by Lord Denning?

12. Is the option under the Licence Agreement of allowing the consumer to return the software if he disagrees with the contract a sufficient concession to prevent a finding of oppression?

13. Could you redraft the Licence Agreement to overcome any potential argument of oppression and surprise?

14. Is it possible to reconcile the two Supreme Court of Canada cases? What do the differing approaches say about the consistency and uniformity of contract principles in Canadian law?

15. Can the Rinehart Ltd. Licence Agreement be construed as having a liquidated damages provision?

16. In the event that a consumer of Rinehart's software suffers a loss, what are the chances that a Canadian court would enforce the contractual limitation in the Licence Agreement?

17. Is there a reasonable basis for distinguishing between commercial and consumer contracts?

18. Has the House of Lords effectively eliminated broad based jurisdiction from the commercial contract cases?

19. Are there legitimate business or commercial reasons supporting the use of exclusionary and liquidated damages clauses that the Supreme Court of Canada has ignored?

Chapter 8 Notes

1. Slawson, *Standard Form Contracts and Democratic Control of Lawmaking Power*, (1971) 84 *Harv.L.Rev.* 529.
2. K. Llewellyn, *The Common Law Tradition* (1960) pp. 360-71.
3. (1934) 2 K.B. 394, 403 per Scrutton L.J.
4. *Ibid.*, p. 406.
5. (1983) 24 C.C.L.T. 6 (B.C.C.A.).
6. See Reiter, *The Control of Contract Power*, pp. 358-61.
7. *Ibid.*
8. See *Templin v. Alles*, (1944) 1 D.L.R. 733 (Ont.C.A.).
9. *Knight Sugar Company v. Webster*, (1930) S.C.R. 50 (S.C.C.).
10. See F. Kessler, *Contracts of Adhesion — Some Thoughts about Freedom of Contract*, (1943) 43 *Col.L.Rev.* 629, 631-33.
11. *Tilden Rent-A-Car Co. v. Clendenning*, (1978) 83 D.L.R. (3d) 400, 405 (Ont.C.A.).
12. *Ibid.* To the same effect, see *Provident Savings Life Ass'ce Society of New York v. Mowat*, (1902) 32 S.C.R. 147, 162.

13. (1977) 79 D.L.R. (3d) 481 (B.C.S.C.).
14. *Can. Bank Commerce v. Foreman*, (1927) 2 D.L.R. 530, 537 quoted in *Tilden, supra* note 11, p. 407.
15. *Jacques v. Lloyd D. George & Partners Ltd.*, (1968) 1 W.L.R. 625, 630 quoted in *Tilden, supra* note 11, p. 408. Also see Waddams, 49 *Can. Bar. Rev.*, pp. 590-91.
16. *Supra* note 11, pp. 408-409.
17. *Supra* note 5.
18. See, e.g., *Craven v. Strand Holidays (Canada) Ltd.*, (1980) 119 D.L.R. (3d) 225, 227 (Ont.H.C.).
19. (1983) 150 D.L.R. (3d) 685, 688 (Co.Ct.B.C.).
20. (1977) 3 W.L.R. 90, 96-98 (C.A.).
21. See, e.g., *Davidson v. Three Spruces Realty Ltd., supra* note 13.
22. See *Gillespie Brothers & Co. Ltd. v. Roy Bowles Transport Ltd.*, (1973) Q.B. 400, 415 (C.A.) cited with approval in *Davidson v. Three Spruce Realty Ltd., supra* note 13, pp. 492-93.
23. See MacNeil, *Contracts, Exchange Transactions and Relations*, (2nd ed. 1978), pp. 445-47.
24. 50 N.J. 101, 110 232 A.2d 405, 410 (1967).
25. See *Photo Production Ltd. v. Securicor*, (1980) 1 All E.R. 556 (H.L.).
26. *Ibid.*
27. See Ogilvie, *Suisee Atlantique Re-Vindicated: How Long, O Lords, How Long?* (1980-81) *Can.Bus.L.J.* 101, 105.
28. (1981) 116 D.L.R. (3d) 193 (S.C.C.).
29. See *Mechanics' Lien Act*, R.S.O. 1970, c. 267, s.5 (1).
30. *Canso Chemicals Ltd. v. Canadian Westinghouse Co. Ltd.*, (1974) 54 D.L.R. (3d) 517, 10 N.S.R. (2d) 306 (S.C. App.Div.); and Ogilvie, *supra* note 27, pp. 112-14.
31. See Ziegel, "The House of Lords Overrules Harbutt's Plasticine," (1980) 30 *Univ.Tor.L.J.* 421, p. 439.
32. (1979) 24 O.R. (2d) 1, 97 D.L.R. (3d) 170 (Ont.C.A.).
33. *Canadian-Dominion Leasing Corp. Ltd. v. George A. Welch & Co.; O'Connor Office Machines Ltd., Third Party*, (1982) 33 O.R. (2d) 826 (Ont.C.A.).
34. (1973) 33 D.L.R. (3d) 13, 25-26.
35. *Ibid.*
36. (1978) 83 D.L.R. (3d) 1 (S.C.C.).
37. *Supra* note 4.

Part II

THE LAW OF TORTS

9 INTRODUCTION TO THE LAW OF TORTS

The Nature of Civil Liability

A tort is a "civil wrong" that entitles the persons harmed by certain conduct to recover compensation for their loss against the tortfeasor, i.e., the person committing the civil wrong. The offending conduct in the law of tort is referred to as a civil wrong to distinguish it from criminal conduct. In some instances, however, there may be overlap. The wrongful conduct may result in both civil and criminal breaches, e.g., Jones punches Smith in the nose. Jones has committed an assault which is a criminal offence. Also, Smith is entitled to recover compensation for his injury — for instance, his hospital and doctor bills. The law of torts provides a number of categories of civil liability to compensate the victim who has suffered some injury, loss, or harm to his/her person, property or business. The categories include negligence, defamation, assault, false imprisonment, trespass, conversion, and negligent misrepresentation.

Distinguished from Contracts

The law of torts is more complex, abstract, and vague than the law of contract. At the heart of contracts is a central interest advanced by the courts: the enforcement of promises. The parties are those who have exchanged promises. They are not "strangers". From the earliest development, the law of tort has contained rules developed by the courts to determine the liability for "civil wrongs" by a party who may be a complete stranger to the person injured.

Strangers to a contract, however, have no enforceable legal claims. Contractual liability follows from a consensual relationship between the parties. The privity of contract rules excludes most other claims arising under the contract. In contrast, the law of torts is based on wrongs; the promises binding parties to a contract are often absent. The courts, through the law of torts, formulate wide-ranging public policy decisions to serve the interest of the general community.

Limits on Tort Liability

The law of torts has evolved to control, limit, and confine an infinite variety of behaviour of persons and businesses. By attaching the label "civil wrong" to certain behaviour, legal consequences are implied. Compensating the victim of the tort acts as a disincentive by increasing a tortfeasor's costs of certain behavior. Accidents are a major source of tort litigation: cars colliding; airplanes crashing; trains derailing; bridges, buildings, and roads collapsing; food, air, and water fouled with contaminated substances; health aids and drugs adulterated; machines maiming and killing workers and others. This is a partial list of things and events that can create casualties. Individuals can later claim damages for their losses or injuries suffered.

Not all casualties of our industrial society will obtain compensation for their losses. An important function of the law of torts has been to define and articulate the nature and scope of interest that will be protected through a judicial system of civil liability. These interests "may be interests in personal security, reputation or dignity, as in actions for assault, personal injuries and defamation. They may be interests in property, as in actions for trespass and conversion; or interest in unimpaired relations with others, as in causing injury or death to relatives."[1] Once the protected interest is violated, compensatory damages act as a conduit, shifting the cost of the loss to the person causing the harm.

There are so many potential circumstances where tort law applies that it is impossible to keep all of the illustrations confined to the operation of Rinehart's business. In this chapter in particular, a broad brush stroke is used to paint some of the more important theories and principles found in tort law that have application in the commercial context.

The Protection of Interests

The judgment to protect a particular interest is not independent of our community values. Underlining the law of torts are important moral, social, political, economic, and cultural values. Courts are left to weigh and balance the competing interests in society based on legal precedent. From our newspapers we have a first-hand account of the consequences of accidents. What is often missing from these accounts are the gaps, inaccessibility, and cost of the common law compensation system.

Public Policy

An important question is whether or not the judicial system is the best institution to make difficult policy decisions often implied in tort claims. Below, two illustrations based on actual cases clearly indicate the type of problems that may overwhelm and overload the common law tort system.

FIGURE 9.1 **THE SOURCE OF VALUES IN TORT LAW**

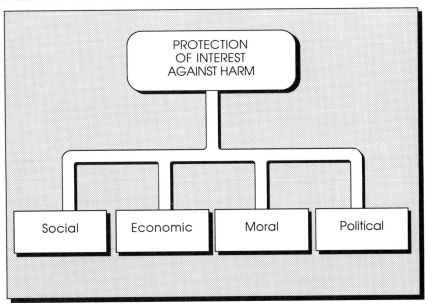

MEDICAL VACCINES

Our first example concerns the manufacturers of whooping-cough vaccine. There has been evidence that the risk of tort actions may be an important reason for drug companies to stop manufacturing whooping-cough vaccine. Of the millions of people who may be vaccinated in a two-year period, fifteen may die and several thousand others may suffer from an illness resulting from the vaccine. By being required to compensate these victims, the manufacturer might decide that the potential economic risk of making the vaccine is too great. The vaccine is removed from the marketplace. Within the next four years, it is predicted that thousands of people without the protection of the vaccine will contract whooping-cough and that a number of these will die.

The medical vaccine cases raise a substantial public policy issue: how to balance the necessity of immunization of a population against a disease with a tort system that compensates those who become victims of the vaccine. Often the only solution is a legislative response that creates a national policy placing the risk on the government.

LETHAL CHEMICALS

Our second illustration is that of the Union Carbide chemical accident in India. After the Union Carbide Corporation plant in Bhopal, India, leaked a lethal chemical killing about 2500 people, tort actions were quickly filed in the United States. The amount of damages requested ran into the billions of dollars. Such a dramatic industrial accident raises extremely complex questions. Is there an ethical obligation on transnational companies dealing with dangerous substances to follow the same safety standards in third-world countries as they do in Western, developed countries? Are local laws that require the use of local workers a contributing factor to the accident? What is the responsibility of government in regulating such industries? What benefits have pesticides brought in terms of better nutrition and health to the millions living in India and other third-world nations? These are some of the issues that have been raised, and later become issues in the tort actions brought by the victims against the chemical manufacturer.

THE IMPACT OF THE PUBLIC POLICY DECISION

The courts, by allowing, withholding, or limiting damages, must take into account global questions that ultimately touch the welfare, health, standard of living, and indeed, the foundation of capitalism itself. The litigation becomes a forum of debate for issues of corporate responsibility, the transfer of technology, training and inspection programs, and education.

It is reasonable to ask whether or not a court is the best institution with the most effective procedures to draw valid conclusions about these questions. Nonetheless, the courts, through the law of torts, are often drawn into such debates. Thus, in the *Westmoreland* case — a former U.S. General sued a television network for a documentary story that stated the General misled the American people on the number of enemy soldiers in the Vietnam War — a court heard considerable evidence about the military and political defeats of a nation at war.

Similarly, in the *Sharon* libel action — an Israeli General sued a magazine for printing a story alleging that he had played a role in the massacre of refugees in Lebanon — broader international issues involving a military leader's action were at issue. In this action, the magazine was not liable to pay damages. The tort action can become a means to write (or rewrite) history as a consequence of determining whether or not reputations of generals have been damaged or harmed. Through newspapers and television, the larger community is allowed to follow the daily evidence of such major cases.

As the above illustrations amply demonstrate, the hard questions are not simply the legal issues of how to protect people against injuries and allocate loss based on notions of fault, but also the larger issues of the value and benefit of certain industries, the structure of trade, the interrelationship of economies, and the standard of living and welfare of millions.

The Allocation of Risks

A major function of the law of torts is to allocate the risks. A damage award allows an injured victim to shift his/her economic loss to the plaintiff. Where the plaintiff is the large manufacturer of the product

FIGURE 9.2 **ALLOCATION OF RISK TO MANUFACTURER**

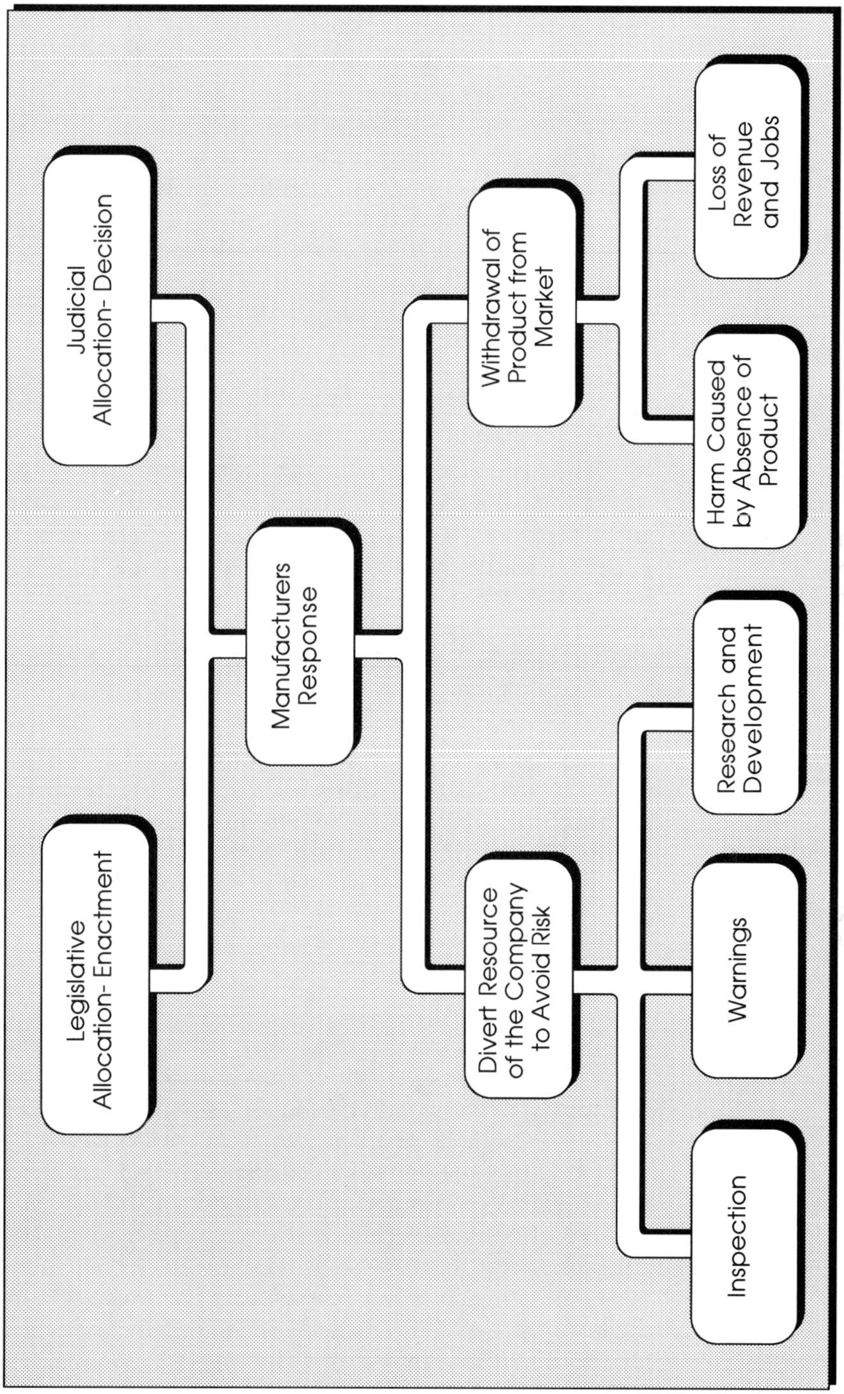

causing the injury, the loss is then allocated to other consumers through a higher price for the product. One by-product, as in the case of the whooping-cough vaccine, is that the increased cost cannot be effectively passed on to the other consumers of the product; in such an instance, the reasonable business decision may be to eliminate the product line or to ask the government to bear the loss. In commercial markets, where the product is required for business use, the flow-through effect of loss allocation is less likely to cause this drastic result.

Effective Precautions

Each manufacturer in the same market is subject to similar risks. The risk can be reduced by increased cost of inspection, supervision, and training of employees; these added expenses are then passed on to the consumer. Allocating the risk to the manufacturer can have the salutary effect of increasing expenditures for research and development in techniques to avoid accidents. This work is carried out by manufacturers who have expertise and knowledge about their product. Thus, airplanes may be, in part, safer because airplane manufacturers have a direct economic incentive in designing, building, and testing airplanes to avoid expensive litigation brought by aircrash victims and their estates.

Why doesn't the crash of a Boeing 727 force Boeing out of the airplane manufacturing business whereas the fifteen deaths and few thousand illnesses caused by the whooping-cough vaccine convince the drug companies to stop manufacturing the vaccine? In large part, the question is answered by whether or not the manufacturer can take effective precautions against a repeat of the same accident and, in part, whether or not the potential risk of liability can be passed along to those who use or buy the product.

Insurance

An important means of distributing the loss is through liability insurance. For a price called a premium, the insurance company agrees to assume the insured's (the person paying the premium) potential risk of loss and to compensate any future victim of an accident caused by the insured. The amount of the premium is dependent on many factors including the safety record of the insured, the potential harm that may result, the number of potential persons who might be harmed, and the means developed by the insured to avoid the risk. In fixing the premium, the insurance company is able to establish a contingency fund that will absorb the loss. The negligent insured's premium rarely will be adequate to pay for the actual amount paid by the insurance company to the insured's victim. But the insurance company has collected many premiums from other insureds seeking to protect themselves against the same risk. As a result, the loss is distributed among all the insureds who have purchased liability insurance covering the same type of risk. (See Chapter 21.)

Insurance is a form of subsidy by the accident-free to pay for the cost of those who are at fault in causing accidents. Why do the accident-free subsidize the accident-causing class? It is unlikely that any insured will be able to predict in advance whether or not his/her conduct will harm others. As there is a risk that this may happen, and the cost of the premium is substantially less than the potential loss from a successful claim, there is an important economic incentive to carry insurance.

Duty

In addition to the preoccupation with a protectable interest, the law of torts has historically required that the plaintiff show that the defendant owed him/her some duty to be careful and cautious. The absence of any such duty will set the negligent defendant free from a damage award. Duty often masks the court's value choice or judgment.

In the nineteenth century, for example, a manufacturer was not liable for harm arising to a consumer of a negligently made product. The consumer purchased the product through a retailer. As a result, the manufacturer, though negligent, was said to owe no duty to anyone other than to those with whom they were in privity of contract. Usually there was no contract between the consumer and the manufacturer; the consumer invariably failed to prove the manufacturer owed him/her a duty of care in producing, storing, shipping, regulating the product, and warning the consumer about dangers in using or consuming the product. This is no longer true in Canada or England.

The most famous statement in Anglo-Canadian law defining, in general terms, what relations give rise to a duty of care is contained in Lord Atkin's judgment in *Donoghue v. Stevenson*:[2]

> The rule that you are to love your neighbour becomes in law you must not injure your neighbour; and the lawyer's question, Who is my neighbour? receives a restricted reply. You must take reasonable care to avoid acts or omissions that you can reasonably foresee would be likely to injure your neighbour. Who, then, in law, is my neighbour? The answer seems to be — persons who are so closely and directly affected by my act that I ought reasonably to have them in contemplation as being so affected when I am directing my mind to the acts of omissions that are called in question.

The Neighbour Principle has been incorporated in Canadian law and is employed to determine whether the defendant owed a duty of care and caution to *this* plaintiff. There are, in fact, two separate issues when the court applies the Neighbour Principle. The first is concerned with the nature of the relationship and the degree of proximity between the parties. The court asks, given the relationship and proximity, was it within the reasonable contemplation of the defendant that his/her actions or conduct would cause harm to the plaintiff? Secondly, assuming the first condition is met, the court is at liberty to determine the extent of the duty between the parties. The door is then open for the court to take into account a variety of moral, social, and economic considerations that might lead to a narrowing of the duty owed, or the size of the class owed the duty.

From the business executive's point of view, the so-called "neighbours" to whom a duty is owed are in a social sense "strangers". It is unlikely that he/she knows these people personally or has contracted with them individually. In the case of a contract, liability is clear in advance; there is no objective Neighbour Principle expanding the potential risk of doing business. Often the contract has a beginning, middle, and end. The time sequence is fixed in advance and the parties are certain. The fear of business people, however, is the expandable notion of duty coupled with the increasing number of interests protected. This will allow "victims" who suffer from a company's negligence compensation awards that can often be substantial.

In a sense, by holding either "duty" or "no duty", the courts are making a significant decision about the way in which business is or ought to be conducted insofar as there is harm or loss to others. Canadian judges, in this way, sit as members of the board of directors and at the right arm of management. Their judgments and wide discretion are important factors in shaping company policy for the manufacture, design, storage, inspection, advertising, and distribution of products.

Standard of Care

The courts have created a test for the standard of care applied to determine whether the defendant's conduct has been negligent. As a general rule, the Canadian courts impose "a reasonable care in the circumstances" principle in defining the defendant's standard of care.[3]

The Reasonable Person

Historically, the courts fixed the standard of care by reference to the reasonable man of ordinary prudence. Today, it is more appropriate to think in terms of the reasonable person, but the old ways of thinking persist with the legacy of the language continuing in the modern context.

This mythical person's prudence is our yardstick to determine whether or not the care employed by the defendant who caused the accident was reasonable. Negligent conduct or activity may occur in a thousand different contexts; but the courts have applied the reasonable person model to all negligence cases. One advantage of the reasonable person model is that the standard of care becomes an objective touchstone. Each defendant is judged in precisely the same fashion.

The reasonable person is an average person without special skills, expertise, or training. Thus, allegations of negligence against doctors, lawyers, accountants, engineers, and similar professionals will bring a higher standard of care. The professional services provided by them cannot be tested by the person who rides the Clapham omnibus — a time-honoured reference to Londoners who rode a double-decker bus as the reasonable person. Further, a manufacturer such as Rinehart, with expert engineers employed in the research and development department, will be held to a higher standard of care when a software product is negligently designed and causes a loss to the user. The standard of care applied takes into account the specialized skills and expertise such a defendant possesses. Judged by this higher standard of care, the defendant's conduct or activity must conform to the practice of a particular profession or industry.

Illustration   Rinehart Ltd. has employed a software engineer, Eric White, a twenty-five-year-old graduate of the University of Toronto. This is Mr. White's first job after graduation. He is assigned the task of testing the Dental Office Management System program developed by Lindsay Software (Figure 1.3). After the testing, Mr. White reports that the program is satisfactory. Later, the Canadian Dental Association, in using the program, discovers a number of program errors. One error has caused the loss of a data bank containing detailed information of billing practices. (We will assume that there is no exemption of liability clause in the contract between Rinehart and the Association.)

The Association claims that the loss resulted from Rinehart's negligence. A reasonably good case of liability can be made on these facts. Mr. White is held to the same standard as a skilled and prudent software engineer. The fact of his inexperience does not reduce the level of care required of him. Moreover, given Mr. White's inexperience, Rinehart Ltd. has an added responsibility to supervise and train Mr. White. The failure to take reasonable precautions would make them negligent.

Strict Liability

Strict liability means that form of civil liability imposed by law without proof of fault or blame against the person causing the harm. Traditionally, the common law required two factors to establish strict liability: i) a non-natural use of land; and ii) as a result of such a use, some substance, e.g., water, chemicals, wild animals, or gas escaped and caused injury to property or persons.[4] An exploding sewage pipe, for example, that damages property or persons would satisfy the common law tests. A peculiar aspect of strict liability is the absence of the reasonable care standard. Although the defendant might have used reasonable care, for example, in the laying of the sewage pipes, this would not excuse his liability.

In the United States, the doctrine of strict liability has been extended to product liability cases. The Canadian courts, however, have been unwilling to go as far as the Americans. It has been suggested that although they cling to negligence and fault principles, the Canadian courts often reach the same result. Rather than directly applying a strict liability standard, negligence, a malleable concept, can be expanded to cover much of the same ground.

Forseeability

What risks must be prevented by the reasonable person? It is clear that almost "any activity is fraught with some degree of danger to others but, if the remotest chance of mishap were sufficient to attract the stigma of negligence, most human action would be inhibited. Inevitably, therefore, one is only required to guard against those risks which society recognises as sufficiently great to demand precaution. The risk must be unreasonable before he can be expected to subordinate his own interests to those of others."[5]

The reasonable person foresees that his/her conduct or activity presents a risk of harm to his/her neighbour. Foreseeable means in a given situation what is likely to result from a particular course of conduct or activity. It is, for example, likely and, therefore, foreseeable, that an inexperienced engineer will lack the specialized skill and experience to adequately test a complicated software program.

Customs and Practices

The customary practices and precautions of an industry or profession are important factors in determining the standard of care. For example, the Canadian Dental Association might show that the general practice of Canadian software manufacturers is to place newly hired, inexperienced engineers in training programs, assign supervisors, and develop methods of review and independent testing procedures. Further, they might have evidence that Rinehart failed to comply with this general practice. A court would attach importance to evidence of this "industry practice", and Rinehart's failure to follow that practice. The standard of care owed by Rinehart would be determined by these issues. Conversely, Rinehart might have complied with the industry practices but the Dental Office Management System program nevertheless caused a loss. A court would conclude that the standard of care required of a software manufacturer was met and that Rinehart, having taken the necessary care, was not liable in negligence.

Proximate Cause

Proximate cause is a legal device to control the ripple effect of negligent conduct or activities. A stone thrown into a lake creates ripples spreading far beyond the initial point of impact. But for the tossed stone there would have been no ripple. The stone is said to have caused the rippling effect. Similarly, in negligence, a particular conduct may cause loss or harm to others over time and at a distance. At some point, the defendant's liability will be cut off. On what basis do the courts draw the line between losses for which the negligent defendant must pay compensation, and those losses for which he does not? A variety of legal conclusions are used: The defendant owed no duty to the plaintiff; the consequences to the plaintiff were not foreseeable by the defendant; another substantial factor contributed to the plaintiff's loss; remoteness prevented liability from attaching.

An Industrial Accident

Take the example of the Bhopal chemical disaster that killed at least 2500 people in India. Assume that, one week later, a religious sect in Calcutta killed two American State Department officials and notified the local media that the killings were in retaliation for the Bhopal incident. Further, assume that, two weeks later, the United States and Canada agreed to impose economic sanctions against India as retribution for the Calcutta killings. Finally, we will assume that Rinehart Ltd. had a transfer of technology agreement with a company located in New Delhi. The effect of the trade embargo caused Rinehart to lose its profit on the agreement with the Indian company. Rinehart argues that but for the negligence of Union Carbide in Bhopal it would not have lost its profitable contract. Similarly, the estates of the two deceased American State Department officials sue Union Carbide claiming that the deaths were caused by Union Carbide's negligence. Is Union Carbide liable to pay compensation to Rinehart and to the deceased Americans' estates?

It is doubtful that either claim would succeed. The predicted legal conclusion might be that the losses were not "foreseeable" by Union Carbide. In essence, the failure to impose liability in such cases is a common sense recognition that the courts must isolate or confine the class of plaintiffs, i.e., those who in terms of time, location, and connection with the defendant, are the most likely to be at risk of harm owing to the negligent conduct or event. Defining the members of the plaintiff class is difficult and troublesome. The courts approach the proximate cause problem with a general question: Is the plaintiff's loss one that the defendant may have reasonably contemplated as a probable outcome of his negligent action?

Burden of Proof

The classic case is *Palsgraf v. Long Island Railroad Company*.[6] At one end of the platform, Mrs. Palsgraf, ticket in hand, waits for her train to Rockaway Beach. At the other end of the platform, two men rush to catch a train headed for another destination. They are late. The train is already moving. One man climbs onto the moving train. The second jumps onto the train but appears about to fall. A guard on the train reaches forward to help him; on the platform another guard pushes the man from behind. Suddenly a small package carried by the man is dislodged and falls onto the rails. Inside are fireworks. There is an explosion. Scales near Mrs. Palsgraf fall from the force of the explosion and strike her, causing her injuries. Mrs. Palsgraf sues the railroad company, claiming damages for injuries on the basis of negligence.

In the trial court, Mrs. Palsgraf succeeded. On Appeal, Cardozo C.J., speaking for a split Court of Appeals of New York, reversed the lower court decision. The following excerpts from his judgment have had an important influence on Anglo-Canadian courts.

> The conduct of the defendant's guard, if wrong in its relation to the holder of the package, was not wrong in its relation to the plaintiff, standing far way. Relative to her it was not negligence at all. Nothing in the situation gave notice that the falling package had in it the potency of peril to persons thus removed. Negligence is not actionable unless it involves the invasion of a legally protected interest, the violation of a right. "Proof of negligence in the air, so to speak will not do." ... The argument for the plaintiff is built upon the shifting meaning of such words as "wrong" and "wrongful," and shares their instability. What the plaintiff must show is "a wrong" to herself; i.e., a violation of her own right, and not merely a wrong to someone else, nor conduct "wrongful" to any one. . . .

Defences

In summary, there are three defences available to the defendant in a negligence action: i) Contributory Negligence; ii) Last Clear Chance; and iii) Voluntary Assumption of the Risk. The first two defences have been substantially altered by legislation in Canada. In this section, a brief outline of each defence is provided.

Contributory Negligence

The common law rule of contributory negligence operated in a harsh fashion by denying a plaintiff recovery if his/her actions had been negligent and contributed to his/her own harm in any way. The courts refused to apportion the negligence between the parties. Thus, in theory, al-

FIGURE 9.3 **DEFENCES TO NEGLIGENCE ACTION**

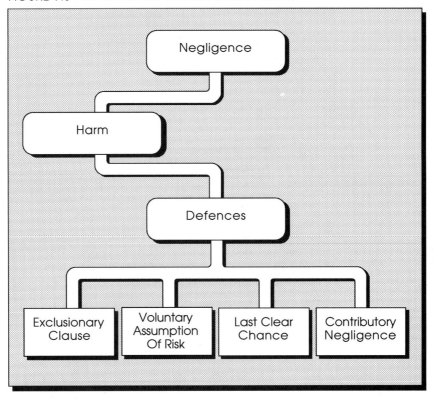

though the defendant's conduct might have been 99 percent responsible for the plaintiff's injury, the plaintiff's 1 percent contributory negligence resulted in the dismissal of the plaintiff's action. The contributorily negligent plaintiff was always left with the entire loss.

In all Canadian provinces the common law rule has been replaced by apportionment legislation. This legislation expressly requires the court to apportion the injury or loss in proportion to the degree of fault or negligence found against the plaintiff and defendant.[7] In a case where it is not possible to determine the degree of relative fault, there is a presumption that each party was 50 percent responsible for the act or event. Under this legislation, the plaintiff who is found to be 1 percent negligent will have his damage award reduced by that percentage.

Last Clear Chance

Another complete common law bar to liability was the defence of Last Clear Chance. The essence of this defence is that the plaintiff, who suffered a loss or injury owing to the negligence of the defendant, had a sufficient opportunity to avoid the accident. In a contributory negligence case, the negligence of each party is concurrent in time. In a Last Clear Chance case, the plaintiff's negligence is subsequent to the defendant's. A clear line can be drawn between the sequence of respective negligent acts of each party.

The defence is often used where the plaintiff's degree of negligence is greater than the defendant's. The major disadvantage of the defence, like contributory negligence, was the "all or nothing" effect of the defence. Rather than comparing the relative degree of fault, and apportioning liability, the plaintiff's case was totally defeated by the Last Clear Chance rule.

In Canada, with the passage of the apportionment legislation, the Last Clear Chance, while still in existence, is only rarely successful. Indeed, a strong case can be made that the rule is no longer an appropriate defence. As the legislation expressly allows for apportionment of negligence, there is little need to resort to the rough and ready Last Clear Chance rule. That rule, in effect, acted as an apportionment device — with one vast difference — by applying apportionment through Last Clear Chance, the plaintiff was not given partial damages; his case was lost. As a result, the Canadian courts prefer to allow apportionment under the statute, and only in the exceptional case will Last Clear Chance apply.

Voluntary Assumption of Risk

As negligence is based on the defendant's fault, it is open for him/her to argue that the plaintiff, with full knowledge of the risk, consented to the risk. An example is the spectator who has attended Vancouver Canucks hockey matches for seven years and one night is injured by being hit by a puck. The hockey spectator knows that this is a risk of watching the sport. Any suit to recover damages will be met with the defence of voluntary assumption of risk.

The defence, however, has been restricted in recent times. One means to this end has been to increase the level of knowledge and awareness of the plaintiff. Did the plaintiff fully understand the nature and character of the risk involved? Secondly, the plaintiff must have voluntarily consented to assume the risk. The modern trend is to look for an agreement between the parties. One Canadian court, quoting English authority, has required, in addition to knowledge, an actual agreement to waive any subsequent claim to negligence.[8] The agreement does not have to be in writing; it can be implied from the situation. With the agreement restrictions, a heavy burden hangs on the defendant to prove this agreement.

Problems for Discussion

1. Discuss the difference between civil liability based on breach of contract and that based on tort.

2. What non-legal factors are important for a court deciding whether or not to award compensation for an injury?

3. What types of interest does the law of tort protect?

4. Give an example of how tort law operates to allocate risks between a consumer and a manufacturer. How does the manufacturer protect itself against such risks?

5. In what circumstances will the potential of tort liability cause a manufacturer to refuse further production and distribution of a product?

6. What is the function of the "duty" concept in a negligence action? Compare the tort notion of duty with the "duty" of a promisor under a contract.

7. Distinguish the concept of "duty" from the principle of "standard of care".

8. In what circumstances will the courts impose a higher standard of care? What standard of care would apply in a negligence action against Rinehart where the plaintiff claimed loss caused by a faulty design in the company's word processing program?

9. Distinguish liability based on negligence and liability based on strict liability.

10. What is the purpose of the proximate cause doctrine?

11. Assume in the *Palsgraf* case that the two men running to catch the train were jewel thieves. As they ran along the platform, a train guard shouted for them to stop. They continued to run. The train guard pulled his service revolver and fired two shots. The first shot struck one of the running men. The second shot struck the train, ricochetted, and struck Mrs. Palsgraf, who was standing at the opposite end of the platform. Would the result in *Palsgraf* have been different if these had been the facts?

12. What was the major defect of the contributory negligence defence? How has legislation eliminated the problem?

Chapter 9 Notes

1. Fleming, *The Law of Torts*, 6th ed. (1983) at 2.
2. (1932) A.C. 562 (H.L.).
3. See *Phillips v. Ford Motor Co.*, (1971) 2 O.R. 537, 553 (Ont.C.A.).
4. These factors derive from the English case of *Rylands v. Fletcher*, (1866) L.R. 1 Ex. 265, Aff'd (1868) L.R. 3 H.L. 330.
5. Supra, note 1, pp. 108-09.
6. 248 N.Y. 339, 162 N.E. 99 (C.A.N.Y. 1928).
7. See, e.g., *The Negligence Act of Ontario*, R.S.O. 1980, c. 315, s. 4.
8. See *Lagasse v. Rural Municipality of Richot*, (1973) 3 W.W.R. 181 (Man.).

10 ECONOMIC TORTS

Introduction

Economic torts are associated with harm, loss, or injury between those engaged in a commercial or business activity. The plaintiff in such an action may not have suffered a physical loss to his/her person or property. Instead, the negligence or intentional conduct of the defendant causes financial loss to a business. That loss may be future profits or expenditures required to repair or remedy the consequences of the defendant's activity.

In the intentional economic torts, the common law has evolved rules to define and control certain types of business misconduct. Often the defendant's action contains an element of fraud, deceit, unfair competition, or a degree of ruthlessness considered beyond the limits of what is acceptable practice in commerce. As the law of contract protects economic relationships where the parties are in privity of contract, the law of tort takes a broader view and imposes liability even though the parties are not bound by a contract. Thus, economic torts expand the potential scope of liability by imposing sanctions against wrongdoers in the marketplace.

The key to understanding economic torts is found in the types of controls the law of torts recognizes as appropriate business or marketplace regulation devices. In other words, through economic torts, the courts define minimal standards of conduct for the participants in a business environment. Taken together, the economic torts are a "code of permissible conduct" that the business community must follow. We discover the basis of this "code" in a piecemeal fashion through learning on what grounds a particular economic tort has been applied to a particular fact or pattern.

The defendant's motive in the intentional economic torts generally falls into one of the following categories: i) to gain a trade or economic advantage at the expense of another business organization; ii) to save an expense; or iii) to punish, harm, or eliminate a third party such as a trade competitor, employee, or trade union. Whether or not the defendant's conduct is a "civil wrong" according to the law of torts, however, does not necessarily turn on motive. The misappropriation of a Rinehart Ltd. trademark by another company is an economic tort per se. Evidence that the misappropriating intended no harm or injury to Rinehart is irrelevant to Rinehart's cause of action in tort.

In recent years, the courts have been willing to extend negligence to cover certain types of business conduct, or activity. In the sections on negligent infliction of economic injury and negligent misrepresentation, we will discover a growing acceptance in Anglo-Canadian law that the general duty of care has an appropriate place in regulating business conduct. The thrust of this chapter is to identify the most common types of economic torts. Care should be taken to distinguish the intentional from the non-intentional tort. The type and nature of economic torts provide an understanding of the range of business interests protected by the courts.

FIGURE 10.1 **TYPES OF ECONOMIC TORTS**

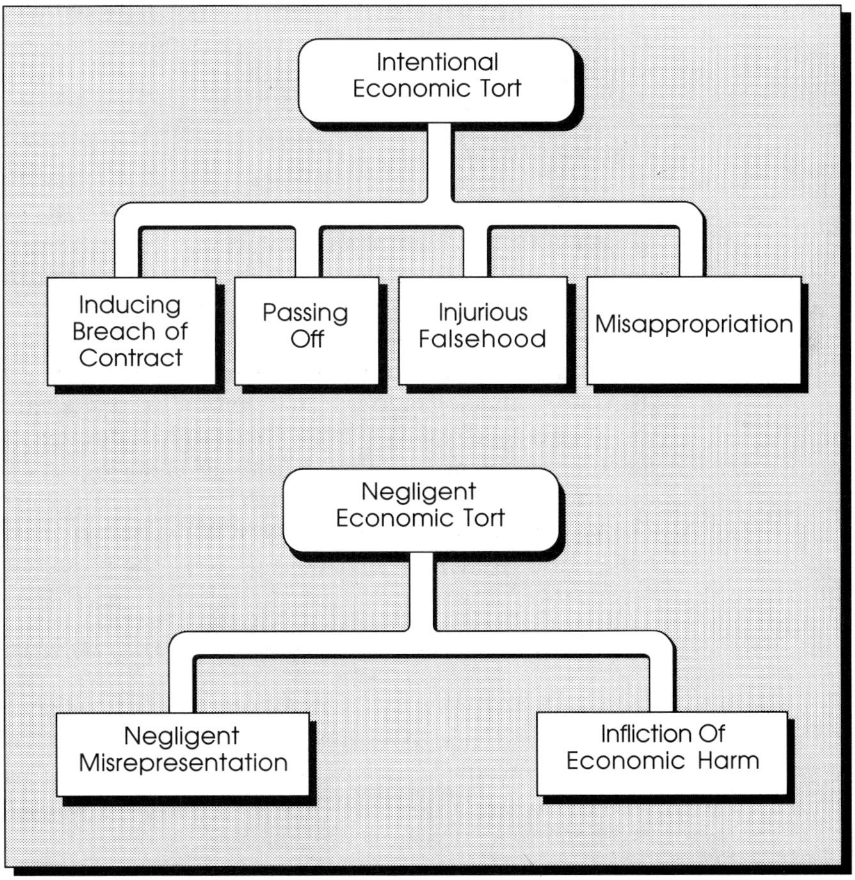

Inducing Breach of Contract

When a person or company intentionally induces — either directly or indirectly — a promisor to breach his/her contract, the promisee is entitled to recover his/her loss against the breach inducer. One of the most common examples is that of one company raiding another company's employees.

Illustration During the distributor's performance of the Software Consulting Agreement (Figure 1.3), Rinehart Ltd. is greatly impressed by the skill, discipline, and expertise of Mr. Tom Winchester. Mr. Winchester, a software computer engineer, has a two-year employment contract with the distributor. The head of Rinehart's Research and Development Department offers Mr. Winchester a 25 percent increase in salary if he comes to work for Rinehart. At the time of the offer, Rinehart has knowledge of Mr. Winchester's employment contract with the distributor. Mr. Winchester accepts the offer and "resigns" from his employment with the distributor. Rinehart's behaviour could be viewed as malicious interference with the contractual relation existing between the distributor and Mr. Winchester. In that case, Rinehart would be liable to pay the economic loss suffered by the distributor.

Elements of the Tort

The legal term for this tort is "procuring a breach". The tort is not limited to procuring a breach of an employment contract: The case law demonstrates that *any* commercial contract is protected by this tort. The crucial elements in proving this tort are the defendant's knowledge of the contract along with evidence that his/her action will cause the promisor to fail or refuse to perform as promised. There is, however, more than one method of interfering with another's contract. In our illustration, the interference results because Rinehart has, through monetary enticement, lured the promisor away from his employment contract. The distributor's employment contract with the software engineer was doomed. The promisor, the software engineer, expressly agreed with Rinehart to nullify his contractual obligations owed to the promisee.

Application to Unions and Government Boards

The tort has been used to control unlawful actions of trade unions and of private and quasi-governmental marketing boards. Thus, tortious liability exists where a trade union wrongfully interferes with the contractual arrangements existing between the company that is the target of the strike and that company's distributor.[1]

In *Gershman v. Manitoba Vegetable Producers' Marketing Board*,[2] the plaintiff had several disagreements with the Board over its decision-making and claim to jurisdiction. After a fire destroyed the plaintiff's produce business, he began working for Stella Company, another Manitoba produce seller. Stella agreed to pay the plaintiff $250 per week and to sell him an interest in the company. The Board forced Stella Company to discharge the plaintiff. The Board had this power because the contracts made by Stella Company, in its business, were regulated by the Board. Stella Company was perfectly aware that unless it discharged the plaintiff, the Board could literally put it out of business.

Solomon J. termed the Board's action a "flagrant abuse of power" and held it liable for procuring a breach of contract.[3] The relevant law is contained in the following passage:[4]

> [A] violation of a legal right committed knowingly is a cause of action, and it is a violation of a legal right to interfere with contractual relations recognized by law if there is no justification for such interference. If the Board, by reason of its special influence, induced Stella Company to discharge plaintiff from his employment, and plaintiff suffered damages as a result of such interference, defendant is liable in law for such damages. In order to succeed in his action plaintiff must prove:
>
> (1) That there was a contract between plaintiff and Stella Company, or there was an agreement to enter into a contract;
>
> (2) That defendant knew of the existence of such contract or of an agreement to enter into such contract;
>
> (3) That defendant intended to procure the breach of that contract or intended to prevent the parties from entering into that contract;
>
> (4) That defendant was successful in inducing Stella Company to breach the contract or prevent Stella Company from entering into the contract with plaintiff; and
>
> (5) That the contract was terminated or the parties were prevented from entering into the contract because of the interference of defendant.
>
> [The Court held that the plaintiff had established all five conditions and awarded him damages.]

Liability in this type of case turns on whether or not the methods used by the defendant are, in themselves, wrongful and unlawful. In this fashion, the courts are able to define the kinds of economic interference that are wrongful, and to provide economic disincentives through damages to discourage specific activities or conduct. As the *Gershman* case illustrates, the tort can be an effective means of preventing abuse of power by government agencies as well as a means of controlling unfair dealings or competition between trade rivals or their trade unions.

Injurious Falsehood

Another intentional economic tort is injurious falsehood. The cause of action arises where the defendant communicates a false statement about the plaintiff to a third party. An injurious falsehood is an untruth about the plaintiff's property or business and results in an economic loss. Because the tort is intentional, the plaintiff, or victim of the untrue statement, carries the burden of showing the defendant intended to make the statement and knew that it was false.

The purpose of the tort is to contain certain types of commercial disparagement. Historically, the typical case involved an untrue statement about a person's interest or title in real property. This statement made by a third party to a perspective purchaser of the property might cause the vendor (the owner and seller of real property) to lose his sale. In the commercial context, the injurious falsehood might relate to the status of the business.

Illustration   Rinehart Ltd., in an attempt to expand the operation of QueTech Ltd., its Ontario subsidary, applied for a $500 000 loan with The Royal Bank of Canada. A competitor, Central Canada Computer Ltd., learned of the application and wrote the president of the Bank that QueTech Ltd. was improperly incorporated under the laws of Ontario. The statement was false and Central Canada Computer Ltd. intended that the false statement would result in QueTech Ltd. being denied the loan. The Royal Bank took an additional three weeks to determine the corporate status of QueTech Ltd., and during this period the interest rate rose by 1 percent. In these circumstances, QueTech Ltd. could recover the increased cost of the loan on the grounds of an injurious falsehood against Central Canada Computer Ltd.

Conspiracy

The tort of conspiracy has been regarded by English and Canadian courts as an anomaly. Nonetheless, civil liability continues to lie where two or more persons combine to cause damage to another's commercial interest. The question of the defendant's intention to cause injury to the plaintiff's commercial interest is of considerable importance in establishing the cause of action. It has been said that the predominant purpose of the conspiracy must have been to injure the plaintiff's commercial interest. On the other hand, if the evidence is that the two or more persons have acted in concert to advance their own self-interest, the civil action for conspiracy will fail.

The problem, however, is proving that the purpose of the defendant's agreement was aimed predominantly at the plaintiff, and this is no easy task. Indeed, in a close case, the courts appear more willing to accept that the defendants' conspiracy was aimed at the public in general.[5] Assuming that the predominant purpose to injure the plaintiff cannot be established, can the element of intent be dispensed with by showing the defendant's conduct was in itself unlawful?

In the *Canada Cement LaFarge* case, the Supreme Court of Canada cited prior cases that found that the intention to injure was irrelevant once the unlawfulness of the means employed by the defendants was established. Estey J. concluded that in Canadian law there were two torts of conspiracy and he provided the test for each:[6]

> Although the law concerning the scope of the tort of conspiracy is far from clear, I am of the opinion that whereas the law of tort does not permit an action against an individual defendant who has caused injury to the plaintiff, the law of torts does recognize a claim against them in combination as the tort of conspiracy if:
>
> (1) whether the means used by the defendant are lawful or unlawful, the predominant purpose of the defendants' conduct is to cause injury to the plaintiff; or,
>
> (2) where the conduct of the defendant is unlawful, the conduct is directed towards the plaintiff (alone or together with others), and the defendant should know in the circumstances that injury to the plaintiff is likely to and does result.

In summary, there are two torts of civil conspiracy. In the first case, liability is based upon the intentional conduct of two or more persons whose predominant intention is to injure some commercial interest of the defendant. The tort occurs whether or not the conduct in itself is lawful or unlawful. Secondly, where there is unlawful conduct by two or more persons directed against the plaintiff and causes injury to the plaintiff, liability is imposed on the basis of constructive intent. Constructive intent is found where the defendants should have known in the circumstances that their conspiracy was likely to injure the defendant and in fact it does so injure him.

Passing-Off

There is an old saying that imitation is the highest form of flattery. In a commercial context, imitation of another's product, wares, personality, or service can become the basis of the tort action called passing-off. The imitator seeks to obtain a "free ride" on the goodwill and reputation in the marketplace that another has already established. There is, however, more than mere imitation involved in the passing-off action; there must be evidence of deception of those who have purchased the defendant's product thinking that it is the product of the plaintiff.

The Common Trade Rule

The plaintiff and defendant must compete in a common trade. The defendant attempts to ride on the coattails of the plaintiff's success and reputation in the trade. The defendant has imitated its competitor's product because the plaintiff has established within the trade a profitable market for its product. Not surprisingly, when the IBM PC gained popularity in a large sector of the microcomputer market, companies located in Hong Kong and Taiwan began manufacturing IBM clones and distributing them in North America. Passing-off is one of the actions available to prevent this unfair trade interference.

Policy Considerations

There are a number of competing policy considerations in a passing-off case. From the consumer's point of view, there is an advantage of wider "free choice" when there are a number of similar products on the market. There is a larger supply and lower price that comes from limiting the monopoly position of any one economically powerful and well-known manufacturer that lays stake to a particular type of good or service. Correspondingly, the consumer may be confused about the origin of the product; associating the quality of a product with one manufacturer.

In many cases, the manufacturer's name is of great importance in the decision to buy. A consumer who buys a pair of Calvin Klein jeans may be as interested in the name of the maker as the price or quality of the product. Passing-off actions must balance, among other things, the desirability of allowing other "free-riding" manufacturers to "disappoint the expectations" of the consumer with the equally desirable goal of ensuring that the consumer has the full benefit of a lively competition in the marketplace.

Other policy considerations centre on the relationship of the plaintiff to its product. There is the desire to protect the original manufacturer's goodwill and reputation attached with the product from unfair competition by the defendant. However, carrying the passing-off action too far in favour of the original manufacturer of the product design, which lacks statutory protection, virtually ensures a form of monopoly over that design. It is a delicate task to weigh the benefits of broader competition with the need to protect the plaintiff's accumulated goodwill in a particular design. Unfortunately, the courts often gloss over these policy considerations.

The Connection to Fraud

The Ontario Court of Appeal has observed[7] that: "The basis of the actionable wrong of passing-off is misrepresentation 'for any business purpose as to the origin of goods or services which the defendant proposes to or does deal in or employs in the course of business. . . .' " In principle, there is a close connection between deceit and fraud. The deception of the product's origin is the ultimate basis of the wrong, and the defendant succeeds through the use of false, misleading, or untrue statements or in the way the product, ware, or service is manufactured, labelled, distributed, and advertised. The scope of the tort includes "any misrepresentation for any business purpose as to the origin of goods or services which the defendant proposes to or does deal in or employs in the course of business, constitutes an actionable wrong."[8]

THE MEANS OF CONFUSION

A common means of confusing the public is for the defendant to use similar shapes, colours, and sizes of the plaintiff's product, and a similar brochure or other advertisement to promote the product. Often, the defendant will use the plaintiff's name or a similar name as an additional means to represent that the product is made by the plaintiff. The effect of such activity is to interfere with the business of the plaintiff. In other cases there may be direct evidence of an intention to injure the plaintiff or to deceive the plaintiff's consumers. One formulation for establishing a passing-off action is contained in the judgment of Cozens-Hardy M.R. in *J.B. Williams Co. v. H. Bronnley & Co. Ltd.*:[9]

> What is it necessary for a trader who is plaintiff in a passing-off action to establish? It seems to me that in the first place he must, in order to succeed, establish that he has selected a peculiar — a novel — design as a distinguishing feature of his goods, and that his goods are known in the market, and have acquired a reputation in the market, by reason of that distinguishing feature, and that unless he establishes that, the very foundation of his case fails.

EVIDENCE OF SIMILARITY

Much turns on the manner in which the defendant has presented its product or service to the consumer. The fact of similarity between the plaintiff's and defendant's product or service is insufficient to establish the cause of action. The plaintiff must take the next step of showing that the appearance of its goods conveys to the consumer that they come from one trade source, and that the defendant's identical product will confuse the buying public into believing that it comes from the plaintiff.

Illustration   Rinehart manufactures and distributes a video game called *Space Attack*. It has been a highly successful product for the company, and is sold throughout North America. In May, 1986, Rinehart discovered that an Alberta company, Visual-Tech Limited, was manufacturing a video game called *Space Attackers*. The essence of both games is for the player to destroy alien space ships. The Visual-Tech game employs spaceships that look identical to the ones used in the Rinehart game; the scoring of "kills" is exactly the same; and other graphics such as the "Earth spaceship", the manner in which the alien space ships crash, and the sound effects are identical. The color, size, and shape of the packaging is also identical. On the front of the package are the following words: "Rinehart's *Space Attackers*". The main difference between the two products is that Visual-Tech's game sells at a lower price. There is evidence that Rinehart has been losing sales since Visual-Tech introduced its game, and consumers have been confused about the origin of *Space Attackers*. On the basis of these facts, it is likely that Rinehart would be entitled to an injunction to stop Visual-Tech from selling *Space Attackers*, and to recover damages. The burden would be on Rinehart to show that the buying public would purchase *Space Attackers* on the assumption that it had been designed and manufactured by Rinehart.

Secondary Meaning

Sometimes a product may acquire a secondary meaning in the minds of the buying public. Because of the distinctive size, shape, and color, the consumer associates the product with a particular manufacturer. The Coca-Cola bottle, with its distinctive size and shape, is a good example. Another soda manufacturer might use the same bottle to give the appearance that its cola is one manufactured by Coca-Cola. In Canada, the courts are required to separate two possible means of deception: i) the confusing name that a product is sold under; and ii) the "get-up" — a technical term meaning the design, shape, color, and size of the product.

In *Oxford Pendaflex Canada Ltd. v. Korr Marketing Ltd.*,[10] the defendant manufactured and sold a desk tray that was a near-perfect copy of the plaintiff's desk tray. The president of the defendant company admitted that he selected the shape of the tray because of the plaintiff's prior success in manufacturing and selling its tray. Also, he admitted that both trays performed the same function, and had the same design and method of stacking. Nonetheless, the plaintiff failed to establish a passing-off case. In both the trial court and court of appeal, it was concluded that the plaintiff's desk tray had not acquired a secondary meaning and was, therefore, fair game for any competitor.

Similarly, in *Ayerst, McKenna & Harrision v. Apotex*,[11] a pharmaceutical manufacturer of a prescription drug called *Inderal* failed to establish a passing-off action against another pharmaceutical manufacturer that made a tablet for the same ailment and in the same form, size, shape, and color. The medical evidence was that the doctors who prescribed the drug were not confused by the identical appearance of the two brands. Also, there were good reasons for making tablets identical in form, size, shape, and color: This would prevent a user from making a "mistake" about the purpose of taking that particular tablet. Given the nature of the product, i.e., that it required a prescription, the court found that it had not acquired any "secondary meaning".

Misappropriation

Misappropriation, or taking without consent or permission the plaintiff's "property", forms the basis of a tort action by the owner against the wrongdoer. A key word in this definition is "property". The courts have given a wide meaning to the word, including confidential information, airspace, identity, profession, news, as well as the traditional chattels, goods, real estate, copyright, patent, and trademark. Once the property label is attached to a thing, the owner is entitled to enforce its ownership against anyone who interferes or appropriates it without permission. Depending on the nature of the property, the owner's remedy is governed either by statute or, in the absence of legislation, by the common law actions of trespass (for real property) or conversion (for personal property).

The tradition of equity, with remedies such as injunction and accounting for profits, also has provided a means to protect certain "interests" against misappropriation. In contrast, the common law courts, with the remedy of damages, built the foundation of tort law. In a unified judicial system such as Canada where a judge can, in the proper case, apply either common law or equitable remedies, it becomes important to distinguish between a "tort claim" for misappropriation, and an "equitable claim" for the same conduct. Three categories should be borne in mind: i) action for damages based on a statute; ii) action for damages based on the common law of tort; and iii) action for equitable relief based on equitable principles.

The Misappropriation of Property

An example of misappropriation of "property" that is governed by a statute is found in *Pro Arts, Inc. v. Campus Crafts Holdings Ltd.*[12] In this case, the plaintiff had a right to sell a poster of Farrah Fawcett-Majors (Farrah) in Canada. This was a very popular poster in the late 1970s because Farrah was a well-known American actress in a television series called *Charlie's Angels*. The defendant sold counterfeit posters of Farrah in Canada. But the counterfeit posters did not appear to be any different from the original one, in the consumer's eye. The court found that: "The counterfeit posters of Farrah were the result of a clear, deliberate and calculated act of piracy of the copyright of the plaintiff, and was clearly against honest industrial or commercial usage."[13]

The court held that the defendant was liable to pay damages for the misappropriation, and applied the *Copyright Act*.[14] Damages for common law conversion based on the value of the article converted at the time of the conversion was disallowed on the grounds that this would have given the plaintiff, already compensated under the statute, double recovery.

Misappropriation of Personality

An action for damages based on common law principles is found in *Krouse v. Chrysler Canada Ltd*.[15] In *Krouse*, the plaintiff, a professional football player, discovered that Chrysler had used his photograph without permission. In the photograph, Krouse is shown in his football uniform blocking a ball carrier. The essence of his claim was that Chrysler had misappropriated his "personality" to sell its cars. The initial question was whether or not he had some protectable right in his image as a football player. Once that right was established, then the transgression of the right would entitle him to damages. The Ontario Court of Appeal observed that those in professional sport attempt to attract notoriety so as to gain the public's attention. There is certainly no complaint when their picture appears in the newspaper or sporting publications.

The problem emerges for the athlete who attempts to exploit his/her individual success by endorsing products. Those who make products pay large fees for such endorsements. Unless the athlete or other celebrity can protect his/her "personality" from misappropriation, any manufacturer would be at liberty to use his/her likeness to sell its product or service. The Ontario Court of Appeal noted that the protection is not within the tort of passing-off. Members of the buying public would not think that the Chrysler car was designed or manufactured by Krouse. Instead, the court said that Krouse was entitled to successfully base his action on the tort of appropriation of one's personality. The manufacturer is liable in damages for using an athlete's or celebrity's likeness, voice, or personality without permission. The invasion of this "commercial interest" is therefore protected against misappropriation.

Misappropriation of a Commercial Interest

The last example illustrates the use of equitable principles to protect a "commercial interest" against misappropriation. In *Canadian Aero Service Ltd. v. O'Malley*,[16] the president and executive vice-president of the plaintiff company took a corporate opportunity for their own personal benefit and thus denied their company a profitable contract. For a number of years the defendants had worked to obtain for their employer, Canaero, a topographical mapping and aerial photographing contract in Guyana. The contract was to be financed by the Government of Canada. Then the defendants resigned from their executive positions with Canaero, formed their own company, and bid for the Guyana contract, which was awarded to their new company.

Equitable principles were essential for the plaintiff to succeed against its former executive officers. For instance, the plaintiff successfully argued that the defendants owed it a fiduciary duty. This meant that the former employees owed their employer loyalty, good faith, and avoidance of conflict of interest. This translated into a prohibition for the company's officers from obtaining any property or business advantage belonging to the company. The misappropriation of the Guyana contract for their personal benefit made the defendants liable to the plaintiff. Because the pressing of a tort action entitles the claimant to damages, the plaintiff's recovery was for the profit made by the defendants. The distinction is between allowing the plaintiff to recover for its loss (common law tort action) and allowing it to recover the defendant's profit arising from the misappropriation (unjust enrichment).

Negligent Infliction of Economic Injury

The law of torts has provided protection against negligent injury to persons or property, but Canada has been slow to recognize a right to recover for pure economic loss. In theory, it should not matter whether or not the loss was due to some physical injury or financial or economic causes. Perhaps the concern of the courts is that granting recovery for pure economic loss will result in problems of remoteness.[17]

Remoteness

In *Weller & Co. v. Foot & Mouth Disease Research Institute*,[18] cattle were infected by a virus that escaped from the defendant's laboratory. Later, a government order prevented the plaintiff, a firm of cattle auctioneers, from selling the infected cattle. In effect, the defendant's negligent handling of the virus caused economic loss to the plaintiff's business. Nonetheless, the court held that the defendant was not liable to compensate the plaintiff for its financial loss. The fear of the court was again one of remoteness. How was the court to draw the line? If the auction firm was entitled to recover its loss, then why not the village butcher, the meat packers, the meat carriers, and indeed, restaurants that must raise the prices of their beef dishes and suffer a loss in their trade?

The strict rule against liability in these cases is an easy way to avoid the hard task of confronting what is at root a policy decision. Denning M.R., in *Spartan Steel and Alloys Ltd. v. Martin & Co. (Contractors) Ltd.*,[19] acknowledged the failure of the traditional resort to "no duty" and "remoteness" to decide the negligent infliction of economic loss cases:

> At bottom I think the question of recovering economic loss is one of policy. Whenever the courts draw a line to mark out the bounds of *duty*, they do it as a matter of policy so as to limit the responsibility of the defendant. Whenever the courts set bounds to the *damages*

recoverable — saying that they are, or are not, too remote — they do it as a matter of policy so as to limit the liability of the defendant. . . .

The more I think about these cases, the more difficult I find it to put into a proper pigeon-hole. Sometimes I say: "There was no duty." In others I say: "The damage was too remote." So much so that I think the time has come to discard those tests which have proved so elusive. It seems to me better to consider the particular relationship in hand, and see whether or not, as a matter of policy, economic loss should be recoverable.

Pure Economic Loss

In *Junior Book Ltd. v. Veitchi Ltd.*[20] the majority of the House of Lords held that the defendant's duty of care included an obligation to take reasonable care to avoid acts or omissions that they ought to have known would cause pure economic loss to another. In that case, the plaintiff built a factory. The main contractor subcontracted the laying of the floor of the production area to the defendant. The factory was built between 1969 and 1970; by 1972, the floor began to crack as a result of poor workmanship or bad materials. As there was no contract between the owner and the subcontractor, recovery had to be based on a theory of tort. It was clear, however, that the negligent acts of the defendant had not caused any physical damage to the plaintiff. What the plaintiff stood to lose was a pure economic loss, i.e., the loss of profits while the factory was closed to repair the floors.

THE ENGLISH POSITION

A major concern in the pure economic loss case is whether or not the harm or injury is too remote. Lord Roskill addressed this problem in the following passage:[21]

I therefore ask first whether there was the requisite degree of proximity so as to give rise to the relevant duty of care relied on by the respondents. I regard the following facts as of crucial importance in requiring an affirmative answer to that question. (1) The appellants were nominated sub-contractors. (2) The appellants were specialists in flooring. (3) The appellants knew what products were required by the respondents and their main contractors and specialised in the production of these products. (4) The appellants alone were responsible for the composition and construction of the flooring. (5) The respondents relied upon the appellants' skill and experience. (6) The appellants as nominated sub-contractors must have known that the respondents relied upon their skill and experience. (7) The relationship between the parties was as close as it could be short of actual privity of contract. (8) The appellants must be taken to have known that if they did the work negligently (as it must be assumed that they did) the resulting defects would at some time require remedying by the respondents expending money upon the remedial measures as a consequence of which the respondents would suffer financial or economic loss.

THE CANADIAN POSITION

Canadian law has not yet fully embraced a tortious action allowing for the recovery of pure economic loss. The leading Supreme Court of Canada case is *Rivtow Marine Ltd. v. Washington Iron Works.*[22] In *Rivtow* the plaintiff bought a crane manufactured by Washington through a local distributor named Walkem. The crane was mounted on a barge and used for logging. Both Washington and Walkem were aware that the crane had design defects, e.g, "cracking in the legs of the pintle masts." Neither defendant warned the plaintiff about the defects. After another crane in an unrelated incident collapsed killing a barge crew member, the plaintiff took its crane out of service for repair. This happened during the busy part of the logging season. The plaintiff then sued both distributor and manufacturer for the loss of the use of the barge during the repair period (its economic loss) and for the cost of repairing the crane.

The majority of the Supreme Court of Canada held that the plaintiff was entitled to recover its economic loss because both defendants had a duty to warn of the defects within their knowledge and had failed to do so. But recovery of the plaintiff's expense to repair the crane was denied. Thus, the failure to warn, even though the plaintiff could not show any physical or property loss suffered, was sufficient to establish its action in tort.

Laskin J.'s dissenting, which the House of Lords has referred to on two separate occasions as "of strong persuasive force", is a brilliant analysis that supports a conclusion that Canadian courts should award for pure economic loss.[23] Laskin J. disagreed with the majority that liability should be based on the defendant's failure to warn of the defects in the crane. The real question in his words were:[24]

> If physical harm had resulted, whether personal injury or damage to property (other than to the crane itself), Washington's liability to persons affected, under its anterior duty as a designer and manufacturer of a negligently-produced crane would not be open to question. Should it then be any less liable for the direct economic loss to the appellant resulting from the faulty crane merely because the likelihood of physical harm, either by way of personal injury to a third person or property damage to the appellant, was averted by the withdrawal of the crane from service so that it could be repaired?

What limits on claims for pure economic loss should be imposed? This question was answered by Laskin J. in the following passage:[25]

> Put another way, liability has been denied on the ground that there is no duty to a consumer or user in respect of economic loss alone. It seems to me that this restriction on liability has in it more of a concern to avoid limitless claims for economic loss from any kind of negligence than a concern for the particular basis upon which manufacturers' liability for negligence rests. That liability rests upon a conviction that manufacturers should bear the risks of injury to consumers or users of their products when such products are carelessly manufactured because the manufacturers create the risk in the carrying-on of their enterprises, and they will be more likely to safeguard the members of the public to whom their products are marketed if they must stand behind them as safe products to consume or to use. They are better able to insure against such risks, and the cost of insurance, as a business expense, can be spread with less pain among the buying public than would be the case if an injured consumer or user was saddled with the entire loss that befalls him.
>
> This rationale embraces, in my opinion, threatened physical harm from a negligently designed and manufactured product resulting in economic loss. I need not decide whether it extends to claims for economic loss where there is not threat of physical harm or to claim for damage, without more, to the defective product.

Summary

In summary, the test for recovery set forth in the majority decision in *Rivtow* is whether the defendant had a duty to warn about structural defects in the crane. The dissenting judgment dismissed this test as inappropriate to form the basis of liability and substituted the test of "threatened physical harm from a negligently designed and manufactured product."[26] In contrast, the House of Lords in *Junior Books Ltd*. emphasized that liability is connected with the plaintiff's reliance on the defendant's skill, judgment, and experience and on the defendant's knowledge that the plaintiff was so relying. The pure economic cases are often complex and divide the judges who decide them. It remains unclear in Canada whether the Supreme Court will ultimately embrace the wider test of liability contained either in Laskin J.'s dissenting judgment, or in the majority judgment in the *Junior Books* case.

Negligent Misrepresentation

The doctrine of pure economic loss, like the doctrine of negligent misrepresentation, builds upon the theory of negligence established in *Donoghue v. Stevenson*.[27] In each case, *Donoghue v. Stevenson* has become a stepping stone for extending the scope of the duty of care to an additional type of case.

There is also a close connection between negligent misrepresentation and negligent infliction of economic loss cases: In each instance, the plaintiff seeks to recover for his/her "pure" economic injury. Historically, the courts carefully restricted liability based on false statement. For instance, liability would be imposed where fraud could be proved against the defendant. Of course, this was of little value to the plaintiff who suffered an economic loss because of the defendant's failure to take reasonable care in making an accurate statement of fact. Also, liability might be founded on the basis of a contract or a fiduciary relationship between the parties.

Negligent misrepresentation must be distinguished from the intentional tort of deceit. Deceit, as the term implies, means that the defendant has intentionally made a false statement or representation; he/she knew that the statement was untrue when made and he/she intended that the victim would act upon this untruth. Evidence that the defendant's false statement was a product of an accident would have defeated the common law action of deceit. There was never any difficulty in imposing liability for the deliberately false statement of fact. No countervailing policy would permit the court from denying jurisdiction in such a case. Our courts never have hesitated to impose liability for fraud.

The "Floodgates" Argument

The courts, however, have been traditionally uneasy about opening the door to liability based on negligent misrepresentation. What was in the back of the minds of the judges who resisted a general right of recovery for negligent misrepresentation (and indeed for pure economic loss) was the fear of 'liability in an indeterminate amount for an indeterminate time to an indeterminate' class per Cardozo J. in *Ultramares Corp. v. Touche*.[28] That is, he recognized that liability for negligent misrepresentation would open the "floodgates" and that the judicial system would be swamped with innumerable cases.

In the leading House of Lords case of *Hedley, Byrne & Co. Ltd. v. Heller & Partners*,[29] the "floodgates" argument was put to the side and liability for negligent misrepresentation was recognized. The liability followed even though the plaintiff was unable to establish its case within one of the traditional categories, i.e., fraud, contract, breach of fiduciary relationship, or physical harm.

In *Hedley, Byrne*, the plaintiff asked its banker for a credit report on one of its customers. The plaintiff's banker then made inquiries from the defendant — the banker for the customer — which gave a favourable reference. The reference, however, had a caveat: It was given "without responsibility." The plaintiff, in reliance on the references, entered into a business transaction with the bank's customer that ultimately resulted in a loss of £17 000. The plaintiff's case against the bank failed because of the "without responsibility" terms in the defendant's reference letter. Nonetheless, *Hedley, Byrne* established the general principle of liability based upon a negligent misrepresentation.

Limitations on Liability

As in *Junior Books* nearly twenty years later, the House of Lords looked for some limiting device to confine the scope of the newly created tort action. Thus, the negligent misrepresentation action generally requires proof that the plaintiff relied upon the skill and experience of the defendant who made the representation or statement. Professionals such as bankers, lawyers, doctors, accountants, engineers, and architects have a duty to make certain that their statements, which may be relied upon by third parties, are accurate and true. Such professionals hold themselves out to the public as possessing certain skills and expertise, and members of the public rely upon those qualities when making decisions based on the expert's statement or representation. The class of potential defendants is not limited to professionals. Any party possessing certain knowledge, skill, and expertise might also be liable for a negligent misrepresentation.

Illustration Rinehart Ltd. produced a brochure for distribution to a dentist who would be using the Dental Office Management System. It will be recalled that the system was the subject of a contract between Rinehart and Lindsay Software (Figure 1.3). Rinehart had another contract with the Canadian Dental Association for delivery of the system. Thus, there is no privity of contract between Rinehart Ltd. and the individual dentist who might use the system. In the brochure, Rinehart represented that the system could be used on IBM-compatible microcomputers. Relying upon the brochure, Dr. Henry Jarvis elected to use the system on his XYZ Computer, which was IBM-compatible. However, the system did not work and, as a result, Dr. Jarvis lost two months of billing records. The total economic loss amounted to $40 000. Subsequently, it is discovered that Rinehart Ltd. was negligent in making the statement in the brochure. The company had not tested the system with all IBM-compatibles, and in particular had not tested it with the XYZ Computer owned by Dr. Jarvis. In these circumstances, it is likely that Dr. Jarvis would be entitled to recover his economic loss based on negligent misrepresentation. The rationale for liability in this case is that Rinehart knew the dentist would receive the brochure containing the representation and would rely upon it. As a result, Rinehart owes a duty of care to the dentist even though there is no contract between the parties.

Problems for Discussion

1. Assume in the *Rivtow* case that the employees of the plaintiff's barge company lost their wages during the period needed to repair the defective crane. Their economic loss, though indirect, was caused because their employer's barge was withdrawn from service. Are the employees entitled to recover their economic loss? Consider the majority and dissenting judgments in *Rivtow* and the House of Lords' decision in *Junior Books Ltd. v. Veitchi, supra.*

2. Holmes drives his car into a hydro-electric power pole. The accident is a result of his negligence. The impact of the crash knocks down electric wires and cuts off Rinehart's electrical supply. At that moment, two of Rinehart's software engineers are testing the Dental Office Management System. When the electricity goes down, the program is lost. To complicate matters, another team, including a Rinehart engineer and a consultant engineer, are testing the back-up program at the same time. The effect of the blackout destroys eight months of work, and Rinehart subsequently claims $175 000 damages against Holmes, the driver. Is Rinehart entitled to recover? See *Heeney v. Best*, (1978) 23 O.R.(2d) 19, varied 28 O.R.(2d) 71 Ont.C.A.).

3. Rinehart places an advertisement in the *Globe and Mail* for a software engineer. Carla Thomson, a software engineer, working under an employment contract with MicroFast Limited reads the ad, and decides to apply for the job. On March 2, Thomson hands her employer a letter of resignation. On March 4, Thomson has an interview with Rinehart and is offered a job at a salary 35 percent higher than the one that she had been receiving from MicroFast. Thomson doesn't tell Rinehart about the employment contract with MicroFast, only that she resigned from her job. On March 5, Rinehart receives acceptances of its offer from Thomson. The following day, March 6, Rinehart receives a registered letter from MicroFast claiming that Rinehart had induced Thomson to breach her contract and demanding that Rinehart fire Thomson. What rights, if any, does MicroFast have against Rinehart? Should Rinehart comply with MicroFast's demand? If so, what legal consequences might follow from firing Thomson?

4. In a new promotional campaign for its word processing program, Rinehart has developed a package for the diskette with a photograph of Saul Bellow, the Nobel Prize winner for Literature, seated behind a computer. The idea was to give the appearance that Mr. Bellow used the Rinehart program for writing his novels. The marketing department has passed along the packaging design to Ms. Bach. The question that Ms. Bach must answer is whether or not Mr. Bellow will have a

cause of action against Rinehart if his photograph is used in this way by Rinehart without his prior permission. Discuss. See *Henderson v. Radio Corp. Pty. Ltd.*, (1969) R.P.C. 218 (Aust.H.C.) and *Krouse v. Chrysler Canada Ltd., supra*, pp. 24-25.

5. On a business trip to Toronto Ms. Bach is introduced to an inventor named Steven Lake. Mr. Lake has invented a printer stand that elevates a printer at a 45° angle, which saves space and allows for a better use of the paper feed on the printer. His market research indicated that the stand would be purchased in the thousands. Mr. Lake wants to know if Rinehart is interested in purchasing his plans for the stand. (He has not yet applied for a patent.) Returning from Toronto, Ms. Bach presents the proposal to Paul Faber, President of Rinehart, who says that the company lacks the funds to purchase, develop, and market such a stand. Later, Ms. Bach sets up her own company called ComputeStand Ltd., purchases Mr. Lake's plans, and goes into production. The stand proves to be a remarkable commercial success, and ComputeStand Ltd. grosses $750 000 in the first year of sales. At this stage, the Board of Directors for Rinehart hires independent outside counsel to determine whether Ms. Bach has misappropriated a corporate opportunity. Discuss the legal consequences. See *Canadian Aero Services Ltd. v. O'Malley, supra*; and *Regal (Hastings) Ltd. v. Gulliver*, (1942) 1 All E.R. 378 (H.L.).

6. As part of the promotional campaign to launch a computer camp for children between the ages of nine and eighteen, Micro-Camp Ltd. prepares and publishes a camp brochure. On the front of the brochure is the Rinehart logo and a display of Rinehart software. The brochure describes the camp as an "Educational Learning Shoppe". Prior to the publication of the brochure, the management of Micro-Camp Ltd. had tried to get Rinehart's consent to use its logo and to display its software. But Rinehart had refused. As a result of the camp's success, Rinehart's enrollment in its Computer Learning Shoppes declines by 25 percent. Discuss whether or not Rinehart has a cause of action to tort against Micro-Camp Ltd. See generally *Athans v. Can. Adventures Camps Ltd.*, (1977) 17 O.R.(2d) 425, 80 D.L.R.(3d) 583 (Ont.H.C.), and *Slumber-Magic Adjustable Bed Co. Ltd. v. Sleep-King Adjustable Bed Co.*, Judgment delivered October 16, 1984 (Vancouver Reg., No. C831864).

7. Rinehart discovers that its outside lawyers, Dobbs and Smith Company, have entered into a contract with LawEdge Ware Ltd. to purchase a law office software system. The president of Rinehart informs the senior partner in the law firm that, unless Dobbs and Smith Company purchases Rinehart's Law Office Management System, it will take its legal business to another law firm. As a result, Dobbs and Smith Com-

pany sends a letter to LawEdge Ware cancelling the contract. LawEdge Ware is now contemplating an action against Rinehart. Discuss what theories it would advance to succeed against Rinehart. See *Fabbi v. Jones*, (1973) S.C.R. 42 (S.C.C.).

8. Earl Smith publishes a financial newsletter for the computer industry. He has three hundred subscribers in North America. Rinehart, although not a subscriber, receives a copy of the November issue when its president attends a computer conference in Hamilton, Ontario. In this newsletter, Smith forecasts that, in order for North American software companies to compete in the 1990s, they would have to establish manufacturing plants in South Korea, which has tax incentives, low-interest loans, and a cheap, skilled labour force. One of the major advantages of locating in South Korea is the possibility of putting together a joint venture with one of the large Korean conglomerates. On the basis of this information, Rinehart's president authorizes a feasibility study on opening a plant in South Korea. One employee is sent to Korea. Altogether, Rinehart spends approximately $15 000 before the study is abandoned. What Rinehart learns, and which Earl Smith's newsletter fails to disclose, is that the Korean government was about to introduce measures to restrict loans to the large Korean conglomerates and that foreign investment was being placed on hold. Most of the information in this part of the newsletter thus proves to be wrong. Ms. Bach is asked whether or not Rinehart may have a tort action against Earl Smith. Discuss. See *Mutual Life & Citizens Assurance Co. v. Evatt*, (1971) A.C. 793 (P.C.), and *Farish v. National Trust*, (1975) 3 W.W.R. 499 (B.C.).

Chapter 10 Notes

1. See *Mark Fishing Co. Ltd. v. United Fisherman & Allied Workers' Union*, (1972) 24 D.L.R.(3d) 585, 601-02 (B.C.C.A.).
2. (1975) 65 D.L.R.(3d) 181 (Man.Q.B.)
3. Ibid., p. 191.
4. Ibid., p. 189.
5. See *Canada Cement LaFarge v. B.C. Lightweight Aggregate*, (1983) 145 D.L.R.(3d) 385 (S.C.C.).
6. Ibid.
7. *Krouse v. Chrysler Canada Ltd.*, (1973) 40 D.L.R.(3d) 15, 24 (Ont.C.A.).
8. Fleming, *The Law of Torts*, 4th ed (1971), p. 702.
9. (1909) 26 R.P.C. 765, 771.
10. (1982) 134 D.L.R.(3d) 271 (S.C.C.).
11. (1982) 36 O.R.(2d) 495 (Ont.H.C.).
12. (1980) 110 D.L.R.(3d) 366 (Ont.H.C.).
13. Ibid., p. 374.
14. R.S.C. 1970, C-30, s. 20(1), (4) and s. 21.
15. Supra, note 6.
16. (1973) 40 D.L.R.(3d) 371 (S.C.C.).

17. See J.C. Smith, "Clarification of Duty—Remoteness Problems Through a New Physiology of Negligence: Economic Loss, A Test Case," (1974) 9 *U.B.C.L. Rev.* 213.

18. (1966) 1 Q.B. 569.

19. (1972) 3 All E.R. 557, 561-62 (C.A.).

20. (1982) 3 W.L.R. 477, (1983) A.C. 520 (H.L.).

21. Ibid., p. 546.

22. (1973) 6 W.W.R. 692 (S.C.C.).

23. See *Junior Books Ltd. v. Veitchi Ltd.*, supra, note 19, p. 544; and *Anns v. Merton London Borough Council*, (1978) A.C. 728, 760 (H.L.).

24. Supra, note 21, p. 712.

25. Ibid., p. 715.

26. Ibid.

27. (1932) A.C. 562 (H.L.).

28. (1931) 255 N.Y. 170, 179; 174 N.E. 441.

29. (1964) A.C. 465 (H.L.).

Part III

THE LAW OF REAL PROPERTY

11 INTRODUCTION TO THE LAW OF PROPERTY

This chapter will explore the classifications of property and the meaning of property. We will consider property ownership as well as the common law and statutes that create, regulate, and define the rights and interest in particular types of property. Remedies provided for the protection of these rights and interest will be reviewed.

Nature of Property

The term property is not a static concept. It has evolved over many years to apply to many types of interests and rights that the courts and legislatures have sought to protect. Historically, land was the most important type of property. Indeed, many of our ideas of property have been shaped by the way that the law has dealt with the ownership and protection of rights in land. Attaching the label of property to a right or interest has important legal consequences: Any interference with that right by another is actionable in tort. The owner of the right is entitled to an injunction that commands the infringer to stop further interference. Unlike many other actions, the property owner does not have to prove that the interference with his property right has caused harm. As the property owner is not entitled to damages in the absence of proving harm, he can enjoin anyone in the world who threatens or actually transgresses his property rights.

Property as a Relationship between People

It can be said that "[p]roperty essentially involves relations between people."[1] The law concerns itself with ordering the relationship between people over a particular thing. This sounds like, and indeed is, an abstract explanation of property. This approach to property, however, permits us to illustrate that the purpose of property law is to determine who has a right to enjoy and benefits from using such property. Later in this chapter, we will see that the ownership of land may be fragmented among a

FIGURE 11.1a   **THE RINEHART BUILDING, AN EXAMPLE OF "REAL PROPERTY"**

FIGURE 11.1b   **A MICROCOMPUTER SYSTEM, AN EXAMPLE OF
"TANGIBLE PERSONAL PROPERTY"**

FIGURE 11.1c   **THE RINEHART COMPANY'S PRODUCTS, EXAMPLES OF "INTANGIBLE PERSONAL PROPERTY"**

number of owners. Although Rinehart may own the building and land in Figure 11.1, the lease of a portion of the building to another creates property rights for the tenant. The mortgage (defined below) gives the lender of money to Rinehart "rights" in the land. The shareholders of the company, through their shares, have an interest in the land. When we piece together this network of different people and institutions, the concept of property becomes more meaningful.

The persons with an interest in land protect and enforce their rights *vis-à-vis* one another by recourse to certain established remedies. For example, the law of property provides the owner with legal and equitable remedies to exclude others and to require others to compensate him/her for any loss for use without his/her permission. Alternatively, to a claim to damages for loss, the owner may recover any benefits obtained by the person using the property without consent.

The Scope of Things That Are Property

What is property? Obviously, land and goods fall within this category. But the category of interest or rights that are considered at law to be property includes confidential information, airspace, identity, profession, and news. The question would have been answered differently in the nineteenth century and earlier where the major source of wealth, power, and influence was land. Land was held in relatively few hands.

Modern property includes much more than land, and is more widely distributed among the population. What these "new" property owners possess is far broader than land. A person's profession or pension is an important kind of property today.

The term "New Property" was coined by Professor Reich in 1964 to describe what he saw as the forms of wealth distribution carried out by the government.[2] The government, through various programs, created this new property by granting licences, subsidies, welfare and unemployment insurance payments, franchises, and many other forms of distribution. The challenge for the courts has been to recognize and integrate the new property into the existing law of property.

In the post-1964 period, there has been a vast increase in the importance of intellectual property — defined as patents, copyright, trademarks, and trade secrets. In subsequent chapters, the specific examples of intellectual property will be examined in detail. In this chapter, it is sufficient to note that, with the growth of the high technology industries, intellectual property has become an important source of wealth for many businesses.

In the balance of this chapter, emphasis is placed on real property. Once the elements of real property have been explained, particularly in relation to personal property, the student will have a better understanding of the traditional rules that the courts and legislatures are adapting to meet the demands of new forms of wealth and either have, or seek to have, attached by their owners, the property label.

The Relationship of Property and Value

As a property must have an owner — there is no such thing as ownerless property — property itself does not necessarily have value. Moreover, property may have no practical use for the owner. An example is found in *Edwards v. Lee's Administrator.*[3] This case involved the commercial development of the "Great Onyx Cave". The only entrance to the cave was on the defendant's land. But the actual cave itself extended under land owned by the plaintiff. The defendant contended that the cave was of no practical use to the plaintiff as he had no access to it. That is, the portion of the cave behind the plaintiff's land lacked any commercial value by itself. It became of value only when the defendant, who owned land adjacent to the cave entrance, decided to develop a tourist attraction.

The defendant's trespass in no way interfered with the surface use or enjoyment of the plaintiff's land. But the law of real property has always been that the surface owner also owns the space below and above the surface. Relying upon this historical incident of property ownership, the plaintiff successfully sued the defendant and recovered one third of the profits earned by the "Great Onyx Cave".

Distinction between Real and Personal Property

A distinction between real and personal property is the type of remedies available to the owner. Real property derives its name from the "real action" that existed to recover land. For example, where the owner of real property was wrongfully dislodged by another, he/she could bring an action compelling the wrongdoer to deliver up possession of the land. The landowner did not have to settle for monetary damages equal to the value of the land taken.

Transfer of Personal Property

A personal action existed to protect the owner of personal property. Unlike the land owner, the owner of a typewriter is entitled to recover the value of the misappropriated chattel. A monetary award was sufficient because the owner could use the award to buy a replacement typewriter. In the case of land, the court viewed each parcel, no matter how common or ordinary, as unique and irreplaceable. The same philosophy applied in the sale of land. Where either the vendor or the purchaser refused to complete the sale of land, one party could compel the other to perform by requesting a decree of specific performance. Typically, a breach of a contract to deliver goods entitled the innocent party to recover money compensation. The seller, in most cases, is not forced to deliver the promised goods. Payment of money to the buyer is sufficient to allow him to cover the loss of non-delivery.

Transfer of Real Property

The transfer of an interest in land is governed by a combination of statutory and common law rules. Many of the common law rules applied in Canada were developed by the English courts during hundreds of years of litigation. The antiquity of these rules provides a reasonable degree of certainty and predictability in the transfer of land. In Figure 11.2, we have two examples of the documents used in Canada to transfer an interest in land.

DISTINCTION BETWEEN *INTER VIVOS* AND TESTAMENTARY TRANSFERS

A transfer during the lifetime of the owner is called an *inter vivos* transfer. Transmission of the property on the owner's death either under his/her will or under the laws of intestacy — which means the property is distributed to the deceased's next-of-kin according to a statutory scheme — is called a testamentary transfer. In this section, we are primarily concerned with the *inter vivos* transfer of real property. In a business setting, the real property is often owned or leased by a company. As the company

FIGURE 11.2 **FORM NO. 23. TRANSFER FOR THE PROVINCE OF BRITISH COLUMBIA**

——————————————— DO NOT WRITE ABOVE THIS LINE, FOR LAND TITLE USE ONLY. ———————————————

		LAND TITLE ACT
PARK FORM NO. LTA 23	**TRANSFER OF AN ESTATE IN FEE-SIMPLE**	FORM 23 [Section 181 (1)]

NOTE: Before submitting this application, applicants should check and satisfy themselves as to the tax position, including taxes of the Crown Provincial, a municipality and improvement, water and irrigation districts.

NATURE OF INTEREST: FEE SIMPLE

HEREWITH FEE OF $ 235.00

Full name, address, telephone number of person presenting application:

MARKET VALUE: $750,000

Address of person entitled to be registered as owner if different than shown in instrument:

JULIA BACH, ESQ.
1250 EAST STREET
VANCOUVER, BRITISH COLUMBIA
V8Z 4Z6

Julia Bach
Signature of Applicant, or Solicitor or Authorized Agent

For Land Title Office Use Only

I/We
(full name, address, and occupation)

DUNCAN ENTERPRISES

1457 WAYVIEW DRIVE
VANCOUVER, BRITISH COLUMBIA V6S 1X3
per: LAWRENCE DUNCAN, PRESIDENT

the owner(s) in fee simple of the following land, in British Columbia:

CITY OF VANCOUVER
LOT   18
BLOCK   63
DISTRICT LOT   2122
PLAN   4921

in consideration of $ 750,000   paid to me/us by:

(full name, address, and occupation)

RINEHART SOFTWARE LTD.
972 ARNOLD AVENUE
VANCOUVER, BRITISH COLUMBIA
V7S 2Y4

(the "transferee") transfer to the transferee all my/our estate and interest in the land.

EXECUTED this   9   day of   MARCH   , 1980

SIGNED IN THE PRESENCE OF:

Signature _J. Caldwell_

Address _221 BAKER STREET_

VANCOUVER, BRITISH COLUMBIA

Occupation _LAWYER_

(Or in the case of a corporation)
The Common Seal of
was hereunto affixed in the presence of:

_____

_____

Corporate Seal

NOTE: 1. If this transfer is executed by a corporation, it must be sealed, see section 16 of the **Conveyancing and Law of Property Act.**
2. This transfer must be witnessed and the execution proved in the manner prescribed by Part 5.

TRANSFER/DEED OF LAND FOR THE PROVINCE OF ONTARIO

Transfer/Deed of Land

Province of Ontario

Form 1 — Land Registration Reform Act, 1984

A

(1) Registry [X] Land Titles ☐	(2) Page 1 of 2 pages

(3) Property Identifier(s)   Block   Property   Additional See Schedule ☐

(4) Consideration

SEVEN HUNDRED AND FIFTY THOUSAND Dollars $ 750,000

(5) Description   This is a: Property Division ☐   Property Consolidation ☐

LOT   58
PLAN 112

IN THE CITY OF TORONTO, IN THE MUNICIPALITY OF TORONTO

FOR OFFICE USE ONLY

New Property Identifiers   Additional See Schedule ☐

Executions   Additional See Schedule ☐

(6) This Document Contains   (a) Redescription New Easement Plan/Sketch ☐   (b) Schedule for: Additional Description ☐   Parties ☐   Other ☐

(7) Interest/Estate Transferred
Fee Simple

(8) Transferor(s) The transferor hereby transfers the land to the transferee and certifies that the transferor is at least eighteen years old and that

Name(s)   Signature(s)   Date of Signature Y M D

DUNCAN ENTERPRISES LTD.

LAWRENCE DUNCAN, PRESIDENT   *L. Duncan*   86 11 7

I HAVE AUTHORITY TO BIND THE CORPORATION.

(9) Spouse(s) of Transferor(s) I hereby consent to this transaction
Name(s)   Signature(s)   Date of Signature Y M D

(10) Transferor(s) Address for Service   3 GLOUCESTER STREET, TORONTO, ONTARIO M4S 1L5

(11) Transferee(s)   Date of Birth Y M D

QUETECH LTD.   N/A

(12) Transferee(s) Address for Service   19 AVENUE ROAD ANNEX, TORONTO, ONTARIO M7L 1S6

(13) Transferor(s) The transferor verifies that to the best of the transferor's knowledge and belief, this transfer does not contravene section 49 of the Planning Act, 1983.
DUNCAN ENTERPRISES
per: PRESIDENT, LAWRENCE DUNCAN
Signature. *L. Duncan*   Date of Signature Y M D   86 11 7   Signature   Date of Signature Y M D

Solicitor for Transferor(s) I have explained the effect of section 49 of the Planning Act, 1983 to the transferor and I have made inquiries of the transferor to determine that this transfer does not contravene that section and based on the information supplied by the transferor, to the best of my knowledge and belief, this transfer does not contravene that section. I am an Ontario solicitor in good standing.
Name and Address of Solicitor   ARNOLD JACOBS   3 GLOUCESTER STREET   TORONTO, ONTARIO   Signature. *Arnie Jacobs*   Date of Signature Y M D   86 11 7

(14) Solicitor for Transferee(s) I have investigated the title to this land and to abutting land where relevant and I am satisfied that the title records reveal no contravention as set out in subclause 49 (21a) (c) (ii) of the Planning Act, 1983 and that to the best of my knowledge and belief this transfer does not contravene section 49 of the Planning Act 1983. I act independently of the solicitor for the transferor(s) and I am an Ontario solicitor in good standing.
Name and Address of Solicitor   MARY CALDWELL   86 HEATON STREET   DOWNSVIEW, ONTARIO   Signature. *M. Caldwell*   Date of Signature Y M D   86 11 7

Planning Act — OPTIONAL
Affix Statement by Solicitor (for Transferee(s) herein if necessary)

(15) Assessment Roll Number of Property	Cty	Mun.	Map	Sub	Par
	19	04	126	312	57213

(16) Municipal Address of Property
6495 BLOOR STREET WEST
TORONTO
ONTARIO M4X 1W7

(17) Document Prepared by:
A. JACOBS
3 GLOUCESTER STREET
TORONTO
ONTARIO

Fees and Tax FOR OFFICE USE ONLY

Registration Fee

Land Transfer Tax

Total

Newsome and Gilbert, Limited
Form LF1327 (1/85)

April, 1985

does not "die" (although it may be liquidated), the law respecting testamentary transfer is of less relevance.

The Torrens and recording systems distinguished   In a Torrens system of registration, such as in the western provinces of Canada, the registered certificate of title is evidence that the person registered is the indefeasible (i.e., cannot be made void) owner in fee simple. A fee simple is defined as the largest bundle or rights that can be owned in real property. For practical purposes, a fee simple estate is the equivalent of absolute ownership. All lesser real property interests such as mortgages, life estates, future interests, or easements are registered on the owner's certificate as a charge. The Torrens system is governed by a complex provincial statute that does everything from defining "land" to providing detailed procedures for registration by the Land Titles Registrar.

In non-Torrens systems, the document of transfer is a deed of conveyance between the grantor or vendor, i.e., the seller of the land, to the grantee or vendee, i.e., the purchaser of the land. A transfer of an interest of land must be evidenced in writing. This writing, or deed of conveyance, is then registered in a provincial recording office. The registered deed of conveyance, however, can be made void. Registration does not — as in the Torrens system — make it indefeasible. The purpose of the recording system is to provide a means of allowing a prospective purchaser to check the vendor's title. The recording system also provides a safe central depository for title documents.

The Torrens system — which was adapted from Sir Robert Torrens' system of registering ships in Australia — provides important incentives for registration. Non-registration of a transfer of fee simple in a Torrens system opens the real property owner to the risk of losing his/her interest in a subsequent sale of the property by the original owner. A third-party purchaser who bought the land without notice of the first sale would defeat the purchaser — even though he/she, too, is innocent. Such a third party is known as a *bona fide* for value.

The registered certificate of title in the name of the owner is a guarantee that this person owns the fee simple interest. There is no need to go behind the registered owner's title. In a recording system, however, the conveyancer, usually a lawyer, must check the vendor's chain of title to make certain that that person has a good and safeholding title to transfer to the purchaser. The fear is that the vendor may have a defect in title and, to ensure against this eventuality, the lawyer representing the purchaser must take precautions to search the prior documents of transfer.

Distinction between Ownership and Possession

In Figure 11.2, Rinehart Ltd., as the purchaser of the land from Duncan Enterprises Ltd., has acquired both ownership and possession of the building and the adjacent land. In some instances, however, there is a separation between ownership rights and rights of possession. For example, there is a five-year lease of floor space in the Rinehart building to Hunt Data Base Ltd. Once this lease is in effect, although Rinehart continues to own the leased space, the right to exclusive possession is vested in Hunt Data Base Ltd. for the five-year term of the lease. In fact, both Rinehart and Hunt own an interest in the same piece of land: i) Hunt has a leasehold interest (discussed below) entitling it to immediate possession; and ii) Rinehart has a reversionary interest in fee simple (discussed below) and will be entitled to possession at the expiration of Hunt's lease.

The separation of ownership and possession applies equally to personal property. Rinehart may purchase an additional computer terminal from IBM under a contract for sale. The title or ownership immediately passes to Rinehart but possession may be retained by IBM, or the carrier used by IBM, until the computer terminal is delivered. Similarly, this separation provides a means of securing payment of goods sold. The seller of the computer terminal may expressly reserve ownership of the goods delivered to the buyer's possession and transfer the title when the final purchase price is received.

A bailment illustrates the separation of ownership and possession of personal property. The bailor — the owner of the personal property — delivers possession to the bailee — the possessor of the personal property. The terms of the bailment determine the conditions on which the bailee will return possession to the bailor. For example, on Rinehart's grounds there is a parking area for employees, tenants of the building, customers, and visitors. A Rinehart customer who leaves a car in the parking lot and pays the parking fee has entered into a bailment with the company. The car owner — the bailor — has delivered possession of the car into the possession of Rinehart — the bailee. Similarly, computer software owned by Rinehart may be the subject of a number of bailments before finally reaching the consumer. The product is shipped by truck or airplane, and the shipper is a bailee. Later, the product is stored in a warehouse where a bailment arises between Rinehart and the warehouseman.

Distinction between Tangible and Intangible Property

In Figure 11.1, we see the difference between tangible and intangible personal property. The computer is a physical object that can be seen, touched, and used for a particular task. The trademark on the computer game, however, is intangible personal property. Other examples of intangible personal property are copyright, patent, and promissory note. In each of these instances, what is owned is an abstract legal right that the law protects and enforces. Thus, to say Rinehart owns the "copyright" (discussed in Chapter 12) means that it can prevent others from using, for example, programs and documentation without prior consent.

In the instance of real property, there is also a separation between tangible and intangible property. Tangible real property is the building and land shown in Figure 11.1. An intangible property right in land is the result of an agreement between the owner of the physical property and another who desires some right of use, access, or security for a loan. Thus, an easement such as a right to use a private road on adjacent land, is an intangible interest in land. Although the road is a physical object, it is not the road that is owned but a "right" to use the road. This right has no physical form.

Similarly, a mortgage (defined below) vests the lender with an interest in the borrower's land. When the load is repaid, the mortgage is discharged; if the borrower defaults, then the lender is entitled to take possession of the land. In the instance of both an easement and mortgage, the interest in real property is enforced and protected against the owner of the tangible land.

Classification of Real Property

The law of real property is in many ways a running history of social, political, and economic developments occurring in England from 1066 onward. The language of real property carries the baggage of time out of mind. "Tenures" in land was the basis of feudal England. The King, by granting a tenure in land, exacted a price from the tenure owner, who was required to deliver up soldiers or agricultural products, or to perform services in the King's Court, or to provide spiritual services. This is, of course, in the distant past.

Modern land law, however, has been significantly shaped by the medieval concept of "Estates". The term "estates" represents property law at its most theoretical and abstract plane. The purpose served by the term was practical. In essence, it meant that all the land in England (and in Canada) had only one absolute owner: the Crown. Every other person held an estate in land. There was more than one type of estate that gave the owner a particular right to use, enjoy, and benefit from the land. The nature of the estate set the time clock for that owner's and his/her heirs' right of enjoyment in the land. In theory, therefore, every estate, regardless of its ultimate duration, would ultimately return to the Crown. Even today, the Crown becomes the "owner" of land when a person who owned the land dies without either next-of-kin or a valid will leaving the land to another.

In this section, we will discuss the various types of estates in land. The basic notion of an "estate" is that the "owner" of land has certain rights in the land for a period of time. The duration of an estate affects its value and marketability. The nature of the estate also affects the type of things that the owner, for the time being, can do with the land. The following illustration of the history of Rinehart's building provides a basis to understand the nature and relationship of various estates and interests in land.

Illustration   Rinehart purchased the fee simple interest — the largest estate in land — in the building and land in Figure 11.2 from Walsingham Enterprises on March 9, 1980. To finance the purchase, Rinehart borrowed $375 000 from the Canadian Imperial Bank of Commerce and gave the bank a mortgage to secure the loan. At the time of the sale, the second floor of the building had been subdivided and leased to John Chivers. The lease was originally made between Walsingham Enterprises and John Chivers on January 2, 1979, and was for a term of ten years with an option to renew for an additional five years. Mr. Chivers, a Chartered Accountant, retained part of the second floor for his own practice and subleased the remaining portion to the law firm of Dobbs and Smith Company. The Chivers-Dobbs and Smith Company lease is for a five-year term and began on August 1, 1981.

To the rear of the property in Figure 11.1 is a warehouse that was also part of the March 9, 1980, sale to Rinehart. Access to the warehouse is over adjacent land owned by Malcolm Hill, who at that time used his land for farming. By contract between Hill and Rinehart, the company was granted a right to use the access road. This contract was made on April 2, 1982, and in return for the access right, Hill received 10 000 shares in Rinehart.

In 1981, with the rapid acceleration of real property in British Columbia, Rinehart subdivided the land into two parcels. On the first parcel was the building, warehouse, and land. On the second parcel were 0.8 h of land. The second parcel was sold to a real estate developer, Dennis Haig, on June 1, 1981, for $500 000. One condition of the sale was that Mr. Haig would not build a structure higher than four stories. The Land Titles in British Columbia registered Mr. Haig as the fee simple owner of this parcel.

Under the terms of Mr. Haig's will, his real property was left to his wife, Helen, for her life and, after her death, to his son John, and to his daughter, Alison, in fee simple, so long as they continued to reside in British Columbia. On August 10, 1982, Mr. Haig died.

For the balance of this chapter, we will refer to the various transactions contained in the above illustration in discussing the interests that the law recognizes in land.

Freehold Interests

Freehold interests include: fee simple, conditional fee simple, life estate, and future interest. The main feature of a freehold interest is that the owner's right to continued ownership lacks any fixed or certain termination date.

Fee Simple Interest

The largest estate that can be owned in land is the fee simple. The fee means that it can be inherited upon the owner's death by his next of kin. It is, in practical terms, the equivalent of absolute ownership. Time, it will be recalled, or duration of the estate, is of considerable value. In the case of the fee simple, the duration is indefinite. At any given time it is impossible to determine when the estate, if ever, will end.

Thus, on Mr. Haig's death, his fee simple interest is not ended. As the owner of the fee simple, he is able, through the terms of his will, to fragment the ownership of that estate amongst his wife and children. Without a will, the provincial law of intestacy would determine the class of persons entitled to claim rights of inheritance. The distribution might have been different than the one contained in his will.

Rinehart Ltd., as a company, may also "die" — the result of bankruptcy when the creditors act to take over, sell the assets, and put the company out of business. In this type of "corporate death", the property of the company is vested in the bankruptcy estate and is for the benefit of creditors. Also, in other situations — such as a sale of the business — the company will have successors who take the fee simple interest at some future date.

Conditional Fee Simple

A conditional or qualified fee simple is illustrated by the devise — the term applies to distribution of real property by a will — to Mr. Haig's children, John and Alison. Upon their father's death, they have a future interest (defined below) in a conditional fee simple. It is conditional because the words "so long as they continue to reside in British Columbia" provide an event that may, at some uncertain date in the future, terminate their interest in the land.

Life Estate

The widow, under Mr. Haig's will, has a life estate in the 0.8-h parcel of land. Both the life estate and the fee simple have a common feature: The duration of the estate is uncertain. Although we are certain that at some date in the future Mrs. Haig will die, we are not certain precisely when that event will happen. As long as she lives, Mrs. Haig is the only person entitled to exclusive possession, which carries with it the full right of enjoyment of the land.

The purpose of a life estate is rarely commercial or business motivated. The fee simple owner who creates a life estate is attempting to provide for support of family members, very often the widow or widower. On Mrs. Haig's death, her estate is automatically extinguished. Thus, unlike the fee simple, it is not an inheritable estate. This does not preclude Mrs. Haig from selling her life estate interest to another. Perhaps the most likely buyers would be her children, who currently have a future interest in the same land. The person who purchases the land will reduce the amount paid for the life estate. The reduction in value will depend on a number of factors, including Mrs. Haig's age and health.

FUTURE INTERESTS

Perhaps one of the most painful subjects in real property for any student of the law is future interests. It is often difficult to wrap one's mind around the notion that a person or company can immediately own an interest in land but must await some future event or date before having a right to occupy and possess the land. The device of future interest, however, plays little role of importance in the commercial or business context. Historically, creating future interest provided landowners with a means of keeping property within one family for generations by fragmentation of the fee simple among the surviving spouse and children.

It would be a highly unusual event for Rinehart to consider creating future interests in its land. In practical terms, future interests are almost always created under a will. It is an estate planning technique, and allows the deceased, in effect, to control his land from the grave. The Rule Against Perpetuities, another nightmare for law students and lawyers alike, was created to place time limits on how long one fee simple owner could keep his/her interest fragmented. In most jurisdictions the rule has been incorporated, with modifications, into statute.

Remainders John and Alison have a future interest in the fee simple called a remainder. A remainder interest generally follows a life estate. As remaindermen, John and Alison have no immediate right to possession and enjoyment of the land. On the death of their mother, their remainder interest is automatically converted into an immediate, present interest in fee simple (in this particular case, a conditional fee simple).

Remainder interests are further divided into vested remainders and contingent remainders. In the above illustration, both John and Alison have a vested remainder in a conditional fee simple. It is vested because the only event that stands in the way of their right to possession is their mother's death. Once that death occurs, there is no further qualification or event that stands in their way.

A contingent remainder interest interjects a further condition beyond the life tenant's death in order for the remainderman to be entitled to a right to possession. Suppose, for example, that, in his will, Mr. Haig had provided the land was to be left to his widow for life, and then to John, provided that he has children at the date of his mother's death, and if he does not, then to his sister, Alison. When Helen Haig dies, John's right to the land depends upon a separate contingency, i.e., that he have children alive on that date. As it is impossible to determine whether or not John will have children alive on that date, his remainder will be contingent until Helen dies.

It is possible that a contingent remainder can become vested before there is an immediate right to possession. This would occur where the will provided that to "Helen for life and then to John, provided that he has children during the lifetime of Helen". Upon the birth of John's child during Helen's lifetime, his contingent remainder is automatically converted into a vested remainder.

Reversions   A reversionary interest is a future interest retained by the grantor of the fee simple estate. A reversion exists whenever the fee simple owner grants a lesser estate to another and does not provide for the disposition of the fee simple upon the expiration of the lesser estate. Thus, in our illustration, John and Alison have a conditional fee simple. Assume that twenty-five years after their father's death, both children have moved to Toronto.

As this event would end their qualified, or conditional, fee simple, the question arises: Where does that estate go? As the will is silent, the law automatically presumes that the estate in fee simple will revert back to the original grantor. In this case the grantor is dead; so, the fee simple would revert to his estate. The will does not provide for this contingency by providing remaindermen and, as a result, there would be a partial intestacy. This means that because the will is silent the statute governing succession will determine who would take the fee simple.

Leasehold Interests

In the "Chivers" lease, the original landlord, Walsingham Enterprises, was the fee simple owner on January 2, 1979, the date on which the lease was made. Chivers is the tenant. The interest vested in Chivers, as tenant, under the lease is a leasehold interest. The leasehold interest is an interest in real property. Unlike a freehold estate, however, a lease has a definite duration. In this instance, it is for ten years, with a possible extension, assuming that the option to renew is exercised, for an additional five years. A lease, therefore, must be for a term certain.

THE COMMERCIAL LEASE
Considering the parties — a company and an accountant — and the purpose of their dealings, isn't the lease just another type of commercial contract? This is a natural question to ask. The courts have had difficulty

FIGURE 11.3 **SAMPLE PAGES FROM A COMMERCIAL LEASE BETWEEN WALSINGHAM AND CHIVERS**

Newsome and Gilbert, Limited
Form 1034

Commercial Lease

𝕿𝖍𝖎𝖘 𝕴𝖓𝖉𝖊𝖓𝖙𝖚𝖗𝖊

made the   2nd   day of December
one thousand nine hundred and seventy-five.

𝕴𝖓 𝕻𝖚𝖗𝖘𝖚𝖆𝖓𝖈𝖊 𝖔𝖋 𝖙𝖍𝖊 𝕾𝖍𝖔𝖗𝖙 𝕱𝖔𝖗𝖒𝖘 𝖔𝖋 𝕷𝖊𝖆𝖘𝖊𝖘 𝕬𝖈𝖙

𝕭𝖊𝖙𝖜𝖊𝖊𝖓

Walsingham Enterprises
1457 Wayview Drive
Vancouver, British Columbia
V6S 1X3

hereinafter called the "Lessor"

OF THE FIRST PART

— and —

Robert John Chivers
3450 West 22nd Avenue
Vancouver, British Columbia
V8D 2J1

hereinafter called the "Lessee"

OF THE SECOND PART

PREMISES

WITNESSETH that in consideration of the rents, covenants and agreements hereinafter reserved and contained on the part of the said Lessee, to be paid, observed and performed, the said Lessor has demised and leased and by these presents doth demise and lease unto the said Lessee

ALL THOSE CERTAIN PREMISES excluding any part of the external walls known and described as

Room 10, on the First floor of the building located at 1457 Wayview Drive, Vancouver, British Columbia V6S 1X3, circled in red on the blueprint of the building Floor plan, attached as Appendix "A" to this lease.

TERM

TO HAVE AND TO HOLD the said demised premises for and during the term of

to be computed from the   2nd   day of   January   1979
and from thenceforth ensuing and to be fully completed and ended on the 1st
day of January   1989.

RENTAL

YIELDING AND PAYING THEREFOR yearly and every year during the said term hereby granted, unto the said Lessor, the sum of $21,000.00
per annum, payable at par at Lessor's address above   in equal monthly instalments of
$1,750.00   each in advance on the 1st
day of each and every month during the said term, the first payment to be made on the
1st day of January, 1979.

The said Lessee covenants with the said Lessor to pay rent.

BUSINESS TAXES

AND to pay all business taxes in respect of the business carried on by the Lessee in and upon or by reason of their occupancy of the premises hereby demised;

Newsome and Gilbert, Limited
Form 1035

Commercial Lease
Page

REPAIRS

AND to repair (reasonable wear and tear, and damage by fire, lightning and tempest only excepted);

AND that the said Lessor may enter and view state of repair;

AND that the said Lessee will repair according to notice in writing (reasonable wear and tear and damage by fire, lightning and tempest excepted);

AND that they will leave the premises in good repair (reasonable wear and tear and damage by fire, lightning and tempest only excepted);

ASSIGNMENT

AND will not assign or sub-let the whole or any part of the demised premises without leave; the Lessee hereby waives and renounces the benefit of any present or future act of the Legislature of Ontario which would allow the Lessee to assign or sub-let this lease, without leave of the Lessor.

AND the said Lessee covenants with the said Lessor, its successors and assigns:

TYPE OF
BUSINESS

(a)   THAT the said demised premises will not, during the said term, be at any time used for any other purpose than that of **Chartered Accountant**.

RIGHT TO
SHOW
PREMISES

THAT the Lessee will permit the Lessor to exhibit the demised premises during the last three months of the term to any prospective tenant and will permit all persons having written authority therefor to view the said premises at all reasonable hours.

NOTICES

THAT any notice which either of the parties is required or permitted to give pursuant to any provision of this lease may, if intended for the Lessee, be given by a writing left at the demised premises or mailed by registered mail addressed to the Lessee at the demised premises, and if intended for the Lessor by a writing left at the premises of the Lessor at

or mailed by registered mail addressed to the Lessor at the Lessor's said premises, and such notice shall be deemed to have been given at the time it was delivered or mailed, as the case may be.

OVER
HOLDING

PROVIDED further and it is hereby agreed that should the Lessee hold over after the expiration of this lease and the Lessors thereafter accept rent for the said premises, the Lessee shall hold the said premises as a monthly tenant only of the Lessors but subject in all other respects to the terms and conditions of this lease.

The words importing the singular number only shall include the plural, and vice versa, and words importing the masculine gender shall include the feminine gender, and words importing persons shall include firms and corporations and vice versa.

Unless the context otherwise required, the word "Lessor" and the word "Lessee" wherever used herein shall be construed to include and shall mean the executors, administrators, successors and/or assigns of the said Lessor and Lessee, respectively, and when there are two or more Lessees bound by the same covenants herein contained, their obligations shall be joint and several.

Harvey Walsingham

Harvey Walsingham
President of Walsingham Enterprises
Lessor

Robert John Chivers

Robert John Chivers, C.A.
Lessee

In Witness Whereof the parties hereto have executed these presents.

SIGNED, SEALED and DELIVERED
In the presence of

in giving the commercial nature of the transaction the same treatment as any other contract. The major reason is historical. The orthodox view of the lease was to perform one central purpose: to vest the tenant with an interest in land. Every other term was incidental to the conveyance function of the lease. This approach would appear strange in many instances to the parties to the lease who considered that it has a business transaction and that the commercial aspect of their relationship was the predominant concern.

A commercial lease is both a business contract and a transfer of an interest in land. Which set of rights is of primary importance? Laskin J. answered this question in *Highway Properties Ltd. v. Kelly, Douglas & Co. Ltd.*[4] In this decision we find a splendid example of a judge willing to update the law so that it realistically reflects the commercial realities of the marketplace. To pretend that a complicated commercial lease has as its primary function the transfer of a legal interest in land from the landlord to the tenant ignores the goal of both parties to treat the transaction like any other commercial contract.

In the *Highway Properties* case, there was a commercial lease between the owner of a shopping centre and a company that was to operate a supermarket. The term of the lease was fifteen years. The tenant had a number of obligations, e.g., to pay rent, taxes, and maintenance costs, to pay into a promotion fund for the benefit of the shopping centre, and to repair premise. One clause provided that the tenant would commence its business thirty days after the completion of the shopping centre and would carry on its business continuously. The shopping centre proved to be a failure. Other tenants moved out. It assumed the appearance of a ghost town. About three years into the fifteen-year lease, the supermarket shut down.

The solicitors for the landlord wrote the tenant a letter advising that the tenant had repudiated the lease and that the landlord would take possession of the building under the terms of the lease and hold the tenant responsible for any damages suffered as a result of the tenant's breaches. The landlord then took possession but was unsuccessful in re-renting the premises for the unexpired term of the lease. An action was commenced against the tenant to recover damages for the prospective loss resulting from its failure to carry on a supermarket business as required under the lease.

The problem facing the landlord was that the law on property did not provide the same rights on repudiation by the tenant as would be generally available in a case involving a breached commercial contract. The common law rule was that once the landlord resumed possession, the tenant's leasehold interest was ended and surrendered to the landlord. The landlord's only remedy was damages up to the date of surrender. If this rule applied then the landlord could not recover for his prospective loss of profit over the outstanding twelve-year period of the lease. Notwithstanding what had been thought of as an established common law doctrine of surrender, Laskin J. found in favour of the landlord.

The Supreme Court decided to look at commercial leases in a different way. The importance of *Highway Properties* is the ultimate restructuring of such leases so as to bring legal rights and remedies available in line with general business expectations. This goal was accomplished by recognizing the modern business realities involved in making and carrying on a commercial lease.

The essence of the landlord and tenant relationship for a commercial lease, like other business transactions, is heavily rooted in expectation found in general contract law. The covenants of a commercial lease illustrate the business relationship, and often contain covenants concerning the tenant's business operation e.g., the use of signs, rent based on sales, and the hours that the business must remain open.

The ancient common law notion emphasized, above all other factors, the conveyancing aspect of the lease. Under this view, the pivotal purpose of the lease was the landlord's transfer of a leasehold estate to the tenant. The "estate" function required the court to consider the transaction as primarily a *real estate* transaction, with the business aspects of the ongoing relationship secondary. *Highway Properties* can be read as a frontal assault on the common law point of view.

The challenge to the common law conveyancing approach was essential before a party to a commercial lease could have full access to contract remedies. Those remedies had been blocked by the common law because they were inconsistent with the overriding notion of the tenant's estate in land.

In *Highway Properties*, the tenant repudiated the lease by going out of business and vacating possession with many years left to run on the lease. How does the landlord go about accepting that repudiation? The common law "estate" rule dictated that if the landlord accepted the repudiation and entered the leased premises, then lease terminated on the *date of re-entry*. Therefore, assuming ten years remained on the lease, the landlord had no right to recover his loss for the remainder of the leasehold term. His damages would have been limited to the loss outstanding at the date the repudiation was accepted and he re-entered the premises for purposes of taking possession. In *Highway Properties*, however, the landlord, was entitled to recover damages for his prospective loss as well as for his accrued loss.

Although the estate function of a commercial lease continues to play an important role, the courts no longer pretend that the lease is not also a contract. In the appropriate case, the breach of that contract entitles the injured party to claim anticipatory loss as if the transaction were any other business agreement.

TYPES OF TENANCIES

Tenancies fall into two general categories: residential and commercial. In most Canadian provinces, residential tenancies are governed by legislation that, among other things, has increased the residential tenant's right to security of tenure, i.e., the right to remain in possession unless cause for removal is made. Also, there are restrictions on the landlord's right to increase rent. Our concern is with commercial tenancies such as the one in *Highway Properties*.

Fixed-term tenancy   A tenancy may be classified by the amount of time that the estate is vested in the tenant under the lease. It is common for a commercial tenancy to provide for a fixed or definite leasehold term — which is for a specific, fixed period of time. For example, in *Highway Properties* there was a definite term of fifteen years. The advantage of the definite term tenancy is the security of tenure that the tenant receives for a certain period of time. In a long-term commercial tenancy, there is an incentive for the tenant to make improvements to the premises. Such improvements, often in the form of fixtures, are personal property attached to the land, e.g., bookshelves bolted to the wall. Fixtures are an expense to the tenant; the long-term tenancy allows the tenant a sufficient period to obtain the full benefit of using them in his/ her business. The long-term tenancy also makes it easier for the tenant to obtain financing for his/her business. The lender has the assurance that the borrower — the tenant — has a right to possession for a considerable period of time and is a more acceptable risk. Finally, the long-term tenancy is an asset to the tenant, who may decide to sell his/her business as an on-going concern.

The negative side of the long-term tenancy is that the tenant remains bound to the lease even though there is a downturn in the tenant's business. Also, the cost of renting similar properties in the same area may decline over time and the tenant is unable to take advantage of the lower rents. The tenant is bound by the higher rental terms of the existing lease.

The periodic tenancy   An alternative to the fixed-term tenancy is the periodic tenancy. Periodic tenancies fall within three categories: i) year to year; ii) month to month; and iii) week to week. The last two classes of tenancies are more common in residential tenancies. In all three tenancies, the periodic tenancy continues to renew itself for a period until either the landlord or the tenant gives a proper notice of termination. A notice of termination is defined as either written or oral communication of an intention to end the tenancy.

The main distinction between a fixed-term and periodic-term tenancy is the degree of security of tenure enjoyed by the tenant. In the periodic commercial tenancy there is less security of tenure for the tenant. As a result, few businesses — nor would their lenders — invest substantial capital and labour in the premises because the landlord has the power to eject the tenant on short notice.

Tenancy at sufferance   In the event that either a fixed-term tenancy expires or a periodic-term tenancy is terminated, and the tenant remains in possession of the premises, he/she is said to have a tenancy at sufferance. The tenancy at sufferance arises by operation of law and not by agreement of the parties. The tenant of such a tenancy has overheld after the period has elapsed when he/she is required to leave the leasehold premises. During this period of continued occupation by the tenant, the landlord and tenant may negotiate for a new lease. Alternatively, a new lease may arise from the conduct of the parties. Thus, where the landlord accepts rent payments from the overholding tenant after the expiration or termination of the lease, a periodic tenancy may be implied from that conduct.

RIGHTS AND OBLIGATIONS IMPOSED BY THE LEASE

The fundamental point of *Highway Properties* is that the commercial lease is a business contract. In many instances, the commercial lease is the basis of an economic union between the landlord and tenant. The respective rights and obligations imposed by the lease will reflect the business integration.

Shared business objectives   A shopping-centre lease, like the one in *Highway Properties*, is a good example of this union, or integration. The tenant, in addition to his/her obligation to pay rent, covenanted to pay taxes and maintenance costs, to repair the premises, and to continually carry on business. Often there are covenants requiring the tenant to pay the landlord a portion of the sales from the tenant's business. Other covenants specify the hours that the tenant's business must be open; the amount to be spent for advertising; the type, placement, and maintenance of signs; and restrictions on the transfer of the lease — in effect the tenant's business — without the landlord's consent.

The anchor tenant   The type of covenants will reflect the respective bargaining power of the parties. In a shopping centre, the developer-landlord usually seeks an "anchor" tenant — a large department store or supermarket with a good reputation. When the landlord negotiates a lease with an anchor tenant such as the Bay or Eaton's, the ultimate terms of the lease reflect the favourable bargaining power of the tenant. Tenants who later negotiate a lease in the shopping centre will have different, often less favourable terms inserted in their leases.

Quiet enjoyment covenant and right of re-entry An important obligation on the landlord is the covenant not to interfere with the tenant's physical possession of the leased premises. This is known as the covenant for quiet enjoyment. The common law rule was that there could not be a lease without a quiet enjoyment covenant. The covenant is closely linked with the concept of the tenant's "estate in land". As an estate owner, the tenant is entitled to exclude any other party, including the landlord, from interfering with his/her possession. In practice, many commercial leases provide the landlord with a right of re-entry, which means a right to enter the premises without the tenant's consent at the time of entry. The right of re-entry is exercised when the tenant has breached a designated leasehold covenant.

For example, if the tenant fails to pay rent, taxes, or maintenance costs, or fails to have gross sales over a certain dollar amount — and the lease specifically makes these breaches a ground for re-entry — then the landlord is entitled to take possession of the premises and end the lease. In the absence of an express covenant, the law will imply a covenant for quiet enjoyment. A covenant granting the landlord with a right of re-entry must be expressed in the lease. The common law does not imply a right of re-entry.

Fitness of the premises: habitability covenant It is well established that unless there is an express covenant that the commercial premises are fit for the particular purposes intended by the tenant's business, such a covenant will not be implied. The law draws a distinction, however, between furnished and unfurnished premises for purposes of habitability. For example, if the premises are commercial and the heating system is inadequate to heat the building, the tenant of furnished premises is entitled to succeed in an action for breach of the implied covenant of habitability.

TRANSFER OF A LEASEHOLD INTEREST

A tenant may transfer his/her interest either by a sublease or assignment. It is common practice in a commercial tenancy for the landlord to require that any transfer is subject to the landlord's approval. There are good business reasons for approval of transfer clauses. The landlord has made a business judgment about the tenant before entering into the lease. The landlord does not want the tenant to have unfettered power to substitute a stranger to that business arrangement. The landlord first wishes to investigate whether or not the proposed subtenant or assignee is financially capable of meeting all the economic conditions required by the lease.

Sublease An example of a sublease is the transfer by Chivers to Dobbs and Smith Company of a five-year term to a portion of Chiver's leased premises. It is a sublease because the head tenant — Chivers — has not parted with his entire interest under the head lease. The head lease is the original lease under which the head tenant has received a tenancy. Under the terms of the sublease, the subtenant is required to comply with all the terms of the head lease. In the event of a breach of the sublease, the landlord has a right to directly sue the head tenant.

Assignment   When the tenant assigns or makes an assignment of the lease, he/she transfers his/her entire remaining leasehold estate to the assignee. The assignee — a tenant by assignment — is now vested with the tenancy. The original tenant — or assignor — however, remains liable on his/her personal contractual covenants with the landlord. In terms of landlord and tenant law, the assignor "drops out" as a property owner. The landlord or his/her successor (in our case, Rinehart) has a right to enforce directly the terms and conditions of the original lease against the assignee. This right of direct enforcement is unavailable by a landlord against a subtenant.

Privity of estate   The landlord lacks privity of contract with the subtenant and privity of estate with the subtenant. Privity of estate is a way the law of property expanded the right to enforce contractual obligations against a third party who was not an original party to the lease. The common law rule was that, as both the landlord and assignee had an estate in the same parcel of land, enforcement of obligations arising from that estate ownership were mutually enforceable. Privity of estate does not exist in the sublease case. The head tenant does not, in a sublease, part with his/her entire estate under the original lease.

The subtenant lacks both privity of contract and privity of estate with the original landlord. Enforcement of the original lease, therefore, is indirect. The landlord must bring an action against the head tenant, and the head tenant against the subtenant.

Restrictive covenants   A restrictive covenant is used to preserve existing amenities in the neighbourhood and ensures that the particular character of the neighbourhood is preserved. Restrictive covenants are used to control density of development, the height of buildings and other structures, and the particular use to which the land is put. For example, Rinehart Ltd.'s restrictive covenant might prohibit the building of residential premises on the land. The reason for the covenant is to preserve the commercial nature of the area. As in the case of an easement — a right of access over another's land — there must be a dominant and servient tenement, and the covenant must be for the better use of the dominant tenement.

Mortgages

A mortgage is a conveyance of land or other property to secure payment of a debt or to discharge some other obligation for which the mortgage was given. The security for the mortgage may be a fee simple, a conditional fee simple, a life estate, or a leasehold interest. The lender of the money is called the mortgagee and the borrower the mortgagor. A mortgage creates an interest in land that vests in the mortgagee. To be valid, the mortgage must be in writing.

A recurring theme in mortgage law is the security nature of the mortgage transaction. This has profound implications on the rights of both parties to the transaction. The reason that the lender requires a mortgage from the borrower is to secure the debt by reference to a specific piece of property. The mortgagee becomes a "secured creditor" — meaning a creditor who is entitled to have his/her claim satisfied from a particular piece of property. The secured creditor has priority over the mortgagor's general creditors, i.e., persons with a general right to recover after the secured creditor's claims have been satisfied.

In our illustration, the Canadian Imperial Bank of Commerce loaned Rinehart Ltd. $375 000 secured by a mortgage on the company's fee simple ownership in land. Should Rinehart seek to raise additional money on a mortgage, the new lender would take a second mortgage. The second mortgagee has a greater risk than the first mortgagee in the event of the mortgagor's default in payment. The first mortgagee will have priority. The second mortgagee must look to the net proceeds realized after the land is sold and the amount owed to the first mortgagee is paid. In some instances, there are third and fourth mortgages on real property. In each succeeding mortgage, the potential risks escalate and the amount of interest and other charges also increase for the mortgagee.

The Equitable View of Mortgages

A considerable difference of opinion existed between the common law and equity courts over the nature of interest created by a mortgage. The common law courts adopted a firm rule that the mortgagee owned the legal estate in the land. Chancery courts considered the debt owed as the principal aspect of the transaction and the conveyance of the legal estate to the mortgagee as incidental to that debt.

The common law courts held that when the mortgagor defaulted in making, for example, payments of principal and interest, the mortgagee was entitled to rely upon the strict letter of the mortgage and exclude the mortgagor from claiming any further right or interest in the land. Chancery, however, intervened and protected the mortgagor from this abrupt seizure of his/her land. The Chancery held that the mortgagor retained an "equity of redemption". This rule of equity provided that the mortgagor, after the mortgage transfer of legal title, still retained an estate in the mortgaged land. With the equity of redemption rule the Chancery was able to hold that the mortgagor was the true owner of the land, and protected the mortgagor from the harsh consequences of the common law approach.

Equity of Redemption

The equity of redemption is the mortgagor's right to redeem the mortgage even though he/she has defaulted. What was the price of exercising the right to redeem? The mortgagor was required to pay, in full, the principal and interest of the mortgage, and the mortgagee's costs and expenses, including the cost of litigation. Once that amount was paid by the mortgagor then his/her obligation under the mortgage was discharged. This meant that the mortgage was at an end. At that point, the legal interest held by the mortgagee was reconveyed to the mortgagor.

The doctrine of equity of redemption is consistent with the Chancery view that a mortgage is merely a means of securing the repayment of a debt. What the mortgagee bargained for was payment of the loan and interest; he/she did not bargain to "buy" the land. Thus, the mortgagee is not prejudiced by a rule that allows the mortgagor to pay off the debt. In some instances, the mortgagee attempts to disguise the transaction as one of purchase and sale. But the courts are quick to look at the substance of the transaction and, notwithstanding the form, treat the transaction as one creating a mortgage.

The equity of redemption cannot be "clogged" or "fettered". For instance, if the mortgage provided that, upon the full payment of principal and interest, the mortgagor could not redeem the mortgage, such a clause would be void. A major incident to the mortgagor's equity of redemption is the right to sell the land to another party. A clause that provided that the mortgagor could not sell, transfer or otherwise dispose of his/her land would be a clog on the equity of redemption and void.

Collateral Advantage

The mortgagee may stipulate some other advantage from the mortgagor other than the repayment of the principal and interest of the debt. This independent performance obligation undertaken by the mortgagor is carefully considered by the court to determine whether or not it operates as a clog on the equity of redemption. A collateral advantage is the mortgagee's way of expanding the purpose of the mortgage beyond the security of money loaned. The loan may be leverage by the lender to obtain a business concession from the borrower. The transaction has a commercial benefit to the mortgagee beyond mere repayment of principal and interest, and the courts have been cautious in making certain that the collateral advantage does not interfere with the mortgagor's rights as the true owner in equity.

A typical example is where the mortgagee requires the mortgagor to exclusively purchase his/her products. Such arrangements are more common where the parties to the mortgage are in the same trade or business. The lender/mortgagee is usually the manufacturer or supplier of goods or services sold by the borrower/mortgagor. The borrower is usually the distributor or retailer of such goods or services, and the market is competitive. By exercising superior financial power, the lender is in a good position to dictate that the borrower purchase his/her goods and services exclusively from the lender. The policy question is whether the lender has legitimately used his/her power as the provider of loan proceeds under a mortgage.

The service station mortgage is a typical example. The mortgagor — the owners of the service station — takes a mortgage from a supplier of petrol products, who demands that the mortgagor purchase only his products. Such agreements have been held valid so long as the duration of the restriction coincides with the duration of the mortgage. In the event that the collateral advantage is extended beyond the redemption date, the better view is that it is invalid.

It is a question of fact whether the collateral advantage is oppressive or unconscionable. Where both parties are experienced business people, this standard is difficult for the mortgagor to meet. The collateral advantage, however, is not always tied to the "exclusive purchase obligation" instances. A collateral advantage may be inserted to protect the real value of money loaned under a mortgage that calls for repayment years in the future. In such an instance, the mortgagor will argue oppression or unconscionability.

Multiservice Bookbinding Ltd. v. Marden[5] is a good example of a hard bargain for a mortgagor but one that fell short of oppression or unconscionability. In this case, the ten-year mortgage provided that the currency of the loan (British pound sterling) was index-linked to the Swiss franc. At the end of the ten-year term, the value of the pound had eroded drastically in terms of the Swiss franc. As a result, rather than collecting the orginal loan of £36 000, the mortgagee was entitled to receive almost £133 000. The decision was supported by the policy ground that lenders would be unwilling to risk long-term mortgage loans unless they could be assured that the true value of the money lent could be preserved for the period of the mortgage.

When the mortgagee inserts a clause postponing the redemption date for a lengthy period of time, the question arises whether this is a clog on the mortgagor's equity of redemption. For example, the mortgage may provide that the mortgage may not be redeemed, i.e., paid off, for a period of twenty years. Again, in the case of experienced business people, this restriction is valid and enforceable against the mortgagor. In *Knightsbridge Estates Trust Ltd. v. Byrne*,[6] the Court of Appeal observed that the mortgage was:

> [A] commercial agreement between two important corporations experienced in such matters, and has none of the features of an oppressive bargain where the borrower is at the mercy of an unscrupulous lender. In transactions of this kind it is notorious that there is competition among the large insurance companies and other bodies having large funds to invest, and we are not prepared to view the agreement made as anything but a proper business transaction.

MORTGAGEE'S REMEDIES

When the mortgagor defaults on an obligation, including the payment obligation, the mortgagee has five options: i) foreclosure; ii) sale; iii) possession; iv) a personal action; and v) transfer of the mortgage. We will briefly consider each of these remedies. In each province, specific legislation alters the procedures and practices used by mortgagees when the mortgagor is in default. For our purposes, a general discussion of the remedies can be made without reference to the laws of any one province.

Foreclosure A foreclosure action is a legal action to extinguish the mortgagor's equity of redemption. This practice was instituted in recognition of the protection the equity courts accorded the mortgagor. Once a foreclosure proceeding is brought, unless the mortgagor pays the outstanding amount owed, an order *nisi* — an interim or temporary order — is made, generally, granting the mortgagor six months in which to pay. At the end of the six months, if the mortgagor is still in default, the court enters an order absolute. This is a final order, and extinguishes all rights and interests that the mortgagor owns in the land by virtue of his/her equity of redemption. In the event that the mortgagee applying for the foreclosure has a first mortgage — and there are second and third mortgages — the foreclosure action will also extinguish these mortgages as well as the mortgagor's equity of redemption.

The rule is "foreclose down and redeem up". Although the first mortgagee may foreclose down on all the subsequent mortgages and on the mortgagor's equity of redemption, any of the junior mortgagees may redeem up by paying off the amount owed to the first mortgagee. In that case, the junior mortgagee, under the doctrine of subrogation — stands in the shoes rule — is treated as having the same position as the first mortgagee. Thus, the second mortgagee who pays off the first mortgage stands in the shoes of the first mortgagee.

Sale A mortgage may expressly reserve in the mortgagee a power of sale. The power will allow the mortgagee to sell the mortgagor's equity of redemption. There are many special rules that apply to such sales to protect the mortgagor. First, a distinction must be made between a sale under the terms of a contract and a court-ordered sale. For example, after a decree *nisi*, the mortgagee is not entitled to sell the land until after the time for redemption expires, unless he/she has received an order from the court. In *Standard Realty Co. v. Nicholson*,[7] the court said:

> The difference is manifest—on a sale after a final order of foreclosure, the mortgagee has a chance of making a gain — he has not to account to the mortgagor; and, if he does not make enough to pay the amount of the debt, he can sue for the balance. When the property is sold under a power of sale, the mortgagee cannot make a gain; he must account for the surplus over his debt, but he can sue if there is a marked difference.

The courts are more likely to intervene when the sale is based on a court decree. Under a power of sale, however, the courts will hold the mortgagee to strict compliance with the terms imposed. If the mortgagee deviates from the terms of the contract power, then the mortgagor can have the sale set aside. It is well established that the power of sale is not a clog on the equity of redemption.

Possession In England it has been said that: "The mortgagee may go into possession before the ink is dry on the mortgage unless there is something in the contract, express or by implication, whereby he has contracted himself out of that right."[8] Unlike the other options, the going into possession is a *right* as well as a *remedy*. In theory, therefore, the mortgagee does not have to await until there has been a default to exercise the right to take possession. Once in possession, however, the mortgagee is under an obligation to manage the property.

In most instances, there is no real economic advantage for the mortgagee to take actual possession of the land. As the mortgagee is only entitled to retain those profits needed to pay the principal, interest, and costs, he/she must account for the balance to the mortgagor. The mortgagor also has an action if during the mortgagee's possession he/she receives less profit than otherwise might have been obtained. The mortgagee is open to the argument that he/she has either through wilful default or neglect failed to obtain the best return on the property. The mortgagee, as a money-lender, may not have the business experience (or the desire) to operate the mortgagor's business; the potential risk of liability, therefore, often outweighs any advantage in taking possession.

The personal action As the mortgage is a contract under which the mortgagor promises to fulfill certain obligations, including the payment of principal and interest, the mortgagee is entitled to bring a personal action against the mortgagor for breach of contract. The mortgagor promised to pay money; the failure to pay is a breach of that promise, and the mortgagee is entitled to recovery based on contract principles. The personal judgment is satisfied out of all the assets — and not just the mortgaged property — owned by the mortgagor. Where the mortgagor is two months in arrears on principal and interest payments, and not in danger of insolvency, the mortgagee has the option to foreclose or to sue the mortgagor on his/her personal covenant in the mortgage contract. A personal action is also available on foreclosure. The mortgaged property may have depreciated in value. On foreclosure and sale, the proceeds may be insufficient to retire the outstanding mortgage debt. In this instance, the mortgagee has a personal action over to recover the outstanding balance from the mortgagor.

Transfer of the mortgage   The mortgagee generally reserves an express right to assign the mortgage to a third party. Until the mortgagor receives notice of the assignment, his/her payment of principal and interest to the assignor — the original mortgagee — is effective to discharge his/her debt owed under the mortgage. The assignee — the subsequent mortgagee — cannot claim that the mortgagor is in default of mortgage payments until the mortgagor has received notice of the assignment and then falls into arrears.

A distinction must be made between the amount loaned on the face of the mortgage, and the amount actually lent to the mortgagor. Harry, a fraudulent mortgagee, for example, may assign a mortgage with the face value of $100 000 to John. The mortgagor, Alison, received only $25 000 from Harry. Even though John is a bona fide purchaser for value (e.g., he pays a discounted price of $75 000) and doesn't have notice of Harry's fraud, John's claim cannot exceed $25 000 against Alison. Of course, John can always sue Harry. This is cold comfort to John, as Harry is likely insolvent, has fled the jurisdiction, or is in prison.

The mortgagor may sell the land to another party while the mortgage remains outstanding. The mortgagor may either use the proceeds from the sale of his/her equity of redemption to discharge the mortgage or the purchaser may assume the mortgage. On the assumption of the mortgage, the purchaser is liable to the mortgagee. At the same time, the vendor, or original mortgagor, remains liable on his/her covenant to repay the principal and interest.

Problems for Discussion

1. How is "property" defined in law?

2. An employee of Chivers discovers a computer terminal owned by Rinehart Ltd. stored in a cupboard adjacent to the leased premises.

The employee removes the computer and begins using it in Chivers' accounting practice. Chivers is aware of the circumstances and uses the computer terminal himself. For a period of eighteen months, the computer terminal is used daily in the Chivers accounting business. When Rinehart Ltd. discovers the computer terminal has been taken by Chivers, it asks for its return and for compensation for the use of the computer over the eighteen-month period. Chivers returns the computer but refuses to pay. Rinehart admits that it had no use for the computer for the period in question; but it claims that Chivers is liable to pay for the fair market value for using the computer terminal. Discuss. See *Olwell v. Nye & Nissen Co.*, 173 P.2d 652 (Wash.Sup.Ct. 1946).

3. Distinguish between the Torrens and Recordings systems for the registration of an estate in land.

4. Distinguish between a fee simple and a conditional fee simple.

5. Define intangible property.

6. Is it possible to have an estate in personal property?

7. What is the difference between a vested and contingent future interest in real property?

8. In the law of landlord and tenant, what is the doctrine of surrender, and did the Supreme Court of Canada abolish that doctrine in the *Highway Properties* case?

9. In a long-term lease such as the Chivers lease, is it possible for the landlord and tenant to insert a clause allowing for premature termination of the tenant's estate?

10. Chivers wants to raise money on a mortgage to expand his business. Rinehart is willing to lend the $75 000 on a mortgage that includes a clause that Chivers will purchase all his computer software exclusively from Rinehart. After the mortgage is made, Chivers claims that the clause is a clog on his equity of redemption and that he is entitled to purchase the software from a competitor of Rinehart. Discuss.

11. John and Alison are joint tenants of a conditional fee simple estate in remainder. Assuming that John dies before the life tenant, his mother, who is entitled to succeed to John's interest in the land? Assume further that prior to his death, Alison sold her interest in land to her mother. How does this change your answer?

12. From the chapter illustrations, provide two examples of reversionary interests in land.

Chapter 11 Notes

1. Cohen, *"Dialogue on Private Property,"* (1954) 9 Rutgers L.Rev. 357, 380-81.
2. Reich, *"The New Property,"* (1964) 73 Yale L.J. 733.
3. 96 S.W.(2d) 1028 (Ky.Ct.App. 1936).
4. (1971) 17 D.L.R.(3d) 710 (S.C.C.).
5. (1979) Ch. 84, 2 All E.R. 639.
6. (1939) Ch. 441, 455.
7. (1911) 24 O.L.R. 46.
8. See, *Four-Maids Ltd. v. Dudley Marshall (Properties) Ltd.*, (1957) Ch. 317.

Part IV

INTELLECTUAL PROPERTY

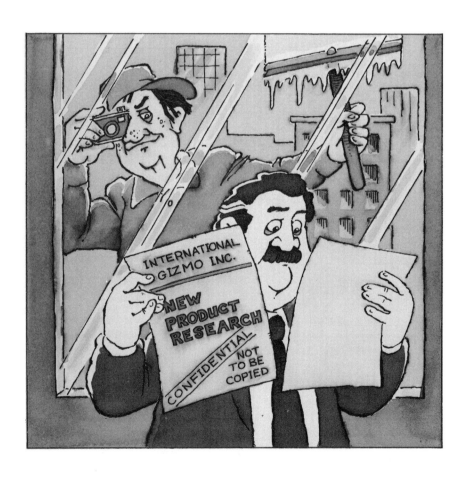

12 COPYRIGHT

Introduction

The term intellectual property is used to encompass the law of patents, copyright, trade marks, and trade secrets. Each heading of intellectual property will be treated in a separate chapter. The common thread running through each chapter will be the specific application of the categories of intellectual property to computer hardware, firmware, and software (defined below).

Scope of the Computer Industry

Few products have so quickly and dramatically touched the activities of companies, banks, governments, schools and universities, hospitals, entertainment, and industry. The computer industry in North America has annual sales in the billions of dollars. The computer has revolutionized our way of thinking, and our ways of communicating, storing, retrieving, creating, and analysing information.

The computer has touched every person's life in profound ways: from the way in which medical and defence research is conducted to the information that business and government have collected on individual citizens. Pundits have told us that the computer has provided the means of changing the industrial age into the information age. Rinehart Ltd. is part of this new commercial age of information. Like many software manufacturers, it is a new business, and — in combination with others — is producing products that will continue to change the type of jobs — and qualifications for jobs — in business, and indeed, may change the very structure and organization of business.

Application of Existing Law

It comes as little surprise that the inventors of hardware, firmware, and software are counting on fitting their creations into the existing legislative and common law umbrella. In this chapter, the focus is on computer programs and the use of copyright to protect the misappropriation of those programs by competitors.

The principles of copyright law, which will be discussed, of course, are applicable to many other products, for example, books, films, and music. This discussion, though centered on computer products, should be considered as illustrative of copyright law.

We begin with the simple premise that computer programs represent items of great commercial value. Without a legal means of protecting software programs, the computer industry would lack the economic incentive to make substantial expenditures of capital and labour for the development of new, complicated, and highly sophisticated programs. Anyone could take advantage of these programs simply by copying them and not paying those who made them.

The Legal Challenge

From a legal point of view, the computer revolution is both exciting and frustrating. It is exciting because the computer has challenged lawyers, judges, and law makers to adapt existing principles and rules of law for the protection of this newly created commercial wealth. Those on the leading edge of technological change worry that they have outstripped the existing capacity of the law, which has few precedents to draw upon. Thus, the computer has brought a degree of uncertainty as to the nature and extent of the legal rights and remedies available when another person threatens to take a "free ride" by appropriating products made at great expense by others.

The Copyright Act

It is frustrating because our copyright legislation was written for the age when a radio was not yet a common household item; this legislation must be expanded to cover computer programs. The courts have had to redefine "literary work" and "fixation", for example, to cover a work never contemplated by the original drafters of the *Copyright Act*. Canadian judges have had the task of putting this new wine into old bottles.

One of the main consequences of the computer revolution has been to challenge what is the outer frontier of "original literary, dramatic, musical, and artistic work" — subjects that the *Copyright Act*,[1] defines as coming under copyright protection. Our pre-existing notions, and those of our judges, have been seriously questioned during this process. Moreover, the dividing line between what is properly the subject of copyright as opposed to a patent has become less clear when the literary work is fixed to a microchip.

Copyright and Patents Distinguished

The law, prior to the computer, was reasonably clear about the distinction between the things subject to copyright and those subject to patent law.

Assume that Ms. Bach writes plays in her spare time. Prior to the computer, she would sit in front of a typewriter, or with a pen and paper, and write a radio script for the CBC. Her finished CBC radio play, *The Semidetached Barrister*, would comfortably fit within the definition of original literary, dramatic, or artistic work. The playwright owns (and licenses to the CBC) the copyright on his/her work. One important feature of the script is that it was intelligible to another person reading the script.

Over time, the expression of ideas in the media of books, film, and paintings shaped our views as to what products of the mind — and what media for communicating those products — were protected by the law of copyright. Indeed, the original purpose of copyright legislation in England was to give the Brotherhood of Stationers a monopoly to publish books. It was only later that the author of the work was said by the courts to have the copyright. Today, the definition of "author" has been expanded to include those who originate computer programs.

What about the status of the standard typewriter that Ms. Bach, as a playwright, used to produce *The Semidetached Barrister*? The actual machine cannot be copyrighted. The typewriter derives its protection from the law of patents. Conceptually, it is not difficult to find a bright line between this machine and the products that a writer might produce in using it.

Replace the typewriter with a computer running a word processing program and suddenly a shadow falls over this bright line. Inside the computer is the software written by a highly skilled expert. This *application program* instructs the computer how to set margins, make paragraphs, adjust margins, number pages.

The *operating systems program* encoded on a microchip in machine language allows the computer to run the application program. The operating systems program controls the internal functions of the computer, and allows the computer to communicate instructions to its various component parts. Without the operating systems program and the application program, the computer will not perform its major function: solving problems and processing information. Both the operating systems and application programs must be ultimately translated, or copied, into an object code.

The major legal problem, however, is that the object code (defined below) is not intelligible to humans; it is little more than a series of 1s and 0s that carry and direct electrical currents inside the machine. Is this object code, which is written solely so that the machine can function, entitled to the same protection as *The Semidetached Barrister*? What are the consequences of requiring the creators of software and firmware to obtain patents to protect their inventions? In the next sections, we will explore these, and other questions. In later chapters on patent, trade marks, and trade secrets, we will examine similar questions from a different angle.

Definitions of Commonly Used Computer Terms

Before we can say anything meaningful about the application of copyright protection to computers, some basic terminology must be explained. Computer terms are often highly technical and their definitions sometimes conflicting. The courts have been required to assimilate the new computer terminology that defines the pattern and process of software creation, and to adapt the language of copyright so that it will be responsive to the new era of "authors" and "literary works".

Firmware

Firmware is the encoding that takes the form of integrated circuitry. This circuitry is on a silicon chip or, as they are commonly known, "microchips". The object code, or machine language, of the problem is fixed in the configuration of the circuits. The firmware is the brain of the computer. By providing information through a series of electrical impulses, the computer hardware is able to process the information and instructions.

ROM and EPROMs

ROM means "Read Only Memory", and this is encoded onto the microchip. The ROM is either an operating system that permits the computer to run a number of compatible software programs, or is a dedicated, permanent application program such as a word processing program.

FIGURE 12.1 **EXAMPLE OF A "MICRO-CHIP"**

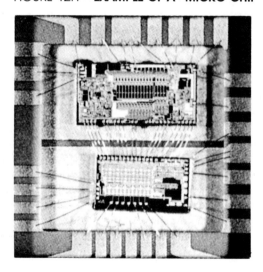

EPROM means "Erasable Programmable Read Only Memory". The EPROMs are like the ROMs stored on a semi-conductor chip. But unlike the ROMs, the EPROMs can be erased and the chip reprogrammed.

Software and Computer Programs

The definition of software is controversial since its meaning can have a direct impact on characterizing the category of intellectual property in which it should be placed. Therefore, in devising a technical definition of software, concern must be taken to employ the legal language of copyright. For example, if software is defined in terms of "algorithm", i.e., the mathematical process that instructs the machine to perform a sequence of instructions, then it has been suggested that it does not fit within the traditional meaning of copyright law.[2] Indeed, it may not be patentable either.

Another approach, one taken by the Patent Appeal Board, is to equate software with a computer program and then define:[3]

The term program is taken to mean a set of ordered steps or list of instructions. . . . This set of steps or list of instructions may be recorded on a variety of media including printed or handwritten lists

FIGURE 12.2 **AN EXAMPLE OF RINEHART'S SOFTWARE AND DOCUMENTATION**

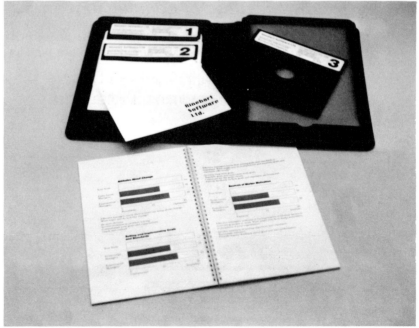

on paper, punched cards or paper tapes, magnetic tapes or electric wiring.

This definition is tailored to fit computer software within the traditional context of copyright law. Information is fixed to a particular medium. This is closer to the writing of an author. One problem with this definition is the failure to separate the program from the algorithms incorporating the program.

In the United States, there is a legislative definition of computer program, namely a "set of statements or instructions to be used directly or indirectly in a computer in order to bring about a certain result".[4] The U.S. definition of software adopts a similar philosophy to that of the Canadian Patent Office. This definition makes it more likely that a court will favour extending copyright protection to computer software.

Hardware

Hardware is the mechanical structure or components designed to carry out the commands and to process the information in the way directed by the firmware and software. In Figure 12.3, the hardware includes the monochrome display, the system unit, the keyboard, and the printer. The hardware falls outside the scope of copyright protection and, as we will see in Chapter 13, comes within the scope of patent law.

The Language of Computer Programs

The basis of firmware and software is the codes or languages used by programmers. The languages are divided into high-level, low-level, and

FIGURE 12.3 **COMPUTER HARDWARE — AN IBM PC MICROCOMPUTER SYSTEM**

machine language. In Figure 12.4, we can discern a considerable difference between the three levels. There are, in other words, three different ways to express the same message or information. But there is only *one* language that the computer understands and can execute: machine language or the object code.

The programmer "writes" a program, not in the English language, but in one of several computer "languages", e.g., COBOL, BASIC, FORTRAN. A program written in one of these computer languages would be understandable to others who knew the language. At this stage, the program has been written in a high-level language. The computer cannot run the program, however, because it cannot understand the language. The program written in the high-level language is also, along with the assembly language, referred to as the *source code.*

In the second stage, the high-level language of, for instance BASIC, is translated in alphanumeric labels. This is accomplished with an assembly program. By using the assembly language, the program remains in a source code, as the assembly state code cannot be understood by the computer.

The process of obtaining a language that the computer can understand is called *compilation.* With the compiler program, the programmer converts his/her *source code* into what is called the *object code.* The object

FIGURE 12.4   **LEVELS OF COMPUTER LANGUAGE**

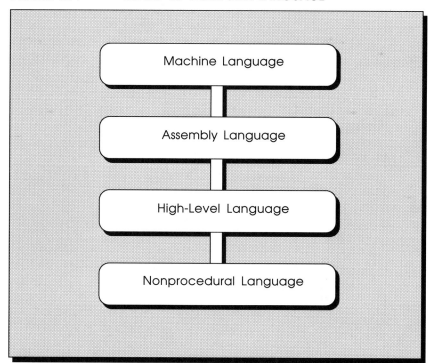

code is written in a binary system of 1s and 0s. A printout of the object code would make very little sense to anyone but the most skilled computer programmer. The object code is synonymous with machine language, and must be placed in the computer's memory. This is accomplished by inserting the object code on a diskette, magnetic tape, or a ROM.

In *IBM v. Spirales Computers Inc., et al.*,[5] Reed J. defined the process of getting the object code into memory:

> The computer's memory is typically composed of semiconductor circuits known as chips. There are two types of memory; ROM (Read Only Memory) and RAM (Random Access Memory). Instructions stored in ROM are permanent; and they can only be read by the computer not changed or rewritten by it, and do not erase when the machine is turned off. Instructions stored in RAM can be changed or rewritten by the operator at any time and are usually erased when the machine is turned off.

Thus, at the end of this process, we see that the object code is the final translation of computer language, such as BASIC, into assembly language, and lastly into machine language. There has been considerable litigation as to whether the object code may be copyrighted. This process has been viewed as one of reproduction. Thus, the assembly language is a copy of the high-level language, such as BASIC, and the object code is a copy of the assembly language. The term "copy" or "reproduction" is significant as it is generally assumed that a source code may be copyrighted; therefore, the term "copy" or "reproduction" allows for the analytical leap that the object code is also protected by copyright.[6]

In the following subsections, we will consider the general requirements of copyright law and the application of these principles to the computer in general and the object code in particular.

The Federal Legislation

Background to the 1924 Copyright Act

In Canada, copyright legislation is by the constitution expressly reserved to the federal government. The foundation of the federal legislation is the *Copyright Act*,[7] which came into force on January 1, 1924. Although there have been, over the years, minor amendments to the federal legislation, it remains largely unaltered in principle and philosophy.

There have been studies recommending new legislation, but the recommendations have not been enacted. Thus, although the English made a major revision of their copyright legislation in 1956, and the Americans in 1976 and 1980, the Canadian legislation patterned after the 1911 English act continues to provide the legislative agenda for the complex copyright issues of the 1980s.

The computer revolution has required the Canadian courts to apply the *Copyright Act* creatively. This is one major difference between the U.S. cases, which have express legislation governing computer programs, and the Canadian cases, which must liberally read legislation drafted for another era. Thus, in *La Société D'Informatique R.D.G. Inc. v. Dynabec Ltée*,[8] Hanna J.S.C. said:

> Protection of the Canadian Copyright Act extends to literary works and account being taken of technological advances since the proclamation of the Act in January, 1924, it must be held that such works (meaning "literary work" defined in the Act) include the computer software packages here discussed.

Key Provisions of the 1924 Copyright Act

In the *Dynabec* case, the following provisions of the *Copyright Act* were set forth as relevant to resolving whether computer software programs could be protected by copyright. For purposes of considering examples of software-copyright cases later, the sections considered in *Dynabec* are reproduced. Also, reference will be made to several other sections that raise specific questions about the nature of copyright ownership in Canada.

SECTION 2
"Every original literary, dramatic, musical and artistic work" includes every original production in the literary, scientific or artistic domain, whatever may be the mode or form of its expression (and then provides examples e.g., books pamphlets, lectures, etc.). . . .

"Literary work" includes maps, charts, plans, tables and compilations. (compare to the American definition: "literary works" include "words, numbers, or other verbal or numerical symbols or indicia." 17 U.S.C. s. 101 (Supp. V 1981).)

"Work" includes the title thereof when the title is original and distinctive.

SECTION 3
SUBSECTION (1)
For the purposes of this Act, "copyright" means the sole right to produce or reproduce the work or any substantial part thereof in any material form whatever . . . ; if the work is unpublished, to publish the work or any substantial part thereof; and includes the sole right,

(a) to produce, reproduce, perform or publish any translation of the work . . . and to authorize any such acts as aforesaid.

SUBSECTION (2)
For the purposes of this Act, "publication" in relation to any work, means the issue of copies of the work to the public. . . .

SECTION 12

SUBSECTION (1)

Subject to this Act, the author of a work shall be the first owner of the copyright therein.

SUBSECTION (3)

Where the author was in the employment of some other person under a contract of service or apprenticeship and the work was made in the course of his employment by that person, the person by whom the author was employed shall, in the absence of any agreement to the contrary, be the first owner of the copyright. . . .

SUBSECTION (4)

The owner of the copyright in any work may assign the right, either wholly or partially and either generally or subject to territorial limitations, and either for the whole term of the copyright or for any part thereof, and may grant any interest in the right by license, but no such grant is valid unless it is in writing signed by the owner of the right in respect of which the grant is made, or by his duly authorized agent.

SECTION 17

SUBSECTION (1)

Copyright in a work shall be deemed to be infringed by any person who, without the consent of the owner of the copyright, does anything that, by this Act, only the owner of the copyright has the right to do.

SECTION 20

SUBSECTION (1)

Where copyright in any work has been infringed, the owner of the copyright is except as otherwise provided by this Act, entitled to all such remedies by way of injunction, damages, accounts and otherwise as are or may be conferred by law for the infringement of a right.

SUBSECTION (3)

In any action for infringement of copyright in any work, in which the defendant puts in issue either the existence of the copyright, or the title of plaintiff thereto, then, in any such case,

(a) the work shall, unless the contrary is proved, be presumed to be a work in which copyright subsists; and

(b) the author of the work shall, unless the contrary is proved, be presumed to be the owner of the copyright. . . .

SUBSECTION (6)
The Exchequer Court of Canada shall have concurrent jurisdiction with provincial courts to hear and determine all civil actions, suits or proceedings that may be instituted for violation of any of the provisions of this Act or to enforce any civil remedies provided by this Act.

The term, or duration, of a copyright in Canada is the lifetime of the author and a period of fifty years after his/her death (Section 5). Twenty-five years after the author's death, the work may be reproduced so long as notice of the intention to reproduce is given to owner of the copyright and a royalty of 10 percent on the published price of the work is paid (Section 7). Unlike, for example the United States, the owner of a literary work has the discretion to register the title of the work with the Registers of Copyright. But registration is not compulsory and a copyright is obtained once the mode of expression is fixed, e.g., a manuscript of a book.

Canada also recognizes an author's "moral right" in his/her work. This right permits the author to prevent distortion or mutilations of his/her work even after the work has been sold to another. Moral rights are contained in Section 12(7) that provides:

Independently of the author's copyright, and even after the assignment, either wholly or partially, of the said copyright the author has the right to claim authorship of the work, as well as the right to restrain any distortion, mutilation or other modification of the work which would be prejudicial to his honour or reputation.

This is generally known as the author's "moral rights". In later sections reference will be made to these sections of the *Copyright Act*.

General Application of the 1924 Copyright Act

The historical purpose of a copyright was to grant a limited monopoly to persons who expressed literary and artistic ideas through such media as painting, writing, and composing. The monopoly allowed the artist, author, or composer to obtain a profit from others who wanted to reproduce his/her work. The community received the benefit of the work. The greater availability of these expressions of the mind increased the body of knowledge, instructed and educated, and entertained. In this way, copyright advanced the larger public interest by providing an incentive to disclose original ideas.[9]

The window of creative expression protected by copyright is narrowed by the express words found in Section 2 of the *Act*, which accords copyright protection to any "original artistic, dramatic, musical or literary work". Once the work falls within one of the categories of Section 2, the author of the work is required to show that the work is original (or not copied from a copyrighted work) and the expression is fixed in a tangible medium. Unlike a patent, there is no further requirement that the work should be novel, useful, or non-obvious. The author's statutory copyright — an intangible personal property right — is in the form of a negative command: No one shall copy or distribute the author's work without his/her permission. Unauthorized copying of the work is an infringement of the copyright and the owner has the right to enjoin the wrongdoer.

TYPES OF PROTECTED WORKS

As copyright protects the great works of art and literature from being substantially copied by others for a period of time, the courts have not hesitated in granting protection to less noble works. Thus, in *Ascot Jockey Club Ltd. v. Simons*,[10] the court held that a horse racing information sheet was protected as an "original literary work". So long as the work is expressed in print or writing, the court will not judge the instrinsic style or quality of the work. If either critical acclaim or enduring importance were the standard, the size of libraries and museums would be considerably smaller. But, of course, that is not the standard. Copyright protects the novels of Saul Bellow as well as the City of Vancouver telephone directory. A telephone directory? Yes, even a telephone directory may be protected by copyright as a compilation of facts. However, bare facts may not.

Copyright of a compilation of facts has great importance for the protection of computer data bases, which have become a multibillion dollar industry. Under Section 2 of the *Copyright Act*, the definition of "literary work" includes compilations. A compilation is a pool of information organized in such a way that it is an original work. Nonetheless, it is not clear whether a computer data base will be defined to mean a compilation for purposes of the *Act*. The courts have considerable discretion in these cases. It may turn, for example, on the respective expenditure of capital, expertise, and labour by the plaintiff compared to that of the defendant. Clearly, the facts in the compilation are not copyrightable. The organization or arrangement of the facts, however, probably will be covered by copyright.

Future decisions will have to determine whether the data base is a computer program or whether to treat the data base as something altogether different. One of the main distinctions between software and a data base is that the latter is updated frequently, often on a daily or even hourly basis. This may prove to be less of a problem in Canada where there is no system of compulsory registration of copyright. But in the United States, where registration is compulsory, the computer data base provides the law with a unique problem.

The infringer does not escape liability because he/she reproduces the original work in another mode or medium. Thus, in *King Features Syndicate Inc. v. Kleeman Ltd.*,[11] the House of Lords held that the plaintiff who owned the copyright in a drawing of "Popeye the Sailor" had a good cause of action for infringement against the company that had reproduced that drawing in the form of dolls and brooches. In the United States, it has been recognized for some years that copyright is available to such consumer items as door knockers and ashtrays.[12]

SCOPE OF COPYRIGHT PROTECTION

The courts have been called upon to define the scope of things that are subject to copyright protection. For example, in *Kenrick & Co. v. Lawrence & Co.*,[13] the plaintiff, with the assistance of an artist, made a sketch of a hand placing an **X** on a ballot. The purpose was to illustrate for illiterate voters how to mark their ballots during an election. The defendant published a similar card with the hand in a slightly different position, and the court assumed that the plaintiff's card provided his inspiration. The plaintiff had sold over a million copies of his card and sought to restrain the defendant from selling his on the grounds of infringement of copyright.

The High Court held against the plaintiff, stating in part:

> It is possible that in this case the proprietors of the drawing registered may have a right to be protected from a reproduction for their picture of a hand drawing a cross in which every line, dot, measurement, and blank space shall be rendered exactly as in the original, or in which the variations from such minute agreement shall be microscopic. But I cannot see how they can possibly make a higher claim, or say that because they have registered a drawing of a hand pencilling a cross within a square that no other person in the United Kingdom is at liberty to draw a hand pencilling a cross within a square for perhaps the next half century.
>
> In the present instance, what the plaintiffs claim is really a right to prevent any one else from drawing the same subject as that of his drawing. If he has a copyright in the *subject*, there is a colourable imitation, because the subject is not altered by changing the position of the hand and adding the indications of a shirt sleeve. But it is clear that there is no copyright in the subject. As for the manner of treating the subject, there can be no copyright in that, for if the thing to be represented at all, it is impossible to treat it in any other way.

In effect, there were only limited ways to illustrate a drawing of how to mark a ballot. The first person who made the drawing expressing an idea does not acquire a monopoly over either the idea or the subject. It is well-settled that no one is entitled to copyright an idea. Thus, a software engineer who created the idea of a spreadsheet program cannot stop another person from using the idea of a spreadsheet.

He/She can, however, prevent another person from copying his/her spreadsheet program that is based on that idea. There is an exception to this rule: Where the idea expressed by the author can only be expressed in one way, then that expression may not be copyrighted. It is said, in such a case, that the idea and expression merge. The merger is sufficient to deprive the author of his/her copyright because the monopoly granted is too large.

ORIGINALITY OF THE WORK

There is no requirement that the author of a work must have expressed original or imaginative ideas. The author is entitled to draw upon a general pool of common knowledge in formulating the ideas that he/she has expressed. A mathematician, therefore, can draw upon the general stock of mathematical knowledge when setting a written examination for students. The questions come from the pool of mathematical knowledge and do not spring wholly from the mathematician's brain. But he/she is entitled to copyright protection in the expression of those mathematical ideas formulated into examination questions.

The test is found in *University of London Press Ltd. v. University Tutorial Press Ltd.*[14] where Peterson J. discussed the relationship of originality and copyright in literary works:

> The word "original" does not in this connection mean that the work must be the expression of original or inventive thought. Copyright Acts are not concerned with the originality of ideas, but with the expression of thought, and in the case of "literary work", with the expression of thought in print or writing. The originality which is required relates to the expression of the thought. But the Act does not require that the expression must be in an original or novel form, but that the work must not be copied from another work — that it should originate from the author.

The standard of skill required to produce the copyrighted work is reasonably small. At the extreme, however, the court will find that "meaningless rubbish would plainly be excluded."[15] So long as there is a "work" and evidence of "some skill, even if very small, applied to preparation", then a copyright will protect the work from misappropriation.

INFRINGEMENT OF COPYRIGHT

Assuming that the plaintiff "owns" the copyright in a literary work, what conduct or acts by the defendant will amount to an infringement of his/her copyright? Lord Diplock in *Francis Day & Hunter Ltd. v. Bron*,[16] provides the following answer:

> [I]t is well established that to constitute infringement of copyright in any literary, dramatic or musical work, there must be present two elements: first, there must be sufficient objective similarity between the infringing work and the copyright work, or a substantial part thereof, for the former to be properly described, not necessarily as identical with, but as a reproduction or adaptation of the latter; secondly, the copyright work must be the source from which the infringing work is derived.

Once the copyright owner demonstrates an objective similarity between his/her work and that of the defendant, and that his/her work was either the direct or indirect source for the defendant's work, a *prima facie* case of infringement is made. It is irrelevant that the infringer of the copyrighted work did not intend to infringe or have knowledge that his/her work would infringe the copyright owner's. In the "unconscious copying" case the defendant is unaware that he/she misappropriated the plaintiff's copyrighted tune. Nonetheless, there is high authority that it is no defence that the infringer honestly did not know, on a conscious level, that he/she had directly or indirectly used the copyright owner's song as the source of his/her own song.

Where the defendant can prove that he/she had no direct or indirect access to the plaintiff's work, he/she will not be liable for infringement even though his/her work is identical to the plaintiff's. In that case, it is a coincidence that the two works are similar or identical. With the chain of causation broken, the action for infringement is lost. The defendant's access to the copyrighted work is always a question of fact.

There must be evidence to convince a judge that the defendant independently reproduced the copyrighted work with the same idiosyncrasies and mistakes. As a pure question of fact, the judge must, on the balance of probabilities, determine whether or not he/she believes from all the evidence that the defendant reproduced the copyrighted work independently of that work.

FAIR DEALING DEFENCE

Fair dealing is a statutory defence to an infringement of copyright action. Section 17(2)(a) of the *Copyright Act* provides that a person is not guilty of infringement for "any fair dealing with any work for the purposes of private study, research, criticism, review, or newspaper summary." The nature of "fair dealing" was considered by the English Court of Appeal in *Hubbard v. Vosper*.[17] The defendant had written a book entitled *The Mind Benders*. The author of the book was a former member of the Church of Scientology and his book, which was highly critical of the Church's doctrines, included substantial passages from books written by the Church's founder. The author of *The Mind Benders* acknowledged using extracts from the founder's books but claimed that this had been fair dealing.

Lord Denning established a two-pronged test for fair dealing: i) the amount of the copyrighted material used by the defendant; and ii) the use to which the material was put. It is not, for example, fair dealing for the defendant to use the plaintiff's copyrighted material to publish a book intended as competition with the plaintiff's. But it is fair to allow copyrighted material for purposes of comment and criticism. The relationship of whether the amount used was reasonable in light of the justified use to which the material is put will always be a question of fact.

Megaw L.J. considered the issue of substantial use in this passage:[18]

It is then said that the passages which have been taken from these various works — in particular, from one of them described as "Introduction to Scientology Ethics" — are so substantial, quantitatively so great in relation to the respective works from which the citations are taken, that they fall outside the scope of "fair dealing". To my mind, this question of substantiality is a question of degree. It may well be that it does not prevent the quotation of work from being within the fair dealing subsection even though the quotation may be of every single word of the work. Let me give an example. Suppose that there is on a tombstone in a churchyard an epitaph consisting of a dozen or of 20 words. Parishioner of the church thinks that this sort of epitaph is out of place on a tombstone. He writes a letter to the parish magazine setting out the words of the epitaph. Could it be suggested that that citation is so substantial, consisting of 100 per cent of the "work" in question, that it must necessarily be outside the scope of the fair dealing provision? To my mind it could not validly be so suggested.

Computer Programs and Copyright Law

The Initial Remedy in an Infringement Action

INTERLOCUTORY INJUNCTION

There have been few Canadian decisions to address the issue of whether software or firmware is copyright protected. And most of these cases have been decided on applications for interlocutory injunction — a temporary order that commands the defendant to stop some conduct until a full hearing can be heard on the merits of the case. As the definition suggests, the interlocutory proceeding is not a full and complete trial on the merits of the case. Instead, the plaintiff, usually on the basis of an affidavit evidence, seeks to restrain the defendant's infringement until the actual trial. The advantage of the interlocutory injunction is the interim protection that the software owner acquires against the "infrin-ger". As the trial may be months in the future, and the "life" of the particular software is relatively short, some immediate step to stop the infringement is required.

As long as the court is persuaded that there is a serious or substantial issue to be tried and the action is not frivolous, an interlocutory injunc-tion will be granted.[19] In practice, once the interlocutory injunction is granted, that is normally the end of the case. The defendant will generally not bother to defend after losing on the interlocutory injunction. This means that in many cases there is no final judgment made on the merits of the full case presented at trial.

In these "stop-gap" interlocutory judgments, the court has not had the advantage of hearing the full evidence. Moreover, in granting the inter-locutory injunction, the court has not necessarily decided that the de-fendant will lose at trial. Thus some caution should be taken in drawing broad conclusions from such a judgment. For our purposes, this causes a problem as most of the English and Canadian judgments from which we must divine the law are on applications for an interlocutory injunction.

ANTON PILLER ORDER

An infringement action might be seriously jeopardized by a defendant who may decide to destroy the offending programs. The Anton Piller order — which takes its name from the case inventing this relief[20] — means that the court authorizes the plaintiff to enter the defendant's premises and to seize and remove the programs. The conditions for obtaining this order are twofold: i) the documents, machines, or equip-ment in the defendant's possession are essential for the plaintiff's case; and ii) there is a serious risk of dishonest destruction of these items by the defendant.[21]

The Means of Expression and Computer Software

It is a well-settled principle of copyright law that only the expression of the idea, and not the idea itself, is protected. A Rinehart software engineer may develop the idea for a graphic and forecasting accounting software program. Although the law of trade secrets may protect this idea, the law of copyright will not. Once the engineer expresses this idea by writing a source code there will be a copyright in *that expression of the idea*. Another software engineer, however, who reads the source code, written in BASIC, may alter or adapt the underlying idea of a graphic and fore-casting accounting package and write another program in COBOL. Rinehart could not succeed in stopping this software engineer from sell-ing his/her version of the idea expressed in a substantially different way.

One way in which the author can protect competitors from gaining access to the underlying idea is by translating the source code into an object code. In its object code state, it is almost impossible for another party to work backward to determine the source code from whence the object code was derived. As a result, the graphic and forecasting accounting package can only be reproduced by someone willing to invest a similar amount of research and development time and independently write the program. At the same time, the company may seek to keep the source code privileged and secret. This tactic may prevent the "free ride" on new ideas gained through access to the original creator's source code.

In most instances, however, the author of the application or operating system program is less concerned with a competitor stealing his/her idea than with misappropriation of the author's expression of the idea. A competitor of Rinehart's Law Office Management System confronts two related problems: i) time lag; and ii) research and development cost. Unless the competitor can quickly enter the market before Rinehart's program has had significant market penetration, the capacity to effectively compete may be lost. Rather than risk a substantial research and development expenditure on the gamble, the competitor may take a shortcut and reproduce Rinehart's program. Rinehart, in this type of case, is using copyright law to prevent unfair competition.

Legal Basis for Protecting the Computer Program

THE FACTS OF THE APPLE COMPUTER CASE

The crucial legal issue facing Canadian, U.S., English, Australian, and South African courts has been whether there can be copyright of the computer programs. In particular, the issue is often narrowed as to whether the object code is protected by copyright. A leading case, which has attracted international attention, is found in American Third Circuit decision of *Apple Computer, Inc. v. Franklin Computer Corp.*,[22] where the court held Apple had copyright in the object code of its operating system programs.

In that case, Franklin Computer manufactured and sold the ACE 100, an Apple-compatible microcomputer. Moreover, Franklin, to achieve compatibility, copied the object code of the Apple's operating system programs, e.g., DOS 3.3, Applesoft, and Apple Integer BASIC. Altogether, Franklin copied fourteen of the Apple operating system programs. Apple estimated that it had taken them forty-six man-months to produce those programs at a cost of $740 000. Franklin made the copies in order to ensure that their computer would be 100 percent compatible with the Apple — an obvious marketing and promoting tool. There was also evidence that Franklin *could have* rewritten the programs but did not, and that there were compatible Apple operating system programs independently written by third parties.

There were three main issues before the court: i) whether there could be copyright in an object code; ii) whether there could be copyright in an object code embedded in ROM; and iii) whether there could be copyright in an operating systems program.

AMENDMENTS TO THE COPYRIGHT ACT AND THE COMMON LAW RULES

As to the first issue, the court heavily relied on the amendment to the *United States Copyright Act* that specifically includes computer programs, and the legislative history of that amendment. The main stumbling block in Apple's case was a prior Supreme Court case, *White-Smith Music Publishing Co. v. Apollo Co.*,[23] that adopted the rule of "human intelligibility". Unless the work could be read by a human reader it could not be copyrighted.

In *White-Smith*, a piano roll containing perforations for purposes of playing could not have been read by a human reader. Even though the perforation was a reproduced copyrighted musical composition, it was deemed not a copy for purposes of the *Copyright Act*. The English case of *Boosey v. Wright*,[24] eight years earlier, had held that the perforated piano roll of copyrighted music was not an infringement. The English judge regarded "the defendant's perforated sheets as part of a mechanical contrivance for producing musical notes; and I cannot think that the manufacturers of musical instruments infringe any person's copyright by so constructing their machines and appliances to be used with them as to produce musical notes indicated on a sheet of music."

The question was whether the eighty-year-old piano roll precedent was going to destroy the copyright foundation of the billion-dollar software industry. The court distinguished the piano roll case and held that copyright protection extended to the plaintiff's object code stored in ROM. The defendant's use of object code on its microchip was a copyright infringement.

The Third Circuit Court observed that "the category of 'literary works', one of the seven copyrightable categories, is not confined to literature in the nature of Hemingway's *For Whom the Bell Tolls*."[25] The decision of Apple's copyright in the object code expanded the definition of "literary works", which includes "numbers or other . . . numerical symbols of indica". The effect of the decision was to avoid the restrictive meaning of "literary works" used in the 1908 Supreme Court decision.

COPYRIGHT PROTECTION FOR ROMS

On the second issue, i.e., whether there is copyright protection for ROMs, the *Franklin* court cited its prior decision in *Williams Electronics, Inc. v. Arctic International, Inc.*[26] In *Williams*, the court decided that the ROM satisfied the statutory rule that the expression of the idea must be fixed. For example, the obvious way of expressing an idea is to write it down on a piece of paper. The expression is fixed on the paper. This analogy can be extended to the object code fixed on a microchip.

COPYRIGHT IN THE OPERATING SYSTEM

The two issues that attracted the most attention in *Franklin* were: i) whether Apple had copyright in its operating system programs; and ii) whether the idea and expression of the idea had merged in the operating system programs. This type of program instructs the machine what to do. For instance, an operating system program will instruct the computer, on a sequence of commands, to activate the printer or to control the operation of the disk drives in the system unit.

Franklin's argument was that the operating system program was un-copyrightable because it was part of either a system, process, or method of operation. Any protection, the argument continued, accorded to Apple was in the realm of patent law. The argument was supported by Franklin's reliance on *Baker v. Selden*[27] in the following passage:[28]

> In *Baker v. Selden*, plaintiff . . . held a copyright on a book explaining a bookkeeping system which included blank forms with ruled lines and headings designed for use with that system. Plaintiff sued for copyright infringement on the basis of defendant's publication of a book containing a different arrangement of the columns and different headings, but which used a similar plan so far as results were concerned. The Court, reversing the decree for the plaintiff, concluded that blank account-books were not the subject of copyright and that "the mere copyright of Selden's book did not confer upon him the exclusive right to make and use account-books, ruled and arranged as designated by him and described and illustrated in said book." *id.,* at 107. The Court stated that copyright of the books did not give the plaintiff the exclusive right to use the system explained in the books, noting, for example, that "copyright of a work on mathematical science cannot give to the author an exclusive right to the methods of operation which he propounds."

Section 102(b) of the *Copyright Act*, the other ground on which Franklin relies, appeared first in the 1976 version, long after the decision in *Baker v. Selden*. The *Franklin* court considered Section 102(b) in this passage:[29]

> . . . Apple does not seek to copyright the method which instructs the computer to perform its operating functions but only the instructions themselves. The method would be protected, if at all, by the patent law, an issue as yet unresolved. (citation omitted)
>
> Franklin's attack on operating system programs as "methods" or "processes" seems inconsistent with its concession that application programs are an appropriate subject of copyright. Both types of programs instruct the computer to do something. Therefore, it should make no difference for purposes of section 102(b) whether these

instructions tell the computer to help prepare an income tax return (the task of an application program) or to translate a high level language program from source code into its binary language object code form. . . . Since it is only the instructions which are protected, a "process" is no more involved because the instructions in an operating system program may be used to activate the operation of the computer than it would be if instructions were written in ordinary English in a manual which described the necessary steps to activate an intricate complicated machine.

. . . [T]hat an operating system program is part of a machine mistakenly focuses on the physical characteristics of the instructions. But the medium is not the message. We have already considered and rejected aspects of this contention in the discussion of object code and ROM. The mere fact that the operating program may be etched on a ROM does not make the program either a machine, part of a machine, or its equivalent.

DISTINCTION BETWEEN THE IDEA AND EXPRESSION

Franklin's second major argument was that the operating system was not merely an expression of an idea but the idea and expression merged. Therefore, to extend copyright protection would violate the long established rule that an idea cannot be copyrighted. The court rejected this argument on the following grounds:[30]

Many courts which have sought to draw the line between an idea and expression have found difficulty in articulating where it falls. (citation omitted) We believe that in the context before us, a program for an operating system, the line must be a pragmatic one, which also keeps in consideration "the preservation of the balance between competition and protection reflected in the patent and copyright laws." (citation omitted) "Unlike a patent, a copyright protects originality rather than novelty or invention." [Citation omitted.] In that opinion, we quoted approvingly the following passage from *Dymow v. Bolton*:[31]

"Just as a patent affords protection only to the means of reducing an inventive idea to practice, so the copyright law protects the means of expressing an idea; and it is as near the whole truth as generalization can usually reach that, *if the same idea can be expressed in a plurality of totally different manners, a plurality of copyrights may result, and no infringement will exist.*" [emphasis added]

We adopt the suggestion in the above language and thus focus on whether the idea is capable of various modes of expression. If other programs can be written or created which perform the same function as an Apple's operating system program, then that program is an expression of the idea and hence copyrightable. In essence, this inquiry is no different than that made to determine whether the expression and idea have merged, which has been stated to occur where there are no or few other ways of expressing a particular idea.

... The idea which may merge with the expression, thus making the copyright unavailable, is the idea which is the subject of the expression. The idea of one of the operating system programs is, for example, how to translate source code into object code. If other methods of expressing that idea are not foreclosed as a practical matter, then there is no merger.

The third Circuit held that, as the trial court had not made any findings of fact on this issue, it should be remanded back for reconsideration on the idea-expression distinction.

APPLICATION OF THE APPLE APPROACH IN CANADA

The *Apple* case has found favour with the Canadian trial level courts that have confronted similar issues. One of the best examples of the approach in Canada is found in *International Business Machines Corporation v. Spirales Computers Inc.*[32], where IBM sought an interlocutory injunction to restrain Spirales from selling a computer imported from Taiwan through its Montreal retail store. IBM claimed that this computer had copied IBM's copyrighted computer program called "IBM Personal Computer Basis Input Output System 1.0" or BIOS. The object code of the BIOS program was stored in ROM for the IBM Personal Computer. The purpose of BIOS was to instruct the computer how to input and output information. Without BIOS, the IBM PC would not work.

The Taiwan computer sold by Spirales contained a copy of the IBM BIOS program stored in ROM. Although the Third Circuit could fall back on recent statutory amendments to the United States *Copyright Act*, Reed J. was left to decide the case based on the 1924 *Copyright Act*. Thus, the BIOS had to be classed as an original literary, dramatic, musical, or artistic work. Reed J. faced the problem of the legislation outstripped by modern technological developments by finding that the language of the *Act* had to be applied in a practical manner that took into account the current needs and concepts.

In granting IBM an interlocutory injunction, Reed J. made a number of crucial findings. First, BIOS, as a literary work, had to be reduced to writing or a printed form. The source code was held to meet this statutory requirement. Second, the language of the writing did not have to be ordinary language. For example, a coyright can exist in telegraph code, shorthand, or in a catalogue of type. Third, by embedding the object code in ROM, the right to claim the program was a literary work still subsisted. The idea that BIOS embedded in ROM had become "part" of the machine held no attraction for the court. Finally, on the issue of human intelligibility, Spirales argued that BIOS was not designed for communication between human beings but only to instruct a computer how to process information. The court held that, as both the source and object codes had been published in a technical manual, the source code could be understood by another human being. Moreover, the object code or machine language embedded in ROM was merely a reproduction of the source code.

Problems for Discussion

1. The President of Rinehart Ltd. owns a videotape recorder (VTR) and, with the aid of this machine and television, has taped the following programs: i) a CBC special report on the Computer Industry in Canada; ii) the Grey Cup game; iii) the feature film titled *WarGames*. The owner of the copyright in each of these three programs brings a copyright infringement action against the President, the retailer, the distributor, and the manufacturer of the VTR. The purpose of the lawsuit is to exclude the use of VTRs in Canada by enjoining the sale of these machines. Has the President infringed the copyright held in the above programs? Is there, in a law, a distinction between the President of Rinehart, as the ultimate user of the VTR and those who manufacture and sell the machine? In reaching your answer consider the "fair dealing" section of the *Copyright Act*, the United States Supreme Court case of *Universal City Studios, Inc. v. Sony Corporation of America*, 220 U.S.P.Q. 665 (1984) (commonly referred to as the *Betamax* case), and the article by Hayhurst, "Copyright and the Copying Machine" (1984) 9 *Can.Bus.L.J.*, p. 129.

2. An artist named Michael Snow requested an injunction against Eaton Centre where his sculpture of sixty geese flying, known as *Flight Stop* was displayed. The Eaton Centre, as part of its Christmas promotion, placed red ribbons around the necks of the sixty geese. The artist contended that the ribbons distorted or modified his work and was prejudicial to his honour and reputation. Did the placing of the ribbons around the artist's work violate his moral rights in the work? See Section 12(7), Copyright Act and *Snow v. The Eaton Centre Ltd.*, (1983) 70 C.P.R.(2d) 105 (Ont.H.C.).

3. Lester Jones copied Rinehart's video game *Space Attack* and sold it as *OuterSpace Attacker* in Ontario. Mr. Jones is a citizen of the United States, and after Rinehart threatened legal proceedings to restrain Mr. Jones from further copying the Rinehart copyrighted program and distributing it, there was evidence that Mr. Jones was preparing to flee the jurisdiction with his inventory of games. What type of relief is open to Rinehart in order to prevent Mr. Jones from leaving the jurisdiction and destroying Rinehart's action of infringement? See *Nin-*

tendo of America, Inc. v. Coinex Video Games, Inc., (1983) 69 C.P.R.(2d) 122 (Fed.C.A.).

4. Jason Smith unlawfully distributed pirated copies of Rinehart's video games *Fight of the Titans* and *Epic Encounters* in British Columbia and Ontario. It is clear that Mr. Smith knew that the copyright in both games belonged to Rinehart. In Ontario, the Crown has charged Mr. Smith with fraud and theft. Under Section 338(1) of the Criminal Code the offence of fraud is defined:

> Every one who, by deceit, falsehood or other fraudulent means, whether or not it is a false pretence within the meaning of this Act, defrauds the public or any person, whether ascertained or not, of any property, money, or valuable security, (a) is guilty of an indictable offence . . .

Mr. Smith's defence is that the fraud must flow from the accused to the victim causing the victim to act in some way to his detriment and that there is no such evidence in this case. Moreover, he claims that the misappropriation of a copyrighted software program is not theft. Discuss whether or not Mr. Smith is liable to conviction on either fraud or theft charges. See *Regina v. Kirkwood*, (1983) 73 C.P.R.(2d) 114 (Ont.C.A.); and cf. *Rank Film Distributors Ltd. v. Video Information Centre*, (1981) 2 All E.R. 76, 81 (H.L.) per Lord Wilberforce.

5. In a proceeding for interlocutory relief, Rinehart has placed in evidence seventy-five lines (a small fraction of the whole) of the program "Law Office Management System" in an action against Great Law Software Ltd. The seventy-five lines were in BASIC language or source code. There is no evidence or samples of the Great Law program titled "Legal Operation Systems". It is conceded that both programs reach ultimately the same result, i.e., providing a system that includes billing, file control, inventory, etc. Great Law Software Ltd. contends that Rinehart has merely shown that the fruits of the two programs are the same but has failed to show any similarities in the programs themselves. The defendant further contends that the burden rests upon Rinehart to place evidence before the court allowing the judge to compare the two programs. Great Law Software has moved for Rinehart's application for an interlocutory injunction to be dismissed. Discuss the merits of the defendant's arguments. See *Thrustcode Ltd. v. W.W. Computing Ltd.*, (1983) F.S.R. 502 (Ch.D.) per Megarry, V.C.

6. The plaintiff had copyright in the game *Trivial Pursuit*, and registered copyright in the game that consisted of the following: playing board, one die, a thousand question-and-answer cards, six player-tokens, thirty-six wedges, and two code-cards giving the colour, categories, and

rules for playing the game. The defendant devised two games: *Golden Trivia* and *Junior Trivia*. The owners of *Trivial Pursuit* alleged that the defendant's games infringed their game by appropriating the same rules, questions, and answers. The plaintiff's evidence showed that the defendant had taken only 20 percent of the time that they had invested in compiling the questions. This led to the inference that the defendant took a shortcut and copied the plaintiff's questions and answers either exactly or with slight variation. Is the plaintiff trying to extend copyright to pure facts? For instance, one question that the plaintiff's claimed copyright for was "Who was on the first cover of *People*?"and the defendant had a question that read: "Who was on the first cover of *People Magazine*?" Have the owners made out a claim for copyright infringement? See *Horn Abbot Ltd. v. W.B. Coutler Sales, Ltd.*, (1984) 77 C.P.R.(2d) 145 (Fed.Ct.).

7. In *Sega Enterprises Ltd. v. Richards*, (1983) F.S.R. 73, 75 (Ch.D.), Goulding J. held that the machine code was entitled to copyright protection because it was "either a reproduction or an adaptation of the assembly code program". Why are the words "reproduction" or "adaptation" crucial for extending copyright to object codes?

8. Ms. Bach's employment contract with Rinehart provided, in part:

   Ms. Bach, as in-house lawyer, hereby consents to be a member of the executive committee and to continue to serve the company as a member of the company's legal staff on the terms hereinafter contained and to perform such services as she may be called upon by the board of directors to perform as such lawyer as far as the same shall be consistent with the duties normally performed by such lawyer ...

   At the request of the President of Rinehart, Ms. Bach gave a series of lectures titled "Copyright and the Computer Age". These lectures were open to the public and were written by Ms. Bach during normal business hours. Rinehart received favourable publicity from these lectures. Ms. Bach was approached by Jason Books Ltd., which offered to publish the lectures in book form. Ms. Bach accepted the offer and signed a publishing contract as author with Jason Books Ltd. The book, *Copyright and the Computer Age*, sold well, and Ms. Bach received royalties of $25 000. Rinehart takes the position that it owned the copyright in the lectures and the book and that Ms. Bach should account for her profits to them. See Section 12(3) of the Copyright Act and *Stevenson Jordan & Harrison Ltd. v. Macdonald & Evans*, (1952) 1 T.L.R. 101 (C.A.). Does Rinehart have any claim to any profits that Ms. Bach made from the book? Assuming that Ms. Bach wrote her play *The Semidetached Barrister* at the encouragement of the President and during office hours, would Rinehart have any claim to the profits from the play?

Chapter 12 Notes

1. R.S.C. 1970, c. C-30.
2. See Palmer and Resendes, *Copyright and the Computer*, Consumer and Corporate Affairs Canada at 9-10.
3. See Patent Office Record, August 1, 1978, at 27.
4. 17 U.S.C. s. 101 (1982).
5. (Unreported Fed.Ct.) T-904-84 (1984).
6. See *Thrustcode Ltd. v. W.W. Computing Ltd.*, (1983) F.S.R. 502; and *Sega Enterprises Ltd. v. Richards*, (1983) F.S.R. 73.
7. S.C. 1921, c. 24.
8. (Unreported, Superior Court, District of Montreal) 1984.
9. See note, *"Copyright Protection of Computer Program Object Code"*, 96 *Har.L.Rev.* 1723, 1739 (1983).
10. (1968) 64 W.W.R. 411 (B.C.S.C.)
11. (1941) A.C. 417, (1941) 2 All E.R. 403.
12. See Note, *"Copyright Protection of Computer Program Object Code"*, supra, at 1740.
13. (1890) 25 Q.B.D. 99 (H.C.).
14. (1916) 2 Ch. 601 (H.C.).
15. See *Apple Computer Inc. v. Computer Edge Pty. Ltd,* (1984) 10 F.S.R. 481, 495 (Aust.Fed.Ct.).
16. (1966) Ch. 587 (C.A.).
17. (1972) 1 All E.R. 1023.
18. Ibid. at 1031.
19. See generally *American Cyanamid Co. v. Ethicon Ltd.*, (1975) 2 W.L.R. 316 (H.L.).
20. See *Anton Piller K.G. v. Manufacturing Processes Ltd.*, (1976) 1 Ch. 55.
21. See Anton Piller K.G. v. Manufacturing Process Ltd., *supra*; and *Nintendo of America, Inc. v. Coinex Video Games Inc.*, (1983) 69 C.P.R. (2d) 122 (Fed. C.A.).
22. 714 F.2d 1240 (3rd Cir. 1983).
23. 209 U.S. 1 (1908).
24. (1900) 1 Ch. 122.
25. *Supra*, note 22, at 1249.
26. 685 F.2d 870 (3rd Cir. 1982).
27. 101 U.S. 99, p. 103 (1879) and Section 102(b) of the *Copyright Act*.
28. *Supra*, Note 22, at 1250.
29. Ibid at 1251.
30. Ibid at 1253.
31. 11 F.2d 690. 691 (2d Cir. 1926).
32. *Supra*, Note 5.

13 THE LAW OF PATENTS

Introduction

The basis of Canadian patent law is contained in the *Patent Act.*[1] The object of this chapter is to introduce certain key concepts in the law of patents: i) invention; ii) subject matter of patents; iii) novelty; and iv) utility. Before considering these specific requirements of patentability, a general introduction to the statutory scheme under the *Patent Act* will be explored. An understanding of these concepts will provide a working knowledge of when and how a patent may be obtained to protect a device or process.

FIGURE 13.1 **LEGAL BASIS OF A PATENT**

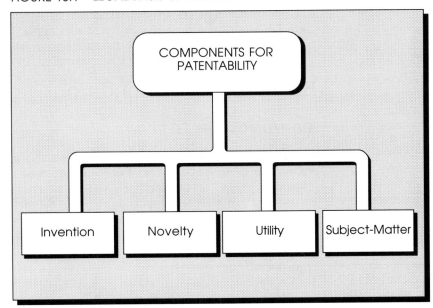

The main advantage of a patent is the economic monopoly that the statute gives to the patent holder. For example, a disk drive system for a computer is patented like any other machine or device. Once patented by Rinehart, however, it entitles the company to the exclusive right to license or sell this device to others. The problem, however, is the software that is inserted into the disk drive and allows the computer to perform certain calculations or tasks. The nature of this problem is often expressed in terms of what is the appropriate subject matter for a patent. And, in the area of computer software, the subject-matter issue often looms as the most significant roadblock to patentability.

As we have seen in Chapter 12, in the computer industry, the line between inventions that are patented and "literary works" that are copyrighted is sometimes unclear. Thus, firmware, such as microchips with encoded object codes, have presented interpretation problems. Most courts that have considered the matter, however, have held copyright and not patent law as the appropriate means of protecting programs on the microchip. But new problems are likely to arise in the future. When one company copies the microcode on a competitor's semiconductor, does this conduct amount to copyright or patent infringement? There is no clear answer. The courts, when applying patent law, often must make important policy decisions about new and novel technologies.

For example, controversy has surrounded the United States Supreme Court decision in *Diamond v. Chakrabarty*,[2] which upheld the patentability of man-made micro-organisms. It takes only a little imagination to anticipate the vision of scientists creating life and obtaining patents for their creations. Again, there is no clear answer in the Canadian cases whether or not a patent would be granted in a similar case. A leading Canadian intellectual property expert, for example, has concluded that "it is probable that man-made life forms are patentable in Canada."[3]

Basic Statutory Conditions

Administrative Structure

In Canada, the Commissioner of Patents plays an important role in the enforcement, interpretation, and administration of the law. The Commissioner receives all the applications, fees, papers, and documents and has the sole authority to grant and issue a patent of invention.[4] The decision of the Commissioner may be appealed to the Exchequer Court — a federal court.[5] An inventor therefore has recourse to judicial review of the Commissioner's interpretations, exercise of discretion, and procedures.

An applicant, called an inventor, who seeks a patent, normally retains the services of a patent attorney. The Patent Office keeps a list of all the patent attorneys who are entitled to represent applicants in the presentation and prosecution of applications before the Patent Office.[6] Who is entitled to a patent in Canada? There are three conditions that the applicant must satisfy about the invention: i) it was not known or used by any other person before he/she invented it; ii) it was not described in any patent, Canadian publication, or in any other country more than two years before the application is made; and iii) it was not in public use or sale in Canada for more than two years before the application.[7] Even though these conditions are satisfied, the applicant still must comply with the other provisions of the legislation.

A patent cannot be obtained for a mere scientific principle or abstract theorem,[8] for example, the scientists who hypothesized a fifth force in the universe called "hypercharge" — which suggests a force that pushes up and works *against* gravity. The discovery of this fifth force is a mere scientific principle in the same fashion that Einstein and Galileo created scientific theories.

The first two conditions ensure that the invention is new and novel. Thus, the concept of novelty is an important condition in obtaining a patent. In the section on novelty below, we will consider the tests that the courts have developed to determine when an invention is novel. The third condition allows the inventor a period of time to test-market a product or process. Before applying for a patent, the inventor may wish to determine whether or not there is a commercial demand for his/her invention. The two-year time limit, therefore, allows the inventor to satisfy him/herself that others find it new and useful. This market information is also persuasive evidence as to the novelty and utility of the invention.

Improvements

A lay person might assume that a patent can be obtained only for an entirely new and novel invention: The law allows a patent for an "improvement" on any patented invention.[9] The *Act* clearly separates the rights of the original patent holder from the rights of the subsequent patent holder of the improvement. The "improver" obtains no independent right to make, sell, or use the original invention. Similarly, the original patent holder of the invention is excluded from making, selling, or using the patented improvement. This indicates a statutory object of protecting each right without diminishing the rights of the other. In the end, it leads the improver and the original inventor to negotiate an agreement together.

Procedure for Obtaining a Patent

The procedure for obtaining a patent requires the applicant to first make an application for the patent to the Commissioner. Along with the application, the applicant includes specifications of the invention. These

FIGURE 13.2 **PROCEDURE TO OBTAIN A PATENT**

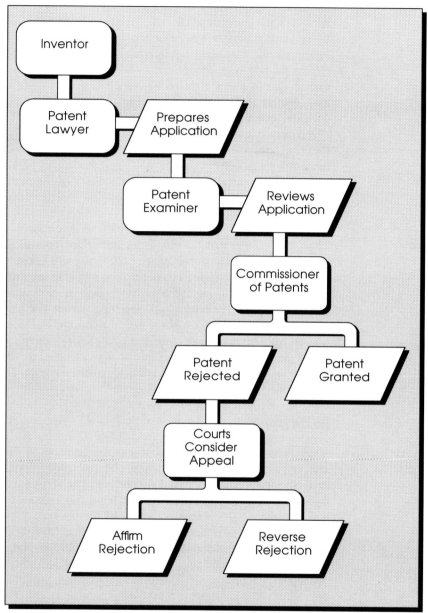

specifications must describe, in full, the invention, its operation, or use. Also, the specifications must detail the steps in the process or method of constructing, making, compounding, or using a machine, manufacture, or composition of matter.[10] In the case of a machine, the applicant must also furnish drawings of the invention.[11] Where the invention can be represented with a model, the inventor must furnish a model of convenient size and in correct proportion.[12]

The application is then reviewed by an examiner who works in the Patent Office. In the event the Commissioner is not satisfied that the applicant is entitled to a patent, then the application is refused.[13] Alternatively, when the application is approved and a patent granted, then the patentee has, by virtue of the patent, the exclusive right, privilege, and liberty of making, constructing, using, and selling the invention to others.[14] These exclusive rights exist for a period of seventeen years.[15] During this period, anyone who uses the invention without the patentee's consent commits an infringement. The patentee may then recover damages,[16] file an injunction against further infringement, or obtain an account, e.g., profits wrongfully gained by the patent infringer.[17]

Definition of Invention

A patent is granted for an invention. Therefore, it is important to understand what is meant by the term "invention". The *Patent Act* defines invention to mean "any new and useful art, process, machine, manufacture or composition of matter, or any new and useful improvement in any art, process, machine, manufacture or composition of matter."[18]

The Policy Reasons

The policy behind granting a patent for an invention is discussed in *Canadian Gypsum Co. Ltd. v. Gypsum, Lime & Alabastine Canada Ltd.* by Maclean J.:

> The design of the patent law is to reward those who make some substantial discovery or invention which adds to our knowledge and makes a step in advance in the useful arts. If there is no novelty there can of course be no inventive ingenuity; but if there is novelty in the sense required in the law of patents, it must be the product of original thought or inventive skill. [T]he inventive ingenuity necessary to support a valid patent may be found in the underlying idea, or in the practical application of that idea, or both.[19]

The Judicial Standard

The statutory definition of "invention" has obtained a judicial gloss. This means that the judges have added their own views to the statutory meaning. This has great importance because the difficulty of what is an invention in any given case vests the court with a considerable amount of discretion. Approaching the question of whether a person has invented something is heavily influenced by the judge's personal view of the degree of ingenuity reflected in the invention. As Fox has observed, "One of the difficulties is that there is no objective standard of invention."[20]

The ultimate decision is based on considerations other than purely legal ones. All the facts and circumstances bearing on the characteristics and quality present in the invention form the substance of the final decision. The concepts surrounding what is an "invention" are elusive and vague, and attempts at definition misleading.

Subject Matter of Patents

We have examined the complexity of the decision-making process that is used to determine whether an invention has been created. In this section, we will analyse the preliminary question of whether the subject matter of the invention falls within the scope of the *Patent Act*. As previously mentioned, an important distinction exists between a patent application for hardware such as a disk drive or printer, and computer software. Another way of expressing the distinction is between inventing a machine and a process that utilizes a machine. It should, however, be stated that it is common to secure patents for both machines and processes.

The Discovery

In the instance of a computer program, however, which uses a mathematical formula called an algorithm, a controversy has arisen as to whether the patent gives the inventor patent over a scientific principle or formula. It is clear that these fall outside the subject matter of what is patentable. Thus, Newton could not have obtained a patent on his principle of gravity. The same would have held true for Einstein's theory of relativity. The way in which inventors have attempted to avoid this characterization has been to apply for a process patent rather than a patent of the software itself. It is clear that a process is patentable. The process may lead to a more efficient or less costly means of production; it may lead to a useful result or a new product. The main issue is whether a process that is based on the use of a software program, and the algorithms in that program, is an application of a mathematical formulae rather than a monopoly by the inventor on the formulae.

In *Schlumberger Canada Ltd. v. Commissioner of Patents*,[21] the plaintiff claimed that the invention was for a computer program used to determine the presence of oil and gas deposits by drilling companies. Prior to the development of the program, instruments were passed up and down boreholes to measure the solid characteristics. This method, however, was not always reliable. The process disclosed in the patent application involved a method of transmitting the measurements to a computer programmed according to a mathematical formula and resulted in the creation of charts, graphs, or tables of figures.

The Federal Court of Appeal held that no patent claim would be upheld on the grounds that a new application had been discovered by using a computer to perform mathematical calculations. The very purpose of computers is to do precisely this type of task. What was new wasn't the use of the computer but the mathematical calculations themselves. It is well established that a mathematical formula or a series of purely mental operations cannot be patented if carried out by a person. The court said that the same rule applied where the mathematical formulae are performed by a computer instead of a person.

The view of the court was that the applicants were trying the equivalent of patenting $E = mc^2$. The new technology was seen as a smokescreen to gain a monopoly on a mathematical formula. The major difficulty in obtaining patents on computer software are the courts' equation of algorithms with mathematical laws. There is some irony that the software, without which a patented computer is useless, has met with considerable opposition as a subject matter for patent law. Legal protection is important to protect the capital investment of the inventor. In the United States, it has been said that "The typical cost of developing most software programs . . . range between \$50 000 and \$500 000, with an average cost of about \$200 000."[22]

It is clear that a process can be patented under Canadian law. Therefore, it would appear that a software program using algorithms to solve problems or make calculations should be patentable. This analysis, however, falls apart once the algorithm is given a definition that limits it to a procedure to solve mathematical problems. Such a definition automatically puts the software program into the unpatentable category of "mere scientific principle or abstract theorem". The basic legal question, still not completely resolved in patent law, is: What is the nature of a computer software program?

A problem arises where the patent application is forced to concede that the only novel feature of the invention is a mathematical formula. For example, in *Schlumberger Canada Ltd.*, the computer program made calculations about oil and gas deposits based on a mathematical formula. Remove that mathematical formula and the software program is useless. A similar approach was adopted by the United States Supreme Court in *Parker v. Flook*[23] where a computer program had been designed to provide a process used in the catalytic chemical conversion of hydrocarbons. As in *Schlumberger Canada Ltd.*, once the Court in *Flook* held that the mathematical algorithm, which was the only novel element in the program, was excluded as non-patentable, the claim for a patent was lost.

The major breakthrough in the United States came with the Supreme Court decision of *Diamond v. Diehr*.[24] In that case, a computer program was used in the process for moulding synthetic rubber. The prior art of moulding raw, uncured synthetic rubber in a final product was accomplished by using a formula called the Arrhenius Equation. The problem in the curing stage, however, was regulating the temperature on a continuous basis. The computer program solved the problem by recalculating, throughout the moulding stage, the cure time based on the Arrhenius Equation. The central problem was whether granting a patent for the process would give the inventor a monopoly over the mathematical formula represented by the Arrhenius Equation. The court, in upholding the patentability of the process, held that the monopoly extended only in so far as to exclude another from using the Arrhenius Equation *and* all the other steps in the process.

The significance of the *Diamond* decision is to establish patentability of a process that used a computer program. The decision, however, stopped short of granting a patent for the computer program itself. Moreover, the decision distinguished a claim to patent a formula of calculation from a claim to a patented process that encompasses such a formula of calculation. This has particular importance for revising the way of dealing with algorithms in a patent claim for a computer software program.

The lesson is that a software program must be viewed as involving the application of a mathematical formula, and as forming an integral part of an industrial process. Once that it is established, the function of the patent is not to pre-empt others from using the algorithms, and the perceived problem in cases such as *Schlumberger Canada Ltd.* can be avoided. The patent of a software program per se remains unlikely. In each instance where an industrial process is the subject of a patent application, a factual determination must be made of all the circumstances in order to determine whether or not the patent has narrowly confined the patentee's use of the software algorithms to the specific process. The limitation on use requires the patentee to show that the infringer has used *both* the algorithm and all of the other steps in the patented process. This leaves open the door for other software inventors to use the algorithms alone. Also, it leaves it open for others to use only the software program without infringing the patentee's process patent.

Novelty

An essential aspect of patentability is novelty. The invention must be new. The issue of novelty is one of fact. This factual inquiry has several components. Novelty may be proved by the success of the inventor in selling the product. For instance, Rinehart develops a 1200 baud modem, and after being introduced onto the market, the modem becomes extremely popular with the public. The fact of this success is an indication of the novelty of the device. The assumption is that if the product is new, then there will be a ready market for it.

Another indication of novelty is knowledge of the subject matter of the invention. It is a well-established principle of patent law that if the subject matter is known by others, then it is not "new" and lacks the novelty required to obtain a patent. There are two related questions: i) whether the knowledge of the subject matter was prior to the claimed invention; and ii) how extensively must this knowledge have been disseminated. The initial inquiry is a factual determination concerning whether the inventor was truly first in making the invention. The second inquiry is more complicated. It requires a determination as to who amongst the general population knew about the subject matter prior to the inventor. Certainly, evidence that the modem was being manufactured by another company would mean Rinehart's modem was not novel. Similarly, if the modem, though not produced and used, had been described in a trade or academic journal, the modem would not be new.

There is, however, a third possibility — that computer engineers knew about this particular type of program prior to the time that one of Rinehart's engineers invented it. So long as a sufficient number of people inside the computer business knew about the particulars of this modem, a patent would be denied on the basis of obviousness of the subject matter. The test, therefore, is not whether the general public had knowledge, but whether people within the trade or business knew of it.[25]

The rationale for novelty is simply that if knowledge is in the public domain then one person or company should not be granted a monopoly of the subject matter of that knowledge. The basis of patent law is to grant patents as a reward for the creation of new and novel articles and processes. Without novelty there can be no invention.

Utility

Utility is closely linked with the earlier concepts of novelty and invention. As is the instance with novelty, the issue of whether the invention has utility is a question of fact. The essence of utility is the usefulness of the invention. For instance, does the Rinehart modem allow computer users to transmit and receive information over telephone lines? If it does, then the modem has a positive benefit and therefore utility. On the other hand, if the modem failed to allow the user to receive information from another computer, then it would not be useful. Similarly, if the modem had a number of "bugs" that made it highly unreliable, and therefore useless, it would again lack utility. An indicator of utility, as well as novelty, is the commercial success of the product.

Problems for Discussion

1. On what grounds have the courts been unwilling to hold that computer software is a proper subject matter for a patentable invention?

2. Why is commercial success of a product or article good evidence of novelty and utility?

3. What procedures are required for an applicant to obtain a patent in Canada?

4. Discuss the policy grounds for granting an inventor a monopoly over the invention. Do these same policy reasons apply to computer software?

5. In what way has the judicial definition of algorithms influenced the courts in deciding the issue of patentability of computer software?

6. In light of the Federal Court of Appeal decision in *Schlumberger Canada Ltd.*, does it remain open for the Canadian courts to follow the result reached by the United States Supreme Court in *Diamond v. Diehr*?

7. As a computer software program may be copyrighted, is the denial of patent protection a disincentive to the development of new software?

8. Chief Justice Burger in *Diamond v. Chakrabarty*, in upholding the patentability of genetically modified micro-organisms observed:

> The briefs present a gruesome parade of horribles. Scientists, among them Nobel laureates, are quoted suggesting that genetic research may pose a serious threat to the human race, or, at the very least, that the dangers are far too substantial to permit such research to proceed apace at this time. We are told that genetic research and related technological developments may spread pollution and disease, that it may result in a loss of genetic diversity, and that its practice may tend to depreciate the value of human life. These arguments are forcefully, even passionately presented; they remind us that, at the present time, human ingenuity seems unable to control fully the forces that it creates — that, with Hamlet, it is sometimes better "to bear those ills we have than fly to others that we know not of."

> It is argued that this Court should weigh these potential hazards in considering whether respondent's invention is patentable subject matter under s. 101. We disagree. The grant or denial of patents on micro-organisms is not likely to put an end to genetic research or to its attendant risks. The large amount of research that has already occurred when no researcher had sure knowledge that patent protection would be available suggests that legislative or judicial fiat as to patentability will not deter the scientific mind from probing into the unknown any more than Canute could command the tides. Whether respondent's claims are patentable may determine whether research efforts are accelerated by the hope of reward or slowed by want of incentives, but that is all. Ibid., at 200.

Discuss the consequences of such patent decisions on moral, social, economic, and political questions raised by the new technology. Do you agree with the assumption made by Chief Justice Burger?

Chapter 13 Notes

1. R.S., c. 203.
2. 206 U.S.P.Q. 193 (1980).
3. See Hayhurst, "Patenting Life", (1980-81) 5 *Can.Bus.L.J.* 19, 34.
4. Section 4(2).
5. Section 17.
6. Section 15.
7. Section 28(1).
8. Section 28(2).
9. Section 34.
10. Section 36(1).
11. Section 39(1).
12. Section 40(1).
13. Section 42.
14. Section 46.
15. Section 48.
16. Section 57(1).
17. Section 59(1).
18. Section 2.
19. (1931) Ex.C.R. 180, 187.
20. See, Fox, *Canadian Patent Law and Practice*, 4th Ed. 1969.
21. (1981) 56 C.P.R.(2d) 204 (Fed.C.A.).
22. Note, "The Policy Implications of Granting Patent Protection to Computer Software: An Economic Analysis", (1984) 37 *Vanderbilt Law Review* 147, 152.
23. 437 U.S. 584 (1978).
24. 450 U.S. 175 (1981).
25. See Fox, *supra* note 20, at 104.

14 TRADE SECRETS AND CONFIDENTIAL INFORMATION

Introduction

An essential goal of any business is to obtain a competitive advantage over others in the same marketplace. One way of meeting this goal is to create or discover some novel idea, process, or formula that can be incorporated into an existing or new product. By keeping secret the basis for the improved or new product, the company has a competitive edge that will exist until others "discover" the secret or expend time and money to duplicate the secret.

The law of trade secrets furthers this basic commercial goal. Others are prevented from taking the secret as a "shortcut" to gain a free ride on the expenditure, talent, creativity, and money of the secret holder. The key element at work is that of secrecy. We start this chapter with several basic working premises: i) certain commercial and industrial secrets are protected; ii) the subject matter of the secret confers some competitive advantage on the holder; and iii) such secrets have economic or commercial value, and their protection stimulates innovative possibilities in both the holder and third parties.

Defining Trade Secrets

The limitations of patent and copyright law make the law of trade secrets of great importance in protecting "inventions of the mind". As the words "trade secrets" and "confidential information" suggest, the courts will protect certain commercial or industrial ideas or processes that have been communicated to another in confidential circumstances. Unlike the law of patents and copyright, which is governed by statute, the law of trade secrets was created by the courts. If a person or company takes the idea or process in breach of confidence, they will be liable to pay compensation, account for profits, or be enjoined from further use.

Types of Secrets Covered

The types of commercial and industrial secrets governed by the law of trade secrets have been described as follows:[1]

> The subject-matter capable of protection may be an industrial secret like a secret machine, process, or formula, or it may be industrial know-how (an increasingly important ancillary of patented inventions); it may be information of any sort; it may be an idea of a scientific nature, or of a literary nature (such as the plot of a story or the theme of a television series), or it may be a slogan or suggestion for a method of advertising; lastly, the subject matter may be the product of work or expenditure of money, or of trial and error, or the expenditure of time.

Patents and Copyright Compared

Although a copyright protects an original expression of an idea, a trade secret may encompass an idea itself. A member of Rinehart's research and development department has an idea for a disk operating system in a central processor that would handle a new and novel type of instruction method. The idea is not fully developed; but the basis of the idea, which the engineer has worked on for several months, appears to hold commercial promise for the company. At this juncture, the law of trade secrets provides protection of the engineer's idea. Even after the idea is fully developed, it may be in Rinehart's interest to retain its secrecy and preserve the market advantage in the manufacture and sale of such a disk operating system.

Many of these ideas or processes might entitle the creator to either copyright or patent protection. This form of protection, however, is not based on secrecy. Indeed, a patent requires the public disclosure of the process. Once disclosed, others may discover ways to explore the basic idea without infringing the patent. Also, as we discussed in Chapter 13, the requirements of patentability are stringent. Thus, the same standards of novelty and uniqueness do not apply to a trade secret. Although Rinehart may obtain a patent for the new disk operating system, the public disclosure of the new system may significantly cut down the lead time required by other software manufacturers to produce a competitive product.

Even assuming that the requirements needed to obtain a patent exist, there are other reasons to seek protection in the law of trade secrets. For example, the duration of the patent, once acquired, is seventeen years. A trade secret does not have a similar time limitation. The law of trade secrets provides a form of non-statutory protection, which, in many instances, may be as effective as a patent without the same risks of public disclosure.

Establishing a *Prima Facie* Trade Secrets Case

The burden of proof on the plaintiff in a trade secrets case requires the satisfaction of the following elements:[2] i) the information communicated to the defendant must have a quality of confidence attached to it; ii) the circumstances of the communication must imply an obligation of confidence on the defendant's use of the information; iii) the defendant must have made an unauthorized use of the information to the detriment of the plaintiff; and iv) the defendant lacks any excuse for his/her action.

The case of *Coco v. A.N. Clark (Engineers) Ltd.*[3] is a good illustration of how the elements of trade secrets cases are applied. The plaintiff designed a moped and began negotiations to sell or license his design for the machine to the defendants. He provided the defendant company with a considerable amount of information, drawings, and other materials about the moped. An agreement was never reached between the parties. Later, the defendant began to produce a moped with the same type of piston and carburetor as the plaintiff's machine. The defendant company employed thirty-five or forty employees to manufacture the moped. The plaintiff, on the other hand, had not begun to manufacture his moped. He requested an injunction to restrain the defendant from further production of the moped until a trial on the merits of the case was held.

The plaintiff's case rested upon the misuse of confidential information

FIGURE 14.1 **TRADE SECRET ACTION**

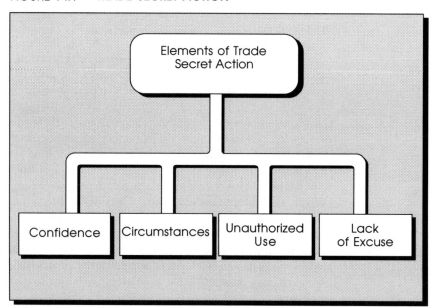

provided to the defendant company during the aborted negotiations. Megarry J. denied the plaintiff request to stop the defendants from making their moped. The plaintiff, however, did not leave the court empty-handed. The defendants were ordered to keep an account of the royalties based on the amount of royalties that they had offered to the plaintiff during the negotiations. After a full trial, on the merits of the plaintiff's claim, the amount owed was based on the defendants' wrongful use of the plaintiff's confidential information.

Megarry J.'s judgment offers an important insight into the nature of the remedy available to protect the unauthorized taking of a trade secret. Considerable emphasis was placed on the fact that i) the trade secret was commercial in nature; ii) the plaintiff had previously negotiated to sell the secret to the defendants; iii) the defendants' conduct, though wrong in law, was not in bad faith or morally unacceptable; and iv) the plaintiff had not commercially exploited his secret and the defendants had begun production. Thus, a plaintiff who has not been deprived of a competitive edge in his/her own production and manufacture of the product incorporating the secret is treated in a different way from the plaintiff who is a true competitive rival.

The Element of Secrecy

An essential requirement for trade secret protection is that the subject matter of the trade secret has not been disclosed to the public. What

FIGURE 14.2   **SECRECY**

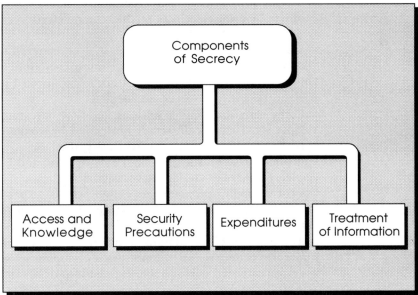

factors are relevant in determining whether the party claiming a trade secret has complied with the secrecy element? An outline of the types of considerations that the courts find relevant includes:[4]

(1) the extent to which the information is known outside the business; (2) the extent to which it is known by employees and others involved in the business; (3) the extent of measures taken to guard the secrecy of the information; (4) the value of the information to the holder of the secret, and to his competitors; (5) the amount of effort or money expended in developing the information; (6) the ease or difficulty with which the information can be properly acquired or duplicated by others; and (7) whether the holder of the secret and the taker treat the information as secret.

What is being kept secret must have an element of novelty (though less than that required for a patent), and the holder must have expended effort and money to develop the subject matter. In some instances, the trade secret may combine public and confidential information. Although the recipient of the combined information is entitled to exploit the public information, he/she must be careful to segregate the public from the private. In *Seager v. Copydex*,[5] Lord Denning, M.R. observed:

When the information is mixed, being partly public and partly private, then the recipient must take special care to use only the material which is in the public domain. He should go to the public source and get it: or, at any rate, not be in a better position than if he had gone to the public source. He should not get a start over others by using information which he received in confidence.

On the issue of the novelty of the subject matter, it has been said that "the mere simplicity of an idea does not prevent it being confidential."[6] On the other hand, "equity ought not to be invoked merely to protect trivial tittle-tattle, however confidential."[7]

In the case of computer software and time-operating systems, the developer may have trade secret protection by combining publicly disclosed concepts. The courts recognize that the specific engineering contained in a software system varies in logic and coherence, speed, accuracy, cost, and commercial feasibility.

Most computer programmers employ known expertise and concepts in developing software, but the novel combination of skills and concepts entitles the program to trade secret protection. The software program and design is far removed from the idle tittle-tattle referred to by Megarry J. Moreover, there is little doubt that developing software programs or systems requires a considerable expenditure of labour and money.

Obtaining Trade Secret Protection

The two major rationales for granting trade secret protection are: i) establishing acceptable conduct in the relationship between business people; and ii) encouraging the economic development of novel ideas and inventions. The law complements important economic considerations. Trade secrets, in other words, do not exist in a legal vacuum. Instead, certain policies are promoted by the enforcement of trade secrets. The consequence of trade secrets is to reward creativity and innovation. This is done by defining the perimeters of business rivalry and protecting the commercial "head start" secured by the secret holder.

Fair Dealing in Commerce

It should be remembered that in most trade secret cases the courts are exercising equitable jurisdiction. This results from the common request by the secret holder for an injunction (an equitable remedy). The tradition of equity is one of greater flexibility in concepts and principles, and more emphasis on the nature of each party's conduct.

Equity is based on broad notions of good faith, good conscience, and fair conduct. In many cases, the holder of the trade secret has disclosed the secret in confidence to the recipient during the course of some commercial dealing to sell or license the subject matter of the secret.

FIGURE 14.3   **BUSINESS JUSTIFICATION FOR TRADE SECRET PROTECTION**

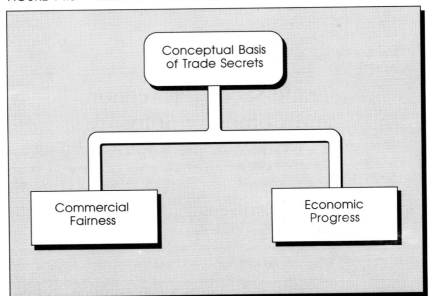

Where the recipient, either consciously or unconsciously, after the negotiations have failed to produce a contract between the parties, uses the subject matter of the secret for his/her own benefit, he/she has taken an unfair advantage. The law of trade secrets encourages honesty and fair dealing by imposing liability on the recipient who uses the trade secret without the holder's consent and to his/her detriment.

Economic Development of Ideas and Inventions

Another way of obtaining trade secrets is through the use of industrial spying, espionage, or hiring away key employees who will divulge the secret. This type of conduct is a form of economic warfare. The cost of diverting funds to make businesses immune from these kinds of assaults reallocates scarce resources from research and development, and production. There are two adverse affects of this commercial misconduct in the computer software industry: i) there will be less software developed; and ii) the higher costs incurred for the software that is developed will be paid from the consumer's purse.

The law of trade secrets provides an important incentive for businesses and individuals to create new ideas and inventions. The products of this mental process are not dismissed simply because the inventor has not obtained copyright or a patent. These products increase our economic wealth and encourage fair competition in the marketplace. The inventor's head start — say, for a new software project idea — is protected. In the instance of the disk operating system for the new generation of central processors, the head start translates into a substantial market advantage over Rinehart's competitors. In time, the competitors may catch up; but, in the interval, Rinehart is allowed to enjoy the fruits of its innovative and secret idea.

Trade Secret Protection and Computer Software

The law of trade secrets has special importance to the computer software industry. As we have seen in Chapter 12, it is only recently that the courts have recognized that a copyright exists in a program object code. The new computer technology has created a degree of uncertainty for lawyers and judges. The use of trade secrets to protect computer software and other products has little express guidance from the Canadian courts. In principle, however, the computer industry will likely obtain the benefits from this area of law. Two circumstances that require analysis are: i) the taking of confidential information from a third party to make software, data bases, or networking systems; and ii) the in-house measures necessary to protect the company's own secrets.

The Taking of Confidential Information

The following illustration shows the nature of the problem when a computer company unsuccessfully attempts to buy know-how or confidential information from another.

Illustration   Dennis Hyde, a thirty-six-year-old computer programmer, has created a number of highly successful programs and has written two books on computer software. He approaches Rinehart Ltd. with a novel idea to place "locks" into the software that would prevent unauthorized copying of software. As software piracy presents a significant loss of revenue, and Rinehart Ltd. has been unsuccessful in developing a fool-proof lock itself, it is keenly interested in Mr. Hyde's idea. During the course of the negotiations, which last for a period of four months, Mr. Hyde discloses to Ms. Bach and to the company's Chief Engineer, Mr. Miller, a locking system that he calls "MasterSafe". Mr. Hyde's idea is neither copyrighted nor patented. In order to test Mr. Hyde's theory, Rinehart allows him access to its mainframe for a three-week period. At the end of this period, Mr. Hyde perfects the "MasterSafe" program. But the negotiations for the sale of the rights to the program break down.

After the negotiations end, Mr. Miller makes alterations to the "MasterSafe" program, and Rinehart renames the program "LockSafe". Rinehart claims copyright for "LockSafe". Rinehart inserts the program in its own software and begins negotiating the licensing of the program to other software manufacturers. Mr. Hyde reads about Rinehart's "LockSafe" software, and several weeks later files an action for an injunction and damages against Rinehart on the grounds it has taken his idea in breach of confidence. Mr. Hyde's "MasterSafe" program has not been commercially produced at the time of the trial.

In this case, a court would likely hold that Mr. Hyde gave Mr. Miller and Ms. Bach information about "MasterSafe" in confidence. He had not made a public disclosure of the information at any time, and the only way that he would have disclosed this information was to a potential buyer. Weight would also be given to the fact that Rinehart had previously attempted to invent its own lock system but had failed. Even though Mr. Miller might testify that he had independently invented a lock system for Rinehart, a court would likely reject this explanation. The coincidences are too strong. On these facts, Mr. Hyde would probably prove that Rinehart had taken an unfair advantage by taking information disclosed during the course of a business negotiation. There is authority that Rinehart is liable to pay a fair royalty for the use of the "LockSafe". At the same time, Mr. Hyde would not be entitled to an injunction to stop Rinehart from producing, distributing, and licensing the software.[8]

In-House Measures to Protect Information and Trade Secrets

Negotiations with "off-the-street programmers" present a particular problem of how a company can protect itself against allegations of trade secret abuse. A more pressing problem, however, is what types of precautions Rinehart Ltd. must take to preserve the necessary secrecy required to claim trade secret protection for programs, formula, patterns, devices, or compilations. The misappropriation of such subject matter by others can eliminate any head start achieved by Rinehart for a particular type of software program. Also, there may be business information that the company seeks to protect.

Unlike the trade secret, business information is often connected with a single transaction. For example, Rinehart may have made a sealed bid for a Marine Weather Satellite software system. The bid, in the hands of a competitor, could ruin Rinehart's chance of obtaining the contract. Thus, secrecy is crucial, and the law permits protection of this type of business information. An ex-employee of Rinehart, with this specific business information could be prevented from disclosing it to his/her new employer. The new employer could be similarly restrained from using such information to the detriment of Rinehart.

General employment information can be used by an ex-employee. For example, Rinehart could not stop a former employee from putting to use his/her general knowledge of software distribution in Canada or the marketing techniques used to sell software, from implementing improvements to the new employer's security system. Such information is generic to the software industry and not specific to Rinehart. The distinction between specific and generic business information is not always as easy to discern. The prudent course for a software manufacturer is to adopt an in-house security system that protects both trade secrets and business information.

In developing in-house security measures, two considerations should be borne in mind: i) what minimal amount of secrecy is required to gain advantage of trade secret protection; and ii) what maximum allocation of resources should be spent, above the minimal amount required by law, to ensure that confidential information is not disclosed to those outside the company. In general, the law of trade secrets requires a degree of secrecy that is reasonable under the circumstances. The burden is to show that reasonable precautions were undertaken to protect the secret or business information.[9] The law does not require total secrecy. The secret is protected even though the information is not kept in a military citadel or fortresslike state.

The second consideration is a business rather than a legal one. The company must balance the risk of an employee or others obtaining confidential information that may be passed on against the cost of preventing that risk. Although trade secrets action represents a deterrent to this type of activity by employees or third parties, it obviously will not prevent the "seepage" completely. It is probably not cost-effective to create a "fortress" that would exclude all possible risks. But certain practical steps are taken in the computer industry to protect trade secrets, and, arguably, a number of these precautions exceed what is required to guard trade secrets in Canadian law.

Illustration   In *Telex Corp v. I.B.M. Corp.*,[10] Telex hired away certain key IBM employees. These ex-IBM employees provided their new employer with trade secrets about a computer control unit. It had taken a team of IBM engineers six years to develop the computer control unit. Telex, using IBM's trade secrets, developed a competing computer control unit in eighteen months. The court held that Telex was liable to pay IBM $10 000 000 for the value of the trade secrets that it had misappropriated.

How had IBM preserved the secrecy of its trade secrets concerning the computer control unit? First, each of the employees had been required to sign an "Employee Confidential Information and Invention Agreement" at the beginning of his/her employment. In this agreement, each employee promised not to disclose the company's trade secrets. Moreover, at the termination of their employment with IBM, the employees had been reminded of their duty to maintain secrecy about confidential and trade secrets that they had learned during the course of their employment. Second, beyond the contractual obligations placed on employees, IBM had created a number of internal security systems. Only authorized employees were given access to areas where the confidential and trade secrets were kept. These doors had magnetic locks. Beyond the limited access rooms and locks, IBM used guards, television cameras, and sensors. The main object of this security program was to strictly control the physical premises where employees worked with secret and sensitive information.

It is also common for software employees to wear ID badges. Care is often taken to limit employees' access to special areas. Sometimes this is done by providing a monitored sign-in and sign-out procedure prior to entering or leaving a restricted area. Inside these special work areas, there are additional procedures. Documents or programs may be numbered. Earlier copies of the materials are destroyed to prevent their reproduction. Highly valued material can only be accessed by passwords known to a few employees. Also, such material may be encrypted. To prevent copying of software, there may be built-in self-destruct features, or time fuses. The first destroys the software when an attempt is made to copy it and the second renders the program useless without a regular coded update. The new technology has created its own system and procedures for protection against unlocking secrets contained within.

Where copying is permitted, it is usually carefully controlled. The confidential information or trade secrets may be divided in different parts with no one employee having access to the whole process or formula. In other words, the company adopts a "need to know" basis for purposes of protecting trade secrets.

These controls, to some degree, are widely used in the software industry. In combination, the number of types of controls may appear to create a highly policed environment. The use of such precautions is a reflection of the nature of the products developed and sold by computer companies. The basis of computer software is the mental labour of highly skilled and knowledgeable employees. Where the thing of major economic value can be carried away inside the head of an employee or another party, the workplace is designed to place barriers to prevent that event.

Ultimately, however, the software computer company licenses or sells its products to consumers. Is it possible for the company to maintain trade secret protection where thousands of units of the software is sold? How does Rinehart enter into a confidential relationship with thousands of its word processing software users? These are two of the questions that Canadian law has yet to answer definitely. There is American authority that suggests that non-disclosure clauses in the consumer licence agreement contained with the software will not deprive the manufacturer from claiming trade secret protection. The fact that the thousands who have "entered" the contract have access to the secret does not mean that the company has made a public disclosure of the secret material. In each case, it is a question of fact whether or not the company has taken adequate precautions to protect confidential information and trade secrets. As relative secrecy, rather than total secrecy, is the test, even mass-marketed software, licensed on condition of confidence, is not automatically excluded.

Problems for Discussion

1. Distinguish between trade secrets and copyrights and patents.

2. What elements are required to establish a prima facia trade secrets action?

3. What advantages would Rinehart Ltd. obtain in protecting an "idea" with the law of trade secrets?

4. What policies are the law of trade secrets designed to promote?

5. What remedies are available to the holder of the trade secret against another who wrongfully uses the secret?

6. How does the holder of a trade secret discharge his/her burden of proof that adequate precautions were taken to protect the trade secret?

Chapter 14 Notes

1. A.E. Turner, *The Law of Trade Secrets*, (1962), p. 4.
2. See *Coco v. A.N. Clark (Engineers) Ltd.*, (1969) R.P.C. 41, 47 (Ch.Div.).
3. Ibid.
4. Vaver, *Civil Liability for Taking or Using Trade Secrets in Canada*, (1981) 5 *Can.Bus.L.J.* 253, 255-56.
5. (1967) 1 W.L.R. 923, 931 (C.A.).
6. *Coco v. A.N. Clark (Engineers) Ltd.*, *supra*, note 2, p. 48.
7. Ibid., p. 49.
8. See *Seager v. Copydex Ltd.*, *supra*, note 5.
9. See *Franchi v. Franchi*, (1967) R.P.C. 149 (Ch.).
10. 510 F.2d 894 (10th Cir. 1975).

Part V

COMMERCIAL
TRANSACTIONS

15 INTRODUCTION TO THE LAW OF SALES

Background Considerations to the Law

Commercial transactions cover a wide variety of transactions in the business environment. The source of law is found in a patchwork of statutes and common law cases (Figure 15.1). Isolating commercial transactions to one specific category, that is, the sale of goods, requires an understanding of the provincial *Sale of Goods Act*. All Canadian provinces and territories have such legislation in force, each drawing substantially from one central source: the 1893 English *Sale of Goods Act*. Thus, there is a uniformity amongst the provincial legislation. For purposes of analysis, the British Columbia *Sale of Goods Act*[1] will be used to examine the impact of the legislation on contracts made by Rinehart.

It is important to understand that the English legislation incorporated many of the judicial doctrines from the nineteenth century. Since then, there have been significant changes in attitudes. Provincial legislatures have a number of other new statutes, including Consumer Protection legislation. Judicially evolved doctrines, including unconscionability, have had an important impact in the traditional area of sale of goods. New technologies, including computers, software, and telecommunications, have challenged the courts to apply nineteenth-century-inspired legislation in a creative and novel fashion. Nonetheless, these changes have complicated the application of *Sale of Goods Act* legislation.

The Concept of Sale

The sale of goods is founded on the existence of a contract. The principles of contract law discussed in Chapters 1 through 8 are, in general, applicable to a sales contract. The main distinction between a sale and other forms of contract is the statutory rules that supplement, modify, or codify rules contained in the common law cases. As the statutory provisions are based upon rules used to sell goods that were widely used

FIGURE 15.1   **COMMERCIAL LAW**

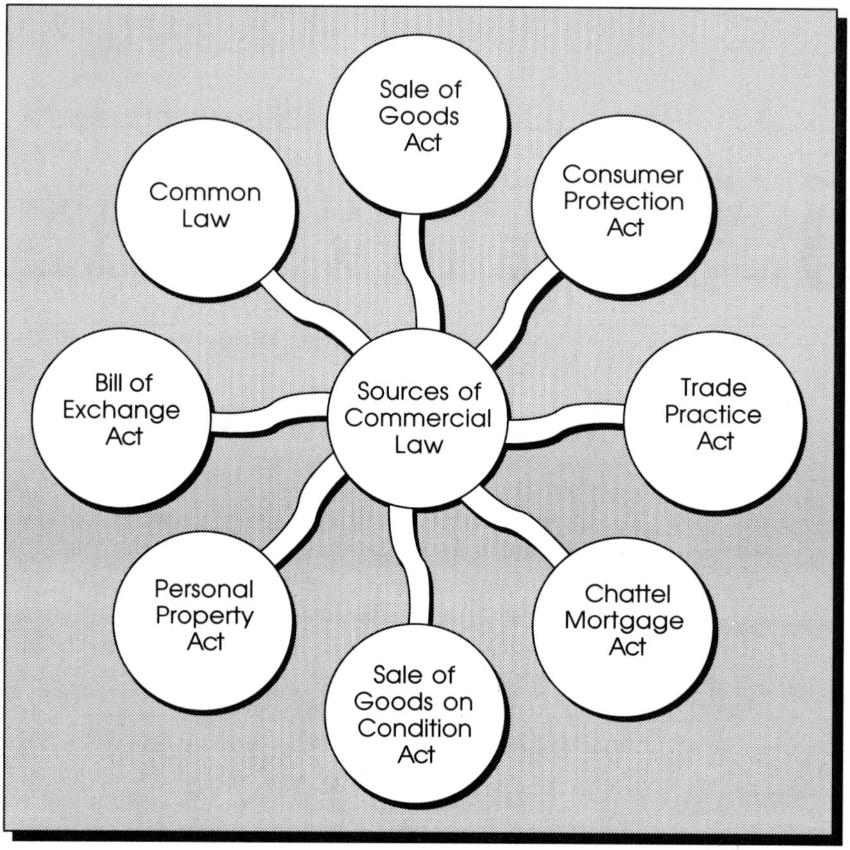

Sale of
Goods
Act

Common
Law

Consumer
Protection
Act

Bill of
Exchange
Act

Sources of
Commercial
Law

Trade
Practice
Act

Personal
Property
Act

Chattel
Mortgage
Act

Sale of
Goods on
Condition
Act

in England at the turn of the nineteenth century, it is not surprising that modern-day courts have had some conceptual difficulty in determining whether, or to what extent, the legislation applies to computer software.

Before addressing the specific problem of computer software as "goods" under the *Sale of Goods Act*, we will consider the fundamental concept of "sale". The starting point is the statutory definition of a contract of sale of goods as "a contract whereby the seller transfers or agrees to transfer the property in the goods to the buyer for a money consideration, called the price."[2] The nature of such a contract includes a transaction between one part owner and another.[3] The contract may be either absolute or conditional.[4] An important distinction also rests upon the *timing* of the passage of the property in the goods from the seller to the buyer. There are two possibilities: i) the property passes to the buyer upon the making of the contract, or ii) the property in the goods passes in the future or is subject to some condition.[5] In the first instance, there is a *contract of sale*. In the second instance, the contract is called *agreement to sell*.

The *Sale of Goods Act* applies to *both* commercial and consumer transactions. The legislation, however, does not apply to every commercial and consumer transaction: only to those transactions involving the sale of goods. The 1893 concept of a contract for sale of goods was tailored primarily for commercial transactions between businessmen of equal bargaining power. Nearly one hundred years later, this assumption is open to challenge. Consumer transactions for the sale of goods have significant problems such as unconscionability (Chapter 4) and, not surprisingly, the *Sale of Goods Act* provides no guidance for resolving many of these problems. Modern legislation such as the British Columbia *Consumer Protection Act, 1967*,[6] the *Trade Practice Act*,[7] sections of the *Chattel Mortgage Act*,[8] and the *Sale of Goods on Condition Act*[9] have introduced provisions that protect buyers in consumer transactions. This legislation indicates that the 1893 concept of equality of bargaining power between all sellers and buyers is absent in most consumer transactions.

Standard form contracts (Chapter 8), often drafted by sellers, may have terms that operate unfairly or harshly on the buyer who has no choice but to accept the contract or forego the goods. In modern times, the courts have evolved equitable doctrines such as undue influence, unconscionability, duress, and misrepresentation (Chapter 4) that apply to contracts for the sale of goods. Thus, the nature of a contract of sale requires an understanding of both the legislation and modern court-made doctrines. Our next step is to consider the types of transactions that are included and excluded from the legislation.

Transactions Included within the *Sale of Goods Act*

A contract falling within the *Sale of Goods Act* has four important elements: i) a sale; ii) of goods; iii) for a price; iv) in which the property in the goods passes to the buyer. Although each element in the formulation may cause problems of construction in a specific case — and has a body of judicially defined rules and exception — all four elements are essential before the *Act* is applicable to a contract.

Goods

The term "goods" is defined as including "all chattels personal, other than things in action and money, and includes emblements, industrial growing crops and things attached to or forming part of the land which are agreed to be severed before sale or under the contract of sale."[10] A problem of construction arises in certain cases, including those involving computer software, and whether the contract is for goods or for work and materials. If the contract is found to be for work and materials, then the *Sale of Goods Act* does not apply.

FIGURE 15.2 **THE SALES CONTRACT**

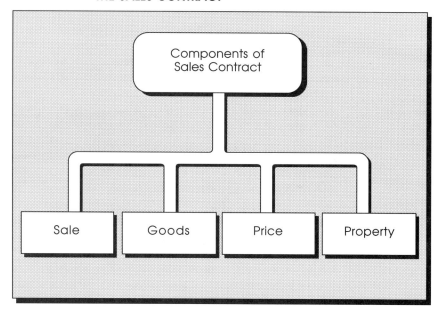

An illustration of this problem of distinguishing between "goods", and work and materials is found in the Australian decision of *Toby Constructions Products Pty. Ltd. v. Computa Bar (Sales) Pty. Ltd.*[11] In the *Toby* case, the defendant sold a combination of hardware and software to the plaintiff. The total price for the "equipment" was $14 390, with $2160 allocated as the cost of the software. The defendant-seller was obliged under the contract to install the equipment and train the plaintiff-buyer's employees in the use of the computer and software. The buyer, however, claimed loss from deficiencies in the computer system. Under the applicable *Sale of Goods Act* (which is similar to that in Canada), the buyer claimed that the seller had breached certain conditions and warranties implied by the *Act*. The buyer, on the other hand, defended on the grounds that the implied conditions and warranties did not apply as the contract was not a contract for the sale of goods but a contract for work to be done and materials provided.

THE NATURE OF THE THING SOLD

The legal question was whether the sale of a computer system, including both hardware and software, was a sale of "goods" within the meaning of the *Act*. The main problem, as we have seen in another context (Chapter 12), is how to characterize the nature of computer software. The

seller in *Toby* argued that the substance of the contract was "the manufacture of and transfer to the plaintiff (buyer) of the command mechanism in the nature of the software designed to make the hardware
work."[12]

What the buyer had contracted to buy was not "goods" but the skill
and labour of the seller to manufacture and transfer a command module.
The premise of this argument is that the intellectual property aspect of
software excludes its characterization as "goods". What is being sold is
the expertise and skill represented in the algorithms. The algorithms
form the program and then are put on a machine-readable medium such
as paper cards, magnetic cards, magnetic tape, discs, drums, or magnetic
bubbles.[13] The buyer, so the seller argued, is paying a price for the algorithms. He would not have paid the same price for the tangible, physical
medium that contains the algorithms or program.

SUBSTANCE OF THE CONTRACT TEST

The court rejected the seller's argument and applied the traditional test
from the English Court of Appeal case, *Robinson v. Graves.*[14]

Robinson adopted a "substance of the contract" test to distinguish
between a contract for the sale of goods and one for work to be done
and material provided.[15] For instance, where the substance of the contract
calls for a dentist to make a denture for sale to his/her patient, the
transaction is a sale of goods.[16] But where the substance of the contract
is the seller's skill and expertise, then the materials that pass to the buyer
become secondary. Such a contract is for work to be done and material
provided. The *Sale of Goods Act* does not apply.

The classic example is a contract made with an artist for an original
oil painting. Here the substance of the contract is the artist's skill and
expertise in making an original representation or likeness. The paint,
canvass, and frame are secondary considerations. The money is paid
primarily for the intangible nature of what the artist brings to the project:
his/her creativity, talent, experience, and training. One further matter of
importance is the uniqueness of what is purchased. Because it is not
something off an assembly line or fabricated on the factory floor for mass
distribution, the transaction might be distinguished from the sale of goods.

In the case of a computer software program, the question becomes
whether the software is like an original oil painting or mass prints of a
painting. The former characterization would mean that software sales
would fall outside the *Sale of Goods Act*, whereas the latter characterization would bring software within the legislation. In the *Toby* case, the
court applied the *Robinson* substance of the contract test, and held:[17]
"At the end of the day what weighs with me is that the system, software
included, whilst representing the fruits of much research and work, was
in current jargon off the shelf — in a sense mass produced."

COMMERCIAL NATURE OF GOODS

The commercial lawyers take the position that the true nature of software is not the algorithms but the embodiment of the program on some physical medium. This views a buyer of software as one purchasing the physical embodiment of the algorithms on, for example, a diskette. Of course, software programs may be transported to a buyer by other means, such as electronic data transmission, or may be incorporated into the hardware.

The commercial lawyer would have little hesitation in finding a contract for the sale of goods in these other methods of transporting the software from the seller to the buyer.

This approach de-emphasizes the intellectual property nature of the product, the means by which manufacturers attempt to protect the product, and the diverse number of software programs ranging in value from a few dollars to millions of dollars. There are two main policy arguments adopted by the commercial lawyers. First, by extending the *Sale of Goods Act* to software, there is one uniform and predictable body of law that will apply to all transactions. Second, the ultimate buyer may take advantage of the implied conditions and warranties that operate to protect consumers. The fact that the form of the transaction is normally a licence rather than a sale has not deterred the commercial lawyer from arguing the applicability of the *Act*. The argument is that the substance of the transaction is more important than the form.

INTELLECTUAL PROPERTY NATURE OF GOODS

The intellectual property approach to software is that the *Sale of Goods Act* should not apply indiscriminately to all sales of computer software. For example, in the Canadian context, it might be argued that a court should distinguish between the consumer transaction evidenced by the contract in Figure 1.4 and the commercial transaction evidenced by the contract in Figure 1.2. The first involves mass-produced software for a general market. The second requires Rinehart to develop a specific piece of software for a particular user. The main argument advanced to exclude the *Sale of Goods Act* is that the essence of what is being sold is intangible intellectual property rather than the diskette containing the algorithms, for example.

The controversy is over what the user of the software intends or expects to buy, and the way that that intention or expectation is formed by the retailers of software. In the case of mass-produced software, the retailer rather than the manufacturer or distributor is making the actual contract of sale with the buyer. What is the essence of what is being sold and bought? The intangible intellectual aspect of the product or the physical embodiment of the product? Part of this debate is over whether software is like recordings of music, films, or books. For instance, does the *Sale of Goods Act* apply to both the sale of a video recording of a film and a software computer program?

Illustration   The setting: A Saturday afternoon in Vancouver. Mr. Jones walks into Dunbar Electronics Ltd. The shop sells a variety of high technology products, including videos and computer software. Mr. Jones buys a video recording of the film *The Grey Fox*; five minutes later, he buys a copy of Rinehart's video game *Space Attack*. Mr. Jones buys both items for his own, or his family's or a friend's entertainment. Yet a distinction might be drawn based on the nature of what rights or remedies Mr. Jones acquires under the *Sale of Goods Act*.

Assume, for example, that Mr. Jones dislikes *The Grey Fox* and thinks that the acting is not very good: he would be unsuccessful in arguing breach of the seller's implied condition as to quality, (s. 18) even though the seller told Mr. Jones that he (the seller) had seen *The Grey Fox* and thought that it was an engaging and entertaining film. The seller made a similar statement about *Space Attack* to Mr. Jones. If, however, the video game or the film did not work or worked improperly, he would have an action. The fear of intellectual property lawyers is that if *Space Attack* were covered by the same implied condition, then the buyer would be entitled to relief not only for the defective diskette but also for failures in the operation of the algorithms or the program. Although there might be less objection to applying the *Sale of Goods Act* to *Space Attack*, the intellectual property lawyer would want the "E.E.C. Accounting System" program excluded.

What is the effect of excluding the *Sale of Goods Act* from all or some computer software sales? The seller's exposure to liability is reduced. Where the buyer has bought work and materials, rather than goods, there is no statutory warranty as to quality or suitability. Instead, the courts apply the reasonable care and skill test from the law of negligence.

In *Greaves & Co. v. Baynham Meikle*,[18] Lord Denning said:

> It seems to me that in the ordinary employment of a professional man, whether it is a medical man, a lawyer, or an accountant, an architect or an engineer, his duty is to use reasonable care and skill in the course of his employment. The extent of this duty was described by McNair J. in *Bolam v. Friern Hospital Management Committee*[19] approved by the Privy Council in *Chin Keow v. Government of Malaysia*:[20]
>
>> " . . . where you get a situation which involves the use of some special skill or competence, then the test as to whether there has been negligence or not is not the test of the man on the top of a Clapham omnibus, because he has not got this special skill. The test is the standard of the ordinary skilled man exercising and professing to have that special skill. A man need not possess the highest expert skill; it is well established law that it is sufficient if he exercises the ordinary skill of an ordinary competent man exercising that particular art."

There is an important and unresolved policy question involved in applying the *Sale of Goods Act* to computer software in general. Those who manufacture, distribute, and sell the software wish to consider their efforts as the exercise of a particular art. On the other side are the end users who want a higher form of protection found in the legislation.

There is *obiter dicta* in *Toby*, which indicates that, where the software is custom made for a buyer, it would not be "goods" within the meaning of the *Act*; this supports the intellectual property lawyer's view of the proper distinction to draw in applying the *Act*. It remains uncertain, however, in Canada, whether the courts will adopt the commercial lawyer's or intellectual property lawyer's view on software as "goods" under the *Act*.

The better view is that software intended for the mass consumer market is "goods", and that the buyer would have recourse to the conditions and warranties under the *Act*. Alternatively, even though the *Act* may not apply, there is case law that suggests that the courts would be willing to imply an equivalent common law warranty.[21]

Sale

There must be a "sale" of goods where the seller agrees to transfer the property in the goods to the buyer. Sale is defined by the *Act* to include "a bargain and sale as well as a sale and delivery." For example, a gift of goods is not covered by the *Act*. Similarly, a bailment of goods is not a sale. In a bailment, the bailor delivers possession (but does not transfer his/her property interest in the goods) to a bailee for a determinable period of time.

Illustration   A bailment occurs when Rinehart delivers an office computer terminal to another company that is in the business of repairing computers. Rinehart instructs the company to repair the faulty disk-drive, and both parties arrive at a price for this service. Although there is a contract between the parties for goods, and a price is agreed upon, there is no sale of goods. After the repairs are completed, the repairer will deliver the computer terminal to Rinehart. Assuming that the repairer's shop burns down and the computer is destroyed, in the absence of negligence, the loss would fall on Rinehart.

The advent of computer software presents a problem of construction where the contract provides for a licence of the software to the buyer. Is the licence such as the one in Figure 1.4 a "sale" within the meaning of the *Sale of Goods Act*? The consequence of excluding this transaction from the *Act* is to deprive the buyer from enforcing the implied-by-law warranties and conditions as to suitability for a particular purpose and merchantable quality. This issue appears not to have been decided in Canada. The main stumbling block is the requirement that the seller transfer title to the buyer; and the *Act* defines property to mean "the general property in goods, and not merely a special property."[22] Therefore, it is an open question in Canadian law whether a licence of a software program is a "sale" within the meaning of the *Sale of Goods Act.*

The better view, however, is that the sale of software under a licence agreement drafted by the manufacturer will not preclude the ultimate consumer who buys it from successfully arguing that the transaction was a sale. One justification for this conclusion is the expectation of the buyer. A buyer of software, who pays money and takes the software away, would consider the sale in the same manner as the sale of a television, a stereo, computer hardware, or the video recording of a film.

The expectation in buying software is not the same as that of renting a car, lawnmower, or VCR. The retailer, as well, treats the sale of software as an outright sale of the "goods" rather than a rental or some other limited form of property transfer. Assuming, for purposes of argument, that the transaction is not a sale within the meaning of the *Act*, it is likely that a Canadian court would draw upon the common law to imply similar conditions for merchantable quality and suitability for a particular purpose.

Property

As discussed above, there is an important distinction between a sale that passes the property interest to the buyer and a rental that merely passes possession of goods for a limited duration — or a particular purpose such as security for a loan. The *Act* does not apply to the rental transaction. Moreover, the *Act* is excluded from a bailment of property. Where the seller retains title to the property until the final installment of the purchase price, there has not been the necessary transfer of property to bring the transaction within the *Act*. Care must be taken to distinguish a sale on credit that is governed by the *Act* from chattel mortgages or financing agreements that provide for the vesting of the property in the goods, upon the borrowers default, in the lender. In each instance, the court considers the substance of the contract between the parties in order to ascertain the true intent either to transfer or withhold the property interest in the goods.

Price

Section 6(1) of the *Act* specifically defines the price in a contract of sale of goods as "money consideration". Where the transaction is a barter, the *Act* does not apply. Thus, where Jones agrees to work for a computer retail outlet for two weekends in exchange for two software programs, the "price" paid for the goods is not a "money consideration". Therefore, Jones, as the buyer, cannot enforce the statutory implied warranties for fitness against the seller. A mixed consideration, which is part in cash and part in exchange, however, is governed by the *Act*.

What if the contract is silent on the amount of money that the buyer is to pay for the goods? In that instance, Section 12(2) requires the buyer to pay a reasonable price. "What is a reasonable price is a question of fact dependent on the circumstances of each particular case." The *Act* leaves open whether the price is to be fixed as of the date of making the contract, the delivery date, the rejection date, or the resale by the seller date. The court, under the *Act*, has the discretion of fixing the price according to the particular facts and circumstances of each case.

Lastly, care must be taken in the situation where no price is contained in the contract. This may be evidence that the parties have not entered into a binding contract. It should be remembered that "consideration" is an important part of contract formation (Chapter 3). In each case, the court must first determine whether the parties have failed to agree upon a price or were simply silent on the issue. Failure to agree on a price will be fatal to the validity of the contract.

Property Interest in the Buyer

The Meaning of Property

The central purpose of the *Sale of Goods Act* is the transfer of the seller's general property interest in the goods to the buyer. The terms "property", "title", and "ownership" are often used interchangeably in this context. Section 1 of the *Act*, however, defines property to mean "the general

FIGURE 15.3 **TYPES OF PROPERTY**

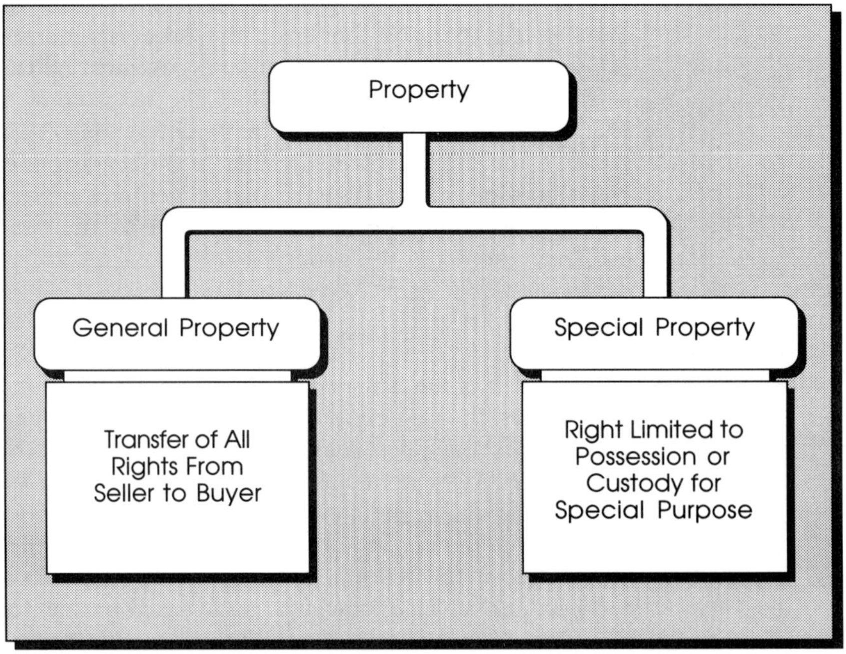

Property		
General Property		**Special Property**
Transfer of All Rights From Seller to Buyer		Right Limited to Possession or Custody for Special Purpose

property in the goods, and not merely a special property." The distinction between "general" and "special" property can be expressed as the difference between ownership and encumbrance. The encumbrancer, who, for example, holds the goods as a pledgee, does not have "ownership" of the goods, but merely retains possession to enforce the pledgor's payment obligation.

What is the effect of attaching the general property label to the goods? It allows us to distinguish between the buyer's personal remedies against the seller and his/her real or proprietary remedies against the goods bought from the seller. As will be discussed later, the proprietary remedy is of considerable importance when the goods have been damaged or destroyed or the seller has become insolvent.

Where the general property interest or ownership has been transferred to the buyer, although possession remains with the seller, the buyer has a proprietary or real action for the goods themselves. In the absence of such an ownership transfer, the buyer's remedy is a personal action for money against the seller. As we will discover in this section, the question of title is of vital significance in a number of different circumstances.

The Benefit of Passing Property to the Buyer

In certain instances, the benefit of passing title to the buyer operates in favour of the seller. The classic case is the destruction or other loss of the goods while in the seller's possession. Assuming that the conditions

FIGURE 15.4   **EFFECT OF PASSING ON BUYER'S RIGHTS**

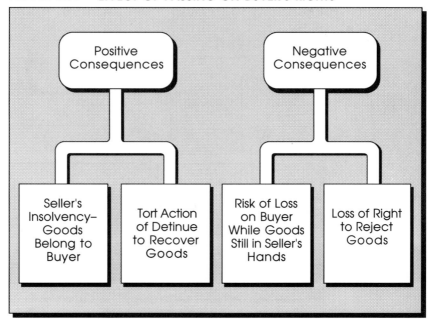

required to pass title have been met, the risk of loss falls on the buyer's shoulders. Thus, where the goods are destroyed by fire on the seller's premises, the question of whether title had passed to the buyer at the date of the loss is crucial in determining who bears the loss of the goods. The practical effect of the risk allocation is to give advance notice that, between the seller and buyer, the buyer is the one who has the economic interest to purchase insurance. It is not always an easy question, however, of when or whether title has been transferred to the buyer. Section 25 provides, in part, that: "Unless otherwise agreed, the goods remain at the seller's risk until the property in them is transferred to the buyer but when the property in them is transferred to the buyer the goods are at the buyer's risk, whether delivery has been made or not."

Should the seller become insolvent while still in possession of the goods, the transfer of title is of great importance to the buyer's rights in the bankruptcy proceeding. In the event that, prior to the seller's insolvency, the title had passed to the buyer, he/she is entitled to call for the goods. Conversely, where property had not passed, and the buyer had pre-paid the purchase price, his/her claim would be a *personal claim* for the money paid. As the buyer would likely be an unsecured creditor, the chance of recovering the full amount of the pre-payment would be remote.

Certain tort actions for the wrongful taking of the goods such as detinue or conversion turn upon the issue of chattel ownership.

FIGURE 15.5 **CONDITIONS FOR TRANSFER OF PROPERTY**

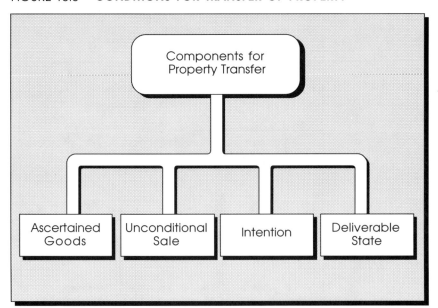

Illustration   Rinehart purchases three filing cabinets from Ajax Office Equipment Ltd. The contract of sale meets all the statutory conditions for the passage of title to Rinehart. While the cabinets are still in the possession of Ajax, a third party, Mr. Smith removes the cabinets without the consent or authorization of either the seller or buyer. He refused, after a request from both Rinehart and Ajax, to give the cabinets to Rinehart.

The remedies available to the buyer turn on whether property in the goods has passed to him/her by the seller. For example, the buyer forfeits his/her right to reject specific goods once property has passed. An exception applies, however, where there is an express or implied contract term preserving the right of rejection. The buyer — in most instances where property has passed — will find that his/her remedy is confined to an action based on breach of warranty and to the recovery of damages based on the breach.[23] The seller's remedy for recovery of the price of the goods also turns on whether the property in the goods has passed to the buyer.[24]

Conditions to the Transfer of Property

GENERAL RULES

The connecting factor in each of the above examples is the pivotal issue of whether the general property has passed from the seller to the buyer under a contract of sale of goods. The *Act* sets forth a number of preconditions to the transfer of the property in the goods from the seller to the buyer.

(1)   A contract for sale must be ascertained.[25]

(2)   The time of the transfer of property to the buyer turns on the intention of the parties.[26]

(3)   Intention is determined from the terms of the contract, the conduct of the parties, and the circumstances of the case.[27]

(4)   The specific goods under an unconditional contract for sale must be in a deliverable state.[28]

Each of these pre-conditions has been the source of considerable litigation. The effect of these rules is to allow the transfer of the property in the goods even though the buyer has not paid for them and the seller retains possession. The buyer becomes the legal owner at the moment that the contract is made. The applications of these rules will vary with the circumstances. An overriding element in many of the reported cases is the intention of the parties to pass the title to goods. The *Act*, therefore, rather than ignoring intention, makes it a central ingredient in the transfer of title formula.

In contrast, the U.C.C. s.2-401(3)(a)(b) — the American counterpart to the *Sale of Goods Act* — provides, in the absence of express agreement, for the passage of *title* in the goods occur when the seller makes actual delivery to the buyer. This eliminates the problem of title passing at the time the contract is made between the parties, and further dispenses with the technical requirements concerning whether the goods are ascertained, in a deliverable state or the contract is unconditional. It can be argued in Canada that similar reforms should be made in provincial sale of goods acts. To illustrate the highly technical problems found in applying the *Sale of Goods Act* provisions to the passage of property, we will consider the main conditions separately.

THE GOODS

The *Act* distinguishes between specific, unascertained, and future goods. The nature of the goods subject to the contract for sale is crucial to the passage of title to the buyer. Therefore, an important preliminary question upon reading the contract is what characterization should be made of the goods being sold.

Specific goods   Unless there are ascertained or specific goods at the time the contract for sale is made, property or title will not be transferred to the buyer. Even when the goods are specific and ascertained, the property in them is transferred only where the parties intended. Our first concern, then, is what is meant by specific goods. Section 1 defines specific goods to mean "goods identified and agreed on at the time a contract of sale is made." Courts have been required to develop rules of identification that apply at the *time the contract of sale is made*.

In *Kursell v. Timber Operators and Contractors, Ltd.,*[29] the court drew a distinction between goods that could be identified at the date that the contract was made and goods that were merely identifiable. In that case, the buyer had a contract to purchase a timber forest. Later, the Latvian Government passed legislation appropriating the forest and annulling all private rights, including the contract in question.

The seller sued the buyer for the price of the forest on the grounds that title had passed before the legislation was in effect and the risk of loss fell on the buyer. Under the terms of the contract, the buyer was entitled to cut merchantable timber defined as "all trunks and branches of trees but not seedlings and young trees of less than 6 in. in diameter at a height of 4 ft. from the ground." Given this term, could it be said there were specific, identified goods at the time the contract was made? If so, property passed to the buyer, who remained liable to pay the price to the seller. The court held that the goods were not identified, but merely identifiable according to the forumlae contained in the contract.

Future goods   As a general rule, future goods may be divided into two categories: i) goods that the seller has agreed to manufacture; and ii) goods that the seller has agreed to acquire from another. (s.1) Section

23(6) provides, in part, that: "Where there is a contract for the sale of unascertained or future goods by description, and goods of that description and in a deliverable state are unconditionally appropriated to the contract, either by the seller with the assent of the buyer, or by the buyer with the assent of the seller, the property in the goods thereupon passes to the buyer."

These rules are complex, and in practice, the reported decisions have further complicated their application by creating subtle distinctions. As a result, it is virtually impossible to reconcile all the cases involving Section 23(6). In each case, there are a number of factors to weigh, e.g., the intention of the parties, whether the goods fit the contract description were in a deliverable state or were unconditionally appropriated to the contract.

Illustration Rinehart places an order to purchase ten office desks from Hayworth-Read Ltd. The desks are to be manufactured according to the specifications supplied by Rinehart. Rinehart pre-pays the purchase price of $12 500 at the time the contract is made — on April 5, 1986. Delivery of the desks is to be made in Vancouver on September 2, 1986. On August 17, after the desks are constructed by Hayworth-Read Ltd. and placed in its warehouse pending final inspection prior to shipment, the company becomes insolvent. In this case, the goods would still be "future goods" and Rinehart would be left to press a claim as an unsecured creditor in bankruptcy and hope to recover part of the $12 500 pre-paid purchase price.[30]

Unascertained goods Although "specific goods" and "future goods" are expressly defined under Section 1 of the *Act*, there is no statutory definition of unascertained goods. The case law developed definition focusses on the absence of anything physically identifiable at the time the contract is made. Where goods such as grain are fungible in nature, the seller may be required to separate part of the grain from a larger amount to fulfill his/her contract with the buyer. Until this separation takes place, the goods remain unascertained and the property in the grain does not pass to the buyer. The intention of the parties is of particular importance in determining when the title to the goods, once ascertained, passes to the buyer. In *Carlos Federspiel & Co. v. Charles Twigg Ltd.*,[31] the court observed:

> [T]he element of common intention has always to be borne in mind. A mere setting apart or selection of the seller of the goods which he expects to use in performance of the contract is not enough. If that is all, he can change his mind and use those goods in performance of some other contract and use some other goods in performance of this contract. To constitute an appropriation of the goods

to the contract, the parties must have had, or be reasonably supposed to have had, an intention to attach the contract irrevocably to those goods, so that those goods and no others are the subject of the sale and become the property of the buyer.

THE DELIVERABLE STATE

Sections 23(3) and (4) introduce the concept of deliverable state as a condition to the transfer of title to the buyer. Where the seller has a contractual obligation to do something to the specific goods, such as repair them, property does not pass until two conditions are met. First, the seller must have fulfilled his/her contractual obligation to do something to the goods. Second, the buyer must have notice that the seller has complied with his/her contractual obligation.

Illustration   Rinehart enters into a contract of sale to buy a used IBM computer hardware system from Pro-Tech Ontario Ltd. Rinehart, at the time of negotiating the sale, discovers that disk-drive **B** is defective. The owner of Pro-Tech agrees to replace the disk-drive before shipping the computer equipment to Vancouver. The task of replacing the disk-drive involves a relatively simple operation, taking little more than ten minutes. Before the disk-drive is replaced, however, the Pro-Tech shop is destroyed in a fire and the computer equipment subject to the contract is also lost. Pro-Tech sued Rinehart on the basis that the property in the IBM Computer system had passed at the time the contract was made. It further argues that the trivial work required of them should not bar the passage of title.

Following the Ontario Court of Appeal decision in *Jerome v. Clements Motor Sales Ltd.*,[32] Pro-Tech would lose its case. In that case, the court observed that: "The fact the things which were required to be done to the [equipment] to put it into deliverable state were trivial in nature does not affect the question." Slightly altering the facts, had Rinehart pre-paid the contract price for the computer system, title would still not have passed. Moreover, had Pro-Tech completed the repair to the disk-drive prior to the fire, it still would have lost because there was no notice of the work done to Rinehart.

AN UNCONDITIONAL CONTRACT

The *Sale of Goods Act* clearly requires that there be an "unconditional contract for the sale of specific goods in a deliverable state" (s.23(2)). Thus, a contract for a sale that is subject to conditions will prevent the transfer of ownership to the buyer. Assume in the above illustration that Rinehart had inserted a term in the contract as follows: "The buyer has a right to test the IBM computer system prior to delivery, and, in the event the test conducted on the system proves to be unsatisfactory to Rinehart, the contract may be rescinded on ten days' written notice to

Pro-Tech Ontario Ltd." Such a condition precedent would make the contract of sale conditional, and, therefore, property in the computer system would not have been transferred at the time the contract was made. Indeed, the term of the contract requiring Pro-Tech Ontario Ltd. to change the disk-drive would have also prevented the property from passing in the computer equipment to Rinehart.

An unconditional contract required under Section 23(2) means a contract that is not subject to either a condition precedent or condition subsequent (see Chapter 6). Typical conditions relate to things to be done to the goods before delivery, to the terms of payment for the goods, or to inspection and rejection rights based on the quality of the goods.

The cases are not always consistent in this area. For example, there is authority that a distinction should be drawn between the transfer of title to goods to the buyer, and the buyer's right to reject defective goods.[33] The condition as to quality of goods, according to this view, does not prevent the passage of title to the buyer. Instead, the seller retains a reversionary interest in the goods. This means that while the title is in the buyer, if he/she rejects the goods based on defective quality, title will be revested in the seller.

Problems for Discussion

1. Rinehart leases a high-quality laser printer from Legend Printer Ltd. The lease is for a one-year period beginning July 1, 1986. At the time of the leasing, a representative of Rinehart explains that the company requires a laser printer for the purpose of printing high resolution quality brochures and pamphlets for the promotion of Rinehart products. A vice-president of Legend knows of these requirements. Within two months, however, it becomes apparent that the printer is not suitable for the use intended. Rinehart now claims that the transaction is governed by the *Sale of Goods Act*, and that Legend is in breach of an implied warranty or condition as to the quality or fitness. Discuss whether or not the contract is covered by the *Act*. See *Blackwood Hodge Atlantic v. Kelly*, (1972) 3 N.S.R. (3d) 49.

2. Ms. Helen Wolf makes a contract with Rinehart on May 2, 1987, for the creation of a software program that would assist her in organizing family-tree data. She desires graphic functions, a data base, a modified spreadsheet, and word processing function. She is informed that such a program would require a great deal of imagination and creativity to develop and that it would be costly. Nonetheless, she agrees to sign the written contract of May 2 and pre-pays the purchase price of $10 000. The price of the diskette is $2 and the balance is labour cost in developing the software. The finished program is to be embodied on a diskette and compatible with an Apple II computer. The delivery

date is set for August 30, 1987, and on that date a representative of Rinehart phones Ms. Wolf to notify her that her program is ready.

a) Is this contract governed by the *Sale of Goods Act*? Is it one for goods or for work and materials?

b) Assuming it is a contract for goods, what was the nature of the goods on May 2?

c) Assume further the agreement was to license the software to Ms. Wolf, will this automatically exclude the contract from the *Sale of Goods Act*?

d) Assume that a fire broke out and destroyed the diskettes and program documentation. Where was the title to the program at the time of the fire that occurred at 5:00 p.m., August 30?

3. "Unfamiliarity with computer programs causes two lingering problems that are clarified by the record album analogy. First, some argue that a program transaction conveys not the software itself, but the "intellectual property" of the program. While this argument may have some validity, it applies with equal force to the sale of music on a record album, which American authority suggests is clearly under the U.C.C.

Secondly, it is argued that the program contract concerns not the transported copy (the software), but the final copy which was made from the software and is contained on the memory devices of the buyer's computer. However, when a record buyer tapes a purchased record, the U.C.C. still covers the record sale. A buyer can consume or dispose of a purchased good in many ways without removing the original sale from the U.C.C. Note, "Computer Programs as Goods Under the U.C.C.," (1979) 77 *Mich.L.Rev.* 1149, 1155.

Are there problems with the analogy between record albums and computer software?

4. In early 1985, an agent of Rinehart's enters into a contract with Comput-Paper Ltd. for the purchase of paper in bulk. The contract is in writing and requires Comput-Paper Ltd. to supply Rinehart with grades No. 1, 2, and 3 bonded paper for office use. The amount of each grade is set at 1000 pounds. A clause in the contract provides that:

It is further agreed by the Buyer, that they will pay to the seller forthwith in the manner in this paragraph provided for and on account of Comput-Paper Ltd. the full sum of ten dollars 100 kg net weight for all paper delivered to the buyer; that is to say, the Buyer to pay the seller for No. 1 bonded paper only.

Later, after all the paper is ready for delivery, the price of all grades of bonded paper increases to approximately $14.50. Therefore, Comput-Paper Ltd. wants to avoid the contract with Rinehart. It argues that there was never a binding contract for No. 2 and No. 3 paper because no price was ever fixed. The seller asserts that there can be no contract unless price, an essential term, is agreed upon by the parties to the contract. There are two issues: i) Whether there is a contract between the parties; and ii) assuming a binding contract, how is the price fixed in this case? See *Montana Mustard Seed Co. v. Gates*, (1963) 42 W.W.R. 303 (Sask.Q.B.).

5. Rinehart enters into a contract with Digtal-Tech Furniture Ltd. for the purchase of ten office desks. Under the terms of the contract, Digtal-Tech is to deliver the ten office desks on August 15. In exchange for the desks, Rinehart agrees to have one of its software engineers adapt Digtal-Tech's current inventory control and billing software program. Rinehart agrees that its engineer is to devote two work weeks to modification and adaption of the Digtal-Tech system. When the desks arrive at Rinehart, an inspection discovers a number of defects. Rinehart claims a right to pursue its claim under the buyer's remedies section of the *Sale of Goods Act*. Digtal-Tech argues, however, that the *Sale of Goods Act* does not apply to the transaction. Discuss.

6. Rinehart enters into a rental agreement for a new Ford van in April, 1985. The period of the rental is one year. The rental company, Jack's Auto, drafts the rental contract but fails to insert a clause concerning the insurance obligation for the van. On May 28, the van, while legally parked on the street, is hit by a drunk driver and is totally destroyed. There is no negligence on the part of Rinehart. Neither Rinehart nor Jack's Auto had insured the van, and the drunk driver causing the accident is uninsured and judgement proof. Ms. Bach receives a letter from the solicitor representing Jack's Auto, who claims that the "right to property or title" passed to Rinehart under the *Sale of Goods Act*. Assist Ms. Bach in preparing a reply to this letter.

Chapter 15 Notes

1. R.S.B.C. 1979, c. 370.
2. Section 6(1).
3. Section 6(2).
4. Section 6(3).
5. Section 6(4).
6. R.S.B.C. 1979, c. 64.
7. R.S.B.C. 1979, c. 406.
8. R.S.B.C. 1979, c. 48.
9. R.S.B.C. 1979, c. 373.
10. *Supra*, note 1, section 1.
11. (1983) 2 N.S.W.L.R. 48 (S.C.).
12. Ibid., p. 51.
13. Ibid.
14. (1935) 1 K.B. 579 (C.A.).
15. Ibid., p. 587.
16. See *Lee v. Griffin*, 1 B. & S. 272; 30 L.J. (Q.B.) 252.

17. *Supra*, note 11, at 51.
18. (1975) W.L.R.1095 (C.A.).
19. (1957) 1 W.L.R. 582, 586.
20. (1967) 1 W.L.R. 813, 816.
21. See *Blackwood Hodge Atlantic v. Kelly*, (1972) 3 N.S.R.(3d) 49.
22. *Supra*, note 1, section 1.
23. Section 15(3).
24. Section 52(1).
25. Section 21.
26. Section 22(1).
27. Section 22(2).
28. Section 23.
29. (1927) 1 K.B. 298 (C.A.).
30. See *Re Wait*, (1926) 1 Ch. 606 (C.A.).
31. (1957) 1 Lloyd's Rep. 240.
32. (1959) 15 D.L.R.(2d) 689 (C.A.).
33. See *Pullman Trailmobile v. Hamilton Transport*, (1979) 23 O.R. 553 (Ont.H.C.).

16 SALES: WARRANTIES AND CONDITIONS

Introduction to Warranties and Conditions

There has been a strong tradition of *caveat emptor* or letting the buyer beware. The modern trend, and one found in the *Sale of Goods Act*, is to expand the buyer's legal protection. Although the doctrine of *caveat emptor* was not abolished by the *Act*, the inclusion of certain warranties and conditions accords with the reality that a buyer has more legal protection than ever before. In this chapter, the purpose is to examine the type, scope, purpose, and application of the statutory warranties and conditions. It should be remembered in each instance that the warranty or condition is intended to protect the buyer in his/her contractual dealings for goods with a seller.

A distinction must be drawn between implied and express warranties. An express warranty is based on a written or oral representation that the goods are, for example, fit for a particular purpose. In other words, it is part of the express agreement made between the parties. An implied warranty is one imposed by law in the absence of an express representation or promise about the fitness of the goods. The legal effect is the same. The seller either expressly or by operation of law is deemed, in the absence of an express exclusion clause, to have warranted that the goods are fit for a particular purpose.

Effect of Breach of Condition and Warranty

A warranty operates as a contractual promise and the breach of that promise gives the buyer a right to recover damages. A condition, on the other hand, when breached, expands the buyer's remedy to ending the contract as well as his/her recovery of damages. Thus, a breach of warranty will not excuse the buyer from his/her future performance under the contract. Instead, he/she is entitled to recover damages for his/her loss. In some instances, such as a products liability case, where the buyer or a third party has suffered injuries because of defects in the goods, damages may be the most suitable remedy. In a strictly commercial context, the buyer who has purchased what turns out to be defective goods may simply not want them. In that instance, where the defective goods are subject to a condition such as merchantable quality or fitness for a particular purpose, then the breach has the advantage of allowing the buyer to reject the goods.

Exemption Clauses

In many contracts for the sale of goods, there is a combination of express and implied conditions and warranties. The source of the seller's obligation arises from the terms of the contract, oral representations, trade usage or custom. It is usually in the seller's economic interest to exclude, in total or in part, conditions and warranties that apply to the goods that he/she sells. The right to include exemption or exclusion clauses in a contract of sale, as we will see, is limited by the *Sale of Goods Act*. At this juncture, there are two issues: i) in what way does the *Act* imply conditions and warranties; and ii) in what way does the *Act* limit the attempts of a seller to exclude the statutory conditions and warranties?

The answer to the second question depends on the nature of the sale. A retail sale of new goods is treated differently from non-consumer sales. Any term of a contract of sale that attempts to limit or destroy the warranties and conditions granted to buyers under the *Act* is void.[1] Exclusionary clauses, by implication, are enforceable against buyers by a company or commercial enterprise, or by a trustee in bankruptcy that purchases for resale or for use in its business (Section 20(1)). Thus, a retail sale of a new Rinehart software program (presuming that the program is a category of "goods") will carry certain statutory warranties and conditions. But the same warranties or conditions may be waived in a contract of sale between Rinehart and IBM for the sale of equipment to Rinehart.

Buyer's Waiver of Condition

Assuming that there is a contract of sale that is subject to a condition by the seller, then the buyer has the right to either waive the condition, treat the breach of condition as a breach of warranty, or repudiate the contract.[2] Therefore, the buyer is given the option of electing his/her remedy on the happening of the seller's breach of a condition. The converse, however, does not apply. Where there is an implied or express warranty that is breached by the seller, the buyer is not given the opportunity of electing to treat the breach as a breach of a condition.

Title and Quiet Possession

Another aspect in the sale of goods is the seller's title to the goods and the buyer's right to quiet possession of the goods. The *Sale of Goods Act* addresses both these problems as a matter of intention between the parties. Unless the parties have expressed a different intention, then there is an implied condition that the seller has the right to sell the goods.[3] Further, there are two implied warranties regarding the buyer's right to exclude others from claiming a competing or conflicting interest in the goods purchased from the seller. The buyer has an implied warranty from the seller that ensures that he/she will have and enjoy quite possession of the goods. Thus, if another party claims ownership of the goods possessed by the buyer, and the claim is valid, the buyer has a good cause of action for damages against the seller. Similarly, the buyer has an implied warranty that the goods are free from any charge or encumbrance in favour of a third party.[4] This is to ensure that the buyer is not prejudiced in purchasing goods that are subject to a security interest that a bank or other lender may enforce against the goods owned by the seller.

Implied Condition of Correspondence with Description

The *Sale of Goods Act* implies a condition that the goods will correspond with the description made by the seller. Section 17 provides that: "Where there is a contract for the sale of goods by description, there is an implied condition that the goods shall correspond with the description. If the sale be by sample, as well as by description, it is not sufficient that the bulk of the goods correspond with the sample if the goods do not also correspond with the description."

Identification of Goods Test

It is well established that the meaning of description is the identification of the goods sold by reference to the class of thing to which the goods belong. For example, a software consumer wishes to purchase a software home math tutor. He/she approaches a retailer who sells the buyer a video game on the pretext that it is Rinehart's Home Math Tutor. The thing that the buyer seeks to buy is not computer software, but a particular class of computer software, i.e., a home math tutorial system. When the retailer sold him/her the video game that he/she described as a home math tutorial, that description was false. What was delivered did not correspond with the contract description. As a result, the buyer is entitled to enforce the implied condition as to description and rescind the contract.

A distinction is drawn between the identification of the goods and the attributes or characteristics of the goods. It is only the inaccurate description, however, that invalidates the contract. Where, for example, the retailer made erroneous statements about features of the Rinehart Home Math Tutor such as the ease of learning how to use the problem or the effectiveness of the program in teaching a child to add, divide, and multiply, there is no breach of the statutory condition as to description. The courts have examined the representations of the seller and the terms of the contract to draw a distinction between the kind of good sold and the quality of the good. Only the former is concerned with the identification of the goods, for purposes of the implied condition, as to description.

Specific Goods and Unascertained Goods

Where the contract is for the sale of unascertained goods, there will always be a sale by description. Without a description of unascertained goods, it would be impossible to determine the subject matter of the contract and the seller's obligation under the contract. In contrast, a sale of specific goods can be made, in theory, without any description to the buyer. Thus, a home math tutor may be sold simply as software without specific description as to the type of software. But it is a rare transaction where the buyer contracts to purchase "software", a "car" or an "animal". In reality, a seller offers for sale a Home Math Tutor, a Ford station wagon, or a Persian cat. Once the seller has made such a representation and the buyer has relied upon the seller's judgment, the implied condition as to description is incorporated in the contract.

It is a question of fact whether there has been a sale by description or the sale of a thing seen by the buyer who has made his/her own assessment, or relied entirely on his/her own judgment in making the purchase. An important factor in deciding this question is the manner in which the seller has offered or displayed the goods. Most goods are described by their package, label, or model. The buyer relies upon the package, label, or model to identify the thing the seller is offering for sale. The fact that the salesman behind the counter is silent will not be a defence where the goods have been falsely described. Thus, a Rinehart Home Math Tutor software package that mistakenly contains the video game *Space Attack* does not correspond with that description. Even though the retailer, or seller, was also deceived by the package and label does not prevent the buyer from rescinding the contract and returning the goods on the basis of a breach of the implied condition as to description.

Fault of the Seller

In certain instances, the inaccurate description may have been an active, intentional scheme to mislead the buyer into believing that the thing delivered under the contract is the same thing as identified in the contract. For instance, Rinehart may contract to buy a new IBM PC system from Computer Acquisition Ltd. The seller delivers a two-year-old model of the IBM PC to Rinehart. The courts have adopted the position that the difference between a new and second-hand good is a difference in kind and not merely a difference in quality.

The buyer's implied condition as to description is not limited to the intentional or deliberate passing-off or substitution of goods that are of a different kind from the goods identified in the contract. Both the seller and buyer may be unaware that the goods sold are of a different kind than that which the contract has identified. The question is where should the loss fall? The courts have held that the seller bears the loss.

Exclusion Clauses

A seller may seek to rely upon an exemption clause to negate the buyer's right to rescind based on the implied condition as to description.

Illustration   Rinehart contracts to sell 2000 copies of the Home Math Tutor to Consumer Software (Vancouver) Ltd., a software distributor. The contract contains the following exemption clause:

> There are no representations, warranties, or conditions, express or implied, statutory, or otherwise, other than those herein contained, nor shall any agreement collateral hereto be binding upon the seller unless it is in writing hereupon or attached hereto and duly signed on behalf of the seller at its said home office.

There is a further clause that says that the goods are not being sold by description. Later, Rinehart delivers 2000 copies of Word Fast, a word processing program. The law is clear that neither the exemption clause nor the clause excluding sale by description will be allowed to alter the subject matter of the sale. As Lord Backburn said in *Bowes v. Shand*,[5] "If you contract to sell peas, you cannot oblige a party to take beans."

Buyer's Remedy

When the seller has breached the implied condition as to description, the buyer's remedy is to reject or return the goods and rescind the contract. The buyer has the right to waive the condition or to treat the breach of the condition as a breach of warranty.[6]

The buyer's right to examine the goods and the rules of acceptance of the goods play an important part in determining what remedies are available in the event of an inaccurate description. Where the buyer has not had a previous opportunity to examine the goods, he/she is not deemed to have accepted them until he/she has had a reasonable opportunity to make the examination and determine whether the goods conform with the contract.[7] Although the goods delivered do not conform with the contractual description, the buyer must take steps to prevent his/her acceptance of the wrong goods.

Acceptance will be, under the *Sale of Goods Act*, deemed to have occurred in three circumstances: i) the buyer intimates to the seller that he/she has accepted the goods; ii) after delivery of the goods, the buyer does any act inconsistent with the seller's ownership in the goods; and iii) after the lapse of a reasonable time, the buyer retains the goods and does not tell the seller that he/she has rejected them.[8]

The courts have construed Section 39 as giving the buyer "try out" time to determine whether the goods conform with the contract description. The length of time varies according to the nature of the goods, the purpose of the goods, and the time at which they are delivered. Thus, a farmer who takes delivery of a second-hand engine in the belief that it is new, although he has the engine from August until the following September, is not deemed to have accepted it. The winter conditions prevent the farmer from "trying out" the machine to determine whether it met the contract description. Further, where the goods appear to comply with the contract description from an ordinary inspection, the buyer is entitled to reject the misdescribed goods when a further inspection by an expert discovers the misdescription. But, there is, however, a time limit on the buyer's right to rejection. The actual amount of time elapsed, the nature of the defect, and the type of goods will influence the court in determining whether a reasonable amount of time has passed prior to the buyer's notice of rejection.

Implied Condition of Merchantable Quality

Statutory Definition

The implied condition of merchantable quality is contained in Section 18(b) which provides: "Where goods are bought by description from a seller who deals in goods of that description, whether he is the manufacturer or not, there is an implied condition that the goods shall be of merchantable quality; but if the buyer has examined the goods there is no implied condition as regards defects which such examination ought to have revealed."

The Meaning of Merchantable Quality

Commercially saleable   The term "merchantable quality" is not expressly defined in the *Act*. The courts have attempted in a number of decisions to supply a workable definition. "Merchantable" has been defined to mean "commercially saleable." Lord Reid, in two House of Lords decisions[9], explained the relationship between merchantable quality and commercially saleable:

> If the description is a familiar one, it may be that in practice only one quality of goods answers that description — then that quality and only that quality is merchantable quality. Or it may be that various qualities of goods are commonly sold under that description — then it is not disputed that the lowest quality commonly so sold is what is meant by merchantable quality; it is commercially saleable under that description.

The composite nature of merchantable quality

Merchantable quality is not limited to problems or misunderstandings between sellers and buyers over the description of goods. The term is a composite of description, purpose, condition, and price of the goods. In each instance, the relative importance of an individual component is influenced by the nature of the goods and the characteristics of the market.

The application of these principles may be illustrated by two actual cases involving the sale of "raw materials" for use or manufacture in the buyer's own commercial enterprise. In the first case, a buyer ordered rayon cloth intending to use it for dressmaking. That intention, however, was not known to the seller and he delivered rayon cloth that was unsuitable for dressmaking, but had other industrial uses. Therefore, the goods ordered by the buyer had more than one quality. Unfortunately for the buyer, he/she assumed that the rayon cloth was only suitable for dressmaking. Much evidence was taken on the issue of whether there was a secondary market for rayon cloth, and the court found that one did exist.

In the second case, the owner of a pheasant-breeding farm bought feed that contained Brazilian ground-nut extraction. A large number of the young pheasants died because the feed was poisonous to them. The ground nut, however, was safe for cattle. As the seller did not know of the use intended by the buyer, and the ground nut had another, safe commercial use, there was no breach of the implied condition as to merchantable quality. The fact that the goods are unsuitable for the buyer's specific and undisclosed purpose does not automatically make them of unmerchantable quality. In this case, there was another market for the ground nut, just as there was for the rayon cloth. The existence of multiple commercial uses for various qualities of goods of the same description is a major obstacle to a successful argument that the seller has breached the implied condition of merchantable quality. The onus is on the buyer to narrow and explicitly detail the description of goods falling within the class of multiple quality goods.

Lord Reid, in *B.S. Brown & Sons Ltd. v. Craiks*,[10] acknowledged that it is impossible for the courts to frame a single, all-encompassing definition that will cover all situations. The courts have adhered to the idea that only a vague definition of merchantable quality will provide the needed flexibility to deal with the potentially wide variety of goods and markets where the implied condition is imposed in contract for sale. Ultimately, the burden is on the buyer to make his/her purpose for the goods known to the seller, and in such circumstances that the seller is aware that the buyer is relying on his/her skill and judgment as the seller of the goods.

There is often a connection between the various components used to judge merchantable quality. For instance, the issues of price, purpose, and description may be closely related. The decision as to whether the goods in a specific instance are of merchantable quality is always a question of fact.

Illustration The University of Toronto places an order with Sauls Computer Ltd. for seventy-five copies of a word processing program. The acquisition officer in the university, however, fails to specify the exact use that the university intends to make of the software programs. One week later, Sauls Computer Ltd. delivers seventy-five copies of Rinehart's Word Fast software program. At the end of two weeks, it becomes apparent that the Word Fast program is unsuitable for the purpose of academic writing. The Rinehart program lacks the superscript and subscript function for footnotes as well as a graphics capability. The university tries to reject the goods and return them to Sauls Computer Ltd. on the basis that they were delivered in breach of the implied condition of merchantable quality. We will further assume that a software package with the additional capabilities required would have cost another $50 per copy. The University paid $350 a copy for the Word Fast software program; and a program with these extra functions would sell for $400 per copy.

In delivering the Word Fast software program, has Sauls Computer breached the implied condition of merchantable quality? As the Word Fast software program could be used for more than one purpose, i.e., academic research and writing, it would be commercially saleable. Since the buyer failed to communicate the specific purpose intended for the goods and used a general description, the seller has not breached the implied condition, because the software can be used for other purposes, e.g., writing business reports, letters. Therefore, as long as the software is saleable at the time of delivery for another purpose than the undisclosed one of the buyer, it is of merchantable quality. The difference in the price of $50 does not make the software of unmerchantable quality. On the other hand, where the difference is so substantial that the goods must be sold at a throw-away price, the goods may be unmerchantable.

The losing contract In some instances, the "merchantable quality" argument may be an attempt by the buyer to rescind what has become a losing contract. The price of the goods, particularly where they are commodities, may have fallen dramatically between the time of the making of the contract and the delivery date. This was the case in *Cehave N.V. v. Bremer Handelsgesellschaft*.[11] Here the buyer tried to reject an entire consignment of citrus pulp pellets. Later, the same buyer purchased the consignment for about 30 percent of the original contract price. The buyer then used the citrus pulp pellets for the same purposes as originally contemplated at the time of making the contract. The drastic reduction in price was caused by two factors: i) damage in shipment of the goods; and ii) a fall in the market price for the goods. The court found that the goods were of merchantable quality in this case. From the facts, it appeared that the buyer was attempting to take full advantage of the market down turn and the issue of "defects" in the goods was merely a smokescreen to make a handsome profit.

The effect of the buyer's inspection of goods   The implied condition of merchantable quality is dependent upon the opportunity of the buyer to inspect the goods at the time that the contract is made. Where the buyer has made such an inspection, and the defects are obvious or apparent from such an inspection, then there is no implied condition for merchantable quality. The patent (or obvious) defect is distinguished from the latent (or hidden) defect. In the latter case, where the inspection would not have revealed the defect because of its latent nature, the implied condition applies to the sale. The buyer has a reasonable time, which will vary according to the nature of the goods and the circumstances, to detect the defect and exercise his/her remedies based on a breach of implied condition of merchantable quality.

Implied Condition of Fitness for a Particular Purpose

The General Rule

As a general rule, there is no implied warranty or condition that goods supplied under a contract of sale are fit for a particular purpose. There are three exceptions where the *Act* imposes an implied condition of fitness: i) the buyer communicates, expressly or by implication, to the seller the particular purpose for which he/she requires the goods; ii) the buyer makes it known that he/she is relying on the seller's skill and judgment; and iii) the buyer contracts for goods that are, by description, in the course of the seller's business to supply.[12]

Definitional Problems

There is overlap between the implied condition for merchantable quality and condition of fitness for a purpose. It is not uncommon to find allegations that the seller has breached both conditions based on the same facts and circumstances. As the term merchantable quality has only a general and somewhat vague definition, the main components contained in fitness for a particular purpose are open to a variety of linguistic acrobatics.

Particular purpose   Much ink has been spilled over the meaning of the word "particular." In *Kendall v. Lillico*,[13] Lord Morris said there is "no magic in the word 'particular'." The definitional problem becomes acute when "particular", which modifies "purpose", is considered in the abstract.

In each instance, there is a factual determination as to whether the buyer communicated the purpose "with reasonably sufficient precision." The buyer satisfied the burden of proof in *Manchester Liners Ltd. v. Rea Ltd.*[14] by requesting that the seller deliver coal to be used on a specific ship. The coal supplied proved unsuitable for use in *that* ship. The seller was held to have breached the implied condition for fitness for a particular purpose on the grounds that he had undertaken to provide coal for one ship and the coal was unsuitable for that particular purpose.

Reliance on the seller's skill and judgment   There is a close conceptual relationship between the terms "particular purpose" and the reliance on the seller's skill and judgment. By specifying or stating the purpose, the buyer communicates his/her intention to rely on the seller's skill and judgment in supplying goods that will meet that purpose. As Lord Reid asked in *Kendall v. Lillico*, "If he [the buyer] does not say which he wants, or at least indicate which he wants by the price which is offering, how can he be relying on the seller to supply something reasonably fit for his purpose?" A reading of the authorities indicates that the scope and meaning of "reliance" is susceptible to change with the views of the court. One view is to consider reliance to be the basis of a contractual obligation for which the seller contracted.[15] Another view is to consider the "reliance" requirement met whenever the seller knows the particular purpose of the goods required by the buyer.

In some instances, these questions are easily determined by the court. An example: a buyer walks into a store and buys a hot-water bottle; the bottle later bursts, injuring the buyer. The purpose of the hot-water bottle is easily determined, as is the extent of the buyer's reliance on the seller's skill and judgment. In the standard retail sale of goods, the courts generally have little difficulty implying the condition of fitness for a particular purpose. The difficult cases usually involve contracts between business persons where the goods are used for a commercial or industrial purpose. In such contracts, there is generally greater knowledge and sophistication by both the seller and buyer.

This leads to a more complicated determination as to whether the buyer, in fact, relied upon the skill and judgment of the seller or his/her own skill and judgment. The general rule is that the reliance may be partial. Or to state it another way, the buyer is not required to show that he/she exclusively or totally relied on the seller's skill and judgment. Thus, even where the buyer has provided detailed specifications and plans that the seller uses to build specially made goods, there is no general rule that the implied condition has been excluded.

Strict liability   The seller's liability for breach of the implied condition for fitness is in the nature of strict liability. For instance, the defects in the goods that made them unfit for the buyer's particular purpose may be latent. That is, even with the exercise of great skill and judgment, the seller may not have discovered the defect. Nonetheless, the seller will remain liable for breach of the condition. The policy reason for such liability is to ensure that the seller deals in goods that he/she knows something about so that buyers can be certain of obtaining in the marketplace goods reasonably fit for their purpose. The implied condition of fitness for a purpose is a risk allocation device that shifts onto the seller's shoulders the economic consequences of selling unfit goods rather than leaving that loss to fall on buyers, who, as a class, would have no or a very small alternative market to dispose of such defective goods.

Illustration   Dawn Products designs and manufactures cable pressurization equipment for the telecommunications industry. In June 1986, Dawn decides to purchase a computer system. A contract is entered into with Rinehart for a system designed to provide six functions; i) accounts receivable; ii) payroll; iii) order entry; iv) inventory deletion; v) provincial income tax; and vi) cash receipts. Rinehart represents to Dawn that the system will solve inventory problems, result in direct savings of labour costs, and be operational by December 1986. However, by that date, only the payroll part of the system is up and running. Rinehart software engineers experience a number of problems in trying to install the balance of the software system. In the contract, Rinehart warrantees the computer system for one year after delivery against defects in material, workmanship, and operational failure from ordinary use. Further, Rinehart represents that the computer system will perform the six functions and that Rinehart will supply the requisite know-how necessary to make the system operational. In February 1987, Dawn sues Rinehart for breach of contract.

The facts in the above illustration are drawn from *Chatlos Systems v. National Cash Register Corp.*[16] In this case, the seller was held liable for breach of express and implied warranties, including that the goods were in good working order and fit for the use the buyer required of them.

Problems for Discussion

1. Ms. Bach has been asked to review Rinehart's standard form software licence agreement for consumer software. The contract is set forth in Figure 1.4. Advise her as to whether the exemption clauses in this agreement are enforceable against a consumer under the *Sale of Goods Act*.

2. By a contract in writing, dated May 23, 1987, Rinehart purchases from Uptown Motors one new Ford van for the price of $17 000 and takes delivery of the van. At the time of the contract, the purchase department neglects to tell the Uptown Motors' salesman of the purpose that Rinehart intends to make use of the van. The intention, undisclosed, is to use the van for moving computer equipment and supplies between the warehouse area and the main office. From the beginning, the van has mechanical problems. Rinehart takes the van in for repairs on two separate occasions, but the engine problems persist. Finally, Ms. Bach, on behalf of Rinehart, writes to Uptown Motors demanding that it provide another new van or refund the purchase price. Uptown Motors' solicitor replies to the letter by refusing both demands, stating that the particular purpose was never disclosed to Uptown Motors and that Rinehart had not relied upon his client's skill and judgment. Discuss. See *Marshall v. Ryan Motors Ltd.*, (1922) 65 D.L.R. 742 (Sask.C.A.).

3. As part of Rinehart's Learning Shoppes, the company commences marketing a line of Computer T-Shirts that say: "I'm computer literate and user friendly." Mr. Alex Bell buys one of the T-shirts at Eaton's. Shortly after he begins to wear the T-shirt, he develops severe dermatitis. The evidence indicates that normal skin would not have been affected by the blend of fabric used in making the T-shirts. Nonetheless, it is clear that the fabric has caused the buyer to develop this disease. Mr. Bell states that he expressly told the sales clerk at Eaton's that he intended to wear the shirt, and that it was sold with an implied condition that it was fit for that particular purpose. Does Section 18(a) apply to this case? See *Griffiths v. Peter Conway Ltd.*, (1939) 1 All E.R. 685 (C.A.).

4. Is the exemption or exclusionary clause contained in Rinehart's consumer software contract (Figure 1.4) enforceable under the *Sale of Goods Act*?

5. Distinguish between a warranty and condition, and provide an example of each as found in the *Sale of Goods Act*. Explain how each specific statutory warranty and condition protects a particular interest of the buyer in a contract for the sale of goods.

6. Assume, based on the transaction in Problem 2 above, that Uptown Motors sells Rinehart a Ford van with a defective steering mechanism. The employee driving the van discovers the defect, reports it to his supervisor, but nothing is done to repair the problem. Three weeks later, the same employee has an accident when the steering in the van fails altogether and hits another car, resulting in the severe injury of that car's driver and passenger. The injured parties sue Rinehart based on its employee's negligence, and Rinehart brings into the lawsuit Uptown Motors on the basis that the goods sold were defective. Will Rinehart succeed in the action against Uptown Motors?

Chapter 16 Notes

1. Section 20(2).
2. Section 15(1).
3. Section 16(a).
4. Section 16(b).
5. 2 A.C. 455, p. 480.
6. Section 15(1).
7. Section 38.
8. Section 39.
9. *Kendal v. Lillico*, (1968) 2 All E.R. 444 (H.L.); and *B.S. Brown & Sons Ltd. v. Craiks Ltd.*, (1970) 1 All E.R. 823 (H.L.).
10. Ibid.
11. (1975) 3 All E.R. 739 (C.A.).
12. Section 18(a).
13. *Supra*, note 9, p. 465.
14. (1922) 2 A.C. 74 (H.L.).
15. See *Cammell Laird v. Manganese Bronze*, (1934) A.C. 403 (H.L.).
16. 479 F.Supp. 738 (D.N.J.), aff'd 635 F.2d 1081 (3rd Cir. 1980), later appeal 670 F.2d 130 (3rd Cir. 1982), cert. dismissed, 457 U.S. 1112 (1982).

17 SALES: REMEDIES

The Buyer's Remedies

The buyer's remedies are contained in the *Sale of Goods Act*. In addition to established common law remedies (damages) and equitable remedies (specific performance and injunction), the buyer has an express right to reject the goods. The rejection of goods is an important, self-help remedy.

FIGURE 17.1   **BUYER'S REMEDIES**

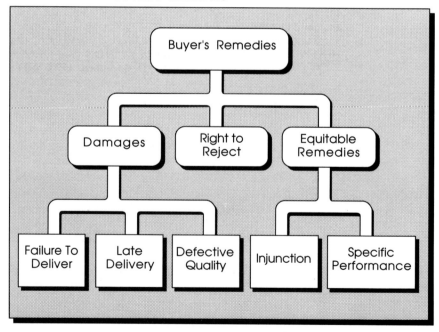

Unlike the other remedies, the buyer does not require a court order to enforce his/her right to reject. In this section, we will discover how the buyer under a contract of sale of goods enforces remedies that are similar in nature and scope to those available at the common law.

The Right To Reject Goods

The buyer's right to reject goods turns on whether the property to the goods has passed under the contract of sale. The question of the passage of property to the buyer depends upon whether the goods are unascertained or specific. Where unascertained goods are concerned, the buyer has a statutory right to inspect and reject the goods after they have been delivered into his/her possession. The real problem is with a contract of sale for specific goods. The general rule is that an unconditional sale of specific goods results in the immediate transfer of the property to the goods to the buyer even though the buyer may not have taken actual possession of the goods. Thus, the buyer's right of rejection is subject to the artificial notion of passage of title.

The courts, however, have created ways to preserve the buyer's right of rejection in the specific goods case. A typical illustration is found in *Polar Refrigeration Service Ltd. v. Moldenhauer.*[1] In that case, the defendant wanted to install air-conditioning equipment in the beer parlour located at his hotel. He entered into a contract for sale with the plaintiff for two air conditioners. The defendant made it clear that he was interested in equipment that would remove smoke from the beer parlour. The brochures used by the plaintiff represented that its air conditioners were suitable for that purpose. After the air conditioners were installed, the defendant found that they were unsuitable for the purpose of smoke removal. The plaintiff then sued to recover the contract price for the equipment, and the defendant claimed a right to repudiate the contract based on the plaintiff's breach of the implied condition as to the quality or fitness of the goods.

The first issue in such a case is whether the seller has breached a *condition*. A breach of a condition entitles the buyer to repudiate the contract and reject the goods. A breach of a warranty, on the other hand, leaves the buyer with only a remedy for *damages*. The obstacle to the buyer's right to reject based on the condition/warranty distinction is contained in Section 15(3) of the *Sale of Goods Act*:

> Where a contract of sale is not severable, and the buyer has accepted the goods or part of them, or where the contract is for specific goods, the property in which has passed to the buyer, the breach of any condition to be fulfilled by the seller can only be treated as

a breach of warranty, and not as a ground for rejecting the goods and treating the contract as repudiated, unless there be a term of the contract, express or implied, to that effect.

In the context of *Polar Refrigeration*, Secton 15(3) means that because the air conditioners, which were specific property, were sold to the buyer, any breach of the condition for fitness for a particular purpose could only be treated as a breach of warranty. The only exceptions are: i) where the contract expressly gives the buyer a right of rejection — a rare clause in a standard form contract normally drafted by the seller; or ii) where there is an implied term allowing for rejection. The crucial phrase, where the court is given considerable discretion to achieve a just and fair result, is "implied term". How does the court go about implying a condition that entitles the buyer to reject the goods? The court determines the main purpose of the contract, for which the buyer was buying the goods, and whether that purpose was communicated to the seller before the contract was made. Where the seller's breach has deprived the buyer of substantially the whole benefit of the contract, then the breach is one of a condition (and not a warranty) and the buyer has the right to reject the goods.

Section 15(3) defines the buyer's right of rejection, in part, according to whether the contract is "severable". A classic illustration of a severable contract for the sale of goods is a contract that obliges the seller to deliver the goods in instalments. Such contracts are generally commercial in nature.

Illustration   Rinehart contracts to sell fifty copies of its Word Processing program to the University of Toronto. Under the terms of the contract, Rinehart is required to deliver ten copies per month over a period of five months. The first delivery is to be made March 1. The first four shipments are delivered, accepted, and paid for by the University of Toronto. The final shipment of ten copies of the program on July 1, however, proves to have a defect. As this is an instalment contract, the University of Toronto is entitled to reject the final instalment. Conversely, if Rinehart had sold fifty copies all at once to the University of Toronto and ten copies prove to be defective, because the contract is not severable the buyer would not be entitled to accept forty copies of the program and reject the defective ten copies.

In general terms, cases such as this involve a question of fact. The court is required to ascertain the terms of the contract and the circumstances of the case, and then to decide whether the breach amounts to a repudiation of the whole contract or a less serious breach giving rise to a claim for compensation by the buyer.[2]

Where the buyer has accepted the goods, the buyer's right of rejection under Section 15(3) is lost and a right to recover damages is substituted. The question of acceptance, therefore, becomes a crucial issue in determining the nature of the buyer's remedies under the *Sale of Goods Act*. The meaning of "acceptance" is found in Section 39, which defines acceptance in terms of: i) the buyer intimating to the seller that he/she has accepted the goods; ii) the buyer doing any act in relation to the goods that is inconsistent with the seller's ownership of them; or iii) the buyer, after a lapse of reasonable time, retaining the goods without intimating to the seller that he/she has rejected them.

Any buyer who falls within one of these three categories of acceptance will not be entitled to exercise his/her right of rejection. For instance, the buyer who resells the goods before determining that the goods are unmerchantable is taking action that is inconsistent with the seller's ownership of the goods. The test is whether, at the time of rejection, the seller can resume possession of the rejected goods forthwith. Where the goods have been sold to third parties and the buyer cannot immediately place the seller back into possession of the goods, then the right to reject is lost and the buyer is left to sue for damages.[3] The right is lost even though, prior to the resale, the buyer did not have an adequate opportunity to examine the goods to determine whether they were merchantable.

Ordinarily, the buyer will lose his/her right to reject the goods very shortly after it becomes clear that they are, for example, unmerchantable. The period of rejection, however, may be extended where the parties attempt to negotiate an amicable settlement. Once the negotiations fail, the buyer must give prompt notice of his/her intention to reject.

The Right To Recover Damages

DAMAGES FOR FAILURE TO DELIVER OR LATE DELIVERY

The notion of damages was discussed in Chapter 7 (See Figure 7.4). In the context of sale of goods, the common law rules have, in large part, formed an important source of remedies that are available to a buyer. Therefore, common law concepts such as measurement of damages and mitigation of damages apply to cases coming within the *Sale of Goods Act*.

A claim for damages may arise where the seller does not meet the delivery date. The buyer may suffer damages because the seller has failed to deliver or delivers after the agreed date. In the instance of failure to deliver, Section 54 provides that the measure of damages, in the absence of evidence to the contrary, is the difference between the contract price and the market or current price of the goods at the time agreed for delivery. The underlying basis of the market rule is that the buyer has available the opportunity to purchase substitute goods in the open market. By fixing the damages on the market price, the court is recognizing that in commercial transactions the buyer has a duty to mitigate his/her loss by entering into the market and buying goods that the seller has failed to deliver. The market rule, therefore, protects the buyer against his/her loss of value for the goods under the contract with the seller who has failed to deliver.

The rule also provides a disincentive for a seller to break his/her contract in a rising market and sell the goods to another buyer for a higher price. Conversely, in the event that the market price falls below the contract price, the buyer has suffered no damages under this rule. The market rule is inapplicable where there is no market for the goods available. In that instance, the basis on which to assess damages is the buyer's loss of profit.[4]

The market rule is not concerned with the buyer's peculiar economic loss because of the non-delivery; instead, the rule is a more objective assessment, leaving the question of damages to the determination of the market price, which, if higher than the contract price at the date of delivery, becomes the basis on which to assess the buyer's loss. The rule has particular application to goods subject to a fluctuating market, such as grain, wood, or other raw materials. It has less importance in the standard consumer transaction where the buyer purchases, for example, a computer, stereo, television, or car.

Illustration Rinehart agrees to buy 1000 cartons of continuous word processing paper from Apex Paper Ltd. The price fixed under the contract dated March 2 is $12.00 per carton plus freight. The delivery date is set for June 22. On April 22, there is an industry-wide strike of pulp mills in Canada, and by June 1 the per carton price of the paper ordered by Rinehart increases to $17.50. On June 22, Apex Paper Ltd. fails to deliver. Rinehart sues Apex Paper Ltd. for damages. Under the market rule, which would apply in this case, Rinehart's damages are calculated as follows: $12 000 (contract price) − $17 500 (market price) = $5500.

There is a second test for measuring damages under Section 54. This test might be referred to as the *Hadley v. Baxendale* rule.[5] Under this rule, damages are the losses directly and naturally resulting in the ordinary course of events from the seller's breach of contract. The market rule is the generally applicable standard of measurement in non-delivery cases. This rule, however, can be displaced and the *Hadley v. Baxendale* rule substituted where there are special circumstances. For example, it can be substituted where the parties contemplate or actually provide for intermediate transactions.

Illustration Vary the facts in the above illustration and assume that Apex Paper Ltd. is aware that Rinehart intends to sell the 1000 cartons of paper to a third party, and that perhaps the third party might sell the paper to a fourth party prior to June 22. Further assume that Rinehart does sell, in a rising market, the 1000 cartons to Halls Distributors for $14.50 per carton on May 15, and that on June 2 Halls Distributors sells its right to the shipment to General Stationery Ltd. for $17.50. On June

6, the pulp mill strike is settled, and by June 22, the price has dropped to $13.00 per carton. On that date, Apex Paper Ltd. fails to deliver the paper to Rinehart, and in turn Rinehart is unable to deliver the goods to Hall Distributors, which in turn is in breach of its contract with General Stationery Ltd. In this case, Rinehart is subject to a civil suit for damages from Halls Distributors, an intermediate buyer, and Halls will in turn be sued civilly by General Stationery Ltd. How are damages assessed in this type of case? As the disappointed buyer, Rinehart is entitled to recover loss based on the market rule, as well as the other losses it sustained in paying claims arising out of the two additional sales.

The general rule is found in the House of Lords decision in *Re R. and H. Hall, Ltd. and W.H. Pim (Junior) & Co.* arbitration[6] where Lord Shaw applied the principles from *Hadley v. Baxendale*:

> [I]f trade losses occur under a contract which points to those goods, then it is in no way unreasonable to charge the seller declining to deliver the goods with the losses which have occurred to the string of dealers which the nature of the contract and of the case provided for supplying in turn. ... A sensible rule clearly covers the loss not only of the original buyer's profit which he has been prevented from earning, but also the loss sustained by him in being saddled with the claims of those to whom he had, in a contemplated course of trade, disposed of the goods.

In summary, where the seller fails to deliver the goods, the general rule for measuring damages is the market rule, i.e., the difference between the contract price and the market price at the date of the breach. This rule is based on the obligation of the buyer to mitigate damages by buying substitute goods. Where there are no substitute goods to buy on the market, then damages will be based on the rule in *Hadley v. Baxendale* which is incorporated in Section 56(2). The *Hadley* rule also applies where: i) there is a fluctuating market for the goods; ii) the original seller and buyer contemplate or actually provide for intermediate sale of the goods prior to delivery; iii) such intermediate sales are made; and iv) as a result of the original seller's non-delivery, the original buyer will be liable for damage claims arising out of the intermediate transactions.

Although Section 54 carefully considers the consequences of non-delivery of goods, the section fails to address the question of whether the same basis for assessing damages applies to late delivery. The rule appears to be that damages for delayed or late delivery are calculated on the basis of the difference between the value of the goods on the date delivery is due and the value of the goods on the date of actual delivery.

DAMAGES FOR DEFECTIVE GOODS

Section 56 gives the buyer a right to maintain an action for damages against a seller for breach of a warranty. The buyer also has the right to treat a breach of a condition by the seller as a breach of a warranty and recover damages. The measure of damages for a breach of a warranty is the estimated loss directly and naturally resulting in the ordinary course of events from the breach.[7] Thus, a buyer who receives goods that are unmerchantable or unsuitable for the particular purpose ordered can sue for damages. Further, the right to damages extends to loss suffered by the buyer as a result of misdescription.

Under this heading of buyer's remedies, damages claims are divided into four distinct categories: i) the cost of the goods reduced by any resale value of the goods; ii) the wasted expense incurred in installing the goods; iii) physical damages to other property or persons; and iv) loss of profits.

In a large number of the cases between commercial sellers and buyers, the buyer claims damages based on a breach of the implied warranty that the goods are fit for a particular purpose. It is not uncommon in such cases for the buyer to argue that there was an express warranty as to fitness, and alternatively, to argue an implied warranty under the *Sale of Goods Act*. The same general common law principles governing breach of contract apply to both a breach of an express contractual warranty and an implied warranty as to fitness under the *Sale of Goods Act*.

Sunnyside Greenhouses Ltd. v. Golden West Seeds Ltd.[8] provides a useful illustration. The sellers, Golden West, sold to the buyer, Sunnyside, roof-covering panels for greenhouses. The buyers were in the business of growing greenhouse crops for resale. The seller represented that the roof panelling installed on the greenhouse roofs would last for seven to ten years. The cost of the roof panels was \$10 472.82 and the cost of installation \$4300. Within two years after installation, some of the panels turned a milky colour, blocking out light. Within a three-year period, most of the panels had discoloured. The defect was deemed latent in nature by the court. The buyers sought damages. On the issue of damages, the court said that the *prima facie* amount is the full purchase price, subject to a set-off for any residual value.

The burden of proving residual value was on the seller by showing that the buyer could sell the defective goods to a third party for a price. In this case, no one would be willing to buy greenhouse panels that were useless for growing plants. Therefore, the buyers were entitled to recover the purchase price of the panels. A second head of damages was the buyer's cost paid to the seller for installing the panels. Here, the court did not allow the buyer to recoup the whole cost of installation. A portion of the cost was disallowed on the grounds that the panels would have had to be replaced at the end of a seven- or ten-year period in any event. Moreover, the buyer had interim use of the panels for a period of time.

The third and final head of damages was a claim akin to the buyer's loss of profits because of the defective panels. The court held that the buyer was entitled to recover the profit that it lost by reason of the seller's breach. At the same time, the problem of economic loss resulting from a seller's breach has raised the issue as to whether damages suffered by a buyer are too remote. In Canada, the problem is further complicated by the rule that a buyer is not entitled to recover for pure economic loss. This means that a buyer must show that a breach has caused physical damage.

On the issue of remoteness, Lord Denning, in *Parson v. Uttley Ingham*,[9] formulated the test as follows: "[T]he defaulting party is only liable for the consequences if they are such as, at the time of the contract, ought reasonably to have [been] contemplated as a *serious* possibility or real danger." In *Parson v. Uttley Ingham*, a pig farmer bought a special-order bulk hopper. The metal hopper was filled with nuts to feed the buyer's herd of pigs. The seller, however, when installing the hopper, failed to open a ventilator door, and the nuts turned mouldy. The buyer's pigs ate the mouldy nuts and later a large number of the herd died after contracting E coli from them. Thus, the buyer sought to recover *substantially more* than the original cost of the hopper, which was £275.

The buyer sought as damages the value of the 254 lost pigs (£10 000) and his lost profits from selling the pigs (£10 000). The court held that the seller was liable for the loss of the pigs and the vet expenses. Damages were awarded on the basis of the seller's breach of warranty that the goods were suitable for the buyer's purposes. Moreover, the seller must have appreciated that there was a likelihood that an unventilated hopper would create a serious possibility that the pigs would become ill. The claim for lost profits, however, was denied, not on the basis of principle, but on the grounds of what potential losses were reasonably within the contemplation of the seller at the time of the sale.

The Right to Equitable Relief

In the *Sale of Goods Act* context, there are two equitable remedies potentially available to a buyer: i) specific performance, and ii) injunction. When a seller breaches an express or implied warranty, the buyer is entitled, as a matter of law, to recover damages. Although there may be issues such as remoteness or the proper measurement of loss, it is well settled that a court cannot withhold damages in a breach of contract case. Equitable remedies, however, are *discretionary* by their very nature, and a buyer is not automatically entitled to such a remedy even though the seller's breach of contract is clear and undisputed.

As a general rule, a court will refuse a buyer's request for specific performance of a contract of sale. The rationale is that in the ordinary instance of the sale of non-specific goods, damages are a sufficient remedy. The buyer with the money recovered from the seller can enter the market and purchase similar goods. In certain instances, a contract of sale may come within the court's equity jurisdiction. For example, in a long-term supply contract, the buyer's need for the goods may be essential for the continuation of his/her business.

In *Sky Petroleum Ltd. v. VIP Petroleum Ltd.*,[10] the buyer, seeking a decree of specific performance, had a ten-year contract for the supply of petroleum with the seller. During the severe oil shortages in 1973 and the rapid increase in the market price of petroleum, the contract was no longer favourable to the seller. The seller sought to terminate the contract on the basis that the buyer had breached a contractual provision respecting credit. The buyer disputed this allegation.

In granting the buyer equitable relief, the court noted two essential factors that justified restraining the seller from withholding the goods: i) there was little prospect of the buyer finding an alternative source for the goods; and ii) there was a serious possibility that if the supplies were shut off the buyer's business would fail. The buyer obtained an interim injunction against the seller, restraining it from cutting off the buyer's supply under the contract. The effect of an interim injunction is to preserve the status quo between the parties to a contract until the court can hear the full facts of the dispute and resolve the merits of the case. Meanwhile, the seller cannot unilaterally terminate its supply obligation, particularly where that act may put the buyer out of business. In the event, after a full trial, the court determines that the seller has a right to terminate the contract, the interim injunction will be lifted. Should the buyer prevail, then the interim injunction will be changed into a permanent injunction in favour of the buyer and consistent, of course, with the terms of the contract between the parties.

What has concerned the courts is a distinction between two separate commands that may be addressed to the defendant/seller: i) Thou shall not cut off the supply of goods to the buyer; and ii) Thou shall supply the buyer with goods. The first command is incorporated into an injunction; the second command lies at the heart of a decree for specific performance. The problem is that the first command is often a roundabout way of achieving the second command. As a general rule, a court will only impose an equitable remedy that acts to place a negative obligation on the defendant. "Thou shall not" is the time-honoured, preferred approach in commercial cases. The courts have generally resisted imposing a positive obligation — "Thou shall" — on the premise that such an order is difficult to enforce. A more fundamental policy reason is that such a positive order infringes on cherished notions of freedom and liberty. In practice, however, the courts recognize that "negative" and "positive" obligations may overlap. In the proper case, the court will not resile from granting an equitable remedy, which in effect places a positive or affirmative obligation on the buyer to supply goods under a contract of sale.

Another exceptional instance is the sale of rare or unique goods. The sales of a famous painting or original manuscript are examples. The buyer is entitled to specific performance of the contract of sale when the goods have no market substitute; that is, they cannot be obtained elsewhere.

Seller's Remedies

The seller's remedies against a buyer may be divided into two categories. First, there are proprietary or real remedies that are, in effect, remedies exercisable against the goods. Second, the seller has personal remedies against the buyer. The personal remedies are a right to an action for the price of the goods or the recovery of damages caused by the buyer's breach. The proprietary claim by the seller is not a substitute for damages. A seller, in the proper case, may be entitled to both exercise a proprietary remedy such as a lien and later sue the buyer for damages arising from the buyer's default.

One major advantage of the proprietary remedies is that they allow the seller to act without seeking the court's approval. Such remedies provide the seller with instant flexibility and quick response time to protect his/her financial stake in the goods sold to the buyer. At the same time, the proprietary remedies tend to be technical and limited in scope. They do not apply in every case, and attention must be focused on the requirements laid out as a pre-condition to enforcement in the *Act*.

FIGURE 17.2   **SELLER'S REMEDIES**

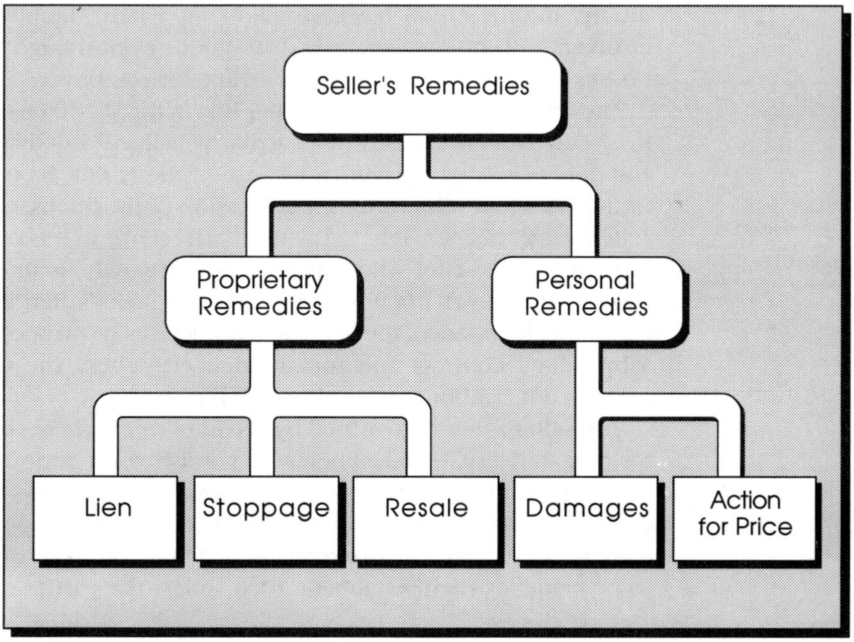

Proprietary Remedies

Proprietary, or *in rem*, means rights to the property itself. The seller enforcing such a remedy does not look to recovery of money against a defaulting buyer. Instead, the right is attached to the very goods that are subject to a contract of sale. There are three proprietary, or *in rem*, remedies expressly provided for in the *Sale of Goods Act*: i) an unpaid seller's lien; ii) the right of stoppage in transit; and iii) the right of resale. The common feature of each of these remedies is that the seller's right is directly concerned with the goods sold to the buyer.

UNPAID SELLER'S LIEN

The seller must demonstrate that he/she is an "unpaid seller" within the meaning of the *Act*. This burden is met by showing that the buyer has not paid or offered to pay the whole price or a negotiable instrument such as a cheque has been dishonoured.[11] Once the unpaid seller's status is established, then the existence of the lien is dependent on the seller's possession of the goods. The lien is a legal right to retain possession until the buyer pays for the goods. The effect of the lien is to "worry" the buyer into paying the price of the goods to the seller. The buyer knows that he/she will not obtain possession until the goods have been paid for, and that if he/she wants the goods, he/she must tender, or pay, the purchase price.

There are three instances where the lien automatically arises in favour of the unpaid seller: i) where the goods have been sold without any stipulations as to credit; ii) where the goods are subject to credit conditions and the credit has expired; or iii) where the buyer has become insolvent.[12] The lien also extends to goods even though the seller holds his/her possession as an agent or bailee for the buyer.

The unpaid seller may lose his/her lien in three circumstances: i) where he/she delivers the goods to a carrier or bailee for delivery to the buyer and fails to reserve a right to dispose of the goods; ii) where the buyer or his/her agent obtains lawful possession of the goods; or iii) where the seller waives his/her right to the lien.[13] The scope of this remedy is limited in nature. The seller's lien, as an *in rem* remedy, is one easily lost. As soon as the buyer obtains possession, the seller's lien is no longer enforceable. In essence, the seller's lien operates to protect the seller from a breach of contract suit for non-delivery where the whole purchase price is not paid or tendered by the buyer.

The seller's lien is governed by separate rules where the contract calls for part delivery, or instalments, of goods over a period of time. In the part delivery instance, the contract is considered non-severable, so the lien may be exercised against the remainder of the goods in the seller's possession. Where the contract is severable and a separate payment is to be made for each instalment, then, unless the parties otherwise agree, the seller cannot enforce a lien for an unpaid instalment by looking to another instalment for which the purchase price has been paid.[14]

RIGHT OF STOPPAGE IN TRANSIT

The seller's right to stop goods in transit has limited scope. The right is contingent upon the buyer's insolvency. Also, the seller must be unpaid for the goods in transit. The term "in transit" means that the goods are in the possession of an intermediary who is neither the agent of the seller nor of the buyer. Where the goods are in the possession of the seller, he/she retains control of his/her agent and can order the shipment stopped without relying on Section 47. Where the goods are in the possession of the buyer's agent, they are not "in transit" even though they have not been actually delivered by the buyer's agent to the buyer.[15]

This *in rem* right of the unpaid seller is exercised by either taking actual possession of the goods or by giving notice to the carrier or other bailee who has possession of the goods.[16] The unpaid seller must give reasonable notice to the person in actual possession or to his/her principal so as to prevent the delivery to the buyer.[17] Once the carrier or bailee has received notice from the unpaid seller, he/she has an obligation to redeliver the goods or deal with the goods as directed by the seller.[18] Should the carrier or bailee fail to act on the unpaid seller's notice, then the seller may have a good action in damages against the carrier or bailee.

RIGHT OF RESALE

The unpaid seller's right to resell the goods is expressly granted in Section 51(2), which provides: "When an unpaid seller who has exercised his right of lien, or retention or stoppage in transit, resells the goods, the buyer acquires a good title to it as against the original buyer." The right of resale exists only where the property in the goods has passed to the buyer.[19] Where the property in the goods has not passed to the buyer, the unpaid seller has a right to withhold delivery, the rights of lien, and stoppage in transit, but no express right to resell the goods.[20] The right of resale may be expanded by express agreement between the seller and buyer. Thus, the seller may reserve the right of resale on a designated default by the buyer.[21] For instance, the seller may reserve the right to resell the goods in the event that the buyer fails to provide a satisfactory credit reference within ten days of the making of the contract.

Once the unpaid seller exercises his/her right of resale, the contract of sale is rescinded. The seller then has a right of action in damages against the buyer to recover the difference between the contract price and the resale price.

Personal Remedies

The seller has two personal remedies against a defaulting buyer of goods under the *Act*. First, the seller has a statutory right to recover the price of the goods. Second, the seller has a right to recover damages for the buyer's non-acceptance of the goods.[22]

ACTION FOR THE PRICE

An action for the price is specifically authorized by Section 52 of the *Act*. The term "price" is, however, not expressly defined. The courts have construed this personal remedy as essentially an action for a liquidated sum.[23] The action for the price is not an action for damages. The seller is not seeking to recover his/her loss but the price of the goods fixed by the contract of sale.

A number of conditions must be satisfied by the seller in maintaining an action for the price: i) the property in the goods has passed to the buyer; ii) the buyer has neglected or refused to pay for the goods; and iii) the goods are subject to a contract of sale.[24] Thus, a contract for the sale of unascertained goods would fall outside the Section 52(1) requirements because the property has not passed until the goods are ascertained.[25]

Nonetheless, under Section 52(2) an action for the price may be maintained against a buyer who has wrongfully refused or neglected to pay on an agreed date to the seller, even though the property in the goods has not passed to the buyer. Where the goods are unascertained, the right of action turns on whether, under the contract of sale, the buyer has agreed to pay for the goods on a certain date. Thus, on the matter of drafting contracts of sale, the seller's draftsmen must take care to protect the seller's position under Section 52(2).

When the seller is unable to maintain an action for the price against the buyer, he/she may have an action for damages based on the buyer's default or breach of the contract of sale. There may be a large difference in monetary terms between the price of the goods and damages awarded for the buyer's non-acceptance of the goods. Thus, in many instances, there is an economic advantage in seeking to recover the price of the goods.

THE RIGHT TO DAMAGES

The basis for determining a seller's right to damages based on the buyer's non-acceptance of goods is identical to the buyer's right to damages based on the seller's non-delivery. Damages are normally assessed based on one of two different methods: i) the Market Rule; or ii) The *Hadley v. Baxendale* rule. The right to charge for storage of the goods is not really a means of assessment but a separate, statutory head of damages allowable to the seller.

The Market Rule is based on a measurement formula: the difference between the contract price and the market or current price at the time the goods ought to have been accepted.[26] The *Hadley v. Baxendale* rule is based on a more subjective ground: the loss directly and naturally resulting in the ordinary course of events from the buyer's breach of

FIGURE 17.3   **MEANS OF ASSESSING DAMAGES**

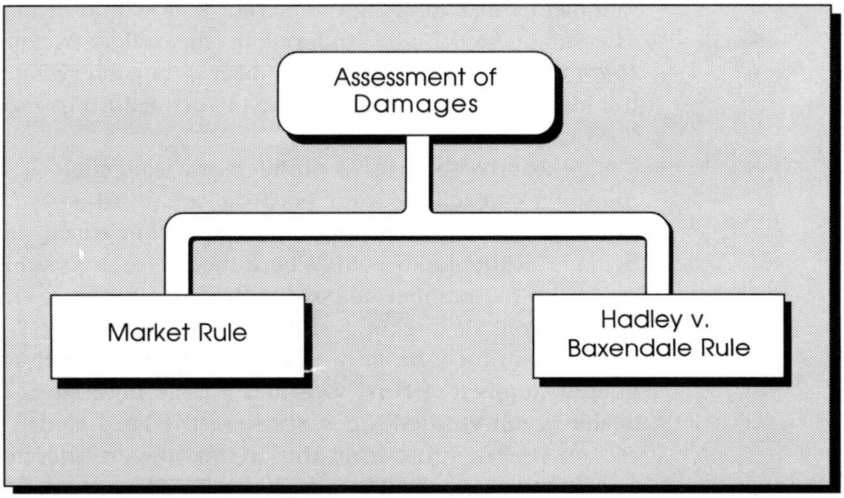

contract.[27] Finally, the seller may recover the reasonable charge for the care and custody of goods for which the buyer, after a reasonable time, has failed to take delivery.[28]

The courts begin with the presumption that the Market Rule applies in the absence of special circumstance. The onus is on the seller to show that the Market Rule works unfairly, and that damages ought to be based on the *Hadley v. Baxendale* rule.

Illustration   Rinehart contracts to purchase a 1986 Ford van from Midtown Motors Ltd. The purchase price is fixed at $14 500. The dealer's profit on the transaction is $3000. Rinehart signs the contract on March 2 and is obliged to take delivery of the Ford van on March 15. However, on March 15, Rinehart notifies Midtown Motors Ltd. that it will not take delivery. On March 22, Midtown Motors Ltd. sells the Ford van to a third party, John Higgins, for $14 500. Midtown Motors Ltd. sues Rinehart for damages based on its $3000 loss of profits from the sale. We will assume there are more Ford vans for sale through Midtown Motors Ltd. than there are available customers. Rinehart argues that the damage action should be dismissed because, applying the Market Rule, Midtown Motors Ltd. has suffered no loss. Conversely, Midtown Motors Ltd. argues that the special circumstances of this case displace the Market Rule and that the $3000 loss of profits based on the *Hadley v. Baxendale* rule should be allowed. There is considerable authority that Midtown Motors Ltd. is entitled to recover the lost profits. This result occurs even though Midtown Motors Ltd. admits that they made a $3000 profit in selling the same new Ford van to Higgins.

The courts have recognized the potential injustice caused by limiting the seller to damages based on the Market Rule in such instances. The rationale is that applying the Market Rule would produce an inaccurate assessment of damages suffered by the seller. By falling back on the *Hadley v. Baxendale* rule of damages, the seller's loss is measured by the lost profit resulting from the buyer's failure to take delivery of the Ford van.

Importantly, the loss of profits is not cancelled or reduced because the seller can sell the same Ford van to a third party at the same price. There is, however, an important distinction based on the supply and demand of the goods sold. Where there is a large number of Ford vans and a limited number of buyers, then the dealer is entitled to recover its lost profit against the first buyer even though the Ford Van is sold at no loss, and for a profit, to a third party. Conversely, where there is a limited number of Ford vans and a large number of buyers, then the dealer is not entitled, upon resale of the Ford van to a third party, to recoup its lost profit from the original buyer. Therefore, in each case such as the one in the illustration, there is a factual issue to be determined. Did the supply of the goods exceed the demand for the same?

Does the same rule apply where the car is second-hand? It has been held that the "new car" rule does not apply because each second-hand car is "different" from the next.[29] In the above illustration, had Midtown Motors Ltd. contracted to sell a second-hand Ford van to Rinehart, and — after Rinehart's refusal to accept delivery — resold the van to a third party at the same or higher price, the seller would not be entitled to recover its lost profit from the Rinehart sale.

Out-of-pocket and overhead expenses may also be claimed by a seller against a buyer who has cancelled certain types of contracts for the sale of goods. Where the *Hadley v. Baxendale* rule applies, then it is clear that the seller is entitled to recover his/her out-of-pocket expenses incurred in the aborted sale. This is of particular importance where the contract of sale requires the seller to specially manufacture the goods subject to the contract. On the other hand, the courts are unwilling, in most other instances, to award, as a head of damages, the overhead expense of the seller. Overhead expense includes a potentially wide range of items such as labour costs, insurance, taxes, rental costs, salaries, and wages. In other words, this includes all the expenses incurred by the seller to run the business that makes the goods ordered by the buyer.

Illustration   Rinehart, as seller, makes a contract of sale with Johnson Associates Ltd., as buyer, for the supply of a tailor-made software program to handle clients with business interests in the timber industry. Johnson, an accounting firm, contracts for Rinehart to install a computer system in its Vancouver office. The contract is made on April 10 with delivery scheduled on September 30. The contract price is $50 000. The price is further broken down as follows:

Materials cost	$ 1 000
Draft plan	$ 2 500
Computer time and labour	$40 500
Profit	$ 6 000
	$50 000

Johnson cancels the contract, without cause, on April 27. At the time of cancellation, Rinehart had already purchased the materials for the project and drafted the plan for the Johnson system. Rinehart brings a damage claim against Johnson on the following basis:

Drafting plan	$ 2 500
Materials cost	$ 1 000
Cost of overhead	$20 000
Loss of profit	$ 6 000
	$29 500

Johnson admits liability for the drafting and materials cost as out-of-pocket expenses, and the loss of net profit. They argue, however, that they are not liable to pay for Rinehart's overhead on the grounds that during the appropriate period Rinehart worked on other projects and recovered its overhead. In a similar case, *Kay-Son v. Atkinson-Harvey*,[30] the court observed:

> The plaintiff is entitled to be put financially in the same position as it would have been had the contract been completed. Had the contract not been cancelled the plaintiff would have enjoyed the profits resulting from it as well as from the work re-scheduled to take its place. In calculating the profits there should be taken into account the expenses of the plaintiff incurred as a result of the contract. Those expenses include the direct costs of labour and material. Overhead is not a factor unless the overhead can be shown to increase by reason of the contract. In the present case, no such increase was shown.

Problems for Discussion

1. It is said that the Market Rule is a more objective basis for awarding damages than the *Hadley v. Baxendale* rule. Do you agree that damages under the *Hadley v. Baxendale* rule are more subjective? In reaching your conclusion, consider the results in *Sunnyside Greenhouses Ltd. v. Golden West Seeds Ltd.*, *supra*, and *Parson v. Uttley Ingham*, *supra*.

2. Give examples of how the *Sale of Goods Act* expands the common law remedies otherwise available to sellers and buyers.

3. Distinguish between the proprietary remedies and personal remedies available to sellers and buyers. What are the advantages of the proprietary remedies? Are the proprietary remedies a substitute for personal remedies?

4. Rinehart purchased an Apple computer from Heyman Computer Ltd. on February 10 and paid $3500 for the system. At the time of purchase, a representative of Rinehart told the sales manager of Heyman that the computer would be used for accounting purposes. Within one week, Rinehart reported to Heyman that the Apple was malfunctioning. The computer was returned to the seller for repairs and re-delivered to Rinehart on February 17. The computer, however, still did not work properly, with problems of resolution in the display monitor and disk drives. Rinehart, on February 28, returned the computer, and Ms. Bach sent a letter rejecting the computer for breach of the implied condition of suitability for the particular purpose of the buyer. The lawyer representing Heyman replied to Ms. Bach's letter, and took the position that Rinehart had accepted the goods and that it was no longer open for the company to reject the computer. Discuss Rinehart's legal position on the right to reject the goods. Would there be a difference if the buyer had been an ordinary consumer? See *Wojakowski v. Pembina Dodge Chrysler Ltd.*, (1976) 5 W.W.R. 97 (Man.Q.B.).

5. Assume in Problem 4 above that Rinehart, after ordering the Apple computer from Heyman on February 10, decided to cancel the order on February 11, and that the reason for cancelling the sale was a last-minute decision to buy an IBM PC On February 13, Heyman sells the same Apple system to another buyer, Mary Aubert. Heyman later contends that Rinehart remains liable to compensate them for the lost profit from the February 10 sale. Rinehart counters that Heyman has not lost any profit because the same system was sold three days later to Mary Aubert. Will Heyman succeed in a damage claim for loss of profits? Would Heyman be entitled to an order of specific performance, compelling Rinehart to take delivery of the computer and pay the contract price?

6. In the above sale of the Apple computer system, in what circumstances would Heyman be entitled to exercise a lien against the goods and resell them to a third party? How would the lien remedy operate differently from the remedy used by Heyman in Problem 5 above? How would you advise a seller such as Heyman to go about exercising a lien?

7. Distinguish between out-of-pocket expenses and overhead expenses in a damage claim brought by a seller against a buyer who wrongfully repudiates a contract governed by the *Sale of Goods Act*.

8. Where a buyer sues for the recovery of the purchase price for goods that are defective, in what circumstances will the court award less than the full purchase price to the buyer?

Chapter 17 Notes

1. (1967) 61 D.L.R.(2d) 462 (Sask.Q.B.).
2. Section 35(2).
3. See *Hardy v. Hillerns & Fowler*, (1923) 2 K.B. 490 (C.A.).
4. See *Mahinder Singh v. Acme Sawmills*, (1958) 14 D.L.R.(2d) 361 (B.C.C.A.).
5. See Chapter 7.
6. (1928) All E.R. 763 (H.L.).
7. Section 56(2).
8. (1974) W.W.R. 420 (Alta. C.A.) affirmed (1973) 3 W.W.R. 288 (S.C.).
9. (1978) 1 All E.R. 527 (C.A.).
10. (1974) 1 All E.R. 954 (H.C.).
11. Section 42(1).
12. Section 44(1).
13. Section 46(1).
14. See *Snagproff v. Brody*, (1922) 3 W.W.R. 432 (Alta. S.C. App. Div.)
15. Section 48(2).
16. Section 49(1).
17. Section 49(2).
18. Section 49(3).
19. Section 43(1).
20. Section 43(2).
21. Section 51(4).
22. Section 53.
23. See *Colley v. Overseas Exporters Ltd.*, (1921) 3 K.B. 302.
24. Section 52(1).
25. Section 21.
26. Section 53(3).
27. Section 53(2).
28. Section 41.
29. See *Lazenby Garages Ltd. v. Wright*, (1976) 2 All E.R. 770 (C.A.).
30. (1979) 12 B.C.L.R. 222 (B.C.S.C.).

18 NEGOTIABLE INSTRUMENTS

Introduction to Negotiable Instruments

Negotiable instruments, or commercial paper, include cheques, promissory notes, and drafts. These instruments provide a form of merchantable currency in commerce. The governing law is found in the law of merchants — the traditional judge-made law, and the *Bills of Exchange Act*,[1] which ensures a high degree of transferability of negotiable instruments.

Transferability, or negotiability, is crucial to business efficacy. In the world of commerce, where business dealings range from province to province and country to country, it is not always practical to exchange cash for goods and services. Also, a negotiable instrument provides a convenient means of credit. For example, Rinehart may exchange goods or services for the buyer's written promise to pay at some certain date in the future. The buyer may promise to pay $2500 for specialized software 120 days after the delivery. Rinehart, however, may require the cash from this transaction before the end of the 120 days.

Assuming that the buyer has given a *promissory note* as evidence of its written promise to pay this sum on the particular date, Rinehart can *negotiate* or sell the note to a third party such as a bank that will pay value for the buyer's promise to pay $2500. The willingness of the bank to accept the note for value is based on its right to enforce the note, when it becomes payable, against the buyer without becoming subject to any contractual disputes that might later emerge between Rinehart and the buyer. An important feature of negotiable instruments is the separation of the contractual rights and remedies enforceable between the original parties to the contract of sale, and the right of a stranger to that contract to enforce payment on the basis of the negotiable instrument alone.

Historical Background

English law did not always recognize the negotiability of commercial paper. In early law, a right to receive a future payment was not generally assignable. Under this centuries-old approach, Rinehart would have no choice but to retain the promissory note until the elapse of the 120-day period and seek payment from the original buyer at that time.

When English law initially recognized the right of assignment, the assignee acquired a legal right that placed him/her in the shoes of the assignor. Thus, in our illustration, the bank taking the note by assignment would have "bought" into any potential lawsuit between Rinehart and its buyer. Any defence arising out of the original contract of sale between the *obligor* — the person obliged to pay the sum due, here the buyer, and the *payee* — the person owed the payment obligation and the assignor of the contractual obligation to pay, here Rinehart, was fully enforceable by the obligor against the assignee. In essence, for purposes of enforcement, the assignee of the negotiable instrument was treated in the same fashion as a party to the original contract.

The conceptual leap between the rule of assignment of a contractual promise to pay and negotiable instruments was made once the transferee or assignee of the instrument acquired a right to payment that, in practice, might be substantially greater than the right of the original payee. With this reduction of exposure to potential defences, parties became willing to purchase a negotiable instrument and to pay value for it.

The major advance in the law of negotiable instruments is based on the doctrine of *holder in due course* — of the transferee who in good faith and without knowledge of intervening equities paid value for the instrument. This is the pivotal doctrine upon which the concept of negotiability is founded. Without a holder-in-due-course status, negotiable instruments would be governed by the general law of assignment.

Sources in Canadian Law

In Canada, the law of negotiable instruments has two main sources. The primary source is federal legislation titled the *Bills of Exchange Act*. Modelled on English legislation, the Canadian act establishes a body of rules that regulate drafts, cheques, and promissory notes. In cases where the *Act* is silent, an important secondary source of law is found in the common law cases.

Another piece of federal legislation, the *Business Corporation Act*[2], expands the scope of negotiable instruments to include share certificates issued by federally incorporated companies.

In this chapter, three aspects of negotiable instruments in Canadian law will be considered: i) the form of negotiable instruments; ii) the negotiation of negotiable instruments; and iii) defences to defeat a holder of such instruments.

The Forms of Negotiable Instruments

There are three commonly used negotiable instruments or commercial papers: i) drafts; ii) promissory notes; and iii) cheques. In this section, each form of negotiable instrument will be examined and illustrated.

The Draft or Bill of Exchange

In a draft or bill of exchange, there are three parties: The *drawer*—Oxford Telecommunication, Inc.—directs the *drawee*—The Royal Bank—to pay a specified sum ($5000) to the *payee*—Rinehart Ltd. In the draft set forth in Figure 18.1, the drawer may have left the line for the payee blank or written "to the order of bearer." In bearer form, the drawee would pay the face amount to whomever presents the draft on the appointed date for payment.

The term "bill of exchange" is used to describe three different types of drafts. The *time draft* is payable after a period of time from the date of the draft itself (see Figure 18.1.). It is common, therefore, for the time draft to provide that the amount is due, for example, thirty, sixty, or ninety days from the date of the draft. The essence of the time draft is the drawer's promise of future payment. It cannot be "cashed" by the drawee prior to that date, but it can be negotiated or sold by the payee or bearer, as the case may be, to a third party who will generally pay a discounted price for the right to later present the draft to the drawee for payment. It is possible that the draft may exchange hands a number of times prior to the due date.

The *sight draft* is payable immediately upon presentation by the holder

FIGURE 18.1 **AN EXAMPLE OF A TIME DRAFT**

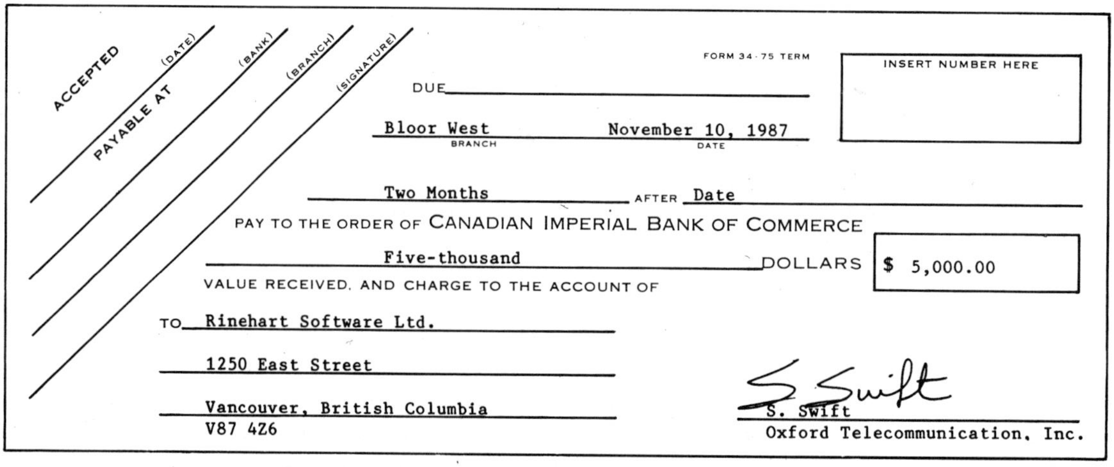
ACCEPTED (DATE)
PAYABLE AT (BANK) (BRANCH) (SIGNATURE)
FORM 34-75 TERM
INSERT NUMBER HERE
DUE
Bloor West — BRANCH
November 10, 1987 — DATE
Two Months AFTER Date
PAY TO THE ORDER OF CANADIAN IMPERIAL BANK OF COMMERCE
Five-thousand DOLLARS $ 5,000.00
VALUE RECEIVED, AND CHARGE TO THE ACCOUNT OF
TO Rinehart Software Ltd.
1250 East Street
Vancouver, British Columbia
V87 4Z6
S. Swift
S. Swift
Oxford Telecommunication, Inc.

Courtesy of the Canadian Imperial Bank of Commerce

to the drawee. In Canada, the drawee of a sight draft has three days to make payment after it has been presented.

The *demand draft* — the cheque is the most common example — is payable immediately without a grace period accorded to the drawee.

The Promissory Note

The promissory note is a two-party transaction between the *maker* — the person making the promise of payment — and the *payee* — the person who is the beneficiary of the promise. Often, the promissory note is found in a debtor and creditor situation. The debtor is the maker and the creditor is the payee. Unlike the draft, there is no drawee that the payee is required to present the note to for payment.

A precondition to a promissory note is the maker's unconditional promise to pay on demand or at a fixed future date a "certain sum of money" either to the order of a named party or of bearer.[3] When the note provides that payment may be paid "on or before" a specified date, the Supreme Court of Canada[4] has held that these words do not create an uncertainty as to the date of payment or introduce a contingency.

Problems have arisen over the meaning of "sum certain in money", a statutory requirement to the validity of a promissory note. A promise to pay $900 with interest at 8 percent per annum until paid *and 10 percent attorney fees* is not a promissory note. The words "and 10 percent attorney fees" makes the amount payable under the note not a sum certain.[5]

The maker must deliver the promissory note to the payee before it is a valid instrument. There are instances where an issue of authority has been raised about the payee's right to complete and dispose of a document that a later transferee seeks to enforce as a promissory note. Thus,

FIGURE 18.2 **AN EXAMPLE OF A PROMISSORY NOTE**

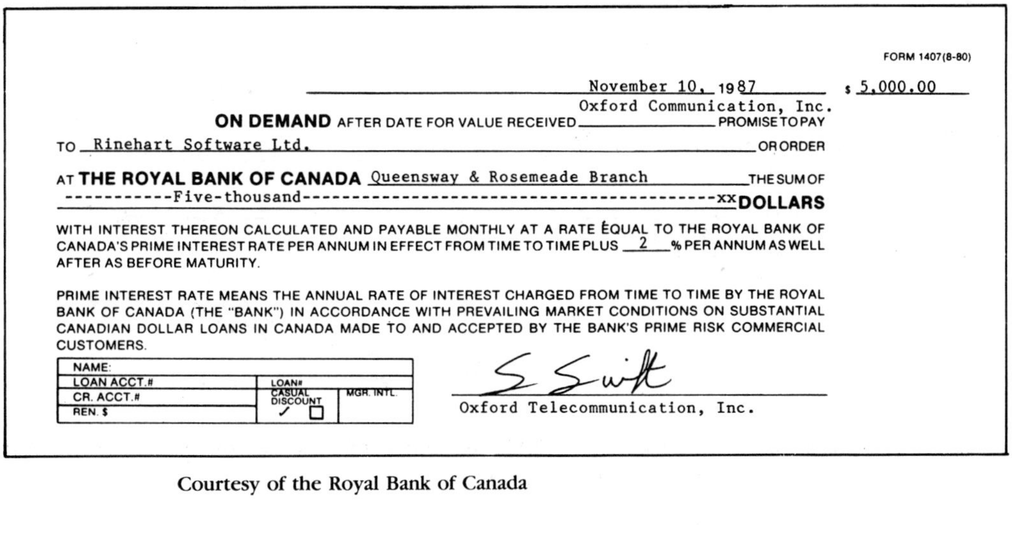

Courtesy of the Royal Bank of Canada

a merchant who persuades a customer to execute a promissory note in blank with the understanding that the merchant will not fill it in or dispose of it has, in fact, a non-negotiable document. In breaking this undertaking, the merchant might fill in the blanks and dispose of the document to a third party. But the third party, in this instance, is not receiving a promissory note, and as transferee of a non-negotiable instrument, his/her claim is limited to an action against the merchant.[6]

The Cheque

A cheque is a specie of draft. Like all drafts, there are three parties: i) the drawer who directs; ii) the drawee (usually a bank) to a payment of a sum certain to iii) the payee.

A cheque is payable on demand by the drawee bank. The payee may deposit the cheque in another bank (the collecting bank) that then sends the cheque to the drawee bank for collection. The cheque carries the drawer's promise that he/she has sufficient funds in the drawee bank to cover the amount of the cheque. A payee who does not want to rely on the drawer's promise may request the drawer to have the cheque *certified* by the drawee bank. With certification, the drawee is committed to honour the cheque and pay the funds. One advantage of certification is to eliminate the drawer's capacity to withdraw his/her promise of payment by placing a *stop-order payment* on the cheque, which orders the drawee bank to dishonour the cheque.

In many instances, the drawer may use a post-dated cheque rather than a time draft. Here, the payee will not be entitled to demand payment from the drawee bank until the actual date that appears on the face of

FIGURE 18.3 **AN EXAMPLE OF A CHEQUE**

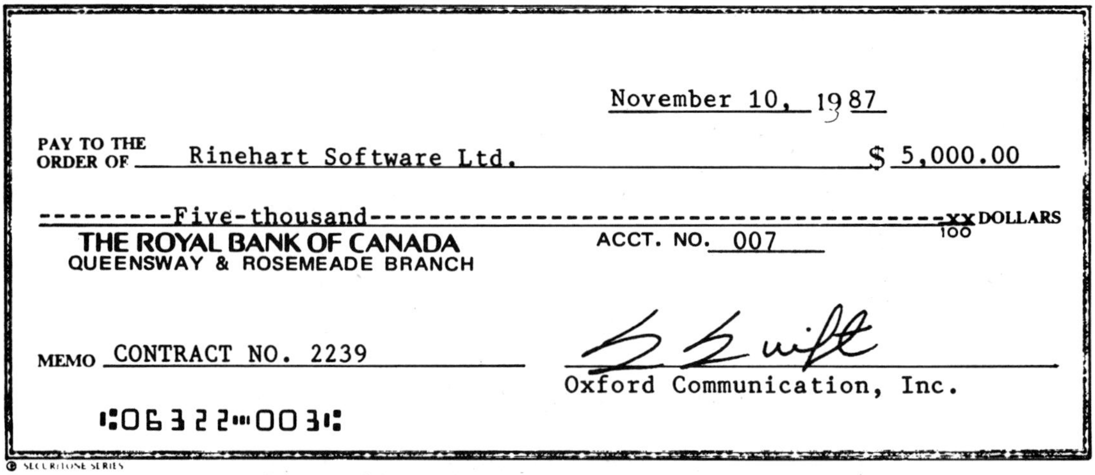
November 10, 1987

PAY TO THE ORDER OF Rinehart Software Ltd. $ 5,000.00

---------Five-thousand------------------------------------xx/100 DOLLARS

THE ROYAL BANK OF CANADA
QUEENSWAY & ROSEMEADE BRANCH

ACCT. NO. 007

MEMO CONTRACT NO. 2239

S Swift
Oxford Communication, Inc.

⑆06322⑈003⑆

SECURITONE SERIES

Courtesy of the Royal Bank of Canada

the cheque. The post-dated cheque, unlike the time draft, is subject to a stop-payment order. Thus, if a dispute over a term of the contract arises between the drawer and payee, the drawer may exercise his right of stop payment. As a result, a post-dated cheque lacks the same level of security as other negotiable instruments in the hands of a third party. The payee is less able to raise money on post-dated cheques. The payee, therefore, may have a liquidity problem. The drawer, nonetheless, retains an important advantage: he/she has financial leverage during the intervening period when problems of delivery, quality, or others of the contract are likely to arise.

Negotiation of a Bill of Exchange or Promissory Note

Once the negotiable instrument is transferred to a third party, the payee is often at a disadvantage because defences available against the original payee depend on the legal status of the new bill or note holder. There are three recognized classes of holders: i) mere holder; ii) holder for value; and iii) holder in due course.

The greatest bundle of rights are obtained by a holder in due course, and, conversely, the least protected is the mere holder. In this part, we will examine the main rules that apply to holders in each of the three categories. In each instance, the determination of who is a holder is essential to working out the rules of negotiability. There are several uniform features amongst all holders. Each is in possession of a negotiable instrument that is either payable to him/her, endorsed to him/her, or in blank or made out to the bearer. Even though the holder was not a party to the original transaction upon which the bill or note is based, he/she acquires rights of negotiation, transfer, and enforcement. These rights exist, in the case of a holder in due course, independently of prior holders or the original payee.

Mere Holder

The mere holder is the most vulnerable of the three types of holders to defences that the obligor has under the bill or note. For example, a transferee of a promissory note payable to a specific payee, and who takes possession of the note without the payee's endorsement, is a mere holder. Assume that Valley View Credit Union ("Valley") acquires the promissory note in Figure 18.2 from Rinehart Ltd., but that the company does not endorse the note. After the transfer, Rinehart Ltd. then releases Oxford Telecommunication from its obligation to pay on the note. On the maturity date, Valley seeks to enforce the note against Oxford. It is clear that in this case, Valley, as transferee without endorsement, has acquired only the title of Rinehart Ltd. Until Valley provides notice of the transfer to Oxford (the maker), then Valley, as transferee, is subject to the subsequent equities between the maker and transferor.[7]

Unless the holder has possession of a note or bill that is endorsed or payable to the bearer, even though he/she provides value and lacks notice of the intervening equities, he/she takes only such title as the transferor has in the bill or note. In effect, the mere holder has the same status as an assignee.

Holder for Value

Unless a holder has supplied valuable consideration for a bill or note, he/she will be deemed a mere holder with the same status as an assignee. At the same time, it is possible for a person to have provided valuable consideration but still fall short of acquiring the preferred status as a holder in due course.

Valuable consideration means: i) any consideration sufficient to support a simple contract or ii) constituted by an antecedent debt or liability.[8] The second statutory definition of valuable consideration has caused litigation. In *Oliver v. Davis*,[9] one party provided a post-dated cheque with a creditor. Later, the debtor's fiancée gave a second cheque for the same amount as the first to the creditor's wife. The creditor was out of town and no explanation was made to his wife as to why the cheque drawn on the fiancée's account had been delivered to her. Later, the fiancée, realizing that she had been deceived about the man she was planning to marry — he was married to someone else — issued a stop-payment order.

After the creditor's cheque was dishonoured, he commenced an action against the debtor and his fiancée. The creditor argued that valuable consideration had been provided for the fiancée's bill, i.e., her cheque, on the basis that it had fallen within the meaning of "an antecedent debt or liability". The courts said that the intent of this phrase was a reference to the antecedent debt or liability of the *promisor*, or *drawer*, of the bill. In this case, the liability was not owed by the fiancée. The court worried about the possibility that a creditor might be entitled to recover on both the debt of the promisor and on the cheque of the drawer.

To prevent the creditor from obtaining double recovery in such circumstances, the court formulated two rules that operate to protect the non-debtor drawer of a cheque: i) Where the debt or liability is owed by a third party, there must be something in the transaction sufficient to connect the drawer's bill with the antecedent debt or liability; ii) The consideration for the bill must be in the form of forbearance or a promise to forbear, implied or expressed, on the part of the recipient of the bill, who agrees not to pursue a claim against his/her creditor.

In the *Oliver* case, the court failed to find evidence that the creditor had forborne, promised to forbear (he was out of town at the time), or ever intended thought of forbearing for an instant in respect of any remedy against his debtor, the drawer's fiancée.

Once the element of valuable consideration has been established, then the holder for value must meet two other conditions under the *Act* before he/she is recognized as a holder in due course. It is this latter status that provides the maximum protection and ensures the negotiability of bills.

Holder in Due Course

The *Bills of Exchange Act* defines a holder in due course as follows: i) a holder who has taken a bill, complete and regular on its face; ii) before it was overdue; iii) without notice that it has been previously dishonoured; iv) in good faith; v) for value; and vi) without notice of any defect in the title of the person who negotiated it.[10]

Once a person acquires the status of a holder in due course, then the circumstances where a court will withhold his/her right to enforce the bill or note are greatly reduced. The holder in due course of a bill or exchange or a promissory note is not considered as an assignee of the payee. A mercantile instrument passes to such a holder in much the same fashion as "money". For instance, one of the conditions to being a holder in due course is that the bill is not overdue.

Illustration   Through the fraud of Rinehart Ltd., an employee, Arnold Stepp, who worked in the accounting department, had another employee, Ben True, who had signing authority, sign a promissory note naming Stepp as payee. Under the terms of that note dated March 5, 1987, Rinehart promised to pay Stepp, on order, at the Canadian Bank of Commerce, Main Branch, Vancouver, British Columbia, the sum of $10 000 with interest annually at 10 percent. After the first periodical payment had fallen due, Stepp transferred the promissory note to the Valley View Credit Union for $7500. Valley had no knowledge of the fact that Rinehart had not paid the interest, and was unaware of Stepp's fraud in obtaining True's signature. When the note fell due, Valley sought to enforce the obligation against Rinehart. The company claimed that Valley was not a holder in due course. If Valley was a holder in due course, then Rinehart — subject to certain defences — would be liable. In such a case, the crucial issue is whether, at the time the note was negotiated to Valley, the note was overdue. The *Act* does not contain an express definition of "overdue". Therefore, the resolution of this issue falls to the general mercantile law.

In *Union Investment Co. v. Wells*,[11] the Supreme Court of Canada, in a case with similar facts, held that the transferee was not a holder in due course. Therefore, for purposes of enforcement, the transferee stood in the same shoes as the transferor — who was a rogue. The requirement that a bill not be overdue is based on the notion that in the common course of dealings, an overdue note raises suspicion. This suspicion then casts an affirmative duty on the intended transferee to make inquiries about the status of the note.

Failure to carry out this duty permits the drawer of the note to raise the same defences against the holder that would otherwise be available against the payee. The custom of merchants concerning such instruments is that such an instrument, after its maturity passes, is no longer regarded as negotiable. In the illustration, the principal was not overdue, only the interest; and the fact that the interest was overdue did not appear on the face of the note. Nonetheless, in *Union Investment Co.*, as the due date for the payment had passed, the Supreme Court of Canada held that the transferee had a legal duty to inquire as to whether the payment of interest had been made.

Where there is an actual default of interest, the failure to make such an inquiry will deprive the transferee of his/her status as a holder in due course. It is the absence of any investigatory duty placed on a transferee that typically distinguishes the negotiable instrument from other kinds of personal property transfers. Yet, even with a bill or note, as the *Union Investment Co.* case indicates, the negotiability rule stops short of applying to overdue or dishonoured instruments.

Defences Effective Against a Holder in Due Course

The *Bills of Exchange Act* provides that a holder in due course holds the bill free from defects of title by prior parties and from mere personal defences available to the prior parties among themselves.[12] A mere personal defence may be, for example, a right of set-off that the drawer has against the payee. In Figure 18.1, although Rinehart is owed $5000 as the payee of the time draft, in the course of other dealings, Rinehart may have incurred a debt owed to Oxford. Assume that Rinehart owes Oxford $2000. Oxford has a right to set off that amount against the $5000 owed to Rinehart under the time draft. Once the bill is negotiated to a holder in due course, however, Oxford cannot set off the $2000 against this holder.

There is a third category called *real defences*. A real defence can be used to defeat the enforceability of a bill or note in the hands of a holder in due course. There are four examples of real defences: i) lack of capacity; ii) material alteration; iii) fraud; and iv) forgery.

Lack of Capacity

The lack of capacity defence is limited to instances where the drawer of the bill is a minor or infant. It is well settled that an infant cannot make himself liable on a bill or note. The infant is only liable for the fair market value of goods and services actually supplied to him/her that are necessaries — food, shelter, clothing, and education. Even though an infant gave a promissory note or accepted a bill of exchange for the price of necessaries, and is later sued on the bill or note, he/she would not be liable on the bill or note. The person supplying the necessaries would be put to his/her proof that the necessaries were supplied and recovery would be on that basis alone.[13]

Material Alterations

The effect of a material alteration of a bill, unless all the parties liable on the bill have consented, is to void it. Where the bill is in the hands of a holder in due course, only material alterations that are apparent on the face of the bill will render the bill void. In the absence of an apparent alteration, even if the bill has been materially altered the holder in due due course has the right to enforce the note as if it had not been altered.[14]

Material alterations include an alteration of: i) the date; ii) the sum payable; iii) the time of payment; iv) the place of payment; and v) the addition of a place of payment with the acceptor's assent.[15]

Thus, for example, where it is obvious that the date of the note has been altered from 1984 to 1987, and an ink different from that of the rest of the note has been used to insert the name of the place where the note was made, and a different ink has again been used to insert 10 percent interest in a blank space, the note is void.[16]

Fraud

The defence of fraud plays a central role in consumer transactions where promissory notes are used to finance the purchase of goods and services. Fraud is often much easier to assert than to prove. In the successful case, the party asserting fraud is usually at some substantial disadvantage, e.g., lack of education, a language difficulty, or being elderly. The seller takes advantage of this weakness or disability to deceive and mislead the buyer. Clearly, in such an instance, there is a strong argument for imposing an equitable solution that may include the voiding of the note. Where a third party has acquired the note, the task of connecting the fraud to the holder can be difficult.

A typical example of this problem is contained in *Nordic Acceptance Ltd. v. Switzer.*[17] In that case, a finance company purchased a promissory note from a home-improvement firm. The finance company sought to enforce the note against the drawers. The drawers lived in a small village and were humble, uneducated people. The wife had never signed a promissory note before. After the husband had left for work, two men working for a home-improvement company came around to the couple's house and offered to do stonework.

The men represented that the work would be done without any cost, and then asked for the wife's signature on a number of documents, including sixty blank cheques. They told her a story about the work involving something to do with the company's income tax. Later, the couple's signatures were crudely forged on a promissory note. Then the note was sold for a large discount to the plaintiff's finance company. The question was whether this fraud and forgery tainted the note in the hands of the holder.

The rule in such a case has a large measure of discretion whether the circumstances and facts are such as to invite the transferee's actual suspicion. Where there is actual suspicion arising from the facts, then, prior to negotiation, the transferee has a duty to make suitable inquiry to remove the suspicion. As the court found that there were a number of reasons to arouse suspicion, and that the holder had failed to discharge his/her duty of inquiry, the defence of fraud could be successfully raised and the drawers' obligation under the note held void.

The court concluded that mere suspicion or speculation that something might be wrong is insufficient to deprive the holder in due course of his/her right to enforce the payment obligation. In each case, it is a question of fact whether, given all the circumstances, the suspicion was actual or vague. Where there is a historical relationship between the payee and the holder, for example, where they have done business over a period of time or share common officers, employees, or offices, it becomes more difficult for the holder to avoid the application of the actual suspicion rule.

In the commercial cases, fraud is more difficult to establish. For example, where employees are asked to sign a "document" on the basis that it will operate to oust a minority shareholder, and the documents are, in fact, a promissory note, later sold to a bank, they cannot escape liability on the ground that they did not know that what they had signed made them personally liable.[18] So long as the bank in this example gives value for the note and has no knowledge of the fraud or misrepresentation, the co-signers are unable to defend against their liability in a suit brought by the holder in due course. The defendants had been careless and negligent. As a result, they have been disentitled from stripping the holder in due course from any enforcement action.

Forgery

Forgery is another real defence that the courts have used to deny the enforcement of a bill or note in the hands of a holder in due course. The case of forgery often arises in the circumstances of the forged cheque. As a general rule, a bill with a forged or unauthorized signature is wholly inoperative.[19] In the case of a forged cheque, the victim of the forgery is entitled to recover the money paid by the bank so long as he/she has given notice within one year after he/she has acquired notice of the forgery.[20]

The bank has a remedy against the forger — but the forgers are usually long gone, broke, or in jail — and against any endorser who endorsed the bill or note after the forgery or unauthorized endorsement.[21] Where the note has passed down a chain of holders in due course, the lawsuit works back up the chain. The last person left "holding the bag" is the first holder in due course who took directly from the forger.

There can be problems where the drawer of the forged cheque presents the cheque to a bank different from the one on which the cheque is drawn. For instance, assume that Arnold Stepp, a payroll clerk for Rinehart, fraudulently causes an officer of the company to sign a cheque drawn on Rinehart's account at the Royal Bank. Later, Stepp negotiates the forged cheque through the Bank of Nova Scotia. The Bank of Nova Scotia, as the collecting bank, then forwards the cheque to the Royal Bank. The Royal Bank, unaware of the forgery, pays the cheque and charges the amount of the cheque against Rinehart's accounts. After Rinehart discovers the forgery, a suit is brought against Stepp and the Bank of Nova Scotia. The *Act*, however, does not apply because it is limited to a suit by the Royal Bank. This action is brought by the drawer, Rinehart. The proper procedure would have been for Rinehart to sue the Royal Bank for the amount of the loss, and then for the Royal Bank to recover the amount in a suit against the Bank of Nova Scotia. A suit against the collecting bank by the drawer will normally fail.[22]

The Canadian courts have recently developed a rule that places a positive duty on commercial customers to employ reasonable accounting and business procedures to minimize the opportunity of forgery. The rule provides an affirmative defence in a subsequent action by the drawer against a bank that has credited the drawer's account to pay the forged cheques.

Illustration   Arnold Stepp, a payroll clerk, works in Rinehart's accounting department. Between March 1, 1985 and August 31, 1987, Stepp forged the name of Rinehart on a series of twenty-three cheques. The Bank of Montreal debited Rinehart's account by the amount of the forged cheques, totalling $39 500. Rinehart commenced an action against the bank after the forgery was discovered. The bank's evidence shows that Rinehart's accounting department failed to follow a number of common business procedures that would have detected the forgery. For instance, Rinehart's head accountant, Helen Voll, admitted that she had not followed the company's procedures regarding the reconciliation of bank statements, and that Stepp's forgery was concealed by his manipulation of the reconciliation statements. Voll also admitted that she did not inspect the cancelled cheques, and that, if she had seen them, she would have questioned them as the companies named on the cheques did not do business with Rinehart. Instead, these duties were assigned to Stepp, and Voll failed to supervise him. This state of affairs inside Rinehart enabled Stepps to commit and conceal his forgery.

The court is faced with the decision of where to place the loss of Stepp's forgery — on Rinehart or on Rinehart's bank. The answer to this decision lies, in part, with the legal relationship between a bank and its customer. Although this relationship is basically contractual, formed by the banking agreement signed by both parties, the contract does not necessarily govern the whole relationship. In *Canadian Pacific Hotels Ltd. v. Bank of Montreal*,[23] a case upon which the above illustration is based, the court observed:

> I cannot see that a large sophisticated bank customer who receives daily statements of account from its bank, whose daily bank trans-actions amount to many thousands of dollars, can be absolved of responsibility for checking the accuracy of those statements in re-spect of cheques bearing forged signatures. If the bank is to be held liable to its customer for honouring cheques bearing forged signa-tures surely it must be considered a part of commercial custom that the customer take steps to identify forgeries and prevent their re-currence as part of normal business practice. The Price Waterhouse report indicated unequivocally that if CP Hotels *had* followed proper accounting practices and procedures, Sigulim [the forger] would not have been able to succeed in his scheme. . . .
>
> In enacting s. 49(1) of the *Bills of Exchange Act*, the Legislature clearly did not intend that strict liability be imposed upon the bank. . . . In a commercial context an efficient internal control system is designed to prevent fraud against the corporation without regard to specific provisions of the *Bills of Exchange Act*. In my opinion a bank dealing with a sophisticated commercial customer has a right to expect that the customer will have such internal controls in place. The customer owes a duty to the bank to operate an acceptable internal control system so that both the bank and its customer are jointly engaged in prevention and minimization of losses occurring through forgeries.
>
> To impose such a duty on a sophisticated customer does not run counter to the spirit of the *Bills of Exchange Act*. The practical approach to take to this issue is [to] assess it on the principle of two innocents. Where two suffer for the fraud of a third, the one who most enables that third party to create the fraud should bear the loss. . . . CP was negligent in failing to properly supervise its em-ployee, Sigulim, and in failing to follow proper accounting procedure with respect to the bank reconciliations. CP being thus in breach of its duty to the bank should bear the loss.

The Law of Negotiation

Under the heading of holders, we considered the question of a person's status for purposes of determining his/her rights to the property in a negotiable instrument or to the enforcement of that instrument against the drawer. In this section, we will consider the methods of negotiating a bill or note. To appreciate the methods of negotiation requires a basic understanding of the statutory requirements defining the terms of negotiability and transferability.

Section 60 of the *Bills of Exchange Act* contains the legal formula of negotiability: i) A bill is negotiated when it is transferred from one party to another in such a way as to confer the status of holder on the transferee; ii) The actual procedure of negotiation depends on the description contained within the bill as to whom the sum certain is payable. There are two possibilities: that the bill is payable to the bearer or that the bill is payable to the order.

A bearer bill is negotiated by *delivery*. Alternatively, a pay-to-the-order bill is negotiated by *endorsement and delivery*. The recipient in either case is the "holder". The *payee* of a bill, who takes actual delivery, is not a holder, and the transfer to him/her is not a "negotiation" within the meaning of the *Act*.

Illustrations   1. A bill payable to Rinehart Ltd. 2. A bill payable to Rinehart Ltd. or order. 3. A bill payable to the order of Rinehart Ltd. 4. A bill payable to bearer. 5. A bill payable to Rinehart Ltd. or bearer.

We will assume in each case that Oxford Telecommunication is the drawer of the bill (in the form of a cheque) and that the Royal Bank is the drawee. In all five cases, upon the delivery of the cheque to Rinehart Ltd., they have an instrument that can be negotiated to a third party or holder. From the holder's point of view, there is a distinction in the method of transfer among the five illustrations.

In the first three illustrations, transfer and negotiation are accomplished by the appropriate signing officer endorsing the cheque and delivering it to the holder. In illustrations four and five, there is no requirement for an endorsement, and in these two cases, the cheques may be validly transferred by delivering them to a holder. Similarly, once the signing officer of Rinehart endorses a cheque payable in illustrations one, two, and three, and if that endorsement is not restrictive — see the types of endorsements noted below — then it becomes a bearer instrument.

As "endorsement" is an important feature of the law of negotiation, it is not surprising that the *Act* deals with the types of endorsements at length. The rights and obligations of endorsers have been the cause of much litigation. First, it is possible for the *holder* (as opposed to the payee) to transfer a bill to his/her order for value without endorsing it.

The person taking the transfer without endorsement, however, takes only such title as the transferor had in the bill.[24] The transferee, therefore, does not have the same rights as a holder. Who must endorse a bill and how they endorse it are two important questions.

Before an endorsement operates as a negotiation, the bill must be signed — usually on the back — and the signing is for the entire bill.[25] A partial endorsement — one that purports only to transfer a part of the amount payable to the endorsee — does not operate as a negotiation of the bill.[26] The endorsement obligation is placed on the payee — as illustrated in the first three illustrations above — and upon subsequent holders of the bill.

The endorsement may be made in several ways under the *Act*: i) an endorsement in blank; ii) a special endorsement; iii) a restrictive endorsement; iv) a qualified endorsement; and v) a conditional endorsement.

Endorsement in Blank

An endorsement in blank specifies no endorsee.[27] Thus, in Figure 18.3, when the signing officer of Rinehart signs the back of the cheque "Rinehart Ltd. per Helen Voll" without more, this is an endorsement in blank and converts the cheque into a bearer instrument. At this point, the cheque can be negotiated simply by delivery to another person. Mr. Stepp, our rogue, might steal the endorsed cheque and negotiate it to a holder in due course. Such a holder would be entitled to enforce the payment obligation against Oxford, and Rinehart's only remedy would be against Mr. Stepp.

Special Endorsement

A special endorsement specifies the person to whom, or to whose order, the bill is to be payable.[28] To protect the company against the potential loss caused by the Stepps of the world, the cheque in Figure 18.3 would be endorsed as follows: "Pay to the order of Rinehart Ltd." or "Pay Rinehart Ltd." Were Mr. Stepp to steal a cheque so endorsed, then he could not negotiate it to a holder in due course. Any further negotiation would require the signature or further endorsement of the signing officer — and head accountant — Ms. Helen Voll.

Restrictive Endorsement

A restrictive endorsement operates either to prohibit any further negotiation of the bill or to limit the authority to deal with the bill as directed, and does not transfer ownership.[29] Rinehart's signing officer, Helen Voll, might employ one of the following three types of restrictive endorsements to the cheque in Figure 18.3: i) "Pay Rinehart Ltd. only, per Helen

Voll"; ii) "Pay Rinehart Ltd., or order, for collection, per Helen Voll"; or iii) "For deposit only, per Helen Voll".

A restrictive endorsement is typically used to make a bill non-negotiable, and as a precaution for a wrongful negotiation by another. As a general rule, a bill with any one of the above restrictive endorsements must be paid to the person endorsing the bill and no other party.[30]

Conditional Endorsement

Although a bill must have an unconditional obligation imposed on the drawer or maker to pay, an endorsement of such a bill may be conditional in nature. The condition may relate to the happening or non-happening of a particular future event. For instance, the promissory note in Figure 18.2 might be subject to a conditional endorsement in the event of negotiation to a third party such as Valley View Credit Union.

Rinehart Ltd. might be concerned about its potential liability should Oxford Telecommunication become insolvent prior to the date on which the bill is payable. In order to avoid liability to Valley, Rinehart might endorse the promissory note as follows: "Pay Valley View Credit Union, but only if Oxford Telecommunication, Inc. is solvent on November 10, 1987." If this phrase had been contained in the promissory note itself, then it would not have been negotiable. But the restrictive endorsement does not make the promissory note non-negotiable.

In the event that Oxford is insolvent on November 10, 1987, then the holder, Valley, will have no right to collect the money owed from either Valley or Rinehart. As a practical matter, Valley might be unwilling to accept a promissory note with such a conditional endorsement or might offer to pay a small sum for the note because of Valley's insolvency risk.

Qualified Endorsement

An endorser of a bill guarantees that payment will be made against it by the obligor. For instance, should Rinehart negotiate the promissory note in Figure 18.2 to Valley with a blank endorsement, and Oxford, on November 10, 1987, is unable or refuses to pay, then Valley may collect the sum owed from Rinehart. Thus, a blank endorsement is an unqualified guarantee of payment by the endorser. The endorser may seek to eliminate his/her exposure to liability to the endorsee by making a qualified endorsement.

A typical method to accomplish this goal is to write on the cheque "Rinehart Ltd., per Helen Voll, without recourse." The words "without recourse" make the endorsement by Rinehart Ltd. qualified. Although the bill may be negotiated in this way, the holder taking such a note is aware that, in the event of default, he/she has no claim or action against the endorser on the note.

Problems for Discussion

1. Assume that the promissory note in Figure 18.2 had the following clause inserted: "Oxford further agrees to furnish security satisfactory to Rinehart at any time required; and if Oxford fails to furnish such security when demanded, or if default in payment is made, or should Oxford sell, mortgage, or dispose of its business, or for any reason Rinehart should consider this note and any renewal thereof insecure, it has the power to declare it in its favour at any time due and payable forthwith." Is a note with such a provision a bill within the meaning of the *Bills of Exchange Act?* See *Gardiner v. Muir*, (1917) 3 W.W.R. 1080 (Sask.C.A.).

2. Assume that the promissory note in Figure 18.2 had the following clause inserted: "The undersigned agrees that Oxford will pay to Rinehart Ltd. an additional 10 percent collection fee upon any default calculated on the balance of capital and interest then due." Is this a note for a sum certain? See *Atlas Thrift Plan Corp. Ltd. v. Di Stefano*, (1964) Que.S.C. 472.

3. Ruth Miyako, A B.C. lawyer, ordered a copy of Rinehart's law office software from Warner Computers in Vancouver. The purchase price was $549.00. The assistant manager asked Ms. Miyako to sign a conditional sales contract and promissory note. Under the terms of the agreement, Ms. Miyako would pay the seller $63.75 per month for twelve months. The payment included 15 percent interest on the original purchase price. One week later, Warner Computers assigned the note and conditional sales contract (which was contained in one document with a perforated line separating the two parts). One term of the conditional sale contract provided:

   Title to the article being sold pursuant to this contract shall remain in the vendor until the full purchase price with respect to this conditional sale has been paid; in the event of default by the purchaser in making payments in accordance with the conditions contained herein, vendor shall have the option of demanding immediate payment of the instalments that have fallen due, or of repossessing the said articles without liability, and without being required to repay money already received by it on account of the purchase price under this conditional sale, in which case the purchaser shall be liable for the balance of the purchase price owing on this conditional sale.

   Before the software was delivered to Ms. Miyako, Warner Computers made an assignment in bankruptcy. Although Ms. Miyako never received the software, the assignee of the note (prior to bankruptcy), Meadowland Finance Company, sought to enforce the note as a holder in due course. Discuss whether Meadowland is entitled to collect the proceeds due on the note from Ms. Miyako. See *Range v. Belvedere Finance Corp.*, (1969) 5 D.L.R.(3d) 257 (S.C.C.). Is the note in this case a bill of exchange? See *Traders Group Ltd. v. Fulkerth*, (1972) 3 W.W.R. 481 (Alta.S.C. App. Div.).

4. Would there be a different result in Problem 3 above if the conditional sales had been detached from the note, and only the note delivered to the assignee upon transfer?

5. Rinehart Ltd. has received a cheque payable to "cash or order" from Oxford in the amount of $10 000. Rinehart wants to treat the cheque as a negotiable instrument and transfer it to Horowitz and Kessler for accounting services furnished to the company. Ms. Bach has been asked to determine whether the cheque is a bill of exchange even though it is not payable to the order of Rinehart Ltd. or bearer. Is it? Compare: *Cole v. Milsome*, (1951) 1 All E.R. 311 (K.B.); and *Judmaier v. Standard Bank*, (1927) 1 W.W.R. 270 (Alta.D.C.).

6. Rinehart received a promissory note from Oxford for the sum of $10 000 due and payable on July 8. The note was delivered to Rinehart by a representative of Oxford on April 7. In return for the promise of payment, Rinehart agreed to develop a computer software program for Oxford. On May 7, Rinehart negotiated the note to Barclay Finance Company by delivery.

   During the month of May, by mutual agreement, Oxford delivered telecommunication equipment to Rinehart. The agreed price for the equipment was $5000. On June 7, Barclay, which had paid valuable consideration for the note on May 7, discovered that Rinehart had only delivered the note and had failed to endorse it. On that date, Rinehart's accountant endorsed the note. Unknown to the accountant, two days earlier, two Rinehart engineers had written a letter to Oxford claiming that the telecommunication equipment was defective.

   The note is now due, but Oxford refuses to pay Barclay the $10 000 on the grounds that Oxford has a set-off against Rinehart for the price of the telecommunication equipment. Barclay claims to be a holder for value and denies that the set-off defence is good as against them. Discuss. See *Aldercrest Developments Ltd. v. Hamilton Co-Axial Ltd.*, (1970) 13 D.L.R.(3d) 425 (Ont.C.A.).

7. In certain cases involving fraud, a contractor or other supplier of goods or services has a close business connection with a finance company. The contractor and finance company may, for example, share office space or have common officers or directors. To what extent will this "business connection" prevent the finance company from claiming rights as a holder in due course against the maker of a note? See *Citizens Finance Co. Ltd. v. Sanford*, 43 D.L.R.(2d) 493, (1964) 1 O.R. 573, aff'd 49 D.L.R.(2d) 216n, (1965) 1 O.R. 660n.

8. The "sophisticated customer" rule from *Canadian Pacific* places a higher duty of care on a commercial enterprise in its supervision of employees charged with handling the company accounts. Would Rinehart Ltd. come under this rule? If so, in what circumstances would the company's bank be liable to compensate the company for a loss caused by the forgery of a cheque by an employee? What would be the duty of care placed on Rinehart and Rinehart's bank in the forgery case?

Chapter 18 Notes

1. R.S.C. 1970, c. B-5.
2. Stat. of Can., 1975, c. 33, section 44(3).
3. *Bills of Exchange*, section 176(1).
4. *John Burrows Ltd. v. Subsurface Surveys Ltd.*, (1968) S.C.R. 607 (S.C.C.).
5. See *The A. MacDonald Company Ltd. v. Dahl*, (1919) 2 W.W.R. 156 (Sask.C.A.).
6. See, *Frontier Finance Ltd. v. Hynes and Niagara Sewing Machine Co.*, (1957) 10 D.L.R.(2d) 206 (C.A.).
7. See, *Aldercrest Developments Ltd. v. Hamilton Co-Axial Ltd.*, (1970) 13 D.L.R.(3d) 425 (Ont.C.A.).
8. Section 53(1).
9. (1949) 2 K.B. 727 (C.A.)
10. Section 56(1).
11. (1907) 39 S.C.R. 625 (S.C.C.).
12. Section 74(b).
13. See, *In Re Soltykoff*, (1891) 1 Q.B. 413 (C.A.).
14. Section 146.
15. Section 146.
16. See, *Clement v. Renaud*, (1956) 1 D.L.R.(2d) 695 (Ont.C.A.).
17. (1965) 50 D.L.R.(2d) 600 (Ont.H.C.).
18. See, *Puffer v. Mastorkis*, (1967) 59 D.L.R.(2d) 427 (Ont.H.C.).
19. Section 49(3).
20. Section 49(3).
21. Section 50(1).
22. See, *Jervis B. Webb Co. v. Bank of Nova Scotia and Reid*, (1965) 49 D.L.R.(2d) 692 (Ont.H.C.).
23. (1981) 122 D.L.R. (3d) 519 (Ont.H.C.).
24. Section 61(1).
25. Section 62(1).
26. Section 62(3).
27. Section 67(2).
28. Section 67(3).
29. Section 68(2).
30. See, *Falconbridge, Banking and Bills of Exchange*, 7th Ed., p. 653.

Part VI

ASSOCIATIONS IN A
BUSINESS CONTEXT

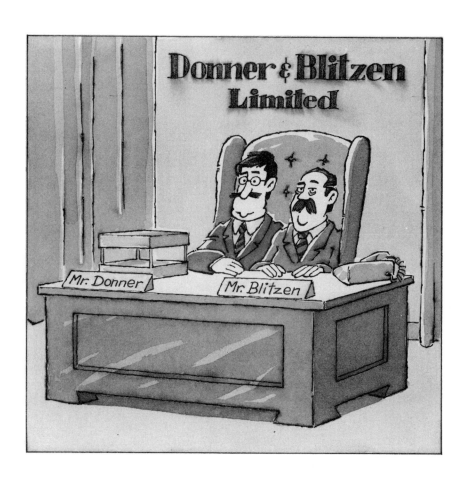

19 THE POWER IN THE COMPANY

Introduction

The traditional approach to company law divides the subject between:

Shareholders

Shareholders own the company. Their role is to elect, at annual shareholder meetings, representatives who are authorized to manage the company.

Directors

Directors manage the business of the company. The directors are the elected representatives of the shareholders and are responsible to the shareholders for their actions.

Officers

The directors delegate the responsibility for the day-to-day management of the company to the officers. For example, the president of the company is hired by the board of directors and the terms of his/her employment contract, compensation benefits, and duties are determined by the board. The president, as other officers in the company, must answer to the board for his/her management decisions.

The relationship between shareholders, directors, and officers is an important part of company law. At the same time, however, the practical realities of *control* are not necessarily determined by the formal legal hierarchy.

In this chapter, we will consider the basic issues of who really runs the modern Canadian company: What type of power do these people have? How does the court limit the exercise of such power? How do those with a diversity of interests go about protecting their interest in the company?

The Shareholders

The traditional view is that a company is operated for the benefit and profit of the shareholders. In a strict legal sense, the company is owned by the shareholders, and the consequences of their ownership is to receive the profits made by the company. This simple notion of "ownership" does not address modern reality, which finds a vast difference between the group of persons who control the company and those who are shareholders.

Control means responsibility for dealing with the assets of the company. To have the capacity to control the purchase, sale, lease, mortgage, or other disposition of assets is to have enormous power over the direction and vitality of the company. The question of control raises another important issue about what a shareholder owns when he/she buys a share in a company.

For example, Alison Faubert owns 200 shares of common stock in Rinehart Ltd. (See Chapter 20 for a full discussion of shares.) The Valley View Credit Union, which operates a trust and pension department, holds 25 000 shares in Rinehart Ltd. These shares are held on behalf of several clients. What exactly does Ms. Faubert's and Valley's ownership of Rinehart Ltd. shares mean? One explanation is that these shareholders have a *property ownership interest in the company* in the same way that they would own land, a car, diamonds, or a computer system. In the case of rental producing real estate, the owner is entitled to receive the profits from his/her land. The profit is directly linked to the land ownership. Does this reasoning follow when a person's capital is placed in shares of Rinehart Ltd.? Does that person in other words, "own" Rinehart Ltd. in the same manner as he/she might "own" a building on Main Street?

There is a significant difference between the interest of shareholders and that of other property holders. The shareholder does not have *legal title* to the company's assets. The assets are owned by the company. The company, for legal purposes, is a separate *legal entity* entitled to exercise property ownership. As the shareholder "owns" shares in the company, which in turn "owns" the assets, the right to profits is indirect. The company, as the legal owner, earns the profits, and those in control of the company —its directors and officers — decide on the quantum of profits that they will distribute to the shareholders.

Whether Ms. Faubert or Valley receive a profit (i.e., a dividend) on their shares depends on two factors: i) the earnings of the company on its assets, and ii) the amount of profits, after expenditures, those in control decide to place at the shareholders' disposal.

Viewed in these terms, there is an appearance that those in control of Rinehart Ltd. may arbitrarily use the assets of the company in any way that they see fit, including for their own personal use, and may dispose of the company's profits without limitation. Of course, legal principles intervene to prevent such an abuse of control. The central basis for protecting shareholders and other security holders (such as lending institutions) is through the equitable principle of *fiduciary relations* — those in control of the company owe an obligation of loyalty and good faith to the company. Shareholders may enforce this duty in the event of an abuse of a fiduciary obligation by an officer or director. The law of fiduciaries — based on equitable principles from the law of trusts — does not place the shareholders in a position to exercise a broad power over those who control the company. Within the confines of the equitable rules, the directors and officers are entitled to exercise power over the company. The law of fiduciaries merely prevents them from exercising their power in *bad faith* or placing their *personal interest* above that of the company.

It has been said that "the stockholder has surrendered control over his wealth."[1] Further, it has been concluded that the shareholder "has become a supplier of capital, a risk-taker pure and simple, while ultimate responsibility and authority are exercised by directors who 'control'."[2] In one study conducted in the United States, for example, out of 200 of the largest companies, 169 were controlled by management, and no one shareholder or group held more than 1 percent of the shares.[3]

The Centre of Control

The centre of control in and over the company has shifted over time. We have already examined the classic separation of ownership and control. This formal separation continues to play an important role in shaping the legal rules that regulate the managers of companies and makes them accountable to shareholders and other investors. Modern trends have shifted control into the hands of new professionals.[4] For example, it is traditional to view shareholders, such as Ms. Faubert, as a group of individual investors who themselves make a critical appraisal about risking their capital by buying shares in a company.

In the nineteenth century, shares were held, accumulated, and disposed of by individual investors, who largely relied upon their own judgment and skill in making these economic decisions. In the 1980s, new forces have intervened, and capitalism has entered "the age of the portfolio manager, and its characteristic institution is the institutional investor, or financial intermediary."[5] In practical terms, this means that the investment decision is being made by professional money managers, who are entrusted with the money of individuals.

There is a handing over of capital to these financial intermediaries, who in turn, are vested with the ultimate decision-making as to whether to put part or all of that capital into the shares of Rinehart Ltd., another company, bonds, gold, or land. The consequence is that the monitoring of professional managers of a company shifts from the person who put up the capital for the shares — the shareholder — to the person who has made the decision to buy the shares, and can, if required, also sell the same shares.

There are new players and new costs for the law to consider. New legal principles are required to take into account the delegation of capital-investment decisions to powerful institutions such as banks, insurance companies, and trust companies. And the professional managers in control of the company must now look over both shoulders — for the unhappy individual investor (a rarer and less potent source of difficulty) and the institutional investor in control of large blocks of shares and representing a collective of many small investors of capital.

Another major trend is the role played by the presence of large trade unions that have negotiated employee pension plans. These plans have great sums of capital available for investment in, among other things, company shares. Here the investment decision is not made directly by the employees who have contributed to the pension or other benefit plans but is generally delegated to a professional manager. The impact has been twofold: i) to widen the class of persons who make a capital contribution to the purchase of shares, and ii) to concentrate the power over investment decisions in the hands of professionals who may be outside of the management control group running a company.

Though the object of control — that of the directors and officers of the company — has remained constant over time, the source of exercising supervision and imposing discipline over the control group has shifted away from the shareholder-individual and has been replaced by professional portifolio managers and savings planners.

The Exercise of Control and the Takeover

The decision to invest or not to invest in the shares of a company reflects, as we have seen, the portfolio managers' or savings planners' assessment of management operation of the company. So long as the control group can satisfy those who have the effective decision-making power to invest capital in their company, and keep them satisfied that their investment is yielding a better return (i.e., making profit and distributing dividends) than an alternative investment, it can be said that the control group is being kept responsible and acting in the best interest of the company. If the control group loses its credibility with this new class of professionals, there may be a move to sell shares, which is a vote of no confidence and, as a result, inefficient management is held accountable and forced out or forced to become more efficient.

The threat of merger and takeover plays a similar function over the control group within the company.[6] The unfriendly takeover group has sufficient capital to purchase a majority of shares in the targeted company, and to replace the controlling group of directors and officers. This take-over group is generally different from the existing individual shareholders, and from the financial intermediates and savings planners. Indeed, those proposing the unfriendly takeover must convince these individuals or institutions to adopt their takeover plan, and, in turn, the incumbent management team, fearing for their jobs, often attempt to devise means to defeat such a takeover.

In any discussion of a company's professional managers, who are in control of the company, and of those who attempt to exert supervision in order to hold them accountable, the question arises as to what "threats" the control team represents to shareholders. The obvious instances of wrongdoing such as misappropriation of corporate opportunity, fraud, or other acts of disloyalty are a problem, but in the general scheme of things these acts occur with comparative rarity.

The more serious problem is in the monitoring of the control group's performance under the classic structure. The profits of the company have become separated between those with the active duty and responsibility for the company — the professional managers — and those who are the passive holders of the company — the shareholders. In order to attract and retain investors in the company, profits must be returned to them in the form of dividends. This means that professional managers do not fully reap the benefit of their labour. The benefit must be shared with the capital risk-takers. There is a tension, therefore, over the allocation of profits and the result is that "No manager will be completely vigilant."[7]

This thesis is based on an assumption that human behaviour and motivation tend to compensate themselves for accepting fewer benefits than they have acquired for the company; thus, the professional manager will even the score. He/she does this in a number of ways: by failing to take on new responsibilities or pushing new ventures, consuming company benefits, and attempting to obtain more than he/she has put out. Rather than wrongdoing, the main problem is the nature of profit sharing within a company that encourages less than optimal performance by the management team.

Managers tend to work in teams or groups, and responsibility is divided and overlaps between groups; it is, therefore, often difficult to point the finger at a single person in management and show that he/she is making too little effort for too much pay. The collective anonymity of the control-group members serves to foster a management system that is exceedingly difficult to monitor or to supervise by the shareholders or by their financial intermediaries. As shares are dispersed among many people and institutions, it is not cost effective for any one shareholder to invest the time, money, and effort to monitor the control group's performance.

The benefit achieved by upgrading management's performance would be shared by all shareholders and not just the one who takes it upon himself /herself to become *active* in monitoring the managers. Moreover, even a shareholder who decides to become involved in supervision has few options should he/she find that the managers are working below their optimal performance. He/she could try and persuade the managers to work harder; but that is unlikely to achieve positive results. Or, he/she might lay his/her case before all the shareholders at the general meeting; but again it is unlikely that, given the passive nature of these investors, any thing of substance will be accomplished. Thus, in the large public company, the professional managers have little fear of being disciplined or supervised by the "owners" of the company.

A hostile tender offer fills this supervision void. It provides a means of disciplining the professional managers who fall below a certain level of productivity for their company. Those who make tender offers have an economic incentive to monitor closely the performance of such managers. A hostile tender offer becomes likely when a wide gap develops between the market price of the company's shares and the price of those shares with the company controlled by more efficient managers. In such a case, there is a strong economic incentive to take over such a company and make a profit by improving the management. A tender offer represents a threat to the control group's job security.

The party making the tender offer — which may be another company — by gaining control of the majority of shares in the target company, can force out the old control group and replace it with personnel who are willing to maximize profit-making. In theory, this greater effort by the new management group creates a surplus benefit — a by-product of full efficiency — that then finds its way into the pockets of the new owners. The threat of a takeover provides, it has been argued, a powerful incentive for professional managers to make their labour and judgment profit-maximizing. They know that should their performance become non-profit-maximizing, this will be reflected in the manager's report card, i.e., the market price of the company share. A majority interest of those shares may be accumulated in the hands of a single person or entity who then has the power, and the incentive, to clean house of the inefficient managers.

The vulnerability of the managers theory of company takeovers lies in the difficulty in determining whether the manager's activity is profit-maximizing or non-profit-maximizing.[8] Little success comes from imposing an objective standard to most of the particular courses of action taken by a manager. Management decisions are often discretionary in nature as there are several options available. It is a matter of business judgment whether any one will increase or decrease the profits of the company.

For instance, Rinehart Ltd. launches a lawsuit against Pitney Burrows Ltd. for copyright infringement arising out of a misappropriation of the company's software. Assume that, on Ms. Bach's recommendation, the Board of Directors agree to settle the $100 000 lawsuit for $25 000. Has the management maximized profit for the company and its shareholders? One might argue that Ms. Bach, as the company lawyer, recommended settlement because she has no personal benefit to gain beyond her salary. As a result, Ms. Bach lacked an incentive to spend the many hours in research and preparation required for the litigation, and she compromised the claim to avoid the extra labour. In this view, Rinehart's shareholders have lost the benefit of the extra $75 000, and should this pattern of conduct continue, then another party, by acquiring the majority of shares in Rinehart, could fire the incumbent managers (including the company lawyer) and hire a new management team to increase the profitability of the company.

This analysis overlooks the discretionary nature of Ms. Bach's decision in recommending settlement of the case. She might rightfully argue that the result of litigation in this type of case is uncertain, that the defendant's ability to pay is limited, and point to the potential cost and expense of litigation that might not be recouped. From her point of view, Ms. Bach may have exercised her best legal and business judgment: The $25 000 settlement indeed has enhanced the company's profit, and the alternative course of action may have been profit-losing.

As the example illustrates, it is not an objective standard that can be applied to a manager's decisions. Assume that Rinehart Ltd. suspects a potential takeover offer is in the wind, would Ms. Bach's recommendation and the Board's decision have been any different? There is a substantial likelihood that it would have been the same. This has led some to conclude: "Accordingly, the idea that they [the control group] are 'disciplined' to act in the 'interest of the shareholders' is simply rhetoric."[9]

The position adopted on the discipline theory will influence one's view as to whether the courts should make it easier or harder for a hostile takeover to occur. In other words, to what extent should the law equip an incumbent manager with the power to resist a corporate takeover of his/her company? How should the courts allow the managers the right to defend themselves while preventing self-dealing that may injure the shareholders? In the following section, we will consider these questions.

The Best Interest of the Company

So far we have concentrated on the techniques, as well as the problems, of disciplining managers or making them accountable to the shareholders. Now we will take the analysis another step and consider *Teck Corporation Ltd. v. Millar*,[10] which illustrates a means to resolve the issue of whether a majority of the shareholders are entitled to exercise control over the conduct of the company directors. In *Teck v. Millar*, we will examine the court's approach to allegations of the control group's abuse of power. Also, the dispute occurs in the setting of a company takeover, with the new majority shareholders asserting that the directors of the company had undertaken a course of action to frustrate their attempts at gaining control of the company.

Throughout the following analysis, the court emphasizes two central problems: i) formulating a rule of business judgment applicable to the control group; and ii) applying the rule, which involves a detailed examination of the purpose or motivation of the directors.

The Facts of Teck v. Millar

Afton Mines Ltd. was a junior mining resource company incorporated in British Columbia. The company had an authorized capital of 5 000 000 shares, but only 2 600 000 had been issued and were trading on the Vancouver Stock Exchange. The dominant figure in Afton was Chester Millar. He was the moving force behind the original incorporation and in the transfer of the company's main asset, namely, copper-mining claims in land near Kamloops, B.C. Millar was one of three members of Afton's Board of Directors, along with Price and Haramboure.

The other two directors deferred to Millar in the main decisions, giving rise to this dispute. To place the lawsuit in perspective requires a basic understanding of the resource market in British Columbia. A company such as Afton, with limited capital, expertise, and marketing capacities, is known as a junior resource company. Its principal functions are to acquire potentially valuable mining claims and to conduct preliminary exploration and drilling to determine, through assays, the presence and amount of minerals on land owned by the company.

Once the junior resource company can prove minerals in commercial amounts have been found, then negotiations are undertaken with established, large resource companies called "majors". The role of the major is to provide the necessary capital for drilling and full-scale mining operations, to provide technical and expert assistance, and to make available marketing and managerial experience. The majors are in a strong position to require the junior resource company to exchange approximately a 50 percent interest for their contribution of capital and expertise.

Afton carried out drilling operations on its lands, and by October 1, 1971, had achieved preliminary results that were encouraging, not only to the company, but to the majors. Millar wanted more money to carry on his drilling operations, but was at a stage where he was unwilling to transfer a large block of the company's shares to a major. Having trouble raising funds, however, he began negotiations with Canex, a wholly-owned subsidiary of Placer, an international mining company. In the initial round of negotiations on March 17, 1972, Placer wanted a 60 percent interest in Afton. Millar was unwilling to sign such a deal.

Another company, Teck, became interested in dealing with Afton. Teck ultimately decided that the best course of action was to acquire a majority interest in Afton; after Millar and the other directors refused to sell their shares, Teck began buying shares on the Vancouver Stock Exchange. Millar had been unwilling to sign an ultimate deal — a term used to describe a contract between a junior resource company and a major, which gives the major a large equity position in the junior — with Teck because that company, unlike Placer, had never brought a mine into production, and lacked the personnel and experience of Placer.

During this period Millar, on behalf of Afton, was negotiating with a number of majors, including Teck and Placer, and was playing one proposed deal off against another. When Teck decided it was futile to make the ultimate deal with Afton, it began purchasing shares on May 8, 1972, along with an associate company called Iso. By May 31, 1972, Teck and Iso had acquired 1 109 312 shares in the open market and now held a controlling interest in Afton.

The man behind Teck, Dr. Keevil, phoned Millar and told him that Teck had one million shares. Presumably, the intent of Teck was to enter into a contract with Afton for the development of the Afton mine. Although Teck had controlling interest in Afton, Millar and his group still ran the company as the Board of Directors. But Millar knew that Teck would soon control the Board. Teck was unwilling to make an ultimate deal, or indeed to discuss precise terms with Millar and his Board, waiting instead until it controlled the Board and Millar and his group were ousted. Before this could happen, however, Teck wanted to make certain that Millar did not bind Afton to a contract with another major.

On May 30, 1972, after Teck had notified Millar that it now owned control of Afton, Millar and Price struck a deal with Canex. Under the terms of that agreement, Canex would obtain a 30 percent interest in Afton. To carry out the contract meant that Afton would allot shares to Canex, in accordance with the terms of the agreement. Also, on May 30, 1972, Teck requisitioned a shareholders' meeting at Afton. The next day, Teck sent a letter to Millar, Price, and Haramboure advising them not to make an ultimate deal without consulting Teck. After receipt of that letter, Millar and his group signed the contract with Canex on the basis that it was in the best interest of the company.

Under the terms of the contract, Canex, if it elected to put the mine into operation, was entitled to require Afton to transfer to it 1 167 437 shares of Afton. Assuming that Canex would exercise this option, the additional allotment of shares would destroy Teck's majority position — a position that had cost Teck $16 000 000 to acquire. The day after the Afton-Canex contract was made public, Teck sought an injunction to prevent the issuance of any shares to Canex and to have the contract held void. Teck's argument was that Millar and his group had entered into the contract, not for the benefit of the shareholders, but for purposes of defeating the majority share position that Teck had acquired.

The Exercise of Management Power

The first question raised by Berger J. in the *Teck v. Millar* case was the directors' power of management:[11]

> [T]he whole case for the plaintiff is that the defendant directors were actuated by an improper motive, and that Canex knew it. That is the footing on which the case had proceeded. ... There is no dispute that under the articles of association the directors had the power to enter into the contract here, and no dispute that they had the power to allot shares pursuant to such a contract. The case alleged against them is that they were actuated by an improper purpose in the exercise of their powers.
>
> The directors' power to manage the affairs of the company is complete. That is, majority of shareholders, even if they pass a resolution at a general meeting, cannot dictate to the directors [cite omitted]. The directors are not the agents of the shareholders. Once given the power to manage the company, they can exercise the power according to their best judgment, until removed from office [cite omitted].
>
> Teck had no right to insist the directors should not enter into an agreement with Canex, Cominco or anyone else. A majority of the shareholders do not by reason of the fact they have a majority, acquire thereby any legal right. Their rights, like those of any other shareholder, are derived from applicable companies' legislation, the company's memorandum and articles and the case law as developed by the Judges. A majority can pass shareholders' resolutions at meetings of the company, they can elect a new board of directors at a meeting of the company, but they do not, by virtue of their majority, enjoy any proprietary right.

The Directors' Fiduciary Duty

The second issue in *Teck v. Millar* was the nature and scope of the directors' fiduciary duty to the company. Related to this issue was the further question of whether, in the exercise of their discretion, the directors had breached their fiduciary duty. Berger J. decided this issue in the following passage:[12]

> Teck had the right, however, like any other shareholder, to challenge the exercise of any power by the directors on the ground that such power was being exercised for an improper purpose. This is not an allegation that the directors acted *ultra vires* [outside their authority and office]; it is rather an allegation of abuse of power [cite omitted].
>
> The cases decided in the United Kingdom make it plain that di-

rectors, in the exercise of their power, must act in what they *bona fide* consider to be the best interests of the company. If they issue shares to retain control for themselves, that is an improper purpose [cites omitted].

Now counsel for Teck does not accuse the defendant directors of crass desire merely to retain their directorship and their control of the company. Teck acknowledges that the directors may well have considered it to be in the best interest of the company that Teck's majority should be defeated. Even so, Teck says, the purpose was not one countenanced by the law. Teck relies upon *Hogg v. Cramphorn Ltd.*[13] In that case the directors of Cramphorn Ltd. established a trust for the benefit of the company's employees and allotted shares to the trust, nominating themselves as trustees to enable them to purchase the shares. Buckley J. [as he then was], found that the directors had done so to ensure that a Mr. Baxter, who was seeking to acquire control of the company, could not achieve a majority. Buckley, J., was persuaded that the directors had acted in good faith, believing they were serving the best interests of the company....

Thus Buckley, J., takes the view that the directors have no right to exercise their power to issue shares, in order to defeat an attempt to secure control of the company, even if they consider that in doing so they are acting in the company's best interests.

... Counsel [for Teck] goes on to say that *Hogg v. Cramphorn Ltd.* lays it down that an allotment of shares, and any transaction connected with it, made for purpose of defeating an attempt to secure a majority is improper, even if the directors genuinely consider that it would be deleterious to the company if those seeking a majority were to obtain control.

This, it seems to me, raises an issue of profound importance in company law. Lord Greene, M.R., expressed the general rule in this way in *Re Smith & Fawcett, Ltd.*:[14] "They [the directors] must exercise their discretion *bona fide* in what they consider — not what a court may consider — is in the best interests of the company, and not for any collateral purpose." Yet, if *Hogg v. Cramphorn Ltd.*, *supra*, is right, directors may not allot shares to frustrate an attempt to obtain control of the company, even if they believe that it is in the best interests of the company to do so. This is inconsistent with the law as laid down in *Re Smith & Fawcett....*

... The Court's jurisdiction to intervene is founded on the theory that if the directors' purpose is not to serve the interest of the company, but to serve their own interest or that of their friends or of a particular group of shareholders, they can be said to have abused their power. The impropriety lies in the directors' purpose. If their purpose is not to serve the company's interest, then it is an improper purpose. Impropriety depends upon proof that the directors were actuated by a collateral purpose, it does not depend upon the nature of any shareholders' rights that they may be affected by the exercise of the directors' powers.

... The classical theory is that the directors' duty is to the company. The company's shareholders are the company [cite omitted], and therefore no interest outside those of the shareholders can legitimately be considered by the directors.

A classical theory that once was unchallengeable must yield to the facts of modern life. In fact, of course, it has. If today the directors of a company were to consider the interests of its employees no one would argue that in doing so they were not acting *bona fide* in the interests of the company itself. Similarly, if the directors were to consider the consequences to the community of any policy that the company intended to pursue, and were deflected in their commitment to that policy as a result, it could not be said that they had not considered *bona fide* the interests of the shareholders.

So how wide a latitude ought the directors to have? If a group is seeking to obtain control, must the directors ignore them? Or are they entitled to consider the consequences of such a group taking over? [cite and quote omitted].

My own view is that the directors ought to be allowed to consider who is seeking control and why. If they believe that there will be substantial damage to the company's interest if the company is taken over, then the exercise of their powers to defeat those seeking a majority will not necessarily be categorized as improper.

... If the directors have the right to consider the consequences of a take-over, and to exercise their powers to meet it, if they do so *bona fide* in the interest of the company, how is the Court to determine their purpose? In every case the directors will insist their whole purpose was to serve the company's interest. And no doubt in most cases it will not be difficult for the directors to persuade themselves that it is in the company's best interests that they should remain in office. Something more than a mere assertion of good faith is required.

I think the Courts should apply the general rule in this way: The directors must act in good faith. Then there must be reasonable grounds for their belief. If they say that they believe there will be substantial damage to the company's interests, then there must be reasonable grounds for that belief. If there are not, that will justify a finding that the directors were actuated by an improper purpose.

... I think that the directors are entitled to consider the reputation, experience and policies of anyone seeking to take over the company. If they decide, on reasonable grounds, a take-over will cause substantial damage to the company's interests, they are entitled to use their powers to protect the company. That is the test that ought to be applied in this case.

Application of the Purpose Test

Berger J. held that the directors of Afton had acted in the best interest of that company by entering into the contract with Canex. In reaching this decision, the purpose test was applied to the directors' conduct in the following fashion:[15]

> The whole case, in my view, turns on the question of Millar's motivation. His was the dominant mind on the board, his purpose was the board's purpose. . . .
>
> I do not think the terms of the contract [between Afton and Canex] afford any ground for saying that the defendant directors made this contract with one overriding purpose, to frustrate Teck's attempt to obtain control. I do not think the terms are such that the defendant directors must be taken to have entered into it without considering the best interests of Afton's shareholders or deliberately putting the shareholders' interest to one side.
>
> So what conclusions ought to be drawn? Now I think Millar was to a great extent acting intuitively. He did not weight the alternatives and consider the implications on a finely balanced scale. People usually do not make decisions in that way. Most important decisions in life contain an intuitive element. . . .
>
> The difficulty of determining a man's state of mind has sometimes been discounted by the Courts. Bowen, L.J., once said that a man's state of mind is as much a matter of fact as the state of his digestion. But like most aphorisms it does not take us very far. I suppose you could determine the state of a man's digestion today, but it is not easy to determine what the state of a man's digestion was six months ago. . . .
>
> [I]t is necessary, then, to disentangle the directors' primary motive or purpose from subsidiary ones. I do not think it is necessary to distinguish motive, purpose or object. The question is, what is it the directors had uppermost in their minds.
>
> The plaintiff's case comes down to this: Counsel says that Millar and Price were wary of Teck, that they were afraid once Teck got control, the possibility of a deal with Placer would be gone, that Teck might very well force a disadvantageous contract upon Afton, that the mining property would not be developed as profitably as they thought it would be under Placer's management. So, he says — and this is the key to the plaintiff's case — the directors made the contract with Placer, their purpose being to ensure the issuance of the shares to Canex, and the defeat of Teck's majority position.
>
> Counsel for Teck relied heavily on the evidence Millar gave that on May 27th he was resigned to a take-over. Mr. Giles says it shows that the deal made the following week with Canex was a last desperate attempt to save himself and the directors. The defendant says

on the other hand, that it was a chance to make a deal that he felt was in the best interest of the company. . . .

I find their [Millar and his board members] object was to obtain the best agreement they could while they were still in control. Their purpose in that sense was to defeat Teck. But, not to defeat Teck's attempt to obtain control, rather it was to foreclose Teck's opportunity of obtaining for itself the ultimate deal. That was, as I view the law, no improper purpose. In seeking to prevent Teck from obtaining the contract, the defendant directors were honestly pursuing what they thought was the best policy for the company.

The defendant directors were elected to exercise their best judgment. They were not agents bound to accede to the directors of the majority of shareholders. Their mandate continued so long as they remained in office. They were in no sense a lame duck board. So they acted in what they conceived to be the best interest of the shareholders, and signed a contract which they knew the largest shareholder, holding a majority of the shares, did not want them to sign. They had the right in law to do that. When a company elects its board of directors and entrusts them with the power to manage the company, directors are entitled to manage it. But they must not exercise their power for an extraneous purpose. That is a breach of their duty. At the same time, the shareholders have no right to alter the terms of the directors' mandate except by amendment of the articles or by replacing the directors themselves.

The purpose of directors in their negotiations with Placer was from the beginning a legitimate one. The purpose was to make a favourable deal for Afton. That purpose continued throughout. Did it become an improper purpose because Teck acquired large shareholdings? Did it become an improper purpose because the directors made a deal with Canex knowing that they had to before Teck acquired the power to stop them? I think on the evidence the answer must be no.

[T]he plaintiff has failed to show the directors had no reasonable grounds for believing that a take-over by Teck would cause substantial damage to the interest of Afton and its shareholders. Indeed, I am satisfied that it has been affirmatively shown that the directors did have reasonable grounds for such belief. . . . Their primary purpose was to see that the ultimate deal the company made was a deal with Placer, not Teck. They were not motivated by a desire to retain control of the company.

Problems for Discussion

1. What does a shareholder "own" by virtue of his or her shares in a company?

2. What legal protection does a shareholder have over those who control the company?

3. Explain the devolution of power from the hands of individual investors to portfolio managers and savings planners.

4. Discuss the conflicting view of those who argue that hostile tender offers discipline professional managers who are inefficient with others who argue that the discretionary nature of management decisions makes an objective assessment difficult. With which view do you agree?

5. When the board of directors exercises its management power against the wishes of the majority and uses those powers to destroy an existing majority or to create a new majority, on what basis will the court intervene on the side of the majority shareholders? On this issue, do you agree with the approach of Berger J. in *Teck* or that of Buckley J. in *Hogg v. Cramphorn.*, (1967) Ch. 254, (1966) 3 W.L.R. 995, (1966) 3 A11 E.R. 420?

6. The Privy Council in *Howard Smith Ltd. V. Ampol Petroleum Ltd.*, (1974) 1 A11 E.R. 1126, 1135 (P.C.) sought to distinguish the *Teck* case by suggesting that it was limited by two important facts: (1) the allotment of shares of Afton to Canex was a common provision in the mining industry; and (2) the purpose was to prevent Teck from getting the ultimate deal and not to defeat its attempt to gain control. To what extent do these factual considerations preclude the application of *Teck* to other similar cases?

7. Discuss whether the purpose doctrine developed in *Teck* is consistent with either the theoretical position of EasterBrook and Fischel or Frug. Would you reach a diferent result based on the English position found in *Howard Smith*? In the latter case, the Privy Council said:

[W]hen a dispute arises whether directors of a company made a particular decision for one purpose or for another, or whether, there being more than one purpose, one or another purpose was the substantial or primary purpose, the court, in their Lordships' opinion, is entitled to look at the situation objectively in order to estimate how critical or pressing, or substantial or per contra, insubstantial an alleged requirement may have been.

8. To what extent must the board, when faced with a situation as in *Teck*, demonstrate that its action was urgent or critical at the time that the decision was made?

9. Are judges competent to sift through the enmeshed facts and motives in a takeover struggle? How difficult is it to 're-create' the climate, pressures, and motives through 'convincing' evidence as to what happened during the critical days before the Board of Directors of Afton acted?

10. Those in control of the company, i.e., the directors and managers, have the responsibility to further the interest of the company; but given the diversity of interest, and potential conflicts among various factions, how does the control group discharge its responsibility? See *Howard Smith Ltd. V. Ampol Petroleum Ltd., supra*; and Berle & Means, *The Modern Corporation and Private Property*, (rev. ed. 1967) pp. 293-313.

Chapter 19 Notes

1. See Beale and Means, *The Modern Corporation and Private Property* (rev. ed. 1967), p. 297.
2. Ibid.
3. See *"Larner, Ownership and Control in the 200 Largest Nonfinancial Corporations,* 1929 and 1963," 56 *Am. Econ. Rev.* 777, 779-81 (1966).
4. See Clark, *"The Four Stages of Capitalism: Reflections on Investment Management Treaties,"* (1981) 94 *Har. L. Rev.* 561.
5. Ibid. p. 564.
6. See Easterbrook & Fischel, *"Responding to Tender Offers,"* (1981) 94 *Har. L. Rev.* pp. 1168-69.
7. Ibid. p. 1170.
8. See Frug, *"The Ideology of Bureaucracy in American Law,"* (1984), 97 *Har. L. Rev.* 1276, p. 1362.
9. Ibid. p. 1362.
10. (1973) 33 D.L.R.(3d) 268 (B.C.S.C.).
11. Ibid. 306-307.
12. Ibid. 309, 311-316.
13. (1967) Ch. 254, (1966) 3 W.L.R. 995, (1966) 3 A11 E.R. 420.
14. (1942) Ch. 304 at p. 306, (1942) 1 A11 E.R. 542.
15. Supra, Note 10, at 317, 324-328.

20 THE SHAREHOLDER AND THE COMPANY

Introduction

The Company as a Legal Entity

An important feature of company law is the rights and liabilities of shareholders. The company is an independent legal entity that can own, trade, and sell property, pay taxes, and enter into binding contracts with other persons. The company is a legal person in the eyes of the law. In the case of legal liability, it is the company that is liable to pay compensation. A shareholder, for instance, is only liable to the limit of the money he/she invested in the company's shares. Thus, should the company become insolvent, the shareholder will lose his/her investment but will incur no additional liability.

The Constitution of the Company

The structure, organization, and government of the company is contained in the company's constitution. The nature of the constitution is governed by statute. In Canada, there are three different types of corporate statutes: i) letters patent, which has its antecedents in eighteenth-century English common law; ii) memorandum of association, which is drawn from modern English registration legislation; and iii) certificate of incorporation, which is drawn from American legislation, specifically from the State of New York.

The last type has now been adopted in most Canadian provinces. British Columbia, however, has blended the registration system with the corporate remedies found in American law. The philosophy underlying the trend toward the certificate of incorporation approach has been articulated as follows:

> The primary purpose of corporation laws is not regulatory. They are enabling acts to authorize businessmen to organize and to operate

FIGURE 20.1 **CERTIFICATE OF INCORPORATION FOR RINEHART SOFTWARE LTD.**

CANADA
PROVINCE OF BRITISH COLUMBIA

NUMBER 25917

Province of British Columbia
Ministry of Consumer and Corporate Affairs
REGISTRAR OF COMPANIES

Certificate of Incorporation

I HEREBY CERTIFY THAT

RINEHART SOFTWARE LTD.

HAS THIS DAY BEEN INCORPORATED UNDER THE COMPANY ACT

GIVEN UNDER MY HAND AND SEAL OF OFFICE

AT VICTORIA, BRITISH COLUMBIA,

THIS   31st   DAY OF   JANUARY, 1975

DEPUTY REGISTRAR OF COMPANIES

their business, large or small, with the advantages of the corporate mechanism. They are drawn with a view to facilitate efficient management of business and adjustment to the needs of change. They provide the legal frame and financial structure of the intricate corporate device by which business can be carried on and in which the combined energies and the capital of the managers and of many investors may work together. They deal with the internal affairs of the organization, the content of the articles of incorporation, the rights of the shareholders, the powers and liabilities of directors, the authorized number and variety of shares, the holding of meetings, restrictions on corporate finance, such as the withdrawal of funds by way of dividends and share purchases, the corporate records, the authorization of organic changes such as amendments, sale of entire assets, merger and consolidation, and dissolution and winding up. Some of the provisions are regulatory, seeking to prevent abuses of management and also of the majority and to protect minority shareholders and creditors.[1]

The Capital of the Company

A company is a creature of statute and is regulated by regulatory bodies created by statute. Although in theory and principle each company has an equal basis in law, in practice, the resources, income, and power of a company depend upon its capital and means of financing. A company with nominal capital and without an effective means of financing is little more than an empty shell. Shareholders — those who own shares in a company — provide an essential means of corporate finance. The money paid for the shares is used by the company to carry on its business operation, including expansion of new product lines or, indeed, the acquisition of other companies. In this chapter, emphasis will be placed on the nature of company shares and how shares provide a means of equity financing.

The Nature and Types of Shares

The Shareholder's Interest in the Company

Initially, a distinction must be drawn between a share in the company and the physical document known as a share certificate. The shareholder derives his/her "bundle of rights" from his/her ownership of the "share". Unlike the share certificate, the "share" is a legal concept. The share, then, is an abstract notion that owes its existence to certain established legal principles. A share, like a "fee simple interest", is not a tangible piece of property that can be seen or held. The share certificate is the physical manifestation of the share in the same way that a deed is the physical manifestation of the real property owner's fee simple interest in land. The share certificate, like the deed, is an indication of title to property. The share certificate, under current Canadian law (excluding British Columbia and New Brunswick), is negotiable — as a negotiable instrument.

Considerable uncertainty has occurred in defining the precise interest owned by a shareholder in a company. In part, the difficulty may be traced to determining whether the company shares entitle the shareholder to claim an ownership interest in the company's assets. There is, however, legal consensus that the company assets are owned by the company and not by the shareholders. The fact that the company is a separate legal entity that can, and, in fact, does hold title to such assets, means that the capital supplied by the shareholder is not, in a legal sense, his/her property. What the shareholder owns is the share in the company, and this share "is a property in a fractional part of the capital", per Lord Wrenbury, *Bradbury v. English Sewing Cotton Co. Ltd.*[2]

When Bettina Jones purchases ten shares of Rinehart Ltd., what is the nature of her interest in the company? As the above discussion illustrates, Ms. Jones does not "own" a portion of Rinehart's assets. Her interest entitles her to a right of participation in the company on the terms of the articles of association. In essence, this means that her power over the company is exercised by voting her ten shares at Rinehart's annual general meeting. For instance, she may exercise her right to vote in favour of a Board of Directors that, in her view, will maximize a dividend return to shareholders such as herself. Whether the Board members for whom she votes are elected, her investment is in the hands of the Board of Directors and management of the company.[3]

As a shareholder does not own the assets of the company it has been well settled that a shareholder lacks an insurable interest in the company's assets. This was the case even where practically all the shares in the company were owned by one shareholder who claimed a right to insurance proceeds upon the destruction of company assets by fire.[4]

In the House of Lords, Lord Buckmaster said:

> Turning now to his position as shareholder, this must be independent of the extent of his share interest. If he were entitled to insure holding all the shares in the company, each shareholder would be equally entitled, if the shares were all in separate hands. Now, no shareholder has any right to any item of property owned by the company, for he has no legal or equitable interest therein. He is entitled to a share in the profits while the company continues to carry on business and a share in the distribution of the surplus assets when the company is wound up. If he were at liberty to effect an insurance against loss by fire of any item of the company's property, the extent to which his share in the ultimate distribution would be

diminished by the loss of the asset — a calculation almost impossible to make. There is no means by which such an interest can be definitely measured and no standard which can be fixed of the loss against which the contract of insurance could be regarded as an indemnity.[5]

The Ontario Court of Appeal in *Kosmopoulos v. Constitution Insurance Co. of Canada*[6] distinguished this House of Lords decision and held that a company with a sole shareholder entitled the shareholder to have an insurable interest in the company's assets.

The Distinction Between Shares and Other Securities

A company may use a variety of different means of raising money for itself. There is, however, a broad distinction between those who lend money to the company and those who invest money in the company. The first class occupies the status of creditors in relationship to the debtor company for a fixed debt owed on specified terms. The second class occupies the status of shareholders who have put up their money to obtain an equity interest in the company. The shareholders' equity is represented by shares issued by the company. The creditors, rather than holding shares, hold a document evidencing the company's debt. The debt document will fall within one of the following classes: i) bonds, ii) notes, and iii) debentures. The precise nature of the debt document is determined by the amount that the company seeks to raise, the company's assets and credit worthiness, the number of potential lenders sought by the company to share the debt burden, and the terms for repayment of principal and interest.

Rinehart may seek to raise $50 000 for short-term financing to acquire office equipment. The Royal Bank of Canada may lend this sum on a promissory note for a three-month period at prime plus one percent, and secure the loan with Rinehart's accounts receivable. On the other hand, Rinehart may plan a major expansion of the Toronto operation and require $2 000 000. Moreover, Rinehart may want five years to repay the principal sum with periodic payments of interest during the interim period. It is unlikely that a promissory note could be obtained on these terms. Thus, Rinehart would seek to raise this sum from a number of different investors, both private and institutional, by issuing bonds. Alternatively, debentures might be issued. The distinction between a bond and debenture is complicated. Basically, bonds are offered to the general public and compete with similar securities issued by other companies and governments. A debenture is a security arranged with institutional lenders and are usually privately placed.

FIGURE 20.2a **SHARE**

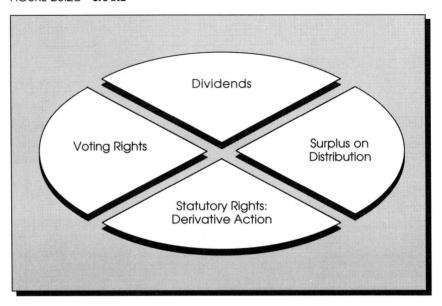

FIGURE 20.2b **A SHARE CERTIFICATE FOR RINEHART SOFTWARE LTD.**

Lastly, a major difference between shares and debts that are used to attract funds is that the shareholder undertakes a greater risk. The shareholder's investment follows the fortune of the company. Should the company prosper, then a return on investment and an appreciation in the value of the shares will have shown the shareholder to be a sound and wise investor. The downside, however, is that the company may fall on hard times. In that situation, no dividends may be paid, or part or all of the investment lost. An institution or person holding a debt security does not share in the profits of the company. At the same time, the amount of the return is fixed in advance and normally secured against the company's assets. In the event of financial difficulty, the debt security holders are paid before the shareholders.

Issuing the Company Share

The terms "issue" and "allotment" are used in Canadian company law to describe the process whereby the directors of the company offer shares in the company with third parties for a price. The law of contract applies to the dealings between the company and prospective shareholders, i.e. there must be an offer, acceptance, and consideration to support a binding contract. In the typical transaction, the prospective shareholder makes an offer to the company for shares, and the company accepts the offer by alloting shares to the offeror.[7] Thus, allotment is the company's means of assenting to an offer for a certain number of shares.[8]

The price of the shares is established by the board of directors, but of course the price shifts according to the financial position of the company. Thus, Rinehart's board of directors may set a price of $10 per share but a willing buyer will pay only $4.50 per share. If the shares are to be sold, they must reflect a reasonable relationship to the market value of such shares, compared with similar shares, in the marketplace. The shares are issued by the directors once the purchase price is paid. The purchase price may be money, property, or past services. Also, the board of directors in most provinces is entitled to issue shares at a discount price. This is a statutory modification to the common law rule that a company is required to receive full value for shares issued.

At the early stages of capital formation, investors who buy shares are taking a greater risk. The company will not have a track record, its products are uncertain of a market, its management team untried, and its competitiveness unclear. Later, as these factors become clearer and more certain, the market value of the shares will reflect the good or bad fortunes of the company. Shareholders who purchase after the company has acquired a track record often undertake a lower risk in their investment, but at the same time may have a lower yield of return than the original investors.

Illustration At the time of the original incorporation of Rinehart Ltd., four principal investors purchase 10 000 shares each for $2.50 per share. Two years later, the market value of the shares is $5.00, and the board of directors decides to issue 40 000 new shares at $5.00 each. Assume that one share of Rinehart's stock yields an annual dividend return of $0.60. This is an attractive 12 percent return for the new investors, and represents a 24 percent return to the original four investors. In addition, the value of the original capital investment by the four early investors has doubled in value. The new investors who pay $5.00 per share also have a hope that, over time, their investment will duplicate the success of the original investors.

Classes of Shares

COMMON AND PREFERRED SHARES

"You must be very pleased to have become a member of our company," said the managing director, March Hare. Alice looked, carefully, at her (preferred) share certificates and the company's regulations. "But I don't see here any right which could properly be said to make me a member," she said. "There aren't any," said March Hare.[9]

FIGURE 20.3 **FINANCING THE COMPANY**

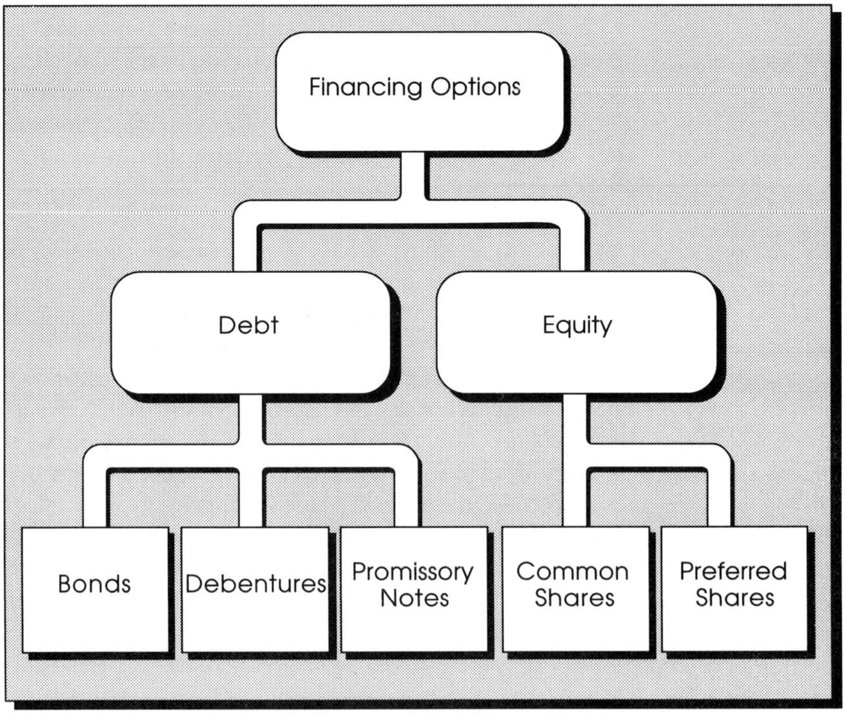

Shares may be divided into two major categories: i) common shares and ii) preferred shares. The distinction between the two types of company shares turns largely on the greater restriction placed on preferred shares. For instance, a preferred shareholder may not have voting rights, although, in practice, all shares in a company will have some voting rights attached.

A preferred share normally entitles the owner to a specified dividend return that has priority over common shares. Similarly, a preferred share usually carries a preferential payment out of the assets of the company in the event that the company is wound up. A preferred share does not carry any automatic rights of preference. The general rule is that, unless preference is expressly given to preferred shareholders, their rights are based on a principle of equality with the common shareholders.

The question of priority between common and preferred shareholders has arisen in instances where the company has sold or liquidated its assets and has gone into voluntary liquidation. In *International Power Co. Ltd. v. McMaster University*,[10] the shareholders disputed the distribution of a $500 000 surplus between common and preferred shareholders. The common shareholders contended that the preferred shareholders were entitled only to cumulative dividends and $100 per share, which represented the par value of a share. The preferred shareholders argued that they were entitled to equal treatment with the common shareholders with respect to the surplus. The court adopted the English rule that the rights of shareholders are deemed to be equal. This presumption may be rebutted by documents forming the constitution of the company that expressly provided for an unequal treatment. This principle of equality or parity of treatment was set forth by Lord Herschell in *Birch v. Cropper*:[11]

> To treat them [preferred shareholders] as partners receiving only interest on their capital and not entitled to participate in the profits of the concern, or to regard them as mere creditors whose only claim is discharged when they have received back their loan, appears to me out of the question. They are members of the Company, and as such shareholders in it as the ordinary shareholders are; and it is in respect of their thus holding shares that they receive a part of the profits.

Applying this principle, Tascheau J., writing the judgment in *International Power Co. Ltd. v. McMaster University*, held that the preferred shareholders had a priority to be repaid at par for their shares, and further a right to share equally with the common shareholders in the distribution of the assets of the company.

PAR AND NO PAR SHARES

Historically, common or preferred shares would be issued at either a par value or no par value. The amount of the par value shares was established by the company. The figure used was often random, e.g., $10, $100 or $150. The par value was not necessarily the market value of the share. One purpose of the par value share was to provide the appearance that every investor was paying the same amount for a share in the company. Another practice, now barred in most provinces, was for the company to issue partly paid shares, taking back a contractual promise from the investor for the unpaid balance. The par value method of financing fell into disfavor with provincial legislatures. There was often confusion for the investor who might conclude that the par value set by the company was consistent with the market value of the shares. Also, given the practice of issuing partly paid shares, there were numerous accounting and disclosure problems. The current practice now required by law is for a company to issue no par value shares.

Limitations and Restrictions Attached to Shares

A share in a company carries certain rights that may be exercised by the owner. The most important rights are: i) to attend and vote at shareholders' meetings, ii) to share in the profits of the company by way of dividends, and iii) to share in the assets of the company upon dissolution.

The scope and nature of these rights vary according to provincial legislation and provisions contained in the company constitution. These rights are distributed among the shareholders of the company. The method of distribution in a number of provinces is left to the discretion of the company.

The Principle of Equality

The principle of equality established in *Birch v. Cropper* has been applied to the right of both common and preferred shareholders' right to vote. Thus, unless there is a specific limitation on that right, it is presumed that the right is attached to the share. Similarly, if the right is excluded in certain instances, it is assumed that the shareholder is entitled to vote in all instances not falling within the exclusion. By statute, the company's power to impose voting limitations is restricted. Thus, where the board of directors has recommended a substantial alteration to the company's constitution, a shareholder is entitled to vote on the recommended change. In most instances, a share enables the owner to one vote.

Legislation governs the rights of minority shareholders who find themselves outvoted by the majority. As a general rule, the decision of the majority rules the day. In certain instances, however, the defeated minority may have recourse to remedies contained in provincial legislation. The two most important statutory remedies are to bring a court action either in the case of oppression or for an appraisal.

Shareholder Oppression

The gist of the statutory action is to provide remedies for a shareholder who complains that the affairs of the company are being conducted in a manner oppressive to some shareholders, including himself.[12] Two other bases for jurisdiction have been added to the *Companies Act*: i) where the powers of the directors are exercised in a manner to oppress a shareholder; ii) where there is some act of the company or resolution of the shareholders that has been done or proposed, which is unfairly prejudicial to a shareholder or shareholders, including the claimant. In a successful oppression action, the shareholder has a number of potential remedies, including the winding-up of the company.

REMOVAL OF DIRECTOR/SHAREHOLDER

An example of a successful oppression action by a shareholder is found in *Diligenti v. R.W.M.D. Operators*.[13] Four individuals entered into the restaurant business and formed two companies for that purpose. Each partner was issued 25 percent of the shares and each became a director of both companies. A dispute arose between Diligenti and the other three directors, and they voted to oust him from his directorship. Afterward, the remaining three directors entered into a management contract with a third company, which they controlled. Under the terms of this contract, the third company was paid a fee by the two restaurant companies for management services. Diligenti claimed that the action of the directors amounted to oppression, and he sought judicial relief. The basis of his action was that the directors' action was "unfairly prejudicial" to him. A major issue in the case was whether the oppression remedy was available to remedy a shareholder's removal from office as a director.

> Regarding the removal of the applicant from his position as director of both companies, there is an impressive line of authorities which have held that where a shareholder has been removed as a director, in some cases holding an equal number of shares with each of those whose combined votes have brought about his removal, an application for relief under the *English Companies Act* provision and the former *British Columbia Companies Act* provision could not succeed because such conduct did not oppress the individual concerned in his status as member but affected his status as director only.
> ... On the face of it it would appear to me that, particularly in a company of the nature of those involved here — private companies, closely held, formed to take over the operation of four individuals who have been equal founders and proprietors of a venture and in which companies each of the four holds the same number of shares — each of its members has a very real interest and concern in the management of the affairs of the company.... In my view, as such shareholder he would have a very real interest in being and re-

maining a director so as to have a voice and a vote in the shaping of the policies and the general business decisions which the board, in its overall responsibilities, will make on behalf of the company. This is not solely a matter of protection of his interests in the narrow sense — for being one of four he can always be out-voted: it is a matter of whether or not he has a right, in the circumstances, to the opportunity for a continued voice and vote in shaping policies. . . .

The question, then, is: Does the addition of the provision regarding the doing of an act that is "unfairly prejudicial" assist the applicant in the circumstances here? In my view, it does. . . .

In considering the whole effect which should be given to the expression "unfairly prejudicial" . . . I agree that it must be borne in mind that the consequences in question must flow to the applicant as a member, and not as a director or employee. Prejudicial, according to the dictionary, means detrimental or damaging to his rights, interests, etc. The question then is: does the applicant have some rights or interests as a shareholder in respect of which he has been unfairly prejudiced?

It is forcefully contended by Mr. Cumming [lawyer for the defendants] that he does not. His rights as shareholder, according to this argument, are determined by the articles of association of the companies, which provide that the shareholders shall elect the directors. In this context, he is not a partner in a partnership, he has no legal right to participate in the management of the affairs of the company — he has no legal right to be a director — and so, the argument runs, it would be wrong to import into the process of decision here principles or rights based upon partnership law, for to do so would in effect be to alter the effect of the articles of the companies by which he is bound, and to give him a legal right which he does not have, that is, to be a director of the companies. . . . The other shareholders, it is contended, have done him no wrong: they have done nothing other than that which, by the articles, all shareholders have the right to do, that is, to determine who shall be directors, and therefore he cannot have been unfairly prejudiced in his status as member.

I consider, however that the new provision is not to be so narrowly interpreted or its effect so narrowly confined, for to do so would be to deal with it as though the words were still "oppressive". I consider that there are rights — equitable rights — attaching to the position of the applicant as shareholder in the circumstances present here, in respect of which he had been unfairly prejudiced, ...

First, in circumstances such as exist here there are "rights, expectations and obligations inter se" which are not submerged in the company structure, and these rights are enjoyed by a member as part of his status as a shareholder in the company which has been formed to carry on the enterprise: amongst these rights are the rights to continue to participate in the direction of the company's affairs. Second, although his fellow members may be entitled as a matter of strict law to remove him as a director, for them to do so in fact is unjust and inequitable, and is a breach of equitable rights which he in fact possesses as a member. And third, although such breach may not "oppress" him in respect of his proprietary rights as a share-holder, such unjust and inequitable denial of his rights and expec-tations is undoubtedly "unfairly prejudicial" to him in his status as member.

The legislation has also been used by a minority shareholder to compel a company to inform him/her, as a shareholder, about the holding of annual general meetings.[14] It is clear from the recent case law that the courts have adopted a flexible and discretionary approach in applying the legislation dealing with shareholder oppression. The size of the company, the prior association of the incorporator-shareholders, and the basis on which the shareholder received the shares are all important factors that have influenced the courts in granting or denying relief.

PROTECTION OF MINORITY SHAREHOLDER

The scope of the statutory remedies for oppression and appraisal do not confer a broad-based jurisdiction to allow the courts to intervene on every application made by a dissenting shareholder. These remedies are limited. The motive or purpose of the majority is not open to judicial review, but abuses of the process or procedure will engage the minority protection rights. The majority, therefore, may be guided by self-interest. They owe no fiduciary obligation to vote in the best interest of the minority.

It would be wrong to conclude, however, that the majority's rights are absolute. They are not. At the same time, it would be wrong to assume that the minority has an absolute right to challenge every decision by the majority in the courts. The minority's protection is limited in nature under provincial legislation. These basic protections can be expanded by the company's constitution. Finally, the minority has the obvious self-help remedy of selling their shares in the face of a majority rule that is politically unacceptable to them.

Dividend Rights

Another important right attached to a share is the right to receive a dividend. Like other shareholders' rights, the payment of a dividend has certain limitations. The payment of a dividend is within the discretion of the control group within the company. Perhaps the early forms of corporations had the primary purpose of increasing the return on capital invested by shareholders. The modern company, however, particularly the large companies, may have priorities other than increasing the shareholders' return on capital. The shareholder typically has no right to compel the company to pay a dividend. The forces of the market place provide an economic compulsion on the control group to pay a competitive dividend return in order to retain and acquire shareholder investment. Whether a dividend is paid, and the amount and the timing of the dividend have become a managerial decision that is influenced by factors such as competitive rates of return for shares in other companies, employee compensation schemes, expansion goals, marketing and promotion plans, and debt load. Ultimately, the question of dividend or no dividend is a complex decision that attempts to promote the overall best interest of the company.

Rights on Dissolution

The last right of shareholders is to a distribution of the company's property after dissolution of the company. Dissolution is the legal death of the company. Afterward, something must be done with the property left remaining when all the company's debts are paid. As we discussed earlier, the Supreme Court of Canada, in *International Power Co. Ltd. v. McMaster University and Montreal Trust Co.*, adopted the principle of equality of sharing between shareholders. The common and preferred shareholders each had equal rights to a distribution of the surplus assets of the company. This judicial rule, in Canadian law, merely creates a presumption as to distribution rights amongst shareholders. The company constitution may vary distribution rights in an unequal fashion. An explicit provision in Rinehart's constitution is that common shareholders are entitled to the exclusive right of distribution of surplus assets upon dissolution, and that preferred shareholders have no right to any part of the surplus assets; this would displace the judicial equality rule. In that case, an important restriction on the preferred shareholder's right would be enforced by the courts.

Insider Trading

Provincial legislation also restricts what is termed "insider trading". In British Columbia, an insider is liable under Section 153 of the *Companies Act*[15] to compensate another person for any direct loss suffered as a result of certain transactions. An insider is a director or senior officer of the company, or a person or company owning more than 10 percent of the voting rights attached to all equity shares in the company. The purpose of the legislation is to prevent an insider from profiting through the use of "specific confidential information". The policy is reasonably clear. Insiders, by virtue of their position, have a greater likelihood of learning about matters that will materially affect the value of the company's shares or debt. For instance, knowledge by a director that the company is about to default on a debt, or be sued by another person, or be taken over by another company, would allow him/her an important headstart in either selling or buying shares of the company. When an insider's transaction occurs, liability is two-fold: i) to any person who suffers a direct loss as a result of the transaction and ii) to the corporation for any direct benefit or advantage received by the insider.

An example of an insider transaction is found in *Pelling and Roberts Projects Ltd. v. Pelling and Don Pelling Insurance Service Ltd.*[16] The defendant controlled the majority shares in Strataco Management Ltd. He received an offer of $200 000 for all the shares of the company. The defendant had fifty-four shares and the plaintiff had twenty-four shares in the company. The defendant, without disclosing the offer, bought the plaintiff's twenty-four shares for $21 500. The court held that the requirement of "specific confidential information" applied not only to corporate information (e.g., the acquisition of an important contract to produce goods) but also to such information available to a shareholder. It was emphasized that the defendant's information was not simply an offer to purchase his controlling interest, but to buy the company.

The plaintiff, however, was denied damages on a pro rata basis. That is, the plaintiff was not automatically entitled to a percentage of the offer price paid to the defendant. The court discounted the plaintiff's loss because the majority shareholder was entitled to a premium for the controlling block of shares that he held. In *Dusik v. Newton,*[17] the court held that the minority shareholder, in a similar type of case, was entitled to damages on a pro rata basis. In *Dusik*, the court found that the majority shareholder had acted in bad faith and in an underhanded way in his dealings with the minority shareholder. The pro rata basis of damages appear to have had a punitive element attached.

Derivative Actions

The insider transaction is a personal, direct action by the affected shareholders and entitles them to individual compensation for their direct losses. A derivative action is brought on behalf of the company and other injured shareholders. It is a class action rather than a personal action. Thus, the term derivative is used to describe an action where a class of shareholders share the benefit of the action in proportion to their share holdings. Derivative actions are common in cases where it is alleged that the management has acted wrongfully. It often involves a conflict between the control group running the company and a minority of shareholders. A dividend may be challenged as improperly distributed. The board of directors may have acted beyond the powers of the company in making a particular contract or in selling or buying property.

Historically, the derivative action was an invention of equity. The equity courts created a cause of action based upon breach of fiduciary duty owed by the management or board of directors to the company. The action, brought in the name of the company, was a judicial means to control the actions of those running the company. The shareholders, with the use of a class action, had an effective method to hold the managers and directors responsible and accountable for their conduct. The equity courts imposed stringent procedural requirements on those bringing a derivative action. Perhaps the most effective means of defeating such an action was to show that the plaintiffs had failed to exhaust all the internal remedies available to a shareholder.

An early example of the procedural problems in a class action is *Foss v. Harbottle*.[18] In that case, shareholders of Victoria Park Co. sued the directors, the lawyer, and the architect of the company. The main allegation was that the directors, acting on behalf of the company, had sold land owned by themselves personally to the company for an inflated price. Also, the shareholders contended that the company had raised the purchase price for the lands in a manner not authorized by the company constitution. The court refused to consider the merits on the plaintiff's class and dismissed the action on the defendant's motion. In the court's view, the plaintiffs had failed to resort to all means and found them ineffectual before commencing their action.

These procedural obstacles have been largely displaced by legislation in a number of provinces. Two preliminary tests are used to determine the jurisdiction of the court in a derivative action. The first test found in British Columbia, Ontario, and under federal legislation is the "reasonable efforts" test, which has been substituted for the more exacting standard found in *Foss v. Harbottle*. The minority shareholder must establish that reasonable efforts were made to convince the company to bring the action on the company's behalf and that, despite these reasonable efforts, the company declined to commence the action.

The minority shareholder's derivative action has a second threshold test: whether the claimant is acting in good faith and in the interest of the company by bringing the action. This test is intended to exclude a shareholder from bringing an action that is in his/her best interest but not that of the company. If the shareholder has suffered some private wrong, then a direct action rather than a derivative action is the appropriate course to take.

Problems for Discussion

1. In what circumstances are common and preferred shareholders presumed to be equal? What, if anything, can be done to provide for a system where there is inequality between these two classes of shareholders?

2. Distinguish between a share and a share certificate.

3. What rights are attached to a share in a company?

4. What is the difference between a personal and derivative action?

5. How has legislation in British Columbia and Ontario modified the equitable rules applied to a derivative action?

6. Discuss whether the court in *Diligenti v. R.W.M.D. Operators*, *supra*, has blurred the distinction between a company and a partnership. Are there dangers in holding that a shareholder has certain equitable rights attached to a share that entitle him/her to retain a directorship in the company? Would the result have been different if the shares had been held in a public company? Again, would the same decision have been reached if the original shareholder had died and the executor of his/her estate had demanded a seat on the board of directors?

7. On March 5, Ms. Bach learns from a lawyer friend employed by Revenue Canada that a ruling is about to be made that would restrict the deductability of computer equipment and software. The ruling is scheduled to be released on April 2. The effect of the Revenue Canada ruling, in Ms. Bach's view, would be to depress the price of Rinehart's stock. On March 6, Ms. Bach tells her husband of the proposed ruling. That same day, he sells 20 000 shares of Rinehart's for $8.00 per share. On April 3, after the Revenue Canada ruling is released to the press, Rinehart's shares fall to $5.00 per share. What remedies would another shareholder and Rinehart have against Mr. Bach? Is he an insider? Would the result be different if Ms. Bach had owned the shares and sold them based on this information? Was the advance warning of the ruling "specific confidential information". See *Company Act*, R.S.B.C. 1979, c. 59, s. 153; and the *Securities Act*, R.S.B.C. 1979, s. 107.

8. Can a case be made that the courts have been increasingly willing to make special considerations for the private, closely held company? If so, how does this affect matters such as insurance liability and company management? See, for example, *Kosmopoulos v. Constitution Insurance Co. of Canada*, *supra*, and *Dusik v. Newton*, *supra*, and *Jackman v. Jackets Enterprises Ltd.*, *supra*. Are cases such as these useful for a shareholder of Rinehart to determine his/her rights and remedies?

Chapter 20 Notes

1. Dickerson, Howard, Getz, *Proposals for a New Business Corporation Law for Canada*, Vol. 1, Commentary, (Ottawa: Information Canada, 1971), para. 8.
2. (1923) A.C. 744, 767.

3. See *Prudential v. Newman Industries* (No. 2), (1982) 1 All E.R. at 366-67.
4. See *Macaura v. Northern Ass'ce Co., Ltd.*, (1925) A.C. 619 (H.L.).
5. Ibid. pp. 625-7.
6. (1983) 149 D.L.R.(3d) 77 (Ont.C.A.).
7. See Cudney and Kingston, *Ontario Corporation Manual*, pp. 2528-31.
8. See *Nicol's case*, (1885) 29 Ch.D. 421.
9. Pickering, "The Problem of the Preference Share" (1963) 26 *Mod.L.Rev.* 78.
10. (1946) S.C.R. 178 (S.C.C.).
11. (1889) 14 App.Cas. 525, 531.
12. See *British Columbia Companies Act*, R.S.B.C. chap. 67, section 221(1).
13. (1976) 1 B.C.L.R. 36 (B.C.S.C.).
14. See *Jackman v. Jackets Enterprises Ltd.*, (1977) 4 B.C.L.R. 358 (B.C.S.C.)
15. R.S.B.C. 1979, c. 59.
16. (1982) 2 W.W.R. 185 (B.C.S.C.).
17. (1984) 50 B.C.L.R. 321 (B.C.S.C.).
18. (1843) 2 Hare 461, 67 E.R. 189 (Ch.D.).

21 INSURANCE

The Purpose of Insurance

Rinehart Ltd., like any business, undertakes a number of risks in carrying on its business activities. The purpose of insurance is to shift the financial consequences of a risk from the corporation to an insurance carrier. In return for the acceptance of the risk, the insurance carrier is paid a *premium*.

The types of risks vary depending on the nature of the corporation's business, location, and products. For instance, a violent storm damages the roof of the warehouse. Computer equipment stored inside the warehouse is water damaged. A key employee, the vice-president in charge

FIGURE 21.1

"All in favor of a cap on our liability?"

Drawing by Stevenson; © 1986 The New Yorker Magazine, Inc.

of research and development, suddenly dies. Another employee, driving a Rinehart van, negligently causes an accident. The Rinehart van is damaged. Personal injuries are suffered by the driver of the other vehicle. The chief executive officer may have failed to read a loan agreement. Later the corporation defaults on the loan, and the bank, under the loan agreement, charges Rinehart a large penalty.

These are only a few of the examples of economic loss that Rinehart or Rinehart's directors or officers might face during the normal operation of business. It is important to recognize that the risks that are insurable include the acts or omissions of those who manage the corporation. It is common for the corporation to insure against the risk of personal liability that a director or officer might face in the management and operation of the business. The failure to carry directors' and officers' insurance may well discourage highly qualified people from becoming board members or officers of the corporation.

There are two means of dealing with the risk of potential liability: i) self-insure and ii) outside insurance. To self-insure means that the corporation accepts the risk of the potential loss and will pay any claim from the corporation assets. In many instances, it is likely that the decision to self-insure against a major risk would be a breach of the directors' and officers' fiduciary duty of care and loyalty to the corporation. Thus, the use of outside insurance through an insurance carrier is the typical means of protecting the corporation against the risk of potential loss. The effect of insurance is to indemnify or make whole the person who has suffered a specified loss or injury.

Assessing the Risk

In order to stay in business, an insurance company must be able to assess, define, and limit the risks that it undertakes. The assessment of risk depends on the nature of the thing insured. For example, Rinehart would carry insurance for fire and theft. In fact, the building owned and occupied by Rinehart may never be damaged by a fire nor the contents stolen. An insurance carrier would want to consider the statistical probability of the risk of fire and theft. The policy issued to Rinehart would be one among many issued to other companies. The likelihood is that the insurance company will have to pay claims to some that are insured for a loss occasioned by fire and theft. Because it can never be accurately predicted which among the pool of insured will incur the loss, the insurance carrier must deal with the probability of loss.

The probability of loss may shift over time. For instance, a thirty-five-year-old man seeking life insurance in 1900 had a greater probability of death at an earlier age than today. Similarly, shareholder actions against corporation directors for negligence has increased sharply, along with claims under directors' and officers' insurance policies. Not surprisingly, insurance carriers have increased the annual premium rates as much as tenfold and raised the deductible amount by a similar percentage.

ASSESSMENT FOR LIFE INSURANCE

Assume that Rinehart has purchased a life insurance policy on the lives of certain key employees. The insurance company would seek to determine its risk. Such factors as the age, current health, prior illness, cause of death of family members, marital status, and life-style factors such as smoking, drinking and drug use are highly relevant in determining the longevity of an employee.

Illustration   Arthur Tevis, the senior software designer of Rinehart, is thirty-five years old. His father died at age forty-nine of a heart attack. Mr. Tevis is eleven kilograms overweight and has high blood pressure. He smokes one pack of cigarettes a day, and drives a high-performance sports car. Rinehart, which hired Tevis for his computer skills, is concerned that, should he die before a major project is completed, several hundred thousand dollars of investment might be lost. A representative of Rinehart seeks a $250 000 life insurance policy on Mr. Tevis' life. Given the above information about Mr. Tevis, it would not be surprising to discover that the insurance company considers Mr. Tevis a greater than average risk. As the degree of risk increases, the amount of compensation demanded by the insurance company correspondingly increases.

In the insurance industry, the assessment of risk is made by an actuary. The function of an actuary is to calculate the probability of injury or loss. Predicting the probability of injury or death to a person, for example, who is part of a larger pool of insureds allows the insurance company to spread the risk of a single death or injury among the pool.

An insurance company does not offer insurance coverage on the life of a single executive or on a single piece of property. Instead, there is a pool of persons whose lives are insured. The actuary attempts to predict the average life expectancy of Mr. Tevis, the thirty-five-year-old employee. The decision might be made that the risk of death is too great and the insurance company would be unwilling to undertake that risk because its exposure to liability is too high.

ASSESSMENT OF DIRECTORS' AND OFFICERS' LIABILITY

In the above illustration, an insurance carrier considers whether to accept the risk of insuring a particular life. Although the insurance for Mr. Tevis might be declined, the insurance carrier would, of course, continue to issue life insurance policies generally. In contrast, directors' and officers' liability insurance has caused insurance carriers to reassess the risk of such insurance coverage for every corporation in the risk pool.

There has been controversy over the abrupt increase in annual premiums for directors' and officers' liability insurance. Some insurance carriers have declined to offer such insurance altogether. The rationale for the substantially higher premiums lies in the more than doubling of claims made under directors' and officers' insurance policies. The assessment of potential risk has changed. Courts have become more willing to impose personal liability on directors and officers who have failed in their duty to meet the disclosure requirements in banking and securities dealings. In a conflict of interest case, the courts impose a high duty of loyalty; self-dealing is a breach of that duty, and liability will follow.

Illustration   Rinehart has been notified by General Insurance Company that its directors' and officers' liability policy will be renewed, but that the premium upon renewal will increase from $10 000 per year to $125 000. The deductible will be raised from $15 000 to $750 000. Four members of the Rinehart board of directors have threatened to resign. Rinehart has the choice of dramatically increasing the board members' compensation in attempt to retain the directors' services. Such an increase, of course, is passed on to the consumer in the form of a higher price for the corporation's products. Also, there is the possibility of lower return to shareholders. And, in the event of the resignations, the corporation faces the prospect of recruiting new board members with less experience and skill.

The assessment of risk is made by the insurance carrier and by the insurance industry. In the case of directors' and officers' liability insurance, this assessment has a direct impact on the economic system. Everyone is affected from the worker on the factory floor to the shareholder. The derivative lawsuit has reshaped the financial risk to management. Management has also discovered that the insurance industry has cut its potential losses by limiting exposure to such risk.

Legislation and Insurance

The law of insurance is highly regulated. Each province has enacted legislation (e.g., *Insurance Act*) that governs a wide range of substantive matters from the provisions of an insurance contract to the licensing of insurance agents and brokers.

Indeed, the term *insurance* is itself the subject of statutory definition. In Ontario, insurance is defined by statute to mean:[1]

> The undertaking by one person to indemnify another person against loss or liability for loss in respect of a certain risk or peril to which the object of the insurance may be exposed, or to pay a sum of money or other thing of value upon the happening of a certain event and includes life insurance ...

The Insurance Contract

Insurance law is a specialized form of contract law. With certain qualifications, the basic principles of the law of contract apply to an insurance policy. In this section, the major characteristics of an insurance contract are considered.

PARTIES TO THE CONTRACT OF INSURANCE

The parties to the insurance contract are: i) the *insurer*, i.e., the party promising to compensate for a loss, and ii) the *insured*, i.e., the party to be compensated in the event of a loss. Not any party, however, is entitled to contract for insurance as an "insured". The "insured" must have an insurable interest in the property or life covered by the contract of insurance.

An *insurance broker* acts on behalf of both the insured and the insurer. The broker, therefore, may be an agent of both parties to the insurance transaction. An insurance broker provides an important service in a business environment, providing expertise for the multiple insurance needs of businesses. The insurance broker, in contrast to the insurance agent, is not a principal of a single insurer. The broker and the agent are subject to licence requirements established by provincial law. Both broker and agent may be personally liable if they form a contract of insurance with an unlicenced insurer.

An important function of an agent or broker is the completion of the insurance application form. In some circumstances, the agent or broker may complete the form and present it to the applicant for signature. Where the insured does not read the form, and the information contained is materially wrong, the insurer is bound by the acts of its agent. Thus, even though the insurer would not have issued a policy had the real risk of loss or damage been known, the completion of the application by the agent or broker with the wrong information cannot be used to defeat a subsequent claim by the innocent insured.

INSURABLE INTEREST

The insured is required to have an insurable interest in the life or property as a precondition to recovering for a loss. The crucial time is the date that the loss occurred.

For example, a shareholder of Rinehart does not have an insurable interest in the assets of the company.[2] The shareholder would have an insurable interest in the share certificates of the company, however.

The concept of insurable interest requires that an insured must have a connection with the person or property covered by the insurance contract such that any loss or damage will result in a direct loss to the insured. The insured must have a direct relationship to the property or

FIGURE 21.2 **THE INSURANCE CONTRACT**

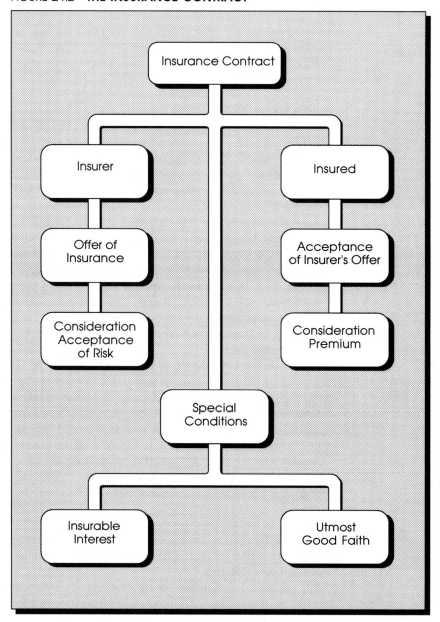

the person insured. The insurable interest concept is consistent with the notion that the purpose of a contract of insurance is to *indemnify*, i.e., pay the loss incurred through an injury to the insured's property or to a person with whom the insured has a direct relationship, such as a spouse or employer.

FORMATION

As a general rule, the applicant offers to enter into a contract of insurance with the insurer, and the insurer accepts that offer. Even though the insurer may have initiated the dealings with the applicant, the *offer* is the applicant's submission of a proposal for insurance to the insurer.

The applicant typically makes his/her offer to an insurance agent or broker. An *insurance agent* acts as a principal of a single insurer. In circumstances where the insurance agent has authority to solicit insurance business, collect premiums, and issue binders or interim coverage, the insurer is bound by the acts of the agent.

UTMOST GOOD FAITH REQUIREMENT

During negotiation neither party is under an affirmative duty to disclose facts to the other side in most contracts. This, however, does not hold true for an insurance contract. The concept of *utmost good faith* requires that the insured fully disclose material facts to the insurer. The primary reason for the heavy burden of disclosure is the need of the insurer to understand the nature of a risk that is being insured against. A non-disclosure of a material fact substantially alters the nature and scope of the insurer's risk.

The utmost good faith requirement evolved in the context of marine insurance. The shipowner seeking insurance was required to disclose not just information requested by the insurer but all necessary and essential information bearing on the extent of the risk insured against.[3] Later, the courts applied the utmost good faith requirement to other areas of insurance. Thus, a general rule emerged imposing a duty of disclosure on insurance applicants to make known material facts that might influence the insurer's opinion as to the risk incurred.[4] The concealment of a material fact that results in a breach of the utmost faith rule entitles the insurer to void the insurance policy. Similarly, a misrepresentation of fact may have the same consequence.

It is not enough for the insurer to prove concealment (another name for fraud) or misrepresentation of fact. To void the insurance policy, the concealment or misrepresentation also must be *material* to the insurance. In turn, materiality is addressed in terms of whether the fact would affect the rate and risk.[5]

STANDARD FORM CONTRACT

The terms and conditions of the insurance contract are contained in the *policy*. In theory, an insurance contract (except life insurance) can be made without the issuance and delivery of a written policy. The execution of the application, issuance of a receipt, and payment of a premium is the basis of a binding contract between the insured and insurer without the issuance of a policy. In practice, the issuance of the policy by the insurer and the acceptance by the insured takes place in the ordinary course of business.

The terms and conditions contained in an insurance policy are not typically the result of negotiation between the parties. The insurer drafts and the insured accepts the draft. As there is a general uniformity of terms and conditions used in similar policies used by most insurance companies, there is little opportunity for the insured to seek different or more favourable terms elsewhere. The insurer's authority to dictate terms is regulated by statute. For instance, in Ontario, statutory conditions are automatically incorporated into every contract. An aim of the statutory conditions is to prevent an insurer from using unjust and unreasonable clauses to avoid liability.

Although the policy of insurance is a standard form contract, there are distinctive terms for each policy, e.g., the subject matter, identity of the insured or beneficiary, the premium rate, and duration of the insurance.

The provisions of insurance policies are uniform with insurance companies in Canada. Thus, for example, in the life insurance sought by Rinehart on Mr. Tevis' life, the terms would be mostly the same regardless of the insurance company. In Ontario, however, the Superintendent of Insurance has authority to prevent unfair or deceptive practices.

PREMIUMS

The consideration paid by the insured for protection against an insurable risk is called a *premium*. The amount and frequency of premium payments is also based on the type of insurance required. Marine insurance may be purchased for a single voyage. Life insurance, on the other hand, may be purchased by the insured at age eighteen and kept in force until the date of death, perhaps sixty years later. The premium paid in each case would be based on very different factors. For life insurance, the mortality rate is a significant factor on which the rate of premium is based. In a marine insurance policy, the destination, the cargo, and type of ship would define the risk.

A second factor influencing the amount of the premium is the face value of the policy. The premium payable on the death of the insured in the amount of $50 000 will be substantially less than on the same insured in the amount of $1 000 000.

Lastly, the amount of the premium is directly connected to the interest rate that an insurer can make on investing premium dollars. In times of high interest rates, the insurer (and indeed the entire insurance industry) may be willing to reduce the amount of the premium. During such a period, the insurer's main interest is pooling an investment fund and making profits from the high interest rates available in the marketplace. The problem, however, is when interest rates decline and the insurer has underwritten a large number of policies based on the theory of low premiums plus high interest. This sequence of events happened in the North American insurance industry in the 1980s, and in 1985 resulted in an estimated $22 billion industry underwriting loss.[6]

Only in rare circumstances is the insured entitled to recover premiums paid to the insurer. A threshold case requires the insured to prove that the insurance contract was never binding, and that the cause for the failure to form a contract was not his/her own fraud. Proof of a non-binding contract of insurance, for which money has been advanced as a premium, entitles the insured to recover on the basis of total failure of consideration.

Types of Insurance

Insurance law makes a distinction between contracts of *indemnity* (e.g., fire and marine insurance) and contracts based on a *contingency* (e.g., life insurance).[7] A contract of indemnity limits the liability of the insurer in two ways: i) to the actual loss suffered by the insured, and ii) to the happening of an unascertained event against which the insurer has insured.

A contract based on a contingency is not based on the insured's actual pecuniary loss. For instance, in the case of life insurance, the insurer pays the face amount of the policy to the beneficiary without any proof that the insured's death caused a financial loss to the beneficiary. Further, a contract based on a contingency assumes that the specific event, e.g., the

FIGURE 21.3   **INSURANCE CONTRACTS**

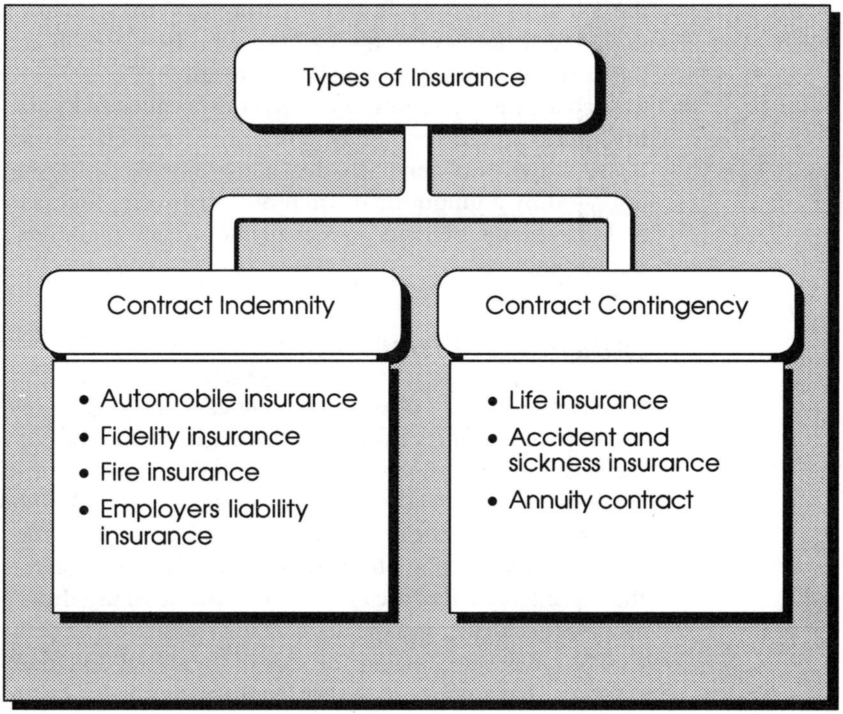

Types of Insurance

Contract Indemnity

- Automobile insurance
- Fidelity insurance
- Fire insurance
- Employers liability insurance

Contract Contingency

- Life insurance
- Accident and sickness insurance
- Annuity contract

death of the insured, will happen in the future. An indemnity contract, such as marine insurance, assumes that, in most cases, neither the ship nor the cargo will be damaged.

Reinsurance means that an insurer has acquired insurance on the risk underwritten on a third party: simply put, insurance on insurance. The purpose of reinsurance is to allow the first insurer to relinquish some of the risk. In return for accepting part of the risk, the reinsurer obtains part of the insurer's premium. One of the best known reinsurers is Lloyd's of London. The reinsurer intends to make a profit by investing the premium dollars obtained from the insurer. Once the potential risk actually occurs under the policy, then both the insurer and reinsurer have an obligation to meet the claim. The insurer's obligation is directly to the insured; and the reinsurer's obligation is to the insurer.

Accident and Sickness Insurance

Accident and sickness insurance is designed to compensate against a loss of injury suffered in accidents or through sickness. This type of insurance is one of indemnity. For instance, when the insured loses an eye in a hockey match, accident insurance would compensate him/her for the loss of the eye, including medical expenses and loss of earnings. Most accident insurance policies set forth the monetary amount to be paid in the event of the loss of an eye, arm, leg, etc. Sickness insurance is also designed to indemnify the insured who becomes ill and incurs medical expenses and loss of earnings as a result.

Such insurance contracts are carefully regulated by statute; for instance, in Ontario,[8] a written policy is required for such insurance. A distinction is also drawn between individual and group plans. A group plan is typically operated by a union for its members or by employers for its employees, and insurance benefits are available to all members and designated dependents.

Automobile Insurance

Rinehart has a fleet of ten company cars and eight vans and trucks. The use of these vehicles by employees creates a number of risks: i) a vehicle may be damaged; ii) an employee may be injured or killed; iii) a third party may suffer death or injury or damage to their vehicle. Automobile insurance covers these type of risks. The amount of the premium would depend upon, among other things, the value of the cars, vans, and trucks, the driving record of the employees entitled to use them, the claim record for prior accidents, and the deductability amount. The deductability amount, a common feature, places the risk of the initial dollar amount loss on the insured. That amount may vary from $50 to $500. The greater the amount the insured is willing to pay in the event of a loss, the lower the premium.

Fidelity Insurance

One business risk is that an employee who handles money or other valuables will become dishonest and commit theft. Fidelity insurance indemnifies the company for the loss through the dishonest act of any of its employees. The legal term *defalcation* means misappropriation or embezzlement. Fidelity insurance shifts the risk of defalcation to the insurer. In turn, the insured must make full disclosure of all relevant facts to the insurer. For example, where the employer is aware that an employee who handles the company's accounts had previously committed a defalcation, that fact must be disclosed to the insurer. Failure to disclose such a material fact regarding the risk insurance would entitle the insurer to void the contract of insurance.

Employer's Liability Insurance

Employer's liability insurance insures the employer against loss arising from an injury or loss of life of an employee. The insured is the employer. Thus, in the event of loss, the employer, and not the employee, is the party compensated by the insurer. An employer has an insurable interest in the life and health of its employees.

Life Insurance

The insurer promises to pay insurance money i) in the event of death, ii) on the happening of an event or contingency dependent on human life, iii) at a fixed or determinable future time, or iv) for a term dependent on human life. The beneficiary of the life insurance, upon the death of the insured, must show an insurable interest in the insured. It is clear that an employer has an insurable interest in the life of an employee. In the above illustration, Arthur Tevis is a key member of the Rinehart research and development team. His death would cause the company an economic loss. The risk of that loss, through the use of life insurance, is shifted onto an insurer.

In the case of an individual life insurance policy (e.g., insuring a single life rather than several, as under a group plan), the insurer agrees to accept the risk only after obtaining a satisfactory medical report on the insured. The risk of death obviously is closely connected with the current state of the applicant's health. Unless the applicant is in sound or good health, it is unlikely that the insurer will accept the risk of insuring against his/her death.

Although there are some limited exceptions, as a general rule the failure to pay premiums when due entitles the insurer to cancel the policy. Exceptions to the rule include: waiver of premium payment by the insurer, statutory grace periods, and any express terms to the contrary set forth in the contract.

Fire Insurance

Fire insurance insures against the risk of damage or loss by fire to property in which the insured has an insurable interest. For example, a company such as Rinehart would typically insure against the destruction of the company building by fire. Indeed, where the building has been purchased, in part, with borrowed funds, the lender (called the mortgagee) may require the borrower (called the mortgagor) to insure the mortgaged premises against fire and name the mortgagee as a beneficiary under the insurance policy.

Fire insurance is an indemnity contract. In the event of a loss resulting from fire, the insured is entitled to compensation to repair or replace the destroyed property. The insurance contract between Rinehart and Pocket Insurance Company is a personal contract between those two parties. Should Rinehart subsequently sell the insured premises to another party, the fire insurance policy would not automatically be held for the benefit of the new owner. After the transfer of the premises, in the event of a fire, Rinehart would not be able to claim indemnity as it no longer had an insurable interest in the premises. And the new owners would fail because they were not party to the original contract for fire insurance.

A duty to disclose material facts is placed on the applicant for fire insurance. Assume, for example, that the fire insurance application asks: How many fires has the applicant had in the last three years? Assume further that the applicant has had one fire during that period but failed to disclose that fact. This suppression of a material fact expressly asked for by the insurer to determine the risk of insuring is fraudulent. The effect of the fraud is to void the insurance.

Problems for Discussion

1. A law firm, Dobbs and Smith, has two insurance policies. One policy is an office equipment floater that covers: "office contents, including all materials and supplies usual to the business of the Insured, including furniture, furnishings, fittings, fixtures, machinery, tools, utensils, appliances, books of accounts, drawings, card-index systems and other records, — generally all office contents of every description, kept or used by the Insured". The policy expressly excludes loss to customer's goods. Dobbs and Smith, the Insured, is burglarized, and eighty-seven originally executed wills belonging to the firm's clients are stolen. The Insured claims that the wills were "records" that were "kept" by them within the meaning of the policy, and that the Insurer is required to pay for the cost of duplicating the wills and having new ones executed by the clients. The Insurer refuses to honour the claim. Discuss. See *Dudelzark & Landry v. Attorney for Non-Marine Underwriters of Lloyd's of London, et al.*, (1985) 38 Alta.L.R.(2d) 110 (Q.B.).

2. Rinehart employees, as part of their compensation, are provided with accident and sickness insurance. One employee, Howard Twist, attends a party with a group of friends. He is not accustomed to drinking. On this occasion, Mr. Twist consumes a substantial amount of alcohol in fifteen to thirty minutes. Not long after drinking the alcohol, Twist enters a car as a passenger and is left to sleep inside. About an hour after leaving the party, he dies. He has drunk a sufficient amount of alcohol to depress the respiratory centre and end breathing. Mr. Twist's wife claims the $50 000 face amount under the insurance policy on the grounds that her husband had died as a result of a "bodily injury caused by an accident". The insurer refuses to pay, claiming that Mr. Twist's death was not an "accident" within the meaning of the policy. Discuss. See *Leontowicz v. Seaboard Life Insurance Co.*, (1984) 36 Alta.L.R. 65 (Alta.C.A.).

3. James Dylan, a truck driver, requests Jean Hern, an insurance agent, for coverage to operate his truck on the highways and for insurance of any trailer that he might be hauling. Ms. Hern has Dylan sign an application form. Four months later, Dylan is involved in a traffic accident and a trailer that he was pulling is damaged. The repairs to the trailer amount to $8 000. He discovers that the insurance policy issued by the insurer does not cover loss or damage to the trailer. Dylan sues Ms. Hern to recover his damages. On what theory, if any, would the insurance agent be liable?

4. Paula Sones requests automobile insurance by telephone to an insurance agent named Karin Smith. Ms. Smith has authority to issue automobile insurance policies that bind Sun Alliance, the insurer. At the time of the telephone conversation Ms. Smith knows that Sones' husband had been in an automobile accident several months before. At the time of that accident, he had been drinking and was driving on a suspended driver's licence. Notwithstanding this information, Ms. Smith completes the automobile insurance application in such a fashion as to mislead the insurer about the circumstances surrounding the husband's accident. Sones signs the application as completed by Smith. Several months later, Sones' husband is in another accident, and Sones claims for the loss on the insurance policy. The insurer relies on the defence of misrepresentation. Discuss whether the insurer is entitled to defeat Sones' claim. See *Gallant v. Sun Alliance Insurance Co.*, (1983) 4 D.L.R.(4th) 180 (N.B.Q.B.).

5. On a remote tract of land owned by Rinehart stands a 30m × 30m Quonset hut. The building is divided into storage and work areas. After some minor repairs and clean-up around the hut, an accumulation of lumber piles up. The foreman in charge of the clean-up puts a small advertisement in a local newspaper that reads: "Pick up all the lumber and wood around 134 Johnson Street building, help

yourself". Over the following weekend, the police notice a number of pick-up trucks around the premises, stop to inquire, and find that the interior of the building has been stripped, including panelling, sections of the ceiling, oil furnace, oil storage tank, and bathroom and plumbing fixtures. People on the scene, however, point to the newspaper ad. The company seeks to recover for the loss resulting from the damage done to the premises. The insurance policy issued by Royal Insurance, however, specifically excludes theft. The insurer resists the Rinehart lawsuit on the basis the loss had been caused by theft. Discuss. See *Reliable Distributors Ltd. v. Royal Insurance Co. of Canada*, (1984) 14 D.L.R.(4th) (B.C.S.C.).

6. Some have proposed that there should be a ceiling on the maximum liability of directors and officers for breach of their duty of care to the corporation. Discuss whether this is an acceptable way to remedy the difficulty that corporations face in obtaining directors' and officers' liability insurance.

Chapter 21 Notes

1. *Insurance Act*, R.S.O., c.218, s.1(30).
2. See *Guaranty Co. of North America v. Aqua-Land Exploration* (1966) S.C. 133 (S.C.C.).
3. See *Bates v. Hewitt* (1867) 2 Q.B. 595.
4. See *Ontario Metal Products Co. v. Mutual Life Insurance Co.*, (1924) 1 D.L.R. 127 (S.C.C.).
5. See *Henwood v. Prudential Insurance Co. of America*, (1967) 64 D.L.R.(2d) 715 (S.C.C.).
6. *New York Times*, Monday, June 9, 1986, "Insurance Industry Under Fire," p. D1.
7. See *Glynn v. Scottish Union & National Insurance Co., Ltd.*, (1963) 40 D.L.R.(2d) 929 (Ont.C.A.)
8. *Insurance Act*, s. 242.

22 PARTNERSHIPS

Introduction

Definition of Partnership

The *Partnership Act*,[1] Section 2, defines partnership as "the relation which subsists between persons carrying on business in common with a view of profit". This same definition is found in other provincial partnership legislation, providing for a uniformity of approach to what is meant by a partnership.

The classic definition of partnership is:[2]

> A contract of two or more persons to place their money, effects, labor and skill, or some or all of them, in lawful commerce or business, and to divide the profits and share the loss in certain proportions; and that it is not essential to a legal partnership that it be confined to commercial business. It may exist between attorneys, conveyancers, mechanics, owners of a line of stagecoaches, artisans or farmers, as well as between merchants and bankers.

A partnership is a form of business association. What follows from this form is a very different structure than that of a company: there is a different means of financing the business operation, and a different group of people entitled to share in the profits and running of the organization. For example, two software engineers may decide to enter a partnership to develop, manufacture, promote, and distribute their product. There is no legal rule that requires them to set up a company.

It is relatively easy to establish a partnership. The partnership can be made by a handshake of two or more persons who agree to carry on business together for profit.

FIGURE 22.1   **MEANS OF PARTNERSHIP CREATION**

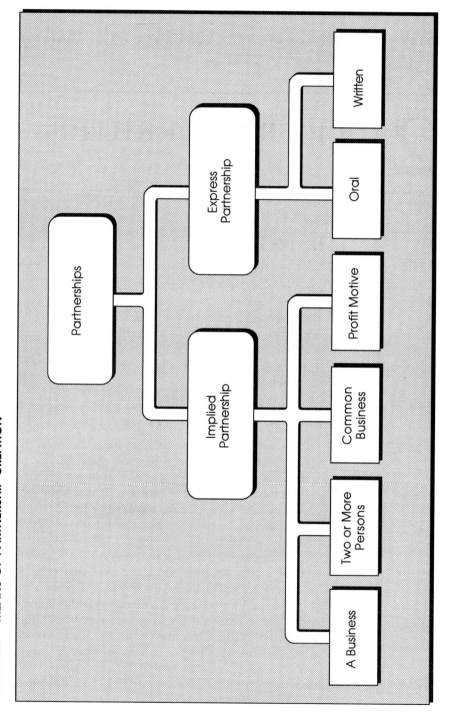

Implied and Express Partnerships

Partnership, unlike a company, may arise either through implied or express terms. In contrast to a company, which requires compliance with a number of formal procedures, a partnership may come into existence without any formal registration, without a written document between the partners, and without the express, formal agreement of the partners. Such a partnership is said to be implied from the circumstances. The partnership legislation sets forth the conditions that must be present before an implied partnership is said to exist.

For activities to be deemed to be a partnership, i) there must be a business, ii) with two or more persons; iii) the business must be in common between these persons; and iv) the purpose of the business must be to make a profit.

As a partnership may be implied from the circumstance of two or more persons conducting an activity that makes a profit, the *Partnership Act* has been carefully drafted to exclude an implied partnership in certain cases. Example: Where two or more persons have a joint tenancy, a tenancy in common, joint property, common property, or part ownership, the common ownership is not, by itself, sufficient to create a partnership. This holds true even where the common owners share the profits from the property. The courts have emphasized the need to find that each owner intends to deal with the land not according to his/her respective interest but as land that is indivisible amongst all the partners. The property is considered as partnership property.

Legal Entity

A company is a separate legal entity. Does a partnership have a legal entity separate from the individual partners? This question has been hotly disputed in court decisions and legal writings. The traditional common law view has been that there is no "entity" but merely individuals called partners. The rights and duties of the partners are not attributed to the partnership. The theory, however, does not always hold up in practice. Large law firms and accounting firms are a good example.

A law firm may list the name of three partners, two of whom may be dead, and have twenty additional partners and fifty associates. This type of partnership would be more like a company in both its internal and external relationships. Internal management, for instance, would be conducted by an executive committee composed of several of the many partners. A large corporate client would consider the law firm to be a legal entity rather than an aggregate of partners. A wide variation in the types of partnerships makes any definitive statement about legal entity status difficult to apply accurately across the board.

FIGURE 22.2 **LEGAL STATUS**

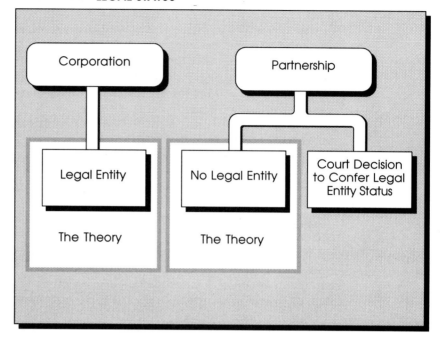

Liability of the Partners and the Firm

The *Partnership Act* is specific about the scope and nature of the partner's and the firm's liability.

Ability To Bind the Firm

Each partner is deemed to be an agent of the partnership and his/her other partners. This means that each partner has the ability to bind his/her firm and other partners for "any act for carrying on in the usual way business of the kind carried on by the firm of which he is a member".[3]

Liability of the Firm

The partnership firm is variously liable for the wrongful acts or omissions of any partner acting in the ordinary course of business of the firm, or with the authority of his/her co-partners.[4] The firm must pay for the loss or injury caused by the partner to another person who is not a partner in the firm. For example, a partner in a law firm might fail to commence a legal action within the period allowed by the *Limitation Act*, so that as

FIGURE 22.3 **LIABILITY OF INDIVIDUAL PARTNERS AND THE PARTNERSHIP**

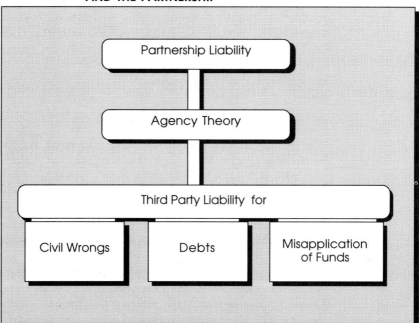

a result, the client's right to recover damages is barred. The client would be entitled to sue the law firm for the negligence of the partner and recover damages for his/her loss. In such a case, every partner in the law firm would be jointly liable for the loss.[5]

Liability for Firm Debts

One of the major differences between a partnership and a company concerns the liability for business debts. The officers and management of the company are not liable for the debts incurred by the company. Moreover, the shareholders stand to lose their investment but lack any liability above their investment. A partner, however, is jointly liable with all the other partners for the debts and obligations of the firm.[6] Should there be insufficient assets in the partnership to satisfy the firm's debts and obligations, then the partners are personally liable. A partner's personal residence, car, investments, life insurance policies, etc. may be looked to by creditors of the firm once the firm's resources have been exhausted when the debt remains unpaid.

Liability for Misapplication

The question of the firm's liability arises when one partner of the firm, acting within the course of business, acquires money or property from a third party and then misapplies it. For example, a client gives Arnold Smith, a partner in Dobbs and Smith, Barristers and Solicitors, a $50 000 retainer. Mr. Smith misappropriates the funds for his own benefit rather than placing them in the firm's trust account. The client is entitled to hold the law firm liable for the loss of the $50 000.[7] Indeed, every partner in the law firm is jointly and severally liable to the client for their partner's misappropriation of the retainer.[8]

Limitations on Liability

The liability of a partner under the *Partnership Act* turns on whether he/she was admitted as a partner at the time that the firm became liable to creditors for a debt. Where the debt was incurred prior to a person's admission to partnership status, he/she is not liable for the debt.[9] An initial question, therefore, must be raised when enforcing a debt or obligation to the partnership: Was each partner a member of the firm at the time the debt was incurred? A collateral question concerns the liability of partners who have retired from the firm. As a general rule, the retirement does not operate to discharge the retiring partner from his/her liability on debts or obligations incurred before his/her retirement.[10] The only way in which the retiring partner can effect a discharge of liability is by an express or implied agreement with the remaining partners and the creditors.[11]

Rights and Duties of Partners

Sources of Rights and Duties

The rights and duties of the partners may be found in three sources: i) the formal agreement between the partners; ii) the *Partnership Act*; and iii) common law and equitable principles. These mutual rights and duties, whether in the agreement or defined by certain sections of the *Partnership Act*, may be varied by the consent of all the partners.[12] In this section, we examine selected rights and duties for discussion.

Fiduciary Obligations of Partners

One of the most important sources of duties is found in the equitable doctrine of fiduciary obligations. As each partner is in practical terms both a principal and agent of the partnership, the possibility of advantage taking is increased. The fiduciary obligation doctrine is a means of ensuring that each partner is loyal and acts in good faith with regard to the other partners. A partner who acts for personal benefit, which robs the treasury of the partnership of a profit or opportunity for a profit, is liable to account for his/her ill-gotten gains to the other partners. The *Part-*

FIGURE 22.4   **SOURCE OF PARTNERSHIP RIGHTS**

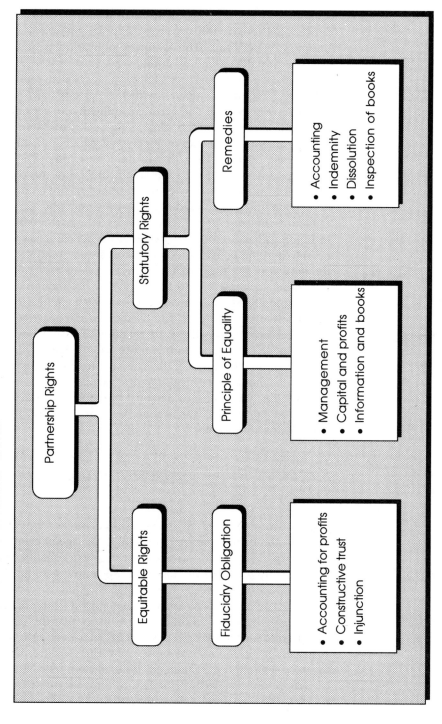

nership Act, Section 22, provides that "a partner shall act with the utmost fairness and good faith towards the other members of the firm in the business of the firm". This statutory obligation is in addition to the fiduciary duty developed by equity.

The breach of the partner's fiduciary duty occurs where he/she either secretly or openly competes with the partnership for contracts, commissions, or property. The partner's obligation to act out of loyalty, good faith, and fairness compels him/her to seek these benefits for the partnership and not for his/her own personal gain. For example, a partnership has a lease on a building that is about to expire. The partners are negotiating a new lease with the landlord. One of the partners, in secret, enters into negotiations with the landlord to obtain a lease for himself/herself on the same building. Assuming that the partner succeeds in obtaining the lease in his/her own name, the partnership would succeed in holding that he/she had breached his/her fiduciary duty to the partnership and the court would order that he/she hold the lease in trust for the benefit of the partnership.

Another example would be a lawyer who, though a partner in a law firm, "moonlights" by accepting work from a client and pockets the fees personally. In such a case, the partner, in the absence of consent from the other partners, is liable to account to his/her law firm for all the profits made by him/her in this transaction.[13] The key is that the partner is carrying on a business of the same nature and competing with his/her own firm. On the other hand, a partner who enters into a book-publishing contract on how to use a personal computer for fun and profit would not be accountable to his/her law firm for the publisher's advance and royalties on the book.

Statutory Rules for Determining Rights and Duties

A major consideration in a partnership is the determination of rights to share in the capital, profits, losses, and management of the partnership. The *Partnership Act* adopts a basic principle of equality between partners. The equality principle establishes a presumption about the dealings that partners have with one another though they may be varied by agreement. For example, every partner may have a hand in the management of the partnership business. In practice, it is likely that the day-to-day management and decision-making, particularly in a large firm, is delegated to a management committee composed of a few of the partners. The management committee, or indeed, the managing partner, as the case may be, has reasonably wide authority to bind the partnership. He/she may have the right to set salaries for employees, compromise claims pursued against the firm, or retain the services of an accountant or law firm.

Each partner is entitled to an equal share in the capital and profits of the business, and must make an equal contribution toward any losses suffered by the firm.[14] There may be, however, provisions of a partnership agreement that provide for an unequal division of profits and losses. Such an agreement is binding and enforceable. In the absence of an agreement, the equality principle applies to distribution of capital and profits and contribution to losses.

Another important rule is that no partner is entitled to remuneration for acting in the partnership business.[15] Once again, however, this rule operates only where there is no express or implied agreement among the partners to the contrary. The economic incentive is generally the division of the firm's profits among the partners. As each partner is both a principal and agent of the firm, he/she is not an employee or servant of the firm and thus cannot receive a salary or wage.

A partner may personally make payments or incur liability on behalf of his/her firm. In such a case, what rights, if any, does the partner have against the firm? The *Partnership Act* is clear that such a partner has a right to indemnity. A right of indemnity entitles the partner to compensation for the payment or obligation undertaken. This right of indemnity applies where the partner has made payments or incurred personal liabilities: i) in the ordinary and proper conduct of the business of the firm, and ii) in or about anything necessarily done for the preservation of the business or property of the firm.[16] The onus is on the partner to establish a legal link between his/her actual expenditure or debt incurred and the business or preservation of the business of his/her firm.

Another important right is access to the firm's books and full information to all things affecting the partnership. Information cannot be kept secret from one or more of the partners. This is a variation of the equality theme that appears in many partnership contexts. Each partner has a right, when he/she thinks fit, to have access to and inspect and copy the partnership books.[17] Beyond the rights to the firm's books, there is a more general right to full information on all things affecting the partnership, and each partner has equal access to this information.[18]

Dissolution of the Partnership

Meaning of Dissolution

"Dissolution" means that the partnership, while it continues to be in existence, is in the process of winding up. Thus, an act or event that dissolves the partnership does not operate to automatically terminate the partnership.

There are a number of provisions of the *Partnership Act* that specifically deal with the events, procedures, and effects of dissolution. Dissolution

FIGURE 22.5 **DISSOLVING THE PARTNERSHIP**

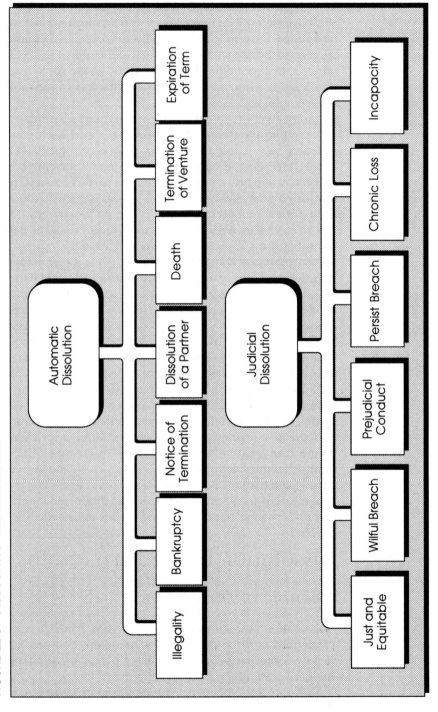

has important consequences for the partners' authority, the firm's assets, and the return of benefits to the partners. In this section, we will examine the main rules governing dissolution. Through the study of the process of dissolution we will discover what must be done to end the partnership.

Statutory Basis for Dissolution

The following statutory grounds for dissolution will dissolve the partnership without recourse to the courts:

1. A partnership for a fixed term that has expired;[19]
2. A partnership for a single adventure or undertaking that has terminated;[20]
3. From the date set forth in a notice of dissolution given by one partner to the other partners;[21]
4. On the death, bankruptcy, or dissolution of a partner where there are two partners;[22]
5. On the death, bankruptcy, or dissolution of a partner where there are more than two partners, subject to agreement among the partners;[23]
6. On the happening of any event that makes it unlawful for the business of the partnership to be carried on.[24]

The following statutory grounds vest a court with discretion to issue a decree dissolving the partnership:

1. Where a partner is declared to be under a mental capacity that makes him/her incapable of managing his/her affairs or discharging his/her duties as a partner;[25]
2. Where a partner in any other way becomes permanently incapable of performing his/her part of the partnership contract;[26]
3. Where a partner's conduct is calculated to affect prejudicially the carrying on of the business;[27]
4. Where a partner wilfully or persistently commits a breach of the partnership agreement or conducts himself/herself in such a manner that it is not reasonably practicable for the other partners to carry on the partnership business with him/her;[28]
5. Where a partnership can only be carried on at a loss;[29]
6. Whenever, in any case, circumstances have arisen that, in the opinion of the court, render it just and equitable that the partnership be dissolved.[30]

The possibility of judicial intervention to cause partnership dissolution allows for an expansion of the grounds otherwise available to bring a partnership to a close. The authority of the courts on dissolution is broad in nature. As ground six indicates, the court has considerable discretion limited only by what a judge finds to be "just and equitable" under the circumstances. The court has further discretion as to the nature of the dissolution decree where there are three or more partners. In such a case, the court may dissolve the entire partnership or order that the partnership be dissolved between the partner whose condition or conduct has given rise to the application and the remaining partners.[31]

Authority of the Partners after Dissolution

As the partnership does not terminate at the moment of dissolution, some mechanism is required in order that the business of the partnership can continue until the final winding-up. The *Partnership Act* provides this interim authority. Each partner, after dissolution, continues to have authority to bind the firm, and the other rights and obligations continue as well.[32] The limitation on the continuation of authority and rights and obligations is that they must be exercised by the partners so long as they are necessary for the winding-up. In essence, the partners are empowered to continue dealing with existing partnership business transactions that are unfinished at the date of dissolution. But they do not have authority to enter into new business transactions, except as it can be demonstrated that the new transaction is necessary to implement the winding-up process. There is one exception to the statutory authority: The firm is not bound by the acts of a partner who has become insolvent.[33]

Distribution of Benefits to Partners

Upon dissolution, the partnership may, after paying outstanding debts, have money or property left for distribution to the partners. The *Partnership Act* provides a rule for the application of assets on dissolution. Once the claims have been settled against the partnership, every partner has an entitlement to the surplus assets.[34]

In certain partnerships, e.g., a law firm, it is not uncommon for a person entering the partnership to pay a premium to the other partners. The existing partners may take the position that they have built up the firm, increased its good will and client base, and acquired assets over the years, and that any new partner should make a contribution, in the form of a premium, to the existing partners. Indeed, the existing partners are also potentially selling a right to future profits that now will have to be shared with the new partner. It should be noted, however, that in most partnership agreements there are express formulae specifying the "share" rights of all partners and, in the case of a large law firm or accounting firm, it is unlikely that the new partner would take the same proportionate share of the profits as a senior partner.

The problem, however, does occur as to whether a partner is entitled to recover all or part of his/her premium on dissolution. Given the wide variety of partnerships and the equally wide circumstances surrounding both the partnership and dissolution, it is not sensible to develop a single, detailed distribution formula for partnership premiums. Instead, the *Partnership Act* has left the quantum of return to the discretion of the court.[35] In deciding whether to order repayment of the premium, the court takes into account the terms of the partnership contract and the length of time during which the partnership has continued.

There are two grounds on which the court will not order a repayment of the premium: i) where the court finds the dissolution was wholly or chiefly because of the misconduct of the partner who paid the premium, or ii) where the partnership agreement contains no provision for the return of any part of the premium. In a well-drafted partnership agreement, the problem of returning a premium will be expressly dealt with. It is only in those circumstances where the partnership agreement is silent on this matter that the court exercises its jurisdiction.

Limited Partnership

The Nature of a Limited Partnership

A limited partnership is a specialized structure or organization that may be formed for any of the same business purposes as an ordinary partnership. The essential structural aspect of a limited partnership is the statutory classification of the partners into separate categories: i) general partners, and ii) limited partners. There must be one or more persons in each category to form a limited partnership.[36] One of the important uses of limited partnership is as a financial mechanism to raise investment capital.[37] Rinehart Ltd., for example, rather than issuing additional shares, may attempt to raise funds by creating a limited partnership with designated officers of the company as general partners.

The limited partnership interest is then sold to investors who participate in the profits that the partnership projects from a particular business venture. In recent years, the limited partnership has been used to finance real estate acquisitions. There have been important tax advantages, in particular the ability to deduct certain costs such as depreciation, that have made the limited partnership form of investment attractive to the high-bracket taxpayer.

Registration Requirement

Unlike an ordinary partnership that may be implied from the circumstances of the business dealing and that involves two or more persons, the formation of a limited partnership requires the registration of a certificate signed by all the persons desiring to form the partnership.[38] This certificate must be filed with the registrar. The certificate operates as a

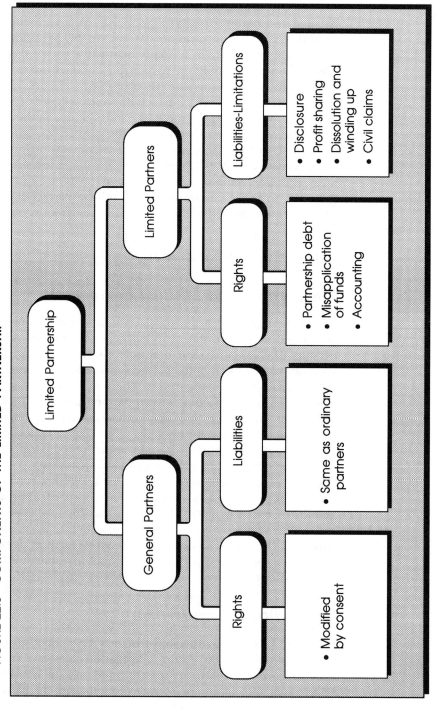

FIGURE 22.6 **COMPONENTS OF THE LIMITED PARTNERSHIP**

disclosure statement that includes information on: i) the general nature of the business carried on; ii) the term of the partnership; iii) the amount of cash, and the nature and fair value of the property, if any, contributed by each limited partner; and iv) the share of the profits or other compensation that each limited partner is entitled to receive as a result of his/her contribution.[39]

Rights of the General Partners

A general partner may, at the same time, be a limited partner in the same limited partnership.[40] The rights and powers of such a general partner are the same as those of a general partner who does not have a limited partner interest. The person with both partner interests also has the same rights as any limited partner against the other general partners in respect to his/her contribution.[41] What, then, are the rights of the general partner? The *Partnership Act* makes it clear that a general partner's rights and powers, including the restrictions and liabilities, that normally apply to partners in an ordinary partnership are equally applicable to the general partner.[42] There are a number of special circumstances, however, where the general partner lacks authority to act without the written consent or ratification of all the limited partners: i) Where the general partner intends to act in such a way that would make it impossible to carry out the business of the limited partnership;[43] ii) Where the general partner desires to consent to a judgment against the limited partnership;[44] iii) Where the general partner intends to possess limited partnership property, or to dispose of any right in such property, other than for partnership purposes;[45] iv) Where the general partner proposes to admit either a general or limited partnership without an express right to do so contained in the limited partnership certificate;[46] and v) Where the general partner intends to continue the partnership business after the bankruptcy, death, retirement, finding of mental incompetence in, or dissolution of a general partner, unless he/she is authorized to do so in the limited partnership certificate.[47]

Limits on the Liability of the Limited Partner

One of the major attractions of the limited partnership arrangement for "investors" is the limitation of their liability as partners. As we discussed earlier, a partner in an ordinary partnership is generally jointly and severally liable for all the partnership debts and losses. Once the partnership assets have been exhausted, then the creditor or claimant, as the case may be, is entitled to look to the personal assets of the partners. Thus, an ordinary partnership carries with it the potential of unlimited personal liability.

In contrast, a limited partner's liability is limited to the amount of property that he/she has either contributed or agreed to contribute to the capital of the limited partnership. Thus, if the limited partnership should be insolvent, the creditors are limited in the quantum that they can recover from the limited partners.[48] The immunity to excess of contribution recovery can be lost, however, where a limited partner takes part in the management of the business.[49] Therefore, it is only the passive limited partner who is entitled to limit his/her liability to others.

The limited partner has a statutory liability to the limited partnership to pay the amount of the contribution that he/she has promised.[50] The *Partnership Act* deems the limited partner a trustee for the limited partnership for any specific property stated in the certificate that he/she has either not contributed or that has been wrongfully returned to him/her.[51]

These provisions are intended to provide a means of enforcing promises to make a contribution by a limited partner. There are two groups given enforcement rights to extract the promise contributions: i) all the partners in the limited partnership, and ii) the creditors of the partnership. Although all the partners can consent to either waive or compromise a claim for the recovery of a promised contribution, such a waiver or compromise is not binding on the creditors.[52]

Rights of the Limited Partner

There are two important sources of statutory rights granted to the limited partner against the partnership: i) disclosure rights, and ii) profit-sharing rights. In order for a limited partner to have knowledge about the business affairs of the limited partnership, he/she requires access to the partnership books and information. The *Partnership Act* gives the limited partner the same right as a general partner to inspect and make copies of the partnership books;[53] to be given, on demand, true and full information about all things affecting the limited partnership;[54] to be given a formal accounting of the partnership affairs where the circumstances are just and reasonable;[55] and to obtain dissolution and winding-up by judicial decree.[56]

The limited partner has a qualified right to share in the profits made by the limited partnership. The qualifications on this right are contained in the *Partnership Act* and the limited partnership certificate. Typically, the right to participate in the profits is set forth in the certificate as entitlement to a share in the profits or by way of a stipulated income. An important statutory qualification requires that, before the distribution of any profits to a limited partner, the limited partnership assets must exceed all the limited partnership liabilities.[57] This restriction is intended to protect outside creditors from being victims of a depletion of partnership assets available for distribution once the limited partnership becomes insolvent.

Problems for Discussion

1. Janice Becker, a software engineer, enters into an oral agreement with Rinehart Ltd. for the use of the company's research facilities for a two-month period. In return, Becker agrees to pay Rinehart Ltd. 25 percent of the gross profits from the ultimate production and sale of her software program called Auto Part Inventory Finder. Does a partnership exist between Rinehart Ltd. and Becker? See *Taylor v. King Cole Theatres*, 183 Va. 117, 31 S.E.2d 260 (1944) and the British Columbia *Partnership Act*, s.4(b).

2. Rinehart Ltd. is approached by a California partnership doing business as Micro-Black Box. After two months of negotiations, Rinehart and the partnership agree to combine their efforts to develop a computer security system for Sprint. Ms. Bach is asked to determine whether Rinehart Ltd., as a company, has the capacity to enter into an express partnership agreement with Micro-Black Box. Discuss whether a company is a person for the purposes of partnership law.

3. Are there circumstances where the two members of a "two-man company" can be considered as partners? See *Bevan v. Anderson*, (1957) 23 W.W.R. 508 (Alta.).

4. Larry Hughes, a lawyer, enters into an oral agreement with Smith and Dobbs, Solicitors and Barristers to become a partner in the corporate department. The law firm has a written partnership agreement. Hughes, however, does not sign the agreement. Three years later, Hughes is killed in an air crash. His estate claims the rights granted to a deceased partner's estate that are contained in the written agreement. The law firm claims that those provisions do not apply to Hughes as he had not signed the agreement. Discuss whether the Hughes Estate will prevail with its argument. See *Green v. Stanton*, (1969) 69 W.W.R. 415 (B.C.C.A.).

5. Rinehart Ltd. enters into an agreement to sell a mini-computer to Alice Hayworth. Ms. Hayworth is a member of an accounting firm doing business under the name of Horowitz and Kessler. She signs a note on behalf of her firm that obliges it to pay Rinehart Ltd. the sum of $25 000. Under the partnership articles, however, Ms. Hayworth has no authority to sign notes for the firm. The mini-computer is for the accounting firm's use. The accounting firm now claims that it is not liable on the note. Discuss whether Rinehart Ltd. will succeed in enforcing the note against Horowitz and Kessler. See *Fairchild v. Ferguson*, (1892) 21 S.C.R. 484.

6. Assume in Problem 5 above that Ms. Hayworth does have signing authority, and signs the note in favour of Rinehart on March 2. On

March 3, Bonnie Karlin is made a partner in Horowitz and Kessler, and on that same date Robert Jacobs retires from the partnership. Discuss whether Ms. Karlin and Mr. Jacobs have liability to Rinehart Ltd. on the promissory note dated March 2. See *G.F. & J. Galt Ltd. v. Cronsberry*, (1914) 16 D.L.R. 105 (Alta.); and *Trust & Guaranty Co. v. Bryden*, (1910) 15 W.L.R. 212 (B.C.).

7. Harry Mandell, a partner in Horowitz and Kessler, makes an unlawful copy of Rinehart Ltd.'s accounting program for use in the firm's business. Mr. Mandell's activity is done without the knowledge or consent of the other partners in the firm. Nonetheless, other partners in the firm also are using the Rinehart program in completing tax returns for clients. Rinehart discovers the misappropriation of its property. Discuss whether the company has a claim against Horowitz and Kessler. See generally *Pitire v. Racey*, (1963) 37 D.L.R.(2d) 495 (B.C.).

8. Steel and Garcia form a limited partnership to finance the development of a computer software system called Select Real Estate Finder. The two become the general partners and ten partnership units are sold to investors at $10 000 each. One investor, Michael Parson, pays $2000 to the general partners and signs a promissory note for the balance. The note is due on February 8. On March 10, the Parson note is still unpaid, and another limited partner, Paula Huber, brings on an action to recover $8000 plus costs against Michael Parson. Discuss whether this action will succeed. See *Lee v. Block Estates Ltd.*, (1984) 3 W.W.R. 118 (B.C.S.C.)

Chapter 22 Notes

1. 1979 R.S.B.C., c. 312.
2. 3 Kent, Comm. 24, 28.
3. Section 7.
4. Section 12.
5. Section 13.
6. Section 11.
7. Section 13.
8. Section 14.
9. Section 19(1).
10. Section 19(2).
11. Section 19(3).
12. Section 21.
13. Section 33.
14. Section 27(a).
15. Section 27(f).
16. Section 27(b).
17. Section 27(i).
18. Section 31.
19. Section 35(a).

20. Section 35(b).
21. Section 35(c).
22. Section 36(1)(a).
23. Section 36(1)(b).
24. Section 37.
25. Section 38(1)(a).
26. Section 38(1)(b).
27. Section 38(1)(c).
28. Section 38(1)(d).
29. Section 38(1)(e).
30. Section 38(1)(f).
31. Section 38(2).
32. Section 41(1).
33. Section 41(2).
34. Section 42.
35. Section 43.
36. Section 50.
37. In the past, substantial tax advantages made limited partnerships a competitive investment.
38. Section 51(1).
39. Section 51(2).
40. Section 52(1).
41. Section 52(2).
42. Section 56.
43. Section 56(a).
44. Section 56(b).
45. Section 56(c).
46. Section 56(d).
47. Section 56(e).
48. Section 57.
49. Section 64.
50. Section 63(1).
51. Section 63(2).
52. Section 63(3) and (4).
53. Section 58(a).
54. Section 58(b).
55. Ibid.
56. Section 58(c).
57. Section 59(2).

23 LABOUR UNIONS

Introduction

In the previous chapters in this part, we have concentrated on business organizations that represent and are controlled by managers and investors. The traditional approach to business law is to exclude any consideration of labour unions as a form of business organization with separate rules and principles governing their formation, operation, purpose, and relationship with companies. This is a serious omission. Labour unions are associations in the business context that represent employees' interests.

In Canada, labour law is a large and complex subject covering diverse issues ranging from political demonstrations to unfair labour practices. A single chapter cannot hope to do justice to the wide spectrum of labour problems. Instead, the objective is to provide a basic introduction to: the structure of labour unions; the statutory obligations and restrictions placed on unions; the certification and decertification of labour unions; bargaining units; and collective bargaining.

Federal-Provincial Jurisdiction Over Unions

In Canada, the jurisdiction over labour law is divided, under the constitution, between the federal and provincial governments. The federal government, under the *Canada Labour Code*, has jurisdiction over industries that are subject to federal regulation. Employers with national business operations such as shippers, airlines, banks, television, and radio fall within the federal jurisdiction. All other business operations come within provincial jurisdiction. The division between the federal and provincial jurisdiction has been expressed in the following fashion:[1]

> In the field of employer-employee and labour-management relations, the division of authority between Parliament and provincial legis-

latures is based on an initial conclusion that in so far as such relations have an independent constitutional value they are within provincial competence; and, secondly, in so far as they are merely a facet of particular industries or enterprises their regulation is within the legislative authority of that body which has power to regulate the particular industry or enterprise . . .

There remains a grey area in the jurisdiction between the federal and provincial governments. It has been suggested that Canadian labour law has moved toward concurrent authority where both governments can apply their respective labour codes without conflict. A provincial labour relations board is sometimes called upon to determine whether a union has been properly certified by the provincial board. In the process of such a decision, the board must take into account the divided and concurrent jurisdiction, and make an assessment as to whether the commercial or industrial undertaking of the employer is within the jurisdiction of the province.

In one case,[2] the British Columbia Labour Relations Board cancelled the union certification because the employer's inter-provincial trucking business was within the jurisdiction of the Canadian Labour Relations Board and the certification had been improperly issued by the British Columbia Board.

Certification of a Union

There are two procedures that will enable a union to represent a group of employees. First, the company, as the employer, may voluntarily recognize the union as the bargaining agent on behalf of a group of "employees". The term "employees" has caused problems of interpretation in some instances. An independent contractor, for example, is not an "employee" within the meaning of the labour codes.[3] The courts have developed a number of different tests to determine whether a person is an employee. One test looks at the questions of: i) control, ii) ownership of tools, iii) chance of profits, and iv) risk of loss.[4]

In British Columbia, the definition of "employee" has been expanded to include what is called a "dependent contractor". The concept of dependent contractor more closely resembles the traditional concept of an employee than it does that of an independent contractor. Thus, owner-operators of trucks have been held to be dependent contractors.[5] The dependent contractor, like the employee, is entitled to union representation.

Second, the most common procedure enabling a union to represent a group of employees is the application for certification as a bargaining agent by either a provincial or federal labour relations board. Certification is an administrative process. Usually, a local of a national or international union will apply for the certification.

FIGURE 23.1 **ENTITLEMENT TO UNION REPRESENTATION**

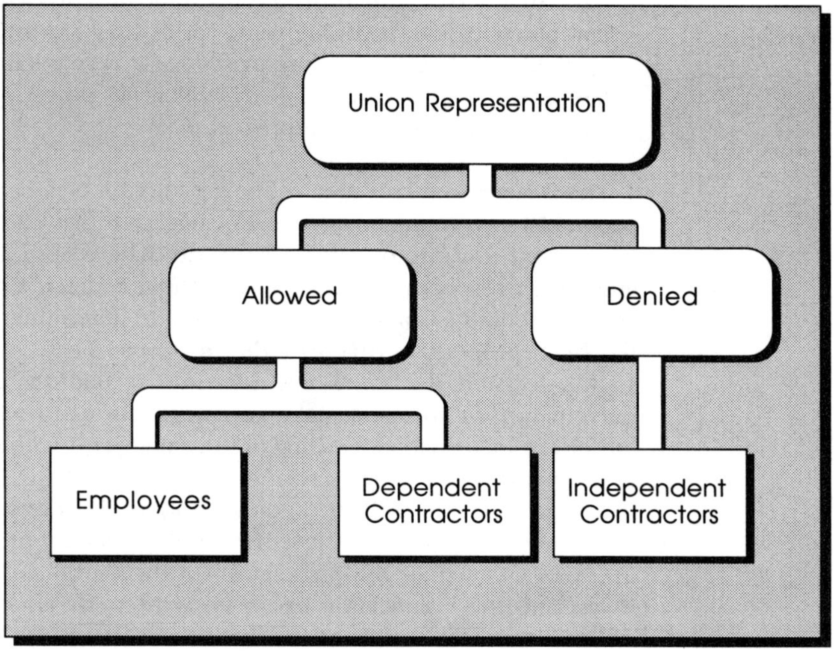

Definition of Trade Union

The first step in the certification process is for the applicant to establish that it meets the labour code definition of "trade union". In British Columbia, the Labour Code, Section 1(1) provides the following definition.

> "Trade union" means a local or Provincial organization or association of employees, or a local or Provincial branch of a national or international organization or association of employees in the Province, that has [as] one of its purposes the regulation in the Province of relations between employers and employees through collective bargaining, and includes an association or council of trade unions, but not an organization or association of employees that is dominated or influenced by an employer.

This definition has been interpreted by the British Columbia Labour Relations Board to establish four elements as a precondition to trade union status:

> First, an organization of employees must be in existence. Secondly, the organization must be local or provincial in character. Thirdly, it must have as one [of] its purposes the collective representation of

FIGURE 23.2 **DEFINING TRADE UNION**

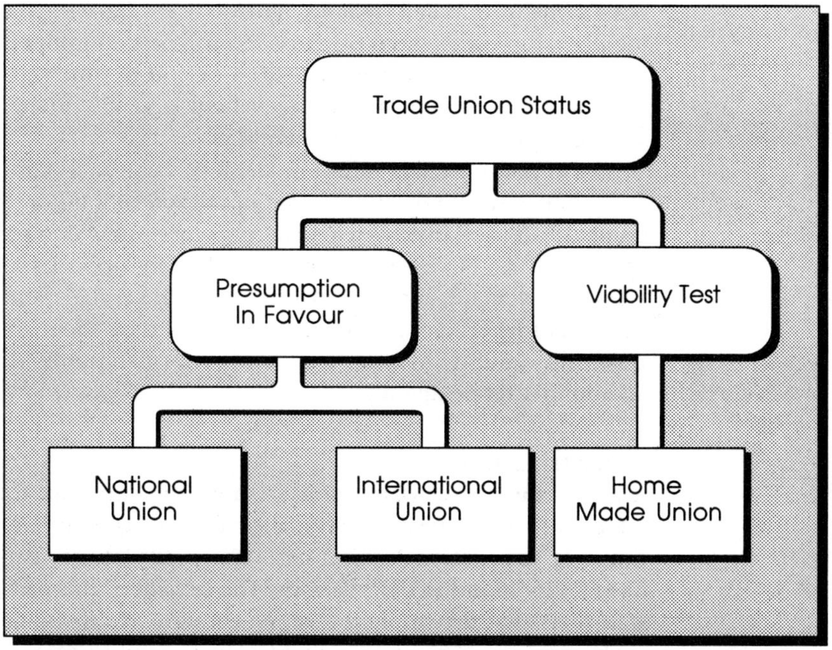

employees within the province. Finally, there must be an absence of employer domination or influence.[6]

The rationale for excluding, as in British Columbia and Newfoundland labour legislation, national or international unions from certification is the perceived difficulty of enforcing the provisions of the provincial labour relations legislation against a union that lacks a responsible governing body located in the jurisdiction. It is not sufficient merely to show the organization has a local or provincial character.

Viability of the Union

The applicant body must demonstrate that it is a viable entity that can carry out its stated purposes. For purposes of assessing viability, associations seeking certification fall within two general categories: i) "home-made" associations that have no affiliation with an established national or international union, and ii) locals of established national or international unions.

HOME-MADE ASSOCIATIONS
The labour relations boards apply a more stringent test to ascertain the viability of a home-made association. The burden is on the association

to demonstrate its viability by showing, among other things, that: i) it has a constitution and by-laws, ii) its officers have been duly elected, iii) membership cards have been issued for new employees, iv) dues have been received from employees for a period of time (e.g., two years), v) regular union meetings have been held, and vi) procedures have been adopted for the initiation of members.

As the above indicia of union viability suggest, a different standard, in law, applies to the formation and operation of a union than applies to a company. It is relatively easy to incorporate a new company, and whether that company is viable is dependent largely upon its ability to acquire financing, develop and promote products or services, and to make profits. These factors are generally ones determined by the marketplace. In contrast, the viability issue for a union is a formal, public decision made by an administrative agency.

AFFILIATED LOCALS

A less stringent standard applies where the applicant for certification is a local of an established national or international union. The parent national or international union has, over a number of years, demonstrated its viability in industrial relations. The benefit of this past experience and stature is that an employee representation is attributable to a local of such a union. The establishment of the viability of an affiliated local is usually done by the applicant merely providing evidence that it is a proper off-shoot of the international or national union.

Employee Membership

The purpose of certification is to enable a union to represent a bargaining unit — a group of employees who enter into a collective contract with their employer on such matters as terms and conditions of employment. An important issue in the certification process is whether the employees, through a vote, have approved of the proposed representation or whether a sufficient number of the employees (55 percent in British Columbia) are already members of the union. The British Columbia Labour Relations Board has discretion to order a representation vote as a precondition to certification even though the applicant has demonstrated that 55 percent of the employees in the bargaining unit are already members.

In practice, however, the British Columbia Labour Relations Board has adopted a policy of granting certification of a union without a vote where the union has more than 55 percent support. This avoids the possibility of a prolonged and messy campaign brought on by a vote, which may include employer intimidation or threats and other unfair labour practices. Moreover, in appropriate cases, where there is an atmosphere of tension and distrust among employees and a representation vote may be an inaccurate reflection of the employees' true wishes, the Board may certify a union without a vote even though it has less than 55 percent support.

In some instances, there may be rivalry between two unions, each competing to represent employees within a bargaining unit and each seeking certification. The contest over union membership can be contentious. Employees may resign from one union and join another. Disputes over the appropriate bargaining unit may further complicate matters. An important issue in such instances is the timeliness of the applicant unions' membership evidence. Union membership is not constant. It may, over time, increase or decrease. In the normal course of events, a three-month rule is applied by the labour relations board. That is, union membership, for certification purposes, is determined for the three-month period prior to the application. The policy behind the rule is to provide some certainty that the union applying for certification has the support of the majority of the employees in the bargaining unit at the time of the application.

The problem can arise where another union raids the applicant's members and seeks to adduce evidence that *during* the three-month period the applicant no longer has majority support. The labour relations board balances the potential restriction on employees who may change their minds during the three-month period and resign from the applicant union with the need for a rule providing some certainty as to the applicant's membership. The balance favours certainty, but the rule is not inflexible or blindly applied.

The Bargaining Unit

THE UNIT FOR COLLECTIVE BARGAINING

Determining the bargaining unit is often one of the most complex issues to be decided during the certification process. The determination has great importance for the union, employees, and employer. Once the union is certified it is the exclusive bargaining representative of all the employees of the unit. The employer is required, by law, to bargain with the union for all the employees in the bargaining unit. The labour relations board is delegated the responsibility for drawing the boundaries around a bargaining unit. The board decides which employees are within the unit and, necessarily, excludes others who fall outside the unit.

Until the bargaining unit is determined, the union, for example, cannot meet the onus of showing that it has a majority support of the employees within that unit. On the question of what standards the board is to apply, the British Columbia Labour Relations Board has observed:[7]

FIGURE 23.3 **FACTORS DETERMINING THE BARGAINING UNIT**

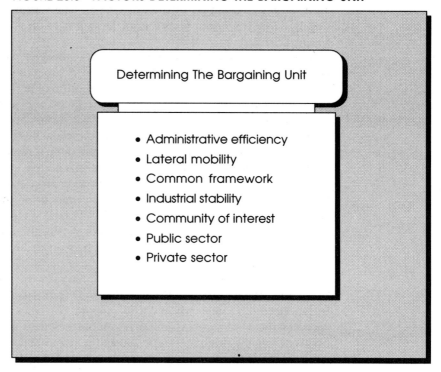

Determining The Bargaining Unit

- Administrative efficiency
- Lateral mobility
- Common framework
- Industrial stability
- Community of interest
- Public sector
- Private sector

[T]he scope of the unit is the key to securing the trade union representation and collective bargaining rights for the employees. Since this is a fundamental purpose of the Code, the Board's definitions must be such as to facilitate organization of the employees. On the other hand, that unit sets the framework for actual bargaining for a long time into the future. A structure is needed which is conducive to voluntary settlements without strikes and will minimize the disruptive effects of the latter when they do occur. Unfortunately, the lesson of experience is that these two objectives often point in different directions.

In British Columbia, the Labour Relations Board has adopted a number of factors to assist it in determining whether the bargaining unit claimed by the applicant union is appropriate. Each of these factors vests the Board with considerable discretion to take into account the peculiar circumstances of each case. There are two preliminary issues that the Board must consider: i) the size of the bargaining unit, and ii) the nature of the industry being organized into bargaining units.

THE SIZE OF THE UNIT

First, the Board must balance the needs and desires of special groups of employees for a separate bargaining union with the advantages of one for all the employee bargaining units. There are a number of factors that the Board has announced that favour the granting of a certificate to a union for a one/all employee bargaining unit:

a) The administrative efficiency and convenience of collective bargaining. Multiple units complicate the bargaining process. Management is forced to negotiate with a number of unions. The day-to-day carrying out of several collective agreements rapidly complicates decisions on the firing, hiring, promoting, and suspension of employees.

b) One unit makes lateral mobility much easier. Where there are several bargaining units the transfer or promotion of an employee between units becomes more difficult.

c) One unit encourages a common framework of employment conditions. Each employee has the same schedule and fringe benefits. A patchwork of different holidays, overtime, sick days, and pension plans, among other fringe benefits, creates ambiguity in the work place.

d) One unit encourages industrial stability. Multiple units increase the likelihood of strikes and shut-downs. It is more likely that an employer will be "whipsawed" by a series of strikes.

Although these factors are important, they are not compelling. It is commonplace for the Labour Relations Board to certify narrow bargaining units. The main goal in the process of drawing a boundary line is to establish the communality of interests of the employees. However, the advantages of stability and simplicity may give way to practical problems in the one-employee-unit approach in any one industry. Some employees may be blue-collar workers with set hours, with similar skills, and located in one geographic area. Other employees, such as salesmen in the same industry — white-collar workers — have different hours, pay, and locations. To place both groups in the same bargaining unit may ignore the distinctive needs and interests of each.

THE NATURE OF THE INDUSTRY

There is an important distinction between public and private sector employees. In the past, the public sector employer was inclined to engage in collective bargaining with a union. A private sector employer, however, who resists the concept of collective bargaining may seek to have the labour relations board draw the boundaries of the unit wide, and this may make it far more difficult for a union to obtain majority support for certification. The board, in the private sector certification case, initially may define the bargaining unit narrowly to allow collective bargaining to take root in a particular industry. But later, once collective bargaining becomes more acceptable, and other unions begin to make inroads by gaining certification within the same industry, the board may require the enlargement or merger of existing bargaining units.

Collective Bargaining

Definition of Good Faith

Where a union is certified as the bargaining agent on behalf of a unit of employees, then it has the exclusive authority to bargain collectively for all members of the unit. The collective bargaining right extends to non-union as well as union members of the bargaining union. Collective bargaining in British Columbia is defined to mean: "negotiating in good faith with a view to the conclusion of a collective agreement or the renewal or revision thereof, or to the regulation of relations between an employer and employees."[8]

The key to the statutory definition is the obligation of "good faith."

FIGURE 23.4 **JUDICIAL SUPERVISION OF COLLECTIVE BARGAINING**

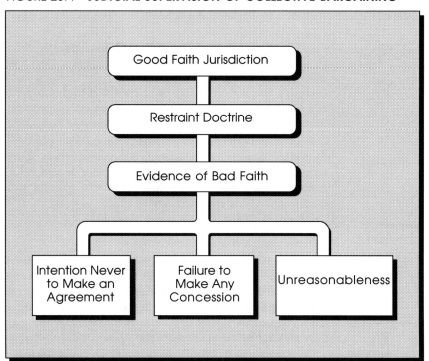

The term is nebulous. By what standard is either party judged to have bargained in good faith? This question has perplexed the labour relations boards in Canada and the United States. A broad definition of "good faith" that includes an assessment of every proposal, counter proposal, or failure to make a requested concession would, in effect, make the labour relations board a third party to every collective bargaining session. The boards have refused to accept such a task. Instead, in British Columbia, the Board has taken the position that "Collective bargaining is not a process carried on in accordance with the Marquess of Queensbury rules . . . ."[9]

The "good faith" jurisdiction of the Board has been narrowed by the "restraint doctrine." The restraint doctrine, first announced in the *Noranda*[10] case, is an attempt to move the Board's consideration of an unfair labour practice away from an inquiry into the reasonableness of proposals and towards an inquiry into the reasonableness of the *conduct* of a party who is alleged to have not bargained in good faith. Thus, the Board has turned the "good faith" standard, with the inherent problems involved in a wide-open invitation to intervene, into a more manageable inquiry into "bad faith" of the participants. In effect, the duty to negotiate in good faith has been interpreted as a duty not to negotiate in bad faith.

Definition of Bad Faith

The true essence of collective bargaining is good faith negotiation between the union and the employer with both sides making a reasonable effort to enter a collective agreement. As indicated above, the obligation to collectively bargain has a statutory source. Where one or both parties do not bargain with a view to concluding a collective agreement, this is a breach of the statutory duty. The question of *bona fides* of intention to reach a collective agreement is one of fact. The Labour Relations Board provides a forum, available to either party to the negotiations, for complaints that the other side is bargaining in bad faith. Evidence of bad faith bargaining is grounds for the Labour Relations Board to conclude that there is an unfair labour practice.

The fact that neither the union nor the employer can conclude a collective agreement is not, in itself, a *prima facie* case of bad faith. Each side may insist on reaching an agreement on terms favourable to its interest, and the positions of each may be far apart. It is not bad faith for one party to "stick to its guns" when bargaining over proposals. There is not a single definition of bad faith. Instead, the Board has developed a number of guidelines to assist in the bad faith inquiry: i) Whether the conduct of one party creates an inference that the party never intended to reach an agreement; ii) Whether one party has failed to make any concession at all; and iii) Whether from the context of a particular proposal an inference of unreasonableness may be drawn.

In applying these guidelines, the Board decides whether one party has shown no desire to reach an agreement on any terms with the other side. The absence of such a desire is bad faith and an unfair labour practice.

Illustration   The Federation of Office Workers entered into collective bargaining with Rinehart on April 24. The bargaining unit represented by the union consisted of the salespersons employed by the company. For over four months the company's proposal on wages and commissions was to retain the status quo — a position maintained even though, prior to the unionization of the sales forces, the company created an expectation of a substantial pay raise, which the company had traditionally given in early January. Moreover, the company's proposals on company cars were substantially inferior to the existing arrangements enjoyed by other employees. There is no evidence of economic justification for the company's positions on wages and company cars. In mid-June, the company unilaterally gave the salespeople a substantial pay rise. The effect of this action was to by-pass the union. Did Rinehart Ltd. bargain in good faith with the union?

In a similar case, the British Columbia Labour Relations Board found that the company had committed unfair labour practices.[11] The Board quoted with approval the United States Supreme Court decision in *N.L.R.B. v. Katz*:[12]

> It is clear at a glance that automatic wage increase system which was instituted unilaterally was considerably more generous than that which had shortly theretofore been offered to and rejected by the Union. Such action conclusively manifested bad faith in negotiations ... though no additional evidence of bad faith appeared. An employer is not required to lead with his best offer; he is free to bargain. But even after an impasse is reached he has no licence to grant wage increases greater than any he has ever offered the union at the bargaining table, for such action is necessarily inconsistent with a sincere desire to conclude an agreement with the Union.

The violation of the duty of good faith collective bargaining may result in a conviction for an offence and the offending party may be subject of a fine.

The Conciliation Option

Under the *Canada Labour Code* and most provincial codes, either party to the collective bargaining has the discretion to request the appointment of a conciliation officer. For example, under federal legislation the Minister of Labour, once notified that the parties have been unable to conclude a collective agreement, has the right to appoint a conciliation officer. The duty of such an officer is to assist the parties in reaching an agreement. The officer lacks any authority to impose an agreement on the party. His/her role is to attempt to bring the parties together on proposals and to suggest compromises. Within two weeks of his/her appointment, the conciliation officer writes a report containing his/her recommendations and findings and then delivers the report to the Minister of Labour.

The conciliation officer provides two important roles: i) as an intermediary between two deadlocked parties, and ii) as a conduit of information about the dispute to the Minister of Labour, who has the right to make the findings and recommendations public. After the conciliation process is completed, then the parties may resort to other options such as strikes and lockouts.

Variations on the federal model may be found in provincial labour codes. In British Columbia, for example, the Minister may appoint a mediation officer, without the written request of one of the parties. As with the federal conciliation officer, the B.C. mediation officer makes findings about the nature of the dispute which are then passed along to the Minister.

Decertification

Decertification, like the original certification process, is an administrative decision concerning the right of a union to represent a bargaining unit. Decertification occurs where, after ten months from the time of the certification of the union, the labour relations board is satisfied that the union has ceased to represent a majority of the employees in the unit. The board conducts an investigation into the support for the union and has the discretion to order a vote of the employees in the union.

The right of decertification is to enshrine the basic policy of majority rule by the employees of a bargaining union. The effect of decertification is to void any outstanding collective agreement between the union and the employer. An employer, therefore, will often have a vested interest in influencing its employees to seek decertification. This would rid the company of an unwanted collective agreement. As a result, the board, in carrying out its investigation, must be satisfied that the employer has not interfered and either overtly or covertly influenced the decision of the majority to decertify the union. That is, the majority of the employees who wish decertification must have reached this decision unconstrained by the interference, encouragement, or sponsorship of the employer.

The policy behind decertification was set forth by the British Columbia Labour Relations Board in *Downie Street Sawmills and I.W.A. et. al.*:[13]

> In addition, Section 27(1) of the Code repeatedly refers to trade unions as the "freely chosen representatives" of the employees. This emphasis is soundly based. The Board's mandate under Section 27

imposes the obligation to "secure and maintain industrial peace and to promote conditions favourable to the orderly and constructive settlement of disputes." Productive and harmonious industrial relations cannot be fostered in an atmosphere of hostility and resentment which must inevitably result where continued trade union representation is imposed on a group of unwilling employees. [In the absence of] at least minimal backing from bargaining unit members, a trade union could easily find itself in a situation where it is unable to obtain a strike vote or ratification of a collective agreement. Effective and constructive trade union representation requires a spirit of co-operation from employees in a unit.

The decertification decision is not based on simple arithmetic but is discretionary and takes into account the circumstances surrounding the application. In other words, although a majority of the employees may no longer wish to be represented by the union, it does not follow that decertification will be automatically ordered. The motives of the employees and the employers, as well as the surrounding circumstances, are weighed by the labour relations board in reaching its decision. For instance, the board may refuse decertification, even where supported by a majority of employees, where there is evidence that the application is an attempt to: i) void an existing collective agreement, ii) raid employees in the unit by another union, iii) interfere with a collective bargaining action such as a strike, and iv) assist the employer who has committed an unfair labour practice or misled or coerced the employees.

Labour Disputes: Definition of Key Terms

Unions are an important part of the law of industrial relations. In this section we will consider four key terms that appear in the context of labour disputes. When the collective bargaining process breaks down and conciliation or mediation fails, the union or employer may resort to other means to exert pressure for a settlement. Strikes, lockouts, and pickets are tools of persuasion brought to bear when agreement across the negotiating table has failed. As the British Columbia Labour Relations Board said in *Adams Laboratories Employees et. al.*:[14]

> We are well aware that labour disputes are not picnics; that picket lines are not tea parties; that feelings and emotions can run high; and that provocation can easily be found or imagined.

Meaning of Strike

A general definition of a *strike* is the voluntary cessation of work by employees. In practice, an intentional slowdown by employees may have the same effect on the employer as a total work stoppage. The major purpose of provincial and federal labour codes is to establish a collective agreement that will regulate the work place. Included within a collective agreement — as an alternative to work stoppage in the case of a dispute — are arbitration procedures. An arbitration panel — typically comprised of one labour, one management, and one person chosen by the other two — listens to both sides of the dispute and reaches a decision based on its interpretation of the collective agreement, legislation, and prior board and court decisions.

In Canada, a strike is legal or illegal depending on the timing of the cessation of work. In Canada, a strike is *legal* only after the statutory procedures for collective bargaining have been satisfied.

The purpose of a strike is to persuade the employer to make a proposed change or to resist a proposed change to the terms and conditions of employment. For instance, the union may be seeking a higher rate of pay than the employer is prepared or willing to concede. The strike, in theory, places economic pressure on the employer to give in to the union's demand.

When the strike is legal, the employer is not entitled to dismiss any of the striking employees. The employer, however, has a number of important remedies, including damages and injunctive relief against those who participate in an illegal strike.

The union's decision to strike is heavily influenced by economic factors. When the economy contracts, as in the case of a recession, and real growth is slow — meaning that there is the possibility of lay-offs, cut-backs in production and hiring, and high unemployment — the strike threat is less effective. The employees in the bargaining unit are also less willing in such economic circumstances to support strike action.

Meaning of Lockout

The employer's counterpart to the strike is the *lockout*. The employer, in order to put economic pressure on employees and the union, may elect to temporarily close its plant, office, or factory. This move may force the other side to accept the employer's proposals. As is the case with a strike, the employer must comply with the collective bargaining procedures contained in the federal or provincial codes before taking lockout action.

Meaning of Picketing

Picketing is industrial action by employees, often in the context of a strike, who station themselves at or near their place of employment with the purpose of turning away from the work place others who seek to work or do business with the employer.

In Canada, picketing is strictly controlled by law. The *Criminal Code* makes picketing (with a limited exception) an offence. The exception to the criminal prohibition is information picketing. Unlike the ordinary picket, where the goal is to maximize disruption in the employer's work place, the information picket is limited to communicating to others who enter or leave the work place the nature of their dispute. Any interference with the free flow of people in and out of the premises picketed is unlawful. In particular, the information picket is restricted from using insults, intimidation, or physical or human blockades in front of the entrances and exits of the premises.

The right to picket is expanded under the British Columbia Labour Code. In the context of a legal strike or lockout, which must occur at the striking employees' place of employment, the union may authorize pickets to attend the sites or places of business of the employer apart from the place of employment. The statutory purpose of picketing is one of persuading others not to work for, enter the premises of, or do business with the employer.

Secondary Boycotts

A *secondary boycott* is the carrying of the industrial dispute to those who either supply or purchase goods or services from the employer, who is the subject of strike action, and the convincing of these suppliers or purchasers to stop doing business with the struck employer. Except for British Columbia, secondary boycotts are unlawful in Canada. The effect of a secondary boycott is to escalate and spread industrial disruption to other businesses not directly involved in the strike or lockout. A secondary boycott, where permitted, is accomplished with the use of on-site pickets.

Problems for Discussion

1. Ten technical workers employed by Rinehart Ltd. decide to form a trade union called the British Columbia Association of Computer Technicians, Local No. 1. The proposed union does not have any affiliation with an international or national trade union in Canada. The workers apply to the British Columbia Labour Relations Board and request certification. In making a decision on whether to grant or deny certification, what issues will the Labour Relations Board raise?

2. Jones Shipping Co. Ltd. is a British-Columbia-based company engaged in the business of carrying freight by truck on an unscheduled basis. Its area of operation includes Western Canada and the Western United States. About 50 percent of the company's freight trucking business occurs outside British Columbia. Ten employees who are mechanics work at the company's maintenance yard in Vancouver. Although a

mechanic is sometimes called upon to travel outside the province to repair a truck, most of the repair and maintenance takes place at the Vancouver yard. The ten mechanics were organized into a bargaining unit by the Machinists Union. Does the British Columbia Labour Relations Board or does the Canada Labour Relations Board have jurisdiction over the certification of the union in this case? See *Arrow Transfer Company Limited et.al.*, (1974) 1 Can.L.R.B.R. 29 (B.C.L.R.B.).

3. Assume that seven computer software engineers who have signed the consulting contract with Rinehart Ltd. (see Figure 1.3.) want to form a bargaining unit. They approach the local of the Computer Technician Workers Union and request the local to make an application for certification. The initial question, which you have been asked to research on behalf of the local, is whether the "consultants" are "employees" or "dependent contractors" of Rinehart Ltd. In reaching your opinion consider: *Fownes Construction Co. Ltd. et.al.*, (1974) 1 Can.L.R.B.R. 453.

4. Discuss the policy behind the doctrine of the viability of unions. Why is such a doctrine justifiable for a union, as an organization in the business context, but not for other forms of organizations such as a company or partnership?

5. Discuss the application of employee support: i) for a certification application, ii) for decertification, and iii) for determining rival claims by two unions for the same group of employees. Are there different policy considerations that apply in each case? To what extent are these policies contrary to the true wishes of the employees?

6. Eight employees of Rinehart Ltd.'s advertising department have been organized by the Graphic Arts Union. The Union has applied for certification to the British Columbia Labour Relations Board. The company contests the application on the grounds that Rinehart has a number of different departments and that the eight employees are only a small fraction of the total work force. Moreover, Rinehart argues that in the event certification is granted, other employees may later seek certification in additional small bargaining units. The result, says Rinehart Ltd., would be the potential for an "unrealistic patchwork" of scores of bargaining units. Much of its time would be taken up negotiating with each faction, and any one labour dispute might lead to the closure of the entire operation. In your view, will the union succeed in a certification bid? See *Woodwards Stores (Vancouver) Limited et.al.*, (1975) 1 Can.L.R.B.R. 551.

7. During the course of collective bargaining with Rinehart Ltd., the B.C. Federation of Sales Workers, Local No. 1, asks the management whether Rinehart has successfully negotiated a contract to develop computer software with NASA for the space-shuttle arm. The company replies

that it has not, in an effort to support the company's proposal for a lower rate of commission for the sales employees in the bargaining unit. In fact, however, Rinehart has withheld this information from the union. The company then takes the position that it had no affirmative obligation to disclose information on sensitive "national defence" contracts to union officials, and that the contract had top-secret status. The union claims, nonetheless, that the company deliberately withheld the information to prevent the union from making an intelligent appraisal of the company's position. The union claims that the company committed an unfair labour practice. Discuss. See *C.A.I.M.A.W. and Noranda Metal Industries Ltd.*, (1975) 1 Can.L.R.B.R. 145.

8. Consider the following observation by S. Bok, the author of *Lying: Moral Choice in Public and Private Life*, (1978, p. 131):

> A factory owner, for example, may falsely predict that the plant will have to close down if the union wins the upcoming representation election. Such deception cannot be condoned as an element of mutually agreed-to bargaining. For all employees clearly will not know the "rules of the game" by which the employer is playing. They are also at a great disadvantage, since there is little they can do to deceive the employer in return. And even if they know the deceptive nature of what is told them, there may be no way for them to leave the bargaining situation if they do not have an equivalent job opportunity elsewhere.
>
> Once a union has been formed, the false statement by the factory owner that he will have to close down the plant — say, if the union insists on a 10 percent wage increase — is often made in a context of possible deception suspected by each side. The union may retaliate by offering deceptive threats at the bargaining table. But while both parties may *know* the rules of the game, neither may have consented to play by these rules. Nor are they free to abandon the bargaining or to change the unspoken rules.

To what extent are these moral concerns addressed in labour law legislation?

Chapter 23 Notes

1. Laskin, *Canadian Constitutional Law*, 4th ed. (1975), p. 363.
2. See *Arrow Transfer*, (1974) 1 Can.L.R.B.R. (B.C.L.R.B.).
3. See *Odin v. Columbia Cellulose Co.*, (1967) 66 D.L.R.(2d) 278 (B.C.S.C.).
4. See *Montreal v. Montreal Locomotive Works Ltd.*, (1947) 1 D.L.R. 161, 169 (P.C.).

5. See *Fownes Construction Co. Ltd. et.al.*, (1974) 1 Can.L.R.B.R. 453.
6. See *Jensen Mushroom Farms Ltd. and Canadian Farmworkers' Union, Local No. 1,* (1980) Decision No. 53/80 (B.C.L.R.B.).
7. See *Insurance Corporation of British Columbia and Canadian Union of Public Employees, Local 1695, et.al.,* (1974) B.C. 63/74.
8. Section 1.
9. See *Canadian Association of Industrial, Mechanical and Allied Workers, and Noranda Metal Industries Limited,* (1975) 1 C.L.R.B.R. 145.
10. Ibid.
11. See *Federation of Telephone Workers of British Columbia and Dominion Directory Company Limited,* (1975) 2 Can.L.R.B.R. 345.
12. (1962) 369 U.S. 736, 743 per Mr. Justice Brennan.
13. Unreported, 16/83 (B.C.L.R.B.).
14. (1980) 2 Can.L.R.B.R. 101.

Part VII

LEGAL ETHICAL PROBLEMS IN THE BUSINESS ENVIRONMENT

24 THE GENERAL FUNCTIONS OF A COMPANY LAWYER

Within the corporate client hemisphere, what are the major functions assigned to the corporate lawyer? In this section, emphasis will be placed on the functions, responsibilities, and roles typically assumed by inside company lawyers. The priority assigned to each will vary from company to company. Indeed, the priority may shift over time as the needs of the company evolve. The overall conclusion that may be derived from a study of the functions is that courtroom advocacy has relatively little importance in the day-to-day dealings of business people with legal counsel. The drama of the courtroom is replaced in most instances with the less dramatic task of monitoring and reviewing the legal aspects of the company's operations.

Company Advisor

A major role played by the inside counsel is that of advisor to the members of the company who are in control of the decision-making process. As advisor, the company lawyer assumes the role of a counsellor.

Predicting Legal Consequences

The company lawyer may be called upon to predict the legal consequences of the action of a third party, a proposed course of action by the company, or the ruling or decision of an administrative agency or a court on a product or on the operations of the company.

Illustration In an American lawsuit between Franklin Computer Corporation and Apple, a federal appeals court decided that the object code developed by Apple was copyrightable. The object code, contained on a diskette, stores the computer instructions as a series of 0s and 1s.

had argued unsuccessfully that the Apple software could only be protected under the law governing patents. A patent is more difficult to obtain than a copyright, lasts a shorter period of time, and the criteria for patentability is more stringent.

The President of Rinehart Software Ltd., Paul Faber, requests Julia Bach to predict whether a Canadian court would reach a similar result. Ms. Bach is also asked what the practical implications of such a decision would be on Rinehart's software lines.

The scope of the advice sought by Mr. Faber is established by his question to Ms. Bach. To ask whether a Canadian court would reach a conclusion similar to the American court is requesting technical legal advice. In rendering this advice, Ms. Bach would survey the existing Canadian cases involving software issues and, consult legal periodical literature, and, given the specialized area of law involved, e.g., intellectual property law, she may seek the opinion of an outside lawyer who specializes in that area. The advice sought in the second question on practical implications is not limited to a legal framework. In effect, Ms. Bach is being asked to analyze the zone of doubt surrounding the protection of the company's software products from a business as well as a strictly legal perspective. She must take into account the business implications and determine the extent to which the decision will directly affect specific operations within the company.

Recommendations Based on Legislative Change

An important aspect of the advisory role is to provide legal advice based on proposed changes to the laws and regulations governing the activities of the company. One specific function assigned to Ms. Bach is the monitoring of pending and proposed provincial and federal legislation, regulations issued pursuant to legislation, research studies, and law reform reports recommending changes to legislation. She then advises the appropriate department of the possible legal and economic impacts of proposed or new legislation or regulations. The legal department would also undertake responsibility for developing the new policies and procedures necessary to implement the new legislative or regulatory changes.

PROPOSED LEGISLATIVE CHANGE

Where appropriate, Ms. Bach will recommend changes to the pending or proposed legislation that would minimize any adverse impact on a department or on the company as a whole. Forming or joining a lobby group as a means of communicating the interest of the industry is a possible avenue. In a proceeding of central importance to the company, such as proposed changes to the *Copyright Act*, Ms. Bach, as company lawyer, may represent the company's interest within a lobby formed by the industry. With the volume of proposed legislative change at the provincial and federal levels, it is not possible for the company to employ only the scarce legal resources for the time-consuming activities of industry lobby groups. Instead, the company lawyer will alert members of the executive department, and the head of the department most likely to be affected, of the significance of proposed changes for the company and the operation of a department. In turn, those within the company communication chain will assist in formulating an appropriate response, if any, for the legal department to make.

LEGISLATIVE CHANGE ILLUSTRATION

Rinehart's wholly owned subsidiary, QueTech Ltd., located in Ontario, employs fifteen people. It is 1983, and a government-sponsored bill, Bill 124 titled *An Act To Amend the Wages Act* is given first reading on November 18. The proposed amendment to existing legislation would exempt from seizure or garnishment, 80 percent of a person's wages. (Garnishment is a court directive to an employer to withhold a certain sum of money from an employee's wage or salary and forward it to the court for distribution.) The exemption would be 50 percent of a person's wages where a creditor sought to enforce an order for support or maintenance. The court would be vested with discretion, taking into account the financial circumstances of the person subject to the writ of execution or notice of garnishment, to either increase or decrease the statutory exemptions.

As a result of the enactment of Bill 124, the company counsel, in conjunction with the personnel and accounting departments, would devise a procedure for handling garnishment orders enforceable against employees of QueTech Ltd. The accounting department, for example, would be required to distinguish between garnishment orders for support and maintenance and all other such orders to determine whether there is a court order altering the statutory exemption, and to establish a system of files and records for the third parties who have received payment under the *Act*.

INTERPRETATION OF LEGISLATIVE INTENT

It is possible that the head of accounting or personnel may seek clarification from the company lawyer about the application of the proposed legislation. For example, the bill uses the term "wages." Does this term include salaries, bonuses, or other forms of compensation paid to employees? Similarly, it is unclear whether the percentage exemptions are to be calculated on the basis of annual, monthly, or weekly "wages." For example, an employee who earns $26 000 is the subject of a garnishment order for $10 000. Is the accounting department to deduct $2 000 per month for five consecutive months, i.e., 100 percent of the employee's monthly wage? This issue turns on whether the bill means annual wages or the wages actually paid on a weekly or monthly basis.

GOVERNMENT REGULATIONS

Not all important decisions by government are contained in legislation. Many government subdivisions have the authority to make regulations within their area of jurisdiction. These regulations, having the force of law, may have important consequences for the company.

Illustration In British Columbia, under the *Workers Compensation Act*, by Order of Council the Cabinet may by regulation set the maximum annual wage rate payable to an employee under the *Act*. By B.C. Reg. 382/83, filed October 12, 1983, a regulation was entered setting the maximum wage rate for the 1984 year at $30 200.

This information would have been communicated from the legal department to the personnel department. In the event of a worker's compensation claim, an employee can then be advised as to the maximum wage rate that he or she would be entitled to receive.

Of primary interest to the legal department will be government reports and pending bills involving changes to the existing *Copyright Act*. As we will discuss in later chapters, there has been doubt that the current *Copyright Act*, enacted in 1924, fully protects the software programs from infringement by others. Thus, the Canadian software industry has taken an active interest in amendments to the *Copyright Act* that would clearly define the scope of protection accorded to computer software.

Illustration In 1982, the Consumer and Corporate Affairs Department of the federal Government published a study titled "Copyright and the Computer." The study concluded that the scope for copyright protection ought to be extended to software programs on the economic ground that "protection for software may increase the net social benefits of copyright or similar legislation sufficiently that Canada would benefit from extending such protection to software both in its traditional form and as firmware." This conclusion conflicts with a 1977 study titled "Copyright in Canada, Proposals for a Revision of the Law," which concluded with a recommendation that computer programs per se need not be protected by copyright.

These studies have important legal and economic consequences for the company. The legal department may be requested by the executive department to play an active role within the industry lobby group that promotes the extension of the *Copyright Act* to software. These developments would be monitored by the legal department, and procedures for consultation and advice, as well as information distribution, would be installed. For instance, the company lawyer may serve on a subcommittee assigned the task of co-ordinating the company response to such studies and recommendations.

The legal advice may be sought in connection with a particular transaction or course of action where the legal consequences are known. The lawyer may be requested to find out whether the proposed transaction or course of action will result in the intended legal consequence. In these circumstances, the lawyer's advice may be sought as to whether the transaction or course of action as proposed will effectively maximize the rights and protect the interest of the company.

Illustration Sam Sones, the Executive Vice-President of the company, has been approached by an American company, J.Q. Productions Inc., that has offered a substantial sum for the rights to use all the characters from the video game *Fight of the Titans*. The Vice-President is aware of the legal consequences of such a licence. In the previous year, he had worked with Ms. Bach on the agreement to sub-licence *Space Attack* to West-Game Worlds, Inc. In the proposed licence agreement with J.Q. Productions, Inc., the American television production company has inserted a clause that provides that J.Q. Productions Inc., as licensee, reserves the right to change, alter, or otherwise modify any of the characters, and to add or delete the characters to be used in the television cartoon series called *Fight of the Titans*. The clause continues by stating that Rinehart Software Limited shall be notified of any proposed action under the clause in advance and that consent in writing shall be obtained prior to the action: but in no circumstances shall the consent of Rinehart Software be unreasonably withheld. Mr. Sones may want advice on whether the clause will ensure that the company can control the artistic integrity of the television cartoon series based on the game characters.

The advice sought may be of a purely technical nature where questions of company policy or objectives are not at issue. For example, using the *Fight of the Titans* illustration, there may be a question as to whether the licence agreement must be notarized or witnessed. In certain transactions, the contract must be in accordance with a form prescribed by statute or regulation, such as a conveyance used to transfer real property. Some transactions must be registered in order to be enforceable against third parties. The issue may be whether a special form is required and it may be whether registration is required.

Evaluator For Third Parties

The company lawyer is asked by third parties for certain information about the company. The third party relies upon the opinion of the company lawyer. For instance, a securities commission may require an evaluation as to whether the securities offered for sale are in compliance with securities legislation. Further, the company's financial auditors may request information about the company in order to complete a financial statement that other parties will rely upon as accurately reflecting the financial situation of the company. The lawyer who undertakes the function of evaluator may be placed in a strained position caused by his/her obligation to the company and also to the third parties who will rely upon his/her evaluation.

Legality of Transaction

The evaluation is often connected with the legality of a proposed transaction by the company—the authority of the company to issue shares, the compliance with securities law in the registration of shares, or the questions about a legal situation raised by the company's financial auditors or lender. As we will discover later, a controversy surrounds the question as to the obligation of the lawyer to conduct an independent factual inquiry beyond the information supplied by the client. When the lawyer makes such an evaluation for the benefit of a third party, he/she owes a duty of care and competence to the recipient of the evaluation where the lawyer knows, or ought reasonably to have known, that the recipient intends to rely upon the opinion. This duty of care exposes the lawyer/ evaluator to civil liability in the event that the evaluation falls below the standard of care placed on the lawyer.

Informal Request

The inside company lawyer may be asked to make informal evaluations by shareholders, investors, distributors, and prospective purchasers who seek a legal opinion that they can rely upon in making some transaction in connection with the company. As a general rule, the lawyer will be extremely careful to avoid making such evaluations. The evaluation may be in conflict with laws that explicitly or implicitly restrict such action. Moreover, this type of evaluation is an informal request for the supply of legal services on behalf of the third party, and the lawyer may not believe that the evaluation is compatible with his/her solicitor-client relationship with the company. In most instances, the inside company lawyer will take precautions against providing such informal evaluations.

Illustration Assume that Rinehart Software Limited has decided to make a limited partnership offer to existing limited partners in the company. The company lawyer, Ms. Bach, has received a phone call from a limited partner seeking an opinion about the offering.

Caller: Ms. Bach, I understand that under the new offer to purchase limited partnership shares I will receive 2000 common shares and 1000 warrants for my 10 limited partnership units. I am not clear on how long I have to take up the offer.
Bach: As you can see from page four of the offer agreement, you have until July 8, 1986 to make your decision.
Caller: What are the advantages for me of trading my units for the common shares and warrants?
Bach: The agreement lists the advantages. You will get shares that are

easier to trade than the partnership units. Also, you have the chance to share in the earnings of the company, including new products that aren't covered by the limited partnership. In addition, the share purchase warrants may be subject to research and development tax credits in the event that you sell or exercise them. We aren't sure whether the federal legislation that includes provisions for the tax credits will be passed.

Caller: I'm worried that the government will pass the legislation. What do you think?

Bach: The answer is that I don't know. I can't advise you as to what will finally happen to the legislation.

Caller: I see. But that makes the warrant part of the deal uncertain.

Bach: The research and development tax credits are only one of the advantages. You have to consider the whole package.

Caller: Then the tax credit isn't that important?

Bach: That isn't what I said. It's one factor to consider. You have to balance the increased tradeability of the shares that you would be receiving and the chance for additional earnings against the possibility that the tax credits won't be approved by the government.

Caller: Okay. But there's something else. I want to know whether you think that *Space Attack* is going to sell in the States.

Bach: We have high hopes for the game. Our marketing people in the States indicate that it should sell well. We are promoting it through a series of 30-second network television ads. But the video-game market is highly competitive and we can't be certain that *Space Attack* will capture the necessary market segment.

Caller: Than you think I should accept the offer?

Bach: I can't make that decision for you. It's something that you ought to take up with your own broker, accountant, or lawyer.

The company lawyer has been asked for an evaluation of the limited partnership offer by a unit holder. She has been asked to make a legal evaluation. The caller also wanted an economic evaluation, and Ms. Bach has attempted to avoid representing to the caller anything that was not contained in the formal offer sent to all partnership unit holders. She has walked a tightrope. Ms. Bach is not merely the company lawyer. She is, in a case such as this, the company spokesman. The caller is a potential investor whose decision concerning the offer will have a direct impact on the success of the offering. As a result, she cannot ignore the caller or treat him/her as a complete stranger. The company wants the offers to be accepted. Ms. Bach, as the company lawyer, wants the company to succeed in obtaining that goal. Nonetheless, because she is a lawyer, her advice must be given with considerable caution. For example, if Ms. Bach had said that in her opinion the video game *Space Attack* is guaranteed to make large profits in the American market, and if the partnership unit holder relied upon that opinion in accepting the offer and converting his/her units into company shares and warrants, civil liability might be imposed against Ms. Bach in the event the game lost money for the company.

Should Ms. Bach become the company salesperson, then she risks a serious contravention of the securities regulations that restrict what a company may represent to a potential investor. All the information contained in the offer is already before the investor. She can lead the investor through this information, but she cannot take the next step of speculating about the company or its products. A company lawyer would not make evaluations for use by an investor in these circumstances.

Formal Opinions

A legal evaluation in the form of an opinion may be required by a bank as a condition for approving a company loan. The loans officer for the bank may require an evaluation by Ms. Bach as to whether the company is in compliance with all provincial, federal, and local laws and requirements in Canada; and on whether its foreign subsidiaries are in compliance with all the laws governing and applicable to a company in that jurisdiction. The bank, as lender, wants to ensure that the company is not in violation of any laws that might make the loan an insecure investment for the lender. An evaluation in broad, sweeping terms regarding compliance would be avoided by Ms. Bach or any other lawyer. In the case of the foreign subsidiaries, she would, as a matter of prudence, consult local counsel within the jurisdiction for such an opinion.[1] In Canada, there is no formal rule governing the lawyer as an evaluator for a third person. In the United States, however, under the *Model Rules of Professional Conduct* — a body of recommended ethical rules for American lawyers — Rule 2.3 provides that:

> (a) A lawyer may undertake an evaluation of a matter affecting a client for the use of someone other than the client if:
> (1) The lawyer reasonably believes that making the evaluation is compatible with other aspects of the lawyer's relationship with the client;
> (2) The terms upon which the evaluation is to be made are stated in writing, particularly the terms relating to the lawyer's access to information, the contemplated disclosure of otherwise confidential information and the persons to whom report of the evaluation is to be made; and
> (3) The implications to the client are disclosed and the client consents.
> (b) In reporting the evaluation, the lawyer shall indicate any material limitations that were imposed on the scope of the inquiry or on the

disclosure of information.

(c) Except as disclosure is required in connection with a report of the evaluation, information relating to an independent evaluation is confidential.

Company Negotiator

The inside company lawyer provides negotiation skills as part of furnishing legal services both inside and outside the company. The lawyer may play an important role in the negotiation of certain types of contracts, including the terms of a lease, a loan, a distributorship agreement, and employment agreements. With an understanding of the legal consequences of such contracts, the lawyer is able to evolve strategies that will enhance the position of his/her client. In the event of threatened or actual litigation, the lawyer will attempt to settle the claim through the bargaining process with those whose interests are adverse to his/her clients.

Alternative to Negotiating a Consumer Complaint

Ms. Bach has received a letter on law-firm stationery. The author of the letter states that he had purchased the video game *Epic Encounters* for his son's birthday. The video game proved to be defective. There was intermediate failure of the point scoring system programmed into the game. He asked for a refund from the retail distributor of the game, but was refused on the grounds that the program malfunction was the result of user mishandling. The letter ended with a request for a new video game or else a refund of the purchase price of $49.50. In the event that a new video game or refund is not made within twenty days of the date of the letter, the lawyer has threatened the company with a small claims action. The Rinehart Licence Agreement (see Figure 1.4) sets out the rights of the consumer, and Ms. Bach reviewed the terms of that contract.

Ms. Bach then had the program tested by the Research and Development Department. Its report confirmed that the video game had been in contact with a magnet that had caused the destruction of part of the game. After reading the report, Ms. Bach requested her secretary to send a new copy of *Epic Encounters* to the writer of the letter.

Solving the Consumer Complaint at the Least Cost

Ms. Bach, given the nature of the dispute and the potential amount of time, effort, and cost involved, is electing one of two possible courses of action: i) to ignore the letter, treating the threat as not serious given the amount of time, effort, and cost that the purchaser would have to expend in pursuing his remedy, and ii) to accept the offer of settlement. The second alternative might have been taken because of the low cost and effort required by Ms. Bach. Also, settlement can be justified as part of the cost of maintaining a good company reputation with consumers. It would have been unlikely, however, that Ms. Bach would have made a "counter offer", which means, of course, future correspondence. Instead, her time and effort is better spent ensuring that the instructions included with video games are "user friendly". If the number of returns increases, she would need to initiate action and advise management of the need to develop a returns policy.

Cost and Benefit of a Long Negotiation

Ms. Bach has learned from Ann Macey, President of Rinehart Software (U.S.) Ltd., that she is having difficulties with the former president of the company, Mr. Jason Hinds. Mr. Hinds was the president before the company was acquired by Rinehart Software Ltd. As part of the acquisition agreement, Mr. Hinds was retained as Executive Vice-President of Marketing of the company. In the past six months, however, Mr. Hinds has shown an unwillingness to follow the directives of the new president. The U.S. subsidiary is an important distribution vehicle for the company's products in the United States. Mr. Hinds is a highly qualified computer engineer, but the point has been reached where his services are a detriment to the company. Until Mr. Hinds is discharged from the subsidiary company, its operations and morale will suffer. Mr. Hinds, as part of the acquisition agreement, also holds a substantial number of shares in the subsidiary. Ms. Bach has flown to Dallas, Texas, where the subsidiary is doing business, and negotiated a formal contract for the withdrawal of Mr. Hinds from his position in the company, and a covenant for him not to set up another company to compete with the subsidiary in Dallas, Texas. The negotiation went on for three days before a contract was signed between Mr. Hinds and Rinehart Software Ltd.

Ms. Bach has spent extensive time and effort. The company has spent considerable money to negotiate an amicable settlement with Mr. Hinds. One rationale is the overall objective of the company to ensure harmony of employee relationships. Though there may have been cause to discharge Mr. Hinds, there could have been a real potential of litigation for wrongful dismissal. The termination arrangements negotiated between Mr. Hinds and Ms. Bach have avoided a lawsuit, ensured that the former employee will not set up a competing business, and retained the goodwill of a shareholder with an important holding in the subsidiary company.

Legal Policy Formulator

A major function of the inside counsel is to formulate policies and procedures for the company that will operate to prevent legal problems from arising. The preventive practice of law avoids the infringement of statutes and regulations governing the company's activities, as well as lawsuits by third parties who are the providers or consumers of services, goods, and materials. Equipped with knowledge of the law, an understanding of the institutions enforcing and interpreting the laws, and knowledge of the object of the law, including the interests of persons to be protected, the lawyer can assist in the establishment of company policies and procedures that will ensure that the company's activities and operations fit within the existing legal framework.

FIGURE 24.1 **COMMERCIAL LAW**

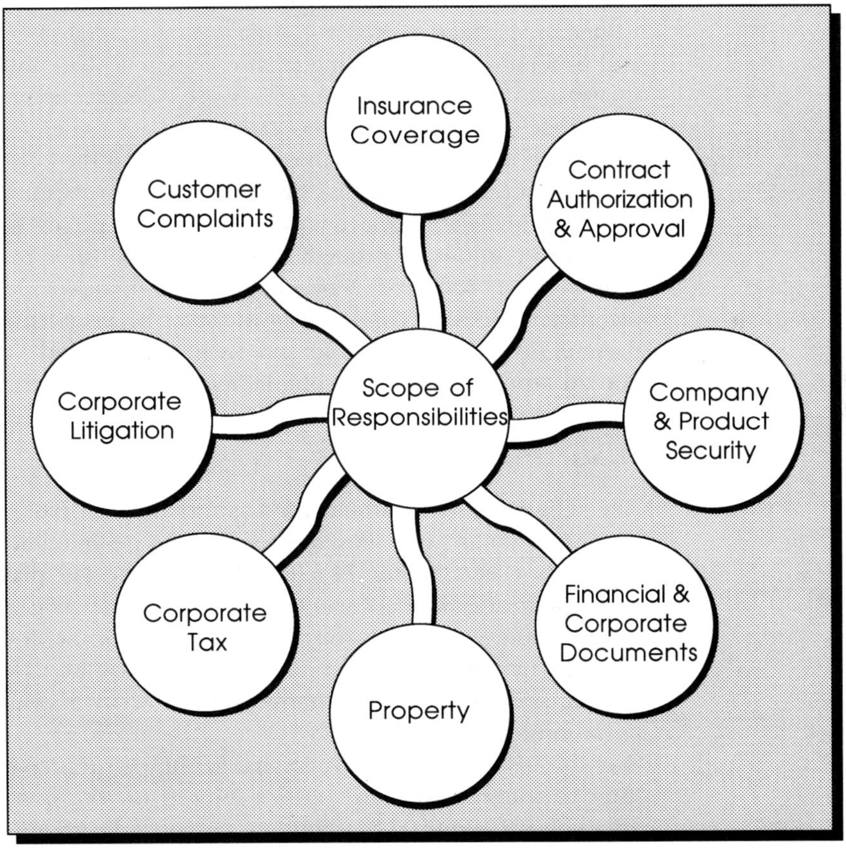

Some of the more common areas for policy and procedure formulation by the lawyer would include: i) customer complaints, ii) insurance coverage, iii) contract authorization and approval, iv) financial and corporate documents, v) corporate litigation, vi) company and product security, vii) intellectual and real property, and viii) corporate tax. In each of these areas, the lawyer will have considerable responsibility in designing the policies and procedures and identifying channels of authority and decision-making. A brief description of these areas will provide a better idea of one of the most important functions of the company lawyer.

Customer Complaints

In any business, disappointed or dissatisfied customers will complain about a product manufactured by the company. Under the heading of Alternative to Negotiating a Consumer Complaint is one illustration of a complaint by an "unhappy" customer, in that instance one who had purchased the video game *Epic Encounters*.

One of Ms. Bach's tasks, as company lawyer, might be to devise policies and procedures for handling such complaints. The policy of handling a complaint from a purchaser of one of the video games will probably differ from that applying to purchasers of the E.E.C. Accounting system. The difference in the policies will reflect the size of the consumer market for the product, the cost of the product, and the relationship between the company and the product consumer. Once a policy has been differentiated for a product, a procedure must be established to record the types of complaints received. A procedure must be developed to process the claims and lines of communication must be established to certain departments, such as Research and Development and Marketing, so that certain types of recurring complaints can be rectified.

Insurance Coverage

The acquisition of insurance for a variety of corporate purposes assumes an overall company policy regarding the type and amount of insurance coverage. (See Chapter 21.) The company lawyer plays a vital role in shaping the insurance coverage. He/she is able to gauge the potential risk of liability arising through the activities of the company. In return for the payment of the premium, the risk of liability is undertaken by an insurance carrier. Some insurance, such as Worker's Compensation, may be required by statute.

Other insurance such as personal liability insurance to cover personal injuries suffered by third parties injured on the company's premises, although not required by statute, is essential. Product liability insurance may be important for Rinehart Software Ltd. as the product line, in the event of malfunction or defect, may result in substantial loss to the customer. However, by contract with consumers, Rinehart Ltd. may include terms to limit or exclude such potential liability. (See Figure 1.4.) Other insurance is required to protect the premises and inventory of the company against theft or damage caused by fire, vandalism, or weather.

In the event of a claim against an insurance policy, the company lawyer will play a major role in determining the cause of the loss, the validity of the claim, the amount of potential loss, whether the loss is one covered by the insurance policy (or one that falls outside the policy or within an exception), and also in filing a claim with the insurance company and working with the claim adjuster to reach a settlement.

Contract Authorization and Approval

The binding legal rights and obligations between the company and others is the subject of a contract. The company lawyer works to develop policies and procedures for the preparation and review of contracts. Some contracts will be standard form contracts. For example, a contract for the video games sold in the mass market will include terms for warranties and guarantees, as well as prohibitions against unauthorized duplication of the game. The same contract written by the company lawyer will be used in all transactions for the same video game. The offer to sell the video game is an offer to sell on the basis of this contract drafted by the company.

Other contracts will be tailored to meet the specific needs of the company: contracts with bankers, insurance companies, suppliers, and distributors, or contracts involving real property such as leases and mortgages are a few examples. The lawyer must be able to draft, interpret, and negotiate contracts on behalf of the company. These skills require expertise regarding the use and limitations of contract law. The company relies upon the lawyer to ensure that its bargain is contained in the contract and that remedies are inserted to protect it against the loss of that bargain.

The policies and procedures are essential because the lawyer does not make or interpret contracts in isolation. A policy must be devised to establish lines of authority and communication within the company respecting the preparation of contracts. A decision must be made as to when to employ outside counsel to prepare contracts. For instance, the company lawyer has, in the case of Rinehart, considerable experience in preparing contracts regarding the sale of computer software to the general public. The lawyer, however, may lack sufficient experience to prepare a lease for renting warehouse space.

In formulating policies and procedures for contracts, three rough divisions can be discerned: policies and procedures for i) the standard form contract; ii) the contract that has a combination of standard form or "boiler plate" clauses common to many such contracts and specially drafted clauses to tailor the agreement to the specific needs of the parties; and iii) the contract that is entirely tailored to meet the needs of the parties.

The standard form contract terms and conditions for video games are used because the nature of the obligations and rights imposed will remain constant even though the identity of the purchaser changes. Other important factors that will affect the policy on standard form contracts include: i) the economic leverage of the company to impose terms and conditions on the other party to the contract, ii) the frequency of the transaction governed by the contract, and iii) the use of similar contracts by the company's competitors.

The contract may not contain standard form terms and conditions if the nature of the transaction is extremely rare, and if the content is specifically tailored to handle one situation. For example, in a previous illustration, Ms. Bach flew to Dallas, Texas, to personally negotiate and prepare a termination agreement with the former president of the subsidiary now forming part of Rinehart Software Ltd. In such situations, the policies and procedures will be formulated to meet the specific transaction. In contrast, in the above-mentioned contractual cases, the policies and procedures are created in advance and govern the most common, repetitive transactions.

In the last two categories of contract, procedures will be adopted after being approved by the other persons within the company who are responsible for reviewing the document. Which officers and employees are designated as part of the review process will depend, in part, on the subject matter of the contract. Once the draft contract has been circulated and any changes incorporated into the final contract, the company lawyer must again circulate the contract to the officers and employees responsible for approval. Procedures for execution of the final contract must be consistent with the articles of incorporation and any relevant resolutions.

Financial and Company Documents

In Rinehart Software Ltd., the accounting department has the primary responsibility for handling the financial affairs. The law department performs a number of functions in conjunction with the company's chief financial officer. Ms. Bach, as company lawyer, has responsibility for reviewing annual and quarterly reports and financial statements. On a periodic basis, there will be dividend reports sent to shareholders, and the company lawyer also will review them. The financial matters, including questions of tax resulting from a proposed acquisition or merger, will require consultation with the company's legal department. Lastly, and most importantly, will be the legal assistance required in a decision to increase the number of shares offered by the company, to make a new offering of shares, or in an offer to convert partnership units for investors.

There are numerous company documents that must be drafted, reviewed, and filed every year. It is likely that the legal department will be vested with the responsibility for these matters. People within the company with defined areas of responsibility and decision-making authority must meet throughout the year. The shareholder and the board of directors meetings require notices, and a record of the meetings to be recorded as minutes. The preparation and filing of the notices and minutes will generally fall within the legal department's jurisdiction. Other statements and filings include proxy statements, statements filed with the Registry of Companies where the company is incorporated, and statements required by provincial and foreign securities commissions.

Labour Relations

The legal department of the company develops, along with the management, policies and procedures for i) hiring and firing practices; ii) the negotiating and drafting of collective agreements with the employees' union; iii) handling employee grievances; iv) complying with worker's compensation laws and other laws governing the conditions of the workplace; and v) developing lines of communication between the personnel department and the legal department for passing on proposed or actual laws that may alter or modify the obligations of the company with regard to its employees.

Intellectual Property

As Rinehart Software Ltd. is in the business of producing "intellectual property", i.e., computer programs contained on diskettes, its intellectual property experience and involvement is greater than that of companies in other industries. Rinehart's legal department undertakes responsibility for copyright, trademark, patent, and "passing off" matters (where another company attempts to sell its products under the trademarks of Rinehart Ltd.). The principles contained in these specialized areas of intellectual property law are the primary means of protecting the company's product.

We have examined the intellectual property principles that guide the legal department in the protection and enforcement of the company's proprietary interest in its products. At this stage, it is important to understand the general responsibility assigned to a company lawyer who handles intellectual property problems. As this area of law is highly specialized, policies will be established to define the areas where outside counsel with expertise and experience can be consulted. Certain general responsibilities can be identified as follows: i) preparing applications.for the registration of a copyright, patent, trademark, or trade name; ii) reviewing the contents of registrations with management; iii) understanding and explaining to management the procedures for registration; iv) devising means to protect the secrecy of applications; v) handling the registration procedure with the statutory registrars; vi) understanding and explaining the statutory jurisdiction and authority of the registrars over the application and the continuing jurisdiction once registration is completed; vii) preparing renewals, licences, or assignments; viii) preparing internal procedures for the enforcement of the rights acquired against third parties; ix) advising on the meaning of ownership of the rights acquired upon registration and on the effect of failure to register; and x) developing schedules of fees and costs of registration and renewals.

This is not an exhaustive list of responsibilities, but rather is intended to be a general guide to the primary functions of the legal department of Rinehart Software Ltd. Copyright issues, for example, also arise in the preparation of catalogues, brochures, and advertisements used by the company to promote the product line. The design and artwork on the package containing the software program requires copyright protection as do the instruction guides or manuals instructing the purchaser on how to use the program.

The Conduct of Top Management and Directors

The company lawyer provides advice to the top management and directors on the type of conduct that may result in civil or criminal liability, e.g. the limitations on conduct imposed by the fiduciary relationship that top management and directors owe to the company. Such individuals, for example, often have access to confidential information, trade secrets, or corporate opportunities that they could exploit for their own personal profit. Alternatively, the company could decide to hire a key employee from a competitor for the purpose of learning confidential information about the competitor's product design, research and development projects, or customer lists.

Conflict of Interest Problems

The legal department plays an important role in the formulation of policies and procedures designed to prevent conflict of interest between the company and its employees, and to prevent the misappropriation of confidential information from a competitor. The first step is to identify the employees of the company to be governed by the policies and procedures. The second is to identify what is meant by "fiduciary relationship" between those employees and the company. Third, procedures must be established to test whether a particular course of action would violate the fiduciary duty of the employee. Lastly, company policy must be established concerning dismissal of employees who fail to follow the policies and procedures.

FIDUCIARY DUTY OF OFFICERS AND DIRECTORS

The fiduciary duty has been defined by the Supreme Court of Canada in terms of a top executive officer's obligation of loyalty, good faith, and avoidance of conflict of duty and self-interest.[2] The rationale for strictly imposing this duty on two particular classes of individuals within the company is explained in the following passage from *Canadian Aero Service Ltd. v. O'Malley:*[3]

> Strict application against directors and senior mangement officials is simply recognition of the degree of control which their positions give them in corporate operations, a control which rises above the accountability to owning shareholders and which comes under some scrutiny only at annual general or at special meetings. It is a necessary supplement, in the public interest, of statutory regulation and accountability which themselves are, at one and the same time, an acknowledgement of the importance of the corporation in the life of the community and of the need to compel obedience by it and by its promoters, directors and managers to norms of exemplary behavior.

BREACH OF FIDUCIARY DUTY ILLUSTRATIONS

Ms. Bach, as the company lawyer, in part, executes her own fiduciary duty by ensuring that the directors and senior management adhere to the company policies and procedures instituted to preclude, or at least reduce the risk of, a conflict of interest and duty. In a rapidly changing and growing industry such as computer software, senior management must be aware of the limitations that the company is entitled to impose on their actions.

Illustration The head of the Research and Development department, Mr. Alan Miller, has been approached by a computer engineer who has developed a software program called *Seagold*. This video game is based on the superpowers searching for minerals on the seabed floor. The engineer has offered to sell his program to Rinehart Ltd. After examining the software program, the head of R&D became convinced that the program would be highly successful in the video game market. Instead of buying *Seagold* for the company, he has resigned his position and, together with the computer engineer, formed a new company called Seagold Video Ltd. The new company marketed the video game in Canada and the United States and grossed $2 000 000 in its first year of operation. One explanation for the successful marketing venture was the use of a confidential customer list owned by Rinehart and photocopied by the head of R&D prior to his resignation. In this case, Mr. Miller has breached his fiduciary obligation to the company, and along with his new company, is liable to account for his profits to Rinehart.

Inside Trading

In *Canadian Aero Services Ltd. v. O'Malley*, two senior management officers of Canaero, along with a lawyer, were found liable to account for profits made from a breach of their fiduciary duty. In that case, the senior corporate officers formed a competing company named Terra Surveys Limited. This new company received a large government contract for the topographical mapping and aerial photographing of parts of Guyana. The owners' prior employer, Canadian Aero, argued successfully that its former employees had spent a great deal of time and effort in Guyana to secure precisely the same contract for Canadian Aero. After four years of working toward securing the contract, the officers resigned from Canadian Aero, and shortly afterward their new company obtained the Guyana contract. The newly formed rival company was held liable in damages that the court indicated were based on an accounting of the profits.

Another potential area of conflict is found with the "inside trader". The insider is generally a top executive or a member of the board of directors. Because of his/her position, he/she has inside information about the company that might be exploited for personal benefit by trading the company's shares.

Illustration   Mr. Jenison, a director of Rinehart Ltd., recently returned from London, England with information that the government was about to announce a major scheme to finance the development of an E.E.C. Accounting system for use in the Common Market. An English company, Rugby Software Ltd., with government financing, planned a major marketing campaign for an "E.E.C. Accounting System" that would likely decrease the market share enjoyed by Rinehart Ltd. in Europe. Armed with this information, Mr. Jenison sold 10 000 shares of Rinehart Software Ltd. for $25 per share. After the news from England was released that Rugby Software Ltd. had received a major government subsidy, the price of Rinehart Ltd. shares declined in value to $10 per share.

The New York Court of Appeal, in a case with similar facts, held the corporate fiduciary liable:[4]

> Just as a trustee has no right to retain for himself the profits yielded by property placed in his possession but must account to his beneficiaries, a corporate fiduciary, who is entrusted with potentially valuable information, may not appropriate that asset for his own use even though, in so doing, he causes no injury to the corporation.

The primary concern, in a case such as this, is not to determine whether the corporation has been damaged but to decide, as between the corporation and the defendants, who has a higher claim to the proceeds derived from the exploitation of the information. In our opinion, there can be no justification for permitting officers and directors, such as the defendants, to retain for themselves profits which, it is alleged, they derived solely from exploiting information gained by virtue of their inside position as corporate officials.

The Company Lawyer as Advocate

As a general rule, the company lawyer does not personally handle litigation involving the company. Trial advocacy is a highly specialized field requiring experience and skill in complex areas of law, e.g., tax, trade regulation, copyright, patent and trademark, securities law, and labour disputes such as wrongful dismissal claims. Some large American corporations with a substantial legal department handle some or all of the litigation on behalf of the corporation. In Canada, however, the trend remains for the company lawyers to retain outside counsel to act on behalf of the company.

The day-to-day responsibilities of the company lawyer inside the company make it highly unlikely that he/she would have the time to undertake the role of counsel in litigation. It is more likely that the company lawyer would appear before an administrative tribunal. An administrative tribunal often is more informal and less adversarial than a court. The final decision by in-house counsel to handle such a problem depends on whether he/she has developed a sufficient standard of competence to effectively represent his/her client before an administrative tribunal.

Policies and procedures, even informal ones, must be worked out between the legal department and executive department in order to guide the company lawyer in the retention of competent and experienced counsel to represent the company in a lawsuit. The referral of a case to outside counsel will involve: i) ascertaining that the counsel to be retained does not have a conflict of interest in handling the lawsuit; ii) judging the experience and qualifications of the outside counsel; iii) setting the fees and disbursements; iv) establishing a reporting system between the company and outside counsel so that the company lawyer can monitor the progress of the case; and v) creating an internal line of communication between management and the company lawyer.

Problems for Discussion

1. "Without the constant advice and guidance of lawyers business would come to an abrupt halt." Stone, "The Public Influence of the Bar", (1934) 48 *Har.L.Rev.* 1, p. 9. Is this statement still true today?

2. "Normally, inside counsel is rendering advice in the context of present or future contemplated conduct. In this context, the word of approval by inside counsel may frequently constitute the 'passkey' by which corporate transactions are consummated. Because of this fact, the responsibilities of inside counsel are substantial. Inside counsel should not only counsel by the strict letter of the law but also by the spirit of the law." Ferrara and Steinberg, "The Role of Inside Counsel in the Corporate Accountability Process", (1981) 4 *The Corp.L.Rev.* 3, pp. 10-11. How is the idea of the "passkey" function of in-house counsel connected with his/her duty to advise according to the spirit of the law?

3. On the insider trading issue, is Mr. Jenison liable for the loss in the value of the shares sold to the third party who purchased them? Would the result be different if Mr. Jenison had told his wife the information and if she had sold shares held in her own name and made herself a profit?

4. In the Rinehart breach of fiduciary illustration above, what is the nature of the duty that the former head of the Research and Development department owed to Rinehart after his departure?

Chapter 24 Notes

1. See, Fuld, "Lawyers' Standards and Responsibilities in Rendering Opinions", (1977) 33 *Bus. Law.* 1295, pp. 1304-07.
2. See *Canadian Aero Services Ltd. v. O'Malley*, (1972) 1 O.R. 592; 40 D.L.R.(3d) 371, 384 (S.C.C.).
3. Ibid.
4. See *Diamond v. Oreamuno*, (1969) 248 N.E.(2d) 910 (N.Y.C.A.).

25 THE PROFESSIONAL RESPONSIBILITY OF THE LAWYER

The Rules Governing Lawyers' Conduct

There is a good reason to devote a major section to professional responsibility in a business law text: The ethical issues involved in many day-to-day decisions or activities of a company provide us with considerable insight as to the role of the company lawyer and his/her duties, responsibilities, allegiances, and loyalties. They allow us to see first hand the larger world in which the company exists. There are third parties, such as suppliers, lenders, investors, and distributors; there are many government subdivisions with regulatory authority, such as securities agencies, tax authorities, human rights commissions, and environmental and consumer protection agencies; and there is the general public that may be adversely affected.

Our concern with professional responsibility is not limited to the legal services rendered by Ms. Bach. The company employs outside counsel who must furnish their services within the bounds imposed by established ethical restrictions. Finally, there are the lawyers employed by the third parties with whom Ms. Bach or outside lawyers will negotiate contracts, settle disputes, arrange financings, or purchase, lease, or mortgage property.

The object of this chapter is not to chart all the potential issues that may raise professional responsibility questions. Instead, it is to provide a general overview of some of the major issues. In the problems, we will canvass the grey areas where Ms. Bach may have no clear answer to a specific problem, or indeed, where there may be several, conflicting answers. By walking the tightrope with Ms. Bach, we will have a better idea of how difficult her task is, and how she carries a particular burden not placed on the shoulders of others within the company. Professional responsibilities put her in a position where she must have a "sense of consequence". Unlike other employees of the company, Ms. Bach must be aware that her many functions comply with the professional standards set by her profession.

FIGURE 25.1 **THE BASIS FOR PROFESSIONAL DISCIPLINE**

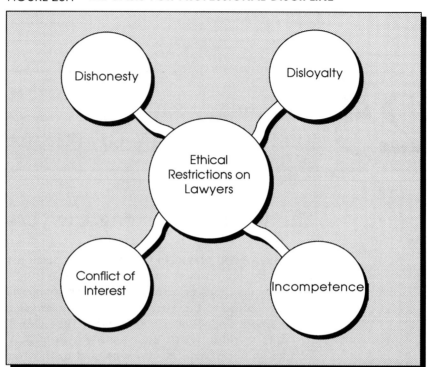

A second object of this chapter is to consider the question of competence. As an infraction of a professional responsibility obligation typically triggers an administrative proceeding before a disciplinary committee of the law society, an allegation of incompetence is generally part of a damage action against a lawyer based on negligence. For instance, the failure of a lawyer to warn a client of the risk involved in a certain transaction is the cause of considerable litigation in Canada. It is essential that we have some concept of the standard of care that the courts impose on the lawyers.

The Rinehart Company depends upon competent, reliable, and efficient legal services. Although the in-house counsel is primarily responsible for furnishing such services, frequent resort to outside counsel is required. By examining the standard of care requirement, we will be able to ascertain the attitude of the courts toward experienced business executives and their retained lawyers. This information will provide an important basis for the business executive in retaining, instructing, and controlling counsel in the future. The major lesson of this chapter is that you, as a future business executive, have an active responsibility to closely monitor the legal services.

In matters concerning the professional responsibility of lawyers, there are many hard questions, and very few clear, easy answers. This much is clear: The definition and scope of the responsibility is more than a matter of applying abstract ideals of what is right or wrong, honest or dishonest, or moral or immoral. Though these ideals may explain a lawyer's professional responsibility, they do not provide specific *rules* or guidelines. Professional responsibility is an area of *law* that does contain such rules or guidelines.

In Canada, the provincial law societies have adopted Canons of Ethics. In British Columbia, the Law Society has adopted Rules of the Law Society that, among other things, govern discipline-related matters and procedures. Second, the Law Society has published, for the guidance of the members of the Law Society of British Columbia, a *Professional Conduct Handbook*. Finally, the Canadian Bar Association has adopted a Code of Professional Responsibility. Although the Code is not binding on members of provincial law societies, it is persuasive and is used as an additional guide to determine the professional responsibility duties of lawyers. The pattern in British Columbia is representative of the approach and content of the professional responsibility duties found in other provinces. Therefore, for purposes of discussion, we will use the British Columbia Law Society as our model. Later, we will examine a radically different approach to professional responsibility contained in the American Bar Association's Model Rules of Professional Conduct. Unlike the Canons, the Model Rules provide a comprehensive, modern *code*. At this stage, however, before discussing the content of the provincial Canons and Rules and the Canadian Bar Association's Code, consideration will be given to the arguments in favour and against codification of the rules of professional responsibility.

The provincial Canons and Rules take a conceptual approach that is substantially different from that found in the American Model Rules. Those who oppose the code approach argue that "morality" and "ethics" cannot be codified like the law of tax or criminal law. Further, that codification encourages lawyers to find "loopholes". The argument is made that a lawyer's conduct is not professional misconduct unless the conduct comes within the precise language of the rule. Finally, it is sometimes said that legal ethics are a matter of common sense and honesty or of a sense of right and wrong; and that the circumstance of legal practice is so diverse that it would be impossible to cover all possibilities. An unstated premise is that the Code, with express prohibitions, limits the flexibility of the lawyer on behalf of the client.

Those who support the code approach have argued:[1]

The goal of . . . [the code] has been to produce standards of professional conduct that are consistent, comprehensive and constitutional: consistent, integrating the competing responsibilities that arise in the conduct of our profession; comprehensive, constitutional, in that they be bottomed on law, constitutional, corporate, criminal, agency, tort, fiduciary — the seamless web — to the end that the law by which lawyers are disciplined is congruent with the law that lawyers practice.

These competing points of view are considered in the following discussion of the Canadian approach to professional responsibility with the Canons of Ethics, the Rules of the Law Society, and with the Canadian Bar Association's Code of Professional Responsibility.

Every lawyer who practices law in Canada must be a member of a Law Society and as such is governed by the Canons, Rules of the Law Society, the *Handbook of Professional Responsibility* (published by the provincial law society) and guided by the Code adopted by the Canadian Bar Association.

It is important to emphasize that the professional responsibility obligations and duties apply equally to inside as well as outside lawyers who represent a company. The fact that Julia Bach is an employee of Rinehart Software Ltd. does not exclude her from operating by the rules governing professional responsibility. She has been employed as a lawyer, and to the extent that she is called upon to render legal advice and opinions, draft and negotiate agreements, or conduct litigation, she is acting as any other lawyer would on behalf of a client. A lawyer's universe is larger than any particular client. The fact that Julia Bach's client is, from a layman's point of view, her "boss", does not mean that the "boss" has a free hand in defining Ms. Bach's responsibilities to her "profession" and, indirectly, to the community as a whole.

The Professional Responsibility of the Company Lawyer

Our focus must be concentrated on the rules of professional conduct governing inside and outside company lawyers. This is not to ignore the professional responsibility governing lawyers in other contexts, or to suggest that there is not a broad overlap of duties owed by a lawyer to any client. Instead, the examination of professional responsibility where the company is the client presents a number of difficulties that require special attention. Without an understanding of the rules governing professional conduct, it becomes impossible to determine the scope of the company lawyer's role and function, and what can be properly demanded and given by the lawyer to the client. Problems of professional responsibility are not a rare occurrence; they are a constant, real feature of day-to-day practice for the company lawyer.

In essence, the rules of professional conduct define the type of things that a lawyer cannot do, may do, or shall do on behalf of a client. Like an invisible referee in a football game, the rules define what is foul or when a play is out-of-bounds. It falls upon the lawyer to know the rules and referee or police the game. The benchers of the law society are not at his/her right hand to interpret the rules or apply the rules to all the potential daily problems that emerge. The penalty for not enforcing or ignoring the rules means that the lawyer is in substantial risk of reprimand, suspension, or disbarment by the law society.

The Canons of Legal Ethics

The Generalized Language

Part **A** of the *Professional Conduct Handbook* contains the Canons of Ethics. The foreword of the *Handbook* warns that "Members should also appreciate that breaches of these rules will have to be considered as unprofessional conduct." Unprofessional conduct — which has no precise meaning — is a basis for disciplining lawyers. A major problem with the "unprofessional conduct" standard is the lack of guidance that it provides for inside legal counsel.

Not only the basis for discipline but also the Canons' view of the function and purpose of lawyers is difficult to reconcile with the modern company lawyer who practises either in-house or in a private law firm. For example, Ruling 1 of the Canons of Ethics provides that "The lawyer is more than a mere citizen. He is a minister of justice, an officer of the Courts, his client's advocate, and a member of an ancient, honourable, and learned profession." This statement suggests that a lawyer is a man, a trial lawyer or counsel, and an educated, honourable gentleman.

FIGURE 25.2 **DIVISION OF ETHICAL OBLIGATIONS UNDER THE CANONS**

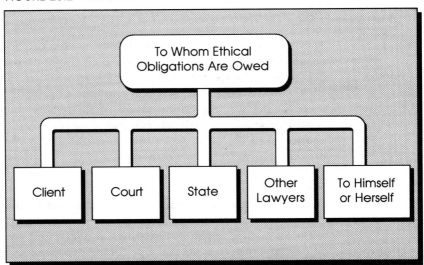

An analogy can be drawn between the 1921 Canons of Ethics and the 1924 *Copyright Act*. The original drafters of the *Copyright Act* cannot be justifiably faulted for failing to anticipate technological advances such as television, computer programs, or computer microchips. Copyright protection had been directed to protection of books, dramatic works, engravings, lectures, maps, charts, plans, tables, compilations, and photographs. Similarly, in 1921, the drafters of the Canons of Ethics could not have anticipated the growth and specialized needs of the company lawyer. The Canadian legal profession in 1921 was smaller, more homogeneous, overwhelmingly male, primarily generalist (rather than specialist), with shared expectations and similar practices. Certainly, this is no longer the case in British Columbia or elsewhere in Canada.

Assuming that it were ever possible to address professional responsibility issues by reference to general and vague terms such as "justice", "courtesy and good faith", "fair and honourable", "honour and propriety", or "unprofessional or dishonest conduct", it is unlikely that these terms of reference are a meaningful guide for a Canadian company lawyer. Indeed, there is an implicit assumption that a lawyer's client is a natural person.

To continue our analogy with the *Copyright Act*, it may be necessary to argue that a software program is "like" a book and should be protected by copyright protection. Would Ms. Bach be violating the Canons by drafting an acquisition agreement that includes terms extremely favourable to the company, and by using the economic advantage of the company's market position as leverage to compel another party to sell his or her software program on the basis of that contract? Would she be maintaining the "high traditions of his profession by being in fact, as well as in name, a gentleman"?

The Framework for the Profession

The limitations of the Canons of Ethics include the broad, general language that defines a lawyer's professional responsibilities, and the preoccupation with the role of the lawyer as an advocate. Nonetheless, until the Canons are updated, they will continue to provide the basic framework for defining the ethical duties of all lawyers, including company lawyers. The lawyers' ethical obligations are divided into five major categories: i) to the state, ii) to the court, iii) to the client, iv) to other lawyers, and v) to himself or herself.

THE STATE

There are four ethical duties owed by a lawyer to the state. The one most directly affecting a company lawyer provides that "He owes a duty to the State, to maintain its integrity and its law and not to aid, counsel, or assist any man to act in any way contrary to those laws." For purposes of analysis, we will assume that "man" includes a client that is a company.

As the company lawyer's functions include giving advice on the many laws and regulations governing the company and its activities, there is an express prohibition against aiding, counselling, or assisting the company to act contrary to the laws.

The Canons place no obligation on the company lawyer, as adviser, to consider the moral, economic, social, or political factors of the intended act. To comply with the letter of the law appears to satisfy the company lawyer's ethical duty to the state even though other considerations may have equal importance for the well-being of the state. Further, there is an implicit assumption that the laws of the state are clear and unambiguous.

There may be more than one interpretation of the law; and reasonable minds may differ as to which interpretation is to be preferred. Later, should the company lawyer's interpretation prove to be wrong, would this mean that he/she has violated his/her ethical duty to the state for advising the course of action adopted by the company? Would he/she be subject to disciplinary proceedings based on this ethical obligation? These are unsettling questions for a company lawyer who works in a highly regulated environment.

The Court

There are four ethical obligations to the court. The lawyer's conduct must be characterized by candour and fairness; he/she must assist in defending judges against unjust criticism and complaint; he/she must not offer evidence that he/she knows should not be admitted; and he/she must not use private influence on judges or curry favour with juries. As the primary role of an inside company lawyer is devoted to matters other than litigation, these ethical obligations have little relevance to his/her practice.

For the outside lawyer retained by the company to conduct litigation, the obligations do not provide answers to some specific problems. There is, for example, no specific obligation to prevent a lawyer from bringing or defending a proceeding although he/she knows there to be no reasonable basis of success. There is no mention of any restricting of dilatory practices for the purpose of frustrating the opposing party's attempt to seek appropriate redress. Although the lawyer is proscribed from offering evidence that he/she knows should not be admitted, the Canons are silent on the matter of the alteration, destruction, or concealment of documents that the lawyer knows, or ought reasonably to know, are relevant to a proceeding. Again, the Canons are silent on trial publicity. Should there be, for instance, a duty on a lawyer to not make extrajudicial statements that he/she knows, or ought reasonably to know, will cause substantial or material prejudice to the result of a proceeding?

The advocate, on behalf of a company, may be appearing in tribunals other than a court. There is nothing in the Canons to suggest that the ethical obligations would apply to an administrative tribunal such as a provincial labour relations board. Most of the administrative tribunals have been created since 1921. This represents an important shift from making the courts the exclusive decision-making institution in Canada. The reality of the 1980s is that quasi-judicial administrative boards play an important, if not dominant, role in the resolution of many legal disputes involving a company. The advocate may provide an important service before non-adjudicative bodies, boards, and councils. The company may retain the service of a lawyer to represent them on specific bills before Parliament. Is there any professional responsibility attached to this type of advocacy? Should the lawyer be required to disclose to the body, board, or council that he/she is representing the company?

The definition of the ethical obligations to the court is inadequate. The silence on many crucial issues arising in judicial proceedings and the total exclusion of any obligations in quasi-judicial proceedings or non-adjudicative proceedings leaves a large opening for important types of misconduct. Lawyers must only answer for a narrowly defined set of duties. The alternative, under the 1921 Canons, is to allow the Law Society to redefine the specific duties by using the catch-all "unprofessional or dishonest conduct" provision as a means of updating the ethical obligations of the advocate. The problem with this approach, however, is that the lawyer will not necessarily know in advance precisely what specific duties will be included in this catch-all provision.

THE CLIENT

The largest group of ethical obligations under the Canons concern the client. There are eleven ethical obligations to the client. Their major preoccupation is with the lawyer's function as an advocate on behalf of a client and with lawyer's fees, trust funds, and valuation of legal services. In Chapter 24, we considered the functions of a company lawyer on behalf of his/her client. The question becomes whether, in carrying out these functions, the lawyer is acting consistently with his/her ethical obligations. Only two of the eleven specific ethical obligations have any bearing on the role occupied by a company lawyer: i) A lawyer "should avoid representing conflicting interests", and ii) "The office of the lawyer does not permit, much less does it demand of him, for any client, violation of law or any manner of fraud or chicanery."

In the succeeding two chapters, attention will be focused on professional responsibility problems arising from the representation of a company. What is important at this stage is an appreciation that neither the lawyer nor the client will obtain very much guidance from the Canons in resolving these problems.

HIS FELLOW LAWYER

The phrase "to His Fellow Lawyer" is taken from the Canons. The language indicates a legal profession composed of men. Obviously, the ethical obligations would not be construed as excluding women lawyers. Leaving aside the semantic problem, there are four ethical obligations under this heading. The key words are "courtesy and good faith" and "honour and propriety". The lawyer is admonished not to be influenced by the ill feeling between clients; that his/her conduct should be characterized by courtesy and good faith; that he/she should strive to suit the convenience of the opposing counsel; that undertakings should not be undertaken unless they can be fulfilled; that communication on a subject in controversy should be through the opposing party's lawyer; and that no "paltry advantage" should be taken when his/her opponent has made a slip or overlooked a technical matter.

The matters raised under this head, by and large, assume an adversary role. They are an attempt to establish a sense of fairness and non-advantage-taking between lawyers. In a way, they are a code of behaviour between gentlemen. This criticism is not intended to disparage the importance of good faith and honour, but to simply recognize that the complex functions carried out by a company lawyer require specific guidelines. Again, where the client is a company, statements that a lawyer "should give no undertaking he cannot fulfil and he should fulfil every undertaking he gives" overlook the relationship that an in-house lawyer has with his/her "client". Moreover, the entire heading assumes that the primary communication by a lawyer on behalf of a client is with an opposing party's lawyer. But in the company setting, as we have noted in our review of the functions of the company lawyer, a great deal of the lawyer's communications on behalf of the company are with non-lawyers.

To Himself

The use of "Himself", as for that of "Fellow", is a reflection of the composition of the legal profession in 1921. Today, a law society would construe this heading as encompassing a woman lawyer. Lawyers are under six ethical obligations to himself or herself. This category contains two generally worded obligations that vest the Law Society with unfettered power to monitor the professional conduct of the lawyer.

> It is his duty to maintain the honour and integrity of his profession and to expose without fear or favour before the proper tribunals, unprofessional or dishonest conduct by any other member of the profession, and to accept without hesitation a retainer against any member of the profession who is alleged to have wronged his client.

> He should also bear in mind that he can maintain the high traditions of his profession by being in fact, as well as in name, a gentleman.

These provisions allow for self-regulation by lawyers of their colleagues whose conduct is unprofessional or dishonest. If a lawyer falls short of the general requirement to "maintain the honour and integrity of his profession", then his/her conduct is unbecoming a "gentleman", and, like a disgraced army officer, he/she is removed from his/her "office". The disciplinary committee of the Law Society sits in judgment to determine whether a lawyer has breached any ethical obligations under this head, or any other head contained in the Canons.

The disciplinary committee performs a crucial role in enforcing the Canons. This might lead to the expectation that the decisions of the disciplinary committee would shed light on the meaning of the Canons in modern legal practice. Yet the disciplinary committee does not provide detailed reasons for its decisions. The justification for disciplining a lawyer is confined to the general conclusion that he/she is guilty of "professional misconduct" or "conduct unbecoming a lawyer."

The Natural Justice Requirement

A lawyer who has been disciplined by the Law Society may appeal the decision to the courts. A common argument advanced on appeal is that the lawyer was denied natural justice. The courts have defined natural justice as requiring "that a person in the position of the solicitor be assured (a) the right to adequate notice and a fair hearing; (b) that the tribunal be free of bias or reasonable apprehension of bias."[2]

The lawyer is entitled to know the substance of the case against him/ her in advance of the hearing. A fair hearing means that the accused lawyer and his/her counsel have a right to be heard, to testify, to call witnesses, and to present his/her defence. While there may be irregularities or defects in the notice or hearing, the lawyer may waive such defects through his/her acquiescence and participation in the hearing.[3] Nonetheless, the disciplinary committee must act within its statutory jurisdiction. Where the committee acts totally without jurisdiction over the subject matter, that defect cannot be cured by the conduct of the lawyer subject to the proceeding.[4]

The question of bias or apprehension or appearance of bias has been raised where the decision of the disciplinary committee is prepared by the prosecutor and not by the members of the tribunal that hear the case. In Ontario, the *Law Society Act*[5] expressly requires that the disciplinary committee that hears the evidence must reach the decision as to whether the lawyer is guilty. The decision must be in writing and contain reasons for the decision, including findings of fact and the conclusions of law, if any. In the case where a third party assumes the role of preparing the decision, it has been held:[6]

It goes without saying that the written decision and reasons of the discipline committee, who are the judges in this process, must be prepared by them personally for transmittal to the solicitor. The

drafting of this document by a third person [in this case, the pros-
ecutor] is a fatal breach of the rules of natural justice; that function
cannot be delegated.

In Ontario, the Discipline Committee reports its finding to a Convocation and, by statute, only the Convocation is entitled to take the appropriate disciplinary action. The decision-making process is, therefore,
divided into two stages.

The Rulings of the Law Society

The second source of the Canadian law governing a lawyer's professional
responsibility is the rulings made periodically by the Benchers of the
Law Society. The threshold question is whether the Law Society, through
its rule-making power, has made the law of professional responsibility
more congruent with the law practised by company lawyers.

An examination of the rulings in British Columbia indicates that, like
the Canons, the main preoccupation is with the lawyer who is practising
in a law firm or as a sole practitioner. Indeed, the first ruling is the
adoption of the Canons of Ethics. Many of the other rulings are irrelevant
for the company lawyer, e.g., Ruling 10, which places duties on the
solicitor preparing: a will; most of the rulings restricting advertisements,
firm name, announcements, letterheads, legal publications and signs, di-
rectories, and referrals; the nature and scope of undertakings addressed
to the private practitioner; it includes a prohibition against appearing
intoxicated in court or acting in an "ungentlemanly" fashion before a
court; and rulings on cross-examination, court attire, meetings with a
judge, and the duty of counsel in divorce proceedings.

In addition to ruling, the law society may enter into a joint policy with
another institution. The Law Society of British Columbia entered into a
joint policy with the Superintendent of Brokers which governs lawyers'
conflict of interest in the securities business. The policy is concerned
with the disclosure by a lawyer of his/her interest in a company that he/
she represents for purposes of filing documents by or on behalf of the
company with the Superintendent or the Vancouver Stock Exchange.
Also, the lawyer must disclose his/her position as a director or senior
officer in the corporation. The disclosure applies to a prospectus, a statement of material facts, a take-over bid circular, a director's circular, and
an information circular sent to members in connection with an amal-
gamation, merger, another business combination, or an offering memorandum. Disclosure applies to a lawyer who has primary responsibility
for the preparation of, or for advice to the corporation or an underwriter
of the corporation with respect to, the contents of any disclosure document.

The Law Society has stopped short of barring a lawyer who owns a
material beneficial interest or who is a director or senior employee for

the corporation from preparing disclosure documents in the provincial securities industry. The purpose of the disclosure requirement is to alert potential investors or others who rely on those documents of the potential conflict of interest of the lawyer who prepared the document.

The Standard of Care for the Competent Lawyer

Our focus has been on the legal rules that the profession uses to monitor and discipline members of the Law Society. In this part, we will concentrate on civil suits for damages against lawyers who have allegedly been negligent in representing their client. The main issue is: what standard of care or level of competence is a client entitled to expect from his/her lawyer? Lawyers are often engaged to assess the risk of undertaking a particular course of action proposed by a client. Most malpractice suits are based on allegations that the lawyer failed to advise, investigate, or disclose certain information or facts to his/her client. As a general rule, the lawyer's omission is the result of oversight, lack of expertise and knowledge, or a conflict of interest. In Chapter 27, we will consider at some length the conflict of interest cases. They will illustrate instances where civil liability for loss suffered by a client and professional discipline often converge.

The idea of incompetence typically translates into a legal action by the client based on either breach of contract or negligence. In England, a barrister is immune from an action by a client for negligent conduct of his client's civil case in court.[7]

In Canada, however, a lawyer is admitted to the provincial law society as both a solicitor and barrister. When a lawyer is engaged to perform legal services that traditionally have been performed by a barrister, is he/she entitled to rely upon the immunity granted English barristers to defeat a negligence action? The Canadian courts have long held that the English immunity doctrine does not apply to a Canadian lawyer.[8] The courts in Canada have distinguished the English doctrine on the grounds that in Canada a lawyer is entitled to sue for his/her fee and that the two professions of solicitor and barrister are joined. Allowing a client to sue his/her lawyer has been held to be in the public interest.[9]

Two sociological factors entered into the decision to extend negligence to lawyers: i) the vast majority of the lawyers who are in private practice are required to carry liability insurance in respect of negligence, and ii) the large number of newly called lawyers entering the profession, each with little experience and working for a competent counsel during their articling year, that will be representing clients in the courts.

A number of issues require analysis when considering a malpractice action against a lawyer. For example, the legal advice may turn upon the lawyer's judgment as to future interpretations of a statute. Where that advice subsequently proves to be mistaken, is the client entitled to throw the economic loss suffered by it on the shoulders of its lawyer? Does it make a difference whether the client is experienced in business? How does the court assess damages against a lawyer who has acted negligently?

The Duty of a Lawyer to His/Her Client

In Canada, the duty of a lawyer to his client has been expressed as follows: "[T]he solicitor contracts with his client to be skillful and careful. For failure to perform his obligation he may be made liable at law in contract or even in tort, for negligence in breach of a duty imposed on him."[10] In the absence of an express promise, a lawyer does not promise that he/she will win the client's case. The legal adviser, however, does promise the use of skill, care, and competence in carrying out his/her undertaking on behalf of the client.[11]

A lawyer who undertakes to provide financial advice must meet the standard of competence expected of an experienced solicitor advising his/her client on such matters. In the context of a company, the line between legal and business advice is often blurred. It is clear, however, that a lawyer who is engaged to provide either legal or business advice must exercise skill, reasonable care, and competence. The main components of a typical negligence case include: i) a solicitor-client relationship between the person seeking advice or information and the person giving such advice, ii) breach of the duty of care resulting from that relationship because of the solicitor's negligence, and iii) reliance by the client upon the advice or information that caused the loss or harm.[12]

The Lawyer's Duty to Warn of Risks

One of the most common allegations of negligence against a lawyer is the failure to warn the client of a risk associated with the transaction or venture. The courts have distinguished between cases where the risks were of consequences unknown to the client and those where the client, because of his/her knowledge and experience, would be expected to know. The issue is often whether in the view of the court, the client was in fact deceived or misled about the possibility of risk.

In *Ormindale Holdings Ltd. v. Ray, Wolfe, etc.*,[13] the plaintiffs were apartment landlords who followed the advice of their lawyers to avoid application of the *Rent Act* legislation. In order to allow the plaintiffs to sell units, the lawyers devised a scheme to take advantage of an apparent loophole in the provincial legislation restricting the conversion of rental accommodation into long-term tenure. Had the scheme worked, the plaintiffs would have stood to make a profit of $5 500 000. The British Columbia Court of Appeal, however, struck down the scheme, and the plaintiffs then commenced a negligence action against their lawyers.

The court concluded that as long as the lawyer applies reasonable skill and knowledge to the task and exercises reasonable care, he/she will not be liable even though he/she makes an error in judgment as to the interpretation of a statute. Does the lawyer have an obligation to warn his/her experienced business clients that a court may disallow the scheme that attempts to take advantage of a "loophole" in the statute? It has been held that a lawyer is not obligated to give a formal warning of risk to experienced business clients.[14] It is presumed that such clients need no advice on the consequences of their plan failing; the result is clear that they will lose their financial investment in the plan.

A lawyer may also give advice to a business client as to whether a contract with a third party should be terminated. In such a case, the courts place considerable emphasis on the experience and knowledge of the client as grounds for finding that the lawyer did not breach his/her duty in failing to mention other remedies that, under the circumstances, would be unsatisfactory.[15]

The duty to warn of risks is greater where the client is inexperienced and relies on the lawyer's expertise to protect his/her interest. Thus, in a real estate transaction where the vendor is a relatively poorly educated person who enters into a contract to sell his/her property, his/her lawyer has a duty to warn of possible deficiencies in taking a vendor's lien as security.

In *Major v. Buchanan*,[16] for example, a real estate transaction was entered into between an inexperienced vendor and a purchaser who owned an interest in an adjacent apartment block. The purchase price was secured by a vendor's lien and the proceeds owed to the vendor were to be paid out of mortgage money secured on the apartment block. The vendor's lawyer failed to determine whether the purchaser had an interest in the apartment house. He also failed to direct the purchaser to require the mortgage company, which was advancing the purchase money, to pay the required amount to the vendor.

Moreover, the lawyer allowed his client, the vendor, to enter the transaction without warning him of the risk of allowing the purchaser to demolish the house on the property. Once the house was demolished, because of zoning laws, the vendor's lien was destroyed. The court found that the lawyer was negligent in failing to advise his client of the numerous risks involved in the transaction, and that if the client had been properly advised he would not have proceeded to close the transaction without reasonable protection.

Goodman J. held:[17]

[A] solicitor has the duty of warning a client of the risk involved in a course of action, contemplated by the client or by his solicitor on

his behalf, and of exercising reasonable care and skill in advising
him. If he fails to warn the client of the risk involved in the course
of action and it appears probable that the client would not have
taken the risk if he had been so warned, the solicitor will be liable.
If he warns the client of the risk involved in the course of action,
then he can only proceed to follow such course if the client instructs
him so to do. If he fails to exercise reasonable care and skill in
advising the client with respect to his risk and the client or solicitor
on his behalf adopts a course of actions which the client would
probably not have taken or authorized if he had been properly advised, again, the solicitor will be liable if the client suffers a loss. . . .
In the present case, I am satisfied that the solicitor failed to advise
the plaintiff of the numerous risks involved in completing the transaction in the manner in which it was completed and that he failed
to exercise reasonable care and skill in advising him with respect
to the closing and the execution of the demolition agreement. I am
satisfied that on the balance of probabilities, the plaintiff, if properly
advised by his solicitor, would not have proceeded to close the
transaction without reasonable protection with respect to obtaining
security for payment of the balance of the purchase price and, in
particular, would not have permitted the demolition of the house.
He has, in my opinion suffered substantial damage as a result of such
omissions on the part of the solicitor.

The plaintiff was awarded $13 000 plus interest of $4680.

Illustration   Ms. Bach retains outside counsel to review a lease on
office space in a building located in Toronto. The outside counsel, Joseph
Sober, is an experienced real estate lawyer who has been retained on
that basis. There were several conferences and letters exchanged between Ms. Bach and Mr. Sober on the lease before it was executed on
January 2, 1983. The term of the lease is for five years with an option to
renew. In early 1984, Ms. Bach was instructed by the company president
to negotiate a sublease for part of the office space. When Ms. Bach sought
to obtain the approval of the landlord, as required by the lease, for the
sublease, it was discovered that a clause allows the landlord's mortgagee
to withhold consent to any sublease. The landlord's mortgagee exercised
its right to block the sublease proposed by Rinehart Company. Is Mr.
Sober guilty of professional negligence for failing to point out the restriction on subletting to his client, the Rinehart Company?[18]
In this illustration, the Rinehart Company would argue that Mr. Sober's
failure to warn it that it ran the risk that the landlord's mortgagee would
withhold consent to a change of user amounted to negligence. In a similar
case, *Sykes v. Midland Bank Executor Co.*,[19] the English Court of Appeal
held that "When a solicitor is asked to advise on a leasehold title it is,

in my judgment, his duty to call his client's attention to clauses in an unusual form that may affect the interests of his client as he knows them."[20]

In the *Sykes* case, the client was a firm of architects and surveyors. Does it make a difference, bearing in mind the *Ormindale* decision, that Mr. Sober was dealing not only with an experienced business client but with another lawyer employed by the company? Finally, on the question of damages arising from the negligence, to what extent is it relevant that the client would probably have entered into the transaction even if the restriction in the lease had been pointed out to it?

Problems for Discussion

1. Courts often award only nominal damages (e.g., $1.00) against the negligent lawyer, on the basis that the client would have proceeded with the transaction in any event. Do you agree with this approach?

2. What is the relationship, if any, between professional responsibility and competency?

3. What relevance has the standard of care requirement for the lawyer employed by, and who acts on behalf of, the company?

4. Do you agree that a different warning of risks requirement ought to apply to a business client?

5. What are the potential dangers arising from the vague language and the priorities found in the Canons?

6. Are the Canons of Ethics an advantage or disadvantage for the company lawyer?

7. How has the assumption of the lawyer's role and function shifted since 1921?

8. Is the Canons of Ethics, and the matter of enforcement, consistent with the rule of law?

9. Are Canadian lawyers being disciplined by a law that is congruent with the law that lawyers practise?

10. Are members of the discipline committee which had found the lawyer guilty of professional misconduct and, in its report to the Convocation, which recommended his suspension, entitled, consistent with the principles of natural justice, to sit in the Convocation to consider the report? See *Law Society of Upper Canada v. French*, (1975) 2 S.C.R. 767, 49 D.L.R.(3rd) 1 (S.C.C.)

Chapter 25 Notes

1. Kutak, Proposed Final Draft, *Model Rules of Professional Conduct* (1981), vi.
2. *Re Emerson and Law Society of Upper Canada*, (1983) 44 O.R.(2d) 729, 738 (Ont.H.C.).
3. Ibid. at 739.
4. See *Essex Incorporated Congregational Church Union*, (1963) A.C. 808, pp. 820-21 (H.L.) per Lord Reid.
5. R.S.O. 1980, c. 233, ss. 33(1)(c) and 33(12).
6. Supra, note 2, p. 760.
7. See *Rondel v. Worsley*, (1969) 1 A.C. 191, (1967) 3 All E.R. 993 (H.L.).
8. See *Leslie v. Ball*, (1863) 22 U.C.Q.B. 512.
9. See *Demarco v. Ungaro*, (1979) 95 D.L.R.(3d) 385, 405-06 (Ont.H.C.).
10. See *Nocton v. Lord Ashburton*, (1914) A.C. 932 (H.L.) per Viscount Haldane; and *MacCulloch's Estate v. Corbett*, (1982) 49 N.S.R.(2d) 663, 671; 96 A.P.R. 663, p. 671 (N.S.S.C. App.Div.).
11. See *MacDonald v. Lockhart*, (1981) 118 D.L.R.(3d) 397, 411 (N.S.S.C., App.Div.).
12. See *Nelson Lumber Co. v. Koch*, (1980) 4 W.W.R. 715, 728-29 (Sask.C.A.).
13. (1980) 116 D.L.R.(3d) 346 (B.C.S.C.).
14. Ibid, p. 357.
15. (1981) 28 B.C.L.R. 342 (B.C.C.A.).
16. (1975) 61 D.L.R.(3d) 46, 59 (Ont. H.C.).
17. Ibid, p. 69.
18. See *Sykes v. Midland Bank Executor Co.*, (1971) 1 Q.B. 113 (C.A.).
19. Ibid.
20. Ibid, p. 124.

26 THE RIGHT OF CONFIDENTIALITY

The Lawyer-Client Privilege

The Modern Canadian Rule

The modern confidentiality rule was formulated by the Supreme Court of Canada in *Descoteau v. Mierzwinski*:[1]

> All information which a person must provide in order to obtain legal advice and which is given in confidence for that purpose enjoys the privileges attached to confidentiality.

The right of confidentiality is perhaps easier to state and apply where the client is an individual than when the client is a company. It is safe to assume, however, that the privilege applies to all clients in respect to all confidential communications between a lawyer and his/her client for the purpose of obtaining or giving legal advice.[2]

PROTECTION AGAINST DISCLOSURES

Our courts have stated that: "The privilege protecting from disclosure communications between solicitor and client is a fundamental right — as fundamental as the right to counsel itself since the right can exist only imperfectly without the privilege."[3] The duty of keeping his/her client's secrets is squarely placed on the lawyer. "[I]t is settled law that any confidential information communicated to a lawyer and received by him in his professional capacity must not voluntarily be disclosed without either the consent of his client or a direction from the Court."[4]

RATIONALE FOR PRIVILEGE

The underlying basis for the privilege is the same in Canada, England, and the United States. Perhaps the best expression of the rationale is found in the decision by Chief Justice Jackett in *Re Director of Investigation and Research and Shell Canada Ltd.*:

[I]t has been recognized from very early times that the protection, civil and criminal, afforded to the individual by our law is dependent upon his having the aid and guidance of those skilled in the law untrammelled by any apprehension that the full and frank disclosure by him of all his facts and thoughts to his legal advisor might somehow become available to third persons so as to be used against him.[5]

Unless the lawyer was entitled to keep his client's secrets in confidence, then the administration of justice and the enforcement of laws would be placed in jeopardy. As we will see later, there are exceptions to the rule that exclude communications by the client that are themselves criminal in nature or for the purpose of furthering a criminal intent.

UNAUTHORIZED DISCLOSURES TO THIRD PARTIES

The privilege also applies where the lawyer makes an unauthorized disclosure of the privileged communication to a third party. Within this category we will consider two separate cases: i) where the client's communication to his/her lawyer concerns the intended commission of a crime or fraud; and ii) where the client's communication to his/her lawyer concerns a transaction, proceeding, or other matters where a real threat against the person or property of another is involved.

Compulsory Disclosure by a Third Party

The term "communication" is broad in nature. Included within the definition would be letters, interviews, telephone conversations, memorandums, notes, questionnaires, and work papers. In *Ott v. Fleishman*,[6] the British Columbia Supreme Court stated: "All information received on behalf of a client in a professional capacity, even if furnished anonymously, is also confidential."

SCOPE OF THE COMMUNICATION

The scope of the communication rule has potential legal consequences for the company. The company counsel, as legal advisor, will be consulted on a wide variety of matters affecting the company's compliance with domestic and foreign laws and regulations. As these communications are sensitive in nature, and may well disclose prior violations of law or regulation governing an aspect of the company's operation, there is the real possibility that another party may attempt to compel disclosure of the communication to assist them in establishing a civil or criminal action against the company.

The question arises as to the basis on which the privilege for confidential communication will apply to preclude the requested disclosure. In the company context, given the highly regulatory environment confronting the company, it is likely that many communications will pass between the company lawyer and those responsible for making decisions inside the company. The Supreme Court of Canada has made it clear that the privilege applies only to communications where the client has sought legal advice and the lawyer has been contacted in his/her professional capacity.

COMPELLING CLIENT DISCLOSURE

It is permissible to compel the defendant to disclose his/her knowledge about certain facts. But the privilege entitles the defendant to refuse a question about what the lawyer told him/her or what he/she told the lawyer. The fact being contained in a letter, for instance, to the lawyer is not a ground for the client to refuse disclosure.

Illustration   It has come to the attention of Ms. Bach that employees of Rinehart Ltd. working in Europe have paid "commissions" or "bribes" to secure contracts on behalf of the company. After consulting with Paul Faber, President of the company, Ms. Bach retains outside counsel. Working with outside counsel, a questionnaire is prepared for purposes of conducting an internal investigation. The questionnaire is sent to the ten sales representatives in Europe and the general manager for Europe. The covering letter is signed by the Chairman of the Board, and requests that all replies be sent to Ms. Bach. The letter also states that the investigation is highly confidential and that the employees should not discuss it with anyone.

Two months later, Ms. Bach receives the completed questionnaires from all eleven employees of the company. These documents candidly disclose a practice of paying bribes in order to obtain contracts for the company. Three weeks later, under the signature of the Chairman of the Board, a letter is sent to all those who filled out the questionnaire instructing them that any future "commissions" are to be paid only after receiving the prior written approval of Ms. Bach. A policy statement is also enclosed stating that in future all company employees are to act in strict accordance with all Canadian and foreign laws and regulations and that a bribe shall not be paid under the guise of a commission.

The potential legal liabilities of the company as the result of such payments are broad and complex. There is the real possibility of violation of securities and tax laws, foreign laws, currency regulations, and breach of fiduciary duty owed to the shareholders of the company. We will assume that Revenue Canada begins an investigation into the bribes, and brings an action against Rinehart Ltd. for violation of the *Tax Act*. Lawyers acting for Revenue Canada ask the court to compel Rinehart Ltd. to produce the written questionnaires sent to its employees and any memorandums or notes of interviews conducted in Canada or abroad with officers or employees of the company. The question arises as to whether the company can successfully raise the privilege and defeat Revenue Canada from securing the questionnaires completed by the company employees.

The Duty to Protect Information Given by the Client

It is important to remember who is Ms. Bach's client. It is Rinehart Ltd. *as an entity*. Has the "client" made a confidential communication to Ms. Bach as the company lawyer for Rinehart Ltd.? Who represents the company? The company lawyer faces these problems frequently. Until it is determined who is the client, it is impossible to apply the privilege. It is unlikely that every employee communication with the company lawyer within a large company entitles the company to raise the privilege successfully. The challenge has been to devise a test identifying those employees and communications for purposes of applying the privilege to a company. In our illustration, for example, the privilege issue may turn on the status of the employees to whom the questionnaire was sent.

The Control Group Test

One solution is found in the Control Group Test. Under this test, employees of the company who have the primary responsibility for making the company's decisions have their confidential communications to the company lawyer protected by the privilege. An American court has expressed the test in this way:

> If the employee making the communications, of whatever rank he may be, is in a position to control or even to take substantial part

FIGURE 26.1 **SCOPE OF LAWYER-CLIENT PRIVILEGE**

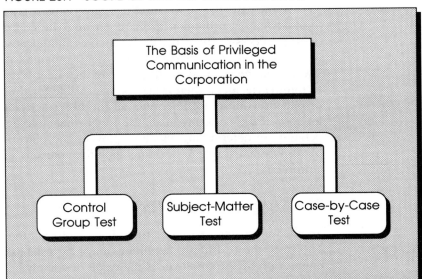

in a decision about any action which the corporation may take upon the advice of the attorney, or if he is an authorized member of a body or group which has that authority, then, in effect, he is (or personifies) the corporation when he makes his disclosure to the lawyer and the privilege would apply. In all other cases the employee would be merely giving information to the lawyer to enable the latter to advise those in the corporation having the authority to act or refrain from acting on the advice.[7]

Unless sales representatives are members of the control group, the questionnaires are not privileged. The experience in the United States has seen the control group test confined to the top-level executives of the company. Membership in the company hierarchical structure then becomes the crucial determining factor as to whether the communication is privileged. The flaw of this approach is revealed by one court in the following passage:

The attorney dealing with a complex legal problem is thus faced with a 'Hobson's choice'. If he interviews employees not having 'the very highest authority,' their communications to him will not be privileged. If on the other hand, he interviews only those with 'the very highest authority', he may find it extremely difficult, if not impossible, to determine what happened.[8]

The United States Supreme Court has rejected the control group test.[9] The problem with the test, as indicated by our illustration, is that the sales representatives are probably not part of the control group of Rinehart Ltd. Indeed, in many cases, middle-level employees are more likely to have the essential information that the company lawyer needs to give legal advice or an opinion to the company. The control group test, by denying access to the privilege for such communication, undercuts the basic policy of encouraging full and frank communication between the lawyer and the client. If the definition of the client is restricted narrowly to top management, then it may be impossible for the company lawyer or outside counsel to determine all the necessary facts to protect the interest of the company. Also, the test is defective because of the uncertainty of determining which employees and officers of the company play a substantial role in deciding upon the company's legal response to a problem.

The Subject-Matter Test

Another approach is based on the subject matter of the communication. To satisfy the test, three conditions must be established: i) the communication by the employee is the result of complying with a direction from his/her superior within the company, ii) the subject matter of the communication is directly related to the employee's performance of his/her duties within the company, and iii) the legal problem is connected with the performance of that employee.[10]

Applying this test, it is unlikely that Revenue Canada would be successful in obtaining discovery of the questionnaires. Although the subject-matter test assists the company in this instance, the question remains whether the test is desirable. It can be argued that this test encourages management to manipulate the rule to protect large amounts of corporate information, and to restrict substantially examination for discovery by any third party who may seek damages or other relief against the company.

The Case-by-Case Approach

When all tests prove defective, the courts often resort to a case-by-case approach. This pragmatic approach leads to uncertainty in the ultimate result of a given case. It makes it difficult for in-house counsel to advise their client adequately as to the scope of the privilege and to formulate a policy that allows the company to take full advantage of the privilege. In *Upjohn v. United States*,[11] counsel decided against applying both the control-group and subject-matter tests, and instructed the courts to decide on a case-by-case basis.

On the facts of that case, which parallel those in our illustration, the U.S. Supreme Court held that the Internal Revenue Service was not entitled to the company's questionnaires. It had other alternatives. For example, it could question the employees of the company who had completed the questionnaire if the company had supplied a list of names to it. Balancing the convenience to the Internal Revenue Service (access to the questionnaire could have saved considerable time and expense), with the policies served by the lawyer-client privilege for confidential communications, the court that held the convenience argument failed.

Unauthorized Communications

In common with all lawyers, a company lawyer may have a conflict between his/her duty to keep the client's confidences and his/her duty to ensure that the administration of justice is not subverted. In this section, we will examine two categories of unauthorized confidential communications by the company lawyer or outside counsel to a third party: i) where the lawyer passes on the communication from the company to a third party to avert a crime or fraud, and ii) where the lawyer, through inadvertence amounting to negligence, discloses the communication to a third party of confidential information that damages the company.

Blowing the Whistle on the Company

The problem arises when the company lawyer, or outside counsel, discovers that the client has committed, or is about to commit, a crime or fraud. Must the lawyer "blow the whistle" on the company? To ask this question is to touch upon an important controversy as to the purpose of confidentiality. Some commentators have suggested that the confidentiality rule is absolute.[12] In contrast, the writers of the Model Rules of Professional Conduct have formulated exceptions to the general rule protecting a client's confidences.

For example, in Model Rules, Rule 1.6(b), a lawyer has the *discretion* to reveal information to prevent the client from committing a crime or fraudulent act that the lawyer believes is likely to cause death or substantial bodily harm, or substantial injury to the financial interest or property of a third party. Where the client's criminal or fraudulent conduct is prospective, the commentary to the Model Rules suggests that the lawyer may be under a moral obligation to make a disclosure to prevent the client from carrying out his/her intended conduct. In the case of murder or substantial bodily injury, the lawyer may be under civil and criminal sanctions if he/she fails to disclose such information.[13]

The Crime and Fraud Exception

The lawyer-client privilege does not apply to prospective crimes and frauds communicated by the client to his/her lawyer. In *Solosky v. The Queen*,[14] the Supreme Court of Canada observed that:

> if a client seeks guidance from a lawyer in order to facilitate the commission of a crime or fraud, the communication will not be privileged and it is immaterial whether the lawyer is an unwitting dupe or knowing participant.

On two occasions, the Supreme Court of Canada has quoted with approval[15] the nineteenth-century English case of *Queen v. Cox*,[16] which establishes the common law exception to the privilege based on intended criminal or fraudulent conduct by the client:

> In order that the privilege may apply there must be both professional confidence and professional employment, but if the client has a criminal object in view ... one of these elements must necessarily be absent. The client must either conspire with his solicitor or deceive him. If his criminal object is avowed, the client does not consult his adviser professionally, because it cannot be the solicitor's business to further any criminal object. If the client does not avow his object he reposes no confidence, for the state of facts, which is

the foundation of the supposed confidence, does not exist. The solicitor's advice is obtained by fraud.

In most of the reported cases, the criminal purposes exception has been applied to individual clients. As a matter of principle, it should also be extended to the company client. This exception to the privilege, however, is difficult to apply to the types of cases that are most likely to emerge inside a company. It is unlikely, for example, that an officer, director, or employee will confide in the company lawyers about his/her intent to murder his/her spouse or a troublesome minority shareholder. It is more likely, given the complex web of laws and regulations governing the company, that the proposed action will cause an infraction of one of many hundreds of laws and regulations governing the company and its business.

As a result, the exception, in the company context, carries the possibility of making substantial inroads in the privilege. The policy question is raised as to how wide the courts are willing to draw the zone of silence over the company's affairs. The issue of fraud, in light of the complexities of the common law's vague definition, makes it uncertain in many cases whether a course of action suggested by the client will be subsequently held to be fraudulent by a court. The uncertainty of applying these exceptions in the company context leads to a case-by-case approach rather than a rigid doctrinal one.

Loyalty Owed to the Client

The client's communication is encouraged by a rule that guarantees the lawyer's loyalty to the client. The confidentiality rule arose out of the adversary system. The purpose of the rule was that a lawyer, in order to conduct the case effectively, had to have access to all of the client's information. If the client thought that the lawyer would testify against him/her, or provide certain sensitive information to others, then the client would be inhibited from disclosing all the relevant information, and the administration of justice would suffer.

EVIDENTIAL NATURE OF THE RULE
It has been said that the lawyer's duty not to disclose the client's confidences is both an ethical duty and an evidentiary privilege.[17] The evidentiary privilege — which prevented an opponent from requiring the other side's lawyer to testify against his/her own client — by its very nature, arises in the limited context of litigation. The ethical duty, on the other hand, is of a wider scope governing the bounds of the professional services rendered by a company lawyer or outside counsel retained by the company.

THE COMMON LAW RULE

Originally, in the evidential context, the privilege was seen as a rule protecting a lawyer's loyalty to the client. The lawyer could not be compelled to testify against the client. Today, the privilege is viewed as belonging to the client. The client can waive the privilege and allow the lawyer to testify. In the Supreme Court of Canada case of *Solosky v. The Queen*,[18] Dickson, J. approved the formulation of the common law rule contained in the following passage from Wigmore:[19] "i) Where legal advice of any kind is sought ii) from a professional legal adviser in his capacity as such, iii) the communications relating to that purpose, iv) made in confidence v) by the client, vi) are at his instance permanently protected vii) from disclosure by himself or by the legal adviser viii) except where the protection be waived."

The common law rule appears straightforward until certain questions are raised within the corporate setting. For instance, Wigmore's definition depends upon a certain understanding as to the identity of the client. Does the privilege extend to members of the board of directors, shareholders, senior management, and company employees? There has been considerable litigation on the definition of "client" when a company is involved.

Another problem is the capacity in which the company lawyer received the communication. Did he/she receive the information in his/her capacity as "lawyer" or was he/she acting in some other capacity, such as secretary of the company? Clearly, the privilege only applies where the lawyer has received the communication in his/her capacity as a lawyer, but it may be a complicated question of fact as to whether he/she was acting in that capacity at the time he/she received the communication.

THE ETHICAL BASIS OF THE RULE

The evidentiary privilege assumes that litigation is anticipated or in progress. Thus, confidential communications that are not connected with anticipated litigation would not be governed by the evidential privilege. Confidentiality, however, is not limited to the evidentiary privilege. It is an ethical duty that restricts a lawyer from disclosing the client's confidence. The ethical duty protects the client against the disclosure of information by the lawyer of information that might be embarrassing or detrimental.

REASONS TO SUPPORT A STRONG RULE

There are three arguments to support a strong confidentiality rule that ensures that the client's communications remain secret. First, to competently advise the client on the possible legal options or consequences, the lawyer must have all the facts before him/her. Second, the privileged communications may have a positive effect on law enforcement. Without such protection, the company may not risk advising its lawyer but proceed on a course of action that is illegal. There is an assumption, largely unproved, that the privilege will enable the company to be the internal law enforcement officer that will ensure that laws are complied with. Third, the privilege is rooted in the traditional role performed by lawyers in providing legal services for their clients. Under this view, the lawyer is not a quasi-public servant whose role is to dictate compliance of the law and to blow the whistle when the law is breached.[20]

DIFFICULTY IN APPLYING THE RULE

The rules of professional responsibility are as vague as are the responsibilities of the lawyer who must determine whether the privilege governs a particular communication from a client. As one commentator has stated: "The corporate lawyer must choose between violating the law and facing protential civil and criminal liability or disobeying a disciplinary rule and facing disbarment or a damage suit by his client."[21] The problem becomes acute once the potential range of issues faced by a company lawyer is understood. Rinehart Ltd. operates in a highly regulatory environment in Canada and elsewhere. There are complex laws governing employment practices, restricting discriminatory hiring policies; there are labour laws restricting conditions and terms of employment; there are other laws respecting restrictive trade practices, securities regulations, and tax laws.

Illustration (of the rule in practice)   Ms. Bach is working in her office when she is approached by one of the senior engineers in the Research and Development Department of Rinehart Ltd. After closing the door, Jack McKay, the senior engineer, asks if he can speak to Ms. Bach in confidence about a matter of some importance. The following conversation takes place.

McKay: Julia, I'm worried about the navigational computer program that we've sold to Air Canada.
Bach: Tom Millar in marketing said it's one our best programs.
McKay: Marketing has been pushing us to get the program on line. But it's not ready.
Bach: What do you mean, 'not ready'?
McKay: There's a bug in the night-landing protocol.
Bach: You mean it's not safe?
McKay: I tried to tell Tom.
Bach: Forget Tom. You should have gone to Faber directly.
McKay: I have.
Bach: Exactly what happens with the bug?
McKay: There's a one in fifty chance that the plane will undershoot the runway. The pilot might be out as much as 150 m.

On Thursday morning, Ms. Bach drops into to see Mr. Faber, the President of Rinehart Ltd. Ms. Bach explains that McKay has expressed concern about the navigational landing program. Faber replies that he has discussed the matter with two other engineers in Research and Development, and that they have assured him that the program has been debugged. Ms. Bach insists that there should be a full meeting of the Board of Directors to consider all of the evidence from R&D, and then a decision made as to whether to recall the program from the market. On Friday, a meeting is held and the evidence reviewed. The Board backs Faber and the navigational landing computer program is left on the market.

Two months later, an Air Canada flight crashes in Toronto killing 150 passengers. It was a night landing. The Civil Aviation Board investigation determines that the pilot had undershot the runway by nearly 100 m. The final report places the fault on pilot error and the accident file is closed. The ill-fated flight was equipped with the Rinehart Navigational landing program.

Relatives and friends of the dead pilot contend that the Civil Aviation Board report is wrong on the cause of the crash. They demonstrate that the dead pilot was a seasoned pilot and that it was unlikely that he would have made such a basic error in judgment. A lawyer representing the pilot's estate brings a civil action against Air Canada and Rinehart Software Ltd. on the basis that the pilot's death was caused by the negligent manufacture of the navigational landing program. There is no clear-cut answer as to the scope of confidentiality rule to this case.

Inadvertent Disclosure of Confidential Communications

A company lawyer, or outside counsel, has an obligation to ensure that matters disclosed by the client in confidence are not revealed to third parties. One of the reasons that the confidence is made to the lawyer is to keep the communication a secret. How long does the obligation imposed on the lawyer last? In *Ott v. Fleishman*,[22] the answer provided was that "[T]he requirement of confidentiality continues indefinitely, even though the solicitor and client relationship may have terminated." Nonetheless, a lawyer may inadvertently disclose the communication to another and, as a consequence, damage may result to the client.

Illustration Because of the pressure of her work load, Ms. Bach retains outside counsel, Dobbs and Smith Company, to negotiate the purchase of the software program "Corporate Tax Adviser". The program has been created by an engineer with an accounting background. Edwin Reynolds, the engineer, first approaches Ms. Bach about the software program in March. The Research and Development Department confirms the reliability and accuracy of the program in early April. By mid-April, the Marketing Department, in a written memorandum, concludes from its market surveys that such a program could gross $75 000 a year for approximately five years.

Howard Dobbs, a senior partner at Dobbs and Smith Company, assigns the file to an associate lawyer, Steve West. Over coffee, West discusses the file generally with another associate, James Elliot. Several days later, Mr. Elliot has a meeting with one of the firm's large clients represented by John Railton. Mr. Railton mentions that his accounting firm is looking forward to someone inventing a company tax adviser. It is something that accounting firms would be able to use. Mr. Elliot says that one of his firm's clients is about to bring out such a program. Mr. Railton asks who has invented the program. Mr. Elliot replies that the inventor is an engineer named Reynolds.

Several days later, Steve West calls Reynolds to come in and sign the licence agreement to sell his software to Rinehart Ltd. Mr. Reynolds says he is no longer interested in selling. Later, Ms. Bach learns that Reynolds has been contacted by Mr. Railton and that they have formed a company to promote the software package. Through further investigation, Ms. Bach discovers what has transpired between Mr. Elliot and Mr. Railton.

Does Rinehart Ltd. have an action against Dobbs and Smith Company for the loss of the contract with Mr. Reynolds?

In *Rademaker, Macdougall and Company v. Number Ten Holdings Ltd.*,[23] on a similar fact pattern, the court held that the law firm had failed to safeguard the client's secrets, and that the unauthorized disclosure of confidential information was a breach of the solicitor-client contract.

Shareholder Derivative Actions

When a shareholder claims that officers or directors of the company have committed a misdeed, can the privilege be successfully asserted by the officers or directors to prevent the shareholders from obtaining evidence of communication given to the company lawyer? The general rule is that, in the event of a lawsuit by a shareholder (or shareholders) based on allegations of fraud or misconduct carried out to the detriment of the company, then the court has the discretion to release the privileged communication to the shareholders. In *Milic v. Bagby*,[24] the court applied the leading English authorities:

> The first of these is *Gouraud v. Edison Gower Bell Telephone Co. of Europe*.[25] That was an action brought by a shareholder of the defendant corporation for an injunction to restrain it and another corporation from acting upon a certain agreement made between the defendant companies, it being the allegation of the plaintiff that

the agreement was made in fraud of the rights of himself and other dissenting shareholders. The plaintiff wished to inspect certain communications between the defendant and its solicitors and this was resisted upon the ground of solicitor-client privilege. It was found as a fact by Chitty J. that the directors of the defendant, when obtaining professional advice, were acting on behalf of the company as a whole and made payments out of the funds of the company for the communications alleged to be privileged. In ordering the communications to be produced, His Lordship referred at p. 499 to:

> "[T]he general principle that obtains in partnership actions, and also in actions by a *cestui que trust* against a trustee — namely, that a party cannot resist production of documents which have been obtained by means of payments from the monies belonging to the party applying for their production. I think that that is the general principle and one which, to my mind, applies as between a shareholder and the directors who manage his property, when the documents are paid for out of his property."

Problems for Discussion

1. On the question of damages, would the *Rademaker* case be distinguishable if the negotiations between engineer and Rinehart Ltd. had not been on the verge of breaking down over the issue of royalty payments?

2. Is Mr. Railton personally liable for using this confidential information?

3. For assessing damages against the law firm, is Rinehart Ltd. entitled to recover the $75 000 × 5 as projected by its marketing department? If not, what is the appropriate amount of damages for the court to award?

4. The plaintiff corporation brings an action against a former director to recover monies that he allegedly has misappropriated. The former director counterclaims, alleging that the resolution authorizing the litigation is invalid. The corporation obtains a legal opinion from its lawyer after the lawsuit is filed. The former director, relying on *Gouraud v. Edison Gower Bell Telephone Co. of Europe*, demands that the corporation reveal the legal opinion to him. The company claims the privilege. What is the appropriate result in this case? See *Woodhouse & Co. v. Woodhouse* (1914), 30 T.L.R. 599 (C.A.).

5. Is Ms. Bach's obligation in this case to maintain the confidence or to disclose the communication to the relevant third parties?

6. What, if any, is the potential civil or criminal liability against Ms. Bach if she fails to disclose the communication?

7. Consider the following quote: "When there is relatively little involvement of the adviser in an improper activity, either because the involvement is slight or the impropriety is unclear, the social harm is not perceived as substantial, the adviser should be permitted to resign, but only if it does not operate to the disadvantage of the client. As the involvement and the perceived social harm become greater, withdrawal should become mandatory. When the involvement is substantial and the social harm grave, an obligation of public disclosure, abandoning confidentiality, might properly be imposed." Lorne, "The Corporate and Securities Advisor, The Public Interest, and Professional Ethics," (1978) 76 Mich.L.Rev. 425, 490. Do you agree?

8. One standard adopted by a New York Court in *People v. Belge*, (1975) 50 A.D.(2d) 1088, 376 N.Y.S.(2d), 771, 772, aff'd (1976) 41 N.Y.(2d) 60, 390 N.Y.S.(2d) 867, provides: "We believe that an attorney must protect his client's interests, but also must observe basic human standards of decency, having due regard to the need that the legal system accord justice to the interest of society and its individual members." Is the human decency standard a useful guideline?

9. The fact pattern in the illustration was inspired by Judge Ferren, who concluded that emphasizing disclosure may be misplaced and, instead, the best solution lies in the threat of withdrawal by the company lawyer. "The lawyer's threat of withdrawal from representation, when permitted or required by the Code, is a powerful weapon against a client whose conduct appears to be irresponsible, if not illegal. If every lawyer were to take that prerogative seriously no greater sanction would be necessary" Ferren, "The Corporate Lawyer's Obligation to the Public Interest," (1978) 33 Bus.Law 1253, 1269. Do you agree with this point of view?

Chapter 26 Notes

1. (1982) 1 S.C.R. 860, 893.
2. See *Susan Hosiery Ltd. v. Minister of National Revenue*, (1969) 2 Ex. C.R. 27, at 33; and *Dusik v. Newton*, (1983) 1 D.L.R. (4th) 568 (B.C.C.A.).
3. *Supra*, note 1, p. 880.
4. See *Ott v. Fleishman*, (1983) 22 B.L.R. 57, 59 (B.C.S.C.).
5. (1975) 55 D.L.R.(3d) 713, 721-22 (Fed.C.A.).
6. *Supra*, note 4, p. 60.
7. See *Philadelphia v. Westinghouse*, 210 F.Supp. 483, 485 (E.D. Pa. 1962) per Judge Kirkpatrick.
8. See *Diversified Industries v. Meredith*, 572 F.2d 596 (8th Cir. 1977).
9. See *Upjohn v. United States*, 449 U.S. 383 (1981).
10. See J. Gergacz, "Attorney-Corporate Client Privilege," (1982) 37 *Bus.Law.* p. 491.

11. *Supra*, note 9.
12. See M. Freedman, *Lawyers' Ethics in an Adversary System*, 27-42 (1975).
13. See *Model Rules, Comment to Rule* 1.6, p. 39.
14. (1980) 105 D.L.R.(3d) 745, 757 (S.C.C.).
15. See *Solosky v. The Queen*, Ibid.; and *Descoteaux v. Mierzwinski, supra*, note 1,
    p. 881.
16. (1884) 14 Q.B. 153, 168.
17. Burke, "The Duty of Confidentially and Disclosing Corporate Misconduct," (1981) 36 *Bus.Law.* 239, 241.
18. *Supra*, note 14, p. 756.
19. Wigmore, *Evidence par. 2292* (McNaughton Rev. 1961).
20. See "Redlich, Lawyers, the Temple, and the Marketplace," (1975) 30 *Bus.Law.* 65, 72; and Cooney, "The Registration Process: The Role of the Lawyer in Disclosure," (1978) 33 *Bus.Law.* 1329, 1337.
21. *Supra*, note 17, p. 255.
22. *Supra*, note 4, p. 60.
23. (1983) 47 B.C.L.R. 376 (B.C.S.C.).
24. (1982) 30 C.P.C. 66, 70-71 (Ont.S.C.).
25. (1888), 57 L.J. Ch. 498.

27 CONFLICT OF INTEREST

Confidence and Secrets

The right of confidentiality is an important consideration when a lawyer represents an opponent of an existing or former client. The client is encouraged to make a full and complete disclosure of information to the lawyer. Confidentiality ensures that confidences and secrets will not be transmitted by the lawyer to a third party without the client's consent. A conflict of interest is often directly defined by the pivotal question as

FIGURE 27.1 **MEANS OF RESOLVING CONFLICTS**

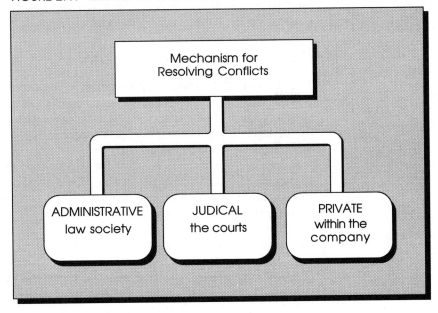

Mechanism for Resolving Conflicts

| ADMINISTRATIVE law society | JUDICAL the courts | PRIVATE within the company |

to whether the lawyer has obtained confidential information from a former client and later acts against that client.

At the bottom of the problem is an ethical consideration. The Law Society of Upper Canada Rules of Conduct and Commentaries provides:

> A lawyer who has acted for a client in a matter should not thereafter act against him (or against persons who were involved in or associated with him in that matter) in the same or any related matter, or when he has obtained confidential information from the other party in the course of performing against a former client in a fresh and independent matter wholly unrelated to any work he has previously done for that person and where such confidential information is irrelevant to that matter.[1]

The essence of the above Ontario position is directly paralleled in the Canadian Bar Association Code of Professional Responsibility, Rule 11. The Code provision has been considered and applied by the Canadian courts in resolving a disqualification motion based on the conflict of interest.[2]

The conflict of interest problem may be the issue in a disciplinary proceeding against the offending lawyer, or alternatively, may arise before the courts on a motion by the client to disqualify his/her former lawyer or law firm from representing an opponent in a lawsuit. In each forum, the resolution of the proceeding against the lawyer will turn on the factual determination of the connection, if any, between the confidential communications with the former client and the current matter adversely pursued by the lawyer against the former client.

Resolution of Conflict Issues

The context of the conflicts problem is an important consideration. In general, there are three spheres in which conflicts of interest are resolved: i) by a judge; ii) by benchers sitting as a disciplinary committee; and iii) by the company lawyer or outside counsel in the day-to-day representation of the corporate client.

It does not, however, necessarily follow that the same test or standard applies equally to a disciplinary hearing based on a breach of professional responsibility and to a judicial hearing based on disqualifying a lawyer from representing a party in that case.

LAW SOCIETY RESOLUTION OF MISCONDUCT CASE

Where a lawyer faces possible suspension or disbarment on the grounds of conflict of interest, the case must be established by convincing evidence.[3] The standard applied to determine whether the lawyer has committed professional misconduct is: has he/she "... done something with regard to which would be reasonably regarded as disgraceful or dishonourable by his professional brethren of good repute and competency."[4]

The same observation applies to the company lawyer who must decide for himself whether a conflict has, or is likely to, emerge from a particular course of action or transaction.

JUDICIAL RESOLUTION OF CONFLICTS

One Canadian court has phrased the question as: "How can they [the clients] have confidence in a just result when their former solicitor acts for the other side in a matter where he advised both parties?"[5] The leading English case establishing the traditional test for one line of Canadian authority is *Rakusen v. Ellis, Munday & Clarke*:

> Solicitors have great privileges and they have corresponding duties. Of their privileges, a better instance cannot be furnished than the absolute privilege which is conferred on them in the matter of giving evidence in the matter of, say, communications which they may make to their clients, or their clients may make to them. We expect, and, indeed, we exact from solicitors, who are officers of the court, a higher standard of conduct than we can enforce against those who are not our own officers. [T]here is a general principle that a solicitor who has acted in a particular matter, whether before or after litigation has commenced, cannot act for the opposite party in the same matter under any circumstances.... [W]e must treat each of these cases, not as a matter of form, not as a matter to be decided upon the mere proof of a former solicitor acting for a client, but as a matter of substance. We must come to a conclusion before we allow any special jurisdiction over solicitors to be invoked, and we must be satisfied that there is real mischief and real prejudice which in all human probability will result if the solicitor is allowed to act.[6]

There is a concern that in allowing a lawyer to act for an opponent against a former client, who has disclosed confidential information, will provide him/her with "an undue advantage".[7] There is, however, no absolute presumption that the client has disclosed confidential information that is connected with the particular subject matter of the former client's opponent. The *Rakusen* case provides the court with broad discretion, in a case-by-case approach, in deciding whether to disqualify a lawyer on the basis of a former client's motion. The linchpin of the motion to disqualify rests upon showing the *probability* of mischief resulting from the lawyer's representation of a client's opponent. The modern trend in

Canadian law has been to apply the conflict of interest rule to disqualify a lawyer where there is any *possibility* of prejudice toward a former client.[8]

Depending on whether probability or possibility of prejudice is applied as the guiding test, the court defines the degree of danger that the former lawyer will abuse the professional confidence that he/she has obtained from the client in the current matter. In the balance is the former client's continuing right to protect his/her confidences and secrets disclosed to his/her lawyer. Against this interest is the right of the lawyer to freely practice his/her profession and the right of the public to choose the lawyer of their choice.

The highest protection of the former client lies in the possibility test. Conversely, the confidentiality of communications interest is diminished in favour of other interest when the probability test is applied. The modern Canadian trend is also reflected in the case law in the United States. In *Westinghouse Electric Corp. v. Gulf Oil Corp.*, the court observed that: "[D]oubts as to the existence of an asserted conflict of interest should be resolved in favor of disqualification."[9]

INTERNAL RESOLUTION OF CONFLICTS BY THE COMPANY LAWYER

For inside counsel, such as Ms. Bach, most conflict of interest problems will rarely be resolved by a court, or indeed, by a disciplinary committee of the Law Society. The very nature of her client multiplies the potential for a conflict of interest. Although she is employed by Rinehart Ltd. and owes her allegiance to the company, she may be called upon to advise a stockholder, director, officer, or employee connected with the company. The interest of persons with such status within the company may not always coincide with that of the company. To the extent that there are differing interests if a conflict arises, inside counsel must remember that the company is the client. Practically, this may mean that confidences confided by an officer of the company will be disclosed by the in-house lawyer to the company client, e.g., to the board of directors.

Loyalty and Duty

The preservation of confidences and secrets is closely related to the more general principle of law governing fiduciary relationships. The lawyer, as a fiduciary, has a duty of absolute loyalty and fidelity.[10] The lawyer-client relationship is not treated as an arms-length relationship between the parties. The model applied is more akin to the trustee-beneficiary relationship created by the Chancery courts exercising equitable jurisdiction.

In another context, Lord Denning, in *Seager v. Copydex Ltd.*, observed that:

The law on this subject . . . depends on the broad principle of equity that he who has received information in confidence shall not take unfair advantage of it. He must not make use of it to the prejudice of him who gave it without obtaining his consent.[11]

This body of equitable principles placed a high duty on the fiduciary to act solely for the benefit of the beneficiary and prohibited the fiduciary from obtaining any personal gain or taking any advantage from the relationship. Simply stated, the fiduciary was precluded from advancing his/ her interest against those of the beneficiary. These equitable principles have been incorporated into conflict of interest cases. Thus, in *Lapierre v. Young*,[12] the following formulation was approved:

> In equity the relationship of solicitor and client is recognized as a fiduciary relationship and carries with it the obligations on the solicitor's part to act with strict fairness and openness towards his client; for failure to fulfil this obligation a solicitor will be liable to make compensation with respect of any resulting loss to his client, though the circumstances are not such as would sustain an action for deceit at common law.

With this approach, the lawyer's relationship with the client is viewed as akin to a trustee's relationship with the beneficiary of a trust.[13] Canadian law has long recognized the importance of the fiduciary relationship and, by virtue of this relationship, has been zealous in safeguarding the "beneficiary" from any conflict of interest that might taint the absolute fidelity and loyalty the trustee is required to possess in carrying out his/her responsibility.[14] The problem of divided loyalty looms large in a number of the conflict cases. "[I]t is clear that the solicitor cannot act on both sides and all the more so when there is superadded to the divided loyalty owed to the two clients adverse in interest, the personal financial interest of the solicitor's senior partner."[15] It is likely that this approach will continue to play an important role in defining conflict of interest in the lawyer-client relationship.

The Appearance of Impropriety

The appearance of impropriety is an important public policy consideration in monitoring the conduct of lawyers in their relationship with clients or former clients. The lawyer who represents a client in a lawsuit against an existing client places the entire judicial system in potential harm. The faith in the integrity and justice of the system depends on an independent judiciary and on lawyers, as officers of the court, discharging their duties with the utmost propriety.

Recent Canadian decisions have emphasized that: "A lawyer should avoid even the appearance of professional impropriety."[16] The use of this rationale in conflict of interest cases is often associated with "any possibility" test of conflicts. Although the previous grounds concentrate on the underlying basis of the lawyer-client relationship, the appearance of impropriety creates an additional interest in the conflict of interest cases.

The concern of the court has been expressed as ensuring "that justice be seen to be done."[17] This interest has strong public policy overtones: " . . . the principles involved herein are designed not only to protect the interests of the individual clients but they also protect the public confidence in the administration of justice."[18]

Freedom of Client Choice

A countervailing policy argument in a conflict of interest case is that the law should facilitate the freedom of clients to retain the lawyer or law firm of their choice. Thus, to disqualify the lawyer or his/her firm destroys a basic right to be represented by the counsel of one's choice. This defence by a lawyer to a disqualification motion appears to rise or fall on the courts view as to whether the broader or stricter test of confidential communications applies. Thus, in *MTS International Services v. Warnat Corp.*,[19] the court, having applied the broader test of "any possibility" of conflict, dismissed the freedom of choice argument. Conversely, the less strict test of "probability" of conflict creates a greater chance that the court will find that the freedom of choice has paramount importance.

American courts have recognized the consequences of disqualification for the client who must seek a new lawyer. Such a client suffers the loss of time, money, and the benefit of its long-time counsel's specialized knowledge of its operations. The ultimate balance is between ensuring reasonable access to legal services without damaging the nature of the relationship that the common law has traditionally applied between a lawyer and client.[20]

Types of Conflicts of Interest

Between the Client and Lawyer

A common type of conflict of interest occurs where the lawyer has financial, business, or personal interest in the subject matter that he/she is handling for a client. "The general law is absolutely and unmistakenly clear that a lawyer must not permit himself to function in an undisclosed conflict of interest. Whenever such a conflict arises the solicitor must either make a full disclosure or withdraw."[21] The conflict between the client and lawyer arose in the *Henfrey*[22] case, when the law firm applied sale proceeds received on behalf of its client to outstanding legal fees. The client had instructed the law firm to deposit the funds in a bank account. The court ordered the law firm to repay the money.

FIGURE 27.2 **CLASSES OF CONFLICT OF INTEREST**

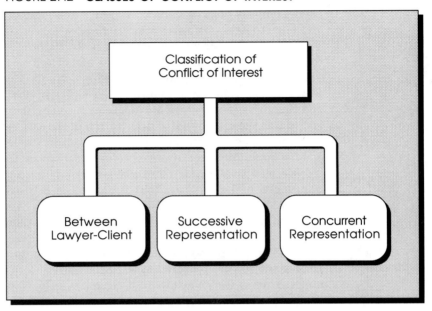

Trouble usually follows when a lawyer becomes financially involved in the business affairs of the client. A heavy onus is placed upon the lawyer, by virtue of his/her having acquired special knowledge from the client, of making a full and proper disclosure of any transaction between himself/herself and the client.[23] Although requiring the client to obtain independent legal advice is not an absolute rule, it is recognized that this course will rebut the presumption that the transaction is invalid. Where the lawyer has placed himself/herself in a conflict and obtained a benefit, then evidence of good faith or the financial inability of the client will not provide the lawyer with a defence in a subsequent action against him/her by the client. Nothing short of consent by the client and full disclosure will save the transaction.[24]

In *MacDonald v. Lockhart*,[25] a lawyer was held liable to account to his client for benefits arising from a series of loans that he advanced in connection with the reorganization of his client's businesses. The personal relationship of the lawyer to one of several business partners may also result in a conflict of interest. Where the lawyer's judgment is clouded by friendship, financial gain, or other undisclosed associations, there is greater likelihood that he/she will fail to warn the client of the risk involved in a course of action.

Another example is found in *MacCulloch's Estate v. Corbett*[26], where a professional negligence action was brought against a solicitor who had been retained by a number of people desiring to incorporate a new company. The lawyer failed to discharge her duties to file the required list of company officers, statutory report, and notices of registered office, and failed to issue qualifying shares to those who were to act as directors. When a dispute erupted between one of the parties and the others, she transferred control of the company to him. The court concluded that: "The respondent allowed her relationship with Mr. Murphy [the person to whom she transferred control] to completely obscure her solicitor and client relationship with Mr. MacLennan and his fellow incorporators, and in this she committed a clear breach of duty to the appellants."[27]

A joint policy statement between the British Columbia Law Society and the Superintendent of Brokers (June 1983) specifically requires disclosure by a lawyer of any material beneficial interest in the securities or property of the company held by him/her in all disclosure documents submitted for filing by or on behalf of the company. Also to be disclosed is information that the lawyer or a partner is a director or senior officer in the company.

The intent of the policy statement is to require the lawyer primarily responsible for the preparation of or for advice to the company or an underwriter of the company to disclose his/her personal interest in the company. The policy statement does not prohibit such a lawyer from acting on behalf of the company in the preparation or filing of a prospectus, a statement of material facts, a take-over circular, a director's circular, or an information circular respecting merger. To do so would effectively exclude in-house counsel from performing securities work for the company. Instead, those who rely upon these disclosure documents are able to judge for themselves that the lawyer who prepared or filed them has a personal interest in advancing the financial position of the client.

Successive Representation

The classic conflict of interest case arises where a lawyer represents a party in a lawsuit against a former client, and the current litigation is substantially related to matters in which the lawyer previously represented the former client. It does not follow, however, that the lawyer can never represent a party who presses an adverse claimant against a former client. The major concern is that the lawyer may have acquired confidential information from the former client that may be used to advance the cause of the new client and, correspondingly, that may operate to the prejudice of the former client.

The recurring theme in the successive representation cases is the danger of confidential information being used by the lawyer against a former client. It is not enough merely to establish that the lawyer-client relationship existed. The onus is on the former client to establish "that there is a genuine threat that confidences revealed to his former counsel will be divulged to his present adversary."[28] The client is not required to be specific about the precise confidence disclosed to disqualify the former lawyer. The genuine threat or probability of mischief can be established by proving that the present and prior representations are substantially related. Once that is done it is presumed that confidential information was disclosed to the former counsel in the earlier representation.

The nature of the prior relationship is one of some importance. Where the former lawyer was general counsel and occupied a pervasive, daily relationship with the client over a lengthy period of time, it is more likely that disqualification of former counsel will succeed.[29] A former in-house lawyer who, while engaged by the company, assisted in the drafting of a share option purchase agreement will be later disqualified from representing the company officer against the company in an action based on the agreement.

One American court[30] has gone a step further and disqualified a law firm which had consulted with the former company lawyer on behalf of its client, a former officer with the same company.

In *Bregman*,[31] the former in-house lawyer had a significant connection in his legal capacity in drafting the agreement that was the subject of the litigation. It was irrelevant that any of the confidences that the former in-house lawyer knew were also known by the former officer. Although the law firm retained by the former officer had no connection with the company, the court felt compelled to disqualify them on the grounds that:

> It may be presumed that Randall [former in-house counsel] possessed confidence of his client ORG, and the possibility that breach of these confidences was committed by Randall is sufficient to make disqualification a necessary and desirable remedy 'to enforce the lawyer's duty of absolute fidelity and to guard against the danger of inadvertent use of confidential information.'[32]

Concurrent Representation

A conflict of interest will arise in circumstances of simultaneous representation of more than one party with potentially adverse interests in the same transaction. The courts apply a more stringent rule of prohibition in the concurrent representation cases. Such adverse representation is *prima facie* improper and will result in a breach of the lawyer's fiduciary relationship to the clients. For the lawyer to act on both sides will divide his/her absolute obligation of loyalty owed to each client. Although, in a real estate transaction, it is not professional misconduct in British Columbia for a lawyer to represent both parties to the transaction as long as he/she obtains both parties' consent and advises them that in the event of a conflict he/she will discontinue his/her representation of both parties.[33]

In many cases, it will be virtually impossible for the lawyer to prove that his/her representation of one party did not divide his/her loyalty to the other. There is the danger of the court finding that the lawyer's allegiance lay with one client over another. Where one of the parties is inexperienced and unsophisticated, the lawyer in such circumstances carries a heavy burden of showing that he/she acted with strict fairness and openness toward the client.

The burden of proof placed on the lawyer is high in all such cases. In *Davey v. Woolley*, Wilson J.A. observed:

> the solicitor unquestionably assumes a dual role at his own risk, the onus being on him in any lawsuit that ensues to establish that the client has had the 'best professional assistance which, if he had been engaged in a transaction with a third party, he could possibly have afforded.'[34]

The concurrent representation may also adversely affect the enforceability of the transaction by one of the parties. Thus, in *Mastercraft Construction Corp. Ltd. v. Baker*,[35] the lawyer was agent and solicitor for the company selling land and also for the purchasers who desired to buy the land. The lawyer failed to advise the purchasers of the advisability of inserting a condition in their offer concerning financing. He was aware of the purchasers' financing problem and still did not advise them adequately.

The conflict is reasonably clear. The lawyer had confidential information about the financial condition of the purchasers and had an obligation to provide his other client, the vendor, an offer without any conditions attached. Though the lawyer was not a party to the ultimate lawsuit, the court made it clear that had he been sued, he would have been liable to the purchasers. The court granted the purchasers the right to the dismissal of the vendor's damage action based on breach of contract. The contract was held null and void.

Internal Representation

Conflict of interest arises for the in-house and outside company lawyer by virtue of the very nature of a company. Who does the lawyer represent? What is the nature of his/her representation? The better rule is that the company lawyer does not represent any one group within the company but the entity as a whole. Further, it has been suggested, that "Indeed, the touchstone for determining the entity interests must be the aggregate interests of the shareholders."[36] A conflict arises when the interest of management no longer advances the interest of the shareholders.

One illustration of the problem arises when a company official makes incriminating statements and expects them to be kept confidential by the company's lawyer. The officer may have wrongfully appropriated a corporate opportunity, paid a bribe to another for a business contract, or violated a law that might be imputed to the company. A conflict arises when the officer divulges his/her conduct or proposed conduct to the company lawyer. The client is the company and not the officer. Thus, the communication from the officer would not be kept confidential, but would be reported to the board of directors. This follows because the privilege belongs to the company and not the officer.

In practice, the problem arises because of the close working relationship often enjoyed between the company lawyer and the executive officers of the company. An assumption is wrongly made that the officer's communication will be kept confidential by the company lawyer. One commentator has observed that:

> It is fundamentally unfair for an official to be lulled into a sense of false confidence that a corporate attorney is acting as his *personal* counsel when, in fact, that attorney may deliver incriminating information to the corporate management, board of directors, or to a government agency for prosecution.[37]

The alternatives in such circumstances place the company lawyer in a dilemma. If he/she treats the officer as the client, the lawyer will be in a conflict of interest within the lawyer-client relationship with the company. On the other hand, advising the officer that any incriminating information will be passed on to management, to the board of directors, or to law enforcement agencies will probably result in the officer not making the disclosure and making it more difficult for the lawyer to obtain important facts to protect the interest of the company. The best course of action is for the company lawyer to refuse any temptation to represent both the officer and the company. The officer should be advised that he/she should retain independent counsel so that any disclosures of a confidential nature will be kept secret.

On the question of whether the company lawyer should disclose any corporate wrongdoing by an officer to the shareholders, there is no clear answer. A case-by-case approach, based on the nature of the risk of disclosure to a potentially large group of shareholders, has been suggested.

Disqualification of a Lawyer

A successful disqualification action will rest on the following factors: i) that the client's former lawyer represents his/her adversary; ii) that the present lawsuit concerns matters in which the lawyer previously represented his/her former client; and iii) that the previous matters are "substantially related" to the matters embraced in the present lawsuit.

Once these factors are proved by the former client, there is a presumption that confidential information was disclosed during the previous representation.

THE SUBSTANTIALLY RELATED TEST

The substantially related test is inextricably linked to the confidential information that the former lawyer obtained in the prior representation and that may be used for the benefit of his/her former client's opponent in the current representation. The use of "possibility" as opposed to "probability of mischief and prejudice" reflects the judicial attitude toward the degree of protection required to prevent the transmission of such information through the lawyer to the opponent of his/her former client.

Illustration (of a disqualification case)   The wholly owned subsidiary of Rinehart Ltd. in Ontario, QueTech Ltd., uses the legal services of Mr. Lloyd from 1975 to 1982. In 1982, Ms. Bach decides to retain the legal services of another Toronto law firm to handle certain legal problems of QueTech Ltd. During the seven years that QueTech Ltd. uses the services of Mr. Lloyd, there is never a formal retainer and all the work is done on a file-by-file basis. The legal work performed by Mr. Lloyd includes rendering legal advice on certain personnel issues, including collection of moving expenses, garnishee of wages of a company employee, and severance pay owing to an officer.

In 1983, Mr. Lloyd brings a wrongful dismissal action on behalf of a former employee of QueTech Ltd. against the company. Ms. Bach decides to instruct local counsel in Toronto to file a motion to disqualify Mr. Lloyd from the lawsuit. The company's position is that Mr. Lloyd is privy to much information respecting the company's policy concerning the firing and dismissal of employees, and that the information is of a confidential nature. Query: Will QueTech Ltd. succeed in disqualifying Mr. Lloyd from the wrongful dismissal case?

In *Schmeichel v. Saskatchewan Mining Development Corporation*,[38] where the facts were identical to those above, the court held that the company had not established a *prima facie* case. The evidence was in conflict. The company asserted that its former lawyer had obtained a great deal of information about the company's policies concerning dismissal of employees. Its former lawyer, however, asserted that his legal advice concerning personnel matters was minimal. There was no evidence that the former lawyer had rendered legal advice to the company concerning wrongful dismissal in general or in this particular case.

The contention by the company that a possible mischief might result if the lawyer was allowed to represent its opponent in the wrongful dismissal case was dismissed. Obtaining confidential information in the prior representation did not exclude the former lawyer from representing an opponent in a matter unrelated to the previous representation. Conversely, if Mr. Lloyd had originally been asked by the company to provide an opinion on the dismissal of its employee, and subsequently the lawyer had sought to represent that employee in a wrongful dismissal action against the company, it is likely that disqualification would have resulted.

Problems for Discussion

1. What is the relationship between the conflict of interest rules and the client's right to confidentiality of communications?

2. Should the Canadian courts adopt a strict or a broad test when deciding a disqualification case?

3. Is a different standard applied in a disciplinary proceeding against a lawyer alleged to have committed professional misconduct because of a conflict of interest?

4. What risk does a company officer or employee undertake by confiding in the in-house lawyer about a potentially wrongful course of action?

5. How should the in-house lawyer resolve conflicts among the individual participants within the company?

6. Should a distinction be drawn, for purposes of disqualification, between a former in-house lawyer who worked inside a company for a substantial length of time and outside counsel who provided work on a case-by-case basis over the same period of time? See *Global Van Lines, Inc. v. Superior Court*, 144 Cal.App.(3d) 483, 192 Cal.Rptr. 609 (1983). Note that in the *Global* case, the former in-house counsel had no personal knowledge from his prior representation concerning the present suit that he commenced against his former client. He was disqualified on the grounds that during his employment with the former client, he had acquired substantial knowledge of the policies, attitudes, and practices of the company's management in entering into the type of agreement that was before the court.

7. What elements must a client prove to disqualify his/her former lawyer in a successive representation case? Are the elements different in a concurrent representation case?

Chapter 27 Notes

1. Commentary to Rule 5.
2. See, e.g., *Can. Southern Ry. v. Kingsmill, Jennings*, (1978) 8 C.P.C. 117, 120-21 (Ont.H.C.); and *Mercator Enterprises Ltd. v. Harris, et al.*, (1978) 29 N.S.R.(2) 703, 710 (N.S.S.C.).
3. *Carson v. Benchers*, (1975) 6 W.W.R. 544, 557 (Sask.C.A.), quoting with approval *Shumiatcher v. Law Society of Sask.*, (1966) 58 W.W.R. 465, 60 D.L.R.(2d) 318, leave to appeal refused 61 D.L.R.(2d) 520.
4. *R. v. Lecaine*, (1983) 22 Sask.R. 57, 59.
5. *MTS International Servides v. Warnat Corp.*, (1981) 118 D.L.R.(3d) 561, 562 (Ont.H.C.).
6. (1912) 1 Ch. 831, 834-35 (C.A.).
7. *Sinclair v. Ridout and Moran*, (1955) O.R. 167, (1955) 4 D.L.R. 468.

8. *Can. Southern Ry. v. Kingsmill, Jennings, supra,* note 2, p. 122, quoting from *Emle Industs. Inc. v. Patentex Inc.,* 478 F.2d 562 (2nd Cir. 1973).
9. 588 F.2d 221, 225 (7th Cir. 1978).
10. See *Nocton v. Lord Ashburton,* (1914) A.C. 932; and *Allison v. Clayhills,* (1907) 97 L.T. 709.
11. (1967) 1 W.L.R. 923, 931; (1967) 2 All E.R. 415 (C.A.).
12. (1981) 30 O.R.(2d) 319, 323 (Ont.H.C.).
13. Also, see *Allin v. Ferguson,* (1912) 5 D.L.R. 19, 21 (Sask.S.C.).
14. See, e.g., *Can. Aero Service Ltd. v. O'Malley,* (1974) S.C.R. 592, 40 D.L.R.(3d) 371 (S.C.C.).
15. *Davey v. Woolley,* (1982) 35 O.R.(2d) 599, 602 (Ont.C.A.).
16. *MTS International Services Inc. v. Warnat Corporation Ltd., supra,* note 5.
17. *Steed & Evans Ltd. v. MacTavish,* (1976) 12 O.R.(2d) 236, 238 (Ont.H.C.).
18. *Goldberg v. Goldberg,* (1982) 141 D.L.R.(3d) 133, 135-136.
19. *Supra,* note 5, p. 565.
20. *Government of India v. Cook Industries, Inc.,* 569 F.2d 737 (2nd Cir. 1978).
21. *Henfrey & Company Ltd. v. A Law Firm,* (1983) 6 W.W.R. 448, 458 (B.C.S.C.).
22. Ibid.
23. *Morkin v. Boras,* (1978) 2 W.W.R. 385, 394 (Alt.S.C.).
24. *Phipps v. Boardman,* (1967) 2 A.C. 46, (1966) 3 All E.R. 721 (H.L.).
25. (1981) 118 D.L.R.(3d) 397 (N.S.S.C., App.Div.).
26. (1982) 49 N.S.R.(2d) 663 (N.S.S.C.).
27. Ibid., p. 673.
28. *Duncan v. Merrill Lynch,* 646 F.(2d) 1020, 1028 (5th Cir. 1981).
29. See *Fund of Funds, Ltd. v. Arthur Anderson & Co.,* 567 F.2d 225, 236 (2nd Cir. 1977).
30. *NCK Organization Ltd. v. Bregman,* 542 F.2d 128 (2nd Cir. 1976).
31. Ibid.
32. Ibid., p. 134.
33. Ruling 1, "Acting for Both Sides," Handbook, The Law Society of British Columbia.
34. *Supra,* note 15, p. 602.
35. (1978) 86 D.L.R.(3d) 121 (Ont.H.C.).
36. "Developments in the Law, Conflict of Interest in the Legal Profession," (1981) *Harv.L.Rev.* 1244, 1336.
37. Gallager, "Legal and Professional Responsibility of Corporate Counsel to Employees During an Internal Investigation for Corporate Misconduct," (1983) 6 *The Corp.L.Rev.* 3, 12-13.
38. (1983) 3 W.W.R. 31 (Sask.Q.B.) aff'd (1983) 5 W.W.R. 151 (Sask.C.A.).

Index of Cases

Subject Index

TO THE OWNER OF
THIS BOOK:

We are interested in your reaction to **Canadian Business Law**. Through feedback from you, we can improve this book in future editions.

1. What was your reason for using this book?

    _____ university course   _____ continuing education course

    _____ college course   _____ personal interest

2. Approximately how much of the book did you use?

    _____ $1/_4$ _____ $1/_2$ _____ $3/_4$ _____ all

3. What is the best aspect of the book?

4. Have you any suggestions for improvement?

5. Is there anything that should be added?

Fold here

Tape Shut